ANNALS OF COMMUNISM

Each volume in the series Annals of Communism will publish selected and previously inaccessible documents from former Soviet state and party archives in the framework of a narrative text that focuses on a particular topic in the history of Soviet and international communism. Separate English and Russian editions will be prepared. Russian and Western scholars work together to prepare the documents for each volume. Documents are chosen not for their support of any single interpretation but for their particular historical importance or their general value in deepening understanding and facilitating discussion. The volumes are designed to be useful to students, scholars, and interested general readers.

The Stalin-Kaganovich Correspondence 1931–36

Compiled and edited by
R. W. Davies, Oleg V. Khlevniuk,
E. A. Rees, Liudmila P. Kosheleva, and
Larisa A. Rogovaya

Russian documents translated by Steven Shabad

Yale University Press
New Haven & London

This volume has been prepared with the cooperation of the Russian State Archive of Social and Political History (RGASPI) of the State Archival Service of Russia in the framework of an agreement concluded between RGASPI and Yale University Press.

Designed by James J. Johnson and set in Sabon Roman by The Composing Room of Michigan, Inc., Grand Rapids, Michigan.
Printed in the United States of America by Vail-Ballou Press, Binghamton, New York.

Library of Congress Cataloging-in-Publication Data

Stalin, Joseph, 1879–1953.
   [Stalin i Kaganovich. English. Selections]
   The Stalin-Kaganovich correspondence, 1931–36 / compiled and edited by R. W. Davies
. . . [et al.] ; Russian documents translated by Steven Shabad.
      p. cm. — (Annals of Communism)
Includes bibliographical references and index.
   ISBN 0-300-09367-5 (alk. paper)

   1. Stalin, Joseph, 1879–1953—Correspondence.   2. Kaganovich, L. M. (Lazar Moiseevich), 1893– —Correspondence.   3. Soviet Union—Politics and government—1917–1936—Sources.   I. Kaganovich, L. M. (Lazar Moiseevich), 1893–   II. Davies, R. W. (Robert William), 1925–   III. Title.   IV. Series.
   DK268.S8 A4 2003
   947.084′2—dc21

                                                                    2002156190

A catalogue record for this book is available from the British Library.

The paper in this book meets the guidelines for permanence and durability of the Committee on Production Guidelines for Book Longevity of the Council on Library Resources.

10 9 8 7 6 5 4 3 2 1

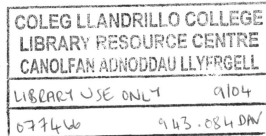

Yale University Press gratefully acknowledges the financial support given for this publication by the John M. Olin Foundation, the Lynde and Harry Bradley Foundation, the Historical Research Foundation, Roger Milliken, Lloyd H. Smith, the William H. Donner Foundation, Joseph W. Donner, Jeremiah Milbank, the David Woods Kemper Memorial Foundation, the Daphne Seybolt Culpeper Foundation, and the Milton V. Brown Foundation.

Contents

1936

Illustrations follow page 244

Preface

The Stalin-Kaganovich correspondence is an important and unique historical source, which no historian engaged in research on Soviet history of the 1930s can ignore. In 1931–36 Stalin entrusted the function of acting as his deputy on party questions to Lazar Moiseyevich Kaganovich, and during the next few years Kaganovich's influence continually increased. Although this post was not authorized by any specific party decision, it was in effect the second most important post in the Central Committee. Kaganovich was in charge of the work both of the Orgburo (Organizational Bureau) of the Central Committee and of several of the most important Central Committee departments, and he managed the sittings of the Politburo during Stalin's absence on vacation and chaired numerous Politburo commissions. Kaganovich consulted Stalin about all Politburo decisions of any significance, and this is the subject matter of a large part of the letters reproduced here.

The present collection continues *Stalin's Letters to Molotov* (Yale University Press, 1995). In the 1920s, Molotov was a secretary of the Communist Party Central Committee and acted as Stalin's deputy on questions concerning the party. During Stalin's vacations Molotov, like Kaganovich in the 1930s, remained in Moscow and was in charge of the work of the supreme party agencies, and prepared the decisions on the most important issues of party and state. These letters covered the years 1925–30 (the small number of letters for 1931–36 included in the collection is fortuitous). In December 1930 Molotov was appointed in place of Rykov as chairman of Sovnarkom, the Council of People's Commissars of the USSR, the supreme government body, and ceased to be a secretary of the party Central Committee. It was at this point that Stalin transferred to Kaganovich Molotov's functions as his deputy in the party.

Stalin's Letters to Molotov included only Stalin's own letters. Molotov's letters to Stalin were located in the Stalin collection (*fond*) in the former Politburo archive (now the Archive of the President of the Russian Federation, APRF), and were inaccessible to historians. In the present book Kaganovich's replies to Stalin are included, and this considerably enhances its value.

The Stalin-Kaganovich correspondence has been brought together from several different archives. Stalin's letters are mainly located in the Kaganovich collection, which was transferred in 1995 from APRF to the Russian State Archive for Political and Social History, RGASPI (formerly RTsKhIDNI), *fond* 81, *opis* 3, *dela* 99–102. (For a description of Stalin's letters in the Kaganovich collection, see Y. Cohen, "Des lettres comme action: Stalin au début des années 1930 vu depuis le fonds Kaganovic," *Cahiers du monde Russe,* 38, no. 3, 1997, 307–46.). Nearly all these letters by Stalin are originals, in pencil or in ink of various colors; a few are typewritten copies. Certain letters were located in other collections of RGASPI, and this is indicated at the beginning of the letter concerned. Some of the letters sent by Stalin to Kaganovich were also addressed to other members of the Politburo, especially Molotov, or to the Politburo as a whole. In these letters Stalin called for a solution to a particular problem, or instructed the Politburo to carry out a particular task.

Kaganovich's letters to Stalin are deposited in the Stalin collection, RGASPI, f. 558, op. 11, dd. 739–43. They are also handwritten originals. When Kaganovich wrote his letters to Stalin, he prepared preliminary versions; then he transcribed in full the final version, which was either clean, or included some amendments. Kaganovich wrote in an almost childish script, notably different from that of Molotov, Stalin, and the other leaders and characteristic of someone who did not write much when he was young. The rough copies are preserved in Kaganovich's personal archive (the family collection), which his daughter Maia Lazarevna Kaganovich presented to RGASPI in 1995. The editors are grateful to her for permitting us to use these documents.

In the present volume the version included is the final one as sent to Stalin. In most cases the rough versions correspond almost exactly to the originals, or vary from them only in insignificant points of style. But the comparison of the preliminary and final versions has enabled us in some cases to find significant variant readings in the rough versions; these have been given in the notes to the documents. A couple of letters are available in rough versions (documents 53 and 111) but not available in the final versions. Perhaps Kaganovich did not send them. They are included here because the information in them is of interest.

The letters were almost always sent between Moscow and the south by special NKVD courier. This took two or three days. In addition to the letters, Stalin and Kaganovich also exchanged ciphered telegrams, usually every day, sometimes several times a day; the telegrams were usually received and deciphered on the day on which they were written. These ciphered telegrams are in twenty files of the Stalin collection, RGASPI, f. 558, op. 11, dd. 76–95. Kaganovich's telegrams to Stalin have been preserved only in the form of the typed deciphers, and it is these which have been used in this volume. Stalin's telegrams to Kaganovich are available both in the original text (Stalin's original or the notes of his secretary) and in typewritten copies on special forms, prepared in Moscow on receipt of the telegram. In this volume we have used the original, which is often simply a note in Stalin's handwriting on Kaganovich's telegram. When sending Stalin's text to be coded, the secretary noted the date of transmission and numbered the telegram. The only telegrams not available to us are those for the period 5–20 October 1935; these are still located in the Presidential Archive and have not yet been declassified. A list of these telegrams, published in the Russian edition, shows that their subject matter is not at all unusual. A few documents were transmitted by telephone—"phonegrams."

A ciphered telegram is described by the transmitters, or by the editors of this volume, as "cipher" or "telegram" at the beginning of the document (the words are interchangeable). A letter is not specially indicated. Except where otherwise indicated, the letters and ciphers translated in this book were handwritten by the authors of the documents.

The Stalin-Kaganovich correspondence is very bulky. Most of the correspondence—862 letters and ciphers—has been published in the Russian edition of this book (*Stalin i Kaganovich: Perepiska, 1931–1936gg.* [Moscow, 2001]). Only ciphers on routine appointments are omitted. For the English-language edition the editors have selected what we consider to be the most interesting letters. Almost all Stalin's letters are included, but we have omitted a number of Kaganovich's letters which deal with minor and ephemeral topics or provide an enormous amount of detail about the Moscow Region, where he was party secretary. For the years 1931–35 we include only a few of the ciphered telegrams, but in the introduction to the chapter for each year, and in the notes to the documents, we include extracts from, or summaries of, the most important telegrams. In 1936 very few letters were exchanged, and most important matters were dealt with entirely by telegram. For 1936 we therefore include translations of a substantial number of telegrams. The first major public trial of the opposition leaders, the Kamenev-Zinoviev trial, took place while Stalin was on vacation in 1936, and Stalin and Kaganovich exchanged many telegrams about it. We include all these in the present volume. They provide a unique account of political repression as seen by the two top leaders.

Some documents directly related to the correspondence are included in the Appendix. Kuibyshev's letter to Kaganovich was found in Kuibyshev's personal files. Stalin's letter to Ordzhonikidze, which Stalin sent to Kaganovich for his information, was found among Stalin's letters to Kaganovich. Stalin's letters to the Politburo about the publication of Engels' article "The Foreign Policy of Russian Tsarism" were located in appendixes to the minutes of sittings of the Politburo. Ilya Ehrenburg's letter discussed by Stalin and Kaganovich in their 1934 letters was found among the Stalin documents in RGASPI. But Kaganovich also mentioned in his letters many documents which he sent to Stalin, and which we have not succeeded in finding; this is indicated in the notes to the letters concerned.

For obvious reasons the correspondence between Stalin and Kaganovich took place only during Stalin's lengthy vacations in the south. During 1933–36 the number of letters exchanged greatly declined, and from 1937 the correspondence between Stalin and his colleagues, characteristic of the 1920s and the first half of the 1930s, ceased more or less completely. This obviously requires investigation.

The simplest explanation of the absence of letters in these later years is that they were destroyed from considerations of "delicacy." A new phase in the repressions was embarked upon in 1935–36, and the explosion of the Great Terror took place in 1937 and 1938. But there is a great deal of evidence, both political and purely technical, to show that these letters never existed.

There is no doubt that with the strengthening of Stalin's personal power his need to discuss problems with his colleagues diminished. The Politburo lost its former importance as a collective leadership. When taking a decision Stalin no longer had to persuade or talk round the members of the Politburo, because he was confident that they would be compliant. This power relation between Stalin and his group was finally established in the course of the Great Terror of 1937–38, when several members of the Politburo were executed and the threat of repression hung over the others.

But the decline in the correspondence between the top Soviet leaders was a result not only of political circumstances but also of the improvement in telephone communication between Moscow and the southern resorts. Over many years letters sent through special couriers were the major means of communication. But this had many defects. The letters took quite a long time to arrive, and, as is clear from the present correspondence, Stalin frequently complained that he lacked up-to-date information. Ciphered telegrams were a parallel means of communication. But it required a lot of work to transmit, receive, and decipher them. Moreover, some issues could not be discussed, because technical staff participated in their transmission. A reliable telephone service would obviate these difficulties. But this was not at first available. On 21 June 1932, Voroshilov wrote to Stalin: "It is unfortunate that there is no link with Sochi by *vertushka* [the secret government telephone network]; it would make it possible to be more frequently in touch directly, rather than by correspondence" (RGASPI, f. 74, op. 2, d. 37, l. 49). And Ordzhonikidze, who was hard of hearing, wrote to his wife from the south in March 1933, "It is difficult to talk on the phone; you have to shout, it is very difficult to hear—though sometimes it can be heard fairly clearly"; "I am sending this letter with Comrade Ginzburg; I tried to phone but I could not get through" (ibid., f. 85 [recent addition]).

A closed high-frequency telephone link between Moscow and the government vacation homes (dachas) in the south was evidently established in 1935. The archives contain several letters addressed by Stalin to Kaganovich and Molotov in 1935–36 which were dictated over the telephone (evidently by Stalin) and noted down in Moscow by his assistant Dvinsky (RGASPI, f. 558, op. 11, d. 789, ll. 171, 172). The present collection includes several of these phonegrams (for an example see document 125). But an increasing number of issues were evidently decided by direct telephone conversations between Stalin and Politburo members. On 14 September 1936, Kaganovich wrote in a letter to Stalin, "I informed you about Spanish affairs by telephone" (document 166). Technical progress thus dealt an irredeemable blow to future historians. As elsewhere in the twentieth-century world, Stalin and his colleagues gave increasing preference to the telephone instead of letters.

In the remaining prewar years, 1937–40, Stalin, according to the diary of his Kremlin appointments, did not travel outside Moscow on vacation (*Istoricheskii arkhiv,* nos. 4, 5–6, 1995; no. 2, 1996). This explains the complete absence of correspondence between Stalin and his colleagues in these years. Stalin did not go on vacation in the south again until the autumn of 1945, after the end of the Second World War (ibid., no. 4, 1996, 113).

The editors do not claim to have made a comprehensive analysis of this collection of documents nor to have made a detailed study of all the problems dealt with. Our task was a more modest one: to make it as easy as possible for historians, and readers interested in history, to familiarize themselves with this material. We have also sought to explain the meaning and content of the documents and to place them in their historical context. This has determined the form of this book.

In the notes to each letter we explain matters specific to the letter. The book also includes introductory essays for each of the years in which the letters were written. Each essay provides a general account of the events of the year and describes those events most frequently discussed in the correspondence. In a general introduction to the book we seek to place these events in the broader context of Soviet history. At the beginning of the book we also provide a brief biography of Kaganovich. The introductory essays and the notes are complementary, and matters explained in the introductory essays are not as a rule discussed in the notes.

In preparing the notes and the introductory essays we have used existing literature and a wide range of new sources. In particular, we have used Politburo documents; it is primarily problems dealt with by this supreme organ of the party and the state which were discussed in the letters. Decisions on issues dealt with in the correspondence appear in the minutes (*protokoly*) of the Politburo (RGASPI, f. 17, op. 3) and also in special minutes—the particularly secret decisions are marked "special file" (*osobaya papka;* ibid., op. 162). Additional materials relating to Politburo decisions are attached to the originals of the minutes (ibid., op. 163) and are also found in the Politburo collection in APRF (f. 3).

Although it was mainly Kaganovich with whom Stalin corresponded in 1931–35, Stalin also communicated with other colleagues during his vacations. In addition to the letters sent to Kaganovich but really intended for other members of the Politburo, from time to time Stalin corresponded with Molotov, Ordzhonikidze, Voroshilov, and other members of the top leadership. This correspondence is located in the personal collections of these leaders in RGASPI, and in the Stalin collection, recently transferred from APRF. These documents were also used in preparing the notes and introductory articles.

All documents are published in full. Points of ellipsis within documents were made by the authors of the letters. Points of ellipsis within square brackets [. . .] were made by the editors; they appear only in our introductory essays and in the notes to the documents. Stalin's letters are published with virtually no corrections. Misprints and minor errors which do not affect the meaning have been corrected without noting this in the documents. Kaganovich's letters contained numerous mistakes in orthography and punctuation. These were corrected in the Russian edition. We have sought to retain in the translation the informality and colloquial language of Kaganovich's letters.

The letters are published in chronological order and numbered in sequence. The authors did not date some letters, and the editors have inserted dates in brackets on the basis of the contents of the letters.

The archival source (fond, opis, delo) is listed above the text of each letter. All the documents in the collection are located in RGASPI unless otherwise stated.

The book concludes with a glossary of terms and abbreviations and with a list of people mentioned in the correspondence, along with their brief biographies. Only very frequently used names of institutions and terms are left in the Russian form (e.g. Sovnarkom, Gosplan, Politburo). The glossary also gives the Russian names of institutions given in the documents in English translation (e.g. AUCCTU; Council of Labor and Defense). Russian terms that appear in only one or two documents are translated in the text or notes of the documents and do not appear in the glossary. The brief biographies deal primarily with activities during the period (1931–36) covered by the correspondence.

Acknowledgments

The editors would like to thank the following for advice and assistance: Marea Arries, our indefatigable secretary; Michael Gelb; Melanie Ilič; Stephen Kotkin; John Morison; Richard Stites; and Stephen Wheatcroft. We would also like to thank Maia Kaganovich, Lazar Kaganovich's daughter, for providing the draft copies of Kaganovich's letters to Stalin and the photographs from the family archive. The editors are grateful to Marilyn Flaig for preparing the index.

The translator would like express his gratitude to Vladimir Solovyov, Elena Klepikova, and Aleksandr Protsenko for their assistance in clarifying some of the abstruse idioms and technical terms in the correspondence.

The research was supported by Grants R 000 23 73 88 and R 000 239 543 from the British Economic and Social Research Council.

A Note on
Soviet Administrative Structure

The Union of Soviet Socialist Republics was divided at this time into six "Union republics." The USSR and the Union republics each had their own government, headed by a Council of People's Commissars (Sovnarkom), with its own People's Commissariats (i.e. Ministries). Some PCs (e.g. of Military and Naval Affairs and Transport) existed only at the USSR, or "all-Union," level. Some (e.g. Finance) existed at both the all-Union and the republic level. Industry was managed until the end of 1931 by the so-called Supreme Council of the National Economy (Vesenkha), to which there corresponded republican Councils of the National Economy. At the beginning of 1932, Vesenkha was split into the PCs of Heavy Industry, Light Industry, and the Timber Industry.

The main unit of local government in the larger republics was the *oblast* or *krai*. The difference between the two was that the krai had subordinate to it *oblasti* and *avtonomnye oblasti* (autonomous regions—for which the term *okrug* was sometimes used instead of *oblast*). For simplicity we have translated both *krai* and *oblast* as "region." In Ukraine, the regions were established in the course of 1932–33. Confusingly, there were also "autonomous republics," with roughly the same status as a region. An autonomous republic or region was thus called because of the presence in it of a substantial number of members of a national minority—for example, the Bashkir Autonomous Soviet Socialist Republic. The term "autonomous" was used to give the national minorities at least a theoretical sense of control over their own territory. Regions and autonomous republics were in turn divided into "districts" (*raion,* plural *raiony*), The village was the lowest administrative unit. Towns fitted into the structure at various levels depending on their importance.

In the course of the 1930s the units of government, including PCs, regions, and districts, were increasingly subdivided. The following table summarizes the position at two dates in the period. "Autonomous and other regions or *okrugs*" are those within an oblast or krai, or within a Union republic not divided into oblasti.

	1930	*1937*
Union republics	6	11
Regions (*oblasti* and *kraia*)	13	39
Autonomous republics	15	22
Autonomous and other regions or *okrugs*	17	52
Districts	2,811	3,307
Village soviets	71,780	62,585

The Sovnarkom of the USSR was nominally appointed by the Central Executive Committee (TsIK) of soviets, which in turn was appointed by the elected Congress of Soviets. In 1930–41 the chairman or president of Sovnarkom was Molotov. The party structure was, broadly speaking, parallel to the government structure. But in practice it was superior to it; it made all major appointments and took all major decisions. The party congress elected a Central Committee which in turn appointed a Political Bureau (Politburo), headed by a general secretary (Stalin), and an Organizational Bureau (Orgburo). The Politburo and Sovnarkom were the effective central working bodies of party and government. Below the all-Union level, every republic had its own Central Committee, TsIK, and Sovnarkom; and in every region and district the principal officials were the secretary of the party committee and the chairman of the soviet executive committee (in that order).

Soviet officials at this time often used the pood (16.38 kilograms, 0.01638 metric tons) as a unit of weight. In this volume we have given the figures in poods as in the original document, but have added the figure in metric tons (tonnes) in brackets.

Finally, it should be noted that the agricultural year, roughly corresponding to the grain harvest, ran from July 1 to June 30 (written as, for example, 1931/32). From 1931 the economic year coincided with the calendar year.

The Stalin-Kaganovich Correspondence

1931–36

Introduction

NOT LONG before Lazar Kaganovich's death, he said of Stalin: "He must be assessed differently according to the time, the period; there were various Stalins. The postwar Stalin was one Stalin, the prewar Stalin was another, and Stalin between 1932 and the 1940s was yet another Stalin. Before 1932 he was entirely different. He changed. I saw at least five or six different Stalins."[1] These comments are confirmed by the evidence of this correspondence. The years 1931 and 1932, and the first six months of 1933 before the new harvest (approximately the end of June or July), were characterized by a severe and mounting crisis, which exercised a tremendous influence on the formation of the Stalinist system, and on Stalin himself. The financial system was disrupted, large-scale inflation occurred, indebtedness to foreign countries reached a critical level, industrial production stagnated. The peak of the crisis was the terrible famine, in which millions of people died. These were years of growing dissatisfaction in the country and in the party with Stalin's policy, and with the burgeoning state terror. It was in this critical period, in November 1932, that Stalin's wife, Nadezhda Allilueva, committed suicide (some say she was accidentally killed by her husband). Her death gave rise to many rumors; and there is considerable evidence that it led Stalin to be even more venomous. The events of those years and their direct consequences in 1933–36 are the theme which runs through correspondence published in this book.

The general process by which dictatorships and dictators are estab-

---

1. F. Chuev, *Tak govoril Kaganovich* (Moscow, 1992), 154.

lished and developed is a major problem for historians. But the process is difficult to investigate and comprehend owing to the paucity of source materials. Usually the documents at our disposal illuminate not the system of dictatorial power but the *results* of policies in the form of decisions, statistics, reports, and speeches. It is even harder to investigate what may be termed the sociology of power. The source materials are almost always such that it is difficult to establish the real process of decision making, which includes the relations within the ruling group, the structure of the ruling stratum, and the relative influence of its various subgroups, and also to establish the methods by which the hierarchy of power is stabilized and supported. These general problems in analyzing all dictatorships are even more difficult to cope with in the case of the Stalin period. Secrecy abounded, and the public speeches and statements of the Soviet leaders were a pale reflection of their real intentions and thoughts. Practically no verbatim and summary records were kept of the proceedings of the Politburo and Sovnarkom.

Moreover, in the Stalin period the leaders did not keep diaries.[2] Khrushchev and Mikoian dictated their memoirs many years later, and they were far from frank.[3] Molotov revealed a little of himself in interviews with his admirer Chuev, a poet.[4] Kaganovich was interviewed briefly by Chuev.[5] He also wrote his *Notes from Memory*.[6] Unfortunately these were a compilation consisting of a few pieces of information about his life and a vast summary of a large number of party documents and of the writings of Lenin and Stalin.

In these circumstances, the correspondence between the Soviet leaders has proved to be the best and most reliable source for understanding their assessment of the situations they were facing, their mutual relations, and their actions. The correspondence includes various official communications (such as memoranda on draft decisions, and reports),

2. The only exception so far are the diary notes of V. A. Malyshev, but these are scrappy and could be more informative (see *Istochnik*, no. 5, 1997, 103–47).

3. Khrushchev's memoirs have been published in various forms in both Russia and the West. The most recent and fullest publication appeared in the Russian journal *Voprosy istorii* in 1990–95, and the previously unpublished part of the memoirs appeared in English as *Khrushchev Remembers: The Glasnost Tapes* (Boston, 1990). Mikoian's memoirs were in his collection in APRF and were recently transferred to RGASPI. They have been published in Russian as A. Mikoian, *Tak bylo* (Moscow, 1999).

4. *Sto sorok besed s Molotovym: Iz dnevnika F. Chueva* (Moscow, 1991); for a version of this book in English see *Molotov Remembers: Inside Kremlin Politics, Conversations with Felix Chuev*, ed. A. Resis and I. R. Dee (Chicago, 1993).

5. Chuev, *Tak govoril Kaganovich*.

6. L. Kaganovich, *Pamiatnye zapiski* (Moscow, 1996).

as well as the ciphered telegrams. These helped the leaders to coordinate decisions. But it is the personal letters which are the most interesting source. They were never concerned with purely personal problems but were rather a form of official communication. They nevertheless provide a great deal of evidence about the informal relations between the Soviet leaders, who expressed far more frankly and fully than in other sources the motives for their actions, and their attitudes of mind. Only a relatively small number of letters of this kind have been preserved. The Stalin-Kaganovich correspondence is the frankest and most complete of the available collections of such letters.

Joseph Stalin, one of the two heroes of this book, was the leader of the people and was known among his associates as *khoziain* ("master" or "boss"). Kaganovich, our second hero, was the faithful assistant of the master and carried out his wishes. During the years in which these letters were written, Kaganovich occupied major posts at the top of the party and state. In 1931–34, when his influence was at its height, he was simultaneously a secretary of the party Central Committee—actually Stalin's deputy in the party—and head of the party organization in the capital city, Moscow, and Stalin's deputy in the Defense Commission, the supreme body concerned with decisions about defense, attached to both the Politburo and Sovnarkom. At the beginning of 1934 he was, in addition, placed in charge of the Commission of Party Control attached to the Central Committee, and the Commission on Railroad Transport, the highest state and party body for the management of transport, an organization similar to the Defense Commission. The correspondence between Stalin and Kaganovich accordingly reflected some of the most important problems in leading the country and the party, and the process of change both in the nature of power and in Stalin's own relations with his colleagues at the important turning point in Soviet history clearly recalled by Kaganovich—1932.

Stalin and His Revolution

Many historians characterize the changes in the political, social, and economic nature of the Soviet regime during the three prewar five-year plans as the Stalinist revolution from above. Although this is a controversial concept in several respects, it is certainly the case that what took place was a fundamental and revolutionary upheaval, and that its prime mover was Soviet state policy, particularly the policies of Stalin himself.

The Stalin revolution began with the events at the end of the 1920s, when the crisis in state grain procurements (*zagotovki*) drove the Stalinist majority in the Politburo to their decision to abolish the New Economic Policy (NEP) by forcibly seizing grain and carrying out repressive acts against the peasantry. This upheaval, described by Stalin as the "great breakthrough," involved a sharp struggle among party leaders. Stalin and his adherents defeated the group of "Right-wingers"—Rykov, Bukharin, and Tomsky, who were Politburo members, and their supporters. The Right-wingers supported more moderate policies and considered that the escalation of violence in the countryside was dangerous.

According to the Russian historians V. P. Danilov and N. A. Ivnitsky, in 1929 over 1,300 peasant revolts were recorded in the USSR as a whole;[7] simultaneously the peasants reduced the area sown to grain and killed farm animals. This peasant resistance drove the Stalin group to adopt even more radical measures. At the end of 1929 and beginning of 1930, in response to pressure from Moscow, local leaders embarked on the establishment of collective farms on a mass scale. By 1 March 1930 as many as 56 percent of peasant households were recorded as members of collective farms, and in certain districts, referred to as "districts of comprehensive collectivization," nearly all the peasants were driven into the collective farms. The most powerful device for creating collective farms was the "elimination of the kulaks as a class." Kulaks, according to the Marxist analysis, were the more wealthy peasants who exploited the mass of the peasantry. But it was not only relatively well off peasants who were subject to exile, arrest, and execution; these measures were liable to be used against all peasants who were opposed to joining the collective farms.

Peasants responded to forcible collectivization with a new wave of uprisings, and by murdering local leaders. The OGPU (political police) registered 402 mass disturbances in the USSR in January 1930, another 1,048 in February, and 6,528 in March.[8] The pressure of peasant resistance led to changes in the initial plans of the Soviet leaders. On 2 March the newspapers published Stalin's famous letter "Dizzy from Success," in which he accused local leaders of "distortions" of policy in carrying out collectivization. But the disturbances did not cease im-

---

7. *Dokumenty svidetelstvuiut: Iz istorii derevni nakanune i v khode kollektivizatsii, 1927–1932 gg.,* ed. V. P. Danilov and N. A. Ivnitsky (Moscow, 1989), 23.

8. L. Viola, *Peasant Rebels Under Stalin: Collectivization and the Culture of Peasant Resistance* (New York, 1996), 138–39.

mediately. Consequently the central authorities sent a directive to the regions that the policy should be less severely enforced and acknowledging that the regime was threatened with "an extensive wave of peasant insurrectionist disturbances" and the destruction of "half the lower-level officials."[9] In spite of concessions the leadership of the country did not abandon the general policy of comprehensive collectivization, which was resumed in subsequent years.

The disturbances in March were the high point in the peasant movement against the regime; the number of disturbances declined, although they continued to the end of 1930. In 1930 the OGPU recorded 13,754 mass disturbances; in the 10,000 of these for which data are available almost two and half million persons took part, so the total number of participants must have been more than three million.[10] The government was able to control the situation only by using terror. Hundreds of thousands of peasants were sent to camps and labor settlements in Siberia and the north. In 1930, according to one source, 20,201 people were sentenced to be executed in cases investigated by the OGPU;[11] it is certain that many of these were peasants.

A major feature of Stalinist policy was the tremendous growth in the plans for industrial construction. Industrial development on the Stalinist model envisaged the mass purchase of advanced capital equipment in the West; the implanting of this equipment into Soviet industry was intended to create a base for the development of modern production, particularly in heavy industry. The Soviet leaders anticipated that this policy would enable the economy to jump over the stage of gradual accumulation of technology and knowhow which had been a feature of industrialization in Western countries; the Soviet economy would rapidly be brought up to the level of the most advanced countries. But these calculations proved to be in large part erroneous. Superindustrialization, even in its first stages, involved many problems and contradictions. As a result of excessive outlays, large amounts were invested in unfinished construction, the return from which was delayed. Existing enterprises, particularly those which produced con-

9. *Dokumenty svidetelstvuiut*, 36–37.

10. Viola, *Peasant Rebels*, 136–40; V. Danilov and A. Berelowitch, "Les documents de la VCK-OGPU-NKVD sur la campagne sovietique, 1918–1937," *Cahiers du monde russe*, XXXV (1994), 673–75; some fragmentary information indicating that the peasant movement was widespread is published in N. A. Ivnitsky, *Kollektivizatsiia i raskulachivanie (nachalo 30-kh godov)* (Moscow, 1994), 143–44.

11. V. P. Popov, "Gosudarstvennyi terror v sovetskoi Rossii, 1923–1953 gg.," *Otechestvennye arkhivy*, no. 2 (1992), 20–31.

sumer goods, reduced production owing to the shortage of raw materials. The cost of industrial production increased, and its quality fell sharply. In the summer of 1930 industry was involved in a severe crisis.[12]

The disruption of agriculture, the concentration of huge resources in heavy industry, and the export of food on a large scale led to a sharp decline in the standard of living. Enormous queues formed for rationed foods even in large towns, even though the government regarded the population of these towns as its main social base and endeavored to ensure them priority in food. Prices on the free market increased rapidly. The food difficulties in the towns led to disturbances.

Mass dissatisfaction with the government increased the political authority of the Right-wing leaders, who had warned that the repression of the peasantry and the abrupt changes in industry would have serious consequences. In this context Stalin renewed the campaign against them. In December 1930 Rykov was removed from the chair of Sovnarkom and from the Politburo; he was the last of the Right-wing leaders to have retained high office in the government and the party. Rykov's place in Sovnarkom was taken by Molotov, and Molotov's function as secretary of the party Central Committee and as Stalin's deputy in the party was transferred to Kaganovich.

By this time forced industrialization and compulsory collectivization had led to further profound changes. In 1930–31 more than 1.8 million peasants were exiled to distant parts of the country in so-called special settlements,[13] and many were arrested and sent to camps. At least a million peasants fled to the towns and the building sites to avoid repression. A further two million may have been intended for exile within their region (the so-called Category III exiles), but after these peasants lost their property many of them also fled to the towns and building sites.[14] Collectivization greatly disrupted agricultural productive capacity.

The industrial and financial crisis developed further.[15] In 1932,

12. R. W. Davies, *The Soviet Economy in Turmoil, 1929–1930* (Basingstoke and London, 1989).

13. V. N. Zemskov, "'Kulatskaya ssylka' v 30-e gody," *Sotsiologicheskie issledovaniya,* no. 10, 1991, 3.

14. *Dokumenty svidetelstvuiut,* 46–47.

15. Except where otherwise stated the information about the economy in the introductory essays in this book is taken from R. W. Davies, *Crisis and Progress in the Soviet Economy, 1931–1933* (Basingstoke and London, 1996).

dubbed the "final" year of the five-year plan, the struggle intensified to complete the main projects of the plan. The capital investment plans approved at the beginning of 1932 were at first increased. Together with other factors, the growth of investment led to greater inflationary pressure. By 1 May prices on the urban free market (the "bazaars") were ten times the 1928 level and 57 percent above the prices of 1 May 1931. From April 1932 production in both heavy and light industry either failed to grow or even declined. The foreign trade deficit reached a critical level. In spite of desperate efforts to acquire foreign currency (even by selling rare books and works of art from museums), the government was compelled to reduce imports sharply. This led to great difficulties even for such priority projects as the Cheliabinsk tractor factory, whose import quota for equipment was reduced by more than 50 percent.

The internal crisis was intensified by developments abroad. In September 1931 the Japanese Kwantung army invaded Manchuria, and a serious military threat appeared on the Soviet Far Eastern frontiers. The 1932 defense budget amounted to 250 percent of actual defense expenditure in 1931, and investment in the defense industries was planned to increase by 45 percent. The expansion of the armaments industries involved the most skilled labor and the most complex materials and equipment—and this intensified economic difficulties.

But it was the reduction in food supplies and the spread of famine which had the most tragic consequences. The harvest of 1931 was low, and proved insufficient to supply both internal needs and the planned export of grain. The state grain procurements imposed an intolerable burden on the peasants. The total amount of grain allocated for internal consumption in the agricultural year 1 July 1931–30 June 1932 increased by 2.5 million tons, but, to achieve this increase, grain export, while remaining high, was reduced as compared with the previous year, and grain stocks were also reduced. In 1931 famine already affected a number of regions. At the same time, in the course of 1931 and 1932, there was a huge increase in the number of manual and office workers and people in other categories of the population receiving bread from the state—enterprises continually increased the recruitment of labor in their efforts to fulfill the overoptimistic plans. The total number of people receiving state food rations increased from 30 to 38 million between January–March 1931 and January–March 1932. This increase could not be sustained, and on 23 March 1932 the Politburo decided to cancel the guaranteed supply of bread for 20 million people in ration Lists 2 and 3; henceforth they received a smaller allocation from the state, and hard-pressed local authorities were expected to make up the difference.

The food crisis increased social tension. Peasants left the collective farms in substantial numbers. Hungry peasants resisted the removal of grain for the state procurements. In many places crowds of peasants attacked state grain stores and distributed the grain. In the spring of 1932 the reduction of food rations in the towns led to antigovernment disturbances, the most significant of which took place in the textile factories of Ivanovo-Voznesensk industrial region. On 5 April a strike took place at the Nogin factory in Vichuga. On 9 April nearly all the factories in the town went on strike. On the following day a crowd of many thousands of people marched on the town soviet, broke into the police headquarters, and occupied the buildings of the local GPU and the party district committee. Disturbances continued the next day. According to official reports now released from the archives, one demonstrator was killed and another wounded in clashes with the police, fifteen policemen were severely injured, and a further dozen policemen and a few district officials received minor injuries. On 12 April Kaganovich arrived in Vichuga. By a mixture of repressive acts and promises the disturbances were brought to an end. Strikes and mass disturbances also took place in a number of other districts of the Ivanovo Region.[16]

The growing crisis led the government to make significant concessions. In a revised plan for the agricultural year 1932/33, adopted on 6 May 1932, state grain procurements were slightly lower than the actual procurements in 1931/32. The plan envisaged that the procurements from the collective farms would be reduced and those from the state farms increased. A further decree of 20 May permitted peasants and collective farms, after they had completed their deliveries to the state, to sell their output at prices formed on the market (previously the state had attempted to fix the prices). These decisions had a clear objective. Compulsory deliveries and centralized supplies had brought the country to the verge of famine. The Stalin leadership, remembering the experience of NEP, attempted to appease the peasants.

These were sensible measures in themselves; but they were too little

---

16. RGASPI, f. 81, op. 3, d. 213, ll. 3–7, 64–65, 77–78, 93; N. Werth and G. Moullec, *Rapports secrets soviétiques* (Paris, 1994), 209–16; J. Rossman, "The Teikovo Cotton Workers' Strike of April 1932: Class, Gender and Identity Politics in Stalin's Russia," *Russian Review*, 56 (1997), 44–69.

and too late. The new harvest of 1932 did not ameliorate the situation. A new wave of severe famine began, and millions of people died. Secret reports contained ample information on widespread cannibalism. Large numbers of peasants and homeless children poured out of the hungry villages into the towns. A typhus epidemic spread through the country, affecting better-placed industrial cities as well as the countryside.

The evidence indicates that Stalin's policy was rejected by many party members, who believed he was responsible for unjustified confrontation with the peasantry. At this time some party members attempted to come together to organize a campaign against Stalin within the party. The best known evidence on this resistance concerns the "Union of Marxist-Leninists," which was inspired by M. N. Riutin, a party member of long standing. He prepared a document entitled "Stalin and the Crisis of the Proletarian Dictatorship" and an appeal entitled "To All Members of the Communist Party of the Soviet Union (Bolsheviks)." The appeal began: "The party and the proletarian dictatorship have been led into an unprecedented blind alley by Stalin and his clique, and are in mortal danger from this crisis."[17]

A particularly alarming symptom of the crisis for the regime was the resistance of many local party officials to the grain procurement plan. The party leaders at lower levels were well informed about the true state of affairs in the countryside, and they witnessed deaths from hunger day by day; in many cases they refused to carry out orders from the center to send for export grain obtained in the state procurements.

During the crisis the Stalin leadership kept itself in power by a policy of severe repression. The main devices for obtaining grain included widespread searches, mass arrests, and executions; whole villages were sent into exile. One important instrument for subjugating the countryside were the political departments (*politotdely*) of the Machine-Tractor Stations (MTS); the political departments were established at the beginning of 1933 and were granted considerable powers. In the towns the OGPU arrested "disrupters of production," "kulaks," and wreckers. In November 1932 new legislation introduced the system of internal passports. Only urban citizens received passports, to hinder the inflow of starving peasants into the towns. Simultaneously with the issue of passports, a population check was carried out, which resulted in the removal of "socially dangerous elements" from large

17. *Izvestiia TsK KPSS*, no. 6, 1989, 109.

towns, particularly capital cities. In April 1933 the Politburo resolved to organize "labor settlements" in addition to the widespread system of camps, colonies, and special settlements. The Politburo proposed to send to the labor settlements, in addition to peasants condemned for sabotage of the grain procurements, "the urban stratum which refused to leave Moscow and Leningrad consequent upon the introduction of passports," and also "kulaks who fled from the villages and were discovered working in industry."[18] During 1933 about 270,000 persons were sent into exile as special settlers.[19] In the same year the number of persons incarcerated in camps increased by about 200,000.

To suppress dissatisfaction within the party a new party "cleansing" or purge (*chistka*) was announced in November 1932. An unprecedentedly large number of party members was prosecuted for failure to carry out the central directives on the removal of grain from hungry villages. During 1932 and 1933 about 450,000 persons were expelled from the party (which had 3.5 million members on 1 January 1933). Dissident party members or former party members who were arrested included Riutin and his supporters.

While terror and compulsion continued to be an inherent part of state policy, a kind of "liberalization" of economic policy also played an important part in overcoming the crisis. In 1933 the plans for industrial growth and capital investment in heavy industry were appreciably moderated. The pressure on the countryside was somewhat reduced. The peasants were granted greater rights to manage their own "personal auxiliary economies" (the private plots cultivated by each collective farm and state farm household). At the same time the large capital investments of the first five-year plan resulted in a huge increase in industrial capacity. From approximately August 1933 to the summer or autumn of 1936 industrial and agricultural production grew rapidly, and the standard of living of a large section of the population increased above the very low level of the years of hunger and deprivation.

There is no reason to suppose that a better coordinated and less extreme policy could not have been pursued in previous years, even within the framework of the policy of rapid industrialization. If the state had not adopted unrealistically high investment plans and had

18. RGASPI, f. 17, op. 3, d. 921, l. 67. In practice there was no significant difference between labor settlements and special settlements, and the terms were used interchangeably (see Zemskov, " 'Kulatskaya ssylka' ").

19. Zemskov, " 'Kulatskaya ssylka,' " 4.

exercised less remorseless pressure on the peasants, the tragic consequences of crisis and famine could have been at least in part avoided or mitigated. The policy of the Soviet leaders, and the conceptions and actions of Stalin personally, were a significant factor in the development of the country and affected the fate of millions of people. This leads us again to the complicated question of decision making, of the relation between the objective restraints on Stalinist policy and those actions which resulted from ill-informed, mistaken, or inhumane decisions by Stalin and his entourage.

On 18 June 1932 a twenty-year-old Ukrainian student, G. I. Tkachenko, wrote to S. V. Kosior, secretary of the Central Committee of the Ukrainian Communist Party. Tkachenko, a member of the Komsomol (Young Communist League), a sincere socialist, was horrified by the famine which menaced Ukraine. He wrote:

> Do you realize what is happening in the lands around Belaia Tserkov, Uman, and Kiev? There are vast areas of land not sown. [. . .] In collective farms in which there were 100–150 horses, there are now only 40–50, and these are dying off. The population is terribly hungry. [. . .]
>
> . . . There are dozens and hundreds of cases when a collective farmer goes to the fields and vanishes—and after a few days his corpse is found, and it is pitilessly buried in a pit as if this were quite normal—and on the following day the corpse is found of the person who did the burial—they are dying from hunger. [. . .]
>
> . . . In Kiev untold numbers of peasant families, already bloated from hunger, sit on street corners and beg and weep for a piece of bread. And who are these people? Collective farmers who had earned hundreds of labor-days. [. . .]
>
> . . . This year we cannot hope for anything better. Things will be even worse because the harvest will be very poor and the grain-procurement plans are imposing even more on the collective farms.[20]

We cite this letter, rather than any of a large number of similar or even more harrowing documents, because on the day on which young Tkachenko wrote it, 18 June 1932, Stalin explained his understanding of the famine and its causes in a letter to Kaganovich, Molotov, and other members of the Politburo (document 35).

In that letter Stalin admitted the existence of "<u>impoverishment</u> and

---

20. *Golod 1932–1933 rokiv na Ukraini* (Kiev, 1990), 183–85, citing archives of the CC of the Ukrainian Communist Party. A labor-day was a unit of measurement of the work contributed by collective farmers to the socialized sector of a collective farm, equaling approximately one day's work of average skill.

<u>famine</u>" in "a number of <u>fertile</u> districts" (such an admission by Stalin was a rare exception). But his analysis of the situation and his proposals were neither objective nor realistic. In Stalin's letter famine was treated as a more or less normal bureaucratic problem, as due to the mistaken distribution of the grain procurement plan and to the need for local leaders to "devote a proper amount of attention" to agriculture. Stalin was particularly incensed by the Ukrainian peasantry—"several tens of thousands of Ukrainian collective farmers are still traveling around the entire European part of the USSR and are demoralizing our collective farms with their complaints and whining." This letter was a kind of program for agriculture, but, like the rest of the Stalin-Kaganovich correspondence, it did not contain any serious discussion of such questions as the food situation in the country, or grain distribution, or the relation of internal consumption and export, or the situation of the peasantry, or the effectiveness of the decisions on collective-farm trade in achieving the aim of increasing peasant incentives to improve production.

Stalin received much information which would have enabled him to know the real situation in the countryside and the existence of widespread famine. But if he had acknowledged these facts and had analyzed the situation on their basis he would have had to recognize his own mistakes and the errors in his previous policy. To avoid this, Stalin constructed for himself and his colleagues—in his secret correspondence as well as in his public statements—a description of events which was far from reality, but allowed the Soviet leaders not to lose their political prestige. This tendency became the rule, resulting in a permanent delay in policy changes and in inconsistent decisions which exacerbated all crises.

Obviously Stalin's ability to take decisions depended to a considerable extent on the information which reached his desk. He received an enormous amount of information. It included drafts of decisions and other official documents, reports from the OGPU-NKVD, memoranda on events sent to him through the party, letters and appeals from numerous state and party officials, reports from various supervisory agencies, information from TASS (the official press agency), reports from Soviet ambassadors, excerpts from the foreign press, and letters from some ordinary citizens. The documents in the archives, including Stalin's personal archive, do not enable us to reconstruct adequately the range of information which Stalin actually received and took seriously in different periods. In any case he could not have devoted equal attention to all these materials; undoubtedly a lot of them were never read.

However, the correspondence with Kaganovich provides grounds for concluding that Stalin based his view of his environment primarily on the reports and communications of his immediate colleagues. A considerable amount of his time was taken up with reading their numerous memoranda and draft decrees, and considerable space in his letters was devoted to discussing them. This concentration on the routine activity of the machinery of party and state fully corresponded to his belief in the power of the state and party machines, and of administrative measures. Such attempts to solve urgent problems by reorganizing the administration are characteristic of many administrators in many countries at various levels of government. But Stalin was a particularly strong advocate of this faith in administration. In his letters in the summer of 1932, when agriculture was undergoing a severe crisis, he devoted a great deal of attention to reorganizing the People's Commissariat of Agriculture. In a long letter dated 17 July (document 47) he criticized the policy of the PC of Agriculture and proposed to hive off the management of state farms into a special commissariat, leaving the PC of Agriculture the responsibility for administering the MTS and the collective farms. On 5 August 1932 (document 55) Stalin even claimed that "the main shortcoming in the work of the leadership bodies (top and bottom) <u>in agriculture</u> consists (<u>at this</u> moment) of <u>organizational</u> lapses." In this connection he proposed to "destroy the system of <u>collective-farm centers</u> from top to bottom, as a system that is already unnecessary, and transfer its functionaries to agencies of the PC of Agriculture and the new state-farm PC." The application of this policy eliminated from agriculture the last remaining quasi-cooperative organizations in agriculture. In addition, Stalin proposed in the same letter a plan which would split up the MTS so that each MTS would belong to a subagency specializing on a major crop (including grain, cotton, sugar beet, and flax). The majority of collective farms, however, produced more than one crop, and the application of this proposal led to even greater organizational problems than before. Belief in the omnipotence of administrative reorganization was a major feature of Soviet policy before Stalin came to power and continued until the collapse of the USSR. It often prevented the introduction of serious reforms.

The documents do not deal with all the important decisions and events of these years. Thus in 1932 Stalin had no correspondence with

Kaganovich about the famous expedition to the Arctic led by Otto Shmidt, or about the opening of the first synthetic rubber factory in Yaroslavl, or about the opening of various metal works. All these events took place during his leave. In 1933, Stalin and Kaganovich did not correspond about the achievement during Stalin's leave of a world air-balloon record, or about the first production of Soviet nickel at Ufalei, or about the first ferro-alloys at Zaporozhe. Almost nothing was said about the expansion of the education system, or its problems. In a letter written in September 1933 (document 67) Stalin reported that he did not intend to read the draft decree on the major reform of the factory technical schools (FZU). This was partly because he concentrated his attention on what he regarded as the key problems of Soviet policy, especially on what was going wrong. And some questions were in practice left to Stalin's lieutenants in spite of their importance to Stalin's vision of Soviet development. In particular, with the exception of some cases of dramatic interventions or interference by Stalin, discussed below, industrial problems were largely left in the hands of the redoubtable Ordzhonikidze.

Although there were important matters with which Stalin did not deal, there were many matters which he took firmly into his own hands. Before the archives were opened, it was generally believed that until the later 1930s Stalin paid little attention to foreign policy. Thus Jonathan Haslam, perhaps the best-informed of Western historians of Soviet foreign policy, wrote that "Stalin himself appears, at least from the documents now available, to have only rarely taken a direct hand in the day-to-day running of diplomacy; it was simply not his forte."[21] The Politburo protocols, and correspondence such as that between Stalin and Kaganovich, reveal, however, that even in the early 1930s Stalin followed and took decisions on Soviet foreign relations, on matters both large and small.

And documents released in recent years, including the present correspondence, demonstrate conclusively that Stalin himself was the main inspirer and organizer of the policy of terror and compulsion. The Stalinist leadership resorted to mass arrests and executions as normal methods of governing the country and overcoming the frequent problems and crises. For example, Stalin's correspondence with Kaganovich finally shows who was the author of the famous law of 7 August

---

21. J. Haslam, *Soviet Foreign Policy, 1930–33: The Impact of the Depression* (London and Basingstoke, 1983), 18.

1932, which became a symbol of the Stalinist era. This law encouraged the introduction of what Stalin himself called "Draconian" measures against the theft of socialist property (document 49). Introduced in conditions of famine, its measures were directed to a considerable extent against starving peasants who cut off ears of grain in the collective-farm fields in order to save their lives (this is why the law became popularly known as the "law on the five ears of grain"). By 15 January 1933, five months after it was introduced, the law had led to the sentencing of 103,000 people. Data are available on 79,000 of these: 4,880, or 6.2 percent, were sentenced to be executed, and more than 26,000, or 33 percent, were sentenced to ten years' deprivation of freedom.[22] Most of those sentenced were peasants. Stalin's letters also show that in addition to being the author of the law, he set out its theoretical justification.

Stalin's colleagues in the Politburo were an obstacle to his drive to establish a personal dictatorship. The Stalin group, emerging as the victor in the fierce struggle within the party in the 1920s, was notable for its cohesion and its subordination to its leader. But at first this subordination did not take the form of absolute dependence on the dictator. The members of the Politburo recognized the primacy of Stalin, but also considered themselves to be political personages in their own right, masters of the departments of state of which they were in charge. In the first phase of the final victory of the Stalin group a residual tradition of "collective leadership" remained in the party; and meetings of the Politburo, Orgburo, and Secretariat were held quite regularly. But after the destruction of the oppositions within the party, the members of the top leadership were the only serious factor in the political system which limited Stalin's undivided power (although he sometimes had to give way to the pressure of the mass of the people).

The elimination of the role of his immediate entourage as an obstacle to his power was one of the major problems which Stalin resolved in the period covered by this book. This outcome was facilitated by the lack of unity in the Politburo, by the growth of conflicts within the Stalin group. Discord between Politburo members was aggravated both by personal factors and by disputes among the government departments for which they were responsible. Each member actively de-

22. I. E. Zelenin, " 'Zakon o pyati koloskakh': Razrabotka i osushchestvlenie," *Voprosy istorii,* no. 1, 1998, 121. Note, however, that the law in its initial extreme form was unworkable, and important modifications to it were introduced on Stalin's authority without being reported in the press.

fended "his" institution and "his" people. There were numerous clashes in the government and the Politburo about the distribution of materials and investment, and about decisions which helped some government departments but harmed the interests of others. There was a permanent state of conflict, an inherent consequence of the system of state administration, between the different People's Commissariats and the leadership of Sovnarkom and Gosplan. While every commissariat sought to obtain more favorable conditions for its work, and demanded increased investment and lighter plans, the government and Gosplan opposed these tendencies, and sought to achieve a balance of major interests. This was the context of the numerous conflicts between Ordzhonikidze and Molotov referred to in the Stalin-Kaganovich correspondence (see, for example, documents 2 and 3). Kaganovich, when he was appointed people's commissar of transport at the beginning of 1935, himself participated as a representative of his commissariat in similar conflicts, as he recalled many years later:

> Khrushchev writes that Molotov and I were on bad terms, at daggers drawn, and that we quarreled. This is untrue. When he and I worked in the Central Committee, we worked in harmony, but when he became chairman of Sovnarkom, and I became a minister [i.e. people's commissar], we had disputes on practical issues. I claimed additional rails [for the railroads] and more investment, and Mezhlauk, head of Gosplan, did not let me have them, and Molotov supported him. [. . .] On the same grounds Khrushchev claims that Ordzhonikidze, like me, quarreled and fought with Molotov. But Sergo [Ordzhonikidze], like me, quarreled with him about investments and his treatment of industry. We argued, and we appealed to Stalin. This offended Molotov—why are we complaining about Sovnarkom? But we considered that the Politburo was the supreme court of appeal.[23]

The correspondence published in the present book confirms that Stalin was in fact the supreme arbitrator in conflicts between government departments. Stalin's great advantage was that he acted as the incarnation and expression of general state interests, that he fought against departmental egoism and bureaucracy, against those he described as "the high-and-mighty bureaucrats, who are seeking medals for their fellow bureaucrat pals" (document 9), and against the "bureaucratic self-importance" and "backwardness and inertia" of the senior administrators (document 8). In his letter of 4 September 1931 (document 9)

---

23. Chuev, *Tak govoril Kaganovich*, 61.

he protested against the attempts of the People's Commissariat of Supply to create its own reserve stock of grain. Shortly afterward the Politburo and Sovnarkom resolved to concentrate the stocks of grain and other commodities in the Untouchable and State Reserves (*fondy*), which were administered by a special Committee on Reserves, which was independent of the People's Commissariats.[24] On 6 September 1931 (document 11), Stalin and Molotov strongly criticized the attempts of Vesenkha to decide on its own responsibility how to use the part of its foreign currency allocation which it had managed not to spend: "The savings of 4 million in hard currency belongs to the state coffers rather than Vesenkha, which does not have and should not have coffers. We are against an anarcho-syndicalist view of the state, under which profits from savings go to Vesenkha while losses go to the state. We believe that the state is above Vesenkha." A few days later Stalin called for an end to the practice that the party Central Committee could approve the decisions of government departments, in place of Sovnarkom; he saw this as an attempt to "to turn the CC from a leadership body into an auxiliary body for the parochial needs of the people's commissariats" (document 13). In October 1933 Stalin suggested that Ordzhonikidze "should be flogged" because, by entrusting the management of the artillery factories to "two or three of his favorite fools, [. . .] he is prepared to sacrifice the state's interests to these fools" (document 82).

In the course of his battles with the government departments Stalin often came into conflict with his colleagues, particularly in 1931. Although the conflicts were fierce, he tried to bring about compromises which would maintain a certain equilibrium and stability in the Politburo. At this time he considered that it was not permissible to undermine the ruling group, "which historically evolved in a struggle against all types of opportunism" (document 2). This attitude was to a considerable extent due to the growth of the crisis of 1931–33, which weakened the position of Stalin. But as the crisis was overcome Stalin's behavior changed. The correspondence with Kaganovich illustrates this change. His letters in the summer and autumn of 1933 became increasingly demanding and caustic. (This may be one of the things which Kaganovich had in mind when he later spoke about a "different" Stalin after 1932.) The members of the Politburo sought to main-

---

24. RGASPI, f. 17, op. 162, d. 11, l. 24 (decision of the Politburo dated 10 October 1931); GARF, f. R-5446, op. 57, d. 16, l. 53 (Sovnarkom decree dated 19 October 1931).

tain their authority, as is shown by the conflict about Vyshinsky's speech, during which Stalin irascibly reproved Kaganovich and Molotov (see documents 62, 64, 65).

In the following years the system of the collective leadership of the party was increasingly disrupted, and the autocratic power of Stalin increased. This was facilitated by the death of two members of the Politburo: Kirov, who perished as a result of a terrorist act on 1 December 1934, and Kuibyshev, who died at the beginning of 1935. In February and March 1935, on Stalin's initiative, the Politburo took decisions which provided much of the organizational framework for the new arrangements in the higher levels of the party. Andreev, a Politburo member, was released from his post as people's commissar of transport and appointed as a secretary of the Central Committee. Kaganovich was appointed in his place; he retained his position as a secretary of the Central Committee but ceased to be chair of the Commission of Party Control (attached to the Central Committee) or secretary of the Moscow party organization. In place of Kaganovich, Yezhov was appointed chair of the Commission of Party Control, and Yezhov had also recently been made a secretary of the Central Committee. Khrushchev was promoted to Kaganovich's previous post as secretary of the Moscow Regional Party Committee. Andreev and Yezhov were placed in charge of the work of the Orgburo, the party body which was second in importance only to the Politburo.[25] Until then it had been Kaganovich's fiefdom.

These changes in personnel at the beginning of 1935 dispersed the influence of Stalin's closest colleagues. With the appointment of Yezhov and Khrushchev began the gradual promotion of a new generation of leaders to the higher levels of power. Kaganovich to a considerable extent lost his position as Stalin's first deputy in the party, which he had occupied for several years. Formally he was replaced by Andreev as the secretary of the Central Committee in charge of the Orgburo. But Andreev's influence on its work was weakened from the outset by the statement that Yezhov was to participate in the management of the Orgburo, and because Kaganovich remained both a secretary of the Central Committee and a member of the Orgburo. Moreover, Andreev, once a member of a party opposition, was a timid and gray figure with few ideas of his own. The correspondence in this book shows

---

25. *Stalinskoe Politbiuro v 30-e gody; Ssbornik dokumentov,* ed. O. V. Khlevniuk, A. V. Kvashonkin, L. P. Kosheleva, and L. A. Rogovaya (Moscow, 1995), 142–33.

that during Stalin's leave in 1935 and 1936, Kaganovich was generally responsible for the work of the Politburo.

In 1935 and 1936 Politburo sittings were no longer convened regularly. On average, they were held less than once a month, and in 1936 only nine sittings were convened, while in 1930–33, seven or eight sittings of different kinds took place every month. Henceforth most decisions were taken by poll, and the practice became widespread of summoning meetings of a few Politburo members. These effectively replaced the regular official sittings.[26]

Unlike the documents for previous years, the documents of 1935 and 1936 no longer contain evidence of the open assertion of their rights by members of the Politburo in such forms as threats to resign or ultimatums about the needs of the government departments for which they were responsible. The Stalin-Kaganovich correspondence is a sensitive indicator of the new relationships within the Politburo. Stalin's letters became more laconic and imperative, and Kaganovich's replies less independent and more flattering. It is noteworthy that in 1935–36 Kaganovich's letters to other members of the Politburo included flattering and often clumsy panegyrics to Stalin. This is shown by three of his letters to Ordzhonikidze:

> Things are going well here. To sum it up briefly, I can briefly repeat what Mikoian and I said to comrade Kalinin when he went off to Sochi. Before his departure he asked us what to tell the Boss? We told him, say that "the country and party are so well charged up with energy that although the chief marksman is resting the army is still firing." For example, what has happened with the grain procurements this year is our completely unprecedented stupefying victory—the victory of Stalinism.[27]

> Unfortunately it was necessary to burden the Boss with a lot of issues, although it is impossible to put into words how valuable his health is for us who love him so much, and for the whole country.[28]

> This, my boy, is the outstanding dialectic in politics which our great friend and father has mastered completely.[29]

26. O. V. Khlevniuk, *Politburo: Mekhanizmy politicheskoi vlasti v 1930-e gody* (Moscow, 1996), 164, 288.

27. *Stalinskoe Politburo v 30-e gody*, 146 (letter to Ordzhonikidze dated 4 September 1935).

28. Ibid., 148–49 (letter to Ordzhonikidze dated 30 September 1936).

29. Ibid., 151 (letter to Ordzhonikidze dated 12 October 1936).

The final stage in the process of eliminating collective leadership and turning the members of the Politburo into powerless senior officials under the dictatorial leader took place in the course of the Great Terror in 1937–38. Ordzhonikidze committed suicide (or was killed) as a result of his conflict with Stalin.[30] In 1938–39 five members or candidate members of the Politburo were executed—S. V. Kosior, Eikhe, Rudzutak, Chubar, and Postyshev—and G. I. Petrovsky was removed from office.[31] Stalin kept even his closest colleagues in a state of permanent tension before the war. He removed Molotov's wife, Zhemchuzhina, from her post as a people's commissar and removed her from the Central Committee for political reasons (after the war she was arrested). Various accusations were made against Kaganovich. Kaganovich's brother, the people's commissar of the aircraft industry, was threatened with arrest, and committed suicide.

Kaganovich and the other members of the Politburo never again held such an authoritative and relatively independent position as at the beginning of the 1930s. And Stalin never again engaged in such a frank and detailed correspondence with his colleagues as in the present correspondence with Kaganovich.

30. See O. Khlevniuk, *In Stalin's Shadow: The Career of "Sergo" Ordzhonikidze* (New York, 1995).

31. See R. Medvedev, *O Staline i Stalinizme* (Moscow, 1994); R. Conquest, *The Great Terror: A Reassessment* (New York, 1990); R. Tucker, *Stalin in Power: The Revolution from Above, 1928–1941* (New York, 1992).

Lazar Kaganovich:
The Career of a Stalinist Commissar

L AZAR MOISEYEVICH KAGANOVICH was one of the most important and colorful figures in the ruling Stalinist group which dominated the life of the Soviet Union from Lenin's death in 1924 until the defeat of the "Antiparty" group in 1957. For most of this time he was a member of the Politburo, and for a critical but relatively short period, which coincides with the period covered by the letters published in this work, he was widely seen as Stalin's heir apparent. Despite his immense importance, Kaganovich's role inside the Stalinist leadership has been relatively neglected by historians.[1] As the last survivor of that leadership, Kaganovich was one of the few who left his own, albeit highly selective, account of these fateful years.[2] The Stalin-Kaganovich correspondence sheds important new light on the inner working of the ruling group of which he was a major player.

Kaganovich was born in 1893 into a poor Jewish family in the village of Kabana, Chernobyl county, Ukraine. At the age of thirteen he completed his formal education and went to work in Kiev, where after spells of unemployment and a series of unskilled jobs he became a shoemaker in a factory. In 1911 he joined the Bolshevik party, follow-

---

1. The best biography to date is by the Italian historian L. Marcucci, *Il commissario di ferro di Stalin* (Turin, 1997). See also the brief sketch in R. Medvedev, *All Stalin's Men* (Oxford, 1983), and the fuller account in R. Medvedev, S. Parfenov, and P. Khmelinsky, *Zheleznyi yastreb* (Yekaterinburg, 1992). And see Yurii Shapoval, *Lazar Kaganovich* (Kiev, 1994). The work by E. Evseev, *Satrap* (Moscow, 1993) is of questionable value, as is the work by the supposed American "nephew" of Kaganovich, S. Kahan, *The Wolf in the Kremlin* (London, 1989).

2. F. Chuev, *Tak govoril Kaganovich* (Moscow, 1992); L. M. Kaganovich, *Moi 20 vek* (Moscow, 1996).

ing the lead of his older brother, Mikhail. He was active in the union of
leather workers, which was renowned for its militancy. In 1915 he and
his wife Maria left Kiev and went to work in Yekaterinoslav, Meli-
topol, and finally Yuzovka, where he became deputy chairman of the
local soviet following the overthrow of the tsar.

Largely self-educated, but widely read, Kaganovich was a model of
the Bolshevik worker-intellectual. His hopes of higher education had
been dashed at an early stage. He was intelligent, lively, quick-witted,
energetic, and ambitious. He had enormous self-confidence and possessed a will of iron. He spoke Russian, Ukrainian, and Yiddish. Until
1917 he had no experience of life outside Ukraine, and he was practically unknown outside the confined circles of Bolshevik and trade
union activists in these centers. Kaganovich came from a warm, secure
family background, which was blighted by poverty. His personal life
remained remarkably stable. He embraced Bolshevism, the most militant wing of Russian Social Democracy, out of conviction.

Following the February revolution in 1917, Kaganovich returned to
Kiev, where he was inducted into the army. In his memoirs he glosses
over this event, which was clearly a source of embarrassment. He implies that he was sent by the party into the army to undertake propaganda work.[3] In the army in Saratov he actively involved himself in agitation. He attended the all-Russian conference of Bolshevik military
organizations in St. Petersburg in June 1917 and was elected to the All-
Russian Bureau of Military Party Organizations attached to the Central Committee. On his return to Saratov he was arrested and dispatched to the front, but was released at Gomel as a result of protests
by local Social Democrats. In the following months he was active in
the party organization in Gomel and Mogilyov and played a key role
in the Bolshevik seizure of power in these centers.

From January 1918 he was a member of the All-Russian Collegium
for Organizing the Workers' and Peasants' Red Army and was responsible for propaganda and recruitment. He had by this stage established
close links with leading Bolsheviks involved in matters of military organization. In May 1918 he was sent by the Central Committee to
Nizhny Novgorod, where he quickly established himself as head of the
Bolshevik party organization. Nizhny was a frontline town, threatened directly by the advance of the Czechoslovak Legion, which in
August 1918 overran Kazan. In 1918–19 the province experienced

3. Kaganovich, *Moi 20 vek,* 98.

dozens of peasant risings, while, at the nearby giant Sormovo engineering complex, Mensheviks and Socialist Revolutionaries led a number of major strikes against the Bolshevik authorities.

In August 1918 Lenin ordered the authorities in Nizhny Novgorod to immediately institute a "mass terror" to extinguish the threat of counterrevolution.[4] Kaganovich as party boss, then just twenty-four years of age, oversaw this policy, which included the execution of bourgeois "hostages." In this campaign he was assisted by the leadership of the Eastern Military Front, headed by Trotsky. Drawing on this experience, Kaganovich elaborated organizational proposals to dramatically tighten up political control in Nizhny and to galvanize the local party organization to ensure its survival. With Machiavellian guile he stressed the need for the party to conceal its role in these terrible events, assigning the public role to the forerunner of the OGPU, the Cheka, and the Revolutionary Tribunal. He also staunchly defended the Cheka against its critics.[5]

In 1919 Kaganovich advanced sweeping measures for the militarization of the Bolshevik party at the national level. At the same time he voiced his full support for the employment of former tsarist officers in the Red Army, albeit under strict political control. This position was remarkably close to that expounded by Trotsky. Lenin remained reluctant to embrace this policy, while Stalin and the leadership of the Southern Front were adamantly opposed. Nevertheless, the VIII party congress in March 1919 adopted the two basic principles—militarization of the party and the employment of tsarist officers—as official policy.[6]

Kaganovich's experiences in Nizhny helped to shape his political development. He emerged as an extremely effective organizer, a man of great energy and implacable willpower. In carrying through the "red terror" he had willingly accepted the demands made to secure the survival of the Bolshevik regime. In 1919 Kaganovich became the most vocal and articulate advocate of centralization in party and state management. In challenging the views of senior party figures on organizational matters he demonstrated that he was a man to be reckoned with. The ideas which he advocated in 1918–19 were to become the prevailing orthodoxy of the Bolshevik party after Lenin's death.

4. V. I. Lenin, *Polnoe sobranie sochinenii*, vol. 50 (Moscow, 1965), 142–43.

5. See Kaganovich's report in *Stenograficheskii otchet 5-i Nizhegorodskoi gubernskoi konferentsii RKP (bolshevikov)* (Nizhny Novgorod, 1918), 68.

6. R. Service, *The Bolshevik Party in Revolution* (London, 1982), 106–10. F. Benvenuti, *The Bolsheviks and the Red Army, 1918–1922* (Cambridge, UK, 1988), 72–74.

In September 1919 Kaganovich volunteered for service on the Southern Front for the defense of Voronezh. In September 1920 the Central Committee sent him to work in Turkestan. The full story of Kaganovich's role in Voronezh and Turkestan remains to be told. Both were centers where the very survival of the revolution was in the balance and where counterrevolution was ruthlessly suppressed. As effective leader of Turkestan in 1920–21, during the illness of Sokolnikov, Kaganovich had oversight of the bloody military campaign to suppress the Basmachi rebellion, although Lenin also charged him with developing a policy aimed at winning the support of the Moslem population for Soviet power.

At the X party congress in March 1921 Kaganovich voted in favor of Lenin's proposals on the trade unions and for the resolution outlawing the "Anarcho-Syndicalist deviation."[7] In Turkestan, prior to the congress, he waged a furious campaign against Trotsky's plans to merge the trade unions into the state apparatus and against the Workers' opposition plans to transfer the management of industry to the trade unions. By 1921, despite his close association with Trotsky in 1918–19, he had resolutely broken with him. Following the congress he was briefly assigned to the All-Russian Central Council of Trade Unions to assist in purging the unions of supporters of the Workers' opposition.

Kaganovich's career received a dramatic boost in 1922, when he was appointed to work in the party Secretariat in Moscow as head of the Organizational and Instruction Department (Orgotdel), and again in 1924, when he became head of the Organizational and Assignment Department (Orgraspred). He was brought into the Secretariat, he recalls in his memoirs, through the influence of Valerian Kuibyshev, with whom he had worked in Central Asia.[8] In the Secretariat he was responsible for the appointment of cadres and for organizing party instructors and inspectors. He worked alongside Molotov, but was directly responsible to Kuibyshev and then to Stalin, with whom he began to forge a close relationship. He played a key role in developing the *nomenklatura* system for the central appointment of state and party officials, which was to provide Stalin with his power base in his struggles with Trotsky and Bukharin.

---

7. *Desiatyi sezd RKP(b), mart 1921 goda: Stenograficheskii otchet* (Moscow, 1963), 770, 775.

8. Kaganovich, *Moi 20 vek*, 251–52.

Kaganovich's career was based on his expertise in party organizational and personnel matters. But he was much more than simply a backroom administrator. In 1923 he spearheaded the successful campaign to discredit Trotsky within the Moscow party organization during the last relatively free discussion within the party.[9]

In 1924 Kaganovich took charge of the "Lenin enrollment," which brought an influx of 200,000 industrial workers into the Communist Party. He was responsible for the admission and political education of the new members. In 1924 he published his pamphlet *Kak postroena RKP(b)* (How the Russian Communist Party Is Organized). This work, which was widely published in the following years, outlined the basic principles of party organization which all new members should know. It took as its basis Lenin's pamphlet *Chto Delat?* (What Is to Be Done?) of 1903, with its uncompromising defense of party centralization, activism, and discipline. It made no reference to internal party democracy, except to cite with warm approval Stalin's comment to the party conference: "our party is distinguished by the fact that it does not fetishize the question of democracy: it does not consider it as 'something absolute, beyond time and space.' On the contrary, democracy is not something given for all times and conditions, for there are moments when it is not possible or wise to implement it."[10]

In 1924 and 1925 Kaganovich also took a major part in the campaign to revitalize the local soviets. Widespread peasant abstentions in soviet elections underlined the Soviet regime's weakness and the alienation of the rural population from its government. This was dramatized by the Georgian peasants rising against Soviet rule in August 1924.[11] In the years following Lenin's death, Kaganovich emphasized the importance of Lenin's final writings, particularly his stress on conciliating the peasants, in providing the guidelines for government policies.

The Secretariat in these years was the forge in which the future Stalinist leadership was shaped. The Secretariat come to dominate the life of the party, and the officials whom Stalin gathered around him came to exert enormous influence. In the 1920s the Secretariat posted officials to the republics and regions to implement central policies: A. A. Andreev to the North Caucasus, Sulimov to the Urals, Bauman to

9. Ibid., 340–45.
10. Kaganovich, *Kak postroena RKP (Bolshevikov): Ob ustave partii* (Moscow, 1924).
11. E. H. Carr, *Socialism in One Country, 1924–1926*, vol. 2 (London, 1970), ch. 22.

Moscow, Vareikis to the Central Black-Earth Region, Sheboldaev to the Lower Volga, and Khataevich to the Central Volga.[12]

In April 1925 Kaganovich was appointed general secretary of the Ukrainian Communist Party. He was nominated by the Politburo in Moscow, and the Ukrainian Central Committee confirmed it, although other, more senior Ukrainian leaders, such as Petrovsky and Chubar, had asked that Molotov be given the post and strongly resented Kaganovich's appointment.[13] This was his first major position. His task was to secure the loyalty of the Ukrainian party to Stalin. He replaced Emmanuil Kviring, who sympathized with Zinoviev. The appointment was a bold one. As a Jew, Kaganovich was the target of anti-Semitic attack, even though he had roots in Ukraine and spoke the language.

As leader of the Ukrainian party Kaganovich initially supported the New Economic Policy and, despite criticism from the left, introduced further concessions to the peasantry as part of the policy of "face to the countryside." However, in 1926 he emerged increasingly as an advocate of industrialization. He supported the plan to build the giant Dnieper hydroelectric station, at a time when Stalin was unenthusiastic, and he pressed for a central role to be assigned to Ukraine in the plan for the industrial transformation of the USSR.

Kaganovich from 1925 onward promoted the policy of Ukrainization, which involved the advancement of Ukrainian cadres and the recruitment of Ukrainians into the party. Ukrainian was made the official language of the party, the state, trade unions, and the army in the republic, and its use was promoted in the schools and in the mass media. This developed the nationalities policy which Stalin had expounded at the XIII party congress. The aim behind this strategy was to create a base of support for the Communist Party among the predominantly peasant population of the republic. It was also intended to be part of a strategy to turn Ukraine into a model socialist republic, which would serve as a beacon for revolutionary movements in eastern Europe.[14]

Ukrainization encountered bitter opposition from the Russian-domi-

---

12. J. Hughes, "Patrimonialism and the Stalinist System: The Case of S. I. Syrtsov," *Europe-Asia Studies*, 48 (1996), 557.

13. "Vokrug stati L. D. Trotskogo 'Uroki Oktyabrya,'" *Izvestiia TsK KPSS*, no. 8, 1991, 180–90.

14. J. E. Mace, *Communism and the Dilemmas of National Liberation: National Communism in Soviet Ukraine, 1918–1933* (Cambridge, Mass., 1983).

nated party and trade union movement in Ukraine and was also opposed by the left wing of the Communist Party. At this time the great
majority of the urban population of Ukraine were Russian speakers.
Kaganovich also clashed with those in the Ukrainian Communist
Party, led by the people's commissar of education, A. Ya. Shumsky,
who wanted the policy of Ukrainization to be implemented with still
more determination. In this struggle, in 1926, Stalin adopted a neutral
stance, even censuring Kaganovich for his conduct.[15] In the end, Shumsky was defeated and disgraced.

In June 1926 Kaganovich was elected a candidate member of the
Politburo of the USSR Communist Party. In 1926–28 he waged an implacable campaign against the United opposition, employing ruthless
tactics to ensure that the opposition were not accorded a hearing in
Ukraine. Like other supporters of Stalin, however, he embraced many
of the policies of the left.

At the end of 1927 Kaganovich further shifted his position. He became a convinced advocate of rapid industrialization. During the grain
procurement crisis of 1927–28 Kaganovich and the Ukrainian leadership adopted a hard line, enforcing a ruthless policy of requisitioning,
and arguing against a policy of grain imports. With the war scare of
1927 the Ukrainian leadership was put on alert, with Kaganovich conducting a tour of the frontier zone. In the spring of 1928, following the
Shakhty trial of mining engineers, a rigorous investigation into the loyalty of the engineers in the Donets Basin was carried out by the Ukrainian GPU with Kaganovich's blessing.

In Ukraine his abrasive and highly authoritarian style of leadership
brought his relations with Petrovsky and Chubar to breaking point. In
June 1928 Stalin resolved to recall him from Ukraine. This appears to
have been part of the price which Stalin had to pay to secure the support of the Ukrainian leadership.

Kaganovich's recall from Ukraine did not signal any decline in his
influence. He returned to work in the party Secretariat, where he again
assumed responsibility for the party instructors and for cadres policy.
This was of critical importance in the developing struggle with the
Right opposition. In 1928 he played an active part in the defeat of
Uglanov in the Moscow party organization, and in December 1928 he
was appointed to the presidium of the All-Union Central Council of

---

15. M. I. Panchuk, "Natsional-ukhil'nitsvo," in *Anatomia problemi: Marshrutami istorii*
(Kiev, 1990), 221–22.

Trade Unions (AUCCTU) to lead the campaign to discredit Tomsky and to reorient the trade unions under the slogan "Face to production." To the charge that this was a violation of proletarian democracy, Kaganovich responded with his stock reply that for Bolsheviks democracy was not a fetish.[16]

The area in which Kaganovich made a decisive impact in these years, however, was agricultural policy. In 1928 he won the enmity of the Right for his uncompromising defense of the "extraordinary measures" for obtaining grain by coercion. Then in 1929 he played a major role in the institutionalization of the "Urals-Siberian method" for obtaining grain, which was approved by the Politburo in March 1929, following Kaganovich's tour of Siberia and his consultation with the Siberian leaders. It involved mobilizing the poor and middle peasants against the kulaks through peasant meetings at which grain procurement targets were allocated to individual households. The peasant meetings were also induced to adopt "self-imposed obligations" for the remainder of the peasants—a measure intended to confer a degree of popular legitimacy on these policies.[17]

The Urals-Siberian method came unstuck in the second half of 1929. In the face of increased state procurement targets and pressure to push the peasants into the collective farms, the policy of splitting the peasants along class lines failed, and the regime was confronted by the opposition of the peasants as a whole. In truth, the Urals-Siberian method was never much more than a cover for the implementation of state policy in the countryside by coercion. In December 1929 the Politburo endorsed collectivization, and in January 1930 it approved the policy of "dekulakization." By 1930 all pretense had been dropped: Kaganovich oversaw the implementation of collectivization in Siberia and in the Volga regions.[18] He led the attack on those institutions which had failed to mobilize the poor peasants—the local soviets, lower party bodies, the poor peasants' committees, and the women's department of the party (abolished in 1930). Kaganovich also actively recruited and rallied urban activists for work in the countryside.

16. E. H. Carr and R. W. Davies, *Foundations of a Planned Economy, 1926–1929*, vol. 1 (London, 1969), 556–63. See Kaganovich's report to the XVI party congress—*XVI s"ezd VKP(b): Stenograficheskii otchet* (Moscow, 1930), 122.

17. Y. Taniuchi, "Decision-Making on the Urals-Siberian Method," in J. Cooper, M. Perrie, and E. A. Rees, eds., *Soviet History, 1917–1953* (Basingstoke and London, 1995), 78–103.

18. J. Hughes, *Stalinism in a Russian Province: Collectivisation and Dekulakisation in Siberia* (Basingstoke and London, 1996), 187–92, 194–97.

Following the defeat of the Right, Kaganovich was propelled to the apex of the party leadership. From 1930 onward he occupied the third place, after Stalin and Molotov. In July 1930 he was elected a full member of the Politburo. With the appointment of Molotov to head the Council of People's Commissars (Sovnarkom) in December 1930, Kaganovich took over the Organizational Bureau of the Central Committee, or Orgburo, and the Secretariat. He also assumed responsibility for managing the affairs of the Politburo, although the sessions of the Politburo were chaired by Molotov, and was involved in the work of a plethora of Politburo commissions. During Stalin's prolonged summer absences from Moscow, Kaganovich signed the minutes of the Politburo.

In April 1930 Kaganovich was also appointed secretary of the Moscow party organization, following the ouster of Bauman. He led an uncompromising struggle to crush all remnants of opposition within the Moscow party organization. Under his vigorous leadership the Moscow party was turned into a flagship organization. The industrial economy of the city and region was transformed. Kaganovich assembled a team of energetic administrators, including Khrushchev, Bulganin, Malenkov, and Ryndin, who oversaw this work. Given Kaganovich's enormous burden of work in the central party apparatus, much decisionmaking power had to be delegated to his subordinates, most notably Khrushchev.

The most dramatic development of these years was the transformation of "Red Moscow" into a modern capital. Kaganovich oversaw the destruction of a large part of the city's ancient architectural inheritance. But he also presided over two new giant construction projects: the building of the Metro, the first section of which opened in 1935, and the building, with GPU convict labor, of the Moscow-Volga Canal. Without Stalin's authorization these projects could not have been realized, but it was Kaganovich who provided much of the energy and drive in developing and implementing them. In 1935 the newly opened Metro was named after Kaganovich in recognition of his contribution.[19]

While holding down his responsibilities in the central and Moscow party organizations, Kaganovich was also assigned other tasks. In July

19. C. Merridale, *Moscow Politics and the Rise of Stalin: The Communist Party in the Capital, 1925–32* (Basingstoke and London, 1990); N. Shimotomai, *Moscow Under Stalinist Rule, 1931–34* (Basingstoke and London, 1991); T. J. Colton, *Moscow: Governing the Socialist Metropolis* (Cambridge, Mass., 1995).

1932 he and Molotov were sent to attend the Ukrainian party conference in Kiev to lay down the law regarding the necessity of meeting the
center's procurement targets for grain.[20] Stalin briefly considered re-
assigning Kaganovich to head the Ukrainian party organization, but
decided that he could not afford to lose him from the Secretariat. At
the end of 1932, as the famine crisis deepened, Kaganovich was sent to
the North Caucasus to quell peasant unrest with military force and to
organize the expulsion of whole Cossack villages.[21]

In 1933 Kaganovich was the architect of the new system of administrative control in agriculture, based on the one developed during the
civil war, of creating political departments (the notorious *politotdely*)
in the state farms and the Machine-Tractor Stations (MTS). In 1933 he
was placed in charge of the party's purge commission to expel disloyal
and unsuitable elements. At the XVII party congress he presented the
proposals for the abolition of the Central Control Commission and the
Workers' and Peasants' Inspectorate and to create a new system of
party and state control. He himself was appointed chairman of the
new Commission of Party Control.

For a period in the early 1930s it appeared as though Kaganovich
had eclipsed Molotov as Stalin's right-hand man. A veritable cult developed around Kaganovich, particularly within the Moscow party organizations. The cult reached its apogee at the Moscow party conference in January 1934, where delegate after delegate poured effusive
praise on him.[22] At the XVII party congress a few weeks later many
delegates coupled the names Stalin and Kaganovich as the embodi-
ment of the party leadership. In the celebrations of the October revolution in 1934 and 1935 the portraits of Kaganovich were second in
prominence only to those of Stalin. Western journalists speculated on
whether Kaganovich would succeed Stalin.[23]

From the mid-1920s onward Kaganovich was a key figure within
the ruling Stalin group. His loyalty was to Stalin above all. It is difficult
to find occasions after 1928 when Kaganovich took a stance on policy
at variance with Stalin's. He closely followed every shift in Stalin's line.

20. H. Kostiuk, *Stalinist Rule in the Ukraine: A Study of the Decade of Mass Terror
(1929–39)* (London, 1960), 18–21.

21. N. Shimotomai, "A Note on the Kuban Affair (1932–1933): The Crisis of Kolkhoz
Agriculture in the North Caucasus," *Acta Slavica Iaponica*, Tomus I (1983), 46.

22. *IV Moskovskaya oblastnaya i III gorodskaya konferentsii Vsesoyuznoi Kommunisticheskoi Partii (b)* (Moscow, 1934).

23. "Is He Driving Towards Supreme Power in Russia?" *Christian Science Monitor*, 1
May 1935.

Given the nature of the tightly knit Stalinist group, it is extremely difficult to disentangle the contribution of individual members, but Kaganovich's influence on policy was clearly considerable. He was one of the first to enthusiastically embrace the "left turn" of 1928, lending weight to Isaac Deutscher's characterization of him as a "left Stalinist."[24]

Although he received little formal education, Kaganovich possessed considerable ability. He was an accomplished speaker. His speeches, though politically orthodox, were invariably powerfully argued and characterized by vitality, originality, and humor. He possessed an almost superhuman capacity for work, an excellent memory, and an ability to quickly adopt new approaches.[25] These talents in part explain Kaganovich's meteoric rise to prominence in the 1920s and his ability to shoulder the enormous burden of work of Stalin's deputy after 1930.

However, his lack of formal education remained apparent. Kaganovich never learned to write grammatically. His letters contain many errors. He had difficulty expressing himself on paper. He wrote his letters to Stalin in rough before making a clean copy. Even then, many mistakes remained.

Kaganovich's abrasiveness won him both the enmity of Trotsky and the hatred of the Rightists.[26] He was not trusted. He was regarded as ambitious and manipulative, as someone who could quickly change his stance on policy and who would ruthlessly abandon erstwhile friends and allies. Piatakov, one of Trotsky's closest allies until he humiliatingly capitulated to Stalin, in 1929 declared: "Stalin is the only man we must obey, for fear of getting worse. Bukharin and Rykov deceive themselves in thinking that they would govern in Stalin's place. Kaganovich and such would succeed him, and I cannot and will not obey a Kaganovich."[27]

Kaganovich shared many of the same characteristics as those who staffed the upper and middle echelons of the Stalinist party-state apparatus. He was of proletarian origin and largely self-educated; he was a

24. I. Deutscher, *The Prophet Unarmed: Trotsky, 1921–1929* (Oxford, 1970), 246.

25. See the assessments of Kaganovich given by contemporaries: B. Bajanov, *Avec Stalin dans le Kremlin* (Paris, 1930), 58; G. Bessedovsky, *Revelations of a Soviet Diplomat* (London, 1931), 219–23; B. I. Nicolaevsky, *Power and the Soviet Elite* (London, 1965), 48.

26. On Trotsky's scathing assessment of Kaganovich see L. Trotsky, *The Challenge of the Left Opposition, 1926–27* (New York, 1980), 270–90, 356, 403, and *Writings of Leon Trotsky, 1932* (New York, 1973), 22, 69.

27. Quoted in B. Souvarine, *Stalin* (London, n.d.), 489.

praktik—a party organizer and administrator—rather than a theorist, and he had impeccable civil war credentials. Already in 1918 a pattern was set in Kaganovich's career which was repeated again and again. He became the party's leading troubleshooter and was given many of the most unpleasant tasks. This role required very strong nerves. Not for nothing did Stalin call Kaganovich "Iron Lazar." If in these tasks Stalin used Kaganovich for his own ends in the full knowledge that this would stoke up the flames of popular anti-Semitism, it is also clear that Kaganovich willingly accepted that role.

Kaganovich's career cannot be understood in isolation from the internal dynamics of the ruling Stalin group and the ideas and policies which drove it. The group itself was formed in the struggle with the various opposition groups of the 1920s and around the common platform of forced industrialization and collectivization. Kaganovich identified himself wholly with that project. In the 1930s he frequently reflected on Stalin's "revolution from above" as an event which in scope and significance eclipsed the October revolution itself. Addressing the XVII party congress in 1934, he declared: "The world-historical significance of the report of Comrade Stalin to the XVII congress consists precisely in the fact that this was the report on the leadership of the greatest revolution (*perevorot*) which human history has known, a revolution which smashed the old economic structure and created a new, collective-farm system on the basis of the socialist industrialization of our country."[28]

The Politburo, bound by loyalty to Stalin, was not free of tensions and personal conflicts. Kaganovich often used to be identified by historians as being associated with a hard-line faction in the Politburo, one which was always pushing for more extreme solutions, with Stalin occupying a mediating position between hard-liners and moderates.[29] This view of the Stalin group is oversimplified. In periods of difficulty, as during the famine crisis of 1932–33, the entire leadership backed hard-line solutions, and in periods of relaxation, after 1933, they all tended to favor moderation.[30]

In the Politburo, Molotov, chairman of Sovnarkom, was closely al-

---

28. *XVII Sezd Vsesoyuznoi Kommunisticheskoi Partii (Bolshevikov): Stenograficheskii otchet* (Moscow, 1934), 525.

29. This view is well illustrated in R. Conquest, *The Great Terror: Stalin's Purges of the Thirties* (London, 1968).

30. *Stalinskoe Politbyuro v 30-e gody: Sbornik dokumentov*, ed. O. V. Khlevniuk, A.V. Kvashonkin, L. P. Kosheleva, and L. A. Rogovaya (Moscow, 1995), 90–91.

lied to Kuibyshev, head of Gosplan. Kaganovich, as party secretary, was closely tied to Ordzhonikidze, head of the People's Commissariat of Heavy Industry, who was a close personal friend. Ordzhonikidze's relations with Molotov and Kuibyshev in the early 1930s were extremely strained. Kaganovich's relations with Molotov were difficult, based on personal rivalry from the time they had been party secretaries, but his relationship with Kuibyshev appears to have remained good. Kaganovich's relations with Voroshilov were also close.

Kaganovich's relationship with Stalin was based on unquestioned loyalty. Contemporaries spoke of his slavish sycophancy. His speeches were larded with praise of the supreme leader—the *vozhd*. His devotion to Stalin was genuine, if also based on calculation. He held Stalin in awe. He could never bring himself to address him other than with the formal you (*vy*), and they addressed each other in their letters as, respectively, Comrade Stalin and Comrade Kaganovich.[31] In conversations with Chuev at the end of his life, Kaganovich compared Stalin with Robespierre—as a great revolutionary who did not flinch from pursuing the goals of the revolution.[32] Molotov, in conversation with Chuev, noted that among the Stalinist leaders, Kaganovich's uncritical admiration of Stalin was exceptional, that Kaganovich was a "200 percent Stalinist."[33]

For Kaganovich there was no dichotomy between Leninism and Stalinism. The fundamental transformations which Bolshevik ideology underwent—the rejection of egalitarianism, the reversal of nationalities policy, the suffocation of the remnants of party democracy, the strengthening of the state's coercive power—caused him no ideological qualms. He, as much as anybody, acted as the party spokesman who justified and defended these changes. In the attacks on the kulaks, the petty traders (the Nepmen), the bourgeois intelligentsia, and other anti-Soviet elements, the party had a dependable and eloquent spokesman in Kaganovich.

Kaganovich's career displays an extraordinary unity and continuity. There is little hint of any political deviation in his career. In 1918 in Nizhny Novgorod he uncompromisingly implemented "mass terror" as part of the class war, and in the Secretariat in the 1920s he defended in unambiguous terms the strictest form of party centralization. In the

---

31. Chuev, *Tak govoril Kaganovich*, 129.
32. Ibid., 56, 140.
33. F. Chuev, *Sto sorok besed s Molotovym* (Moscow, 1991), 53, 54.

struggle with the opposition he was implacable, reserving particular scorn for groups like the Workers' opposition, the most resolute defenders of proletarian democracy. Immensely proud of his own proletarian background, Kaganovich had an unsentimental attitude toward the working class, and his view of human nature was essentially pessimistic.

Kaganovich helped create the Stalinist system and played a key role in elevating Stalin as the supreme leader. At the same time, however, Kaganovich as a leader was himself caught up in a process of party construction and state building which had a dynamic of its own. Kaganovich articulated, perhaps more clearly than almost any other Stalinist leader, the changes which the regime underwent. He never questioned the wisdom or necessity of these policies. Kaganovich was no Trotsky and no Bukharin. His conception of socialism was unashamedly statist.[34]

The Stalinist regime evolved out of the establishment of the Bolshevik one-party state after October and the ruthless suppression of internal dissent. Kaganovich became one of the principal promoters of this trend. His model of administration for the party and the state apparatus was derived from military models and shaped by the experience of the civil war. This was reflected not only in his writings on party organization in 1924 but also in his major speeches to the XVI and XVII party congresses on party and state organization.

For Kaganovich, as for Stalin, efficient administration meant centralization and strict control. In this scheme there was little room for dissent, debate, or disagreement. In a world where the leadership knew what was best, control by party and state was extended to suffocate real politics. During the 1930s this obsessive preoccupation with control developed its own inherent logic, extending its reach, searching ever farther to root out internal dissent and opposition. The leadership became still more secretive, more closed and unaccountable. In this process Lenin's conception of party organization and his conception of the role of Marxism as a scientific ideology was commandeered by the emergent Stalinist leadership for its own ends. Alternative systems of thought were excluded, and the ideology itself, in the course of struggle with the Trotskyists and Rightists, was still more narrowly circumscribed.

34. See particularly Kaganovich, "Dvenadtsatyi let stroitel'stva sovetskogo gosudarstva," *Sovetskoe gosudarstvo i revolyutsiia prava*, no. 1, 1930, 15–41.

The years covered by the documents in this book coincide with the apogee of Kaganovich's career. Kaganovich, who had striven to make himself indispensable to Stalin, was to find in the following years that even he was not irreplaceable. In 1935 he took over the leadership of the Soviet railways as head of the People's Commissariat of Transport. He was succeeded as leader of the Moscow party organization by Khrushchev, whilst the Commission of Party Control was taken over by Yezhov. Kaganovich's influence within the party Secretariat also declined after 1935. As head of the People's Commissariat of Transport in 1935–36, he achieved considerable success in improving the performance of the railways, which had been languishing in a state of crisis since 1930.[35] In 1937 he took over the People's Commissariat of Heavy Industry. In 1938 he combined the leadership of both these prestigious commissariats.

During the Great Terror of 1936–38 the Soviet railways and heavy industry, the two sectors for which Kaganovich was responsible, were ruthlessly purged. He was directly implicated in the terror, signing denunciations of his colleagues to the NKVD and issuing orders demanding further arrests. Kaganovich himself signed death warrants for some 36,000 individuals.[36] In these terrible years he also undertook a series of visits to regional party organizations (Ivanovo, Western Region, Donets Basin) and played a major part in accelerating the purge process in these areas.

After the years covered by this book Kaganovich's political career underwent a dramatic decline, especially after 1941, and the second half of his career was an anticlimax. His fall from grace was associated with the rise of a new generation of younger leaders in Stalin's entourage. It was associated with an upsurge of anti-Semitism in official circles, following the Hitler-Stalin pact of 1939, which in part claimed his brother Mikhail, who committed suicide in 1941. But it appears also to have stemmed from policy failures for which he was held responsible. The Soviet railways performed badly during the Soviet-Finnish War in 1939–40. Kaganovich was also criticized for shortcomings in organizing evacuations in 1941. During the war he was twice removed from the leadership of the People's Commissariat of Transport. The most dramatic evidence of his fall from grace was that

---

35. E. A. Rees, *Stalinism and Soviet Rail Transport, 1928–41* (Basingstoke and London, 1995), chs. 5, 6.

36. O. B. Nebogin and M. D. Slanskaya, "Nelziia ostavit v riadakh partii," *Voprosy istorii KPSS*, no. 5, 1989, 100.

from 1941 to 1947 Kaganovich only rarely attended the meetings in Stalin's office.[37]

Contemporary accounts suggest that these experiences had a coarsening effect on Kaganovich's personality. He became notorious for his foul language and his brutal handling of subordinates.[38] Khrushchev, one of Kaganovich's protégés, broke with his former mentor. Having earlier been a great admirer of Kaganovich's drive and energy, he depicts him in his memoirs as a toady, an intriguer, and an unprincipled careerist who was intent on saving his own skin at all costs.[39]

After 1948 Kaganovich's political fortunes revived, but he never occupied a position of influence within the leadership again. He survived the wave of anti-Semitism in Stalin's final years by following the course he had long adopted, of distancing himself as far as possible from his own ethnic roots. Even with the death of Stalin in March 1953, Kaganovich failed to stage a comeback, unlike Molotov. It was Molotov who became the spokesman of conservative Stalinist positions in opposition to Khrushchev's "de-Stalinization" policy. In the Antiparty group in 1957 it was Molotov who took the leading role. Along with Molotov and Malenkov, Kaganovich was disgraced and expelled from the Politburo and the Central Committee. At the Central Committee plenum in June 1957 Kaganovich's role in the terror of the late 1930s was denounced, most vocally by Marshal Zhukov.[40] In 1961 he was condemned by delegates to the XXII party congress for his crimes and expelled from the party. Until his death in 1991 he remained an unreconstructed and unapologetic Stalinist.

---

37. "Posetiteli kremlevskogo kabineta I. V. Stalina," *Istoricheskii arkhiv,* nos. 5–6, 1995, nos. 1–3, 1996.

38. V. Kravchenko, *I Chose Freedom* (New York, 1946), 270, 275–76, 400.

39. N. Khrushchev, *Khrushchev Remembers* (London, 1971).

40. *Istoricheskii arkhiv,* no. 3, 1993, 42–44.

1931

Introduction

IN 1931 Stalin departed on a lengthy vacation. According to his appointment diary, he did not receive anyone in his Kremlin office between 6 August and 11 October.[1] This was the first occasion on which he entrusted the day-to-day management of the work of the Politburo to Lazar Kaganovich. But he had no intention of giving up his own control of affairs; he regularly received information, and continued to guide his colleagues who remained in Moscow.

In 1931 there were already serious symptoms of the crisis which reached its peak in 1932–33. By the time Stalin went on leave, the Soviet economy was experiencing considerable problems. In December 1930, in its effort to achieve the ambitious goals of the first five-year plan, the plenum of the Central Committee of the Soviet Communist Party approved the most optimistic of all Soviet annual economic plans. It proposed that industrial production should increase by 45 percent in a single year and that capital investment in the socialized sector of the economy should increase by 70 percent. The plan proposed to combine these targets with strict financial control. Currency in circulation had increased by 55 percent in 1930, but in contrast the 1931 plan stipulated that no net currency issue should take place in the year as whole.

In the first six months of the year the plans were substantially underfulfilled. In June, as a result of budgetary difficulties and the growing

---

1. *Istoricheskii arkhiv*, no. 6, 1994, 37.

amount of overdue wages, the authorities tacitly relinquished the decision not to issue additional currency. By this time a severe crisis had developed in the foreign trade balance. Although imports were only slightly more than exports in 1930, in the first six months of 1931 imports amounted to about 517 million gold rubles, while exports were less than 366 million rubles.[2] On 20 July 1931 the Politburo set up a commission to investigate the situation and to seek means of reducing the foreign debt.[3]

In spite of these difficulties the Soviet leaders categorically refused any attempt to lower the targets of the plan. Addressing the leaders of industrial enterprises on 23 June, Stalin attacked those who called for more realistic plans: "Drive away all those so-called wise men who talk to you about realistic plans and so on."[4] But Stalin combined this demand for the unconditional fulfillment of the 1931 plan with a program of mini-reforms, which became known as "Stalin's six conditions." The six conditions proclaimed the necessity for a much more extensive use of economic incentives. These included the encouragement of incentives to workers to increase their productivity by eliminating "equalization" in wage payments and by improving living conditions; increased authority and incentives for engineers and technicians; and supervision of the economic results of the work of enterprises by "economic accounting" (*khozraschet*). But these innovations had only a minor effect on the economic difficulties.

In agriculture a new collectivization campaign was launched in the first six months of 1931, accompanied by a second wave of dekulakization. By 1 August 1931, 58 percent of peasant households were collectivized, as compared with 24 percent on 1 January. In 1931 about 300,000 "kulak" households were exiled, most of them during the spring sowing and the harvest. These upheavals undoubtedly had a negative effect on agricultural production, and the harvest also suffered because of a serious drought in the main grain regions. As a result, the grain harvest in 1931 was substantially less than in the previous year. But the authorities did not recognize this in time, and in the agricultural year 1931/32, following the 1931 harvest, they forced through a plan for state grain procurements which was even higher than in 1930/31.

    2. See R. W. Davies, *Crisis and Progress in the Soviet Economy, 1931–1933* (Basingstoke and London, 1996), 22–24, 536.
    3. RGASPI, f. 17, op. 162, d. 10, l. 122.
    4. Ibid., f. 85, op. 28, d. 7, ll. 207–208.

The Stalin-Kaganovich correspondence displays an understanding of some of these problems, but other problems are misrepresented or ignored. Although Stalin frequently emphasized the unconditional need to fulfill the plan, he paid surprisingly little attention to the realization of the famous six conditions, which he had announced only a few weeks before his departure on leave. Thus he virtually ignored the work of the special commission on wage reform headed by Postyshev, a secretary of the Central Committee. In a letter of 4 September (document 9) he merely remarked: "I haven't read the resolution on wages in metal and coal. Tell Postyshev that I am voting <u>for</u> them on trust." Stalin's lack of interest at this time in currency issue, which was increasing considerably in these months, is also remarkable.

At the center of Stalin's attention was the foreign trade deficit. Stalin discussed it in seven of his letters. On 6 September (document 11) he frankly stated that "our foreign-currency situation is desperate," and predicted that it would worsen because exports to the major countries would decline. A feature of these letters surprising for historians is that Stalin did not at this time call for increased grain exports. On 4 September (document 9) he strongly criticized Kaganovich's efforts to increase the export of grain when "grain fetches <u>pennies</u> [groshi]," and insisted that the export of butter and eggs would be more profitable.

Stalin's main prescription for dealing with the foreign trade problem was to reduce imports. This was a quite realistic policy in view of the difficulty of securing exports during the world economic crisis and the fact that international terms of trade were unfavorable to agricultural exports. On 25 August (document 6) he even proposed that all imports from the United States should cease in view of the "<u>draconian credit terms</u> that America practices." On 14 September (document 16) he wrote that the import plan for the fourth quarter (October—December 1931) "should be reduced as much as possible," and he repeated this injunction on 24 September (see document 20).

The Politburo considered the question of economizing on hard currency and cutting back import items several times in the fall of 1931. On 10 October it banned the use of funds obtained from savings on export quotas to make additional purchases.[5] On 25 October the Politburo considered the question of quotas for equipment to be imported by Vesenkha, the Supreme Council of the National Economy of the USSR. According to the Politburo resolution, "In view of the radically

5. Ibid., f. 17, op. 162, d. 11, l. 25.

changed situation for foreign trade, it is to be considered absolutely imperative to revise the supplementary resolutions by the Politburo, the Council of Labor and Defense, and Sovnarkom [Council of People's Commissars] on imports with a view to reducing imports as much as possible." A commission consisting of Rudzutak, Ordzhonikidze, Rozengolts, Piatakov, and Kuibyshev was assigned to identify within two days those items on order and those quota items "that are absolutely essential." On the same day the Politburo considered the issue of "fabrications by the foreign press" that the USSR was insolvent. It was deemed inadvisable to issue an official denial of these reports. *Izvestia* however, was instructed to print an article against rumors of insolvency.[6] On 1 November the Politburo considered proposals by Rudzutak's commission identifying priority orders. A total of 30 million rubles was approved for orders of imported equipment in the fourth quarter. Vesenkha was instructed "to issue an immediate directive to its agencies abroad to review orders that had already been placed but not yet confirmed, canceling orders for less necessary items so as to concentrate imports on top-priority plants and construction projects."[7]

These efforts were not at first successful. Imports as a whole even increased in July—December and did not decline until the beginning of 1932. The balance of foreign trade continued to show a large deficit in every quarter until July–October 1932. There were several reasons why it was so difficult to reduce imports. Stalin's intention to reduce imports was overcome by the pressure of the real need to carry out the technological transformation of industry, and in any case it would have been necessary to pay substantial fines if contracts which had already been agreed to were canceled. Departmental interests, which also played a significant role, were themselves determined by the realities of economic policy. After a time lag, however, the stringent measures to reduce imports took effect. By the end of 1932, the foreign trade crisis was overcome. But the substantial reduction in the purchase of foreign machinery caused further problems for Soviet industry.

On agriculture, Stalin was also sometimes quite flexible. He insisted in the middle of August (document 2) that disturbances in western Georgia should be dealt with not only by repression but also by supplying more grain, arguing that the "reckless 'grain-procurements pol-

6. Ibid., l. 33.
7. Ibid., l. 40.

icy'" of the Georgian authorities had brought these districts to a state of famine. But this did not indicate any general shift in the harshness of his grain policy. He affirmed that the existing policy must be applied in Ukraine and other grain-producing regions, and his complacency about the state of agriculture (in spite of the warnings of his experts) is revealed by his remark that "we have already solved the grain problem." In general, his 1931 letters pay little attention to agriculture; he evidently assumed that the grain collections would proceed without too much trouble.

In this period Stalin paid a great deal of attention to the situation in the Far East. Early in 1931 the Soviet leaders were informed that influential circles in Japan were advocating aggression against the Soviet Far East. Then on 18 September, Japan invaded Manchuria—the first major act by one of the fascist powers, which in retrospect was a prelude to the Second World War. The Soviet Union was too weak to take action against Japan; and Stalin pursued a cautious line. On 14 September (document 16), a few days before the Japanese invasion of Manchuria, he instructed Kaganovich to follow firm but flexible, more circumspect tactics in questions of Soviet-Japanese relations. Stalin's first comment on the Manchurian situation was made in a cipher of 23 September to Kaganovich and Molotov. According to Stalin, it was probable that Japanese intervention was being carried out "by agreement with all or several of the great powers" and that "several influential militarist Chinese groups" had agreed to it. He stressed that "military intervention by us is of course ruled out, and diplomatic intervention is at present inexpedient because it might unite the imperialists." However, "we must behave in the press so that there is no doubt that we are heart and soul against the [Japanese] intervention."[8]

But Stalin's caution was not shared by everyone. On the same day, 23 September, on which Stalin sent his cipher, the poet Demian Bedny published a poem entitled "What Next?" in *Izvestia* (evidently not on his own initiative). Bedny went so far as to treat the "silence of Moscow" about the Japanese invasion as incomprehensible:

> Always ready to resist
> Moscow is mysteriously silent
> And even I at such a time
> Am not very sparing with my words.

8. Ibid., f. 558, op. 11, d. 76, 76, 76ob.

On 29 September (document 22) Stalin instructed that Demian Bedny, I. M. Gronsky (the editor of *Izvestia*), and Maksim Litvinov (the people's commissar of foreign affairs) should all be called to account.

Stalin, supported by the compliant Kaganovich, continued to keep a close eye on the former members of the Right opposition. In 1931 his correspondence with Kaganovich contained strong criticisms of Bukharin. On 26 August 1931, Bukharin, as the person responsible for science and technology in industry, gave a lengthy report to a meeting of managers and officials, entitled "Socialist Reconstruction and the Struggle for Technology: On Technical Propaganda and Its Organization." About this time he also addressed a large crowd in Sokolniki Park, in the north of Moscow, on the same subject. It was this address which Stalin criticized in document 8, a letter to Kaganovich dated 30 August. Bukharin wrote a letter of apology and explanation to Stalin, which said in part: "I was invited one day to an enormous rally for technical propaganda (in Sokolniki Park). When I saw the perspiring crowd, thousands of people wilting under the heat and waiting for a concert to follow the rally, I naturally decided not to give a dry technical report but to talk 'in general.' And I mentioned in passing there that we had been late with food and light industry (because of the problem of personnel and their skills). When one comrade complained to me, I cited, so as to avoid misunderstandings, the decisions of the XVI congress, articles in *Pravda*, etc. [. . .] I should also point out that the transcript that was circulated was uncorrected by me, and it took me a long time to get hold of it."[9]

Meanwhile, on 31 August, the day after Stalin wrote his letter about Bukharin, Kaganovich wrote to Stalin criticizing Bukharin's formal report of 26 August. Kaganovich complained that while Bukharin had added to the report some passages "about the Central Committee and the struggle with deviations, it includes a number of incorrect details." According to Kaganovich, Bukharin "suffers from a lot of Bogdanovite confusion [. . .] the report claims to discover America [. . .] but produces nothing but a schematic approach, mechanistic philosophy, and Bogdanovism." For this reason the report had not yet been published in *Pravda*, although it had begun to appear in *Za industrializatsiiu*.[10] The report appeared in the latter newspaper in two parts on 29 and 30 August 1931, but was never published in *Pravda*.

9. Ibid., d. 709, ll. 82–83.
10. Ibid., d. 739, ll. 56–64; this letter is not included in the present collection.

Two weeks later, on September 16, Kaganovich again criticized Bukharin in a letter to Stalin (document 10). He compared Bukharin's complaints about the soap shortage to his famous statement about bricks in his attack on excessive industrialization in his "Notes of an Economist" in September 1928 (Bukharin wrote that "you cannot make a present building out of future bricks, even according to Böhm-Bawerk"). However, in spite of Stalin's and Kaganovich's comments, the report of 26 August was reprinted a few months later in Bukharin's collection of essays, *Etiudy* (Moscow, 1932).

Stalin also displayed mounting dissatisfaction with the work of other Soviet leaders, including some of his closest colleagues. The letters reveal his strongly critical attitude toward the principal officials of the People's Commissariat of Transport, particularly Rukhimovich. Rukhimovich, a long-standing industrial manager and old Bolshevik, who was appointed people's commissar in charge of the railroads in the summer of 1930, strongly argued in public that new investment was needed. Behind the scenes his criticism evidently went further. In his letter to Kaganovich on 4 October (document 23) Stalin claimed that Rukhimovich "[has conducted] (even now!) the most malicious agitation <u>against</u> the practical line of the CC (on the question of growth rates and so forth)." In the same letter he compared Rukhimovich to Frumkin. Frumkin, another old Bolshevik, was a deputy people's commissar of finance in the 1920s, and in 1928, even before Bukharin, he criticized party policy toward agriculture, and excessive industrialization.[11]

The background to his strictures was that Stalin had been strongly criticizing Rukhimovich in letters to Kaganovich from the end of August 1931. But it was not until 30 September that the Politburo, having received Kaganovich's report, decided to replace Rukhimovich with Andreev as people's commissar of transport, and to appoint Blagonravov, head of the transport department of the OGPU, as a deputy people's commissar.[12] One reason why it took so long to resolve the question, in spite of Stalin's frequent reminders that Rukhimovich should be replaced, may have been the support given to Rukhimovich by several members of the Politburo. Stalin's letter of 4 October (document

11. See E. H. Carr and R. W. Davies, *Foundations of a Planned Economy, 1926–1929,* vol. 1 (London, 1969), 74–75, 321–23.

12. RGASPI, f. 17. op. 3, d. 851, l. 3. For details about the situation in the commissariat in 1931 see E. A. Rees, *Stalinism and Soviet Rail Transport, 1928–1941* (Basingstoke and London, 1995), 38–56.

23) reveals that even after Rukhimovich had been dismissed Molotov proposed to appoint him as head of Gosplan (the State Planning Commission) of the USSR (which would have automatically made him a deputy chairman of Sovnarkom).[13] Ordzhonikidze wanted to offer the demoted Rukhimovich a post as his deputy in Vesenkha. Stalin indignantly rejected these proposals and categorically insisted that Rukhimovich should be sent "to work outside Moscow in the Vesenkha system." Stalin's colleagues had to accept this, and on 12 October 1931 the Politburo confirmed the appointment of Rukhimovich as head of the coal corporation Kuzbassugol in Siberia.[14] It was not until June 1934 that Rukhimovich, now back in favor, was appointed a deputy people's commissar of heavy industry responsible for fuel (this was one of the commissariats which had replaced Vesenkha). Documents indicate that both Ordzhonikidze and Molotov supported this appointment. Molotov proposed to go further, and separate out from the People's Commissariat of Heavy Industry a special commissariat to administer the fuel industry, with Rukhimovich as its head.[15]

In spite of these irritations and disagreements, the dismissal of Rukhimovich was one of the easiest of the problems which Stalin had to resolve in the summer of 1931. It was far more difficult for him to tame his closest colleagues in the Politburo. The Stalin-Kaganovich correspondence for 1931 contains important information about this.

Immediately after his departure on vacation Stalin had to deal with an ultimatum from Valerian Kuibyshev, member of the Politburo and head of Gosplan. On 10 August 1931 Kuibyshev sent a memorandum to Kaganovich (printed as Appendix: document 1) in which he informed him about the process for the preparation of the directives on the second five-year plan (for 1933–37) and the control figures (that is, economic plan) for the development of the economy in 1932; he also requested leave from 20 August to 5 October "in view of my illness." A statement offering to resign formed part of this memorandum. Kaganovich sent this statement to Stalin and on 12 August met Kuibyshev to discuss the question of his resignation. He immediately

13. A Politburo decision of 30 September 1931 on the change in the leadership of the People's Commissariat of Transport resolved "to entrust to the Secretariat of the Central Committee, jointly with Comrade Molotov, discussions with Comrade Rukhimovich about his future work" (RGASPI, f. 17, op. 3, d. 851, l. 3).

14. Ibid., d. 854, l. 7.

15. *Stalinskoe Politbiuro v 30-e gody; sbornik dokumentov*, ed. O. V. Khlevniuk, A. V. Kvashonkin, L. P. Kosheleva, and L. A. Rogovaya (Moscow, 1995), 140–41.

reported the outcome of his conversation to Stalin (document 3). It emerged that Kuibyshev's statement was prompted by several factors. The most important was his conflict with the party organization of Gosplan, especially about its opposition to the proposal to appoint S. Strumilin to a leading post in Gosplan. Strumilin was a leading Soviet economist, but in 1929–30 was under a cloud as the author of a relatively moderate draft of the first five-year plan. Soon after Kuibyshev took over Gosplan on 8 December 1930, Strumilin had been removed from the vice-chairmanship of Gosplan, though appointed a member of the presidium,[16] and he remained a member of the presidium until the 1937–38 purges. K. Rozental, one of Kuibyshev's closest colleagues, supported Strumilin. The attacks on Rozental by the party bureau of Gosplan were thus political in character and were implicitly an attack on Kuibyshev himself. Kuibyshev stated that another reason for his statement was the aggressive attitude of heads of government departments, particularly Ordzhonikidze, the unrestrained and fiery head of Vesenkha.

Stalin, as his letter shows (document 2), was dissatisfied with both Kuibyshev and Ordzhonikidze. But as was normal in this period he tried to calm down the conflict by persuasion and compromise. It was undoubtedly at Stalin's request that Molotov, who was with Stalin on leave in the south, wrote to Kuibyshev on 14 August: "Comrade Kaganovich sent Koba [Stalin] your letter to the Central Committee, and I read it. [. . .] There cannot be any question of your leaving Gosplan. I am sure that everyone would be decisively against it. [. . .] What you need is a break. I think this could happen soon, from the beginning of September. I therefore strongly advise you to drop the question of leaving Gosplan and not to ever raise it again. It is not the time for this—what's needed is to get down in earnest to the improvement of Gosplan. We must help you here, and I think that in the fall things will begin to get better, with success."[17] On 16 August the Orgburo, on Kaganovich's proposal, fully supported Kuibyshev in his conflict with the editors of *Pravda,* which had been dragging on since the beginning of July 1931.[18] On 30 August 1931 the Politburo granted Kuibyshev six weeks' leave, starting on 5 September. But in spite of all these attempts to keep Kuibyshev at the head of Gosplan, the question

16. *Sobranie zakonov,* 1931, vol. 2, no. 62, art. 426.
17. *Stalinskoe Politbiuro v 30-e gody,* 121.
18. For details see O. V. Khlevniuk, *Politbiuro: Mekhanizmy politicheskoi vlasti v 30-e gody* (Moscow, 1996), 80–81.

was not finally resolved; as already mentioned, even at the end of September Molotov proposed to replace Kuibyshev with Rukhimovich as head of Gosplan.

Stalin's criticism of Ordzhonikidze in connection with Kuibyshev's statement was one of the first steps in an extensive attack on Ordzhonikidze which Stalin launched in 1931. Stalin evidently found Ordzhonikidze's independent (and not always sensible) conduct irksome and used any pretext to put him in his place. But at this stage his criticisms were quite careful. While on vacation Stalin reproved Ordzhonikidze for the mistaken attitude of Vesenkha to the question of orders of capital equipment from the United States (document 6). Then, via Kaganovich, he removed Ordzhonikidze's protégés from leading posts in Transcaucasia (document 7). He strongly criticized Vesenkha's proposals about the import of iron pipes (document 8). He also called for the punishment of Vesenkha officials who were responsible for inefficiency (document 14).

But the most dramatic clash between Ordzhonikidze and Stalin at this time concerned the additional import of axles and wheels for railway wagons, and of high-quality steel. At Politburo sittings on 28 and 30 July 1931, just before Stalin went on vacation, the final figure for the import allocation for ferrous metal was adopted: Vesenkha could import 1,300,000 tons of rolled steel in 1931, in addition to the 100,000 tons of pig iron already being imported.[19] But on 30 August the Politburo approved a decision of the foreign-currency commission to place additional orders in Germany for wagon axles and wheels, and for the import of high-quality steel to the value of 15 million rubles; both decisions were adopted on the proposal of the leadership of Vesenkha, including Ordzhonikidze.[20] When Stalin and Molotov were informed about this, they sent a telegram to Moscow condemning the decision, and Stalin reinforced this with a letter to Kaganovich (document 9). On 5 September, in response to the protests of Stalin and Molotov, the Politburo instructed Rudzutak, Kaganovich, and Ordzhonikidze to prepare a telegram to Stalin and Molotov; until an answer was received from them a moratorium was placed on the placing of orders for high-quality steel and wagon wheels and axles. The leaders of Vesenkha and the People's Commissariat of Foreign Trade

19. RGASPI, f. 17, op. 162, d. 10, l. 131. The actual import of rolled steel in 1931 was 1,289,000 tons (*Vneshniaia torgovlya SSSR za 1918–1940 gg.: Statisticheskii obzor* [Moscow, 1960], 316).

20. RGASPI, f. 17, op. 162, d. 10, l. 179.

were also instructed to "present today a precise estimate of the allocations of Vesenkha which have not yet been utilized."[21] The telegram in
response by Kaganovich, Rudzutak, and Ordzhonikidze argued that
the proposed purchases were within the agreed import allocations to
Vesenkha for these purposes.[22] But Stalin and Molotov replied with a
caustic ultimatum (document 11): "If you disagree, we propose a special session of the Politburo to which both of us should be summoned." In the face of this pressure, on 8 September the Politburo canceled its decision of 30 August on the import of high-quality steel,
wagon wheels, and axles, and requested the People's Commissariat of
Foreign Trade to cease all negotiations about placing these orders.[23]
On the following day, 9 September, however, with the caution which
was characteristic of him in this period, Stalin sent letters to Ordzhonikidze and Kaganovich reprimanding them in a conciliatory tone
(document 13; Appendix: document 2). The context of this dispute
was of course the urgent need to reduce imports in view of the state of
the foreign-trade balance.

A few days later Stalin had to deal with another resignation statement by a member of the Politburo—Mikoian, the people's commissar
for supply: "Dear Stalin! Your two telegrams about warehouses were
such a severe blow to me that for several days I could not start work (it
was after an illness). This is because I can take any criticism and reproach, except the reproach that I am not loyal to the Central Committee and to you personally." Complaining that he could not work at
such a complicated post as the people's commissar for supply without
the confidence of the Central Committee and the personal support of
Stalin and that he had held the post too long, Mikoian requested to be
released from the post: "I am ready for any work which the Central
Committee requires, and would undertake local work with particular
pleasure."[24]

We do not yet know the terms in which Stalin rejected this proposals, but the letters published here illuminate the conflict which gave
rise to Mikoian's statement. When Stalin arrived in the south on his vacation, he received information about the difficult food situation in
Georgia and demanded that Kaganovich should deal with the matter,
and should oblige Mikoian to increase the supply of grain (document

21. Ibid., l. 182.
22. Ibid., f. 558, op. 11, d. 76, l. 1 (6 September 1931).
23. Ibid., f. 17, op. 162, d. 11, l. 3.
24. Ibid., f. 558, op. 11, d. 765, ll. 72–73.

2). On 14 August 1931 Stalin sent a telegram to the Central Committee addressed to Mikoian (with a copy to Kaganovich in the Politburo): "We are informed from Abkhazia and Mingrelia that there are no grain warehouses there to supply the tobacco and tea farmers and that none are being built. Mikoian alleged to the Politburo that a whole number of grain warehouses have already been built. Who is right and who is deceiving the CC [Central Committee of the Communist Party]? Surely you can find out how many warehouses have already been built, where precisely they are located, how many are being built and when they will be completed, how many poods of grain have already been sent to the warehouses, and how much will be there by the end of September. It is impossible to put up with deception any longer. Surely an honest and direct answer can be obtained."[25]

In a reply telegram sent to Stalin and Kaganovich on 18 August Mikoian rejected these accusations. He insisted that warehouses were built in 1930 and were being built in 1931. It was difficult to send grain to them because of the need to fulfill the export targets. "I am unable to establish who is deceiving the Central Committee and why," Mikoian wrote, "but I can see that the attacks on the People's Commissariat for Supply are unjustified and without foundation."[26]

On 20 August 1931 the Politburo considered Stalin's further telegram in reply to Mikoian, in which he insisted that "there are no limits to the bureaucratic self-justification" of the People's Commissariat for Supply.[27] The Politburo noted in its decision that the People's Commissariat for Supply had not carried out the decision of the Politburo on building warehouses in Georgia. The commissariat was asked to "immediately undertake work on the accelerated construction of new grain warehouses for the tea and tobacco farmers in western Georgia; all the construction of these warehouses must be supervised by Rabkrin [the Workers' and Peasants' Inspectorate]." The Secretariat of the Central Committee was instructed to send five people to the building sites within three days, and Beria, head of the GPU in Transcaucasia, was "to arrange maximum assistance to the building of new warehouses, so that all the new warehouses shall be completed and handed over for use by 5 November." The Politburo also agreed that "the accelerated transfer of grain to Georgia from the North Cau-

---

25. Ibid., f. 39, op. 1, d. 134, l. 2; ibid., f. 558, op. 1, d. 76, l. 8, 8ob.
26. Ibid., l. 5.
27. Ibid., f. 558, op. 11, d. 76, ll. 14–18 (dated 19 August).

casus is necessary"; the amount of grain to be sent was to be decided within two days by Mikoian jointly with the secretary of the Transcaucasian Regional Committee of the party, L. I. Kartvelishvili. Mikoian was also instructed to resolve the question of grain procurements in Transcaucasia and report on this to the Politburo on 25 August.[28] On 25 August the question was postponed, evidently because of Mikoian's illness.[29] Eventually, on 5 September, the Politburo heard Mikoian's report and accepted his proposal that grain procurements in Transcaucasia should be kept to the plan already approved. The People's Commissariat for Supply and Soiuzkhleb (the grain corporation) were instructed to increase the supply of grain to Transcaucasia so that the entire quarterly supply plan would be achieved no later than 20 September.[30] Mikoian's resignation statement of 12 September was submitted soon after these events.

The conflicts and clashes between Stalin and his colleagues reached their apogee in 1931. In subsequent years they were less frequent and less tense.

Documents 1–23

· 1 ·

Kaganovich to Stalin
[11 August]

F. 558, op. 11, d. 739, ll. 19–25.

Greetings dear Comrade Stalin!

At yesterday's Politburo meeting we considered a number of questions (we are sending you the minutes). On some of them we did not adopt final decisions, and it would be good to get your comments on the most important ones before the 15th:

1. On orders in Germany. Above all on the abuses by companies, they often ship equipment that is clearly no good, and it is downright criminal of them. For example, a single shaft welded from three pieces and so forth.

Vesenkha [Supreme Council of National Economy] adopted a resolution, approved by us, to dispatch inspectors, but that is not enough. We in-

---

28. Ibid., f. 17, op. 3, d. 843, l. 5.
29. Ibid., d. 844, l. 8.
30. Ibid., d. 846, l. 1.

structed them to come up with other measures by the 15th to fight companies perpetrating abuses that even capitalist morals do not justify. Expose them [publicly] and even take the step sometimes of refusing the orders. Then the main issue regarding orders at present is the interest rate, it keeps leaping upward, and now it has already reached 17 percent. There were proposals at the Politburo meeting, on the one hand, that we cancel the orders now, and, on the other, it was proposed that we continue in the same vein regardless of the interest rate. We adopted the decision that you know about. Piatakov is not leaving yet, until we get an answer from you. It turned out that the soaring int[erest] rate covers not only the orders that we are placing now, but also a large number of previous orders. Some said that they cover a range of orders totaling up to 500 million marks, nobody can say exactly, so we gave instructions that a precise accounting be submitted to us.[1]

2. On Japan. We considered the proposal from the PC of Foreign Affairs on a reply to the statement by the Japanese ambassador. We must edit it, our reply (the draft) is too sugary. While the Japanese, for example, are leveling a charge at us that the USSR is pursuing a policy of completely driving the Japanese out of our waters, the reply by the PC [People's Commissariat] of Foreign Affairs keeps adopting a defensive tone. Shouldn't we point out, for example, that there is sentiment in Japan for revising the treaty that was concluded and for an illegitimate expansion of its rights.[2] Since we are going to edit this draft, which was approved in the main by the Politburo, it would be good to get your instructions by wire.

3. On Argentina. Rozengolts made a proposal that a telegram be sent in his name announcing the cessation of purchases and imports of goods of Argentine origin and an end to the use of Argentine ports, transit routes, etc. I am sending you a draft of his telegram, we have deferred the issue in order to ask for your opinion.[3]

4. We have deferred until the 15th consideration of the issue of ensuring customer participation in drawing up orders. The commission that the Politburo set up some time ago has done virtually no work. There is a draft by Comrade Akulov, who proposes turning over day-to-day management of the importation of equipment to the relevant corporations of Vesenkha, and to leave the regulation, control, and supervision of the work of import organizations with the PC of Foreign Trade and trade missions. This seems to conform with the so-called "Berlin agreement" between Piatakov and Liubimov.[4]

5. On nonferrous metallurgy. So far we have approved the roster of directors. We arranged that we would get into substance on the 15th, since we still have to hear the relevant comrades speak on aluminum issues. The main issue in dispute in the aluminum production program for '32–'33 is

this: 8,000 tons is planned for '32—obviously too little—and 50,000 for '33. You yourself pointed out the need for getting up to 70,000–80,000 tons. With regard to every other section the resolution is acceptable. We agreed with Sergo [Ordzhonikidze] that we would discuss this one more time.[5]

6. We considered the issue of revising the contracts on technical assistance. Apparently the situation is still bad. There is not enough supervision of this matter. The foreign companies often violate the contracts, and our people fail to file complaints. We often receive design drawings that are obsolete, whereas in some areas we have already advanced further ourselves. Tolokontsev has particularly distinguished himself when it comes to bad contracts. We have approved a draft resolution and assigned the editing to Sergo and me. I think that the editing should strengthen some points to require greater supervision and responsibility of corporations.[6]

7. We approved the resolutions on cooperatives and public eating facilities, which were completed by the commission. They seem to have captured the main points. We have sent these drafts to you and Comrade Molotov. We will not publish them until we receive your instructions.

We have broken down the opening of stores by month, the pace is demanding, but they (the people in the cooperatives and at the PC for Supply) have agreed to accomplish it. In the section on improving the work of the trade network we put emphasis on economic accountability and on using the ruble to pull up the network.[7] In the resolution on public eating facilities consistent with our currently limited supplies we outlined in addition to organizational changes specific measures to further develop the network not in terms of the quantity of dishes but in the number of people it covers and in establishing a stockpile of supplies, including spoons, knives, forks, etc.[8]

8. We deferred the issue of the fuel and coal budget since Kuibyshev was absent. At the next meeting this issue will be one of the first that we deal with and we will study it thoroughly. The fuel situation is obviously serious.[9]

9. And finally, on the rather odd letter from Comrade Kuibyshev that I received after the Politburo meeting this evening. I am sending you the letter.[10] I spoke with him by telephone about the totally incomprehensible reasons for his proposal to resign. I wanted to meet with him right away, but he asked to do it later, and later I couldn't find him anywhere.

The telephone conversation was rather incoherent, he just told me that "I will make sure I leave no matter what the cost." He seems to have written the letter and spoken with me on the telephone in a state of "particular inspiration." In any case the letter has been written and it will have to be discussed. I will try to talk with him tomorrow, it probably isn't necessary to convene the Politburo now. I will wait for your instructions on this matter, it would be good to wire them.

I will end here for now. As much as I dislike wearing you out, especially during the first few days of your vacation, I will have to do this more often than usual, because it is hard for us to govern without you.

Regards to Comrade Molotov.

Regards to Nadezhda Sergeevna.

Yours, L. Kaganovich.

P.S. After reading my letter I see that I failed to fulfill your directive to master punctuation marks, I started to, but it didn't take, despite the workload it can be done. I will try to have periods and commas in future letters.

L.K.

1. On 10 August the Politburo considered several problems about placing orders in Germany. It took note of Piatakov's report on this subject and approved a decision to send Soviet representatives abroad to inspect equipment that was being purchased. The Politburo instructed Piatakov and Rozengolts to draw up measures "to combat abuses by companies in filling orders." "In view of the fact that the situation with German orders is growing more complicated owing to the instability of the interest rate and its continuing rise," the Politburo decided to send Piatakov to Berlin "to examine, along with Comrade Liubimov, the situation on the spot and to raise the issue with German industrialists of the need for establishing a fixed, maximum interest rate. Concurrently Comrades Piatakov, Liubimov, and Khinchuk are to explore the atmosphere for raising this question with the German government and report their judgments in this regard immediately to the CC." The PC of Foreign Trade was instructed to submit a memorandum stating the total amount of Soviet orders in Germany that were affected by the increase in the interest rate (RGASPI, f. 17, op. 162, d. 10, l. 149). On the same day Kaganovich reported this development to Stalin by cipher (ibid., f. 558, op. 11, d. 76, l.30b). In a cipher dated 14 August Stalin instructed Kaganovich "act more boldly, up to the point of immediately canceling orders" (ibid., l. 7). See note 4 to document 5.

2. On 25 June 1931 the Japanese ambassador to the USSR, Hirota, handed to Karakhan, a deputy people's commissar of foreign affairs of the USSR, a statement by the government of Japan asserting the need to begin negotiations about the complications that had arisen over the fishing issue. On 10 August 1931 the Politburo decided "To adopt the proposal of the PC of Foreign Affairs to convey to the Japanese our assent to discuss disputed issues on the basis of normal diplomatic negotiations rather than on the basis of a conference." A commission comprising Kaganovich, Mikoian, Litvinov, and Karakhan was instructed to do final editing on the draft of the reply (ibid., l. 150). On 14 August a cipher from Stalin instructed Kaganovich to conclude a three-year fisheries' agreement with Japan (ibid., l. 7). On 18 August 1931 the USSR government statement to the government of Japan was handed to Hirota (see DVP, vol. XIV, pp. 473–76).

3. On 31 July 1931 the Argentine police arrested staff members of the Soviet organization Yuzhamtorg (South American—Soviet Trading Company) in Buenos Aires. After completing an investigation, the police submitted a report to the Argentine government which accused Yuzhamtorg of "covertly managing communist propaganda" and pursuing a dumping policy. On 14 August Stalin told Kaganovich by cipher that "it is better to wait a bit" (RGASPI, f. 558, op. 11, d. 76, l. 7). On 20 August 1931 the Argentine government stripped Yuzhamtorg of its rights as a legal entity (DVP, vol. XIV, pp. 807, 808). The Politburo dis-

cussed the issue on 3 September and adopted a decision, "To transfer the Center for Trade with South American Countries to Uruguay. [. . .] In order to preserve the possibility of returning to Argentina, measures are to be taken for the formal preservation of Yuzhamtorg, to which end legal proceedings are to be initiated, if necessary, in the Supreme Court of Argentina to have the decree liquidating Yuzhamtorg declared unlawful" (RGASPI, f. 17, op. 162, d. 10, ll. 182–183).

4. On 14 August Stalin told Kaganovich by cipher that "it is possible to wait a little in regard to the participation of consumers in drawing up orders; Akulov's draft is inadequate" (ibid., f. 58, op. 11, d. 76, l. 7). The Politburo considered this matter in Stalin's presence on 20 October. It was decided "to adopt the draft submitted by Comrade Rozengolts as a basis, with a view to softening it in terms of granting maximum rights to Vesenkha and its corporations in the matter of placing orders, overseeing their fulfillment, and in the matter of inspecting them." A commission comprising Molotov, Kaganovich, Piatakov, Rozengolts, and Akulov was instructed to develop and submit concrete proposals for Politburo approval (ibid., f. 17, op. 3, d. 855, l. 2). On 25 October 1931 the commission's proposals were approved (ibid., op. 162, d. 11, ll. 33, 35).

5. On 14 August Stalin told Kaganovich in a cipher that "eight thousand tons of aluminum next year is ridiculously small; the minimum must be twenty thousand tons" (ibid., f. 558, op. 11, d. 76, l. 7) See note 4 to document 4.

6. On 10 August 1931 the Politburo approved the new proposals on revising the contracts and the procedure for negotiating them (ibid., op. 3, d. 841, ll. 2, 10–11). On 14 August Stalin told Kaganovich by cipher that "draconian measures must be taken" against the careless attitude of Soviet officials to technical assistance (ibid., op. 11, d. 76, l. 7).

7. On 10 August 1931 the Politburo approved, with revisions, the draft resolution on reorganizing consumer cooperatives and developing Soviet trade, including in it a clause to the effect "that one of the deputy directors of each enterprise must be appointed to the board of the workers' cooperative" of the enterprise. Final editing of the draft resolution was assigned to a commission comprising Kaganovich, Mikoian, and Zelensky (ibid., f. 17, op. 3, d. 841, l. 3). See documents 2, 4, 6.

8. On 10 August 1931 the Politburo approved, with a revision, the draft resolution on the condition and development of public eating facilities, "including in it a clause to the effect that cafeterias, in addition to standard lunches, are to have higher-priced lunches." Final editing of the draft resolution was assigned to a commission comprising Kaganovich, Mikoian, and Zelensky (ibid.). The document was published in the press in its final form on 20 August as a CC resolution "On Measures to Improve Public Eating Facilities," dated 19 August 1931. See also documents 2, 4, 6.

9. See note 2 to document 4.

10. Kuibyshev's letter to Kaganovich dated 10 August is printed as Appendix: document 1. For more details, see the introduction to this chapter. See documents 2, 3.

· 2 ·

Stalin to Kaganovich
[later than 11 August]

F. 81, op. 3, d. 100, ll. 101–102.

Greetings, Comrade Kaganovich:

1) I am returning the draft resolution of the CC on <u>public eating facilities</u> with my comments and corrections in the text.[1]

2) I have not received the draft resolution of the CC on <u>cooperatives</u>.[2]

3) I advise that Comrade Syrtsov's memo about timber be discussed. It may contain some sensible elements.[3]

4) I suggest that the question of Ramishvili's departure abroad (to emigrate) be deferred to the fall, until Politburo members return from vacation.

5) Comrade Kuibyshev's memo has created a bad impression; in fact, so does his behavior in general.[4] He seems to be trying to avoid work. On the other hand, Comrade Ordzhonikidze is still misbehaving. The latter is apparently not aware that his conduct (which is aimed against Comrades Molotov and Kuibyshev) objectively leads to the undermining of our leadership group, which historically evolved in a struggle against all types of opportunism—and creates the danger that the group may be destroyed. Is it really possible that he doesn't realize that he will find no support from us <u>whatsoever</u> <u>on this path</u>? What foolishness!

6) It is now clear to me that Kartvelishvili and the secretariat of the Georgian CC, with their reckless "grain-procurements policy," have brought a number of districts in western Georgia to the point of <u>famine</u>. They do not understand that the Ukrainian methods of grain procurement, which are necessary and expedient <u>in grain-surplus</u> districts, are unsuitable and damaging in <u>grain-deficit</u> districts, which have no industrial proletariat <u>whatsoever</u> to boot. They are arresting people by the hundreds, including <u>party</u> <u>members</u> who clearly sympathize with the malcontents and do not sympathize with the "policy" of the Georgian CC. But arrests will not take you very far. The shipment of grain must be strengthened (accelerated!) immediately, without delay. Otherwise we may <u>face bread riots</u>, even though we have already solved the grain problem. Immediately upon receipt of this letter, let the Politburo make it incumbent upon Mikoian to strengthen the shipment of grain to Western Georgia and to personally monitor fulfillment.[5] Otherwise we are sure to face a political scandal.

1. See note 8 to document 1.

2. See note 7 to document 1.

3. The Politburo resolved on 20 August 1931 to discuss Syrtsov's memo on timber-export expenditures at a meeting on 25 August during consideration of the issue of timber exports as a whole (RGASPI, f. 17, op. 3, d. 843, l. 5). The discussion, however, did not take place on 25 August. Based on a poll of Politburo members, a decision was adopted on 25 August to turn over questions of exports and timber-export expenditures to the foreign-currency commission for preliminary consideration (ibid., d. 844, l. 12).

4. See note 10 to document 1. On 14 August Stalin commented to Kaganovich by cipher "Kuibyshev must be overtired; he should be given leave to first September" (ibid., f. 558, op. 11, d. 76, l. 7).

5. A Politburo decision on accelerated grain shipments to Georgia was adopted on 20 August, after a reminder (see the introduction to this chapter). See document 5.

· 3 ·

Kaganovich to Stalin
12 August

F. 558, op. 11, d. 739, ll. 1–7.

Greetings Comrade Stalin!

I had a talk today with Comrade Kuibyshev.[1] He attributes his request first of all to the fact that there has been an organizational breakdown at Gosplan: Rozental wants to leave Gosplan, the party cell is trying to run things and continues to pick at Rozental, particularly for proposing that Strumilin be invited to manage the work in drawing up the [second] five-year plan.[2] Second, the poor relationship of Gosplan with government departments, especially with Vesenkha, he gives the example where a directive was issued throughout Vesenkha to provide material only to Kuibyshev, but not to the Gosplan bureaucracy, other government departments are also starting not to cooperate, so for lack of materials it is paralyzed. And the PC of Finance isn't showing a very good attitude either, as it is more or less competing with Gosplan. All this, Comrade Kuibyshev stated, shows that it [Gosplan] is not coping with the work. I pointed out to him that it was wrong to take this view of the issue, that the CC can both help with people and tell the party cell not to interfere in management and that the attitudes of the government departments can also be straightened out by the Central Committee if there is something abnormal, in any case he should have spoken with you rather than wait until three days after you left on vacation before submitting such a request.

He asked me to authorize a vacation for him now, and I turned him down, explaining that he had linked the vacation to his resignation, that I had forwarded his request to you and we would await your instructions.

My impression is that his request was not thought out and that he will take it back, maybe it would be helpful for him to go see you in Sochi.

Now a few practical questions:

1) Stanislav Kosior came to visit, he complained that the deterioration in the harvest had covered a number of grain-growing regions, like Zinoviev, Krivoy Rog, Kherson, Odessa, Nikolaev, etc., that the shortfall in the gross harvest will reach 170 million poods [2,785,000 tons]. In response to my point that the Right Bank, at least, had had a better harvest than last year, Comrade Kosior said that that would not close the gap. They are not raising the question of a revision of the plan now, but apparently they are laying the foundation for it, so far their procurements are going pretty well, the south in general is not doing badly. The Central Volga is doing well, the Lower Volga is lagging, and a request has come in from Bashkiria and Tataria for a revision of the plan. Bashkiria is asking

that it be given [a target of] 28 [million poods] instead of 44, we are think-ing of flatly rejecting the request and giving them a firm directive.[3] In gen-eral we need to take a firm tone, to the effect that we are not going to re-vise any plans again, otherwise the procurements will start to unravel. On the 15th we will raise the questions of grain procurements with the Polit-buro,[4] and evidently we will need to keep a vigilant eye on grain procure-ments in every region, as was the case last year.

2) The Donets Basin is in bad shape with regard to supplies, both tech-nical (spikes and so forth) and food. On the 15th we will propose that the Politburo adopt a number of practical measures to improve supplies and increase production.[5] On wages we will hear a report by Comrades Posty-shev and Gurevich,[6] we will adopt a final decision after getting your ad-vice, this increase in coal and metal will cost about 70 million until the end of '31, and about 200 million next year, but we will have to do this.

3) On railroad transport, evidently right after the report by Kishkin and Blagonravov (on the 15th) we will need to organize an inspection of the preparation of the railroads for fall. Judging by preliminary information, the situation is not very good. How do you feel about the idea, after some inspection by CC members, of putting on a report by the PC of Transport at the Politburo session and summoning about 20 people from the rail-roads to attend it. We have postponed water transport until the 25th so that the CC can prepare its co-report.

4) I am sending you the Politburo agendas until the 25th. Now we are preparing a list of the principal questions for five or six sessions so that we can send them to you in advance.

Regards to Comrade Molotov.

Yours, L. Kaganovich.

12 August 1931.

P.S. We have decided to meet on the 14th to discuss the second five-year plan,[7] we are sending you the material. L.K.

P.S. [*sic*] A few more additional words about the talk with Comrade Kuibyshev.

When I made the point that we have a body that can resolve all ques-tions in dispute, including the issue of setting up normal relations with Vesenkha and Comrade Sergo [Ordzhonikidze], Comrade Kuibyshev re-plied: "If there has been no success in repairing Sergo's relationship with Molotov, it definitely won't be possible to repair his relationship with me, after all the whole affair (the conflict between Sergo and Molotov)," says Comrade Kuibyshev, "ended in Sergo's triumph and victory, after all he did not take back his words." Needless to say, it is laughable to speak of some victory and triumph, but this sort of approach is rather typical. Your L.K.

1. See note 10 to document 1.
2. On 3 September 1931 the Politburo confirmed Rozental's appointment as a member of

the collegium of the PC for Supply and relieved him of membership of the presidium of Gosplan (RGASPI, f. 17, op. 3, d. 846, l. 12).

3. On 18 August 1931 the Politburo rejected the proposals by the Bashkir Regional Party Committee for a reduction in its plan for grain procurements for 1931, and the Bashkir leaders were instructed "to cease all discussion of the plan for procurements of grain and to develop energetic work to fulfill the plan for grain procurements" (ibid., d. 843, l. 6).

4. See note 5 to document 4.

5. See note 2 to document 4.

6. On 15 August 1931 the Politburo heard a report by Postyshev and Gurevich on the restructuring of the wage system in the coal and iron and steel industries and approved, in the main, the commission's work. Postyshev, Gurevich, and Shvernik were instructed to prepare the final draft (ibid., d. 842, l. 3). See also note 7 to document 9.

7. See document 4.

· 4 ·

Kaganovich to Stalin
[15 August]

F. 558, op. 11, d. 739, ll. 8–18.

Greetings Comrade Stalin!

1) On the 14th we had a conference on the second five-year plan, and after a rather lengthy exchange of opinions we came to the conclusion that the draft directives are not good enough and that they have to be reworked. First of all, they contain a lot of incorrect formulations and goals, for example the idea that we will be able to catch up to the advanced cap[italist] countries and overtake them already in the second five-year-plan period. There was a good reason you allowed ten years for achieving this objective, because the exertions that achieving this goal will require cannot be underestimated, and the Gosplan people decided to jump "ahead" from "realism" to maximalism. Hence their program for metal calling for 45 million tons in '37. We proceeded from the guideline that you once set. We rejected the figure of 45 and adopted 25–30 million tons. We instructed that this draft directive be reworked, assuming, first, a uniform distribution of productive forces around the country, both in industry and in agriculture. Second, there must be a particular elaboration of issues and measures pertaining to the financial position and living standards of workers. The point is not so much to have a six-hour workday as to clearly tell workers (on the basis of calculations) what their situation will be, then they will go to the plant more quickly. The issue of eliminating shortages of goods and the issue of the urban economy must be elaborated, the issue of personnel must be elaborated in particular, and the general section should not get away with phrases, and incorrect ones at that, to the effect that in the second five-year plan there will be no classes, and

only a small-owner mentality, bureaucratism, and self-seeking will remain. Evidently we will have to adopt a shorter directive in the Politburo at the outset so that the control figures of the second five-year plan will be based on this directive and they will probably become the reference document for the CC plenum and the party conference.[1]

2) Today in the Politburo we mainly discussed a number of issues related to fuel and the Donets Basin. The fuel situation requires energetic measures. We established a commission to which we gave a number of assignments, both in fuel distribution and in organizing production.[2]

We had a dispute about the delivery of fuel by foreign ships to Leningrad by sea. Those in favor of this were Kuibyshev, Sergo in part, and the Leningraders. But the Politburo rejected this proposal and resolved to rely on our Volga water transport, evidently we will have to send representatives of the CC and Sovnarkom there, as we did with rail transport.[3]

3) We adopted a resolution on nonferrous metals and in the section on aluminum adopted 20,000 tons in '32 and 70,000 tons in '33, although our industrialists did all they could to prove that this is unrealistic and unfeasible. It looks like we will have to exert more pressure in order to enforce the decision.[4]

4) The progress of grain procurements in the first half of August is cause for some alarm. Procurements are going badly in the Lower Volga, and not very well in the Northern Caucasus and in other places (in the first 10 days of August, 20% of the plan for the USSR as a whole was fulfilled). We decided to send directives to each region individually and in general get into more specific day-to-day management of grain procurements. We are not sending any people now. Let the localities prove themselves in the work on procurements, perhaps we will have to send a few CC members only to certain regions, depending on how things go.[5]

5) The meat situation is extremely bad. I got into a scrap with Mikoian today. Instead of specific proposals to strengthen procurements, he submitted only one proposal to reduce consumption and immediately added orally that it probably won't be possible to meet the reduced ration. We adopted the reduction in consumption even in Moscow, but instructed him to draw up and submit to the Politburo a specific plan of economic measures, especially for procurements of poultry.[6]

6) On the 20th we will have to discuss the situation with the export and import plan and foreign currency. A few days ago, in the Vesenkha commission on the foreign-currency plan for August, we had to decide, on the one hand, to increase payments in America above what Rozengolts had proposed, and, on the other, to curtail Vesenkha's demands. We are not placing new orders now, but we have to pay for the old ones, which are already 40 percent paid. Vesenkha demanded 8–9 million rubles. After calculating what must really be paid, we arrived at 6 million, but the foreign-

currency situation is extremely strained. I must tell you, Comrade Stalin, that the whole manner in which the import situation is organized has made a very bad impression on me, they can't answer the question of what equipment we are importing specifically in August, and as a result maybe we are rushing to import things in August that will then become idle capital for six months, which is the case at a number of plants. We do not know what our payments are on a quarterly basis, whom we are paying and for what. One gets the sense that there is no unity between an order, the movement of equipment, and the movement of payments. If you find it expedient, maybe we would deal here with these issues of the proper organization of the situation at Vneshtorg [PC of Foreign Trade] and at Vesenkha.[7]

7) We deferred the issue of cotton procurements. The point is that we contracted for 40 million poods [655,000 tons]. Now it turns out that the data on crop areas were overstated by about 18–20 percent. And a debate is being conducted, by Shadunets among others, about how much cotton to procure. One person says 32 million, another 22 to 24, and so forth. For us just to give a general directive in these circumstances, to stick to the framework of what was contracted and fail to specify a precise figure, is to ignore the fact that a debate is under way that will demoralize cotton-procurement agents. We must issue a firm directive on how much to procure (a figure) and forbid any debate or babble, so we decided to defer until the 20th in order to get your opinion. Please send it to me by wire.[8]

8) We adopted a resolution today on OGIZ [Corporation of State Publishing Houses]. We are not going to publish it now. You and Comrade Molotov may have some revisions.[9] We deferred the issue of schools, it proved to be very important. It was raised in the Politburo at an extremely opportune time. It came out in the commission that some harebrained schemers were taking the schools along a path of destruction. I will write about it in detail next time.[10]

9) We are sending you the edited text on cooperatives and public food-service facilities. If you have no revisions, please let us know by wire so that we can publish it. If you have revisions, please send them to us.[11]

Well, with that I will conclude this protracted letter, Comrade Stalin. I don't know, maybe I am overburdening you with questions and I am not letting you relax, especially in the first few days, but the need is still great.

Regards to Comrade Molotov.

How are you enjoying your vacation. Are you getting better.

Regards to Nadezhda Sergeevna.

Yours, L. Kaganovich.

1. On 21 August Stalin replied by cipher that the plan for pig iron should be not 25–30 but 25 million poods [a slip for "tons"]: "our dear comrades have obviously not yet abandoned rhetorical leftist attitudes" (RGASPI, f. 558, op. 11, d. 76, ll. 21–23). For the contro-

versy about the pig-iron targets for the second five-year plan, first described by the Soviet historian V. I. Kuzmin, see Davies (1996), 123–24. At the August 1931 conference on the five-year plan Kuibyshev had already reduced the original plan to produce 60 million tons in 1937 to 45 million tons. Directives for drawing up the second five-year plan (1933–37) were approved by the XVII Conference of the VKP(b) in January–February 1932, including a pig-iron plan for 1937 of only 18 million tons. In Kaganovich's draft letter, " 'realism' " was described as "Bagdatiev's 'realism' "; Bagdatiev was a Gosplan official.

2. On 15 August the Politburo approved a draft resolution, submitted by Ordzhonikidze, on providing labor for the coal industry and housing construction in the Donets Basin, an order from Vesenkha dated 14 August, and a resolution by the PC for Supply, dated 11 August, on supplies for the Donets Basin. The PC for Supply was instructed, along with Tsentrosoiuz (the All-Union Central Union of Consumer [Cooperative] Societies), to devise, within 15 days, "a procedure for supplying the Donets Basin that would guarantee against any future interruptions in supplies" (f. 17, op. 3, d. 842, l. 5). A commission headed by Rudzutak was established to finish work on the resolution; the Politburo approved the commission's decisions on 25 August (ibid., d. 844, ll. 3, 14–17). See also document 3.

3. On 15 August 1931 the Politburo rejected the proposal for oil deliveries to Leningrad by sea, confirming the Politburo decision of 16 June on deliveries of all fuel oil via the Volga (ibid., d. 842, l. 2). By a Politburo decision on 20 August, representatives for oil shipping of the CC and Sovnarkom were appointed: Blagonravov for Astrakhan and Baku; Pylaev and Zhdanov for Nizhny Novgorod; Krinitsky for Samara and Saratov (ibid., d. 843, l. 3). See also note 5 to document 8.

4. On 15 August 1931 the Politburo approved a draft resolution on nonferrous metals, gold, and platinum. It said: "Because of the change in the figure for aluminum production (to as much as 20,000 tons in 1931 and as much as 70,000 tons in 1933), Vesenkha is instructed to work out measures to ensure fulfillment of this decision" (ibid., d. 842, ll. 8, 28–34). Actual aluminum production reached 900 tons in 1932 and 4,400 tons in 1933 (*Promyshlennost' SSSR* [The Industry of the USSR] [Moscow, 1936], 525). See also document 1.

5. On 15 August 1931 the Politburo instructed the Secretariat of the CC of the VKP(b), along with Mikoian, to draw up a draft directive for local organizations "both for quantitative indicators of procurements and with reference to their character and methods." The Secretariat was instructed, when necessary, to schedule the dispatch of CC members to districts where the grain-procurement situation was exceptionally bad (RGASPI, f. 17, op. 3, d. 842, l. 7). See also document 3.

6. On 15 August 1931 the Politburo authorized the PC for Supply, in connection with the cutback in the plan for livestock procurements, to reduce the meat rations for the third quarter (ibid., d. 842, l. 6). On 30 August the Politburo approved a draft resolution, submitted by the PC for Supply, on organizing the new livestock-procurement campaign "so that the PC for Supply will concentrate the work of its agencies on actual fulfillment of this decision and on supplying the main workers' districts, above all Moscow and Leningrad, with meat" (ibid., d. 845, ll. 2, 15–20).

7. On 21 August Stalin wrote to Kaganovich by cipher that "it seems to me you have given too much American currency to Vesenkha"; "all orders to America should be cut as much as possible" (ibid., f. 558, op. 11, d. 76, ll. 21–23). See also document 5.

8. On 21 August Stalin informed Kaganovich by cipher that cotton procurements should amount to 34 million poods [557,000 tons], including 28 million poods [459,000 tons] from Central Asia without Kazakhstan (ibid.). On 25 August the Politburo approved this figures, and instructed the Central Asian Bureau of the CC to discontinue any debates on the procurements plan and to develop work as intensively as possible in fulfilling the decisions of the CC (ibid., f. 17, op. 3, d. 844, l. 2).

9. On 15 August the Politburo approved a draft resolution on the report by OGIZ (ibid.,

d. 842, ll. 8, 50–56). The document was published in its final form in newspapers on 3 September 1931 as a CC resolution "On Publishing Work."

10. A resolution "On Elementary and Secondary Schools" was adopted by the Politburo on 25 August 1931 (ibid., d. 844, ll. 8, 22–29) and publkhed in newspapers on 5 September. It condemned "attempts to use the so-called 'project method' as the basis of all schoolwork," which "was leading, in effect, to the destruction of schools." See also document 5.

11. See notes 7 and 8 to document 1. On 14 August Stalin told Kaganovich by cipher that he had talked with Yakovlev, who would bring new proposals to the Politburo which "must be approved unconditionally" (ibid., f. 558, op. 11, d. 76, l. 7). On 17 August he replied to Kaganovich that "you did not send the resolution on cooperation, so I cannot tell you my opinion" (ibid. l. 13).

· 5 ·

Kaganovich to Stalin
20 August 1931

F. 558, op. 11, d. 739, ll. 28–39.

———————————

Greetings dear Comrade Stalin!

Today we had a Politburo meeting on several issues, and we deferred a decision so that we could query you.

1) On the CER [Chinese Eastern Railroad]. In connection with the railroad's difficult financial situation, the Rudzutak commission has drawn up a number of proposals, which focus on putting the railroad's financial operations in order, but they include items that could cause complications with the Chinese. For example, the requirement for an immediate drastic cutback in the railroad's outlays on providing credit to Chinese government institutions and issuing outright grants, the maintenance and transport of troops to defend the railroad, etc. If we add organizational issues to this, such as the question of the rights of the manager and his Chinese deputy, all this can cause an exacerbation of relations. We ask that you let us know your opinion whether we should take the step toward some exacerbation. The draft has been sent to you.[1]

2) On closing a contract with the Belgian firm for the sale of Soviet grain. In the past the Politburo rejected this proposal in view of the high interest on warrant credits (16 percent), now a new offer has come in from the Belgians for 12 percent annually, but instead of 500,000 pounds sterling they would give us 200,000. The commission would be 1 percent instead of the 1, $1\frac{1}{4}$ and $1\frac{1}{2}$ percent, depending on the amount of grain sold, that was previously proposed. Eksportkhleb [the state grain export agency] is placing two representatives at the firm, who will participate in the sale on a day-to-day basis, and if the sale is unsatisfactory, they (the Eksportkhleb representatives) have the right to sell the grain themselves, and so forth. Since the sale of our grain exports will run into significant diffi-

culties this year, the question arises of whether we should refuse these new conditions. We await your opinion, it would be good to wire it.[2]

3) The third issue, which has become very thorny, is the issue of new orders in America. Specifically we decided to query you about the new orders for Magnitogorsk and Kuznetsstroy. Based on the Politburo resolution of 20 July, today we gave permission to supplement the orders in America for Avtostroy [the Gorky auto-plant project], the Khark[ov] Tract[or] Plant, and Dneprostroy [Dnieper Hydroelectric Station project] by 3,900,000 rubles, as for the Magnitogorsk project and the Kuznetsk project we deferred the issue. Point E of the Politburo resolution makes a distinction between these plants (I am sending you the resolution). I must say that we have had a substantial overexpenditure for the first set of plants as well. For example, quotas were set for Avtostroy at 19,160,000 [rubles], and purchases already amount to 22,356,000. Now they have asked for an additional 5,180,000. We gave them 3,364,000. We cut out, for example, 40 lathes that for some reason were transferred from Europe to America. Likewise we cut out various equipment amounting to 800,000 rubles that was transferred from Europe to America, and so on. During the discussion of all these issues the temperature as usual went up very high. It started already in the morning at the foreign-currency commission, actually it started already at the commission about a week ago during the discussion of the August plan for Vesenkha's foreign-currency payments in America. Rozengolts proposed setting it at 2 million, that turned out to be obviously untenable, because the orders were already placed, 40 percent was already paid, and a refusal to make further payments would mean big trouble in America. Vesenkha demanded 8 million, and we settled, as you know, on 6 million. The exchange of courtesies between Rozen[golts] and Sergo was very unpleasant, but it didn't end too badly, because we allocated 6 million. But while our hand was forced in that case because the orders already had to be paid off, in the future we need the utmost restraint in placing new orders, which is actually what the Politburo wrote into point 3.

And so when we got together at the commission today, the attacks and counterattacks started. We wanted to discuss export issues—the fulfillment of the plan, the report on forthcoming payments, etc. Sergo demanded that we first discuss the issue of the new American orders, on the grounds that Rozengolts had acted outrageously by sending a telegram to America that forbade new orders until a directive was issued. We agreed and took up this issue first, but instead of delivering a report on the substance Sergo began trying to prove that the plants were important, the orders should be placed, otherwise the program would be ruined and he essentially boiled it down to the point that we had a quota approved of 80 million for America + 8 million left over from the special qu[arter] and that we should proceed on the basis of the 88 million rubles. I proposed that we be told calmly, with figures and itemized lists of the orders, which factories they are for, what they want to order, and what could be transferred to Europe, so that we don't decide blindly but only after sorting things out. Then Sergo was intolerably tactless, saying, for example: "You are afraid of forcing Rozengolts to carry out the decision and so forth. If you are afraid yourselves we will ask the comrades who have gone away" (as if we have to send an inquiry only if we are afraid of deciding the issue). Sergo had no grounds to make such a statement, because he had not raised this question in the Politburo. I replied that we can inquire regardless of the way the issue was framed, but this statement of his was wrong because the Politburo can force any people's commissar to carry out the Politburo's decisions, even somebody like Sergo.

At the commission we later adopted a number of decisions by way of preparing the issues, because Rozengolts proved to be unprepared both on exports and on the calculations of forthcoming payments. As for the issue of immediate orders in America, we gave instructions to estimate how much the orders add up to for the four plants in the first group: AMO [the Moscow auto-plant project], Avtostroy, Dneprostroy, and the Kharkov Tractor Plant, and for the two plants [in the second group] (the Kuznetsk project and the Magnitogorsk project) and transferred the matter to the Politburo.

At the Politburo meeting, after a proposal that we decide now about the orders for the first group of plants, i.e. orders amounting to 3,900,000 and defer the Magnitogorsk and Kuznetsk projects, we decided to take another look at what we are ordering and simultaneously to query you. Comrade Sergo absolutely out of the blue brought the matter to a head again, I am not going to set forth his entire argument, for example he pompously declared: "You here he said want to play the role of backers of a strong state [*gosudarstvenniki*], but when the plants break down I will have to answer for it, and not the people who are holding a 'serious discussion' here." Why did Sergo need to create this atmosphere, how can he not realize that the Politburo cannot agree to meet all of his needs, that we must be objective. The harder it is for us without you, the more everybody must restrain themselves. He concluded with a laughable statement that I (Kaganovich) was shouting at him and he would not allow it. This laughable claim is not even worth denying, because besides the fact that he will outshout everybody, everybody knows my [positive] feelings about him, but it is true that I did not agree to satisfy all of his Vesenkha demands for new orders [omission here because the edge of the page is cut off] without end and to prevent a situation in which nobody could object to an incorrect proposal by Sergo.

Maybe I described all this in too much detail, but, Comrade Stalin, this upset me very much.

Essentially we are asking you to answer us, first, about the orders for Magnitogorsk and the Kuznetsk project, maybe some of the orders can be ordered in Europe, and some in America. Second, Sergo is raising the question of the orders for the Cheliabinsk project, but this was not part of the quotas. Third, pipe stills and other oil equipment have been ordered from America, so we will have to pay for this, but there are also a number of further demands for new orders. What should we do about them. Evidently they will have to be cut back.[3]

4) We heard a report by Piatakov today on the German orders. They easily knocked down the discount interest rate to 10 percent, because as Piatakov says, they need our orders very badly. They spoke with him about the possibility of granting us a new loan of 200 to 300 million marks, especially for metal orders.[4]

5) Telegrams are coming in from the Central Volga and Siberia about the dimensions of the crop failure. Eikhe has arrived and is raising the question once again of revising the plan. He is requesting that we lower the plan from 100 million [poods] to 63. I severely criticized him for such counterplans, but he is requesting that we discuss his request. So far we haven't discussed it. It will probably be best to refuse now. Maybe the issue will become clearer later on.

The Central Volga people are also requesting a furth[er] reduction. Them we can certainly turn down.[5] We also decided about grain for Georgia today. I sent you our resolution on warehouses today. I will personally keep track of its implementation.[6]

6) I am sending you the resolution on publishing work (based on the report by OGIZ [the Corporation of State Publishing Houses]) and on elementary and secondary schools.[7] Since there has not been a single detailed resolution on schools since the program, we included an introductory section, which begins by taking note of achievements. When it goes on to shortcomings it stresses the basic idea that you stressed in framing the issue, that the fundamental shortcoming is the unsatisfactory level of general-education knowledge. We had very big arguments. Apparently all sorts of leftist and rightist elements, which the party squeezed hard in every other area, have set up a refuge for themselves in the educational agencies and in teaching. That is why we have stressed the task of fighting these elements in this resolution.

I guess I will end here. Good-bye. Yours, Kaganovich.

20 August 1931

1. On 25 August Stalin told Kaganovich by cipher, "You can wait a little with the CER" (RGASPI, f. 558, op. 11, d. 76, ll. 33, 34). Between April and October 1931, 22 sessions of the Soviet-Chinese conference were held. The Soviet delegation proposed a draft for resolving the disputed issues, including: the financial situation of the CER and measures to increase its profitability; providing credit to Chinese government institutions and transporting de-

fense troops; operations of the office of the chairman of the board/managerial director of the railroad, and other items. Agreement was reached only on the introductory section and some items in this list. At this point, because of the Japanese aggression in Manchuria in September 1931, the Soviet-Chinese conference discontinued its work (DVP, vol. XIV, pp. 786–88).

2. On 30 July 1931, in discussing the sale of Soviet grain in Belgium, the Politburo instructed the PC of Foreign Trade to reply to the Belgian firm that the high interest rate was unacceptable to the USSR (RGASPI, f. 17, op. 162, d. 10, l. 132). On 25 August Stalin told Kaganovich by cipher that he did not object to the proposed contract with the Belgians (ibid., f. 558, op. 11, d. 76, ll. 33, 34), and on 25 August the Politburo agreed to the proposal of the PC of Foreign Trade "to conclude a contract with the Belgian firm for the sale of our grain in Belgium, with the granting of warrant credit" (ibid., f. 17, op. 162, d. 10, l. 170).

3. See note 1 to document 6.

4. On 20 August 1931 the Politburo noted Piatakov's report and approved "the measures taken by him to implement the Politburo resolution on setting a fixed, maximum interest rate." The Politburo also decided to hear a report by Piatakov and Rozengolts on 25 August on measures to combat abuses by firms in fulfilling orders. (ibid., l. 164). See also note 1 to document 1.

5. On 25 August 1931 resolutions on the plan for grain procurements for Western Siberia and the Central Volga were adopted by a poll of the Politburo members. The plan for grain procurements from Western Siberia was lowered by 15 million poods (246,000 tons) (the final annual plan was 85 million poods [1,392,000 tons]), and from the Central Volga, by 20 million poods (328,000 tons) (final plan: 100 million poods [1,638,000 tons]) (ibid., l. 170). These figures had been proposed by Stalin in a cipher dated 22 August (RGASPI, f. 558, op. 11, d. 76, l. 26). Actual procurements in Western Siberia totaled 65.3 million poods [1,070,000 tons], i.e. roughly the level of Eikhe's proposals, and in the Middle Volga, 76.6 million poods [1,255,000 tons].

6. See note 5 to document 2.

7. See notes 9 and 10 to document 4.

· 6 ·

Stalin to Kaganovich
25 August

F. 81, op. 3, d. 99, ll. 4–6.

---

25 August [1931]

Greetings, Comrade Kaganovich:

I received your latest letter yesterday. I have given my answer to your questions in ciphers.

1) I think the question of the American orders is more serious than some comrades think. The foreign-currency shortage is not the only problem. The main problem is that if we don't drop the new orders placed to America <u>on the draconian credit terms</u> that America practices, we may <u>lose</u> the <u>preferential</u> terms that we have secured in Germany, Italy, and Britain (and will secure in France). The comrades at Vesenkha fail to understand this. Of course, there <u>can</u> be exceptions, say, for the Cheliabinsk construction

project or military industry. But that is a separate issue that the Politburo must decide on a case-by-case basis.[1]

I have written about this to Comrade Ordzhonikidze.

2) I am not sure that the resolution on cooperatives should be published in the name of the Sovnarkom and the CC. Why can't it be released in the name of the Fulfillment Commission? It would also not be a bad idea to defer the question until the end of the month, when I will already be in Sochi and will have a chance to talk with Molotov about the final text of the resolution.[2]

Best wishes, I. Stalin.

1. See document 5. On 20 August 1931 the Politburo approved a figure of 3.9 million rubles until the end of 1931 to cover orders placed in America for equipment to be shipped to AMO, the Kharkov Tractor Plant, the Gorky auto-plant project, and Dneprostroy. Regarding orders placed in America for Magnitogorsk, the Kuznetsk project, and other enterprises, it was decided to ask for Stalin's opinion (RGASPI, f. 17, op. 162, d. 10, l. 165). In response Stalin sent a telegram addressed to Kaganovich: "In view of the hard-currency problems and the unacceptable credit terms in America, I am opposed to placing any new orders whatsoever in America. I propose that we impose a ban on new orders in America, break off any negotiations for new orders that have already begun there, and, where possible, call off contracts already negotiated for old orders and transfer those orders to Europe or to our own factories. I propose that we allow no exemptions from this rule for Magnitogorsk, the Kuznetsk project, the Kharkov project, Dneprostroy, and AMO and the Gorky auto-plant project. I propose that all previous Politburo decisions at odds with this decision be revoked" (ibid., l. 173). The Politburo adopted these proposals by Stalin on 25 August. The foreign-currency commission was instructed to elaborate, on an urgent basis, concrete measures to implement Stalin's proposals and submit them for approval by the Politburo. People's Commissar for Foreign Trade Rozengolts was instructed to suspend the placing of orders in America (ibid., l. 170). On 30 August the Politburo approved a resolution by the currency commission containing instructions to Vesenkha that it submit to the Politburo by 5 September a report on orders that were transferred from America to Europe and the USSR. The Foreign Trade PC was to report to Vesenkha within four days on which American orders were suspended and to submit a list of contracts that could be canceled. It was stipulated that the contracts would be canceled only by permission of the Politburo (ibid., l. 179). See also documents 4, 15.

2. See note 7 to document 1.

· 7 ·

Stalin to Kaganovich
26 August 1931

F. 81, op. 3, d. 99, ll. 7–11.

Greetings, Comrade Kaganovich:

I am writing about Transcaucasian affairs. A few days ago members of the Transcaucasian Regional Committee, secretaries of the Georgian CC, and several Azerbaijani functionaries (including Polonsky) visited me. They are in the midst of unbelievable infighting, and it seems to be a long way from being over. As far as I can see, the reason the infighting is going on for so long and the squabblers are so tenacious is partly because they are sure their antiparty "work" will go unpunished, since they assume that in case of "trouble" Sergo [Ordzhonikidze] will "rescue" them.

I reconciled them to some extent, and things have settled down for now, but not for long. Almost everybody lies and tries to outsmart the other, beginning with Kartvelishvili. Beria, Polonsky, and Orakhelashvili don't lie. But Polonsky makes a number of gaffes and mistakes. The most unpleasant impression is left by Mamulia (secretary of the Georgian CC), who substitutes for Kartvelishvili by some rule unknown to me. Sukhishvili, the chairman of the Georgian Sovnarkom, makes a comical impression— he is a hopeless nitwit. It is downright astonishing that both of these characters were recommended by Sergo.

If we don't intervene, these people in their stupidity may wreck everything. They have already ruined the situation with the peasants in Georgia and Azerbaijan. Kartvelishvili and the Transcaucasian Regional Committee in general are powerless to improve the situation without serious intervention by the CC of the VKP, assuming that they will want to improve the situation.

What should we do?

We must:

1) Schedule now, for the end of September (by my arrival), a report to the Orgburo of the Transcaucasian Regional Committee, the Georgian CC, and the Azerbaijan CC on the state of affairs;[1]

2) Thoroughly purge them at an Orgburo meeting and remove a number of individuals, such as Mamulia;[2]

3) Appoint a third secretary of the Transcaucasian Regional Committee (I propose Meerzon) and give him appropriate instructions.[3]

4) And so forth along these lines.

Without such measures, the situation in Transcaucasia will fester.

I. Stalin.

26 August 1931.

1. See note 6 to document 16.

2. See note 13 to document 15.

3. Polonsky was appointed third secretary of the Transcaucasian Regional Committee. See note 6 to document 16.

· 8 ·

Stalin to Kaganovich
30 August

F. 81, op. 3, d. 99, ll. 12–14.

Comrade Kaganovich:

I received your letter of 26 August.

1) Why don't you say anything about the <u>Polish</u> draft pact (on nonaggression) that Patek passed on to Litvinov? This is a very important matter, which almost determines the issue of peace (for the next two or three years), and I am afraid that Litvinov will yield to so-called "public opinion" and will dismiss it as a trifle. Give serious attention to this matter and let the Politburo place it under special supervision and try to carry it to a conclusion by every possible means.[1] It would be laughable if we surrendered in this matter to the common, narrow-minded mania of "anti-Polandism" while forgetting, even for a minute, about the fundamental interests of the revolution and socialist construction.

2) What is the situation with Mezhlauk and the orders placed in France? Why have things gotten bogged down there? Why are all the orders placed in Germany and Britain while no one wants to give orders to the French?[2]

3) You have evidently given in to the pressure of Vesenkha regarding the iron pipes, especially since the municipal-economy people are laying on the pressure and are demanding imports. Both you and Vesenkha are wrong, since: a) the CC directive on control figures for 1932 <u>strictly defines</u> the 1931 figure for metal imports, and with regard to 1932 it says that the import figure must be <u>less</u> than the 1931 figure, whereas Vesenkha <u>wants to overturn this CC decision</u>, and you are parroting Vesenkha; b) the arguments that we will not have to pay this year are not convincing, because we will have a more difficult time with hard currency in 1932 and 1933 than this year (the efforts of the USA are aimed at emptying our hard-currency coffers and uprooting our hard-currency position, and the USA now is the main force in the financial world and our main enemy), so consequently we must take care of our hard currency not only for 1931 but also for the years to come;[3] c) instead of pressuring its own organization and making it produce more pig iron, Vesenkha is putting pressure on the state coffers (i.e. on the state, i.e. on the working class), forcing the working class to pay with its own hard-currency resources for the ineptitude, sluggishness, and bureaucratism of Vesenkha organization.[4]

That is where matters stand, Comrade Kaganovich.

4) This is why I don't think we should go easy at all on people (or insti-

tutions) who try to squander the working class's hard-currency resources just for the peace of mind of their organization's functionaries.

5) Assignments for drawing up the second five-year plan may be formalized through the Politburo if Gosplan or the Sovnarkom so requires.

6) Concessions to those who want to transport oil by sea would mean a demobilization of the entire transportation system. We cannot agree to such a concession.[5]

7) Let the Politburo and the Secretariat of the CC take the PC of Water Transport and the PC of Transport under <u>special</u> and <u>systematic</u> supervision and force them to work. Both people's commissars are captives of their bureaucracies, especially [people's commissar of transportation] Rukhimovich, whose bureaucratic self-importance is the reverse side of his backwardness and inertia in regard to a Bolshevik-style structuring of work at the PC of Transport.

8) There is <u>no</u> need for any <u>law</u> by TsIK [the Central Executive Committee of Soviets] on restoring the rights of certain former kulaks <u>ahead of schedule</u>.[6] I just knew that the jackasses among the petty bourgeoisie and the philistines would definitely want to crawl into this mousehole. Please put off this issue until the fall.

9) I read Bukharin's speech (the transcript). It is an empty, non-Bolshevik speech that is out of touch with real life. At the same time, it is an inept, amateurish attempt to "outline" a platform for the former rightists against the CC of the VKP [All-Union Communist Party] with regard to a host of economic issues and worker supply. A strange person, this Comrade Bukharin! Why did he have to put on this act?

I think the CC put Bukharin in charge of the technical propaganda department of Vesenkha not so he could deliver a speech about technical propaganda, about the need for technical propaganda, but so he would organize lively and specific technical propaganda. If he fails to accomplish this task, we will have to look for somebody else.

If Bukharin asks, or the situation demands it, you can tell Bukharin this is my opinion.[7]

Well, that's enough.   I. Stalin.

30 August [1931]. Sochi.

1. See note 1 to document 19.

2. See document 10.

3. See the introduction to this chapter.

4. On 25 September 1931, on the basis of a report by people's commissar of the municipal economy Komarov and Ordzhonikidze, the Politburo considered the issue of the supply of water pipes to the municipal economies of industrial centers. A special commission chaired by Piatakov was charged with submitting proposals on this issue by the 30 September session of the Politburo (RGASPI, f. 17, op. 3, d. 850, l. 5). At the following Politburo session, on 5 October, the issue was deferred (ibid., d. 851, l. 3). Based on a poll of Politburo

members on 15 October (Stalin had already returned to Moscow by this time), the issue was turned over to the Council for Labor and Defense for consideration (ibid., d. 854, l. 9).

5. In a letter to Stalin dated 26 August, Kaganovich reported that the proposal was to transport the oil on foreign ships, and expressed the view that this would result in "considerable demobilization of our river transport" (RGASPI, f. 558, op. 11, d. 739, ll. 48–55). On 5 September 1931 the Politburo approved a resolution on acceleration of oil shipments along waterways (along the Volga) (ibid., d. 846, l. 8, 27–30). See also note 3 to document 4.

6. On 10 August 1931 the Politburo approved a resolution, dated 7 August, by the commission on special settlers. The resolution specified measures for the "full utilization of the special settlers' workforce and their attachment to places of settlement, especially for purposes of creating permanent worker cadres in the timber industry of Siberia, the Urals, the Northern Region, and other areas" (the allocation to special settlers of land for vegetable gardens and crops and of livestock, tax benefits, the organization of housing construction, etc.). Clause 31 of the resolution read: "Taking into account the necessity of separating, as soon as possible, the young people among special migrants from the counterrevolutionary segment of the kulaks, it is to be deemed possible to restore rights to young people who have reached the age of 18 prior to expiration of the five-year period in those cases in which these young people have shown themselves in a positive light. Such restorations shall be carried out by departments for special settlements through the Central Executive Committees of Union and Autonomous Republics or through regional executive committees, and they shall be granted the right of free residency" (*Istoricheskii arkhiv*, no. 4, 1994, 164–69). On 26 August, Kaganovich wrote to Stalin in favor of a directive circular from TsIK, rather than publishing the law (RGASPI, f. 558, op. 11, d. 739, ll. 48–55). Following Stalin's letter printed above, on 8 September 1931 the Politburo revoked the contentious clause of the resolution (ibid., f. 17, op. 162, d. 11, l. 5).

7. For details, see the introduction to this chapter.

· 9 ·

Stalin to Kaganovich
4 September

F. 81, op. 3, d. 99, ll. 16–19.

---

4 September [1931]

<u>Greetings, Comrade Kaganovich:</u>

I received your letter.

1) I think the tractors from the PC of Agriculture will have to be put to <u>every possible</u> use for the timber industry during the winter period. If you have a serious talk with Yakovlev, I don't think he will raise any objections.[1]

2) I don't understand how the Politburo could agree with Vesenkha's proposals for additional imports of railroad-car axles and wheels and high-quality steel. Both proposals represent a direct circumvention of the July decision by the CC (adopted in the presence of Sergo [Ordzhonikidze], Piatakov, Bron, Molotov, and Stalin) on the <u>final</u> program of metal imports for 1931. As I understand it, you and Rudzutak were sim-

ply tricked. It is deplorable and disgusting if we start tricking each other. We have already sent the appropriate telegram to the Politburo.[2]

3) I strongly object to the Politburo decision to <u>replace</u> butter and egg exports with other food exports. This is senseless from the standpoint of current market conditions. You push grain exports as hard as you can when grain fetches <u>pennies</u>, and you want to hold back and do away with butter and egg exports, which are <u>more profitable</u> export commodities. What sense does that make? Wouldn't it be better to hold back grain exports and increase butter exports, or even to increase <u>both</u>, if you really want to make some hard currency and not just play some export game?[3]

4) The Politburo has decided, as the minutes indicate, to allocate 18 million poods [295,000 tons] of grain to bolster livestock procurements.[4] This is probably not a bad idea. But it is odd that 6 million of these 18 million poods (one-third!) are being <u>set aside for the "reserve" of the PC for Supply</u>. What PC for Supply "reserve" is this? What was it needed for? What is the basis for such boundless <u>trust</u> for the PC for Supply and such boundless <u>distrust</u> for the state, which actually is supposed to be the sole custodian of such large reserves? What did the state do to earn such distrust on the part of the PC for Supply? How could you allow such a perversion to occur? Can't this "PC for Supply reserve" be transferred to the reserve of the State (the USSR Sovnarkom) so that it is drawn on only by permission of the Politburo or the Sovnarkom?[5]

5) Don't ask about my health. If you wish me good health, be as vigilant as you can and don't allow the heroes of bureaucratism to lead you around by the nose.

All the best, I. Stalin.

6) The Politburo decision to award the Order of Lenin to <u>various</u> individuals gives a bad impression. You have started to award medals too easily. If this continues, the medal will be cheapened, and it will lose all of its moral force. This cannot be allowed to happen under any circumstances! Tell Postyshev not to give in to pressure from the high-and-mighty bureaucrats who are seeking medals for their fellow bureaucrat pals.[6]

7) I haven't read the resolution on wages in metal and coal. Tell Postyshev that I am voting for them on trust .[7]

I. St.

<u>P.S.</u> Comrade Kaganovich:

1) Please <u>wait</u> until I arrive before making new appointments for Rukhimovich, Kviring, and other PC of Transport people.[8]

Don't you think that Postnikov, Rukhimovich's closest friend and fellow bureaucrat, should also be removed or—better—transferred to one of the railroads (say, the Moscow-Belorussian-Baltic line) to replace Poliudov?[9]

2) Sheboldaev came to see me and asked me for five functionaries from

outside (the local functionaries, i.e. the old Northern Caucasus functionaries, have gotten too settled there and are no longer right for the job). I think we should do what he asks. We could give him Kviring for the regional planning committee, for example.

I. St.

   1. On 5 September 1931 a CC resolution on timber procurements and timber hauling was adopted. It noted that "party, Soviet, and economic organizations are failing to give this matter the proper attention. As a result, the haulage of lumber and other wood [. . .] between 1 July and 20 August amounted to only 17.4 percent of the plan for the third quarter." The PC of Agriculture was instructed to allocate 500 crawler tractors and 1,000 tire tractors for timber hauling for the period from 15 December to 15 February (RGASPI, f. 17, op. 3, d. 846, ll. 31–34).

   2. See documents 10, 11, 13, and 14 and the introduction to this chapter.

   3. On 30 August 1931 the Politburo examined the export-import and hard-currency plan for September and instructed an ad hoc commission "to work out the issue of the possible replacement of butter, egg, poultry, and codfish exports with other food exports for the same sum" (ibid., op. 162, d. 10, l.176). In his reply to Stalin dated 6 September, Kaganovich pointed out that the Politburo had merely instructed the commission to investigate the possibility of the proposed replacement (RGASPI, f. 558, op. 11, d. 739, ll. 88–90). On 8 September 1931 the Politburo resolved "not to allow changes in the established export plan for butter, eggs, and berries" for September (ibid., d. 11, l. 3). See also document 15.

   4. The decree of the board of the PC for Supply on organizing a new livestock-procurement campaign, about which Stalin writes, was approved by the Politburo on 30 August 1931 (RGASPI, f. 558, op. 3, d. 845, ll. 15–23).

   5. Following Stalin's letter, on 6 September Kaganovich wrote to him that the Politburo decision of 30 August had been "formulated inaccurately" (ibid. op. 11, d. 739, ll. 88–90). The Politburo decided on 8 September to amend the 30 August resolution and deem the 6 million poods in grain reserves for meat procurements to be not a PC of Supply reserve but a reserve of Sovnarkom, which was to be used in accordance with Politburo resolutions (ibid., d. 847, l. 7). On 10 October the untouchable reserve (*nepfond*) and the mobilization reserve (*mobfond*) were declared to be reserves (*fondy*) of the Council of Labor and Defense (ibid., op. 162, d. 11, l. 24). On 19 October 1931 the two reserves were placed under the authority of the Committee of Reserves of the Council of Labor and Defense (GARF, f. R-5446, op. 57, d. 16, l. 53).

   6. Postyshev headed the Politburo commission on awards, which reviewed petitions by various agencies and local authorities to issue USSR decorations. On 24 August 1931 Postyshev submitted for Politburo approval the minutes from the latest session of the commission, which contained a proposal to award the Order of Lenin to 44 individuals and the Order of the Red Labor Banner to 18. The individuals to be decorated were mostly functionaries in industrial enterprises (GARF, f. R-3316, op. 64, d. 1128, l. 47). On 25 August the Politburo approved this list of awards (RGASPI, f. 17, op. 3, d. 844, l. 1). On 6 September, Kaganovich replied to Stalin's reproof, "you are quite right, it came out badly, we will be more vigilant" (ibid., f. 558, op. 11, d. 739, ll. 88–90). Despite Stalin's criticism, the commission continued to be active. The torrent of requests for awards was so great that on 29 January 1933 Postyshev made the following request to A. S. Yenukidze, secretary of the USSR Central Executive Committee: "I am sending you all of the commission's materials regarding awards. Insofar as I cannot do this job on a daily basis, please instruct your staff to review and prepare the materials for later consideration by the commission" (GARF, f. R-3316, op. 65, d. 73, l. 9). By October 1935 the number of individuals awarded orders of the USSR exceeded 16,000 (ibid., d. 144, l. 5).

7. The resolution on restructuring the wage system in metallurgy and the coal industry was approved by the Politburo on 10 September 1931. It was decided to publish it in the name of the CC of the VKP(b), Vesenkha, and the AUCCTU [All-Union Central Council of Trade Unions] (RGASPI, f. 17, op. 3, d. 847, l. 2). On 20 September, following Stalin's letter (document 13), the Politburo resolved to amend this decision and publish the resolution in the name of Vesenkha and AUCCTU alone (ibid., d. 849, l. 1). See also note 6 to document 3.

8. See note 2 to document 23.

9. See note 2 to document 22.

· 10 ·

Kaganovich to Stalin
6 September

F. 558, op. 11, d. 739, ll. 76–87.

---

6 September [1931]
Greetings Comrade Stalin!

1. We received your cipher on France today. Your instructions completely coincide with the attitude of the Politburo members toward the French proposals. Tomorrow we will convene the Politburo and will issue a directive to our negotiators in accordance with your instructions.[1]

2. On Poland. The intelligence assignment has been given. On the 10th we will hear Litvinov, we will not adopt any decisions, everything we find out, I will report to you.[2]

3. At yesterday's Politburo meeting we heard a report on grain procurements. First, as of 1 September a total of 373,834,000 poods [6,123,000 tons] of grain procurements had been procured, i.e. 23.7 [percent] of the annual plan. Last year 202 million poods [3,309,000 tons] were procured, [so this year] is 85 percent ahead of last year. What is especially gratifying is that the last sixth five-day period [i.e. 26–30 August] has produced a big spurt. About 78 million poods [1,278,000 tons] have been procured during these five days. Still lagging behind in grain procurements are the Middle Volga, the Lower Volga, the Bashkir Republic, Siberia, and the Urals. The procurement of wheat and especially oats is going poorly. We took note of this in the Politburo resolution.[3] Since grain procurements are not going badly so far, we have not adopted any special decisions.

4. The issue of grain procurements was closely linked for us to the issue of the supply of [consumer] goods, but in view of the fact that no precise data were provided either on available amount of goods nor on their distribution, we set up a special commission, which we instructed to clarify the whole situation and submit specific proposals to the Politburo within five days.[4]

5. On the issue of preparing for the fall fishing season we had an ar-

gument. Mikoian proposed reducing the plan for the second half of the year. We rejected his proposal and approved the fishing-catch plan of 13 million tsentners.[5] At the same time we adopted a resolution to break up Soiuzryba [the All-Union State Corporation of the Fishing Industry and Fisheries] into Vostokryba [Eastern Corporation of the Fishing Industry and Fisheries] (Khabarovsk), Sevryba [Northern Corporation of the Fishing Industry and Fisheries] (Leningrad), and Soiuzryba (Moscow). Incidentally I can report to you that we have worked up your proposal for organizing and developing fisheries in the Moscow Region. The Moscow Committee has adopted a detailed resolution, which I am sending you just in case. The project turned out to be a very big one. We are setting a goal of achieving 1,200,000 poods [19,660 tons] of fish annually by '34.

6. The situation in the iron and steel industry is not too good. We heard reports from Vesenkha—Myshkov and Ivanchenko. Vesenkha uncovered shortcomings at the enterprises and outlined a number of practical measures, and we approved these measures, but I must say that neither Myshkov nor Ivanchenko completely comprehend the subjective shortcomings of the economic management. The question also came up of separating out the new construction projects from the existing corporations so that the corporations can concentrate entirely on operating existing plants, but we took the issue off the agenda in order to ask you. Please let me know your opinion.

7. On the Kharkov Tractor Plant and the Moscow auto-plant project we set firm deadlines for opening and starting up the plants on 1 October. The issue of imports was raised, but we dropped it, not without arguments.

8. I am sending you draft resolutions on r[ail] and water transport. We deferred the issue until 10 or 15 September. We drew up the resolution on rail transport in battles with the PC of Transport people. In addition to the issues of steam locomotives and double-team operation, the issue of railroad cars was especially prominent. The cars are falling apart, and the efficiency of their use is declining. As a result, a significant portion of the cars are listed on paper but in practice are not being used for transport. The cars have no master. The railroads are not only failing to take care of repairs but are trying to get rid of cars needing major or minor repairs to other railroads. The situation with repair shops at exchange sites for rail-cars has become worse than the situation with depots; the shops have been almost completely eliminated. That is why we adopted a resolution attaching the fleet of rail-cars to the railroads and assigning them responsibility for the condition of cars. Of course there is a difference here from locomotives, the cars can be used over a much larger territory and they run on different railroads, but these difficulties can be solved: first, by establishing an appropriate system of accounts between railroads and, second, by properly organizing the planning of shipments, especially by expand-

ing the practice of trains running on specific routes. It seems to me that eliminating the lack of personal responsibility for rail-cars will force the PC of Transport and the railroads to plan shipments better, to prevent empty runs, and to fight for efficient use of cars and actual implementation of economic accountability.

Two sections were excluded here. In one section Rukhimovich proposed listing the new construction projects that must be deferred because of a shortage of rails. We deferred this issue. We instructed STO [the Council of Labor and Defense] to work out the issue so that we can discuss it around the time you arrive.

It seems to me that Rukhimovich wants to divest himself of responsibility in advance for the failure to fulfill the construction plan. The second section that was left out deals with imports. The subcommission on capital construction and equipment supply submitted a number of proposals on imports for the PC of Transport. We took them off the agenda right away. We instructed Antipov and the PC of Foreign Trade people to carefully work on them in terms of a decisive cut. In any case, at the Politburo meeting we will not deal with this now, but as soon as it is ready, I will send it to you. To counterbalance these hopes for imports we inserted a point on mobilizing all domestic transport resources. As for the sections that have been drawn up, I think they respond to the most important issues of transport. Please do give us your opinion either by letter or by wire.[6]

9. In just the same way we deferred the issue of the capital construction plan for nitrogen plants. Doubts overcame us about whether the plan target might be too high, whether we might end up with the same thing as the Gosplan projects in metal. Please do let us know your opinion, or we can easily defer this until you arrive.[7]

10. You will see in the Politburo minutes a resolution on a question raised by Gorky on publishing a history of factories and plants. The history and crux of the issue are as follows: on the eve of the Politburo meeting Gorky called me to say that he had a proposal for publishing a history of factories and plants. He requested that the issue be discussed and right away asked if he could come to the Politburo meeting. I gave my assent. Gorky did not send in the promised material. During the discussion of the issue at the Politburo meeting I had to raise several objections to the guidelines that Gorky laid down and in passing took a poke at Bukharin as well. First, the very idea of the publication is vague and ill defined. Second, based on Gorky's summary this will be primarily a history of plants in technical terms. In fact, that is the justification for publishing the history at a scientific and technical publishing house. He proposed the following editorial staff: [in alphabetical order,] Averbakh, Aleksandrov, Bukharin, Gronsky, Gorky, Yenukidze, Zhiga, Vs. Ivanov, Krzhizhanovsky, Lebedinsky, Leonov, Postyshev, Piatakov, Sverdlov, Seifulina [*sic*], Tikhonov, Troit-

sky, Chubar, Chumandrin, and Shvernik. This list alone is a graphic illustration of the vagueness of this whole history, and there are fewer technically qualified people here than anyone else. I pointed out that the objectives of this history must be defined more precisely, that it cannot be concerned mainly with factory technology, that it will rather consist of specific material about factories as an example for the history of the workers' movement and the change in the psychological makeup, socioeconomic situation, and everyday life of workers.[8] I stressed that technical propaganda cannot be interpreted in a way that separates it from politics, that, for example, Comrade Bukharin has this tendency because, on the one hand, he opens a new phase of our revolution, namely the "technological" revolution, and, on the other, when he does link it to politics, he does it inappropriately, as was the case in his speech in Sokolniki. Oh yes, I also pointed out that Bukharin's speech published in *Za industrializatsiiu* [For Industrialization] contains elements of "Bogdanovism." We approved Gorky's proposal and instructed the Secretariat to formulate a resolution and establish an editorial board, the proposed editorial board, of course, will not do. It seems to me that Bukharin is pushing something of his own here through Gorky. I found out that Gorky made this proposal for publishing a history of factories and plants at the plenum of the RAPP [Russian Association of Proletarian Writers], and he seems to have proposed Bukharin to the RAPP members as editor of the publication. By the way, Bukharin also spoke at the RAPP plenum. Contact in general between Gorky and the RAPP members is apparently taking shape, and Bukharin in some way is attaching himself to this contact. This spurred me even more to strike at Bukharin. He immediately wrote me a note in which he complains with "bitter" tears about the hostile atmosphere, and, he says, "So you have decided to bash me again, could all this really be because of the soap (Sokolniki)" and so forth. He is pretending he doesn't understand that his [reference to] soap now is the same as his bricks in *Zametki ekonomista* [Notes of an Economist].[9] I am firmly convinced that he is not to be trusted, that he is hostile to our line—the party line.

    11. At a closed meeting of the Politburo we discussed the issue of the importation of steel and axles in connection with the your telegram. We had to get into another quarrel, because Sergo demanded that we should not suspend placing the orders, but we insisted on suspending the orders until the issue is clarified irrespective of our sending a telegram. This latter is precisely what the Politburo agreed. As for the substance of the issue, based on all of the figures of the PC of Foreign Trade, Vesenkha still has 156 million within the limits of the quota. The remainder, affording an opportunity to order steel within the limits of the quota. When we adopted this resolution I made a point of insisting that we would place the orders

not as a supplement but within the limits of the quota. In any case, we have now suspended the order.[10] Well, that's enough.

Good-bye. I leave you with a handshake. Yours, L. Kaganovich. Regards to Molotov.

1. In negotiations with representatives of French industrialists, the director of Petrofine, Vangère, proposed that Soviet orders in France be guaranteed with the foreign-currency receipts from the export of Soviet oil to France (DVP, vol. CIV, p. 817). On 8 September 1931 the Politburo in its resolution "On France" adopted the proposal in the telegram from Stalin and Molotov that "We must reject outright Vangère's principle and, in general, any thought of a collateral guarantee on our part. Piatakov's old agreement with the French no longer makes any sense in the current situation, when we have better credit terms in Germany, Italy, and Britain. Either the French accept the Italian-German credit terms, or they can go to hell. If the French government cannot bring itself to guarantee credits, we can propose to them, as the final concession, the British terms, whereby credits for us are provided satisfactorily, but without a direct guarantee from the Brit[ish] gov[ernment]" (RGASPI, f. 17, op. 162, d. 11, l. 6). Simultaneously the Politburo proposed to negotiate specific orders with individual industrialists, without signing contracts until a trade agreement was concluded. Piatakov, Rozengolts, and Krestinsky were instructed to draw up a draft text for a statement to French industrialists (ibid., l. 4).

2. See note 1 to document 19.

3. On 5 September the Politburo instructed the PC for Supply and local party organizations to increase the procurements of wheat and oats (ibid., op. 3, d. 846, l. 4).

4. The commission comprised Postyshev, Mikoian, Zemliachka, R. Ya. Levin, Ya. A. Yakovlev, Yeryomin, Zelensky, Kritsman, and Shvernik (ibid., l. 5).

5. On 5 September the Politburo decided "not to change the annual production plan of the fishing industry," instructing the Council of Labor and Defense to set a production program for fish catch for the second half of the year and to submit it to the Politburo (ibid., l. 4). On 10 September 1931 the Politburo approved the plan of 12 million tsentners for fish catch in the second half of 1931, which had already been adopted by the Council of Labor and Defense on 6 September (ibid., d. 847, l. 11).

6. See note 1 to document 21.

7. The capital-construction plan for nitrogen plants was on the agenda repeatedly at Politburo meetings in early 1931. On 15 October 1931, after Stalin returned from vacation, the Politburo resolved to transfer the matter to the Council of Labor and Defense (ibid., d. 854, l. 9).

8. On 5 September 1931 the Politburo approved Gorky's proposal to prepare the publication of a history of factories and plants (ibid., d. 846, l. 2). On 18 September, following a reminder from Kaganovich, Stalin wrote in a cipher that "the idea of publishing a history of factories and plants is a good one" (ibid., f. 558, op. 11, d. 76, l. 69). On 20 September Kaganovich and Postyshev proposed the names of the editorial board to Stalin. On the following day he replied, objecting to some of the names and proposed to add people well informed about the major old factories and Shvernik, Kaganovich, and Postyshev; he added that "Yenukidze, who has a good knowledge of old factories in Leningrad and Baku, would be very useful." (Ibid., ll. 73, 730b.) On 10 October the Politburo adopted a more detailed decision. This stated that the series entitled "The History of Factories" "should provide a picture of the development of old factories and the establishment of new ones, their role in the economy, the situation of workers before the revolution, forms and methods of exploitation at the old factories, the workers' struggle against entrepreneurs, living conditions, the

genesis of revolutionary organizations and each factory's role in the revolutionary movement, the factory's role and the change in social relations at the factory after the revolution,
the change in the type of workers, the shock-worker movement, socialist competition, and
the upsurge in production in recent years." The editorial board was to consist of: Gorky, L.
Kaganovich, Postyshev, Andreev, Yenukidze, Stetsky, Bukharin, Piatakov, Shvernik, and others (ibid., f. 17, op. 3, d. 853, l. 12).

9. This is a reference to Bukharin's article in *Pravda*, 30 September 1928, in which he
criticized attempts to increase the pace of industrialization, commenting that "it is impossible to build 'real' factories from 'bricks of the future' " (see E. H. Carr and R. W. Davies.
Foundations of a Planned Economy, 1926–1929, vol. 1 [London, 1969], 317–19). In his unpublished speech at Sokolniki Bukharin evidently criticized the lag in light industry and referred to the shortage of soap. Kaganovich suggests that Bukharin's criticism of the soap
shortage in 1931 is similar to his criticism of the brick shortage in 1928.

10. See documents 9, 11, 13, and 14 and the introduction to this chapter.

· 11 ·

Stalin and Molotov to Kaganovich, Rudzutak and Ordzhonikidze
[6 September]
F. 82, op. 2, d. 1424, ll. 66–73. Signatures of Stalin and Molotov.

To Comrades Kaganovich, Rudzutak, Ordzhonikidze.

1. You did not answer the question about whether the Politburo's July
decision on a final program of metal orders in 1931 remains in effect or is
considered revoked. It is clear to us that your decision to import 5 million
rubles' worth of metal means that new metal orders will have to be placed
above and beyond the program that was determined by the Politburo with
the participation of Sergo, Piatakov, Rozengolts, Bron, and Mezhlauk.
This represents a veiled abrogation of the Politburo decision of July and a
breach in our hard-currency front. We object to this.

2. The Politburo set the program of metal imports in tons rather than
rubles. Both of your decisions on additional imports ignore the Politburo
decision defined in tons. The sum of 156 million rubles for imports that
you mention is unknown to us and was not approved by the Politburo.
The replacement of the computation of metal imports in tons with computation in ruble terms is wrong because it makes the circumvention of the
Politburo's July decision easier.

3. The savings of 4 million in hard currency belongs to the state coffers
rather than to Vesenkha, which does not have and should not have coffers.
We are against an anarcho-syndicalist view of the state, under which profits from savings go to Vesenkha, while losses go to the state. We believe
that the state is above Vesenkha.

4. The unused 5 million cannot be used for metal imports, since the
metal imports program for 1931 remains in effect and is broken down by
country. The issue of how to use this money should be discussed separately

while taking account of the interests of the state as a whole, and not only Vesenkha.

5. It should be kept in mind that our foreign-currency position is desperate. It should not be forgotten that this problem will be even graver in the next two years because of an accelerating reduction in our exports to Italy, Germany, Britain, and America. It should also be kept in mind that North America, the current master [*gegemon*] of the financial world and our chief enemy, is making and will make every effort to undermine our hard-currency position. Are you taking this prospect into account? After all, we cannot operate with our eyes closed. How do you plan to deal with these difficulties? How do you plan to carry out the Politburo decision on building up a minimum quantity of hard-currency reserves?

6. We insist that both of your decisions on orders for steel and for railroad-car axles and wheels be revoked. If you disagree, we propose a special session of the Politburo to which both of us should be summoned.[1]

Stalin. Molotov.[2]

1. See the introduction to this chapter.
2. The document is annotated "6 September 1931. Sochi." It is not clear whether it was sent as a letter, a ciphered telegram, or a telegram *en clair* (there is no copy of it in the file of ciphered telegrams).

· 12 ·

Stalin to Kaganovich
7 September

F. 81, op. 3, d. 99, ll. 21–23.

Greetings, Comrade Kaganovich:

1) I received Patek's draft and Karakhan's "discussion" with Patek. I am returning both documents. It appears that Karakhan's behavior during the "discussion" was stupid and indecent. Karakhan failed to realize that after the affair with the French (the TASS denial of a month and a half ago) no state will dare to take the initiative regarding a nonaggression pact without getting into "trouble" with the "opposition." Karakhan failed to realize that the Poles are trying to begin negotiations with us on a pact, but to begin them so that the formal initiative does not come from them. Karakhan failed to realize that in the end we don't care by whose initiative negotiations take place, as long as the pact we need is signed. And so instead of seizing the pretext provided by Patek and his draft, Karakhan—in his stupidity—rebuffed Patek and ruined everything. As for Patek's draft, it is no worse than the original draft by the French, which served, as we know, as one of the bases for negotiations between us and the French.[1]

It is clear to me that Karakhan and Litvinov made a flagrant error, which will take quite a long time to repair.

Incidentally, why was Patek's draft delivered to Karakhan rather than to Litvinov or Krestinsky? Be sure to clarify this matter and please let me know.[2]

2) Please find out the following: a) the volume of industrial output (including the food industry) for August compared with July 1931, b) the volume of industrial output for August compared with August 1930, c) the volume of industrial output (including food) for the first eight months of the year compared with the first eight months of last year—and let me know by telegram.

Regards, I. Stalin.

7 September [1931]

1. After lengthy negotiations, a nonaggression pact between the USSR and France was initialed on 10 August 1931 (DVP, vol. XVI, pp. 452–54).

2. See note 1 to document 19.

· 13 ·

Stalin to Kaganovich
9 September

F. 81, op. 3, d. 99, ll. 25–26.

Greetings, Comrade Kaganovich:

1) I am sending you a copy of my letter to Sergo on steel imports and everything related to that matter.[1] Sergo doesn't know that a copy has been sent to you—I didn't tell him, for the sake of his vanity (you know that he is vain to the point of foolishness). But you should know about this letter, which is of some interest with regard to the CC and its economic policies.

2) You must have already received a copy of my telegram to Tiflis about Transcaucasian affairs. I am sending you several documents[2] which served as the basis for my telegram to Tiflis.[3] I think Polonsky committed a major gaffe by attacking the Transcaucasian Regional Committee and [A. I.] Yakovlev. This gaffe must be rectified.

3) The Vesenkha resolution on the iron and steel industry that was published in the press makes a strange impression. An equally strange impression is left by the statement in the *Pravda* editorial that the Vesenkha resolution was approved by the CC.[4] The same odd impression is left by the resolution of the PC for Supply on livestock procurements, which was also approved by the CC.[5] Why did we need this innovation? Why is all this approved by the CC rather than the Sovnarkom? Why is the Sovnarkom

being bypassed and ignored? Why do people want to make the CC a participant in this completely unjustified tendency to ignore the Sovnarkom? Second, what kind of behavior is this, turning the Politburo <u>into a rubber-stamp body</u> for decrees by the Vesenkha, the PC for Supply, the PC of Agriculture, etc.? Can't we stop these attempts to turn the CC from a <u>leadership</u> body into an <u>auxiliary</u> body for the parochial needs of the people's commissariats?[6]

Well, that's all for now.   I leave you with a handshake.

9 September 1931. I. Stalin.

1. See Appendix: document 2.

2. The documents are not published in this collection. RGASPI, f. 81, op. 3, d. 99, ll. 29–30.

3. See document 15.

4. The resolution of the Presidium of Vesenkha on the work of the iron and steel industry was approved by the Politburo on 5 September 1931 (RGASPI, f. 17, op. 3, d. 846, ll. 6, 17–23) and was published in *Pravda* on 8 September. See also document 4.

5. See note 6 to document 4.

6. Stalin's demand was heeded. See note 7 to document 9.

· 14 ·

Stalin to Kaganovich
[12 September]

F. 81, op. 3, d. 100, ll. 112–113.

———————

Greetings, Comrade Kaganovich!

I received your letter.

1) Your arguments designed to justify the Politburo decision on steel imports do not hold water. The problem is not the calculation of the state's "debt" to Vesenkha leaders in monetary terms but that instead of counting in tons (as is customary in the Politburo) they have pushed you into counting in monetary terms and . . . have confused the so-called foreign-currency commission, the so-called PC of Foreign Trade, etc.[1] There are at least two inevitable conclusions to be drawn from this whole affair with the imports: 1) the <u>foreign-currency commission</u> is crap, not a state organization, and Rudzutak is a worthy chairman of this manure; 2) the <u>Foreign Trade Commissariat</u> is not protecting the state's interests, getting any benefit out of it is like trying to get milk out of a billy goat, and in general, it is rotting on the stalk.

2) I am sending you a clipping from *Izvestia* about the <u>outrageous, criminal</u> attitude of our economic agencies toward metal imports. Vesenkha is trying to rob the state's hard-currency coffers because of metal imports, and the metals already imported for the Cheliabinsk project are ending up

in nobody's charge, as a result of which they are being squandered and practically sold off at auction. Those criminals and vermin! I propose: a) running an article in *Izvestia* for discussion by the Politburo; b) requiring *Pravda* (which is now writing all kinds of rubbish) to check on the situation and write an editorial about the hooliganlike attitude of "communists" toward the state's imported property; c) putting the guilty people <u>on trial</u> without fail and <u>punishing</u> them.[2]

3) The American writer [Upton] Sinclair has written a letter, it turns out, to Khalatov, and then to Kalinin, where he asks for support for some enterprise launched by Sinclair and Aizensteid [*sic*] ("our" well-known filmmaker who fled from the USSR, a Trotskyite, if not worse). Apparently Aizensteind [*sic*] wants to hoodwink us through Sinclair. In short, the whole thing smells fishy. I propose: a) putting off the matter until my arrival; b) suggesting to Khalatov and Kalinin that they refrain from answering Sinclair until the issue as a whole is resolved in the CC.[3]

Regards, I. Stalin.

1. See documents 9, 11, 13, 14, and the introduction to this chapter. The omission marks appear in the original document.

2. See note 3 to document 19.

3. The Soviet film director Sergei Eisenstein left for the United States in the summer of 1929 and returned to the USSR in the spring of 1932. During 1930–31 he worked in Mexico on the film *Que Viva, Mexico!* with the financial assistance of the American socialist novelist Upton Sinclair and his wife. In issue number 3 of 1931, the journal *Inostrannaia literatura* (Foreign Literature) carried an extremely critical article by Ivan Anisimov about the whole corpus of Eisenstein's films. On 10 August 1931 the Politburo considered "Sinclair's letter asking for $25,000 for Eisenstein's work in the cinema" and resolved to turn the issue over to the Secretariat of the CC for a decision (RGASPI, f. 17, op. 3, d. 841, l. 3). On 16 August, evidently in response to an inquiry from Kaganovich, Khalatov reported to him: "Upton Sinclair has written me a letter requesting that we pay him an honorarium in order to fund the work of the Soviet film director Eisenstein in America." On 17 August the issue was considered by the Orgburo. It assigned Stetsky to negotiate with the board of the Filmmakers Corporation (Soiuzkino) to have Eisenstein return to the USSR and decided not to answer Sinclair for the time being (ibid., op. 114, d. 252, ll. 39–40). On 20 August the Politburo approved this decision by the Orgburo (ibid., op. 162, d. 10, l. 166).

In a letter dated 26 October 1931, Sinclair told Stalin that he had financed the Mexican film, and appealed about the arrest of the father of a Russian technician in the USSR. By this time the financing originally made available by Sinclair was considerably overspent. On 21 November Stalin sent Sinclair a cable (in English) defending the arrest and continuing: "Eisenstein loose [*sic*—lost] his comrades confidence in Soviet Union STOPP He is thought to be a deserter who broke off with his own country STOP Am afraid the people here would have no interest in him soon STOP Wish you to be well and to fulfill your plan of coming to see us STOP My regards Stalin." This telegram was not publicly mentioned by Sinclair or in the Soviet press. It was published in 1965. A photocopy of the telegram is included in M. Seton, *Sergei M. Eisenstein: A Biography* (London, 1978), 517.

On 4 December 1931 the Politburo adopted a decision "On Eisenstein":

"1. Rebuke Comrade Rozengolts for allowing Amtorg to get out of hand, for losing control of it and enabling it to engage in philanthropy and patronage of the arts at the state's expense and enabling it to squander $25,000 in favor of Eisenstein, who deserted the USSR, instead of forcing Amtorg to engage in commerce.

"2. Issue a severe reprimand to Comrade Bogdanov for unauthorized expenditure of the people's funds ($25,000) to sponsor the deserter from the USSR Eisenstein, with a warning to him that the slightest attempt by him to violate discipline in the future and to allow the squandering of state funds will lead to his expulsion from the party.

"3. Require Comrades Rozengolts and Bogdanov to immediately dispose of the Eisenstein affair" (RGASPI, f. 17, op. 3, d. 864, l. 9).

On 8 April 1934 the Politburo returned to this issue and resolved: "In view of new circumstances that have emerged, revoke the Politburo resolution of 4 December 1931 on Comrade Bogdanov regarding the Eisenstein affair" (ibid., d. 943, l. 26).

Sinclair became involved in disputes with Eisenstein and withdrew his financial support. Eisenstein returned to Moscow. Sinclair refused to hand over to Eisenstein the extensive Mexican footage. In 1932, as a result of these events, Eisenstein fell into a serious depression (see N. Lovgren's article in *Eisenstein Rediscovered,* ed. I. Christie and R. Taylor [London, 1993], 126).

· 15 ·

Kaganovich to Stalin
11 September

F. 558, op. 11, d. 739, ll. 96–105.

---

11 September [1931]
Greetings Comrade Stalin.

At yesterday's Politburo meeting we discussed a number of issues related to the PC of Foreign Affairs.

1. On Poland. The PC of Foreign Affairs so far has proved powerless to carry out our instructions—to explore the real intentions of the Polish government more deeply. The memorandum they sent in is limited to general judgments rather than [offering] a concrete analysis of the facts and situation in Poland. The PC of Foreign Affairs has submitted a proposal that we present an official written reply now to Patek's maneuver. We did not adopt this proposal. You are absolutely right in your assessment of the glaring error that the PC of Foreign Affairs made and that it will take a long time to rectify it. So it is hardly expedient to make a statement now already without an appropriate sounding. We deferred it until the 20th, giving instructions to the PC of Foreign Affairs to submit by 16 September (so that we can send it to you to study before the 20th) a substantive report, and then decide whether to make a statement or not. I found out why Patek wrote to Karakhan. They attribute this to the fact that Karakhan filled in for Stomoniakov in the Western section during the latter's vacation.[1]

2. We had to defer the directives for the coordinating commission. The PC of Foreign Affairs people were foaming at the mouth as they tried to

prove that it was impossible to reject their proposal, that it could cause a conflict. We were already going to reject their proposal, but then to be cautious decided to defer and query you once again. I summarized the crux of their arguments in a telegram, so I will not repeat it now.[2] They of course exaggerate any threats. It seems to me that the PC of Foreign Affairs people are being too obliging toward Germany. They also acted this way on the issue of Poland, when their main argument was a desire to soothe German public opinion. They are ignoring the fact that we don't have a situation now that would force us to curry favor with Germany, more likely Germany needs us most of all at present.

3. We heard a report by Rozengolts on the progress of placing our orders in Britain. The placing of orders is progressing well. It turned out that 80–90 percent of the orders for the Cheliabinsk project can be placed in Britain. Rozengolts proposed that we approve all the steps being taken there and accelerate the placing of orders there. We confined ourselves for now to noting Comrade Rozengolts' report. I am sending it to you and I ask you to let us know if you have any suggestions; then we would raise this issue again around the 15th or 20th.

4. Concerning America there is no new substantive material, other than the fact that Bogdanov is still sitting in Berlin because the American consul is not issuing him a visa until he submits proof that in the event of his deportation from America, the USSR will take him back. The word now seems to be that Bogdanov will get a visa. We have instructed Krestinsky and Rozengolts to submit a report to the Politburo on the evolving situation in America with regard to us, especially since we suspended our orders. At one point after your telegram we gave instructions to prepare for the possibility of canceling some orders, but it turned out that a cancellation of orders would entail substantial losses of foreign currency and, second, would greatly complicate the situation, and there would be an uproar, so we confined ourselves to noting it.[3]

5. We deferred a very important issue in order to query you about Japan. The Japanese responded to our closing of the Chosen Bank, which caused them as much as 4 million in losses, with a sharp increase in duties on the timber we are exporting, which of course will lead to substantial overpayments on our part.[4] Rozengolts submitted a proposal that we take a number of measures that would compel the Japanese to revoke these duties. He proposed the following: reduce imports of goods (tea) from Japan, impose duties on green teas, demand that the timber duties be revoked when we conclude treaties on the catch and sale of crabs, launch a campaign in the press not to enter into agreements on territorial waters until the Japanese revoke the duties, etc. Of course, such measures on our part could cause serious complications in our relations with Japan, which,

as it is, are not especially good because of the fishing question. We deferred the issue until the 20th and ask that you let us know your opinion.[5]

6. The Austrians are squeezing our exports. The PC of Foreign Trade submitted a proposal that all orders be suspended. We resolved to begin with an official warning to the Austrian government and industrialists that we will discontinue all orders unless their policy changes. After that, if there are no changes in the shortest possible time, we will stop placing orders.[6]

7. The PC of Foreign Affairs submitted a rather "original" and in our view not altogether serious proposal on Latvia. Since new elections are approaching in Latvia and there will be a struggle between rightist groups and leftists, in the opinion of the PC of Foreign Affairs we for our part should help the leftists come to power. To this end it proposes that we send a note about the shortcomings of the commercial treaty (which has been in force already for more than three years) and hint that we may not enter into anything else with them in addition to the commercial treaty. Thereby providing the "leftist" groups with grounds for attacking the government. In other words, the PC of Foreign Affairs is proposing that we provide a "platform" for these groups. What's the point of that? Why should we get our hands dirty? We therefore resolved to drop the issue, and we will discuss the treaty when the time comes, regardless of the Latvian elections.

8. We deferred the issue of the commercial treaty with Afghanistan. The proposal by the PC of Foreign Affairs and the PC of Foreign Trade seems to be acceptable. Please let us know your opinion.[7] I am sending you Karakhan's memorandum.

9. A few days ago we sat over the foreign-currency plan for the fourth quarter at the foreign-currency commission. What was proposed to us proved to be unsatisfactory. Net revenues of 182 million, expenditures of 178 million, savings of 4 million, and if we take account of noncommercial expenditures [i.e. invisibles], then we end up with no increase in foreign currency.

The PC of Foreign Trade included the entire annual plan for grain exports in the fourth-quarter export plan, which is hardly acceptable. It is probably better to push flax. In the final distribution of the plan for flax procurements by region we added 20,000 tons, i.e. 320,000. Last year we procured 180,000, therefore we can now produce more both for industry and for export.[8] On butter, eggs, bacon, and poultry we adopted the proposal of the PC of Foreign Trade, although this of course is not an easy thing to accomplish. Mikoian strongly protested, but you are absolutely right in saying that we must do this.[9] In addition, we propose pushing various exports—medicinal herbs, industrial crops, utility waste, rags, bristles, intestines, etc. Recently this area has clearly declined. At one time there used to be special state trade organizations in the regions to procure these items. Now it is in the hands of the PC for Supply, and it has no time to deal with this. We think it would be more correct to turn this over to the PC of Foreign Trade, restore the state trade organizations in republics and regions, and put Veitser directly in charge of them. In addition we should give the regions a real stake, if, for example, we would give a district executive committee even a bonus of 1 or 2 typewriters and in some places a little Ford, then it would bend over backwards and help procure intestines and bristles and the like. We haven't seen the fourth-quarter import plan yet, we will have to cut it, but the problem is that most of the payments are already predetermined by previous orders. As soon as the plan is ready in rough form I will send it to you before approval in the Politburo. We are at present either deferring or dropping altogether all proposals for imports. One thorny issue now is about the import of supplies and equipment for the PC of Transport. The Antipov subcommission set up by the Politburo commission did a good job of cutting the requests from the PC of Transport people, but the total that is left is still sizable, about 9 million [rubles]. The transport situation is serious, we should support them with something. Of course, after cutting Antipov's proposals one more time. I am sending you these proposals and ask you to give us your advice. What should we do?

The Chekists [the OGPU leaders] have raised the question of implementing the resolution already adopted by the Politburo on the purchase of patrol ships. The terms in Italy are such that we will not have to pay anything until 1935, but we postponed it, first, because now we are pressuring the Italian government with a statement canceling the orders, second, we need to get your opinion from you, we are inclined to go through with this order after waiting a little.[10]

The PC of Foreign Trade submitted a proposal for the purchase of 25,000 tons of <u>rubber</u> at a cost of 8 million rubles, with delivery in the second and third quarters of 1932. Foreign-currency outlays under this deal will begin only in the second quarter of 1932. Rubber prices have now fallen to 2 pence a pound, which is 7 percent of the 1919 price and 4 percent of the 1925 price. We have deferred the issue in order to get your opinion either by letter or by wire.[11]

10. I have sent out Mezhlauk's letter to the Politburo members. Rozengolts asked that we defer it for five days, but we are planning to adopt Mezhlauk's proposals on the 15th.[12]

11. We confirmed Kartvelishvili as first secretary of Georgia immediately upon receiving your telegram.[13] This decision is appropriate, especially at this stage, until fresh people are promoted. You did very well in taking Polonsky down a notch, because he is getting carried away. The Transcaucasians are asking us to defer their report to the Orgburo by

about 10–20 days. I think we could agree to put it off until the 6th or even the 16th of October.[14]

12. The situation with grain procurements is this: the first five-day period in September shows a fairly sharp slowdown. Compared to almost 80 million procured in the last five-day period of August, 45,500,000 poods were procured in the first five-day period of September. Especially sharp decreases are coming from: the Northern Caucasus, where 4,466,000 poods [73,150 tons] were procured, compared to 15,855,000 poods [259,700 tons] in the previous five-day period; the Ukraine, 17,476,000 poods [286,260 tons] procured, 28,817,000 poods [472,020 tons] in the previous five days; the Central Black-Earth Region, 5,487,000 poods [89,880 tons], 8,052,000 poods [131,890 tons] in the previous period; the Low[er] Volga, 5,111,000 poods [83,720 tons], 9,400,000 poods [153,970 tons] in the previous period; the Cen[tral] Volga, 3,965,000 poods [64,950 tons], 4,604,000 poods [75,410 tons] in the previous five-day period. Procurements are going especially badly in Siberia, the Urals, and Kazakhstan: Eastern Siberia is at 3.7 percent of the annual plan, Western Siberia 4.6 percent, Kazakhstan 5.3 percent, the Urals 2.7 percent. Even though the total amount of procurements is much greater than last year—by 76 percent— the procurements now are apparently going to be more of a strain, and management of this issue will have to be strengthened. It looks as if we will have to send CC representatives to some districts.[15]

I will stop here regarding CC business and am writing you separately as secretary of the Moscow Committee about Moscow business.[16]

Regards, L. Kaganovich.

1. See document 12 and note 1 to document 19.

2. Under the convention on coordinating procedures between the USSR and Germany signed on 25 January 1929, a coordinating commission was established for the settlement of differences "arising in the interpretation of bilateral agreements." The Statute on the commission said that it "is not a standing commission but shall be formed especially for each session. It shall convene once a year, approximately in the middle of the year, for a regular session, whose precise timing shall be set in each instance by agreement between the two governments" (DVP, vol. XII, pp. 44–47). On 2 September 1931, in connection with the impending opening of the second session of the Soviet-German Coordinating Commission in Berlin, Deputy People's Commissar of Foreign Affairs Stomoniakov sent Stalin a memorandum on German grievances. The most serious issue was that the Soviet authorities were preventing foreign currency from being taken out of the country by German citizens who were moving out of the country and selling off their property. The PC of Foreign Affairs proposed that permission be given to export foreign currency obtained by the sale of personal movable property (APRF, f. 3, op. 64, d. 660, ll. 7–13). On 8 September 1931 Stalin sent Kaganovich a cipher in which he rejected these proposals (ibid., l. 5). On 10 September the issue was taken up at a Politburo meeting (RGASPI, f. 17, op. 162, d. 11, l. 1). The same day Stomoniakov sent the Politburo a new memorandum in which he pointed out that the amounts to be transferred were insignificant, and he proposed again that concessions be made to the Germans. Kaganovich apparently reported this information to Stalin by wire. On 12 September,

in a wired response, Stalin again rejected the proposals: "We must fight for every ruble of foreign currency. I insist on my opinion, and you can decide as you please" (ibid., f. 558, op. 11, d.76, l. 60).

3. See note 1 to document 6. On 10 September 1931, based on a report by Rozengolts and Ordzhonikidze, the Politburo returned again to the issue of placing orders in America. It noted the statement by the people's commissar of foreign trade that "it is not possible to cancel deals that have been concluded for orders already placed in America" and that it had been forbidden to place new orders in America beyond those already placed and formalized as of 25 August (ibid., f. 17, op. 162, d. 11, l. 2).

4. The operations of the Vladivostok branch of the Chosen Bank were halted by a decree of the USSR PC of Finance dated 13 December 1930 (DVP, vol. XIII, pp. 721, 722).

5. See note 1 to document 16.

6. See note 2 to document 16. Opposite this paragraph in the letter is Stalin's notation "Without a ruckus."

7. See note 3 to document 16.

8. The actual amount of flax procured in 1931/1932 was 256,000 tons, as opposed to 183,000 tons in 1930/31.

9. See note 3 to document 9.

10. On 1 December the Politburo returned to the issue of the purchase of patrol ships and instructed the PC of Foreign Trade "to place the order in Italy for two patrol ships for the OGPU" (RGASPI, f. 17, op. 162, d. 11, l. 71). On 8 December the Politburo revised its decision and authorized the purchase for the OGPU of three patrol ships on condition that the previous foreign-currency limit was preserved (ibid., l. 84).

11. See note 5 to document 16.

12. Mezhlauk's letter was taken up at the Politburo meeting on 20 September. A decision was adopted to appoint M. Gurevich as trade representative in France and Ozyorsky in Britain and to recall Bron back to the USSR to work at the PC of Foreign Trade (ibid., op. 3, d. 849, l. 5).

13. See document 13. On 10 September, based on a report by Kaganovich, the Politburo "agreed to the proposal by the Transcaucasian Regional Committee and the CC of Georgia to dismiss Comrade Mamulia from his job as secretary of the CC of Georgia and to approve Comrade Kartvelishvili as first secretary of the CC of Georgia jointly with his work as secretary of the Transcaucasian Regional Committee" (ibid., d. 847, l. 4). See also document 7.

14. See note 6 to document 16.

15. On 10 September the Politburo instructed the Secretariat to nominate the CC representatives to be sent to districts in which grain procurements were declining (ibid., l. 1). See also note 8 to document 17.

16. On 11 September Kaganovich sent Stalin an eight-page letter on developments in Moscow (ibid., f. 558, op. 11, d. 739, ll. 106–113, not published in this collection).

· 16 ·

Stalin to Kaganovich
14 September

F. 81, op. 3, d. 99, ll. 32–33.

Greetings, Comrade Kaganovich!

I received your letter of 11 September. Let me answer each question in turn.

1) We have to be a little more careful with Japan. We have to hold our ground firmly and unshakably, but the tactics should be more flexible, more circumspect. Rozengolts wants to act on impulse. That won't do right now. The time for an offensive is not here yet.[1]

2) If Austria becomes pigheaded about the orders placed there, we can stop them, but we must do so quietly and in a businesslike manner, without new decrees, without demonstrative articles in the press.[2]

3) I can't say anything about the commercial treaty with Afghanistan, since I haven't had a chance to read the material.[3] I think we can take our time with this matter.

4) The import plan for the fourth quarter should be reduced as much as possible. Don't give in to screaming and hysterics—we won't get anywhere unless we perform thorough surgery. In terms of exports we should push flax, butter, oil cakes, and the like. We can't push grain anymore, since we have to sell it "for nothing," even while we badly need it inside the country.[4]

5) Rubber can be imported, as the PC of Foreign Trade is demanding.[5]

6) The Transcaucasians' report to the Orgburo can be put off until 16 October.[6]

7) Get to work on Moscow's urban economy (firewood, housing, road building, etc.).

That's all.   Regards, I. Stalin.

14 September 1931

---

1. At a session on 10 September the Politburo considered the questions of commercial ties with Japan and negotiations with Japan on fishing issues. It was decided to defer the question of commercial ties with Japan and to ask for Stalin's opinion (RGASPI, f. 17, op. 162, d. 11, l. 1). The issue was not on the agenda of the 20 September session of the Politburo. An agreement on fishing issues was signed on 13 August 1932 (DVP, vol. XV, pp. 469–71). See also document 15.

2. On 10 September 1931 the Politburo considered the question of trade negotiations with Austria and adopted a decision: "Assign the plenipotentiary and the trade representative in Austria to state categorically to the Austrian government and Austrian industrialists that we will stop placing any orders in Austria unless their policy toward our exports changes" (RGASPI, f. 17, op. 162, d. 11, l. 2). See also document 15.

3. The question of a commercial treaty with Afghanistan was not considered at Politburo sessions until 1932. Trade between the USSR and Afghanistan in the years that followed was conducted primarily by the Sovafgantorg trading corporation and by individual Afghan companies by means of commercial contracts (DVP, vol. XV, p. 796). See also document 15.

4. See note 1 to document 20.

5. The Politburo considered the question of rubber after Stalin returned from vacation, on 10 November 1931. It was decided to form a commission that would devise measures to streamline the use of rubber, to reduce imports, and eliminate rubber wastage (RGASPI, f. 17, op. 3, d. 859, l. 1). The import plan for the fourth quarter of 1931 provided for a cutback in hard-currency outlays for rubber imports (ibid., op. 162, d. 11, l. 36). See also document 15.

6. After several postponements, reports by the Transcaucasian Regional Committee

(TRC) and the Central Committees of the Georgian and Armenian Communist Parties were considered by the Orgburo on 19 October 1931. The Orgburo meeting, with Stalin's participation, essentially turned into another session to clear the air between the squabbling Transcaucasian leaders (for the transcript of the meeting, see ibid., op. 114, d. 265, ll. 75–137). The discussion resulted in the establishment of a commission, chaired by Kaganovich, to draw up a draft decision (ibid., l. 1). On 31 October the decision (prepared and approved the day before by the Orgburo) was approved by the Politburo. The resolution said in part that "certain individuals among the leading cadres of both Transcaucasia and the republics are waging an unscrupulous struggle for influence (displaying elements of 'atamanism'), and as a result, the selection of leading cadres and the appointment of functionaries are, in a number of instances, based not on party-oriented, practical criteria but on whether someone is allied with one group or another" (ibid., op. 3, d. 857, ll. 9, 12–19). On the same day, 31 October, the Politburo adopted related personnel decisions. Kartvelishvili was relieved of his duties as secretary of the TRC and appointed second secretary of the Western Siberian Regional Committee. Orakhelashvili, chairman of the Transcaucasian Sovnarkom, was appointed first secretary of the TRC; Beria, chairman of the Transcaucasian GPU, was appointed second secretary of the TRC; and Polonsky, first secretary of the CC of the Azerbaijan Communist Party, was appointed third secretary. Beria was also appointed first secretary of the CC of the Georgian Communist Party. (Ibid., l. 9.) See also documents 7, 15.

· 17 ·

Kaganovich to Stalin
16 September

F. 558, op. 11, d. 739, ll. 114–122.

---

16 September [1931]
Greetings, Comrade Stalin!

I received your last letter.

1. I am not going to attempt to justify a decision that we have already revoked. You are right that our mistake was that we became entangled in calculating quotas, instead of counting in tons we counted in money. That is first, and second, we failed to take account of the overall foreign-currency situation, and we agree completely with your assessment of it. I recall you saying once that we need some kind of unusual jolt to force the economic leaders and others to put all their emphasis on domestic production and stop placing their hopes and expectations on imports. And this whole episode with steel imports played the role of a jolt. In any case you gave us a good lesson, now we must hope that there will be a more frugal attitude toward foreign currency.

I completely agree with you that at present the foreign-currency commission is not displaying this frugal attitude toward foreign currency, and the PC of Foreign Trade sees minutiae but overlooks a lot when it comes to the more important things. In particular, the PC of Foreign Trade is failing to guarantee that the approved quota is not actually exceeded in the ordering process. Just a few days ago we heard the first preliminary reports on the results of a check on how the placing of orders is proceeding. It turned out that the information that more had been ordered already than the approved quotas allowed was incorrect. Specifications have been sent abroad for 300 million more than the quotas, [but] it goes without saying that specifications do not yet constitute an order but rather reference material for the customer; but recordkeeping of orders is so poorly organized at the PC of Foreign Trade that customers could easily go beyond the quotas. As of today such a serious danger does not exist; 390 million has been ordered out of 560 million in quotas (and according to the data of the PC of Foreign Trade a little less). In any case, about 150 million worth has yet to be ordered. We wanted to examine the remaining orders on their merits, but unfortunately there are no data yet on what has been ordered and what hasn't been ordered (according to Piatakov's statement they have material on the orders that he placed, but so far they haven't given even that to us). Therefore we instructed the PC of Foreign Trade and Vesenkha to submit to us precise, specific data, not general statistics, on what has been ordered so that we can, if need be, cancel certain orders, i.e. make some cuts in the quotas. Please let us know your opinion about whether we can make some cuts in the quotas that are still not utilized.[1]

2. The question of the *Izvestia* clipping you sent in about the criminal treatment of imported metal was raised at the Politburo meeting, and an appropriate resolution was adopted. We gave instructions to Roizenman, in five days I will report the results to you.[2]

3. We rejected yesterday a proposal by the PC of Foreign Trade that we change the procedure for the signing of commercial and monetary commitments by trade missions. The restriction was adopted as a result of the betrayal by Savely Litvinov and Yerzikian.[3] Now they propose that we extend the list of those who can sign bills of exchange, agreements, etc., as if we are already guaranteed at present against betrayal. Moreover, extending the list of signers will create an even bigger mess in the recordkeeping of orders and will make it even more possible to order more than the quotas allow.[4]

4. We rejected Zelensky's proposal for increasing the differentiated membership payments in consumer cooperatives. People have still done very little to mobilize the internal resources of cooperatives, and at the same time they want to increase the dues from members.[5] Incidentally, about the resolution on cooperatives Comrade Molotov told me that you expected a reply from us to your revisions, but there was a misunderstanding here, since we were expecting revisions from you to the text of the draft resolution. We completely agree with your proposals (on prices and so forth). We could issue this resolution in the name of the Fulfillment Commission. Please let us know whether to issue it or wait for you to arrive.

5. We discussed the question of how the construction of power stations is progressing. Despite the fact that the total amount of capacity that is being put into operation is incomparably greater than last year's, electric-power construction is not making very good progress. The rapporteurs stressed the need for importing copper, we didn't accept it and pointed to the need for maximum mobilization of resources within the industry. Let them search a little to see if copper is lying around, just like the steel for the Cheliabinsk Tractor Plant that was cited in the *Izvestia* article. The rapporteurs Krzhizhanovsky and Flakserman played down the difficulties and shortcomings of the construction, they made everything sound too pat. But Sergo stressed the seriousness and need for mobilizing all resources to fulfill the plan. We set up a commission to work on the draft resolution.[6]

6. We heard a report on the progress of the fall sowing, although 5 million more hectares have been sown than last year in the same period, we still have only 43 percent fulfillment of the plan. So we did not praise the successes yet, but, on the contrary, put emphasis on the fall plowing because the fall plowing situation so far is poor.[7]

7. Regarding grain procurements, the last ten days have seen a drastic, alarming slowdown. The Northern Caucasus produced 18 percent of the monthly plan in ten days, the Ukraine 22 percent, and thing are especially bad in Western Siberia and the Urals.

We dispatched Sulimov to the L[ower] Volga, Nikolaeva to Bashkiria, Ilyin to the Urals, and Khlopliankin (from the PC for Supply) to the Cent[ral] Volga.[8]

8. We are doing everything we can now to press ahead with log rafting. We adopted a resolution yesterday,[9] we had an argument about the imposition of a labor and carting duty, there was a proposal to impose it, but the Politburo rejected the proposal.

9. Kartvelishvili keeps bombarding us with regard to a secretary for the Transcaucasian Regional Committee to replace [A. I.] Yakovlev, but we will decide that when you return.

10. The Kazakhstanis protested the decision to incorporate eight state farms from Kazakhstan into the Western Siberian Trust. Isaev arrived. In view of the Kazakhstanis' particular long-standing wariness toward Siberia we half yielded to the Kazakhstanis based on considerations of nationalities policy and decided to establish a single Kazakhstan Trust, but we will move this trust to Petropavlovsk or a nearby area, since the bulk of state farms are situated in this district.[10] Yakovlev agreed to this.

11. We have a bad situation at the Communist Academy, it is coming apart. We found out at the Orgburo that the Communist Academy proved powerless to carry out even a tiny bit of the tasks that you set for them at the conference of agrarian specialists, even though they made a great

many declarations and promises. It cannot be left in that condition any longer; we must strengthen it and in a way that brings it closer to the CC. We could put together a leading nucleus consisting roughly of the following comrades: of the current ones keep Pokrovsky (chair[man]), Pashukanis (dep[uty]), dismiss Miliutin as deputy chairman, he doesn't do anything anyway, and add these new members: Stetsky as deputy jointly with his Culture and Propaganda post, Bubnov and Krinitsky as members of the presidium, and Comrade Roshal as secretary for organizational and administrative affairs.[11] Please let us know your opinion.

Your rebuke about the app[roval] of the resolution on the iron and steel ind[ustry] and livestock procurements was correct; we need not have approved it. What was especially regrettable was that *Pravda* printed it without asking anybody. But there was no intention of ignoring Sovnarkom, of course.[12]

Well, I will stop here. I leave you with a handshake. Yours, L. Kaganovich.

P.S. I just received Litvinov's dispatch on Poland, I am sending it to you. He of course feels that he took a "great" diplomatic step with his denial. Please wire your instructions by the 20th as to whether we should postpone the question until your arrival, if we don't get a telegram, we will postpone it to the 25th.[13] I must tell you that I came away from a discussion with Litvinov even more convinced that he is a kind of "Germanophile," since there is nothing happening so far with the French. He does not understand that we cannot subordinate our diplomacy just to relations with Germany, and in general, since he returned from Geneva he leaves the impression of a man who is overly vain and sure of his "greatness," but for "God's" sake, who cares about him, the most important thing was his mistake in substance. All the best.

L. Kaganovich.

1. See note 2 to document 9, and document 20.

2. See note 3 to document 19.

3. The reference is to abuses by Soviet officials related to foreign trade. Savely Litvinov, the brother of Maksim Litvinov, the people's commissar of foreign affairs, worked at the Soviet trade mission in Paris and was prosecuted by the French authorities in 1930 for fraud. In a letter dated 24 November 1930, the Soviet plenipotentiary in Finland, reporting to Kaganovich on the situation at the Soviet trade mission in that country, mentioned that former trade representative Yerzikian was under arrest in a Helsinki prison on charges of forgery and fraud (RGASPI, f. 17, op. 120, d. 39, l. 20).

4. On 15 September 1931 the Politburo rejected a proposal by the PC of Foreign Trade to amend the Sovnarkom decree of 13 October 1930 on the procedure for the signing of commercial and monetary commitments by trade missions (ibid., op. 3, d. 848, l. 4).

5. On 15 September 1931 the Politburo instructed an ad hoc commission to examine the directive of the presidium of Tsentrosoiuz, the Central Union of Consumer [Cooperative] Societies, dated 25 August 1931, on special dues to be paid to the cooperatives by kulak and well-to-do peasants. Zelensky was instructed to raise the issue of the financial situation of Tsentrosoiuz at the Council of Labor and Defense (ibid., l. 2).

6. Later, on 2 October 1931, in discussing power-station construction, the Politburo decided to take the issue off the agenda (ibid., d. 852, l. 9). Capital investment in electrification for 1931 was planned at 850 million rubles but actually amounted to 550 million rubles (E. Zaleski, *Planning for Economic Growth in the Soviet Union, 1918–1932* [Chapel Hill, 1971], 365, 370).

7. At its meeting on 15 September the Politburo noted Yakovlev's report on the progress of the fall sowing campaign. The PC of Agriculture, its local agencies, and party organizations were instructed to mobilize all resources for the complete fulfillment of the sowing plan and especially the fall plowing plan (RGASPI, f. 17, op. 3, d. 848, l. 5).

8. On 15 September the Politburo resolved: "a) In view of the lag in grain procurements in the Urals, the Lower Volga, the Central Volga, and Bashkiria, which jeopardizes the fulfillment of the entire annual plan for procurements, to dispatch as CC representatives, in order to assist local agencies in strengthening grain procurements, Comrade Sulimov to the Lower Volga, Comrade Nikolaeva to Bashkiria, Comrade Ilyin to the Urals and Comrade Khlopliankin to the Central Volga; b) To reject the proposal by Comrade Bergavinov for a revision of the grain-procurement plan for the Far East Region" (ibid., l. 5). See also note 15 to document 15.

9. The resolution adopted by the Politburo on log rafting stated: "Owing to the extraordinary conditions that have occurred as a result of delay, to agree to the proposal of the Chief Administration of the Timber Industry to initiate the unbound floating of 50 percent of all remaining logs that have not been rafted" (ibid., l. 13).

10. On 15 September, as a result of Goloshchokin's protest against the incorporation of Kazakhstan's northern grain-growing state farms into the Western Siberian Trust, the Politburo decided: "To incorporate the northern state farms into the Kazakhstan All-Union Grain Trust and move its center from Alma-Ata to one of the northern grain-growing districts of Kazakhstan" (ibid., l. 3).

11. The conference of agrarian specialists met on 20–27 September 1929. For Stalin's speech see R. W. Davies, *The Socialist Offensive* (Basingstoke and London, 1980), 197–98, 391–92, and *The Soviet Collective Farm* (Basingstoke and London, 1980), 87. In the fall of 1931 the question of the Communist Academy was repeatedly discussed at meetings of the Orgburo and the Secretariat. On 5 December 1931 the Orgburo approved in the main a draft resolution on the structure and work of the Communist Academy, prepared by the Kaganovich commission, and instructed the commission to refine the draft and then submit it for Politburo approval (RGASPI, f. 17, op. 114, d. 266, l. 2; d. 269, l. 1).

12. See note 4 to document 13.

13. See note 1 to document 19.

· 18 ·

Stalin to Kaganovich
19 September

F. 81, op. 3, d. 99, ll. 35–36.

Greetings, Comrade Kaganovich!

I regard transport—above all, railroad transport—to be the most important issue in the coming months.

The principal threat to the national economy now comes from transport, and it is transport that must be improved above all.

The situation cannot be saved with decree-type resolutions by the CC, although such resolutions are of considerable value. Why not? Because as long as a gang of self-enamored and self-satisfied bureaucrats like Rukhimovich are sitting in transport, mocking CC resolutions like Mensheviks and sowing pernicious skepticism all around, CC resolutions <u>will be pigeonholed</u>.

We must smash this gang if railroad transport is to be saved. If my help is needed in this matter, let me know. If you can manage without my help, smash the gang before it's too late. If we look for them in earnest, we can always find new people who believe in our cause and can successfully replace bureaucrats.[1]

Regards, I. Stalin.

19 September 1931

1. This letter continued an exchange of ciphers between Kaganovich and Stalin in which Kaganovich asked whether the draft resolutions on rail and water transport could be approved and published, and Stalin replied in similar terms to those in the above letter (RGASPI, f. 558, op. 11, d. 76, l. 69). See document 19, note 1 to document 21, and note 1 to document 22.

· 19 ·

Kaganovich to Stalin

21 September

F. 558, op. 11, d. 739, ll. 123–128.

---

21 September[1931]

Greetings Comrade Stalin!

1. Yesterday we listened to a report on the issue of Poland. You have probably received Litvinov's memorandum. Litvinov is proceeding entirely from his old position that it is inexpedient and disadvantageous to enter into a pact with Poland. We deemed his standpoint to be incorrect. We adopted no decisions in substance, we instructed him to do some more work on the issue within 20 days and we will probably discuss it when you are already present.[1]

2. We heard a report on the Japanese-Chinese situation. There were proposals, especially on Litvinov's part, that we make an official inquiry and take a sharp tone toward Japan in the press.

Since the information available to us was extremely limited, we did not adopt any decisions. We proceeded on the premise that the situation requires caution and restraint from us.

3. You will read in the minutes a resolution that the contract for orders of pipe stills in America should not be canceled. This is caused by the fact

that a cancellation of this contract would cause substantial losses of foreign currency and would create serious complications for us, so we are
compelled to go through with the order.[2]

4. The article in *Izvestia* on metal imports proved correct. Comrade
Roizenman investigated it. We adopted an appropriate resolution. The article in *Pravda* was delayed for a couple of days because the first article
given to me for review turned out to be poor and is now being redone.[3]

5. Yesterday we gave Popov a big tongue-lashing for his article of the
19th of this month, "On Some Specific Features of the Current Stage."
The article is unquestionably muddled, it contains a number of formulations that incorrectly characterize the present, specifically it depicts collective farms incorrectly and presents the danger from the advance of capitalist elements in a panicky manner. At the end of the second section it
frames the issue of the triumph of socialism in our country incorrectly.
Postyshev and I summoned Mekhlis and Popov, gave them the appropriate instructions, and we adopted the following resolution in the CC Secretariat: "It must be pointed out that the general tone of Comrade Popov's
article is incorrect, that the article contains a number of incorrect formulations in substance. The editors of *Pravda* and Comrade Popov are instructed to write a new article on the same topic in accordance with oral
instructions." They should deliver the article tomorrow.[4]

6. We are doing everything to press ahead with getting oil out of Astrakhan. Oil shipments out of Astrakhan have increased, but mostly to
nearby districts. Delivery up to Nizhny [Novgorod] and Rybinsk has not
been achieved, and therefore we are pushing precisely this aspect of shipments. They are doing all they can to revert to shipping oil to Leningrad by
the circular maritime route, but we are decisively rebuffing them.

7. I received your telegram and letter on rail transport.[5] You are absolutely right that transport is the most important issue for the immediate
future and this is where the national economy is in danger. My second experience in the commission with the PC of Transport people, including
Rukhimovich, has shown that the main thing, of course, is the people, the
leadership of the PC. We devised a number of necessary measures in the
draft resolution, but we did not draw a conclusion from the fact that CC
decisions that were adopted are not being carried out by the PC of Transport and that the trouble lies not only in an inability to carry them out but
in a bureaucratic and skeptically right-wing attitude toward party directives. I completely agree with you that we must smash this group of people
headed by Rukhimovich, who could put us back to a difficult situation. I
just received your letter, I haven't thought through yet how to handle this
issue, but I think I will convene the commission for editing the draft resolution tomorrow, and we will deem the work unsatisfactory since the CC
decisions are not being implemented by the PC of Transport. On the 25th

we will raise the issue of replacing the leadership. The sooner the better for transport and for the country.[6]

Goodbye. I leave you with a handshake.

Yours, L. Kaganovich.

Regards to Comrade Kirov. L.K.

1. On 23 August 1931 Poland's emissary to the USSR, Patek, handed the USSR deputy people's commissar of foreign affairs Karakhan the text of a nonaggression treaty. The leadership of the PC of Foreign Affairs was skeptical. In the record of Karakhan's talk with Patek on 23 August, Karakhan reported in part: "As he [Patek] left, he remarked that he would like to hope that his talk would provide a certain impetus that would advance the cause of the pact. I immediately remarked to him that I didn't think that this could be an impetus or could advance the matter since what he handed me did not contain anything new, but was merely a statement of what we had been unable to agree on" (DVP, vol. XIV, pp. 441–44, 484–89, 498). After Stalin's letter of 7 September (document 12), the Politburo, on 10 September, instructed the PC of Foreign Affairs to submit by 16 September "a substantive, comprehensive report in writing on the issue of how serious Poland's intentions are in the negotiations of a nonaggression pact, with reference to the general situation in Poland and to groups in government and social circles" (RGASPI, f. 17, op. 162, d. 11, l. 1). On 20 September the Politburo heard reports from the leaders of the PC of Foreign Affairs. Litvinov vigorously opposed the immediate opening of negotiations with Poland for a nonaggression pact. But the Politburo rejected "Comrade Litvinov's standpoint, as set out by him in a memorandum of 15 September of this year to the Politburo of the CC regarding Poland" and, "based on previous Politburo decisions on the necessity of seeking a nonaggression pact with Poland," instructed the PC of Foreign Affairs to submit within 20 days its proposals for necessary measures (ibid., l. 9). For the report of the PC of Foreign Affairs and Litvinov's memorandum, see O. I. Ken and I. I. Rupasov, *Politbiuro TsK VKP(b) i otnosheniia SSSR s zapadnymi sosednimi gosudarstvami (konets 1920–1930kh gg.), 1928–1934* (St Petersburg, 2000), 259–65. After lengthy negotiations a nonaggression treaty between the USSR and Poland was signed, on 25 July 1932. See also documents 8, 10, 12, 15, 17.

2. On 20 September 1931 the Politburo decided that the order for pipe stills in the United States should remain in force "in view of the fact that its cancellation would entail a substantial forfeit payment"(RGASPI, f. 17, op. 162, d. 11, l. 11)

3. On 15 September 1931 the Politburo considered the article in *Izvestia* of 9 September, "Imported Metal Is Being Squandered." Their decision instructed Central Control Commission deputy chairman Roizenman to investigate the circumstances in which high-quality imported metal earmarked for construction of the Cheliabinsk Tractor Plant was sent to the wrong place and used improperly, to find the guilty individuals so they could be prosecuted, and to report on the results to the Politburo no later than 20 September. *Pravda* was instructed to publish an editorial on the disgraceful treatment of imported metal and equipment (ibid., op. 3, d. 848, l. 7).

On 20 September the Politburo heard Roizenman's report. The decision set out the facts of the case in detail. The Politburo noted Roizenman's report that all material on the case "has been turned over to the Prosecutor of the Republic in order to hold the guilty individuals strictly accountable" (ibid., d. 849, ll. 9–10). See also documents 14, 17.

4. The 20 September decision on Popov's article to which Kaganovich refers is missing in the minutes of the Secretariat meeting. On 21 September, by a poll of members, the Secretariat adopted a decision to grant a leave of absence to Popov from 20 September to 1 November 1931. On 21 September the Politburo endorsed the Secretariat's decision (ibid., op. 114, d. 260, l. 14; op. 3, d. 850, l. 7).

5. See document 18.
6. See note 1 to document 21 and note 1 to document 22.

· 20 ·

Stalin to Kaganovich
24 September

F. 81, op. 3, d. 99, l. 38.

———————

<u>Greetings, Comrade Kaganovich!</u>
   I received your letter.
   1) You are right that import items will have to be <u>revised</u> and <u>cut back</u>. This is <u>inevitable</u> for many reasons (including the financial crisis in Britain, Germany, and so forth).[1]
   2) People say that the square on the Arbat (where there used to be a church, in front of the movie theater) has not yet been covered with paving blocks (or asphalt). This is shameful! One of the busiest squares, and it's full of potholes! Put pressure on them and make them finish up the square.
   My health is definitely improving.
   Well, that's all for now. I leave you with a handshake. I. Stalin.
   24 September 1931.
   P.S. I will be in Moscow in early October. I. St.

   1. Stalin sent a similar letter on the same day to Molotov (*Stalin's Letters to Molotov, 1925–1936*, ed. Lars T. Lih, Oleg V. Naumov, and Oleg V. Khlevniuk [New Haven, 1995], 228). See also the introduction to this chapter and documents 15, 16, 17.

· 21 ·

Kaganovich to Stalin
26 September

F. 558, op. 11, d. 739, ll. 129–140.

———————

   26 September [1931]
Greetings Comrade Stalin.
   1. You already know from our telegram that we have already discussed the question of the PC of Transport. Everybody agreed that we should do this. I showed the comrades only your telegram where you framed the issue in general terms. We adopted the resolution, which was reported to you, unanimously. You have made your choice from the nominated candidates, and essentially most of the Politburo members were inclined to this candidate.

Today we summoned Rukhimovich, and as soon as he arrives, we will raise the issue officially. Regarding the general resolution on transport—Andreev considers it very good and necessary. The editorial commission inserted a paragraph in the introductory section deeming the work of the PC of Transport unsatisfactory. We have not put the resolution in official form yet, I am personally inclined to do so, but I am awaiting word from you. Now, after the organizational decision, it will already be full-blooded.[1]

2. We adopted a decision on the plan for the fourth qu[arter], we had to reduce the reserve from the contemplated 800 million [rubles] to 585 m[illion]. We added 70 million for the PC of Agriculture, 50 [million] for Vesenkha, etc. Molotov and I were assigned to edit the draft of a long, politicized resolution by Sovnarkom for publication based on the model of last quarter.[2] I doubt that such a resolution is needed. Please do wire your opinion personally to me.

3. The grain-procurement situation is not very good, the pace is slowing. At the Politburo meeting there was a proposal to convene a conference of secretaries of regional party committees on 30 September. But that would be hasty: first, preparations must be made for this conference, second, since this conference will probably also touch on other rural issues I felt that it would be better to wait until you arrive. That is what the Politburo decided, we deferred the question of the conference, but we are sending out telegrams to regional committees to step up grain procurements.

4. We are sending you a report of a new case of flogging of collective farmers in the Lower Volga. It seems to me that this case is of great political importance.

5. At a special Politburo meeting today we discussed the question of the grain-fodder budget and the supply of consumer goods. On both issues we had to adopt a decision only in the form of a guideline.

Regarding the grain-fodder budget, Gosplan provided material that is totally worthless. We established the general Fund of grain for distribution of 1,450,000,000 [poods], we will decide on the remaining Fund in six weeks or two months, when the picture gets clearer. On the issue of the supply of goods it was determined that although we have more goods than last year, less is coming into the supply network and going on sale, because an enormous amount of goods is being diverted to special Funds and to state agencies (special-purpose clothing and so forth). We instructed the Council of Labor and Defense to devise a number of measures and adopted your proposal for a committee on prices, on price reductions at commercial stores, etc.[3]

6. We have not adopted any special resolutions on China; we are proceeding in accordance with your telegram. Please read in *Izvestia* of the 23rd Demian Bedny's poem, I think it contains a direct attack on our pol-

icy, it refers there to the British events and to the Chinese-Japanese conflict and ends, "Moscow, always ready to issue a rebuff, is enigmatically silent," etc. It turns out that Litvinov, who in the Politburo demanded we actively intervene, vetted the publication of this poem by Demian.[4]

7. The insistence by the Secretariat of the CC of the German [Communist] Party on acceptance of Sewering's conditions leaves a very unpleasant impression. Piatnitsky told us that there have been other instances of this sort. We approved the proposal by the Comintern people that the proposal by the Secret[ariat] of the CC of the Communist Party of Germany be rejected. Is this some sign of more serious processes in the German party.[5]

8. We are opening the Moscow auto plant on 1 October, although they will start producing autos a little later, but they should produce a sizable number in October. The auto-plant people (Likhachev) kept hedging, they wanted to delay the opening even longer so that they start off right away in style, producing at full capacity, but we put on the pressure and made them open on 1 October.

Well, I will end here. I am very glad that your health is improving. I leave you with a firm handshake. Yours, L. Kaganovich.

1. The cipher referred to in this paragraph was dispatched by Kaganovich and Molotov to Stalin on the previous day. It proposed that Andreev, Kaganovich, and S. Kosior would be suitable for the post of people's commissar. On the same day Stalin and Kalinin replied, supporting the candidature of Andreev, "who knows transport and transport workers well"; Blagonravov should be freed from his work in the transport OGPU to act as one of Andreev's deputies. (RGASPI, f. 558, op. 11, d. 76, ll. 78, 780b.) The resolution of the Politburo commission on rail transport, approved by the Politburo on 5 October 1931, dealt with a broad range of issues: the use and repair of steam locomotives and railcars; the organization of loading and unloading operations; capital construction and equipment supply; and wages and food supplies for railroad workers. Certain sections of the resolution were to be issued in the form of an order by the PC of Transport. The work of the PC of Transport was described as "unsatisfactory" in the resolution (ibid., f. 17, op. 3, d. 852, ll. 1, 14–24). See also documents 8, 9, 10, 18, and 19; notes 1 and 2 to document 22; and note 3 to document 23.

2. On 21 September Kaganovich and Molotov sent a cipher to Stalin about the plan for the fourth quarter, proposing that finance should be provided for capital investment sufficient to enable the annual plan to be completed, with a state budget reserve of 800 million rubles; Stalin agreed to this proposal on the same day (ibid., f. 558, op. 11, d. 76, l. 72). The Politburo adopted a resolution on the plan for the fourth quarter, incorporating a reserve of 585 million rubles, on 25 September 1931 (ibid., f. 17, op. 3, d. 850, ll. 2–3).

3. On 26 September 1931 a Politburo meeting convened with two issues on the agenda: the grain-fodder budget and the supply of consumer goods and price policy. The issue of the grain-fodder budget was deferred, but the Politburo established a general Fund of grain for distribution to the amount of 1,450,000,000 poods (23,750,000 tons). In discussing the supply of consumer goods the Politburo adopted Stalin's proposals: to establish a Committee on Prices attached to Sovnarkom, to reduce prices at commercial stores by 30 percent, to set fixed prices for bread, and to work out the prospects for collective and state farms and industrial corporations to sell on the market (ibid., op. 162, d. 11, l. 16; op. 3, d. 851, l. 1).

4. See note 3 to document 22.

5. On 25 September 1931 the Politburo resolved: "The following proposal by the Russian delegation to the Executive Committee of the Comintern is to be adopted: 'After hearing the telegram from the Secretariat of the CC of the CPG [Communist Party of Germany], which proposed that, in order to resume the publication of 14 party newspapers, the publisher of com[munist] newspapers accept Sewering's conditions that the publisher print a statement expressing regret over the publication by the CC of the CPG of a manifesto to British sailors and containing a pledge not to violate German laws in the future, the Political Commission resolves to reject this proposal by the Secretariat of the CC of the CPG'" (ibid., op. 162, d. 11, l. 12).

· 22 ·

Stalin to Kaganovich
29 September

F. 81, op. 3, d. 99, l. 40.

Greetings, Comrade Kaganovich!

I received your letter.

1) Please don't hold up the CC resolution on the PC of Transport until I return to Moscow. The main thing is to remove Rukhimovich and Co. from their jobs in the PC of Transport, and this issue has already been decided.[1] The rest is either trivial or not so important.

Incidentally, it would also be a good idea to remove Poliudov (the director of the Belorussian Railroad).[2] He's not a functionary, he's a crook, an antiparty man, a toady, an ignoramus, and a loafer. He will ruin a railroad that is highly important in military terms unless we replace him with another functionary.

2) I haven't read Demian's poem and I don't intend to read it, since I am sure it is not worth reading. He's another problem: he's trying to get into politics, yet politics is where he is shakiest. I am sure he could have written the foolishness about "Moscow"—he is brazen enough for it. We should hold accountable, first, the editor of *Izvestia*, second, Demian (and Litvinov). Why shouldn't they really be held accountable?[3]

Well, so long. Regards.

29 September 1931   I. Stalin

1. The Politburo adopted a decision to relieve Rukhimovich of his duties as people's commissar on 30 September 1931 (RGASPI, f. 17, op. 3, d. 851, l. 3). See also note 1 to document 21 and documents 8, 9, 10, 18, 19, 23.

2. Poliudov, the director of the Moscow-Belorussian-Baltic Railroad, was dismissed from his job by a Politburo decision of 2 October 1931. As Stalin suggested (see document 9), Postnikov was appointed to replace him (ibid., d. 852, l. 7). On 25 October the Politburo agreed to a request by the PC of Finance of the RSFSR to approve Poliudov as a member of the board of the PC of Finance (ibid., d. 856, l. 12).

3. See document 21. On 5 October 1931 the Secretariat of the CC adopted a decision that

criticized Gronsky, the editor in chief of *Izvestia*, for having mistakenly published a poem "which falsely characterizes the position of the Soviet government in the Manchurian events" and stated that Demian Bedny's poem was "incorrect and politically erroneous." Litvinov was rebuked for giving his approval to publish the poem (ibid., op. 114, d. 264, l. 11). See the introduction to this chapter.

· 23 ·

Stalin to Kaganovich
4 October

F. 81, op. 3, d. 99, ll. 42–43.

Greetings, Comrade Kaganovich!

I received your letter.

1) I was astonished by Comrade Molotov's proposal to appoint Comrade Rukhimovich chairman of Gosplan and consequently, a vice-chairman of Sovnarkom. For <u>failing</u> at the PC of Transport and conducting (even now!) the most malicious agitation <u>against</u> the practical line of the CC (on the question of growth rates and so forth), Rukhimovich is made a vice-chairman of Sovnarkom, a promotion! What kind of nonsense is this!? Is that any way to <u>educate</u> cadres? No question about it, that is some "education."

The same must be said of Sergo's proposal to make Rukhimovich a vice-chairman at Vesenkha. These people don't realize that <u>Rukhimovich is a carbon copy of Frumkin</u>, the only difference being that Rukhimovich is more dangerous, since he is, unfortunately, a member of the CC.[1] I have already written Sergo about this.

Rukhimovich should be <u>demoted</u> and sent to a job outside Moscow, in the Vesenkha network.[2] Then everyone will realize that the CC is not joking and not just engaging in idle chatter about the general line. They will realize it and shape up.

2) I have read your telegram about the makeup of the board of the PC of Transport. It seems to have come out pretty well. I would take another step forward and put more Chekists on the board. The PC of Transport cannot get on its feet at this stage without Chekists and Rabkrin people. But we will discuss this in Moscow. It is also good that Blagonravov became the second deputy commissar.[3]

3) Under no circumstances is Postyshev to be assigned to Sovnarkom. He is needed and is <u>more valuable</u> in the CC Secretariat than in Sovnarkom. I don't think Molotov has done a proper study of Postyshev yet.

Well, that's all. Regards. See you soon.

4 October 1931   I. Stalin

1. On 15 June 1928 Deputy People's Commissar of Finance Frumkin sent the Politburo a letter criticizing the policy of emergency grain procurements, which marked the beginning of the retreat from the New Economic Policy. Stalin responded to Frumkin with a letter in which he accused him of protecting the kulaks (I. V. Stalin, *Sochinenia,* vol. 11 [Moscow, 1949], 116–26).

2. On 1 October in a cipher to Stalin, Kaganovich wrote that with Rukhimovich as its head "Gosplan will not be militant but putrefied"; the proposal was "simply laughable" (RGASPI, f. 558, op. 11, d. 739, ll. 136–140). On 12 October the Politburo approved Rukhimovich as manager of the Kuzbass Coal Corporation (ibid., f. 17, op. 3, d. 854, l. 7).

3. On 2 October the Politburo approved the board of the PC of Transport (ibid., d. 852, l. 7). On 13 October, after Stalin returned to Moscow, the Politburo adopted a decision to transfer further functionaries to transport. Kishkin was appointed as a deputy people's commissar of Transport (and director of the chief inspectorate of the PC of Transport). Kishkin had just been approved on 30 September as director of the transport department of the OGPU in place of Blagonravov. The decision placed in leading posts in the PC of Transport 15 directors of roads departments of the GPU, 12 highway-transport party organizers, at least 50 regional functionaries of the transport GPU, at least 50 regional party organizer-secretaries, and 50 functionaries of railroad trade unions (ibid., d. 854, l. 7). "Rabkrin people" refers to staffers of the People's Commissariat of the Workers' and Peasants' Inspectorate. Following these appointments, a policy of repression was pursued in the PC of Transport for several years.

1932

Introduction

ON 1 JUNE 1932 the Politburo authorized six weeks' leave for Stalin.[1] According to the appointment book for visitors to Stalin's Kremlin office, however, he did not receive visitors between 29 May and 27 August 1932, an absence from Moscow of nearly three months.[2] This was one of the leader's longest periods of leave, and it began two months earlier than in previous years. The reason for this was probably his poor state of health. In the spring of 1932 the foreign press published rumors that Stalin was suffering from a serious illness. On 3 April *Pravda* reported that Stalin had informed the correspondent of the Associated Press that his health was good; this was an unprecedented step. On 13 April he permitted an American journalist to photograph him.[3] The evidence indicates that Stalin really had problems with his health. This is referred to in the correspondence below (see, for example, document 38). The year 1932 was certainly one of the most difficult in his personal and political history.

During the winter and spring preceding Stalin's vacation a general crisis developed in the country. Hunger increased, the production of many major industries declined, the financial system was disrupted, and inflation greatly increased. The expansion of military expenditure worsened the crisis. Stalin's cautious attitude toward Japanese aggression, reflected in his letters for 1932 as well as 1931, was a matter of

1. RGASPI, f. 17, op. 162, d. 12, l. 156.
2. *Istoricheskii arkhiv,* no. 2, 1995, 145–46.
3. J. E. Abbé, *I Photograph Russia* (1934).

tactics and not of principle. At the session of TsIK, the Central Executive Committee of soviets, in December 1931, Molotov spoke in strong terms about the "growing danger of military intervention against the USSR." During the first months of 1932 substantial resources were switched to the production of armaments and to the conversion of civilian facilities for military production.

But the most important problem was the considerable exacerbation of food difficulties during these months. Food riots took place in a number of towns. In the countryside in the previous two years compulsory collectivization and the mass deportation of peasants had disrupted production; and, as we have seen, the low harvest of 1931 was accompanied by increasing pressure for grain from the state. Hunger was widespread in the countryside and led to mass departures of peasants from the collective farms, and to peasant disturbances.

In this situation the Soviet leadership undertook a series of reforms in agriculture and industry. In May the grain procurement plan for 1932/33 was somewhat reduced, and free trade in grain was permitted, provided that deliveries to the state had been completed; and, a matter of considerable significance, the state control of prices on the markets was abolished. These and related measures became widely known at the time as "neo-NEP," though this characterization was vigorously rejected by the authorities.

It is significant that in the lengthy correspondence between Stalin and Kaganovich in 1932 the problem of the collective farm market was hardly mentioned. Historians have noted that the reforms of May 1932 were never attributed to Stalin in Soviet publications; and his lack of attention to them in these letters may confirm that he did not pin many hopes on them. He discussed the bazaars and markets only in terms of keeping strict control over "profiteers and resellers" (see documents 49 and 52). Similarly he did not display any interest in plans to carry out a kind of neo-NEP in industry by giving enterprises the right to sell production in excess of the plan independently on the market (document 37). The only positive mention of economic reform in the letters was in connection with Mongolia, where a widespread uprising resulted in the abandonment of the previous policy, now castigated as "leftist." The Politburo condemned the application of comprehensive collectivization and the repression of private trade in this less advanced country.[4] But Stalin refrained from comment when re-

4. RGASPI, f. 17, op. 162, d. 12, l. 133 (decision of 16 May).

ferring to this issue, and merely supported "changing the political course" (document 25).

Stalin's own favorite prescription for providing incentives to the peasants was to increase the supply of consumer goods, and to direct more of them to the countryside. His role in this was publicized widely in the press. This improvement was to be achieved partly by seeking to increase output, and partly by reducing the supply to "nonmarket" (i.e. state) organizations. On 15 February 1932, the Politburo had established a commission chaired by Stalin to organize this campaign, which became known as "the commission of Comrade Stalin." The commission was instructed to check the actual division of the gross production of mass consumer goods between the so-called "market fund" (supplies sold to individual consumers at state prices) and the "nonmarket fund" supplies to state organizations.[5] The commission adopted a number of not very effective decisions, and on 1 April the Politburo resolved that its work had been completed.[6]

But then on 8 May a further Politburo commission was established to check the fulfillment of decisions about mass consumer goods (*shirpotreb*).[7] A considerable proportion of the correspondence between Stalin and Kaganovich was devoted to this subject. Stalin insisted that the supply of mass consumer goods to the countryside should be increased, and even when investment plans in industry were substantially reduced in July and August, he insisted that the allocations to the light and food industries should not be cut (documents 49 and 50). Stalin's demands were put into effect, at least in part: the percentage of mass consumer goods sent to the countryside considerably increased during these crucial months. But the hope of using the flow of goods to encourage agricultural deliveries to the state at low prices proved futile.

The change in the policy toward capital investment was equally belated and taken under the pressure of circumstances. These letters published below show how this major change in policy took place. On 8 June the Politburo resolved that the allocation for capital investment in July–September should not exceed the April–June level, 6,800 million rubles.[8] But nine days later, on June 17, the Politburo increased the July–September plan to 250 million rubles above the April–June

5. Ibid., f. 17, op. 3, d. 872, l. 6.
6. Ibid., d. 878, l. 4 (item 11 on Politburo agenda).
7. Ibid., d. 883, l. 1.
8. Ibid., d. 887, l. 9.

allocation; 150 million of this was allocated to the People's Commissariat of Heavy Industry.[9] Stalin reacted swiftly in a dry postscript to a letter to Kaganovich (document 38). He complained that "the PC of Heavy Industry was given too much money for the third quarter. They should have been given less. They are drowning in money." Then a few days later, on 24 June (document 39), he sent a special letter to Kaganovich, Molotov, and Ordzhonikidze in which he insisted on the dangerous nature of the decision to increase investment. On 29 June, however, he agreed not to change the plan for July–September, as it had already been approved (document 42).

What seemed to have started as an attempt to restrain the PC of Heavy Industry escalated into a general reduction of investment and marked the beginning of a shift from overambitious to more sober planning generally. From the correspondence we now know how this important decision was taken. Grinko, the people's commissar of finance, proposed that investment in the July–September quarter of 1932 should be reduced forthwith by as much as 1.5 billion rubles; Molotov and Kaganovich supported a cut, though smaller than that proposed by Grinko (document 48). On 17 July Kaganovich sent the request to Stalin. On 20 July, over a month after the original decision to increase investment in the July–September quarter, Stalin replied, roughly in agreement with Molotov and Kaganovich, that capital investment in the quarter must be reduced by a "<u>minimum</u>" of 500 million to 700 million rubles (document 49). A reduction of 700 million rubles was approved.

But all these measures could not prevent the growth of the crisis, the driving factor in which was the spread of famine. The 1932 harvest was certainly worse than the poor harvest of 1931, but Stalin did not recognize this. He even claimed in his letter of 25 July that "the harvest prospects will become clear (they have already become clear!), that they are undoubtedly good for the USSR as a whole" (document 51). In June, before the state collections from the 1932 harvest had begun, he called for the convening of a conference of party and soviet officials from the key regions to discuss the grain collections. The conference met on 28 June. Molotov read out a letter from Stalin which had been endorsed by the Politburo, and which insisted that the first party secretaries in the regions should be personally responsible for the success of the collections (document 35).

9. Ibid., d. 889, l. 13.

The letters show that Stalin was greatly concerned about Ukraine. On 25 May 1932, on the eve of his departure on vacation, the Politburo decided to send a commission headed by Molotov to Ukraine forthwith. This commission was instructed to adopt all necessary measures in connection with the critical position of the grain sowing in the republic.[10] In the very first letters from vacation to his colleagues Stalin returned to the situation in Ukraine. At the beginning of July, on his insistence, Kaganovich and Molotov again traveled to Ukraine (document 44). But the position in the republic rapidly deteriorated. On 11 August he posed the question sharply in a remarkable phrase in a letter to Kaganovich: "we may lose the Ukraine" (document 57).

At first Stalin was prepared to make certain concessions in Ukraine. In his letter of 25 July he acknowledged that conditions in some parts of the republic were such that the grain collection plan should be reduced, although Ukraine should not be told about this reduction until the middle or end of August for tactical reasons (document 51). And on 11 August he informed Kaganovich of his intention "[to transform] the Ukraine [. . .] into a genuinely exemplary republic" and to "be unstinting in providing money" (document 57). Following his usual assumptions, Stalin placed his main hopes on personnel changes, proposing to dismiss the Ukrainian leadership and appoint Kaganovich as the first secretary of the Ukrainian Communist Party (document 57). Kaganovich approved this idea (document 59), but Stalin decided he needed him as party secretary in Moscow. The top Ukrainian leaders remained in their posts. It was not until the beginning of 1933 that another secretary of the Central Committee, Postyshev, was appointed as second secretary of the Ukrainian Central Committee with extraordinary powers.

In the midst of the grain collections of 1932, Stalin approved decisions affecting the USSR as a whole which would ameliorate the agricultural situation. Ever since 1928 a determined effort had been made to maximize the sown area, with harmful effects on land management, and especially on crop rotation. On 17 July (document 47), in one of Stalin's scathing criticisms of the PC of Agriculture, he agreed that the policy of indiscriminate expansion of sown area should be abandoned in favor of a consistent attempt to raise yields. In August Yakovlev visited Stalin in Sochi and proposed that crop rotation should be introduced (or rather reintroduced) in all collective farms and state farms.

10. Ibid., op. 162, d. 12, l. 153.

On 17 August Stalin wrote to Kaganovich that he accepted this proposal.[11] A Sovnarkom and CC decree to this effect was eventually approved on 29 September.[12] But these sensible decisions were far too late to affect the 1932 harvest and the catastrophe which followed it.

Of more far-reaching significance than these measures, and the dispatch of various emissaries and commissions to the provinces, was Stalin's increasing inclination in conditions of rapidly growing crisis to a sharp increase in repression. One indication of this was his proposal in his letter of 20 July to adopt laws on the theft of railway and collective farm property, and on profiteering, which soon emerged as the notorious decrees of 7 August on socialized property and of 22 August on the struggle against profiteering. The decree of 7 August imposed the death penalty or a minimum of ten years' imprisonment for the theft of state or collective farm property.[13] The letters provide us with valuable information about the circumstances in which these decisions were adopted. They show, for example, that the decree of 7 August met with opposition in the Politburo. Unfortunately the rough draft of Kaganovich's letter (document 53) omits the names of the members of the Politburo who expressed criticisms of the decree, and the Stalin files do not contain this letter. It is possible that Kaganovich failed to send it to Stalin. Another previously unknown development is that after the adoption of the decree Stalin sent Kaganovich an ambiguous letter (document 57) which resulted in the preparation immediately after his return from leave of an instruction, approved by the Politburo, which in practice somewhat softened the effect of the 7 August decree.[14]

In 1932 Stalin continued to pursue a cautious policy toward Japan, following its invasion of Manchuria. Behind the scenes, the Soviet authorities even put pressure on Japan to sign a nonaggression pact. Thus on 20 June 1932 Stalin wrote to Kaganovich in a coded telegram that the Soviet Union "must frighten the Japanese with the prospect of our drawing closer to the Chinese, and thus compelling them to hasten the signing of the pact with the USSR."[15] He was, however, fully aware that Japan was a major threat to Soviet security. The Soviet

11. Ibid., f. 81, op. 3, d. 99, ll. 157–160. This document is not included in this collection.

12. Ibid., f. 17, op. 3, d. 902, ll. 7, 31–32. It was published as *Sobranie zakonov,* 1932, art. 436.

13. *Sobranie zakonov,* arts. 360, 375.

14. RGASPI, f. 17, op. 3, d. 898, 1 (item 2, high on the Politburo agenda); d. 900, ll. 33–4 (instruction dated 13 September).

15. Ibid., f. 558, op. 11, d. 77, ll. 76, 76ob.

Union took urgent steps to strengthen its Far Eastern defenses.[16] And Stalin actively sought closer relations with the United States in face of the common danger. In spite of the grave Soviet foreign trade crisis, he encouraged deals with American businessmen. For example: in a ciphered telegram to Kaganovich dated 7 June he criticized as too rigid the directive of the people's commissar of foreign trade about negotiations with Western oil companies: "It does not take into account that it is advantageous for us to more or less neutralize the Anglo-American group politically, if we really want to preserve peace, at least for the next two or three years."[17] Document 30 succinctly sums up Stalin's fresh assessment of the US attitude: he anticipated that the decline of American influence as a result of the increased power of Japan and France will lead the United States to "seek ties with the USSR."

In the United States itself, the continued world economic depression meant that many businessmen eagerly sort to export to the USSR. This correspondence discusses, for example, the visit of Colonel Pope to the USSR in June 1932 on behalf of his company.[18] But the political climate in the United States looked much bleaker. President Herbert Hoover, in office from 1929 to January 1933, always presented himself as an implacable opponent of Bolshevism and of American diplomatic recognition of the USSR. In his memoirs he explained at length that he had opposed recognition because it implied "the public condoning of Russia's unspeakable evils"; he insisted that as a result of the recognition of the USSR after Roosevelt assumed the presidency in 1933, "the four great pillars of free men were weakened."[19] The American biographer of Henry Stimson, Hoover's secretary of state, similarly claims that "Stimson was opposed to recognition."[20] In the presidential campaign of 1932 the rival public views of Hoover and Roosevelt about the recognition of Russia were ventilated. In a conversation with Roosevelt when the new president took office in January 1933 Stimson explained that he rejected recognition because of Russia's failure to conform to "the fundamental principle of the family of nations."[21]

16. See R. W. Davies, *Crisis and Progress in the Soviet Economy, 1931–1933* (Basingstoke and London, 1996), 169, 171–73.

17. RGASPI, f. 558, op. 11, d. 77, ll. 22–23.

18. See document 40; this visit was reported in the American press.

19. *The Memoirs of Herbert Hoover: The Great Depression, 1929–1941* (London, 1953), 360–63, 484.

20. E. E. Morison, *Turmoil and Tradition: A Study of the Life and Times of Henry L. Stimson* (Boston, 1960), 312.

21. L. C. Gardner, *Economic Aspects of New Deal Diplomacy* (Madison, WI, 1964), 33.

Behind the scenes, however, Hoover and Stimson were less inflexible. As early as 1929 Hoover apparently showed interest in a practical economic approach to the question of recognition.[22] In 1931 Hoover and Stimson jointly embarked on what they described as their "Russian investigation," to establish whether to increase trade with the USSR. According to Hoover's biographer, he "hinted privately at recognition," but "he and Stimson backed away in 1931."[23]

But in June 1932 William B. Lancaster, a prominent American banker, visited Moscow, spending six weeks there. His visit occupies a prominent place in this correspondence. Lancaster was a director of the National City Bank of New York, which held a considerable amount of the tsarist debt abrogated by the Soviet government. Until 1932 the bank was one of the sources of hostility to recognition.[24] But in 1932, following discussions with the State Department, it evidently had serious hopes of getting some of its money back as part of a recognition package. According to the Soviet record, Lancaster, at his first meeting with the Soviet officials Mezhlauk and Andreichin, informed them that before his departure for Moscow he had met his old friend Stimson. Stimson (quite contrary to his public stand) had unofficially advised Lancaster to inform Moscow that if the Soviet government in some form were to raise the question of renewing diplomatic relations with the United States, this would "not be met with a crude refusal." Lancaster suggested to the Soviet officials that after the US presidential elections an approach from the USSR would be met favorably if the USSR declared that it would abstain from communist propaganda and was ready discuss the regulation of the debts to the United States.[25] This statement obviously assumed that recognition would be on the cards even if Hoover won the election.

The course of the negotiations with Lancaster may be followed in documents 27, 30, 32, 34, 38 and 45. This exchange of correspondence was accompanied by number of ciphers. Stalin took Lancaster's visit very seriously, as evidence of the new American attitude to the Soviet Union (see document 30). And on 9 June he formulated in a cipher to Kaganovich and Molotov quite precise offers which could be made

---

22. M. L. Fausold, ed., *The Hoover Presidency: A Reappraisal* (Albany, NY, 1974), 184.

23. D. Burner, *Herbert Hoover: A Public Life* (New York, 1979), 297.

24. See W. A. Williams, *American-Soviet Relations, 1781–1947* (New York, 1952), 224.

25. APRF, f. 3, op. 66, d. 290, ll. 72–80; the interview was with Mezhlauk and Andreichin. Unfortunately Citigroup, the successor to the National City Bank, has not retained any records of Lancaster's visit to Moscow (information from Mr. Jack Morris).

to Lancaster about settling the tsarist debt in return for a substantial credit or loan:

> [Andreichin's] memorandum and the second interview with Mezhlauk attest that the question of recognizing the USSR and offering us a credit or loan is ripening in America, or has already ripened. Mezhlauk, Piatakov, and Kalmanovich should make roughly the following statement to Lancaster: first, we agree as an exception to go against a tradition which is justified by experience—we will negotiate about a loan before the official recognition of the USSR; second, they could give us a loan of 100–200 million rubles for eight years at seven percent; third, they could add five percent annually to this interest to satisfy the claims of the bank, so we would pay annually a maximum of twelve percent during eight years, which must satisfy all the claims of the bank; fourth, in these conditions we agree that part of the orders will immediately be placed in America, if prices and credit conditions are acceptable, and the interests of the National [City] Bank will be taken into account in obtaining orders with particular firms.[26]

As the correspondence shows, numerous variations on these proposals went to and fro between Lancaster and the Soviet negotiators, all of them closely monitored by Stalin. But Lancaster apparently obtained authority from New York only to offer quite a small loan. On 1 July Stalin rejected Lancaster's proposals as "unacceptable," insisting that "we can agree to the partial satisfaction of the claims of a private bank only on condition that we receive a large loan."[27] On the following day Kaganovich wrote to Stalin that "by all indications, Lancaster has come to sound things out," rather than make a definite commitment (document 45).[28] The negotiations failed, and Lancaster left the USSR in the middle of July. No publicity was given to the visit either in the USSR or in the United States.[29]

A couple of weeks later Colonel Cooper arrived in Moscow, and claimed to Kuibyshev that "he is empowered by decisive American business circles to carry out negotiation on the mutual relations of the

---

26. RGASPI, f. 558, op. 11, d. 77, ll. 47–48.

27. Ciphered telegram to Kaganovich and Molotov (ibid., ll. 129–130). See also note 2 to document 45.

28. A rough draft of Kaganovich's letter preserved in the family archives, written on 26 June—before Stalin's cipher of 1 July—stated more positively, "he came to sound us out, though seriously."

29. The National City Bank published a monthly economic newsletter. While it sometimes mentioned the state of the Russian economy, Lancaster's visit to Moscow is not mentioned in the issues for 1932.

USSR and the USA." Cooper asked to meet the whole Politburo and Stalin![30] Stalin was evidently disillusioned with such proposals by this time and sharply replied: "Cooper is a very impudent fellow [. . .] I am almost certain that he has no specific authorization, either political or commercial. Most probably he wants to attach himself to the construction of our new hydroelectric stations on the Volga. He must not be indulged." Stalin refused to meet Cooper. But, in spite of his strictures, Stalin added in the same telegram that Cooper "must be received politely, and listened to attentively; and write down every word, reporting everything to the Central Committee."[31] The door to recognition by the United States, and to loans, must be left ajar.

Relations with Cooper were further complicated by his discovery while traveling by ship to the Soviet Union that a large group of black Americans was also traveling to Moscow to make an anti-American film. On 31 July, Molotov and Kuibyshev reported to Stalin in a cipher that Cooper had harangued them on this subject for an hour, warning them that "the journey of the Negroes to the USSR and—even worse—the making of the film as an example of anti-American propaganda would be an insuperable obstacle to recognition." Moreover, "Cooper himself would not consider it possible on his own part to undertake further work in the USSR or to participate in the campaign for recognition if the film were to be produced."[32]

The outcome of this incident provided further evidence of the Soviet anxiety for good relations with the United States. On 3 August Kaganovich wrote to Stalin: "as for the substance of the question of the Negroes, we have authorized Postyshev to clarify things, I think we can do without this film; they, the International Workers' Aid, made it without any permission from the Central Committee."[33] Then, on 22 August, a Politburo decision, "On the Negroes," taken by poll and recorded in the top-secret special papers, concluded that "a complete cancellation of the production of the film 'Black and White' is not to be announced," and authorized "Comrades Postyshev and Piatnitsky to examine the screenplay of the film with a view to a major change in the

30. Cipher from Kaganovich, Molotov and Kuibyshev to Stalin, dated 29 July (f. 558, op. 11, d. 78, l. 101).

31. Ibid., l. 100 (dated 30 July).

32. Ibid., ll. 104–5. The poet Langston Hughes was employed as a consultant to the film (see A. Blakely, *Russia and the Negro: Blacks in Russian History and Thought* (Washington DC, 1986), 93–94).

33. From the Kaganovich family archive.

film, corresponding to the exchange of opinions which has taken place."[34] The actors learned from the newspapers that the film had been canceled, and were never told the reason. The film was never made.[35]

Documents 24–59

· 24 ·

Kaganovich to Stalin
2 June

F. 558, op. 11, d. 740, ll. 10–12.

---

2 June [1932]

Greetings Comrade Stalin!

Yesterday we held the first Politburo session to draw up the agenda. We had to resolve in principle a number of issues that had accumulated, especially urgent international issues.

1) Since the terms of the agreement with the Germans for orders have worsened, we decided to send Piatakov to Germany for a short time.[1] Rozengolts suggested that we simply adopt a resolution to prolong the negotiations all the way to the month-and-a-half mark, while totally discontinuing the placing of orders at present, but that is hardly acceptable. At any rate it will be a better idea if Piatakov himself sizes up the situation, especially now that the political situation has become more complicated for us. Judging by its makeup, the new government is highly hostile toward us, we must be especially on our guard now.[2]

2) The telegrams coming out of Japan, including today's interview with Saito, show what seems to be an increase in peaceful sentiment, but at the same time there are telegrams reporting that Japanese airplanes are circling very close to our border, and there even seem to have been instances (not yet verified) of planes flying across our border on the Amur, though not very far. Bliukher sent Voroshilov a telegram in which he proposes shooting at the Japanese airplanes as soon as they fly across the border, i.e. across the middle of the Amur River. Voroshilov replied that shots may be fired only if they really fly across the border or fly in the vicinity of our fleet. We convened the Far Eastern Commission and decided to categori-

34. RGASPI, f. 17, op. 162, d. 13, l.79.

35. For the background see Blakely, *Russia and the Negro*, 93–96; E. Lyons, *Assignment in Utopia* (London, 1938), 508–9. One of the actors, "sizzling with indignation," told Lyons that "American race hatred has reached across the ocean and hit us in the face."

cally forbid shooting and provide Moscow with precise information on every incident. We adopted this because the commander of a company or platoon cannot be allowed to determine when to shoot and when not to. We have no guarantee that some minor little group of Japanese fascist military men may not try to provoke us into war, and the decision on such questions must be in the hands of the center. I think we made the right decision. Unfortunately it was marred by an incident with Voroshilov: the problem was that he did not find it necessary not only to raise this issue for discussion but even to inform us or send us a copy of the telegram. When I found out about this, I proposed that a meeting of the Far Eastern Commission should be convened.

Even though we did not emphasize this aspect of the question but discussed it on its merits, Voroshilov declared: "I am not going to run to you over trifles, you decide a lot of issues here, yet I can't send a telegram out." Some trifle! Whether to shoot at Japanese airplanes or not! Well, of course, we got into a scrap. I think we did the right thing in convening the commission and adopting this decision, this is precisely the way to handle issues that we learn from you every day.[3]

We queried you about Mongolia by wire, the situation there has become much more complicated.[4] I will end the first letter here.

How was your trip there?

All the best. Yours, L. Kaganovich.

1. On 16 May 1932 the Politburo adopted a resolution on the agreement with German industrialists: "It is to be deemed desirable to conclude an agreement with German industrialists for one year[; . . .] it is to be deemed possible to agree to [. . .] concessions with regard to the term of the credit" (RGASPI, f. 17, op. 162, d. 12, l. 140). On 1 June 1932 the Politburo instructed Piatakov to leave for Berlin no later than 4 June and "to seek an improvement in the conditions of the agreement" with Germany on import credits. Piatakov was instructed to "suspend the preparation of orders" until negotiations were completed (ibid., l. 153).

2. In May 1932 the Brüning government in Germany resigned. The new cabinet was headed by von Papen. On 5 June in a cipher to Kaganovich Stalin criticized the "incorrect," very hostile tone of Soviet newspapers about the new government, a tone that was "in practice profitable for those who want to bring about a break between the USSR and Germany" (ibid., f. 558, op. 11, d. 77, l. 14). On the following day Kaganovich informed Stalin by cipher that the editors and functionaries concerned had been summoned and given the required instructions (ibid., l. 18).

3. See document 26.

4. See note 1 to document 25.

· 25 ·

Stalin to Kaganovich (for members of the Politburo)
4 June

F. 81, op. 3, d. 99, ll. 49–52.

---

4 June 1932. <u>Sochi.</u>
Greetings, Comrade Kaganovich!
   (<u>For members</u> of the Politburo)
   1) You should have already received my reply about Mongolia. The best thing would be to manage without sending troops in. Mongolia should not be confused with Kazakhstan or Buriatia. The main point is that we must compel the Mongolian government <u>to change its policy at its root.</u> We must (temporarily) <u>force out</u> the <u>"leftists"</u> and replace them as ministers and leaders of the Mongolian CC with people who are <u>capable of pursuing a new political course</u>, i.e. <u>our policy</u>. The only "leftists" who should be kept in their jobs are the most capable and reasonable (from the standpoint of our policy) and who have retained their authority among the Mongolian masses. The <u>rejuvenated</u> Mongolian government should <u>publicly</u> declare that mistakes were made in <u>domestic</u> policy (the economy, religion, and so forth) and that these <u>mistakes</u> will immediately be rectified. It should declare that the rebel <u>chiefs</u> are agents of the Chinese and especially the Japanese imperialists, who are seeking to strip Mongolia of its freedom and independence, and that in view of this it will wage an uncompromising struggle against them until they are completely destroyed. It should declare an <u>amnesty</u> for all <u>rank-and-file</u> rebels who surrender their weapons to the government and affirm their submission to it. All this, as well as the changes in the makeup of the government, must be done through the <u>Great Hural</u>, and its urgent convocation must be prepared <u>carefully</u> and <u>sensibly</u>.
   That is the main thing now, not sending in troops.
   Of course, if the situation in Ulan Bator is hopeless (which I doubt, because I don't consider Okhtin's report to be objective), we can decide to send in Buryat and Mongolian units, but we can do this, as a <u>temporary</u> measure, only <u>as a very last resort</u>, while bearing in mind that sending in troops is <u>secondary</u> and <u>ancillary</u> to the <u>principal</u> measure—changing the political course.[1]
   2) Everything I have seen and heard in the last few days (and I have seen and heard quite a bit) points to the fact that <u>the main thing</u> now in the relationship between the city and the countryside is <u>consumer goods</u>. Farm produce <u>will be</u> available. There are not enough consumer goods. Push the consumer goods, push them hard, and don't worry about temporarily

short-changing the <u>people's commissariats</u> and (to a certain extent) the <u>cities</u> in favor of the countryside.[2]

3) Take note of Eisenstein, who is trying through Gorky, Kirshon, and some <u>Komsomol members</u> to get himself back among the <u>top</u> filmmakers of the USSR. If he achieves his goal because the CC's department of culture and propaganda is asleep on the job, his triumph will look like a prize for all future (and present) deserters.[3] Warn the CC of the Komsomol.

Well, that is all for now. I am well. Regards. I. Stalin.

P.S. Hurry up with sending Eliava to Mongolia.[4]

1. An antigovernment rebellion broke out in Mongolia in the spring of 1932, and it spread over a substantial part of the country. On 16 May 1932 the Politburo adopted a decision "On Mongolia," which affirmed the principles for amending the political course in that country. The decision criticized the Mongolian leaders for "blindly copying the policies of Soviet rule in the USSR." It recommended that they "adopt a policy" that is "appropriate for a bourgeois-democratic republic" and abandon full-scale collectivization and the elimination of private trade (RGASPI, f. 17, op. 162, d. 12, l. 133). Following Stalin's letter, the Politburo resolved on 10 June 1932 to send a telegram to Eliava, a member of the Politburo's Mongolia commission, and Soviet ambassador Okhtin, who were both in Mongolia, which incorporated all the proposals in Stalin's letter (ibid., l. 188). Meanwhile, on 4 June Molotov, Kaganovich, Voroshilov, and Ordzhonikidze asked in a cipher to Stalin whether the detachment of ten aircraft sent to Ulan Bator should remain there. Stalin replied on the following day that "all ten aircraft or a section of them should be stated to be Mongolian." For this purpose a [backdated] agreement should be concluded with the Mongolian government that they had purchased them in the USSR at the beginning of 1931; the agreement should state a price, and that part of the cost had already been paid. (Ibid., f. 558, op. 11, d. 77, ll. 8ob. 8.) See also document 27.

2. On 8 June 1932 the Politburo adopted a decision on the verification of fulfillment of the decisions on consumer goods. Industrial people's commissariats were given assignments for the production of consumer goods. The countryside's share in the total volume of goods for the second half of 1932 in terms of twelve major items (including cotton fabrics, footwear, woolen articles, kerchiefs, threads, knitwear, sewn goods, soap, cigarettes, *makhorka* [common tobacco]) was set at a minimum of 55 percent (ibid., op. 3, d. 887, ll. 17, 29–33). See documents 27, 28, 31.

3. See documents 14, 27.

4. The first page contains the note, "Have read. M. Kalinin," followed by the signatures of Molotov, Ordzhonikidze, Mikoian, Voroshilov, Andreev, and Rudzutak.

· 26 ·

Stalin to Kaganovich
5 June

F. 81, op. 3, d. 99, ll. 54–56.

---

5 June 1932

Greetings, Comrade Kaganovich!

I received your letter of 2 June.

1) Comrade Piatakov's business trip to Germany is the correct step.[1]

2) The decision by the Far Eastern Commission regarding <u>a categorical ban on shooting without permission from Moscow</u> (i.e. Sovnarkom and the CC) is <u>absolutely correct</u>. It is clear that such issues and "incidents," which carry the risk of "suddenly" unleashing a war, must be handled, down to the tiniest details, by Moscow <u>alone</u>. I advise that you follow this principle <u>to the end</u> and don't give in (under any circumstances!) to the howls of protest from Comrade Bliukher.[2]

3) What is the situation with consumer goods? How many goods have already been sent to the countryside, when were they sent or when are they scheduled to be sent, and which goods specifically? Pay special attention to mass consumer goods. Tell Liubimov and Sergo that the fate of the union [*smychka*, between the cities and countryside] depends on the development of consumer goods, and decisions on consumer goods are to be fulfilled on schedule, unconditionally and precisely. Don't let Zelensky and the functionaries at the cooperatives sleep or take it easy. You and Postyshev must breathe down the necks of Zelensky and the functionaries at the cooperatives <u>all the time</u> and <u>make them</u> set up lively Soviet trade with the <u>countryside</u>. That is the task now.[3]

4) Make *Pravda* publish summaries <u>every day</u> on the production of the Moscow and Gorky auto plants. This is the only realistic way to make both these plants and the PC of Heavy Industry, which is not supplying the metal, shape up. Once again: make *Pravda* (I think Mekhlis has a special phone line to the staff of the PC of Heavy Industry) issue daily summaries on the Moscow and Gorky auto plants.[4]

Regards. I. Stalin.

1. See note 1 to document 24.
2. See document 24.
3. See note 2 to document 25.
4. See note 3 to document 33.

· 27 ·

Kaganovich to Stalin
6 June

F. 558, op. 11, d. 740, ll. 13–21.

6 June [1932]
Greetings, Dear Comrade Stalin!

I received your three ciphers and letter today, I am rushing to write you back today as well, both on these issues and on others.

1) On Mongolia:[1] Judging by the telegrams that are being received now,

the situation there is better than Okhtin reported. We have retained control of Tsetserleg. Ulan Bator is not in direct danger now. Just to be on the safe side, however, we issued a directive for Okhtin to clear the mission of secret documents, in accordance with your instructions. Eliava left on the 4th, and we sent on your telegram to him on an airplane, so that he could study it (and immediately return it), and gave him instructions to step up political measures.

You are right in your letter to make the point about promoting new people, tomorrow we will prepare an additional directive for Eliava and Okhtin both on a introducing new personnel and on a public declaration about mistakes that have been made and so forth. If we just begin by dispatching troops without taking these measures, it will make matters worse, so the Politburo has completely adopted your standpoint that troops should not be dispatched. We are taking the necessary steps to approve the airplanes. Today Okhtin sent in a telegram to the effect that they are forming a regiment in Ulan Bator consisting of 600 Soviet citizens, mostly colleagues, i.e. members of our party, I think we should forbid this move. Yesterday we sent him a sharply worded telegram in reply to his extremely stupid report. He reported that somebody named Muntsuk [Puntsuk], a Mongolian Communist who graduated from the Communist University of Working People of the East, had arrived from Inner Mongolia and told him that a mutiny was being prepared there among the troops, that all they needed was cartridges, etc. He added his own opinion that such a mutiny would be very useful and so forth. We believe that this is a provocation, that this Muntsuk is a provocateur. We instructed him to deliver this Muntsuk to us immediately, and he himself was rebuked for his intolerable gullibility. Apparently he became completely panicky.[2]

2) We received a report that the commander of the Japanese flotilla protecting the Japanese fishing grounds, Captain Kawoshe, sent a rather insolent letter to the commander of our patrol ships threatening that unless we ensure normal fishing conditions, he will be compelled to take appropriate measures himself. A proposal was made in the Politburo that we send a note, but we adopted a more cautious decision: since Karakhan was supposed to meet with Hirota today, the 6th, we instructed him to call Hirota's attention to the fact that the captain's statements were unacceptable and limit himself to that.[3]

3) Dirksen came to see Grinko regarding the Druzag concession in the Northern Caucasus. He referred in passing to the changes in Germany. Dirksen said he did not believe there would be any changes in relation to us, and he expressed satisfaction with the restraint of our press, apparently he is, first, not especially happy himself with the changes, and second, he probably is making comparisons with the American, and in part the British and French press, which is behaving pretty harshly, but your

telegram is absolutely right in pointing out the need to maintain absolute self-control and to avoid stridency. Today I had a second discussion on the telephone with the com[rade] editors and gave them strict instructions along these lines. I am sending you Radek's memorandum on his discussions with Dirksen—isn't he too willing to accept everything he was told there at face value?[4]

4) The Lancaster matter is not over. The first discussion was inconclusive, he did not make any statements and mostly listened instead, but then yesterday we received [a report] from the Amtorg representative in Moscow, Andreichin (incidentally he is not especially trustworthy), on Lancaster's discussion with him. It is clear from this discussion that Lancaster is seeking something and quite persistently. We resolved that Mezhlauk should meet with him again and hear him out without getting into a discussion of the substance of the issues and without making any promises. I am sending you both letters,[5] and I will write you about the results of Mezhlauk's new discussion. In view of the fact that something substantial is possible here, please let us know how we should proceed from here.[6]

5) In the negotiations with the oil representatives, we seem to have messed up and outsmarted ourselves. Rabinovich reports that as soon as they were notified of our new conditions, they declared that their conditions had been final and they were now withdrawing them and breaking off the negotiations. Now the *Daily Mail* and other newspapers have launched a campaign against us.[7] Sokolnikov proposes that we make our own announcement in the press, but if we get into polemics with them, it may ruin any chance for a resumption of negotiations, or we should make an announcement that suggests a way to resume the negotiations, but it is too early for that, it is better to wait a bit. This issue is on the agenda for the Politburo on the 8th, if there is no answer from you to the telegram, we will defer the issue.[8] Maybe somebody new should be assigned to begin talks again? (Maybe Veitser or somebody else.)

6) About consumer goods for mass supply. We are turning up the pressure as much as we can, and now after your letter I will push even harder, next time I will write you already about the results of our work in numerical terms rather than in resolutions. At present I don't have any exact figures at hand. In any case the shipment of goods to the market in May, especially the second half, was much greater than in April and in the first half of May. But until now we have kept pressing for the movement of goods into the market in general, and now we must start focusing on the dispatch of goods to the countryside.[9]

7) You know the figures on the sowing, if it were not for the Ukraine, we would be running 3 million hectares ahead of last year, we put pressure on the Urals, they are way behind, we sent them a chastising telegram,[10] the Northern Caucasus is 400,000 hectares behind last year as well, but we

haven't sent them anything yet. We will have to give Nizhny Novgorod, because of the <u>hailstorm</u>, 700 tons of millet to resow the crops damaged by the hail, and we added 1.6 million poods [26,200 tons] of grain to supply the Ukraine for the supply network. Everybody else who has sent in telegrams, we are refusing.

8) With regard to Eisenstein, I have taken the appropriate measures.[11] The patrons of the arts who act like liberals at the expense of the state's interests must be stopped.

9) On Yaroslavsky's article, I told Mekhlis the day after publication that it is no good. You are absolutely right that it is an outrage. I think it would be best to dismiss Yaroslavsky from *Pravda,* because he is combining it with Central Control Commission activity, and the result is not what we need.[12]

Well I will end here.

I leave you with a firm handshake. Yours, L. Kaganovich.

1. See document 25.

2. On 5 June 1932 the Politburo decided to send Okhtin a telegram on behalf of the PC of Foreign Affairs: "We consider Puntsuk's report a provocation. We consider your gullibility intolerable. Arrest Puntsuk immediately and send him to Moscow" (RGASPI, f. 17, op. 162, d. 12, l. 175). On 19 August the Politburo reviewed the matter of Puntsuk and adopted a decision to bring Puntsuk to Moscow; the OGPU and PC of Foreign Affairs were instructed to look into his background (ibid., d. 13, l. 77).

3. The Politburo instructed Karakhan, when he met with Hirota, to call attention to the fact that the statements by the commander of the third Japanese flotilla were unacceptable (ibid., d. 12, l. 75).

4. The memorandum is missing.

5. The letters are missing.

6. For details about Lancaster's visit to Moscow see the introduction to this chapter. See also documents 30, 32, 34, 38 and 45.

7. The *Daily Mail* is a conservative British newspaper which at that time had a strongly anti-Soviet orientation.

8. See note 3 to document 29.

9. Se note 2 to document 25.

10. On 5 June 1932 the Politburo approved a telegram to the leadership of the Sverdlovsk Regional Party Committtee and Regional Executive Committee, signed by Kaganovich and Molotov, which called the state of sowing in the region "threatening" (ibid., op. 3, d. 887, l. 28).

11. See document 25.

12. See note 3 to document 28.

· 28 ·

Kaganovich to Stalin
7 June

F. 558, op. 11, d. 740, ll. 22–29.

7 June [1932]
Greetings Comrade Stalin!

1) The conference of Politburo members with people's commissars about the third qu[arter] just ended. We haven't put our resolution in official form yet, we are sending it to you as a cipher so as to get your opinion.[1] Gosplan was proposing a reduction in capital projects of 1 billion [rubles] from the second qu[arter], but we supported the amount of the second qu[arter]. Usually this third qu[arter] runs ahead of the second, but we took into consideration both food resources and the inadvisability of going too far with the printing of money. We agreed on the second qu[arter] figure, no lower and no higher. The situation is very bad with regard to economy measures and construction costs. I stressed that a very poor job is being done of carrying out your instructions in this respect, which were issued during the discussion of the second quarter. The most important and dangerous thing is that economic leaders are showing little concern for rubles.

We also proposed that a portion of the money be allocated to enterprises that supply consumer goods. In a discussion with members of Moscow artisan cooperatives they stated that if they are given a small sum in credit for some improvements of their enterprises, they will be able to increase their output significantly. I promised them to do this, but this support must be provided to the artisan cooperatives as a whole. I think Comrade Stalin, that the PC of Heavy Industry and others should assign some of their enterprises specifically to consumer goods while making use of all the other enterprises.

2) We have set up a commission to work out the issues of preparing the harvest campaign. As soon as a draft is ready, I will send it to you immediately.[2]

3) Today we discussed the question of Yaroslavsky's article. We called in the bureau of the editorial board. For his part, despite our statements and explanations, he has not realized his mistake that he aided the enemies with his article. After discussing the article, we adopted the following resolution: "a) Comrade Yaroslavsky's article is to be deemed flagrantly erroneous, factually incorrect and politically harmful; b) It is to be pointed out to the bureau of the *Pravda* editorial board that it has made a mistake by publishing this article in *Pravda;* c) Comrade Yaroslavsky is to be relieved of his duties as a member of *Pravda*'s editorial board.[3]

I think we did the right thing in relieving him from *Pravda,* and relieving *Pravda* of him. He mixed the functions of secretary of the TsKK [Central Control Commission] with the functions of a member of the editorial board by working at *Pravda* as a TsKK member and at the TsKK as a journalist. You are absolutely right that he does not know how to use the newspaper as a weapon, he failed to realize his political mistake till the very last minute.

4) I am sending you an OGPU memorandum on a counterrevolutionary group on the battleship *Marat* and material that deserves attention and requires an increase in our vigilance.[4]

5) A telegram has been received from Slavutsky in which he reports that Ohashi is insisting again on behalf of Manchukuo that we recognize the Manchurian government. This persistence is rather suspicious, since Ohashi himself belongs to a group of fascists. According to available information Saito issued just the opposite directives to his representatives in Manchuria, he is proposing that this issue not be pressed, since if we recognize Manchukuo before they, the Japanese, do it themselves, it will complicate the situation. He plainly proposes that the USSR not jump ahead with recognizing Manchukuo. According to available information, Ohashi received this telegram from Saito after talking with Slavutsky, but he may raise this issue again. We haven't discussed this issue yet, please write what we should do. It seems to me that we shouldn't rush ahead with this recognition.[5]

Well, I will end here. Tomorrow, the 8th, we have a regular Politburo meeting, after which I will write again.

Goodbye. Regards. Yours, L. Kaganovich.

1. On 7 June 1932 Kaganovich and Molotov sent Stalin a cipher: "A conference of Politburo members today outlined the following directives for drawing up control figures for the third quarter: 'a) Gosplan is to be issued a directive to stay within the limits of the second quarter (6,800,000 rubles) on the issue of capital investments when drawing up the national economic plan for the third quarter; b) A certain priority in investments is to be predetermined for the PC of Transport in the third quarter over the second quarter; c) When drawing up the food program for the third quarter, there is to be special consideration of the interests of the harvest campaign; d) The PC of Heavy Industry, the PC of Light Industry, the PC of the Timber Industry, the PC for Supply, the PC of Agriculture and the PC of Transport are to be instructed to work out measures toward reducing construction costs and to convene narrow, specialized business conferences for this purpose and, in a month, reports are to be heard from the aforementioned people's commissariats, along with a co-report by the USSR Workers' and Peasants' Inspectorate; e) All econ[omic] people's commissariats are to be instructed to allocate, within the limits of third-quarter appropriations, more special funds than in the second quarter for the needs of consumer goods and to report to the commission on consumer goods; f) Gosplan is to examine, in addition, the question of developing consumer-goods production through the artisan cooperatives; g) At least 70,000 tons of metal is to be set aside out of the total metal reserves in the third quarter for consumer-goods production.' Please let us know your opinion. We are not putting this resolution in official form until we

receive your answer" (RGASPI, f. 558, op. 11, d. 77, l. 29). Stalin approved the directives on the same day and the resolution was recorded in this form in the minutes of the Politburo meeting (ibid., f. 17, op. 3, d. 887, ll. 9, 10).

2. The commission members were: Molotov (chairman), Kaganovich, Kalinin, Ordzhonikidze, Mikoian, Yakovlev, Mezhlauk, and Krinitsky (ibid., l. 9).

3. In his article "There Must Be Immediate Restructuring," published in *Pravda* on 31 May 1932, Yaroslavsky criticized the former party leadership of the Ivanovo Region, where mass disturbances by the workers of textile enterprises had taken place in April (the article did not mention this). On 5 June Stalin sent a cipher in strong language to the Politburo protesting about "the publication in *Pravda* of Yaroslavsky's article on the disturbances by workers in Ivanovo-Voznesensk," which had enabled foreign correspondents to write about a "new Kronstadt" (ibid., f. 558, op. 11, d. 77, l. 80b.). The decision reported by Kaganovich was adopted by the Politburo on 7 June 1932 (ibid., l. 9). See also document 27).

4. The memorandum is missing.

5. See note 2 to document 30.

· 29 ·

Stalin to Kaganovich
7 June

F. 81, op. 3, d. 99, ll. 58–60.

Greetings, Comrade Kaganovich!

1) I finally had a chance to read Demian Bedny's play *How the 14th Division Went to Heaven* (see *Novy Mir*). I don't think the play came out very well—it is mediocre, rough around the edges, exudes a bawdy atmosphere, and is full of barroom-type jokes. If it is of any educational value, it is most likely of the negative kind.

We made a mistake in putting the Politburo seal on this flat and inartistic piece of work.[1] This is a lesson for us. From now on we will be careful, especially with regard to the works of Demian Bedny.

2) *Novy Mir* is printing Sholokhov's new novel, *Virgin Soil Upturned*. An interesting piece of work! Sholokhov has obviously studied the collective-farm system on the Don. I think Sholokhov has great artistic talent. In addition, he is a profoundly honest writer: he writes about things he knows well. Not like "our" frivolous Babel, who keeps writing about things of which he knows nothing (for example, *The Cavalry*).

3) Almost every day *Pravda* prints two "bottom-of-the-page crawlers" (feuilletons) that deal with various trivialities. Can't *Pravda* be compelled to discard one of the "crawlers" and use the freed-up space for a section (introduce such a section!) called "Letters from workers and collective farmers." The bureaucrats at *Pravda* have replaced letters from workers and collective farmers with letters from professional correspondents and "plenipotentiaries." But the bureaucrats have to be reined in. Otherwise *Pravda* runs the risk of completely falling out of touch with live human be-

ings at factories and collective farms. So go ahead and try to rein in the bureaucrats at *Pravda*.[2] Regards.

7 June 1932   I. Stalin.

P.S. I just received your letter of 6 June. 1) Try to renew negotiations somehow with the <u>oil representatives</u>.[3] 2) It would be better to dismiss <u>Yaroslavsky</u> from *Pravda*.[4] 3) It seems to me that <u>Okhtin</u> should be removed, but this move, i.e. Okhtin's replacement, should be prepared carefully.[5]

Regards. Stalin.

1. The Politburo gave permission on 19 April 1932 to stage Bedny's play *How the 14th Division Went to Heaven* (RGASPI, f. 17, op. 3, d. 881, l. 8).

2. See note 11 to document 32.

3. In May 1932, at the First International Oil Conference in New York, British and American oil companies proposed that the USSR refrain from independent participation in the world oil markets. In return, they pledged to purchase from the USSR 5 million tons of oil a year (the amount of Soviet oil exports in 1931) at a fixed price for ten years. No agreement was reached at the time. Negotiations continued in New York. On 1 June 1932 the Politburo instructed the Soviet delegation to make counterproposals in the talks (ibid., op. 162, d. 12, ll. 152, 157–158), which caused them to break down. Upon receiving word that the negotiations had broken off, Stalin intervened in the matter. On 5 and 7 June in ciphers to Kaganovich he criticized Rozengolts' proposals as "too severe," commenting that "the Anglo-American oil group must be more or less neutralized if we really want to preserve the peace for at least two or three years" (ibid., f. 558, op. 11, d. 77, ll. 17, 22, 23). On 8 June, after considering Stalin's telegrams, the Politburo resolved: "Revising a previous Politburo decision of 1 June on instructions for negotiations [. . .], to deem it possible to enter into negotiations with the oil representatives on the basis of the proposals submitted by the oil representatives. [. . .] To direct the PC of Foreign Trade to outline ways to explore possibilities for a resumption of negotiations with the oil representatives and report on the outlined steps to the CC within two days" (ibid., l. 172). Despite these efforts, no agreement was reached with the Western oil companies (J. Bowden, in *Journal of European Economic History*, vol. 17 [1988], p. 660). See documents 27, 37, 38, and 42.

4. See note 3 to document 28.

5. See note 10 to document 32.

· 30 ·

Stalin to Kaganovich
[before 12 June]

F. 81, op. 3, d. 100, ll. 142–145.

Greetings, Comrade Kaganovich!

1) I received your letter of the 7th. We <u>must not</u> recognize a de jure Manchurian state. By insisting that we extend recognition, the Japanese are hoping to get us into a quarrel with China or Manchuria: if we recognize Manchuria, we get into a quarrel with China, if we refuse to recognize

it, we get into a quarrel with the Manchurian government. That is how the Japanese reason it out with their shallow but cunning minds. But this game doesn't call for great minds. If recognition is so essential and so sensible, why aren't the Japanese themselves in a rush to recognize their own creation? We must reply to the Japanese that we are studying the question of formal recognition, as well as the question of why the Japanese themselves aren't in any rush to recognize a <u>Manchurian state</u>. Once we finish studying the questions, a process that unfortunately is being delayed somewhat by the vacations of members of the session of the Central Executive Committee, without whom the question of recognition cannot be decided, we will inform the Japanese of the results. Not only Hayashi [i.e. Ohashi] should be informed but also—<u>simultaneously</u> and <u>without fail</u>— the Manchurians themselves. To mollify the Japanese and Manchurians, we should tell them at the same time that <u>in principle</u> we have never rejected and do not reject de jure recognition, but that <u>in practice</u> such issues are not decided in a single stroke and require study. That this is correct is clear from the fact that we agreed to receive consuls from the Manchurian government, refused to allow [the 2d Earl of] Lytton[1] to travel to Manchuria, and are pursuing a line of strict neutrality. And so on in this vein.[2]

2) The Politburo is apparently failing to take account of the big changes that have taken place recently in the international arena. The most important of these changes is that the influence of the USA has begun to decline both in China—<u>to Japan's benefit</u>—and in Europe (especially since von Papen came to power)—<u>to France's benefit</u>. This is a very important factor. As a result of this the USA will seek ties with the USSR. And they are already seeking them. One bit of evidence is the arrival of Lancaster, a representative of one of America's <u>most powerful banks</u>.[3] Take this new factor into account.

Regards. I. Stalin.[4]

1. A commission chaired by Lord Lytton of Great Britain, established by the Council of the League of Nations in December 1931, was charged with undertaking an on-site study and reporting to the council on all the factors which threatened to breach the peace between China and Japan. Between February and July 1932 the commission visited Japan, China, and Manchuria. The commission's report, published on 1 October 1932, contained a plan for Manchurian "autonomy," recognition of Japan's "special interests" and establishment of the principle of "open doors" (DVP, vol. XV, pp. 734–36).

2. See document 28. On 16 June 1932 the Politburo instructed Slavutsky to give Ohashi this response: "The Soviet government at present is studying the question of formal recognition of Manchukuo and, in this connection, the question of Japan's failure to recognize Manchukuo. Once we finish studying the question, a process that unfortunately is being delayed by the departure for summer vacation of members of the Central Executive Committee, without whom a decision on this question cannot be adopted, we will report the results. The Soviet government in principle has never rejected and does not reject de jure recognition of Manchukuo, but in practice such issues are not decided immediately. That this is so is clear from the Soviet government's treatment of Manchukuo. Manchukuo can judge this by the

Soviet government's policy on the Chinese Eastern Railroad, by the fact that we agreed to the appointment of Manchurian consuls in the USSR, and by our policy of strict neutrality, which was reflected, in part, in the Soviet government's treatment of the Lytton commission, which wanted to travel to Manchukuo across Soviet territory." Slavutsky was instructed to convey this response simultaneously and directly to the Manchurians, and Troianovsky was instructed to convey it to the Japanese government (RGASPI, f. 17, op. 162, d. 12, ll. 180, 182). See also document 32.

3. See note 6 to document 27.

4. The first page contains the notation "Have read. Voroshilov" and the signatures of Kalinin, Mikoian, Rudzutak, and Postyshev.

· 31 ·

Stalin to Kaganovich
[12 June]

F. 81, op. 3, d. 100, ll. 120–124.

Greetings, <u>Comrade</u> <u>Kaganovich</u>!

1) Why aren't the summaries on the Moscow and Gorky auto plants being published <u>every day</u>? Who are you being merciful to—the bureaucrats? Are the bureaucrats' interests really above the interests of the cause? So this is the disgrace we have lived to see . . . [1]

2) Why did tractor output <u>decline</u> at the Stalingrad Tractor Plant? They got an Order of Lenin and eased up? And the CC can put up with such an outrage! . . . [2]

3) What is the situation with regard to plan fulfillment in the production of tanks, airplanes, engines for them, tank guns, and antitank guns? Was the May plan fulfilled or not? What are the prospects for the June plan?

4) When is the CC thinking of convening a plenum? It would be a good idea to convene it on 1–2 August.[3]

5) I just received your letter of 9 June. Here are my responses:

a) On consumer goods. By decision of the CC we must have not only quarterly but also <u>monthly</u> plans of deliveries for the market—that is first, and then second, we must <u>ship</u> a certain percentage of the <u>total</u> amount of output for the market (and the countryside) and allocate <u>only the remainders</u> to <u>nonmarket</u> consumers.[4] What happened to these decisions? Why aren't they being carried out? If you really are seeking the truth, write me what percentage of total output in certain industries is being allocated to the market (<u>by month!</u>) or should be allocated to the market (by month!) and how much to nonmarket consumers. Come on, try it!

6) As for the Tsentrosoiuz [Central Union of Consumer Cooperative Societies], there is no need to point to how weak it is: its weakness is common knowledge. The Politburo commission on consumer goods was es-

tablished so that you and Postyshev would manage Tsentrosoiuz.[5] That was the point of establishing the commission. From now on any reference to the weakness of Tsentrosoiuz will be (and should be!) regarded as the weakness of Kaganovich and Postyshev. The immediate task is, in May, June, and July, to send the largest possible quantity of mass consumer goods to the grain-growing, sugar-growing (sugar-beet), and cotton-growing regions—in the expectation that the goods will be there already in July and August. If this is not accomplished, the commission deserves to be buried alive. Well, that is all.

Regards. I. Stalin.

1. See note 3 to document 33.

2. On 23 April 1932, at Stalin's suggestion, the Politburo adopted a decision to propose to the Presidium of the CEC of the USSR that the Stalingrad Tractor Plant (STP) be awarded the Order of Lenin (RGASPI, f. 17, op. 3, d. 881, ll. 1, 16). Tractor production declined to 1,697 in May 1932 from 2,997 in April and did not return to its former level for several months (although 28,882 tractors were produced in 1932 as a whole, compared to 17,536 in 1931) (N.T. Dodge, *Trends in Labor Productivity in the Soviet Tractor Industry: A Case Study in Industrial Development*, Ph.D. dissertation [Harvard University, 1960], 608–14). On 16 September 1932, on Stalin's initiative, the Politburo adopted a decision: "To assign Comrade Ordzhonikidze to report to the CC within two days on what is going on at the STP, why it is failing to operate normally and what needs to be done so that normal production is urgently restored" (RGASPI, f. 17, op. 3, d. 900, l. 2). In the newspaper *Za industrializatsiiu*, 17 October 1932, this decline was attributed to the metal shortage and the need to repair worn-out equipment. See document 33.

3. On 16 June Kaganovich informed Stalin by cipher that the Politburo was planning a plenum of the CC for 5 August which might discuss three of the following: consumer goods; timber; iron and steel; possibly state farms; and grain procurements (RGASPI, f. 558, op. 11, d. 740, ll. 53–63). See documents 37, 38.

4. On 10 February 1932 the Politburo proposed drawing up a plan for the distribution of consumer goods for 1932 in which the share of the market would be at least 80 percent of the gross output of these goods (ibid., f. 17, op. 3, d. 872, l. 6). The Politburo subsequently considered on a number of occasions the elaboration of plans for consumer-goods supply and distribution of goods between the market and state customers. See documents 25, 27, 28. In his letter of 9 June (not published in this collection) Kaganovich reported to Stalin at great length the failure of the production of consumer goods to increase sufficiently (ibid., f. 558, op. 11, d. 740, ll. 30–31).

5. On 8 May 1932, at Stalin's suggestion, the Politburo formed a commission to monitor implementation of the decisions by central agencies on consumer goods; it comprised Molotov, Stalin, Kaganovich, Postyshev, Rudzutak, and Yagoda (ibid., f. 17, op. 3, d. 883, l. 1).

· 32 ·

Kaganovich to Stalin
12 June

F. 558, op. 11, d. 740, ll. 37–42.

---

12 June [932]

Greetings Comrade Stalin!

I received your letter of the 7th yesterday and just received your next letter today.

1) Tomorrow I will familiarize all Politburo members with your proposals on the issue of recognizing the Manchurian government and we will adopt a directive to our diplomatic representatives in accordance with your instructions.[1] There is absolutely no question that it is inadvisable for us to go further right now than we already have. The only question that may come up is the following: since we know that Saito is not especially sympathetic to our recognizing Manchukuo, shouldn't Troianovsky inquire of Saito in a discussion how he views this matter before we reply to Ohashi and the Manchurians. If necessary, we will ask you tomorrow by cipher in order to receive an answer by wire. In connection with this question I would like to ask your opinion about what we should do with Znamensky? I remember you once said that it is awkward to remove him right now,[2] but Karakhan in proposing to remove Znamensky is citing some serious facts, for example: despite being categorically forbidden to meet Wellington Koo, and especially Lytton, Znamensky met with Wellington Koo, and with Lytton and other members of his commission.[3] By all indications he wants to "create" some kind of "high" policy there, but is unable to conduct even a simple policy. Wouldn't it be better to remove him? This may also prove diplomatically useful. We deferred Karakhan's proposal that we remove him. So please tell me your opinion.

2) We queried you yesterday about Nanking by telegram.[4] The form the Chinese have chosen is unacceptable without a resumption of diplomatic relations: they begin with a nonaggression pact in which they presumably will try to insert a clause about the treatment of Manchukuo. We know that they are instructing their delegation member in Moscow Mo-de-Guya to privately and secretly sound out our mood and attitude to their counterproposal. All this so far makes a less than serious impression. Perhaps the Nanking people are here reflecting sentiment in America, but this is not yet known. In any case it seems we should hardly rush ahead.

3) About America. It really must be acknowledged that your criticism is correct. We really did underestimate the significance of Lancaster's visit and the overall trend that is building in America. This is especially evident in light of the analysis of the change in the situation in America that you

provided in your letter. A number of new facts show that indeed in America "the matter of recognizing the USSR is taking or has already taken shape." I am sending you a memorandum from Radek and Andreichin on their discussions with Bullitt, quite a major political figure, and with the engineer Pope.[5] The memoranda are very interesting and show that the issue of recognizing the USSR is being framed more and more realistically from various standpoints. Today a report was received that Cooper has organized a trip to the USSR by eight prominent businessmen (we don't know the names yet). We will of course take now take account of all these circumstances, we will arrange a meeting for Lancaster with Kalmanovich, Piatakov, and Mezhlauk, the basis of the talks will be your directives. But the question now arises: is this enough? Shouldn't we sound out some issues in America itself? We await your advice about this.[6]

4) About oil. We arranged for coverage in *Izvestia* and *Pravda*. Neither Gubkin nor other major figures were in Moscow, we got in touch with them and managed to obtain a summary of Gubkin's speech at the Academy of Sciences [in the Urals]. It was not bad, naturally, and today we already received an interview with Gubkin from Novosibirsk as well. But we decided to wait a day or two before publication, so as not to offer only Gubkin. Tomorrow, depending on how the foreign correspondents react to this, we will issue an appropriate report for the foreign press through Foreign TASS.[7] A new conference will presumably take place soon.

5) I am sending you the letters from Petrovsky and Chubar. Chubar's letter is more businesslike and self-critical, it doesn't have the rubbish that was in Petrovsky's letter. Petrovsky starts from the very first lines to shift blame to the CC of the VKP(b), he declares that "I understood the necessity of fulfilling the directives of the CC of the VKP(b) on grain procurements" as if they couldn't have come to the CC of the VKP(b) and raise all their issues in a timely and honest manner. He (Petrovsky) argues with those who tell the truth, that they were out of touch with the countryside and did not know the situation, but then he has to admit that they [the Ukrainians] concealed the truth from the CC of the VKP(b) and began to talk only when the CC pointed out the flagrant outrages to them from Moscow. Essentially his letter boils down to an effort, first, to lay the groundwork for rejecting grain procurements this year, which is absolutely inadmissible, and second, he and Chubar raise the question of providing grain assistance for food needs. In this respect we will have to provide partial assistance, the only question is the quantity. Please write your thoughts on this point?[8] Kosior has written <u>nothing.</u>

6) There is nothing new on the sowing yet, the summary will come in on the 14th, but judging by some data on this five-day period about 6 million hectares will be sown. With regard to the final calculation of the area sown the question of corrections for the area sown by individual peasants

comes up, last year and the year before upward corrections amounted to 10–15 percent. This year we have the same kind of cases, in which individual peasants are concealing a portion of their areas. There are even instances in which individual peasants sow at night so that their sown areas are not counted. I think we can make a correction for the individual sector, like last year, of 10–15 percent, which will amount to about 2 million hectares. Please write your opinion.[9]

7) We will search for a candidate to replace Okhtin. When we find one, we will tell you.[10]

8) I have given appropriate instructions to *Pravda,* and in a day or two we will set up the "department of letters from workers and collective farmers." This will be wonderful.[11]

9) Regarding the assessment of "Demian's fish soup" I completely agree with you, I have read both the new and the old one, and the new one is even worse and cruder. Being a people's proletarian writer in no way means sinking to the level of the negative qualities of our masses as Demian Bedny does. I am simply astonished that Voroshilov, for example, could be delighted with the thing, especially because Demian has many ambiguities in his play. Unfortunately, I haven't read Sholokhov yet.[12]

Well, I will end here. How is your vacation? How is your health?

All the best. Regards. Yours, L. Kaganovich.

1. See note 2 to document 30.
2. See note 1 to document 34.
3. See note 1 to document 30.
4. On 12 June 1932 Molotov and Kaganovich sent the following cipher:

"1) We know from reliable sources known to you that Nanking has decided to restore relations with us. Nanking has decided to enter into negotiations with us on a nonaggression treaty. Nanking believes that the restoration of diplomatic relations will occur through the signing of a nonaggression treaty. An official of the Chinese delegation who has remained in Moscow, Wang, has been instructed, on the basis of 'personal opinion, secretly and officially' to ascertain the opinion of the Soviet government. It was obviously to carry out these instructions that Wang made a request to be received by Kozlovsky, the head of the Far East Department at the PC of Foreign Affairs.

"2) We believe that Nanking's decision stems mainly from fears that we are drawing closer to Manchukuo. The purpose of restoring relations, and through signing a nonaggression pact to boot, will be to make it harder for us to establish the relations with Manchukuo that we need. We can be sure that the Chinese will openly include some clauses in the nonaggression pact that openly tie our hands in our Manchuria policy.

"3) We consider it expedient that Kozlovsky avoid a meeting with Wang right now and that Wang be sent to a staff member of the department, who will suggest to Wang that if he has inquiries, to make them in writing. Please let us know your opinion." (RGASPI, f. 558, op. 11, d. 77, l. 54.) On 13 June Stalin sent a reply by cipher: "Regarding the proposal by the Nankingese for a nonaggression pact I agree with you. If Wang makes a written proposal, wire a copy" (ibid.). On 16 June the Politburo adopted the proposals of Molotov and Kaganovich as they were formulated in their telegram to Stalin and in Stalin's reply (ibid., f. 17, op. 162, d. 12, l. 180). In addition to this decision, on 29 June 1932 the Politburo authorized Kozlovsky to state to Wang that if the latter raised the issue of a pact and recognition, then in his [Kozlovsky's] opinion, the Soviet government "would not object to the immediate restoration of relations without any conditions, after which a nonaggression pact will come as a natural result of the restoration of relations" (ibid., d. 13, l. 4).

5. The memorandum is missing. See note 3 to document 34.

6. See note 6 to document 27 and note 2 to document 34.

7. See note 4 to document 34. In a cipher of 9 June Stalin instructed Kaganovich and Molotov to "immediately start a campaign in the press about the very real prospects for Sterlitamak, Ukhta, and Emba oil"; this might "compel the Anglo-American oilmen to renew negotiations and make concessions to us" (ibid., f. 558, op. 11, d. 77, l. 31).

8. The letters are missing. See note 5 to document 34.

9. See note 6 to document 34.

10. The new ambassador to Mongolia, Chutskaev, was confirmed by the Politburo only on 15 August 1933 (ibid., f. 17, op. 3, d. 928, l. 5). See document 29.

11. On 13 June 1932 the Secretariat adopted Stalin's proposal to establish a department of letters from workers and collective farmers in *Pravda* and reduce to a minimum the number of feuilletons printed in *Pravda* (ibid., op. 114, d. 302, l. 13). See documents 29, 33.

12. See document 29.

· 33 ·

Kaganovich to Stalin
14 June

F. 558, op. 11, d. 740, ll. 43–52.

14 June 1932

Greetings Comrade Stalin.

First of all I want to report to you about the work on foreign currency.

1) Our commission's work is proceeding in two directions, first to ensure fulfillment of the 1932 plan and, second, to work out the issue and measures that secure the transition to 1933.

On the first task we considered the issue of ensuring timber exports in conformity with the 1932 plan and adopted a number of operational measures.[1] We considered the issue of the work of the gold industry and adopted a number of operational measures, especially to ensure the supply both of equipment and of food.[2]

Tomorrow we are convening all suppliers at the CC, i.e. the economic organiz[ations] that are required to fulfill orders and contracts with the gold industry, in order to drum into people the need for a serious attitude toward supplying the gold industry (naturally without disclosing unnecessary facts and figures).

With respect to the second task, i.e. 1933, the subcommissions are still working on the question. Above all, here it is imperative to reduce and partly delay the import plan in 1932, but the Rudzutak commission, instead of working directly for a reduction, confined itself to instructing

Ordzhonikidze and Rozengolts to reach an agreement!! And of course we would have to wait a long time for them to reach an agreement. It was therefore necessary as a result of the report by my subcommission on the balance of payments to set limits in figures so as to make Rudzutak's task of cutting imports easier. We resolved: "Comrade Rudzutak's commission is to be instructed to limit payments in 1932 by a sum of no more than 67 million [rubles] (set already by the Politburo), including payments under the entire supplementary import plan set out in all special decrees including the purchase of grain for the Far Eastern Region, plus payments provided for under the 1932 plan and to be made in 1933 that amount to no more than 85 million rubles."

We could not get by of course without arguments and "compliments," but we insisted and this was adopted.

You will see the key figures in the tables of calculations of our debts and payments that are being sent enclosed to you, we have carefully verified and accurately established them, although even before them you accurately determined our deficit and difficulties. Based on the calculations of payments we determined an assignment for the subcommissions to work out and set an export plan that provides foreign-currency revenues in 1933 of at least 620 million rubles, and at least 290 million rubles in the first half of the year. Of course these figures were drawn up with some margin, all the more so since Rozengolts still has some margin for delaying payments and saving about 40 million, but this 40 m[illion] does not figure yet in our calculations, and we preferred to propose figures with some margins in hand rather than a deficit; so far this is merely an assignment for the subcommissions, and we are still going to examine the specific plans.

2) In your letter that I received today you ask why the summary reports [*svodki*] are not being published. Now this matter has been nailed down and the reports will appear.[3] The *Pravda* people explain that they were not being published because the Gorky Auto Plant was not producing autos but engines for combines, and the Moscow Auto Plant was producing intermittently, but they were able to successfully publish reports both on the engines and on the trucks produced intermittently by the Stalin plant. Yesterday I had a very big talk, if you can really call it a talk, with Mekhlis and Popov, I chewed them out hard both for not printing the reports and for their incorrect attitude toward the proposal to set up a department of letters from workers and collective farmers. They wrote in the form of a report to the CC what they were doing to implement this resolution and devoted a whole page at the beginning of the report to claiming that they have been printing letters to this very day, both individually and in summary and so forth, i.e. they wrote an obvious falsehood, and I pointed out to them, using actual issues of *Pravda,* that they replaced letters from

workers and collective farmers with feuilletons by Ryklin, Agranovsky, Vasilkovsky, and Koltsov.[4] The upshot was that I had quite a scrap with Mekhlis and Popov, in general I think that you are more likely to get complaints about me for being merciless rather than for being merciful. In any case, I will take your comment into account.

3) About the Stalingrad plant: right now they are producing engines for combines, they produced 622 engines in the first 10 days of June and 418 tractors, but that is below the program and you are right that we have to get the plant to shape up.[5] Right now they intend to put the plant on leave from 15 June, I had doubts about the expediency of doing it right now, but Sergo said he coordinated this issue with you.

4) About the production of tanks and airplanes and their engines, cannons, etc., I will write you in detail next time. I received your letter in the evening and was unable to obtain precise inform[ation]. Right now I can say that, according to the information available to me, the program is being fulfilled fairly well.

5) About consumer goods: for almost the entire past two days I have sat over these issues, we mainly considered the specific distribution of the allocation for the third qu[arter]. We have finished with cotton fabrics, what we adopted coincides completely with your instructions in the last letter. We sharply shifted goods toward the countryside. It is now already very late, but next time I will write you in detail with figures for each sector, especially for cotton-fabric production.

6) I am sending you three documents received from Balitsky.[6]

7) The loan campaign is developing fairly well.[7] Moscow finished 100 percent today, the workers' attitude is not bad, at most plants the subscription is proceeding with enthusiasm. One old worker at the Podolsk plant made this statement: "Now," he says, "people are arguing here can you win or not, but I will ask you, I have two sons, both are already engineers, did I win or not. Of course I already won." These words express the full force of how convinced proletarians are of the rightness of our cause, of our actions.

Well I will end here. I leave you with a handshake. Yours, L. Kaganovich.

P. S. 1) In the last five-day period 5,300,000 hectares were sown, making a total of 87,717,000, or 1,900,000 less than at the same point last year. The machine-tractor stations have nearly finished sowing. Now we have to put the emphasis on industrial and kitchen-garden crops.

2) The regions are pushing hard on the problem of grain, and we are refusing the overwhelming majority. Chubar also came in to get some grain, we haven't decided anything yet, we provided 50,000 poods [819 tons] for Moldavia only. They are asking for about 1.5 million, of course there is no way we can give them that much, but we will have to help, especially the

beet-growing districts. Please do let us know your thoughts on this point, how much we can give them.[8]

Right now we are preparing the issue of ensuring a successful harvest campaign.

Regards. L. Kaganovich.

1. On 16 June the Politburo approved a decision on the fulfillment of the export plan for logging in 1932 and adopted a resolution submitted by the Politburo commission on foreign-currency reserves (RGASPI, f. 17, op. 3, d. 888, ll. 1, 18–22).

2. On 16 June the Politburo considered and took decisions on a group of topics concerned with the gold industry (ibid., ll. 10, 38–46).

3. On 12 June Stalin sent the CC of the VKP(b) the following telegram: "I submit to the Politburo four proposals: (1) To require *Pravda* to print daily summary reports on motor-vehicle production at the Moscow and Nizhny Novgorod auto plants. (2) To require *Pravda* to print daily reports of tractor production at the Stalingrad and Kharkov tractor plants and not to be afraid that for certain reasons the Kharkov plant will initially produce fewer than 100 units a day. (3) To require *Pravda* to launch a systematic barrage against the management of our metallurgical plants, which, despite the introduction of gigantic new blast furnaces, have still failed to raise pig-iron production to 20,000 tons a day. (4) To require *Pravda* to launch a systematic barrage against the enterprises of the PC of the Timber Industry and the PC for Supply, which, despite huge outlays of state funds, are still making no headway." (Ibid., f. 558, op. 11, d. 77, l. 57.) On 13 June the Politburo adopted the text of the telegram as an official decision of the Politburo (ibid., f. 17, op. 163, d. 945, l. 121). Reports on the daily production of motor vehicles and tractors began to be published in *Pravda* on 15 June. See also documents 26, 31.

4. See note 11 to document 32.

5. See note 2 to document 31.

6. The documents are missing.

7. On 16 May 1932 the Politburo approved the issue of a new mass loan for 1932 totaling 3.2 billion rubles (ibid., op. 3, d. 884, l. 5).

8. See note 5 to document 34.

· 34 ·

Stalin to Kaganovich
15 June

F. 81, op. 3 , d. 99, ll. 62–63.

---

15 June 1932

Greetings, Comrade Kaganovich!

I received your letter of 12 June.

1) A formal recall of Znamensky would be inadvisable. He should be summoned (without delay) for a <u>personal report</u>, in order to discuss the circumstances, and then settle the question one way or another.[1]

2) Out of all the conversations, "negotiations," "reports," and "statements" on Soviet-American relations, the most interesting development is

Lancaster's appearance, his desire to clarify the terms of the loan and the procedure for settling the bank's claims. Let Mezhlauk, Piatakov, and Kalmanovich have a thorough chat with him.[2]

As for Pope, Bullitt, and the others, with them we must also be tender (remember what the Ukrainians say: "Be tender"!) and attentive.[3] We should deflect the reference by these gentlemen to the "Comintern" with a reference to the <u>fact</u> that we <u>have</u> diplomatic relations with France, Germany, Britain, and Japan, and tell them about the vexation Soviet people feel when they see that the Germans, British, French, and Japanese have long since grasped the difference between the Comintern and the Soviet government, while the Americans have not yet matured to the point of grasping it.

I don't think we should send our people to the USA yet to take "soundings."

3) Regarding the clamor over oil, you handled it pretty well. Be sure to add to the new oil sources in the East that were named in *Pravda* another source—Yakutia. I am sending you the relevant report by the CC's Organizational Department on oil in Yakutia. I think Starovatov's point is <u>not without</u> grounds. Besides the clamor over oil, it seems to me that the oil in <u>Yakutia</u> (and there <u>is</u> oil there) is a real boon for us, a valuable find. Give this matter <u>serious</u> attention.[4]

4) I did not like the letters from Chubar and Petrovsky. The former works up some "self-criticism"—<u>in order to get new millions of poods of grain from Moscow</u>, while the latter plays the hypocrite who has sacrificed himself to the "directive by the CC of the VKP"—<u>in order to obtain a reduction in the plan for grain procurements</u>. Neither one is acceptable. Chubar is mistaken if he thinks that self-criticism is needed not in order to mobilize forces and resources in the Ukraine but to get "assistance" from outside. In my opinion, the Ukraine has been given more than it should get. There is no reason to give it more grain—and there is nowhere to take it from. The worst aspect of this situation is Kosior's silence. What is the explanation for this silence. Does he know about the letters from Chubar and Petrovsky?[5]

5) I <u>don't</u> think the sowing summaries for individual peasants should be amended. <u>It will be better that way.</u> If you and Molotov insist on amendments, they can be made as a last resort, but not by 10–15 percent, rather by a maximum of <u>5–8 percent</u>.[6]

Regards. Stalin.

1. In 1930–32 the Central Control Commission (CCC) conducted an investigation in connection with a collective statement that had come in from a group of Communists who were working in Mukden. In November 1932 Znamensky returned to Moscow. In early 1933 the CCC delivered a severe reprimand to Znamensky, forbidding him from working abroad. See also document 32.

2. See note 6 to document 27. On 10 June 1932 the Politburo approved the suggestions on Lancaster that Stalin had made in a special telegram. The Politburo assigned Mezhlauk, Kalmanovich, and Piatakov to receive Lancaster when he returned to Moscow and to negotiate with him on the basis of Stalin's instructions (RGASPI, f. 17, op. 162, d. 12, l. 183). See document 32.

3. The reference is to a visit to the USSR by Colonel Frederick Pope, the president of the Nitrogen Engineering Corporation of New York, which had technical-assistance agreements with the Soviet chemical industry. On 28 June 1932 the Politburo authorized Mezhlauk to hold a lunch for Pope, with the participation of Osinsky, Piatakov, Radek, and an official from the Anglo-American desk of the PC of Foreign Affairs, and then to arrange for Krestinsky to receive him. The Politburo authorized giving Pope the response "that we are ready to receive an official or semiofficial representative of America in exchange for our equivalent representative in America" (ibid., d. 13, l. 3). See also document 32.

William Bullitt was President Wilson's unofficial representative in Soviet Russia in 1919, and an old friend of Franklin D. Roosevelt. He was appointed first U.S. ambassador in the USSR at the end of 1933. At first enthusiastic about Soviet developments, he later became extremely hostile to the Stalin regime.

4. On 12 June 1932 *Pravda* published an article headed "Sterlitamak, a New World-Class Oil Region. Earmark the bulk of the oil products from Baku, Grozny, and Maikop for export." This reported the discovery of a new "highly abundant oil source" in Bashkiria, which provided the opportunity to allocate for export the reserves of the southern regions (Azerbaijan, Northern Caucasus) situated close to ports. In the days following, reports on the development of the new deposits were published almost every day. Five days after Stalin's letter, on 20 June, *Pravda* ran an editorial in which it reported the new deposits, including those in Yakutia. On 21 June *Pravda* carried an extensive article headed "Oil in Yakutia." See also document 32.

5. On 16 June 1932 the Politburo considered Chubar's statement and adopted a decision to allocate to the Ukraine 2,000 tons of oats for food needs from the unused seed loan, 100,000 poods (1,638 tons) of corn for food needs from what had been allocated for sowing in the Odessa Region but had not been used for the purpose, 70,000 poods (1,147 tons) of grain for the food needs of beet-growing state farms and 230,000 poods (3,767 tons) of grain for the food needs of collective farms in the beet-growing districts of the Ukraine (RGASPI, f. 17, op. 162, d. 12, ll. 180–181). On the following day, 17 June, Kaganovich wrote in a cipher to Stalin "we entirely agree with your characterization of Chubar's and Petrovsky's letters" (ibid., f. 558, op. 11, d. 740, ll. 64–68). On the same day the Politburo of the CC of the Ukrainian Communist Party adopted a decision: "To send Comrades Kaganovich and Molotov at the CC of the VKP(b) the following telegram: 'On the instructions of the CC of the VKP(b), Chubar petitioned for the allocation to the Ukraine of food assistance for districts that are in grave condition. We urgently request another 600,000 poods (9,828 tons) [of grain] in addition to the 220,000 poods which has already been allocated for the cultivation of sugar-beet and for food assistance." On 21 June a telegram signed by Stalin and Molotov was sent to the CC of the Ukrainian Communist Party and the republican government, stressing the necessity of fulfilling "at any cost" the plan for grain deliveries covering July to September. On 23 June, in response to Kosior's telegram requesting assistance, the Politburo adopted a resolution: "To remain within the limits set by CC decisions already adopted and to bar any additional grain deliveries to the Ukraine" (*Golod 1932–1933 rokiv na Ukraini* [Kiev, 1990], 183, 186–87, 190). See also documents 32, 33.

6. On 21 June 1932 *Pravda* published a PC of Agriculture report on the progress of spring sowing as of 15 June 1932. It noted that individual peasants had fulfilled 74.2 percent of their plan, while collective farms had fulfilled 93.2 percent of theirs. See also document 32.

· 35 ·

Stalin to Kaganovich and Molotov (for members of the Politburo)
18 June

F. 81, op. 3, d. 99, ll. 65–68.

_____

For Kaganovich
To Kaganovich and Molotov (for members of the Politburo)
  I urge you to take note of the following.

As you recall, in connection [with] the resolutions of the CC and Sovnarkom on a reduction in the plan for grain procurements[1] the regions sent a request to the CC for permission to give villages the revised plan for grain procurements. We refused the regions, telling them that the plan reduction must be used for the time being only to stimulate sowing operations. It is now clear to everybody that we were right in making the functionaries concentrate on sowing operations.

But we were right about more than that point. We were also right in not allowing the provinces to mechanically allocate the grain-procurement plan among the districts and villages (collective farms) based on the equalizing "principle" and thereby undermine both the grain-procurement work and the economic situation of the collective farms. The principal error of our grain-procurement work last year, especially in the Ukraine and the Urals, was that the grain-procurement plan was allocated among districts and collective farms and was carried out not in an organized manner but spontaneously, based on the equalizing "principle," it was carried out mechanically, without taking account of the situation in each individual district, without taking account of the situation on each individual collective farm. This mechanical equalizing approach to the matter has resulted in glaring absurdities, so that a number of fertile districts in the Ukraine, despite a fairly good harvest, have found themselves in a state of impoverishment and famine, while the regional party committee in the Urals has deprived itself of the capacity to use the districts with good crops in the region to assist districts with bad harvests. Moreover, a number of first secretaries (in the Ukraine, the Urals, and part of Nizhny Novgorod Region) became preoccupied with the giants of industry and failed to devote a proper amount of attention to agriculture, forgetting that our industry cannot advance without a systematic growth in agriculture. This, incidentally, showed how out of touch with the countryside the secretaries are. The results of these errors are now having an effect on the sowing situation, especially in the Ukraine, and several tens of thousands of Ukrainian collective farmers are still traveling around the entire European part of the USSR and are demoralizing our collective farms with their complaints and whining.

What must be done to avoid repeating last year's errors?

The districts and collective farms must get a revised plan, but revised with reference to the distinctive features of each district and each collective farm rather than in a mechanical and equalizing manner. Since the present condition of our organizations does not allow for absolutely precise record of these features, we should add an extra 4–5 percent to the plan in order to cover inevitable errors in the records and fulfill the plan itself at any cost.

I propose that:

1) A conference be convened no later than 26–27 June, to be attended by secretaries and executive-committee chairmen (or Sovnarkom chairmen) of the Ukraine, the Northern Caucasus, the Central Black-Earth Region, the Lower Volga, the Middle Volga, Nizhny Novgorod, Moscow, Tataria, Bashkiria, the Urals, Kazakhstan, Western Siberia, the Western Region, and Belorussia on questions of the organization of grain procurements and the unconditional fulfillment of the grain-procurement plan.

2) The errors made last year in our grain-procurement performance be criticized at the conference and ways be outlined for organizing grain procurements so that the districts and collective farms are given plans revised with reference to the situation in each district and on each collective farm.

3) Responsibility for the condition of agriculture (in a region or republic) and for successes and shortcomings in grain procurements this year be entrusted personally to the first secretaries of the Northern Caucasus, the Ukraine, the Central Black-Earth Region, the Lower Volga, the Central Volga, the Moscow Region, the Western Region, Belorussia, Tataria, Bashkiria, the Nizhny Novgorod Region, the Urals, Kazakhstan, Western Siberia, Eastern Siberia, and the Far Eastern Region, which should in no way, of course, exempt the corresponding chairmen of executive committees and of Sovnarkoms from responsibility.

4) The relevant decisions of the CC be sent to the bureaus of regional party committees and Central Committees of national republics.[2]

I. Stalin. 18 June 1932.

1. The reference is to the 6 May 1932 resolution of Sovnarkom and the CC "On the Plan for Grain Procurements from the 1932 Harvest and the Development of Collective-Farm Trade in Grain," which approved a reduced procurements plan as compared with the plan for the previous year.

2. On 21 June 1932 the Politburo adopted a decision to convene on 28 June 1932 a conference of secretaries and chairmen of the executive committees of the Ukraine, the Northern Caucasus, the Central Black-Earth Region, the Lower and Middle Volga, Nizhny Novgorod, Moscow, Tataria, Bashkiria, the Urals, Kazakhstan, Western Siberia, the Western Region, and Belorussia on the organization of grain procurements and the fulfillment of the established plan for grain procurements (RGASPI, f. 17, op. 3, d. 889, l. 16). On 28 June the Politburo decided not to have a general report delivered at the conference, but instead to assign Molotov to open the conference by outlining its tasks and reading Stalin's letter. Molotov

was to stress that Stalin's proposals had been adopted by the Politburo and must form the basis of the decision on grain procurements. There was also to be a discussion at the conference of the harvest campaign and the distribution of the harvest. (Ibid., d. 890, l. 8.) See also documents 37, 38, 40.

The Russian term *natsionalnye TsK* refers to the Central Committees of autonomous republics, established on the basis of a national (ethnic) minority living in the territory.

· 36 ·

Stalin to Kaganovich, Postyshev and Ordzhonikidze
20 June

F. 81, op. 3, d. 99, ll. 69–70.

To Kaganovich, Postyshev, Ordzhonikidze

Well, dear friends, there is more squabbling. I am referring to Beria and Orakhelashvili and am enclosing two letters from Orakhelashvili: one addressed to me, the other to Ordzhonikidze.[1]

My opinion: as clumsy as Beria's "actions" have been, the one who is wrong in this matter is Orakhelashvili. Orakhelashvili's request should be denied. If Orakhelashvili disagrees with the decision by the Georgian CC, he can appeal to the Transcaucasian Regional Committee, and ultimately to the CC of the VKP. But he has no reason to quit. I am afraid that Orakhelashvili's chief concern is his vanity ("his" people were wiped out) rather than the interests of the cause and positive work.[2] Everyone says positive work is proceeding well in Georgia, and the peasants have gotten into a good mood. And that is what is most important in the work.

Regards. I. Stalin.

20 June 1932

1. The letters are missing.
2. See also note 11 to document 37 and note 3 to document 58.

· 37 ·

Kaganovich to Stalin
23 June

F. 558, op. 11, d. 740, ll. 76–81.

23 June [1932]
Greetings Comrade Stalin!

1) Today we adopted a decision at the Politburo meeting to convene a CC plenum at the end of September. We put on the agenda the three issues that you referred to in the telegram. These are indeed the most important

issues right now. We will take up the issue of grain procurements in a businesslike, concrete manner on the 28th of this month at the conference of party secretaries and soviet chair[men] of regions and republics. We are preparing the draft resolution right now. I think we will have to put a brief introductory section in the resolution with an assessment of the results of the sowing along the lines of the second point of your telegram. This is especially important because as well as the outright lackeys of capitalism we have elements which are more or less rightwing deviationist and more or less Trotskyite elements, marsh frogs who croak over the slightest difficulties, who are ready to rush to extremes, who forget and fail to take account of the actual immense achievements that this spring sowing has brought us. At the same time we will have to include in the draft resolution sharp criticism of shortcomings in the work of local organizations along the lines of your letter, emphasizing the Ukraine, the Urals, etc. Then there will be a number of practical clauses that guarantee successful completion of the grain procurements, without excesses. When the draft resolution is ready, we will send it to you, but please, if you already have additional instructions now, send them by wire so that we can have a more productive conference on the 28th.[1]

2) We did not adopt the resolution on the harvest campaign today, we deferred it until the conference. I am sending you the draft resolution, the discussion at the Politburo meeting focused on the question of issuing advance payments in grain to collective farmers, first of all, whether they should be based on the number of family members or on the number of labor-days, evidently the latter is more proper, second, how much should be issued and when, part of it will have to be issued in the beginning, especially in the Ukraine, where there is a danger of theft, but this portion should be small, 60 percent is too much. We will discuss all these questions at the conference with people from the regions.[2] It would be good to get *Vashu dumku, iak kazhut na Ukraine.*[3]

3) Yesterday S. Kosior came in to talk about the report on tanks. Although he admits that they were out of touch with the districts, he doesn't seem to be aware of the full seriousness of their mistakes in leadership. I warned him that we will have to hold them up as an "example" of how not to do your job. He is proposing the immediate creation of two more regions: the Donets Basin and Chernigov. As regards the first, this is proper, after all, the CC has been proposing this from the very beginning, but it is doubtful whether the second should be created now, whether we should reorganize on the eve of grain procurements, since they are requesting an answer from the CC of the VKP(b), please do let us know your opinion on this issue.[4]

4) The PC of Foreign Trade included in the export-import plan for the third qu[arter] the export of 60 million poods [983,000 tons] of grain and

in addition the delivery to ports of another 50 m[illion] poods [819,000 tons] as security for sale in October. It proposes that the annual plan for exports from the '32 harvest be increased to 4 m[illion] tons. We have not yet resolved this question. Of course it is imperative to export [the grain] without fail immediately, and we should reject the attitudes that have taken shape on the basis of some difficulties in the last couple of months, to the effect that we shouldn't export, but the question is how much to export in the third qu[arter]. I think the PC of Foreign Trade's figure will have to be cut back a little. Please let us know your opinion.[5]

5) We have not yet adopted a resolution on the sale by enterprises of goods produced in excess of the approved plans. The draft submitted by Liubimov is pretty weak. We will still have to do some work on the issue, I am sending it to you.[6]

6) We deferred the proposal to convert the Red Putilov plant to produce Buicks. The problem is that Yakovlev is arguing that the situation with regard to engines for combines is bad, both this year and next, so we have set up a commission, and in the meantime, I hope to get your opinion on this issue, I know that you have spoken in favor of this, but not for this year I think.[7]

7) We discussed fighter planes, tanks, Kurchevsky and cannons at the last meeting of the Com[mission] of Defense. We had an argument, especially over tanks and Kurchevsky. We should expect a turnaround in July.

8) Regarding oil we are sending Rabinovich and Riabovol abroad to resume negotiations on the basis of the latest guidelines. I am sending you the memorandum from Riabovol-Rabinovich and Veitser.[8]

9) Litvinov is not reporting anything. Today there is a message that he made a statement welcoming Hoover's message.[9] We will have to query him about what he is doing there and <u>why he did not send an inquiry before his statement,</u> as soon as he finds himself among ministers and prime ministers, he loses his balance and forgets that we don't have a bourgeois parliamentary system but a Bolshevik leadership.

10) Troianovsky is acting stupidly. Even though he was forbidden he is negotiating with Fujiwara for the Japanese to buy out the CER and for the Japanese to renounce Japanese fishing rights and so forth, we are thinking of sending him a sharply worded telegram telling him to stop these talks.[10]

11) A new squabble is indeed flaring up in Transcaucasia. You are definitely right that reason is on Beria's side, especially in practical matters, while Orakhelashvili reflects the whining, unbusinesslike circles of the party activists. But the affair did not end just with a letter from Orakhelashvili himself, Maria Orakhelashvili arrived here and submitted an official request to the Central Control Commission that it review the question of the reprimand issued to her. Yaroslavsky passed along the request to me. I think the CCC should consider her request under the usual proce-

dure, without blowing up this affair or encouraging a further factional struggle against the Georg[ian] CC.[11]

Well I will end here. Regards. Yours, L. Kaganovich.

P.S. M. Gorky requested that the CC permit Babel to travel abroad for a short time. Even though I already sent the message that we have doubts about the expediency of this, people are calling me up for him every day. Evidently Gorky is fairly intense about this. Since I know that you treat him with particular sensitivity in such cases, I am reporting this to you and I am asking you what to do.[12] L. Kaganovich.

1. On 22 June Stalin in a cipher to Kaganovich proposed that the plenum should meet either at the beginning of August, or at the end of September. If it met at the beginning of August, it should discuss only grain procurements and trade questions. Alternatively it might be postponed to the end of September because grain procurements had already been discussed at the conference of party secretaries at the end of June. In that case, it should discuss trade, consumer goods and the iron and steel industry. (RGASPI, f. 558, op. 11, d. 77, ll. 83–85.) These were the items actually discussed at the plenum, which met from 28 September to 2 October. See note 2 to document 35 and note 3 to document 38.

2. See note 2 to document 35.

3. "Your opinion, as they say in the Ukraine" (Ukrainian)

4. See note 2 to document 41.

5. See note 3 to document 41.

6. The issue of the right of enterprises who have overfulfilled the production plan to sell their output in the market (aside from centralized distribution) was repeatedly considered at Politburo meetings between June and August 1932. On 8 June the Politburo instructed Ordzhonikidze, Liubimov, and Mikoian to submit a single draft resolution (ibid., f. 17, op. 3, d. 887, l. 7). On 9 June Kaganovich wrote in a letter to Stalin about the proposal, asking him "how far can we go here." Kaganovich commented that "of course we must not unleash our enterprises, but it seems to me that if the incentive permitting part of the output to be placed on the market is added to the pressure from the CC for sending goods to the market, we will more easily and rapidly increase the quantity of goods on the market. This is particularly the case with the artisan industry." (Ibid., f. 558, op. 11, d. 740, ll. 30–36.) Stalin does not seem to have replied to this. On 10 July the Politburo instructed the same commission to examine the draft submitted by Liubimov and submit a coordinated proposal to the Politburo (ibid., f. 17, op. 3, d. 891, l. 4). On 23 July the draft resolution submitted by the commission was turned over for additional elaboration to the commission chaired by Liubimov (ibid., d. 893, l. 4). On 8 August the Politburo instructed a commission chaired by Postyshev to draw up a draft resolution, directing it "to determine the industries that should be granted the right to sell their output produced above the plan" (ibid., d. 895, l. 3). On 16 October 1932, when Stalin was back in Moscow, the Politburo resolved to take the question off the agenda (ibid., d. 903, l. 15).

7. See note 2 to document 39.

8. The memorandum is missing. See note 3 to document 29.

9. On 22 June 1932, proposals by US President Hoover for arms reductions were announced at a meeting of the General Commission of the Conference on Arms Reduction and Limitation. The Soviet delegation came out in support of Hoover's plan. (DVP, vol. XV, pp. 776, 777.) See document 40.

10. See note 12 to document 45.

11. See document 36. On 21 June the manager of the organizational and instructional department of the CC, Meerzon, sent CC secretaries Stalin, Kaganovich, and Postyshev a mem-

orandum "On Instances of Factionalism in the Transcaucasian Party Organization." It said that on 10 June 1932 the Bureau of the CC of the Communist Party of Georgia had discussed the issue of factional activity by Maria Orakhelashvili and others, "who by spreading false rumors attempted to turn the CC of Georgia against the Transcaucasian Regional Committee and to discredit certain leaders of the CC and the Tiflis Committee (Comrade Beria in particular)." Maria Orakhelashvili received a reprimand and was dismissed from her position. On 23 June 1932 Yaroslavsky sent Orakhelashvili's request to Kaganovich (RGASPI, f. 17, op. 120, d. 82, ll. 88, 117). See also document 58.

    12. See document 41.

· 38 ·

Stalin to Kaganovich
[after 21 June]

F. 81, op. 3, d. 100, ll. 126–128.

Greetings, Comrade <u>Kaganovich</u>!

    1) With regard to Germany and the general strike I agree with you.[1]

    2) We should insist on the <u>second</u> version of the proposal for Lancaster ($100 million, a 10-year term, 3 percent (<u>and not 5 percent</u>) additional interest, 15 to 20 percent of the $100 million to be used to cover orders). This plan is advantageous to us. It is also advantageous to Lancaster, since it gives him 40 million <u>rubles'</u> worth of orders, as opposed to 5 million to 7 million rubles under the first plan, and it increases his total claims to 60 million <u>rubles</u> (as opposed to 40 million <u>rubles</u> under the first plan). As a last resort we can agree to an increase in orders to 25 percent of the total credit, while not retreating under any circumstances from the other terms of the second plan. I think Lancaster will be forced to agree to this plan, since the main issue for Lancaster (and his bank) is to attract large orders for the factories that are being shut down in America, to revive industry and rescue factories from collapse.[2]

    3) Please don't be concerned about my health. Send me more inquiries—I will be happy to answer them.

    4) Are you calling the conference of secretaries on the organization of grain procurements? If the conference takes place, the plenum can safely be postponed, since the principal issue of the plenum—grain procurements—will have already been settled.[3]

    Regards. I. Stalin.

    P.S. It seems to me that the PC of Heavy Industry was given too much money for the third quarter. They should have been given less. They are drowning in money.[4] I. St.

---

    1. Stalin is alluding to a call by the Communist Party of Germany for social-democratic workers and all members of trade unions to stage "mass proletarian demonstrations and a

mass political strike." On 17 June Kaganovich wrote to Stalin that "we have all formed the impression that the comrades from ECCI [the Executive Committee of the Communist International] are too hasty [. . .] especially with regard to the general strike" (RGASPI, f. 81, op. 3, d. 120, ll. 43–44).

    2. See note 2 to document 45.

    3. See note 2 to document 35 and note 1 to document 37.

    4. See note 1 to document 39.

· 39 ·

Stalin to Kaganovich, Molotov and Ordzhonikidze
24 June

F. 81, op. 3, d. 99, ll. 71–76.

24 June 1932

To Kaganovich, Molotov, Ordzhonikidze:

    1) You gave too much money to the PC of Heavy Industry for capital construction in the third quarter, and by doing so you have jeopardized the whole situation and risked corrupting the functionaries at the PC of Heavy Industry. Why did you overturn your own decision to remain within the limits of the second-quarter totals?[1] How can you possibly not understand that by overfeeding the PC of Heavy Industry with capital investments and thereby creating <u>a cult of new construction</u>, you are killing not only the cult but even <u>the simple, elementary desire</u> of economic functionaries <u>to make rational use</u> of enterprises that are already <u>operational</u>? Take the Stalingrad and Kharkov tractor plants, the Moscow and Gorky auto plants. People built them and completed them with great enthusiasm. And that, of course, is very good. But when the time came to start up these plants and make rational use of them, people lost their enthusiasm, preferred to run for cover—and clearly let down the country in the most unacceptable manner. Why do such things happen in our country? Because we have a cult of <u>new</u> construction (which is very good), but no cult of <u>rational utilization of operational</u> plants (which is very bad and extremely dangerous). And by overfeeding the PC of Heavy Industry with capital investments, you are reinforcing this abnormal and dangerous situation in industry—not to mention that in doing this you are creating the threat of new food difficulties . . .

    2) I strongly oppose giving the Putilov plant 2,900,000 rubles in <u>foreign currency</u> to convert the tractor-assembly unit to an automobile-assembly unit.[2] As it is, we have a lot of debts abroad, and we must learn sometime to economize on foreign currency. If we cannot provide domestically produced machine tools for this project right now, let's <u>wait</u> a year, until we are able to provide these machine tools—what is our rush? Never mind

the fact that we don't know whether we will have enough steel for 20,000 Buicks. We don't have enough steel for the tractor and auto plants—what guarantee do we have that we will have enough of it a year from now for both operational plants and for a Putilov auto plant? There were no guarantees in this regard in Comrade Ordzhonikidze's note.

3) The Politburo adopted a decision that the PC of Heavy Industry should submit a plan of specific measures to establish a well-supplied metallurgical facility for the Moscow and Gorky auto plants and the Cheliabinsk tractor plant. Where are these measures and when will they be submitted? Well, that is all for now.

Regards to all of you! I. Stalin.

24 June 1932

1. On 7 June 1932 the Politburo adopted a decision on the national economic plan covering July to September 1932. Gosplan was given a directive: "when finalizing the national economic plan for the third quarter on the question of capital investment, remain within the limits of the second quarter (6.8 billion rubles)" (RGASPI, f. 17, op. 3, d. 887, l. 9). But on 17 June the Politburo revised this resolution, setting the volume of capital investment at 7.050 billion rubles (ibid., d. 889, l. 13). See documents 28, 38, 40, and 42 and note 1 to document 49.

2. On 23 June 1932 the Politburo considered the question of converting the tractor section of the Red Putilov plant to the production of Buick-type passenger cars. The Politburo passed the issue to an ad hoc commission chaired by Ordzhonikidze for further study (ibid., l. 3). See also document 37.

· 40 ·

Kaganovich to Stalin
26 June

F. 558, op. 11, d. 740, ll. 84–86.

---

26 June [1932]

Greetings Comrade Stalin!

1) I received your last two letters[1] and followed all your instructions: I passed along the message about Germany to the Comintern people, we gave the appropr[iate] instructions to Mezhlauk on the new conference with Lancaster that is to take place in a few days, we have already decided about the plenum, and we will heed your viewpoint on the Red Putilov plant; now on the question of appropriations for capital construction for the PC of Heavy Industry the three of us tried to compose a telegram to you together, but it didn't work out, and we decided that each of us would write something. We reduced appropriations for the PC of Heavy Industry for the third qu[arter] by 84 million [rubles] as compared with the second qu[arter], whereas Gosplan proposed a reduction of 234 million for the

PC of Heavy Industry. The volume of capital investment, 7.05 billion, set by the Politburo for the third quarter, however, exceeds the second quarter by 156 million rubles, which went mainly to the PC of Transport.

A question comes up: did you take account of the fact that we cut the PC of Heavy Industry by 84 million, or did you think that we gave it more, the way I interpreted it was that you assumed that we made a cut, but considering that they ended up with 83 percent of the annual plan, you found it possible to propose a reduction. What should we do next? The question came up because we raised the question of practical conclusions from your letter. So we await a new additional resolution of the issue from you.[2]

2) We sent you several telegrams on international issues today, but there is one more international issue I would like to ask you about. Shouldn't we give additional instructions to Litvinov in Geneva, particularly about Hoover's declaration. We are not proposing anything specific here, but our people seem to have become a little timid right now.[3]

3) I am sending you Bogdanov's letter on America, his conclusions are narrow, but the facts he reports are very interesting and confirm your analysis: that America's inclination to recognize us has developed in earnest—and [your analysis] of the importance of Lancaster's visit.[4]

4) I am sending you a short memorandum received from Balitsky.[5] Although the memorandum does not make a serious impression, America may be acting in different directions just to stir up a war.

5) I am sending you the material received from Comrade Voroshilov on accidents in the air force. Accidents have indeed increased, especially outrageous are the TB-1 crash and the destruction of two large airplanes.[6] But my personal opinion is that this draft resolution does not go deep enough into the causes. We need to carefully study the shortcomings in the system of training, administration and conduct of flying personnel, in both command and the rank and file, and indicate appropriate measures. But this draft, on the one hand, provides only general instructions, and on the other, is merely punitive in nature, and besides, should all the reprimands come from the CC. The issue will be on the agenda on the 1st. Please let us have your comments for the Politburo either in a letter or by wire.[7]

6) We printed the article in *Pravda,* they had to redo it several times and this version could have been done better, but we decided not to hold it up anymore.

7) We will open the conference on grain procurements on the 28th at 6 o'clock. We plan to conduct it in a businesslike manner. A large number of people's commissariat staffers are already putting in for participation in the conference. We don't think we will allow them, but will restrict participation as much as possible, otherwise the conference will be turned into a parliament. We think it will be better to work out the resolution during the conference with the participation of people from the regions.[8]

8) Radek keeps asking for the materials from the PC of Foreign Affairs (surveys, ciphers from plenipotentiaries and so forth) so he can have a chance to orient himself. What do you think?[9] It seems to me that we could do this through the secret department of the CC, except for top secret material. Well I will end here.

Regards. Yours, L. Kaganovich.

1. See documents 38, 39.

2. See note 1 to document 39, and document 42.

3. See note 9 to document 37.

4. The letter is missing.

5. The memorandum is missing.

6. The heavy bomber TB-1 had a crew of seven; mass production began in 1929.

7. See note 2 to document 42.

8. See note 2 to document 35.

9. On 1 April 1932, on Stalin's proposal, a Politburo decision was adopted to establish under the CC an Information Bureau on International Affairs headed by Radek (RGASPI, f. 17, op. 3, d. 878, l. 5). Its functions included the verification and reporting of information on international affairs, and the collection of such information from the foreign press, literature, and other foreign sources, etc. (ibid., op. 162, d. 12, l. 143).

· 41 ·

Stalin to Kaganovich and Molotov
[26 June]

F. 81, op. 3, d. 99, ll. 81–87.

To Kaganovich, Molotov:

Comrade Sheboldaev raises a very timely question in his memorandum. He is right in saying that the role of consumer cooperatives both in the procurement of agricultural produce and in the sale of goods from urban industries, especially in the countryside, should be expanded (the "intermediary" role of cooperatives). He may also be right in saying that cooperatives should be relieved of their state-procurement functions and that they should concentrate on local, "decentralized" procurements. The only thing is that the question must be studied as to whether the state procurement organizations can handle procurements without the cooperatives. Sheboldaev is definitely right in saying that consumer cooperatives should be relieved of excessive taxes, "confiscations," and other such collections.

But Sheboldaev, in my view, is wrong on the matter of procurement prices (in the countryside) and sales prices (in the cities). I am afraid that if the cooperatives are allowed to procure produce in the countryside at free prices, our procurements will be undermined at their root. Sometime we may have to raise prices on state procurements. But this year there is no reason even to think about it. We could declare state procurements with their low prices to be a <u>state tax</u>, a <u>state obligation</u>. But we cannot do that without repealing direct taxes on the countryside. Besides, <u>we cannot</u> carry out this procedure <u>this year anyway</u>, even if a study of the question shows that it is the proper procedure. <u>In any case one thing is clear, and that is that we cannot relieve the cooperatives of all controls and regulation by the state with respect to prices.</u> Obviously, the cooperatives will have to carry out their own procurements at <u>state</u> prices, and only after <u>state</u> procurements are completed (15 January 1933) can the cooperatives be permitted to procure and buy at prices about 5 percent <u>above state prices</u>.

Comrade Sheboldaev is also wrong on the matter of <u>sales</u> prices in the cities. I do not object to sales of urban goods in the countryside by the co-operatives at average commercial or even at commercial prices. But I do oppose increases in <u>sales</u> prices in the cities by the cooperatives to obtain "normal" profits. I oppose this because this would signify a price increase on bread and other agricultural produce. We need <u>Bolshevik</u> cooperatives, as an <u>intermediary</u> organization between the city and countryside, and co-operatives with <u>large profits</u>.

Clearly Comrade Sheboldaev must not be scolded under any circumstances for several excesses in his memorandum. On the contrary, he should be praised for raising a very essential question in an open and timely manner—especially since a large portion of the <u>practical proposals</u> in his memorandum are quite correct.[1]

Well, that is all for now. Regards. I. Stalin.

P.S. I just received your letter of 23 June 1932.

Here are my answers.

1) We can limit ourselves to establishing one more region [*okrug*]— Donbass in the Ukraine.[2]

2) In grain exports I suggest a <u>substantial</u> reduction in Rozengolts's plan (for the third quarter).[3]

3) In my view, Babel is not worth spending foreign currency on a trip by him abroad.[4] I. St.

---

1. Sheboldaev's memorandum, with Stalin's comments in the margins, has survived in the original copy of the Politburo minutes in view of the fact that the Politburo considered this memorandum on 10 July 1932 and assigned the commission on consumer goods to draw up a draft resolution (RGASPI, f. 17, op. 163, d. 948, ll. 4–20). See document 45.

2. On 29 June 1932 the Politburo authorized the establishment of a region (*oblast*) for the Donets Basin, comprising 36 districts (ibid., op. 3, d. 890, l. 10). See document 37. In his letter Stalin used the term *okrug* rather than *oblast*—the okrugs were territorial divisions larger than a district (*raion*) that existed until the administrative reform of 1930.

3. See document 37. On 10 July 1932 the Politburo decided to reduce the planned figure for grain exports in the third quarter and to set a final figure on 16 July (ibid., op. 162, d. 13, l. 11). At the 16 July session the Politburo set grain exports for the third quarter at 31.5 million poods (516,000 tons) (including legumes), 20 million poods (328,000 tons) for war-

ranted grain and 10 million poods (164,000 tons) of carryover stocks, for a total of 61.5 million poods (1,007,000 tons) (ibid., l. 30). On 20 October 1932 the Politburo adopted a decision to reduce exports from the 1932 harvest from 165 million to 150 million poods (2,703,000 to 2,457,000 tons; ibid., op. 162, d. 13, l. 133). Actual grain sent for export in the agricultural year 1932/33 amounted to 1,626,000 tons.

4. See document 37.

· 42 ·

Stalin to Kaganovich
29 June

F. 81, op. 3, d. 99, ll. 78–79.

Greetings, Comrade Kaganovich!

1) Since the decision on the third-quarter plan for the PC of Heavy Industry has already been adopted, it is not worth changing it now, lest we cause confusion among the economic managers and give them a pretext to speculate about a policy of cutting back construction.[1]

2) I have already sent you a cipher regarding Voroshilov's draft on the air force. In my view, we can confine ourselves for now to Voroshilov's draft, with the corrections I have set forth in my cipher.[2]

3) I have read the material on the negotiations with the Anglo-American oil representatives. The observations by Veitser and Ozyorsky are correct. If the negotiations resume, it would be a good idea to limit the term of the contract to five or six years.[3]

Regards. I. Stalin.

29 June 1932

1. See note 1 to document 39 and see document 40.

2. On 21 June 1932 Voroshilov reported in a letter to Stalin: "I am literally beside myself these days over the accidents in the Air Force. Not a day goes by without information coming in about accidents and even horrible disasters with casualties either in one [military] district or another. Suffice it to mention that from 5 June to 20 June alone 11 planes crashed [. . .] and 30(!!) people were killed. [. . .] There has been an increase in flying and technical personnel, and although the staffing is coming from our politically reliable people, they are extremely young, have little experience (which is natural), and most importantly, they are really undisciplined. Daredevil behavior, bravura displays of flying stunts [. . .] that do not encounter fierce resistance from the commanders; a low level of authority projected by the young commanders, poor work by the political bodies and party organizations—these are the principal sources of our miseries [. . .]. I have already asked the Politburo to hear my report and to help me whip the party organizations and political staff into shape. I am thinking of kicking out several 'distinguished,' but absolutely undisciplined air-force commanders who consciously and often violate all orders and statutes of the Workers' and Peasants' Red Army [WPRA]" (RGASPI, f. 74, op. 2, d. 37, ll. 49–50).

In response Stalin wrote Voroshilov on 24 June: "The most alarming thing is the accidents and the deaths of our pilots. The destruction of planes is not as terrible (to hell with them!)

as the death of live human beings, of pilots. Live human beings are the most valuable and important part of our entire cause, especially in the air force. Shouldn't we—besides everything else—establish a special position of <u>deputy</u> commander <u>for the air force</u> under the district commanders, assigning to these deputies <u>direct</u> responsibility for the condition of the air force in the district, which, of course, should not relieve the commander—<u>in the least!</u>—of responsibility for the air force in the district. I think we should" (ibid., d. 38, ll. 69,70).

On 28 June Voroshilov in a cipher to Stalin asked him whether the faults of industry should also be mentioned—"the quality, the lack of communication facilities on the aircraft, the lack of parachutes and braking wheels," etc. (ibid., f. 558, op. 11, d. 77, l. 121). On the following day Stalin replied that "the question of the quality of the aircraft must not be glossed over, it must be posed prominently" (ibid., l. 120).

On 3 July 1932 the Politburo approved the draft resolution of the CC and Sovnarkom, proposed by Voroshilov, "On the Pattern of Accidents in Air Force Units of the WPRA" (the final version was completed on 5 July). Among other measures, it formalized Stalin's proposal for the introduction of the position of deputy district commanders for the air force (*Otechestvennye arkhivy*, no. 6, 1995, 32–39). On 4 July a cipher from Kaganovich reported to Stalin that the Politburo had also adopted a special decision on the quality of aircraft production, asking the PC of Heavy Industry to present a plan for its "decisive improvement" to the Commission of Defense within twenty days (RGASPI, f. 558, op. 11, d. 78, l. 8). See documents 40, 45.

3. See note 3 to document 29.

· 43 ·

Stalin to Kaganovich
[before 2 July]

F. 81, op. 3, d. 100, l. 147.

Comrade Kaganovich!

We cannot afford to ignore the criminal violation of the CC directive on the unacceptability of subversive operations by the OGPU and the [military] Intelligence Bureau in Manchuria. The arrest of some Korean subversives and the involvement of our agencies in this affair creates (or could create) a new risk of provoking a conflict with Japan. Who needs this, other than the enemies of Soviet rule? Be sure to send an inquiry to the Far Eastern leaders, find out what is going on and punish the violators of the USSR's interests as an example. We cannot put up with this outrage any longer!

Have a chat with Molotov and take Draconian measures against the criminals at the OGPU and the Intelligence Bureau (it is quite possible that these gentlemen are agents of our enemies in our midst). Show them that there is still an authority in Moscow that knows how to punish criminals as an example.[1]

Regards. I. Stalin.

1. See note 13 to document 45.

· 44 ·

Stalin to Kaganovich and Molotov
2 [July]

F. 81, op. 3, d. 99, ll. 45–47.

To Kaganovich, Molotov.

1) Give <u>the most serious</u> attention to the Ukraine. Chubar's corruptness and opportunistic essence and Kosior's rotten diplomacy (with regard to the CC of the VKP) and criminally frivolous attitude toward his job will eventually ruin the Ukraine. These comrades are not up to the challenge of leading the Ukraine today. If you go to the Ukrainian conference (I insist on it), take every measure in order to improve the functionaries' mood, isolate the whining and depraved diplomats (no matter who they are!) and ensure genuinely Bolshevik decisions by the conference. I have formed the impression (probably even the conviction) that we will have to remove both of them from the Ukraine—Chubar and Kosior. Maybe I am mistaken. But you have an opportunity to check this situation at the conference.[1]

2) I am returning the draft of the CC's message of greeting for the jubilee birthday of Klara Zetkin. The tone of the draft is too rhapsodic and somewhat too falsely classical. I have moderated the tone somewhat with my corrections.[2]

Regards. I. Stalin.

2 June 1932[3]

1. See note 4 to document 45.
2. The greetings from the CC of the VKP(b) to Klara Zetkin for her 75th birthday were published in the newspapers on 5 July 1932.
3. Stalin's dating of the letter is incorrect. The letter was written in July 1932.

· 45 ·

Kaganovich to Stalin
2 [July]

F. 558, op. 11, d. 740, ll. 2–9.

2 June [1932][1]

Greetings Comrade Stalin.

1) We received your cipher about Lancaster, and I immediately passed it to Mezhlauk. By all indications, Lancaster has come to sound things out. He cannot come up with serious, decisive answers on his own, and this makes your proposal to stay with our plan all the more correct.[2] Should

we report something in the press, perhaps just a report that he is in our country, or is it not worth it. Please write your opinion.

2) We have sent you the draft resolution on the grain-procurement and harvest campaign. I think it conforms with your standpoint, and our speeches at the conference also fully adhere to your counsel that we direct the main thrust against the Ukrainian demobilizers.[3]

Tomorrow we have a session of Politburo members on the accidents in the air force and we will resolve the question of our trip to the Ukraine, although Comrade Molotov doubts that he must go, but you are absolutely right in saying that two people should go and the Politburo will adopt this. At their conference [in the Ukraine] they will discuss only one topic: agriculture. We will have to use specific examples to develop the question of the leadership's being out of touch with agriculture and the uneven distribution of grain procurements, due to a lack of familiarity with the districts, which has led to unhappy consequences.[4]

3) Regarding the accidents in the air force we have set up a commission to investigate the specific causes of the accidents, especially the accidents of the last two days. Yesterday a TB-3 crashed outside Moscow.[5] Today, it was two R-5s.[6] Tomorrow we will hold a closed session of Politburo members where we will discuss Voroshilov's proposal,[7] as well as the issue of the quality of output.

4) We heard Comrade Sheboldaev speak yesterday in the Politburo on consumer cooperatives. The Politburo members read your letter, but they did not have time to read Comrade Sheboldaev's memorandum, so the discussion had to be put off to the next session. Having read the memorandum myself, I feel that while he does raise an important and substantial issue, he is doing just that, raising but not solving it. His proposals seem simple, but they are extremely complicated. Since the very outset of collective farm trade, the members of our cooperatives have been raising the issue of both of procurements and of sales at market prices, and this actually resolves in advance the question of their development of decentralized procurements on a large scale. The parts of his memorandum that you consider positive are certainly correct and they should be adopted, as for prices, and this is the key point, here we can allow some deviation from general procurement prices only with regard to cafeterias that are under cooperative management. We can allow widespread procurement of dairy products and that only with small price increases in certain districts. When we draw up the draft, I will send it to you.[8]

5) The question of finances is closely related to this. Last month an unusually large amount of money was printed. There are many reasons for this: the budget deficit, sluggish sales of manufactured goods and so forth. I am sending you the note from Grinko and Mariasin,[9] the adoption of their proposal alone does not solve the problem, this requires taking a

look at the specific goods, which we will have to do, looking at the economic bodies that stray from the established guidelines, and so forth. One issue they raise is a thorny one—it concerns setting commercial prices for manufactured goods sold in the countryside. We will have to do this, but the question is whether we need to do it for all goods. We have not yet discussed the entire issue, please write down your views on this entire question.[10] At the next Politburo [session] on the 8th we will hear [a report on] the question of construction costs for economic people's commissariats.

6) With respect to consumer goods, we have had, after all, a significant improvement. For the third quarter we have planned 690 million rubles in goods for the countryside. The dispatching problem is getting better. Now the whole trouble lies with the regions and districts, because it will already be easier for us in the center to track down a shipment if it gets stuck somewhere. That is why we had to deliver some strong criticism to regional party committees at the conference on grain procurements for failing to devote enough attention to this problem. I pointed out that while here in the center you have dealt with this personally and have turned all of our minds to this matter, the secretaries in the regions are not even thinking yet of getting to work on this. I think there will be some turnaround, but to consolidate it we will have to summon and hear reports from the regions.

We have drawn up a resolution on the reorganization of industrial cooperatives in the direction of developing their initiative in increasing the quantity of manufactured goods. In view of the importance of this resolution, I am sending it to you so that you can review it before we adopt it.[11]

7) With regard to the foreign-currency plan for 1932–33, we are working hard on a regular schedule, we have not yet finished drawing up the export plan, because the fighting is naturally not only over imports but over exports as well. In particular, please let us know your opinion on the following issue: the plan for iron-ore exports for 1932 is 1.5 million tons and for 1933 we propose 750,000 tons, which will yield about 3 million in hard currency, and roughly the same applies to magnesite. It was stated at the commission session that you are in favor of exporting no ore and no magnesite. We deferred the matter, but personally I would think that half of the ore, i.e. 750,000 tons, could be exported, the revenue after all would be 3 million.

8) Troianovsky has sent a letter requesting that he be replaced there with somebody else, I am sending it to you.

He is holding specific talks about the CER [Chinese Eastern Railroad] —about the sales price and so forth, he should be given more specific instructions, otherwise he could unwittingly become confused there.[12]

9) A few days ago a purported representative of the Chinese People's Army appeared at our border post with a letter for Bliukher, seeking weapons and so forth. We gave instructions to send him back immediately and

not to allow any crossings in the future by such representatives, or by specially sent provocateurs, or by persons objectively playing a provocative role, it makes no difference.

10) In regard to the excerpted report about the Koreans that you sent us, I have cleared it up. Unfortunately, your conjecture proved to be true—it was the OGPU (remnants of the old one). In the event of an inquiry from Hirota (he has instructions), we have given instructions to Karakhan.[13]

11) The All-Union Conference of the Komsomol opened yesterday. Komsomol greetings that were indeed heartfelt were conveyed to you. Since I have to leave for the Ukraine, I doubt that I will be able to deliver a speech to them, but we will set a direction for their work.

12) A joint plenum of the Moscow Regional Committee and the secretaries of district committees opened here today. We are discussing consumer cooperatives, agriculture, and collective farms, and a report by the coal miners' cell, a textile factory and a railroad-car plant. The secretary of the miners' cell delivered a very fine report, it will have to be printed in *Pravda,* you will be able to read it.

13) Gorky keeps asking us to approve the editors of *The History of the Civil War,* I am sending you the list just in case, or we might wait until you return.

14) I am sending you a letter from Litvinov, it does not offer anything of note, but I am sending it just in case.[14]

Well, I will close here, as it is I have made this letter to you too long.

Regards. Yours, L. Kaganovich.

P.S. Your directives on the negotiations with the oilmen in your letter of the 29th—we are issuing the appropriate directives. Rabinovich has left here, but has not yet reported anything new.[15]

1. Kaganovich dated the letter incorrectly. The letter was written in July 1932.

2. See documents 27, 30, 32, and 38 and the introduction to this chapter. In June 1932 Soviet representatives were negotiating with Lancaster about the possibility of partially satisfying his bank's claims on the condition that a large loan would be granted. Under discussion were the size of the loan and the interest, as well as the portion of the loan that would be used to place orders in the United States. At a meeting on 27 June 1932, however, Lancaster rejected the proposal by the Soviet leadership and put forth his own plan for repayment of the loans to the bank. On 1 July Stalin sent Kaganovich and Molotov a telegram in which he rejected Lancaster's proposals. "We can agree to partially satisfy the claims of a private bank only on condition that we receive a large loan. This is our main precondition. Without this combination an agreement is out of the question. So we must stick firmly to the framework of our plan as proposed to Lancaster on 27 June," wrote Stalin. On 2 July this position of the Soviet leadership was conveyed to Lancaster, who again rejected it. In mid-July Lancaster departed from the USSR (APRF, f. 3, op. 66, d. 290, ll. 112–123).

3. See note 2 to document 35, document 44.

4. See document 44. On 3 July 1932 the Politburo adopted a decision to send Kaganovich and Molotov to the Ukrainian party conference (RGASPI, f. 17, op. 3, d. 891, l. 10). On 6 July Kaganovich and Molotov participated in a meeting of the Ukrainian Politburo.

They reported to Stalin by cipher on the same day that "all the members of the Politburo, including Skrypnik, spoke in favor of a reduction of the plan [. . .] We categorically refused." (ibid., f. 558, op. 11, d. 78, l. 6). The Ukrainian Politburo agreed "to deem correct the plan for grain procurements set by the CC of the VKP(b) for the peasant sector in the amount of 356 million poods [5,831,000 tons] and to adopt it for unconditional fulfillment." This resolution served as the point of departure for the proceedings of the III Conference of the Ukrainian Communist Party (6–9 July 1932), which considered Kosior's report. Molotov and Kaganovich spoke at the conference. The resolution of the conference also required unconditional fulfillment of the grain-procurement plans. (*Golod 1932–1933 rokiv na Ukraini,* 36–40, 194–97.)

5. The TB-3 heavy bomber, with a crew of 11, went into batch production in 1932.

6. The R-5 two-seater plane was used for land-based reconnaissance and as a light bomber.

7. See note 2 to document 42.

8. Cf, note 1 to document 41.

9. The memorandum is missing.

10. See note 3 to document 48.

11. See note 7 to document 48.

12. The question of the sale of the CER was discussed in Troianovsky's conversations with the Japanese industrialist Fujiwara in May 1932. On 28 June 1932 the Politburo sent Troianovsky the following telegram: "Tell Fujiwara in the form of your personal opinion that the negotiations with him have clarified a great deal and have laid out various possibilities for settling the CER issue, but that they must be made more effective and to this end they must be conducted by people who are vested with the proper authority [. . .] We call your attention to the fact that you continue to insist on your error concerning the possibility of compensating for the CER with fish, contrary to the instructions given you. We instruct you henceforth to desist from these discussions of compensation with fish" (RGASPI, f. 17, op. 162, d. 13, l. 10). On 3 July the Politburo instructed Kaganovich and Molotov to compose a telegram asking for Stalin's opinion (ibid., l. 13). On 5 July the following telegram was sent to Troianovsky: "We believe that until you receive Fujiwara's answer, which you expect on 6 July, it is inadvisable for you to make any new statements on the substance of your conversations. Upon receiving Fujiwara's answer we will adopt a decision on how to proceed next" (ibid., l. 14). See document 37.

13. See document 43. A message from the Japanese government, conveyed on 7 July 1932 by a counselor at the Japanese embassy in the USSR to the PC of Foreign Affairs, said that a Korean named Lee who had been arrested by Japanese authorities had given testimony that he along with three other Koreans were recruited by the Vladivostok GPU, supplied with explosives, and sent to Korea with the assignment of blowing up a number of bridges. On 10 July 1932, after hearing Karakhan's report "On the Koreans," the Politburo decided to turn over the issue for discussion by the Far Eastern Commission (ibid., l. 12). On 16 July the Politburo instructed a commission consisting of Molotov, Kaganovich, and Karakhan "to compose the text of a reply to the inquiry from the Japanese government about the Koreans and to coordinate it with Comrade Stalin" (ibid., l. 28). On the same day the Politburo, in a decision on "The Question of the Far Eastern Region," stated: "The attention of the OGPU is to be directed to the fact that the affair was very poorly organized; the people selected were not properly checked." The OGPU agent who was directly responsible for the affair received a reprimand and it was decided to recall him from Vladivostok. The OGPU was instructed to strengthen its military operational sector with personnel.(Ibid., l. 33.)

On 26 July 1932 Karakhan, on the instructions of the Soviet government, made a statement to Ota, the Japanese ambassador to the USSR. According to the statement, an investigation had shown that "the entire report by the Korean Lee from start to finish is a malicious and provocative fabrication[. . .]. The Soviet government hopes that the Japanese authorities will both deal with the author of the provocative statement in the proper fashion and will take all necessary and energetic measures to identify the inspirers and organizers of this provocative affair, which is undoubtedly aimed at aggravating relations between the USSR and Japan." (DVP, vol. XVI, p. 814.)

14. The letter is missing.

15. This is a reference to a cipher from Stalin stating: "if negotiations are renewed iit would be good to limit the period covered by the agreement to five—six years" (RGASPI, f. 81, op. 3, d. 99, ll. 78–79). See also documents 27 and 29.

· 46 ·

Stalin to Kaganovich and Molotov
[no later than 15 July]

F. 81, op. 3, d. 99, ll. 167–174.

Greetings, Comrade Kaganovich!
(Read this letter to <u>Molotov</u>)

1) <u>Voroshilov</u> came to see me.[1] We agreed on the following points (although the Politburo, of course, has the final word):

a) The 1933 <u>military budget</u> (covering <u>everything</u>, including <u>salary increases for Red Army soldiers and the commanders for 1933)</u> should be drawn up within a limit of 5 billion to 6 billion rubles, and only in case of extreme necessity can it be pushed to 6 (six) billion. Klim reminded me that I spoke about two months ago of possibly pushing the figure to 7 (seven) billion. But I deflected that point by saying that the situation is different now.[2]

b) <u>The plan for deploying the army</u> (in 1933) <u>in the event of war</u>, as presented by the General Staff, is inflated, outrageously inflated and very burdensome for the state. It must be reworked and <u>cut back</u> as much as possible.

c) <u>The size of the peacetime army</u> for 1932 (based on the General Staff's plan) is inflated (it goes as high as 1,100,000 soldiers). The Staff forgets that the <u>mechanization</u> of the army in every country leads to a <u>reduction</u> in its manpower. The Staff plan implies that the mechanization of our army should lead to an <u>increase</u> in its manpower. This is an absurdity, which demonstrates that our people are hopeless at reorganizing the army on the basis of mechanization. I realize that reorganization takes time, a certain transitional period is needed. But what needs to be done then is, first, determine the length of this transitional period, making it as short as possible. Second, <u>in addition</u> to a decision on manpower numbers, a decision must be adopted regarding <u>calendar time frames for reductions</u> in the size of the army as mechanization proceeds. Without such a parallel decision, it will be impossible to adopt the Staff's draft on manpower numbers for 1932.

d) <u>The resolutions on combat training</u> (for the Staff leadership, artillery, and navy) are <u>unspecific</u> and need to be reworked. The resolutions should be drawn up in such a way that their implementation by the Revolutionary Council can be verified <u>point by point</u>, point by <u>specific</u> point (<u>how many</u> proving grounds will be set up and <u>when</u>, etc.).

e) The issue of the Kremlin school should be resolved in the spirit of leaving the current procedure intact, i.e. the order of the Revolutionary Military Council should be canceled.[3]

2) The situation in the Ukraine is clearly not very good. The only person we could replace Kosior with is Kaganovich. I don't see any other candidates. Mikoian is not suitable: not only for the Ukraine, he is not even suitable for the PC for Supply (he is a bumbling and disorganized "agitator"). But Kaganovich cannot be sent to the Ukraine now (it is not expedient!): we would weaken the Secretariat of the CC. We will have to wait awhile. As for Chubar, we can leave him in place for now and watch how he works.

3) I am sending you an extremely offensive diatribe by the foreign correspondent Basseches against Soviet economic policy. Basseches is a correspondent for *Neue Freie Presse*. He once wrote a vile article about forced labor in the timber industry. We wanted to kick him out of the USSR, but because he repented, he was left in the USSR.[4] Later he wrote vile things about the policy of economic accountability. But we stupidly overlooked these vile things. Now he is outdoing himself with regard to loans and collective-farm trade. Yet we are keeping quiet like idiots, and are putting up with the slander from this pup of the capitalist shopkeepers. Bol-she-viks, ho-ho . . .

I propose:

a) dragging this capitalist scum through the mud in *Pravda* and *Izvestia;*

b) a short time after that, expelling him from the USSR.[5]

That's all. Regards. I. Stalin.

1. The Politburo authorized Voroshilov to make a trip to the Northern Caucasus Military District from 4 to 15 July 1932 (RGASPI, f. 17, op. 162, d. 13, l. 6).

2. The 1933 military budget that was ultimately approved amounted to 4.718 billion rubles (GARF, f. R-8418, op. 8, d. 137, ll. 11–12; R. W. Davies, *Crisis and Progress in the Soviet Economy* [London, 1996], 318).

3. On 16 June 1932 the Politburo assigned Voroshilov to submit a plan for reorganization of the Kremlin School (RGASPI, f. 17, op. 162, d. 12, l. 179). On 21 June Voroshilov reported to Stalin: "I once told you, and it seemed to me that you did not object to some reorganization of the school of the All-Russian Central Executive Committee [VTsIK]. I began to carry out this reorganization, i.e. 500 students had already been selected, and suddenly the Politburo began to have doubts about this measure, or rather, it simply found this reorganization to be wrong. I am being attacked especially fiercely by Kalinin. The reasons: an enhanced type of school where the students are not taken from the Red Army rank and file or the Komsomol membership but are already middle-level commanders, this kind of school does not fully meet the objective that has been set for the Kremlin School. [. . .] My arguments that this school [. . .] will now be stronger in every respect, that discipline in the

school will not be weaker but stronger, had no effect, and the matter has not been settled but has almost been predetermined, and that is to have the same school in the Kremlin as before" (ibid., f. 74, op. 2, d. 37, l. 51). On 26 June Stalin replied to Voroshilov: "It seems to me that in view of the persistent objections of Comrade Kalinin and others (I know that other members of the Politburo also object), we can give way, especially since it is not an important issue" (ibid., d. 38, l. 73). On 1 August the Politburo adopted a decision to leave the Kremlin School in the form it was in 1931 (RGASPI, f. 17, op. 3, d. 894, l. 1).

4. On 10 April 1931 the Politburo adopted a decision: "For the deliberately slanderous report abroad in *Neue Freie Presse* that convicted prisoners supposedly worked in timber procurements in the north and then were supposedly transferred from the north to other localities as a result of a campaign in the foreign press, a report that was designed to provide new 'material' for an anti-Soviet campaign, to expel the correspondent of *Neue Freie Presse* Basseches" (ibid., d. 820, l. 4).

5. Nicholas Basseches was expelled from the USSR in June 1937 (see Eugene Lyons, *Assignment in Utopia* [London, 1938], 336).

· 47 ·

Stalin to Kaganovich
17 July

F. 81, op. 3, d. 99, ll. 91–104.

Greetings, Comrade Kaganovich!

1) I read the note about Münzenberg and the Reichsbanners.[1] We should not get the Comintern involved in this situation. Local military agreements by the GCP [German Communist Party] should be allowed without getting the CC of the GCP involved officially in the situation. That is under the condition that the actual leadership of the organization is by the GCP. We must have nothing to do with Otto Bauer: no matter what kind of "Communist" he pretends to be, this character was and remains a social chauvinist. If he wants to corrupt the Second International, let him corrupt it to his heart's content by himself, with his own resources.

2) It would be a good idea to publish in *Pravda* the resolution of the Second International on the threat of war in the Far East. The resolution is not worth a damn (it opposes other imperialists while saying nothing about its own imperialists, it advocates "peace" but not the outright defense of the USSR, and so forth and so on), but it is targeted at the Japanese imperialists, and that is advantageous to us, i.e. the USSR, in every respect. We should rip the resolution to pieces (if it is published) as a social-reformist evasion of the issue, but since it makes a stride from preaching intervention (Kautsky's position!) to preaching favorable neutrality and psychological defense of the USSR, we must characterize it as the result of pressure from the masses of Social-Democratic workers on the Second International (the fear of losing the masses forced the Second International to alter its position somewhat).[2]

3) I read the resolution of the all-Union cotton conference. I disagree with the line of the PC of Agriculture regarding the expansion of crop areas, especially <u>sovkhoz</u> crop areas, for the second Five-Year Plan. The PC of Agriculture wants to increase the cotton area of state farms from 168,000 hectares this year to <u>415,000</u> hectares in 1937. This is madness and a schoolboy fascination with figures by the PC of Agriculture bureaucrats. This increase would mean an outlay of billions of rubles at a time when the cotton state farms are operating at huge <u>losses</u> (the production costs are astronomical!) and manpower on the state farms will more than likely be in <u>short supply</u> (not only in the present but even more so in the <u>future</u>). Who needs this rotten schoolboy caper? Wouldn't it be better to expand the area on the collective farms, where there are <u>plenty of workers</u>, the state has <u>invested less</u>, and cotton is many times <u>cheaper?</u>

I think we should increase the area of state farms by the end of the second Five-Year Plan to (at most!) 250,000 hectares. This will be enough to have technically equipped and model sovkhoz <u>centers</u> that are capable of producing <u>exemplars</u> of new, <u>top-grade</u> cotton technology <u>for collective farms</u>. The rest of the area should be turned over to collective farms.

I also think the <u>general</u> plan for expanding cotton areas (including <u>collective-farm</u> tracts) for the second Five-Year Plan should be reduced from 3.4 million hectares <u>at least</u> to 3 million hectares. The task now is not to expand cotton areas but to raise crop yields, improve cultivation and develop cadres. The center of gravity should be moved here forthwith. We don't need crop areas per se, even if they are expanded, we need <u>cotton, more cotton</u>.[3]

4) I must say in general that the PC of Agriculture, as an economic PC, <u>has failed the test</u>. Local functionaries deride the PC of Agriculture as completely inept in terms of economic <u>leadership</u>. <u>Expanding areas</u> (for all crops) indiscriminately and crudely (as indiscriminately and crudely as possible!) and <u>wheedling all the money they can from the government</u> (as much money as possible!) is all that the PC of Agriculture now has on its banner. As for the issues of <u>raising</u> crop yields, <u>improving</u> cultivation, <u>reducing</u> costs, establishing <u>economic accountability</u>, the PC of Agriculture deals with them only <u>in passing</u>, to clear its conscience. Meanwhile the PC of Agriculture <u>fails to understand</u> that when areas are <u>indiscriminately</u> expanded and incredible sums are handed out <u>without any controls</u>, functionaries cannot have either the desire or the time not only to improve their work and raise crop yields but even to give any serious <u>thought</u> to this. Moreover, the PC of Agriculture so underestimates the problems of the quality of work and raising crop yields that it has yet to get around to figuring out <u>which crop</u> needs <u>which fertilizer</u> from the standpoint of experience and science, <u>how</u> to use a specific fertilizer and so forth (it's a fact!). All this has resulted in large expenditures and a lot of equipment on

the one hand, and a deterioration in field cultivation and a minuscule economic effect on the other.

These shortcomings are a great economic (and political!) danger to us. They could demoralize the field-cultivation state farms. They could discredit our collective farms and make peasants leave the collective farms because they operate at a loss.

We must:

1) Abandon the policy of indiscriminate expansion of crop areas both with regard to collective farms and (especially!) state farms (especially for labor-intensive crops);

2) We must drastically reorient all of the attention of the PC of Agriculture and its functionaries, without delay, to the issues of improving the cultivation of fields, raising crop yields, developing and improving cadres, efficiently managing the current work of MTS [Machine-Tractor Stations] and so forth;

3) We must systematically and thoroughly train and retrain the leadership personnel and workers at all of our MTS, making them permanent employees of the MTS;

4) We must decentralize the leadership of our MTS and ensure a certain amount of participation by our regional bodies in this leadership;

5) We must unburden the PC of Agriculture and separate all the grain-growing and livestock-breeding state farms from it into a separate people's commissariat, leaving the PC of Agriculture everything related to collective farms, everything that is produced in collective-farm fields, and making the MTS system, which is the backbone of the collective farms, i.e. of peasant-based (nonstate) agriculture, into the linchpin of the PC of Agriculture's work.[4]

I think these and similar measures are absolutely essential in order to bring agriculture out of its current organizational impasse.

That is all for now. Regards. I. Stalin.

17 July 1932

P.S. I just received Vareikis' letter on improving the work of the MTS. It is a good letter. Vareikis' proposals are correct.[5]

For now you don't have to send our regional leaders the report by Vareikis on the departure of peasants from collective farms. These departures are a temporary aberration. There is no point in shouting about it. I. St.

Give the letter to Molotov to read.

1. The Reichsbanner was a paramilitary organization established in 1924 at the initiative of the German Social Democratic Party, the German Democratic Party and the party of the Center for Defense of the Weimar Republic Against Leftist and Rightist Extremism. Membership in the Reichsbanner reached 1 million at the end of the 1920s.

2. On 30 July 1932 *Pravda* published the resolution of the Second International on the sit-

uation in the Far East and an accompanying editorial headed "A Social-Reformist Evasion Under the Pressure of the Masses."

3. On 8 August 1932 the Politburo adopted the decision "On the Cotton Conference at the PC of Agriculture": "a) To deem excessive the preliminary figures of the cotton conference for increases in cotton areas. b) To assign the PC of Agriculture to study the issue of increasing cotton production, especially by raising crop yields" (RGASPI, f. 17, op. 3, d. 895, l. 8).

4. See document 55.

5. On 23 July 1932 the Politburo approved, in the main, the proposals by Vareikis on improving the work of the MTS. Final editing of the draft resolution was assigned to a commission chaired by Molotov (ibid., d. 893, l. 6).

· 48 ·

Kaganovich to Stalin
17 July

F. 558, op. 11, d. 740, ll. 91–97.

---

17 July [1932]

Greetings, Comrade Stalin!

1) Today we sent you a number of ciphers on international issues. I am now sending you in a letter the draft of a report with commentaries in *Pravda* regarding a statement by the semi-official Japanese agency Shimbun Rengo. We definitely need to go at them for their provocative report. Please let us know your opinion by wire.[1]

2) I am sending you some OGPU documents of interest. Please take note of the fact that the approaches to us by representatives of various Chinese groups asking for assistance have become frequent. It seems to me that we must exercise great self-control and austerity here and not yield to sentimental feelings but regard them, irrespective of their subjective attitudes, as people who are provoking war. We should instruct our people in this vein.[2]

3) We are having a very difficult time resolving the question of the balance sheet for nonferrous metals. We succeeded with enormous effort in reducing the payments for '32–'33 on imports, but now everything must be changed again because of the large payments for nonferrous metals, without which it is hard to manage. Apparently we will be forced to go a little beyond the payments that have been planned.

4) I have sent you Grinko's memorandum on the financial situation. This is now already confronting us as the issue for today. The situation now is pretty difficult. The need for banknotes is growing every day and is approaching a demand of 150–160 million a day, while the capacity for meeting it is 30–40, or a maximum of 50 million rubles. Arrears on wages are already building up. Grinko is proposing a reduction in appropria-

tions for capit[al] construction of 1.5 b[illion] rubles, Comrade Molotov considered 1 billion possible. I personally think, firstly, that we don't need to proclaim new policies involving a mechanical reduction but must, in a practical and specific way, go from trust to trust, compare financial appropriations with the actual output of building materials and in this way without dragging it out achieve a reduction for now of about 500 million. That we have to cut is beyond dispute. because there are economic bodies that are really swimming in money and that do not value it. Comrade Molotov is now leaning toward 500 million. Please do write us what we should do.[3]

5) At yesterday's Politburo meeting we discussed the issue of purchasing ships. Veitser reported that there is an opportunity to purchase ships very cheaply with credits for up to three years, and here the most important thing is that total payments in 1933 do not exceed the total we will spend on cargo. We have set up a commission to verify the calculations. We of course will also have to verify the quality of the ships.

Please let us know at least as a guideline whether we should <u>buy them</u>. If Veitser's calculations are correct, we are inclined to think <u>we should buy them</u>.[4]

6) Sokolnikov came in, he is vigorously pushing to be relieved.[5] I have not promised him anything. Please let us know your opinion.

7) I received your last letter.[6]

a) Regarding military matters we will follow all your instructions.

b) Regarding Basseches we will take appropriate measures.

Regards. Yours, L. Kaganovich.

P.S. I am sending you the draft on industrial cooperatives.[7] L. Kaganovich.

1. The previous day, on 16 July 1932, the Politburo instructed Karakhan to "draft a telegram for publication in the press summarizing the *Shimbun Rengo* report about explosions on the CER with commentaries." It was decided to coordinate the draft telegram with Stalin (RGASPI, f. 17, op. 162, d. 13, l. 28). For the ciphers sent by Kaganovich and Molotov, see ibid., f. 558, op. 11, d. 78, ll. 52, 55.

2. The documents are missing. On 16 July 1932 the Politburo, after considering the question of the representatives of Chinese generals who had come to Vladivostok, resolved "to deem it necessary to send them back to China without conducting any negotiations with them. Comrade Stalin's opinion is to be sought" (ibid., f. 17, op. 162, d. 13, l. 28). On 17 July Kaganovich and Molotov in a cipher to Stalin reported the cases in which the Chinese military had crossed the Far Eastern frontier seeking assistance; on 18 July Stalin agreed that they should be sent back (ibid., f. 558, op. 11, d. 78, ll. 48–49, 47)

3. On 17 July 1932, in a letter to Stalin, Molotov raised the question of currency issue in connection with a memorandum from Grinko. Citing Grinko's information to the effect that 1.3 billion rubles had already been issued since the second quarter of 1932, Molotov wrote that the situation was becoming abnormal and required a cutback in expenditure and an increase in revenues. Molotov reported that Grinko proposed a reduction in expenditure of 1 billion rubles. "You will probably give me a real tongue-lashing, but I am inclined to think

we should do this, but not as much as 1 billion, a little less—500 million rubles," wrote Molotov (APRF, f. 45, op. 1, d. 769, ll. 92–93). See also document 45, and note 1 to document 49.

4. See document 49 and note 1 to document 52.

5. On 1 September 1932 the Politburo relieved Sokolnikov of his duties as plenipotentiary in Great Britain in accordance with his request (RGASPI, f. 17, op. 162, d. 13, l. 82).

6. See document 46.

7. On 20 July Stalin replied by cipher "I do not object to the resolution" (ibid., f. 558, op. 11, d. 78, ll. 58–59). The draft resolution "On the Restructuring of the Work and on Organizational Forms of Industrial Cooperatives" was adopted by the Politburo on 23 July 1932 (ibid., op. 3, d. 893, ll. 5, 41–45). See document 45.

· 49 ·

Stalin to Kaganovich and Molotov
20 July

F. 81, op. 3, d. 99, ll. 106–113.

To Kaganovich, Molotov:

I am writing to both of you together since there is not much time left before the courier leaves.

1. <u>Capital construction</u> must definitely be reduced by a <u>minimum</u> of 500 million to 700 million. We cannot make any cuts in light industry, the iron and steel industry, or the PC of Transport. <u>Everything else</u> (even certain items in the military), especially in sovkhoz construction and so forth, must definitely be cut back <u>to the utmost</u>.[1]

2. I am against purchasing ships abroad. It would be much better to purchase equipment for enterprises in nonferrous metallurgy (copper, tin, aluminum, magnesium, gold, zinc, etc.).[2]

3. Recently there has been an increase in the frequency, <u>first of all</u>, of thefts of freight on the railroads (the thefts amount to tens of millions of rubles), and <u>secondly</u>, of thefts of property belonging to <u>cooperatives</u> and <u>collective farms</u>. The thefts are mostly organized by <u>kulaks</u> (dekulakized persons) and other <u>antisocial</u> elements who are trying to <u>undermine our new system</u>. Under the law these gentlemen are viewed as common thieves, they get two or three years in prison (nominally!), but in reality they are amnestied six to eight months later. This kind of procedure with regard to these gentlemen, which cannot be called <u>socialist</u>, merely encourages what is essentially their real <u>counterrevolutionary</u> "work." It is unthinkable to continue tolerating this situation. I propose that we promulgate a law (while withdrawing or repealing current laws) that would:

a) confer the same status on <u>railroad</u> freight, <u>collective-farm</u> property and <u>cooperative</u> property as on <u>state</u> property;

b) make the theft (or stealing) of property in the above-mentioned categories punishable by a <u>minimum</u> of ten years' imprisonment, and as a rule, by <u>death</u>;

c) revoke the use of amnesty for criminals in such "professions."[3]

Without these (and similar) Draconian <u>socialist</u> measures, it is impossible to establish a new <u>social</u> discipline, and without such discipline, it is impossible to uphold and strengthen our <u>new</u> system.

<u>We must not delay</u>, it seems to me, the promulgation of such a law.

4. The decree on collective-farm trade will undoubtedly revive <u>to a certain extent</u> kulak elements and <u>profiteering</u> resellers of goods [*spekulianty-perekupshchiki*].[4] The former will try to stir up the collective farmers and incite them to leave the collective farms. The latter will slip through the loophole and try to convert trade to their own practices. Clearly, we must eradicate this scum. I propose instructing the OGPU and its local agencies:

a) to place the countryside under strict surveillance and <u>remove all active</u> agitators against the new collective-farm system and active proponents of leaving the collective farms and send them to a <u>concentration camp</u> (on an individual basis);

b) to place bazaars and markets under strict surveillance and <u>remove</u> all profiteers and resellers of goods, <u>confiscate</u> their property, and send them to a <u>concentration camp, unless they are collective farmers</u> (it is better to turn over collective-farm profiteers to the collective-farm comrades' court).

Without these (and similar) measures, it is impossible to strengthen the new system and new, Soviet trade.

The OGPU and its agencies must, <u>without delay</u>, start <u>training</u> its forces and studying the enemy. As for <u>operations</u>, they can begin in a month, no earlier.[5]

5. I wrote you about the reorganization of the PC of Agriculture and the establishment of a new people's commissariat. I think that if you agree with my proposal, we can schedule implementation of this task for the fall, and for now do preparatory work (select leadership personnel, etc.).[6]

Regards. I. Stalin.[7]

20 July 1932

1. See document 48. On 23 July 1932 the Politburo formed a commission chaired by Kuibyshev to examine the question of reducing construction costs. It was instructed "to outline a plan of practical measures for reducing construction costs" and to cut back the funding of capital projects in the third quarter of 1932 by 700 million rubles. At a session of the commission on 26 July, Kuibyshev proposed the necessary draft resolution. Reductions affected every industry, but most of all heavy industry (in the amount of 405 million rubles). Commission members who represented the government departments tried to resist. For example, Piatakov, a deputy people's commissar of heavy industry, insisted that the maximum possible figure for cutbacks at the PC of Heavy Industry was 310 million rubles. Ordzhonikidze, who was on vacation, sent in a telegram of protest. But on 1 August the Politburo

adopted Kuibyshev's proposals. Investments for the PC of Heavy Industry (including the military industry) were reduced by 405 million rubles, and investments for the PC of Agriculture by 150 million rubles (including 80 million rubles in the case of state farms). To mollify Ordzhonikidze, Kaganovich wrote him on 2 August: "On the cutbacks in capital investments: we were compelled to do this, my friend, the financial situation requires it [. . .] We wrote to our chief friend [Stalin] and he deemed it absolutely correct and timely to reduce investment by about 700 million, which is what we did" (R. W. Davies and O.V. Khlevnyuk. "Gosplan," in *Decision Making in the Stalinist Command Economy, 1932–37,* ed. E. A. Rees [London and Basingstoke, 1997], 43.)

2. See document 52.

3. See note 2 to document 52.

4. A decree of the Central Executive Committee and Sovnarkom on collective-farm trade, dated 20 May 1932, lifted many restrictions on trade by collective farms, collective farmers and individual peasants at markets. Price regulation on these "collective-farm markets" was repealed, and trade was allowed at "prices formed in the market."

5. See note 3 to document 52.

6. See document 55.

7. The first page is marked "MK"—Kalinin's signature.

· 50 ·

Stalin to Kaganovich and Molotov
[before 24 July]

F. 81, op. 3, d. 100, ll. 137–140.

Comrades Kaganovich, Molotov:

1. If there are any objections to my proposal on promulgating a law against the theft of cooperative and collective-farm property and freight on transport, give the following explanation. Capitalism could not have smashed feudalism, it would not have developed and solidified if it had not declared the principle of private property to be the foundation of capitalist society and if it had not made private property sacred property, with any violation of its interests strictly punished and with the creation of its own state to protect it. Socialism will not be able to finish off and bury capitalist elements and individualistic, self-seeking habits, practices and traditions (which are the basis of theft) that shake the foundations of the new society unless it declares public property (belonging to cooperatives, collective farms or the state) to be sacred and inviolable. It cannot strengthen and develop the new system and socialist construction, unless it protects the property of collective farms, cooperatives, and the state with all its might, unless it prevents antisocial, capitalist-kulak elements from stealing public property. That is why a new law is needed. We don't have such a law. This gap must be filled in. It, i.e. the new law, could be called something like: "On Protection of the Property of Public Enter-

prises (collective farms, cooperatives et al.) and the Strengthening of the Principle of Public (Socialist) Ownership." Or something like that.

If the proposal is accepted, send me an advance draft law.[1]

2. In reply to your letter I wrote at one point that capital investments must be reduced by 500 million to 700 million rubles for all industries, with the exception of the PC of Transport, the iron and steel industry and light industry.[2] To avoid misunderstandings, let me say that in referring to light industry, I also meant the food industries (sugar, preserved food, etc.).

Regards. I. Stalin.[3]

1. See note 2 to document 52.
2. See note 1 to document 49.
3. At the top of the first page of the letter are the inscriptions: "in favor—Molotov, Kuibyshev, Voroshilov, Kalinin."

· 51 ·

Stalin to Kaganovich
25 July

F. 81, op. 3, d. 99, ll. 115–119.

Greetings, Comrade Kaganovich!

1) Yesterday I wrote to you in cipher about a partial reduction of the grain-procurements plan for collective farms and individual peasants in the Ukraine that have especially suffered. After the speeches at the conference of secretaries (at the end of June) and the Ukrainian party conference, my proposal may have seemed strange to you (and Molotov). But there is nothing strange here. The end of June (the secretaries' conference) and the beginning of July (the Ukrainian party conference) were a period of organization of grain procurements and deployment of forces to fulfill the grain-procurements plan. To have discussed a reduction of the plan during this period (even as an exception) in front of everyone and in the presence of the regional secretaries would have been totally demoralizing for the (already demoralized) Ukrainians, would have disorganized the regional secretaries and disrupted grain procurements. That was the situation at the end of June and beginning of July. The situation will be different in mid-August or late August. During this time, first of all, the harvest prospects will become clear (they have already become clear!), that they are undoubtedly good for the USSR as a whole, second, the party and Soviet forces will have already been mobilized and deployed to fulfill the plan, third, closer scrutiny of the Ukraine's affairs during this period has already

revealed the need for assistance to Ukrainian collective farms in the form of a partial reduction of the plan, <u>fourth,</u> the end of August (I insist on the end or at any rate the second half of August) is the most suitable moment to provide assistance to stimulate winter sowing and autumn operations in general.

I think 30 million poods [491,000 tons] of grain is enough for this purpose. <u>At most</u> we could agree to 40 million poods. The Ukrainians may demand that this amount be divided among <u>all</u> the collective farms, or that individual peasants be provided with the <u>same</u> assistance as the collective farms. If such demands are made, they should be rejected. We must take only the collective farms that have <u>suffered</u>, slashing an <u>average</u> of 50 percent off the plan for them. For individual peasants, only one-third or even one-fourth of the plan should be slashed.[1]

2) I have read Grinko's memorandum. He (along with Mariasin) has some exaggerations, institutional one-sidedness and so forth. But for the most part Grinko and his functionaries are right and they <u>should be supported</u>.[2]

Regards. Stalin.

25 July 1932

1. In his cipher of 24 July to Kaganovich and Molotov Stalin stated: "it is necessary to make an exception for the specially suffering districts of the Ukraine, not only from the point of view of justice, but also in view of the special position of the Ukraine, its common frontier with Poland, etc."; a similar exception might need to be made for Transcaucasia (RGASPI, f. 558, op. 11, d. 78, ll. 79–81). On 16 August Stalin wrote in a cipher to Kaganovich "I think the time has come to inform the Ukrainians about the reduction of their grain procurements plan. summon Kosior and tell him" (ibid., d. 79, l. 74). On 17 August the Politburo accepted "Stalin's proposal to reduce the grain-procurements plan in the Ukraine by 40 million poods as an exception for the districts of the Ukraine that have particularly suffered, so that the plan for collective farms in the districts that have particularly suffered can be reduced by half, and the plan for individual peasants, by one-third." Kuibyshev, Kosior, and Kaganovich were assigned to determine the districts for which this reduction was proposed, without allowing equalization to occur in the process. (Ibid., f. 17, op. 162, d. 13, l. 76.)

2. See note 1 to document 53.

· 52 ·

Stalin to Kaganovich
26 July

F. 81, op. 3, d. 100, ll. 1–7.

<u>Greetings, Comrade Kaganovich!</u>

I received your letter of 24 July.

1) If the ships can be purchased with a payment <u>no earlier</u> than 1934, I do not object to purchasing the ships.[1]

2) I spoke in my letter about the purchase not of nonferrous metals but of <u>equipment</u> for the production of nonferrous metals. As is well known, that is not the same thing. I think the production of nonferrous metals will be one <u>of the top</u> items in the control figures for 1933. That is what I had in mind when I referred to equipment for nonferrous metals.

3) I think it would be more expedient to <u>combine</u> in a single law the issue of protecting <u>collective-farm</u> and <u>cooperative</u> property and <u>railroad</u> freight with the issue of protecting <u>the collective farms themselves,</u> i.e. combating the elements that use <u>violence and threats</u> or <u>preach</u> the use of violence and threats to <u>collective farmers</u> in order to make them quit the collective farms, in order to bring about the forcible destruction of the collective farms. The law can be broken down into three sections, of which the <u>first</u> section will cover <u>railroad</u> freight and water-transport cargo with the respective punishments specified, the <u>second</u> section will cover <u>collective-farm</u> and <u>cooperative</u> property with the respective punishments, and the <u>third</u> section will cover the protection of the collective farms themselves from acts of violence and threats by kulaks and other antisocial elements, and will specify that crimes in such cases, i.e. in the latter cases, will be punishable by imprisonment for five to ten years, with subsequent confinement in a concentration camp for three years and without the possibility of amnesty.[2] I think that on <u>all three of these points</u> we must act on <u>the basis of a law</u> ("the peasant loves legality"), and not merely in accordance with the <u>practice</u> of the OGPU, although it is clear that the OGPU's role here will not only not diminish but, on the contrary, it will be strengthened and "ennobled" (the OGPU agencies will operate "on a lawful basis" rather than "high-handedly").

As for the struggle against profiteers and resellers both at bazaars and markets and in the countryside, what is needed here is a <u>special</u> law (here, too, it will be better to operate on the basis of a <u>law</u>) that, while referring to the previous law on collective-farm trade, which points <u>to the eradication</u> of resellers and profiteers, will order OGPU agencies to exile profiteers and resellers to a concentration camp for five to eight years without the possibility of amnesty.[3]

Is that clear?

It is along these lines that my proposals laid out in previous letters should be changed.

4) There are abominations occurring in the supply of metal for the Stalingrad Tractor Plant [STP] and the Moscow and Gorky auto plants. It is a disgrace that the windbags at the PC of Heavy Industry have still not gotten around to straightening out the supply system. Let the CC place under its <u>continuous</u> supervision, without delay, the plants that are supplying the STP and the Moscow and Gorky auto plants with steel (<u>Red October and others</u>) and make up for this disruption.[4] It is time to begin <u>holding ac-</u>

<u>countable</u> the management of plants that are obligated to supply motor-vehicle and tractor enterprises with steel. If Ordzhonikidze starts to make trouble, we will have to brand him a rotten slave to routine who supports the worst traditions of the rightwing deviationists at the PC of Heavy Industry.

5) I am sending you Kavtaradze's letter.[5] I think you should call him in and <u>help</u> him.

Regards. I. Stalin.

26 July [1932]

1. On 1 September 1932 the Politburo adopted a draft resolution, proposed by the PCs of Foreign Trade and Water Transport, on the purchase of ships in the European market (RGASPI, f. 17, op. 162, d. 13, ll. 84, 86.). See also documents 48, 49.

2. Stalin's proposals were embodied in the famous law of 7 August 1932 "On the Protection of the Property of State Enterprises, Collective Farms and Cooperatives and the Strengthening of Public (Socialist) Ownership" (*Pravda,* 8 and 9 August 8 1932; *Sobranie zakonov, 1932,* art.360). See documents 49, 50.

3. On 2 August 1932 the Politburo instructed the OGPU "to submit to the CC within three days specific measures to combat profiteering, profiteers and resellers of grain" (RGASPI, f. 17, op. 162, d. 13, l. 52). On 13 August 1932, on Kaganovich's proposal, the Politburo adopted a decision to approve a decree on combating profiteering and to publish it on 23 August, and to take note of Menzhinsky's letter to OGPU agencies on combating profiteering and to send a copy of it to every member of the CC (ibid., op. 3, d. 896, l. 13). A decree of the Central Executive Committee and Sovnarkom of the USSR on combating profiteering provided for the confinement of profiteers and resellers in a concentration camp for five to ten years without the possibility of amnesty. See documents 49, 59.

4. On 8 August 1932 the Politburo adopted a resolution on the issue of supplying the motor-vehicle and tractor industry with high-quality steel. The resolution instructed the PC of Heavy Industry "to submit, within two days, month-by-month plans for supplying motor-vehicle and tractor plants with steel, with orders precisely allocated to each plant and deadlines specified for their fulfillment" (ibid., op. 3, d. 895, ll. 7, 21–23).

5. The letter is missing.

· 53 ·

Kaganovich to Stalin

2 August

From Kaganovich family archive.

---

2 August 1932

Dear Comrade Stalin.

Yesterday we sent you a number of telegrams on issues that we discussed in the Politburo. I want to explain our decisions on some of these issues in this letter in more detail.

1. On financial measures. We adopted a number of resolutions which I have already written you about and which were already partly summa-

rized in Comrade Grinko's memorandum.[1] In addition to this there is an additional new measure: first is the reduction of staffs, even if it were not related to financial measures, we should do this because the staff has become impossibly bloated, especially in nonbudgetary economic organizations. Of course in doing this we must avoid, as you once said at a Politburo meeting, a purely mechanical approach. A reduction must by no means turn into a purge. The RKI [Workers' and Peasants' Inspectorate] was supposed to concentrate on this task.[2] This job would have proven helpful to the RKI itself, which, frankly, is doing very little right now for the economy drive and is out of touch with economic institutions, and with those that are part of people's commissariats. The second measure is riskier and more controversial. I personally, to be honest about it, had doubts about its advisability, but we more or less all agreed that we could probably go through with purchases for 20 million [rubles] with the credits, with receipts of up to 500 million and payment in 1934.[3] I repeat, this is the least desirable measure. We find your objections quite understandable, we will, of course, drop this issue. Given our difficulties with foreign currency it will probably be better to drop this venture.

2. On the issue of nonferrous metals there turned out to be really a very unpleasant misunderstanding, i.e. to put it bluntly a mistake. You indeed wrote about equipment for the production of nonferrous metals, but by mistake, apparently because of an optical illusion, we mistook your listing at the bottom—copper, aluminum, tin, etc.—as indicating that it was possible to purchase nonferrous metals, especially since the pressure on us in this direction is extraordinary. The situation really is very grave with nonferrous metals. We have already drawn from the reserve fund several times and all this just in a few weeks. That is why we were forced to take the step of increasing purchases of nonferrous metals, partly by reducing other imports, partly by increasing the payment limit somewhat. As a result we have ended up with 71 million in payments for '32 instead of the planned 67,573,000 and 89.5 million for '33 instead of the planned 85. We squeezed hard, but believe me, we just couldn't squeeze out any more. I am sending you detailed material on this matter and ask that you write your opinion.

2 [*sic*]. We just had a special meeting to discuss the issue of the draft decree. The draft decree comprises the three sections along the lines of your instructions. There was an objection to the third section yesterday by . . . [*sic*] today he wasn't there, he went out of town. There were also doubts and even objections about the second and third on the part of . . . [*sic*] but ultimately we settled on this text in principle.[4] I am sending it to you. The decree is undoubtedly timely, many people in the regions have the notion that unless they talk firmly they will allow the kulaks to walk all over them and corrupt the collective farms, so it should be issued as soon as possible.

If the proletariat fails to utilize all the might of its concentr[ation] of econ[omic] and polit[ical] power to strengthen the new eco[nomic] system, the kulaks may achieve some success.

3. We heard a report on the harvest campaign and grain procurements. The harvest went better in the last five-day period, but I can't say it was satisfactory. We have outlined a number of practical measures, specifically we have proposed that people who are familiar with agriculture be taken from the cities but not from factories and plants to give temporary help to state farms for about 10–15 days. The situation with beets is bad, especially with the digging and preparation in the fight against the second round of infestation by caterpillars. There is still something we can do here, specifically with regard to weeding and the fight against the second round of caterpillars. We have asked the CC of the Communist Party (Bolsheviks) of the Ukraine and the Central Black-Earth Region what they are doing and what measures they propose. There have been proposals to announce that a peasant will get 5–6 poods [80–100 kilograms] of grain for each hectare of beets that is weeded and preserved from caterpillars. Counting a million hectares sown, we come up with 5–6 million poods [80,000–100,000 tons], but we have not taken this measure yet, although we were inclined to think that we could take this step, because the beet sowers get none of the benefits from collective farm trade that grain sowers get.

Regarding the question of grain procurements we have approved the plan. The July plan was fulfilled very poorly, and for August we adopted 285 million poods. We resolved to strengthen the grain-procurement staff by selecting 300 people for full-time work.

4. We approved the numbers for fall sowing and fall plowing, and proceeded in this matter from the absolutely correct guideline you gave us that increasing the amount of crop area to be expanded is impermissible. Therefore we increased the expansion [*sic*] by 1 million for state farms and left the entire rest of the collective farm and peasant sector at last year's level. We think we did the right thing.

5. The PC of Heavy Industry has submitted a number of proposals on the issue of the opening of Dneprostroy. We have deferred the issue. I think we must get your thoughts on this issue. In my opinion, we could open it not on the 25th, and besides it's too late, we won't make it, we could open around 10 September. They are asking 2,750,000 for bonuses and expenditures—that is a bit much. And, of course, the proposal that the entire Politburo membership travel there is absolutely not acceptable, some of the Politburo members will have to go. Please do write your opinion.[5] I am sending you materials.

6. We discussed some international issues yesterday. We heard a report on the proposal by the French trade minister to resume trade negotiations.

For the moment we have taken the report under advisement, no practical decisions are required, since the negotiations will not begin before September.[6] Krestinsky has submitted a proposal that we give the French government a memorandum on the issue of the White Guards, considering the present moment most favorable. We did not adopt this proposal, since we feel that in fact it is untimely.

I am sending you a short note from Karakhan on the inquiry from the Jap[anese] maritime ministry to our military attaché Bologoy. There were two types of proposals at the Politburo meeting: there was a proposal that Bologoy be instructed to reply to the Japanese that they should make their inquiry of the trade agency and that he hopes the trade agency will consider their proposal and look on it with favor, and another proposal was to instruct Bologoy to reply simply that this is a trade and economic matter and that they should address this question to the trade agency.

I think the second proposal is more correct.[7] We must agree to any trade and economic deal, we sell oil to everyone, but not under the kind of arrangement, linked to America, that they have proposed.

7. I am sending you two memoranda, the transcript of the conversation between Aleksandrovsky and Niedermaier and Vinogradov's conversation with Reventlow. Both memoranda are of interest.[8]

8. I am sending you material received from Piatnitsky. Piatnitsky raised the question of establishing a commission, but we have deferred this matter until we get your thoughts from you. P[iatnitsky] may be exaggerating, but where there's smoke there's fire, and besides, the letter shows that N[eumann] really did slap something together.[9] Judging by the letters there is something factional, but should we be blowing this up, especially at a time when our German comrades can be congratulated on their election success.

Regards to you. Yours, L. Kaganovich.

1. On 28 July 1932 the Politburo authorized the Gosbank (State Bank) to print 150 million rubles (RGASPI, f. 17, op. 162, d. 13, l. 51). On 1 August, after hearing Grinko's report on financial measures in the third quarter, the Politburo resolved: "It is to be firmly predetermined that the budget for the fourth quarter must absolutely not only be without a deficit but have an excess of revenue over expenditure." It was directed that arrears on wages for workers and office employees be eliminated by 15 August (ibid., ll. 49, 50). On 2 August the Politburo authorized the Gosbank to issue currency to eliminate wage arrears of 200 million rubles (ibid., l. 53). See documents 48, 51.

2. On 1 August Kaganovich asked Stalin in a cipher whether the administrative staff should be reduced by at least 10 percent by 1 September (ibid., f. 558, op. 11, d. 78, l. 119). Later the issue of reducing administrative staff and abolishing corporations was considered at a Politburo meeting on 8 October 1932. The USSR RKI [Workers' and Peasants' Inspectorate] was instructed to reduce all representative offices of local, regional and republic economic and soviet organizations in Moscow; to establish staff commissions for people's commissariats, consisting of representatives of the RKI, the CC, the appropriate people's

commissariat and the CC of the trade union, requiring them to fix a firm level for the staff establishment, which would be prohibited from growing without RKI approval, and to reduce the number of office employees by 10–20 percent, etc. (ibid., op. 3, d. 902, l. 3).

3. This refers to a proposal sent by cipher to Stalin on 1 August to import raw materials for the food and consumer goods industries, to be sold at commercial prices within the USSR for 500 million rubles. On 2 August Stalin replied "I decisively object." (Ibid., f. 558, op. 11, d. 78, 119, 1190b.)

4. The second section of the resolution of 7 August 1932 provided for executions or, under extenuating circumstances, ten-year prison sentences for theft of collective-farm property. The third section provided for sentences of five to ten years in camps for "kulak and capitalist elements" who "use force and threats or advocate the use of force and threats against collective farmers for the purpose of compelling the latter to leave collective farms."

5. See document 54.

6. Soviet-French trade negotiations resumed on 20 October 1932.

7. On 7 August 1932 the Politburo approved the text of a telegram to Troianovsky that instructed Bologoy to reply to the Japanese that "it is best to resolve the issue of oil by entering into a agreement for us to deliver oil for many years ($3\frac{1}{4}$ and more years). The agreement may be concluded as an ordinary, commercial contract between the Maritime Ministry and our Trade Agency in Tokyo or a representative of Soiuzneft [the All-Union Trust for the Design and Construction of Oil and Gas Enterprises]" (ibid., op. 162, d. 13, l. 53). Cf, document 54.

8. The memoranda are missing. O. von Niedermaier (a Wehrmacht officer) and Count zu Reventlow (a Right-wing politician) were Germans with an "Eastern orientation"—see Brief Biographies.

9. See note 4 to document 59.

· 54 ·

Stalin to Kaganovich
4 August

F. 81, op. 3, d. 99, ll. 121–123.

<u>Greetings, Comrade Kaganovich!</u>

1) I am returning the draft decree on protecting public property with corrections and additions. As you see I have expanded it a bit. Publish it as quickly as you can.

2) I have no objections to your import plan, although it would be better to reduce it.[1]

3) Comrade Karakhan's memorandum on a reply to Japan's maritime department is correct.[2]

4) The plan for inaugurating Dneprostroy is too grandiose. Why the hell do we need so much pomp? It must be cut back by <u>two-thirds</u>. The list of individuals to receive decorations and to be put on the board of honor can be adopted. If Kalinin opens the proceedings, and Molotov and Chubar give speeches, that is already quite a lot.[3]

5) There are outrages taking place on the railroads. Employees along

the routes are being raped and terrorized by hooligans and homeless children. The agencies of the Transport OGPU [TOGPU] are <u>asleep</u> (it's a fact!). We cannot put up with this outrage any longer. Call the TOGPU to order. Make them keep order on the routes. Give a directive to the TOGPU to have armed people on the routes and to execute hooligans on the spot. Where is the TOGPU? How can Comrade Blagonravov put up with all this anarchy and these outrages?[4]

Regards. I. Stalin.

4 August 1932.

1. On 16 August 1932 the Politburo approved the draft resolution, submitted by the Molotov commission, on the import plan for 1932 (RGASPI, f. 17, op. 162, d. 13, ll. 59, 66–71).

2. See note 7 to document 53.

3. On 8 August 1932 the Politburo adopted a decision to send Kalinin and Ordzhonikidze to the opening of the Dnepropetrovsk Hydroelectric Station. A commission established to consider the inauguration program was assigned "to reduce the proposals of the PC of Heavy Industry by two-thirds to three-quarters" (ibid., op. 3, d. 895, l. 6). See also document 53.

4. On 7 August 1932 the Politburo considered the issue of hooliganism on transport. Deputy people's commissar of transport Blagonravov, along with the transport section of the OGPU, was assigned to submit to the Politburo within two days a report on "what they are doing to combat hooliganism on transport, what directives they have issued to combat hooliganism and thefts, and what measures are being taken to protect railroad freight" (ibid., l. 13). On 16 August the Politburo heard and approved a report by Menzhinsky and Blagonravov on the progress of the fight against hooliganism on transport (ibid., d. 896, l. 8).

· 55 ·

Stalin to Kaganovich, Molotov, Voroshilov,
and other members of the Politburo
5 August

F. 81, op. 3, d. 99, ll. 125–131.

<u>To Kaganovich, Molotov, Voroshilov, and other members of the Politburo.</u>

The main shortcoming in the work of the leadership bodies (top and bottom) <u>in agriculture</u> consists (<u>at this</u> moment) of <u>organizational</u> lapses. Defects in the organization of the PC of Agriculture, defects in the organization of the Traktorotsentr [the All-Union Center for Machine-Tractor Stations] and the MTS, defects in the training of cadres for the MTS and state farms, defects in the deployment of forces, the redundancy of the Kolkhoztsentr [the All-Union Council for Agricultural Collectives] and its local agencies—these are the organizational lapses. Many think that the organizational issue is a trivial issue. This is a glaring error. Once the correct policy has been worked out, the organizational issue is the <u>decisive</u> issue, since the organizational issue signifies the <u>implementation</u>, the <u>fulfillment</u> of the requirements of the correct policy.

How are we to solve—to eliminate this discrepancy between the existence of a correct policy and the <u>absence</u> of a correct <u>organizational</u> implementation of it?

It is imperative:

1. To detach grain-growing and livestock-breeding <u>state farms</u> from the PC of Agriculture into a separate people's commissariat, and let the PC of Agriculture concentrate on the collective-farm economy as its principal work.

2. To <u>split</u> Traktorotsentr and the MTS according to the principal crops [for which the MTS are responsible] (grain, cotton, sugar beets, flax, etc.) and make skilled MTS personnel <u>permanent</u>, salaried employees.

3. To increase the role of <u>regional</u> MTS agencies and to establish <u>real</u> supervision of them by the regional party committees.[1]

4. To see to it that MTS directors are not merely <u>technicians</u> (who are familiar with tractors and farm machinery) but also <u>agronomists</u> and <u>politicians</u>—public-spirited activists who know how to deal like real Bolsheviks with "muzhiks." To this end:

a) reorganize "Sverdlovka" [the Sverdlov Higher Party School in Moscow] and regional communist higher educational institutions, which now produce know-it-alls we don't need, into agricultural schools of a <u>new type</u> that can provide us with <u>completely modern and economically grounded directors</u> of MTS, <u>secretaries</u> of district party committees, <u>chairmen of district executive committees</u>, and section <u>managers</u> for grain-growing state farms, collective farms, and livestock-breeding state farms;

b) set the capacity of these agricultural schools (the Moscow school and regional schools) at 15,000–20,000 students, and recruit the latter from brigade leaders, assistant MTS directors, chief functionaries of district party committees and district executive committees, functionaries of collective-farm centers, and so forth.

c) organize these schools with <u>three-year</u> programs for <u>secretaries</u> of district party committees and <u>chairmen of district executive committees</u> (including a broader <u>political</u> component) and with <u>two-year</u> programs for everyone else <u>plus</u> six months of <u>preparatory</u> work for people with a low literacy level (i.e. two-<u>and-a-half-year</u> programs).[2]

5. To destroy the system of <u>collective-farm centers</u> from top to bottom, as a system that is already unnecessary, and transfer its functionaries to agencies of the PC of Agriculture and the new state-farm PC, making the district party committees, the district executive committees, the MTS, and the district agricultural departments the main instruments for exerting influence on the countryside.[3]

6. Set up at both people's commissariats clear and well-qualified instructional sessions in agriculture (in <u>all</u> branches of it).

That is all for now. Regards.

5 August 1932. I. Stalin.

P.S. Comrade Yakovlev came to see me and he has read this letter. He also spoke about a number of issues, about which he will report to you orally. I. St.[4]

1. On 1 October 1932 the Politburo adopted a decision to detach grain and livestock-breeding state farms from the system of the PC of Agriculture and to establish a People's Commissariat of Grain and Livestock-Breeding State Farms of the USSR. The PC of Agriculture and the entire system of agricultural agencies were assigned to concentrate "mainly on serving and managing the collective farms." The resolution provided for reorganizing Traktorotsentr and forming a number of specialized tractor centers in the PC of Agriculture (RGASPI, f. 17, op. 3, d. 902, l. 9). Stalin's proposals were realized in full in January 1933, when political sections (*politotdely*) were established in the MTS. See documents 47, 49, 59.

2. These proposals by Stalin were implemented in large measure in a CC resolution of 21 September 1932 "On the Establishment of Communist Higher Agricultural Schools" (*KPSS v rezoliutsiiakh* . . . [The CPSU in Resolutions . . .], vol. 5, pp. 418–20).

3. Kolkhoztsentr and republic, regional and district collective-farm unions [centers] were abolished by a decree of Sovnarkom of 29 November 1932 (GARF, f. R-5446, op. 57, d. 21, l. 97).

4. The first page of the letter contains the signatures of Voroshilov and Rudzutak.

· 56 ·

Stalin to Voroshilov, Kaganovich and Molotov
7 August

RGASPI, f. 81, op. 3, d. 99, ll. 132–137.

Greetings, Comrade <u>Voroshilov</u>, Comrade <u>Kaganovich</u> and Comrade <u>Molotov</u>:

Yenukidze came to see me.

1. I agree with you that it is better to build the banks of the Moscow River on an incline.

2. Yenukidze says the experts have adopted the deep-drilling plan for the subway. If this is true, I welcome it.

3. Of all the plans for the "Palace of Soviets," Iofan's plan is the best.[1] Zholtovsky's project smacks of "Noah's Ark." Shchusev's is just another "Cathedral of Christ the Savior," but without the cross ("so far"). It is possible that Shchusev hopes to "add on" the cross <u>later</u>. We should (<u>in my opinion</u>) require Iofan: a) not to separate the small hall from the large one, but to <u>combine</u> them in accordance with the government's assignment; b) to give the top of the "Palace" a <u>shape</u> by extending it upward in

the form of a <u>tall</u> column (I mean a column of the same shape that Iofan had in his <u>first</u> project); c) to place above the column a <u>hammer</u> and <u>sickle</u> that will be electrically lit from within; d) if for technical reasons the column cannot be hoisted <u>on top </u>the "Palace," to place the column <u>next to</u> (near) the "Palace," if possible, as tall as the Eiffel Tower, or a little taller; e) to place three statues (of Marx, Engels and Lenin) <u>in front</u> of the "Palace."

4. I am depressed at the thought that Molotov's vacation is being ruined or may be ruined because of me (how many times now?). Let Molotov leave immediately on vacation.[2] I will be in Moscow soon, very soon. I have decided this <u>irrespective</u> of everything else.

Regards, I. Stalin.

7 August 1932

P.S. I just received a letter from Kaganovich and Molotov.

1) Concerning the decree on industry (the organizational issue) I will reply tomorrow (once I have examined the draft decree).[3] I will also answer Molotov regarding the other questions.

2) I will reply about the draft decree on profiteering tomorrow (once I have examined it).[4]

3) Concerning the agreement with Hirota—ditto.[5]

4) I would not advise you to simply and "politely" send Barlow packing from the USSR.[6] <u>All</u> foreign bourgeois specialists are or may be intelligence agents. But that does not necessarily mean that they should be "politely" sent packing. No, it doesn't! I advise you not to cut off ties with Barlow, to be considerate of him, toss him some money, take his drawings, but don't show him our achievements (you can say that we are backward people and are ready to learn from Barlow, on a paid basis, of course—of course!).

I will deal with the rest of the questions later (the courier is rushing me). St.[7]

1. On 5 June 1931 the Politburo adopted a decision to build a Palace of Soviets on the site of the Cathedral of Christ the Savior in Moscow. The plan called for the construction of two halls with capacities of 12,000–15,000 and 4,000–5,000 people. (RGASPI, f. 17, op. 3, d. 828, l. 17.) This is the site on which the Cathedral of Christ the Savior was rebuilt in the 1990s.

2. On 12 August 1932 the Politburo granted Molotov a vacation beginning 14 August, for a month and a half (ibid., op. 162, d. 13, l. 63).

3. A commission chaired by Molotov, which also included Stalin, was established on 8 May 1932 to examine the management of industry (ibid., op. 3, d. 883, l. 2). A draft resolution was ready in early August. After sending it to Stalin, Molotov submitted the draft to the Politburo on 8 August (without waiting for Stalin's reply). The Politburo approved the draft resolution and assigned Molotov to prepare a final version of it. But on the same day, 8 August, Stalin criticized the draft in a letter to Molotov: "The draft resolution '<u>On the Organization of Management of Industry</u>,' in my opinion, does not do the job. It is too general and

all-inclusive. It is schematic and unspecific. The issue of the organization of <u>the sale of output</u> was dashed off in a slipshod manner, yet it is an important issue that varies from industry to industry. The issue of <u>supplying</u> the enterprises (distribution of <u>metal, building materials</u>, etc.) has also been dashed off in a slipshod manner and turned over to the control of the PC of Heavy Industry. We cannot allow the PC of Heavy Industry to distribute metal, building materials, etc. (these are supplies!), at its own discretion. I am afraid that if we issue such a resolution, we will set back the work of industry by at least six months, since the esteemed 'Bolsheviks' will neglect this task and will use up all their energy on endlessly moving people from place to place. Wouldn't it be better to cover each industry separately, determining in the process the staff of each trust and the number of functionaries to be transferred to enterprises from a corporation that is being disbanded? Can't this matter be put off until the fall?" (ibid., f. 82, op. 1, d. 1421, ll. 258–260.)

4. See note 3 to document 52.

5. On 5 August Kaganovich reported to Stalin in a letter that Karakhan had reached a fisheries agreement with Hirota which the Politburo found satisfactory (ibid., f. 558, op. 11, d. 740, ll. 122–148). On 10 August 1932 the Politburo resolved to sign the draft of a fishing agreement with Japan, proposed by Karakhan (ibid., f. 17, op. 162, d. 13, l. 63). The agreement on fishing issues was signed by deputy people's commissar for foreign affairs Karakhan and by Hirota, the Japanese ambassador to the USSR, on 13 August 1932 (DVP, vol. XV, pp. 469–71).

6. The American inventor Barlow made a proposal to the Soviet government that he turn over his invention—a new plane, a long-distance combination fighter-bomber—to the USSR. At Stalin's suggestion, Barlow was invited to Moscow. On 16 July 1932 the Politburo assigned Piatakov, Tukhachevsky, and Loganovsky to supervise arrangements for Barlow's reception and clarify all issues related to his proposals (RGASPI, f. 17, op. 162, d. 13, l. 33). Barlow held lengthy negotiations in the USSR, reported to Stalin by Kaganovich in a series of letters and ciphers (ibid., f. 558, op. 11, d. 740, ll. 112–116, 117–121; d. 78, ll. 96–98, 95, 92). Barlow did not turn over the drawings for the plane, but he made a number of political proposals involving support for Roosevelt in the forthcoming U.S. presidential election. In the letter of 5 August to which Stalin is replying Kaganovich noted that Barlow, "evidently a quite experienced intelligence agent," tried to obtain information on Soviet bombs; Kaganovich proposed that the USSR should refuse to pay Barlow to prepare drawings in America, because he would not be allowed to do this—it was impossible to believe that "Roosevelt will defend him and he will be able to prepare a military invention in America for another country" (ibid., d. 740, ll. 122–148).

7. The first page contains the signature of Voroshilov.

· 57 ·

Stalin to Kaganovich
11 August

F. 81, op. 3, d. 99, ll. 144–151.

<u>Greetings, Comrade Kaganovich:</u>

I received your letter of 9 August.

1) The decree on the protection of public property, of course, is good and it will soon have an impact. The decree against profiteers is also good and timely (it should be promulgated soon). But all of this is not enough.

We still must issue separately a <u>letter-directive</u> from the CC to party and judiciary and punitive organizations about the <u>point</u> of these decrees and the <u>methods</u> for implementing them. This is absolutely imperative. Tell the appropriate people to draft such a letter. I will be in Moscow soon and will review it.[1]

2) We will discuss the plenum of the Executive Committee of the Comintern, the utilization of grain and fodder crops, and diesel locomotives when I arrive in Moscow.

3) <u>The most important issue</u> right now is the Ukraine. Things in the Ukraine have hit rock bottom. Things are bad with regard to the <u>party</u>. There is talk that in two regions of the Ukraine (I think it is the Kiev and Dnepropetrovsk regions) about <u>50</u> district party committees have spoken out <u>against</u> the grain-procurements plan, deeming it <u>unrealistic</u>. The situation in other district party committees, people say, is no better. What does this look like? This is not a party but a parliament, a caricature of a parliament. Instead of <u>leading</u> the districts, Kosior keeps <u>maneuvering</u> between the directives of the CC of the VKP and the demands of the district party committees—and now he has maneuvered himself into a total mess. Lenin was right in saying that a person who does not have the courage to swim against the current when necessary cannot be a real Bolshevik leader. Things are <u>bad</u> with the soviets. Chubar is no leader. Things are <u>bad</u> with the GPU. Redens is not up to leading the fight against the counterrevolution in such a large and distinctive republic as the Ukraine.

Unless we begin to straighten out the situation in the Ukraine, we may lose the Ukraine. Keep in mind that Pilsudski is not daydreaming, and his agents in the Ukraine are many times stronger than Redens or Kosior thinks. Keep in mind, too, that the Ukrainian Communist Party (500,000 members, ha-ha) has quite a lot (yes, quite a lot!) of rotten elements, conscious and unconscious Petliura adherents, and, finally, direct agents of Pilsudski. As soon as things get worse, these elements will waste no time opening a front inside (and outside) the party, <u>against</u> the party. The worst aspect is that the Ukraine leadership does <u>not</u> see these dangers.

Things cannot go on this way.

We must:

a) remove Kosior from the Ukraine and replace him with you while <u>keeping</u> you as a secretary of the CC of the VKP(b);

b) <u>right after</u> this, transfer Balitsky to the Ukraine to the post of chairman of the Ukrainian <u>GPU</u> (or plenipotentiary in the Ukraine, since I don't think the position of chairman of the Ukrainian GPU exists) while <u>keeping</u> him as vice-chairman of the OGPU, and make Redens the deputy to Balitsky for the Ukraine;

c) <u>several months later</u>, replace Chubar with another comrade, say,

Grinko or someone else, and make Chubar the deputy to Molotov in Moscow (Kosior can be made a secretary of the CC of the VKP);

d) set the goal of transforming the Ukraine as quickly as possible into a real <u>fortress</u> of the USSR, into a genuinely exemplary republic. We should be unstinting in providing money.

Without these and similar measures (the economic and political strengthening of the Ukraine, above all its <u>border</u> districts, etc.), I repeat, we may lose the Ukraine.

What do you think about this?

We must get to work on this matter as soon as possible—immediately after I arrive in Moscow.[2]

Regards, I. Stalin.

11 August 1932

P.S. I have already spoken with Menzhinsky about Balitsky and Redens. He agrees and welcomes this move in every respect.[3]

---

1. In his letter of 9 August (located in the Kaganovich family archive) Kaganovich stated that the decree had been published and "most workers received it favorably," though some Communists objected to the used of the word "sacred" to characterize socialist property. Stalin himself handled the preparation of the proposed further "letter-directive" after he returned to Moscow. A Politburo session on 1 September established a commission headed by Akulov, a vice-chairman of the OGPU, and assigned it to "consider specific instructions to implement the decree of the Central Executive Committee and Sovnarkom of the USSR on the protection of public property both with regard to the OGPU and with regard to the judiciary and the prosecutor's office" (RGASPI, f. 17, op. 3, d. 898, l. 1). On 8 September, the draft instructions prepared by the commission were approved in the main by the Politburo. Final editing of the document (taking into account the exchange of opinions at the Politburo session) was assigned to the Akulov commission and to Stalin (ibid., d. 899, l. 2). The instructions "for applying the decree of the Central Executive Committee and Sovnarkom of the USSR of 7 August 1932" were approved on 16 September. They defined the crimes covered by the law of 7 August and established categories of thieves and penalties for each of them, the procedure for examining cases, the time frames for conducting investigations, etc. One of the purposes of the instructions was to mitigate the sanctions of the law of 7 August, which were extremely brutal (and therefore caused difficulties in their implementation). Specifically, executions were prescribed for systematic thefts, but not for petty larcenies of socialist property (ibid., d. 900, ll. 33–330b). The instructions also contained a top-secret section, classified as "special file," which provided for a simplified a procedure for approving death sentences (*Stalinskoe Politbiuro v 30-e gody* [Stalin's Politburo in the 1930s], 61–2).

2. See document 59 and the introduction to this chapter.

3. Stalin's proposal was implemented gradually. In November 1932 Balitsky was appointed special representative of the OGPU in the Ukraine (while Redens remained leader of the GPU of the Ukraine). In February 1933 Balitsky officially replaced Redens as chairman of the GPU of the Ukrainian SSR and plenipotentiary of the OGPU in the Ukraine (Shapoval, Yu., V. Pristaiko and V. Zolotarev, *ChK-GPU-NKVD v Ukraini* [The Cheka-GPU-NKVD in the Ukraine] [Kiev, 1997], 47–48, 436).

· 58 ·

Stalin to Kaganovich
12 August

F. 81, op. 3, d. 99, ll. 153–155.

Greetings, Comrade Kaganovich:

1. You must have already received my letter about the Ukraine. Please keep the details of the plan set out in my letter secret for the time being.

2. Representatives of the town of Poti, Georgia, are pleading to be given three or four buses. It turns out that Molotov promised them five buses, but could not keep his promise because Moscow (yes, Moscow!) grabbed up (grabbed up!) the entire reserve of buses. Let them have a few.[1]

3. Beria makes a good impression.[2] He is a good organizer, an efficient, capable functionary. As I take a closer look at Transcaucasian affairs, I become increasingly convinced that when it comes to selecting people Sergo is an incorrigible bungler. Sergo pushed Mamulia's candidacy for secretary of the CC of Georgia, but it is now obvious (even to the blind) that Mamulia is not worth Beria's left leg. I think Orakhelashvili will have to be relieved (he keeps asking for this). Although Beria is not a member (and not even a candidate) of the CC, we should nevertheless promote him to first secretary of the Transcaucasian Regional Committee.[3] Polonsky (his candidacy) is the wrong person, since he doesn't speak any of the local languages.

Regards.

12 August 1932. I. Stalin.

1. See note 7 to document 59.

2. On 13 July 1932 Beria wrote Kaganovich: "I went to see Comrade Koba twice and had a chance to inform him in detail about what we are doing" (RGASPI, f. 17, op. 120, d. 75, l. 15).

3. On 9 October 1932 the Politburo satisfied "the request of Comrade Orakhelashvili to be relieved of the duties of first secretary of the Trancaucasian Regional Committee" and named Beria as first secretary while keeping him as first secretary of the CC of the Georgian Communist Party (ibid., op. 3, d. 903, l. 8). See also documents 36, 37.

· 59 ·

Kaganovich to Stalin
16 August

F. 558, op. 11, d. 740, ll. 153–160.

---

16 August [1932]
Greetings dear Comrade Stalin!

1) We felt that it would be better to decide issues of the reorganization of the PC of Agriculture in your presence. Your program of measures is absolutely correct. The PC of Agriculture has become mired for too long in the initial phase. It is impossible to include such an enormous bulk in a single people's commissariat and in a single tractor center without differentiating it by sectors and crops. I consider especially timely your proposal about Sverdlovka [the Communist Party higher education establishment named after Sverdlov] and communist higher educational institutions in general. The culture and propaganda department is working on this matter right now and by your arrival there will already be specific proposals.[1] If you feel that we can adopt a number of decisions here now, please write us.

2) Regarding the decree and the OGPU letter about fighting profiteers we did as you advised. It will be published around the 23rd, and we sent out Menzhinsky's letter to all CC members.[2] I am now drafting a letter to party and judiciary and punitive organizations—as you wrote—about the last two decrees.[3] It is rather difficult to stay within the framework of just these two decrees. We will have to touch on general issues at least in passing.

3) Regarding Neumann I have passed along your opinion to the Comintern people. They of course completely agree that it is necessary to give Neumann and his group a rap on the knuckles, probably even that they would like to hit them harder.[4]

4) Regarding Ukrainian matters:[5]

a) I completely and fully agree with your assessment of the state of affairs in the Ukraine. The problem is that among some of the active members the issue of grain procurements and their statements that the plan is unfulfillable have grown into a question of their attitude toward party policy. Lack of confidence, a lack of vision, confusion and a formalistic performance of "duty"—these are the main bacilli that are eating away at some of the active members right now and are even having an impact on the leadership *troshki* (a little).[6] The theory that we Ukrainians are innocent victims creates solidarity and a rotten cover-up for one another not only at the middle level but also in the leadership. I believe that regardless even of practical conclusions, the moment has come when the CC of the VKP(b) must officially issue an assessment in a political document and call on the organization to make a decisive turnaround. They are not taking the resolution of their conference seriously, since they consider it partly coerced.

This kind of official political decision by the CC will quickly straighten out a sizable segment of the active membership and would easily facilitate the general improvement of the situation in the Ukraine.

You are also right in linking the issue to the international situation, to Pilsudski's work and the extreme danger of this kind of drifting condition of the party organization and weak ideological militancy, combined with rottenness and a lack of principle. I myself found it pitiful to look at the Ukrainian active members when I was at their conference.

b) As for the question of replacing Kosior, I agree that he has displayed <u>big</u> weaknesses and shortcomings. As the leader of the largest organization in the party he has simplified the task of leadership. Can he be straightened out? It is harder for me to judge than for you. Maybe if we were to take him firmly in [. . .] [illegible—eds.] and give him a tongue-lashing, he might learn some lessons, but of course the situation in the Ukraine right now is so complicated that there is no time for training.

c) Regarding the question of myself I can say the following: having a considerable amount of experience in the distribution and disposition of personnel and in analyzing the state of affairs, I realize that there seems to be no alternative. It will be easier for me, of course, to work on the situation firsthand, because I know the country, the economy, and the people. True the people are no longer the same, when I left them they were different, they have gotten a little worse, I suppose they have changed a lot as a result of the "mild-mannered" and easy-going administration based on the principle "don't insult anyone" and on mutual amnesty. This, by the way, is one of the aspects that are so annoying, again we have to start from scratch with people in the Ukraine! But, Comrade Stalin, you have framed the question so broadly and clearly from the standpoint of the party's interests that there cannot be any serious hesitation. And besides lastly you have not only the official political right, but also the comradely and moral right to direct those you have molded as political leaders, i.e. me, <u>your pupil</u>.

d) Regarding the other possibilities I agree with you, there may be a question of timing, but about that we will talk in person (Grinko for Chubar). In particular right now I feel so worn out physically (desperate headaches) that without a vacation and treatment I will find it hard to take on a big new load.

e) I am also concerned, of course, about Moscow, whom we can put in here, after all quite a lot of tasks have been laid out, but we will talk about that too in person.

f) Evidently, we will also have to think a bit about other functionaries, about fresh blood (at least a little) for the Ukraine.

5) Menzhinsky passed along your letter today. I did not tell anyone, of course, about your letter.

6) Beria came to see me. He does indeed make a good impression as a top-level functionary. We already discussed a number of his questions at today's Politburo meeting, specifically, we reduced [procurements in] Georgia by another 300,000 poods [4,900 tons] of grain and other questions. We will give them buses <u>at Moscow's expense</u>. But Comrade Stalin, we really and truly did not grab too much, we even gave [ourselves] less out of what belongs to Moscow.[7]

Well permit me to close here.

I leave you with a firm handshake. Yours, L. Kaganovich.

Regards to Comrade Molotov.

1. See document 55.

2. See note 3 to document 52.

3. See note 1 to document 57.

4. Neumann and his supporters were fighting against the German party leadership headed by Thälmann. In April and May 1932 the leadership of the Comintern Executive Committee denounced Neumann's group as factional and sectarian. On 8 August Stalin in a letter to Kaganovich wrote about Neumann "It is clear that he has a group and is undertaking factional work. He must be brought to account. As a first step, in my opinion, this should be limited to a serious warning, and depriving him of candidate membership of the [German] Politburo" (RGASPI, f. 558, op. 11, d. 99, ll. 139–142). In the summer of 1932 Neumann took a vacation in Sochi, where he had meetings with Stalin. In the summer and fall of 1932 Neumann came under fresh criticism and was denounced once and for all as a factionalist. (M. Buber-Neumann, *Mirovaia revoliutsiia i stalinskii rezhim* [World Revolution and the Stalin Regime], ed. A. Vatlin [Moscow, 1995], 7, 161–62.) See document 53.

5. See document 57 and the introduction to this chapter.

6. *Troshki*—a little (Ukrainian).

7. See document 58. On 16 August 1932 the Politburo at its meeting considered questions raised by Beria, including proposals to reduce the grain-procurements plan for Transcaucasia, grant Georgia a seed loan, and allocate motor vehicles (RGASPI, f. 17, op. 3, d. 896, l. 9; op. 162, d. 13, l. 62). On 13 August the Politburo decided to allocate to Georgia in the third quarter 10 buses, 10 Ford cars, and eight trucks (ibid., d. 897, l. 21).

1933

Introduction

ACCORDING to Stalin's appointment book, he was absent from his desk in the Kremlin from 17 August to 4 November.[1] On 18 August he traveled to Sochi in the south together with Voroshilov. The journey took seven days. Stalin visited several regions of the country by train, ship, and motor car. Voroshilov wrote about the journey in a letter to Yenukidze: "new ideas came up and specific decisions were made on the spot. Koba [Stalin] absorbed everything like a sponge, thought it over, and immediately proposed a number of decisions."[2] The result of this journey was a series of instructions which Stalin sent to Kaganovich and the other members of the Politburo in Moscow; the topics included the transport of oil on the Volga and the construction of a bridge across it (see document 61).

Stalin's vacation in 1933 was relatively untroubled. The worst of the social and economic crisis was over, although the consequences of the famine, which had resulted in the deaths of millions of people, continued to be felt. We do not yet have a complete picture of the way the famine was overcome. But it is evident that in a number of regions serious food problems continued even after the peak of the famine in 1932–33 was past. In the closing months of 1933 problems of epidemic diseases, including typhus and malaria, were on the agenda of the

1. *Istoricheskii arkhiv,* no. 2, 1995, 188–93. The Politburo did not take the formal decision that Stalin should be granted leave for six weeks until 20 August—i.e. after he had already left Moscow (RGASPI, f. 17, op. 162. d. 15, l. 46).
2. RGASPI, f. 667, op. 1, d. 16, l. 9 (letter dated 27 August 1933).

Politburo. The peak of a typhus epidemic was reached in 1933, when more than 870,000 cases were registered as compared with 233,000 in 1932 and 437,000 in 1934.[3] But in spite of all difficulties the spring sowing was reasonably satisfactory, and the 1933 grain harvest was greater than in the previous two years. This made it possible to increase substantially the supply of bread and flour to the towns. The last few months of 1933 also saw an increase in foodstuffs supplied by the peasants to the collective farm market; the improved situation was reflected in the decline of market prices for food.

The greater stability of the situation in the countryside facilitated the abatement of the level of repression. During the period of famine and extreme pressure for the grain procurements the terror was conducted against the peasants on a huge scale. Following the usual pattern, the mechanism of repression acquired its own inertia. Arrests continued to be made on a mass scale, without specific authorization, by such officials as heads of collective farms, heads of village and district soviets, plenipotentiaries of different kinds, and secretaries of party cells. As a result the prisons and interrogation points were vastly overcrowded; the typhus epidemic started in these places. The absence of a legal foundation for the social order and the arbitrariness of local officials threatened to undermine the regime. The government, while continuing repression, sought to control the terror and bring about a gradual rapprochement with the population, particularly the peasantry. On 7 May 1933 the Politburo adopted a decision which forbade the triumvirates of the OGPU in republics and in regions (except the Far Eastern Region) to impose "the supreme penalty" (i.e. the death sentence).[4] On the following day, 8 May, the Politburo approved the famous instruction to party and soviet officials, OGPU bodies, the courts, and the prosecutor's office. This banned the mass exile of peasants: henceforth exile should be imposed only on an individual basis, only for active "counterrevolutionaries," and below a limit of 12,000 households in the whole of the USSR. The instruction also forbade persons not entitled to do so by law to make arrests, and banned the practice of imprisoning people before trial in the case of "minor crimes." The total number of persons to be confined in the prisons of the People's Commissariat of Justice, the OGPU, and the Chief Administra-

3. GARF, f. R-5446, op. 26, d. 81, l. 115.
4. *Stalinskoe Politburo v 30-e gody: Sbornik dokumentov*, ed. O. V. Khlevniuk, A.V. Kvashonkin, L. P. Kosheleva, and L. A. Rogovaya (Moscow, 1995), 63; the decision was approved by poll.

tion of the Militia (the civilian police) was fixed at 400,000 as compared with the 800,000 actually in prison when the instruction was adopted; this figure excluded those in camps and colonies. The instruction also provided that in the case of sentences of up to three years imposed by the courts deprivation of freedom should be replaced by compulsory work for up to one year, the rest of the sentence being suspended.[5]

There was also a definite degree of stabilization and even growth in industry. Beginning in the April–June quarter of 1933 the performance of heavy industry, including the crucial iron and steel and coal industries, considerably improved. According to official statistics, production in December 1933 was 12 percent greater than in December 1932 and exceeded the low point of January 1933 by as much as 35 percent.[6] The confidential Annual Report of the British Foreign Office for 1933 stated that "there seems to be a certain justification, in the light of the progress made in the basic industries in the closing months, for the increasing optimism with which the authorities regard the future."[7]

Another reason for confidence in the economic situation was that the severe restrictions imposed on state expenditure from the end of 1932 succeeded in bringing about financial stability. Currency in circulation declined by 19 percent between 1 January and 1 July, and did not increase during the rest of the year. And in every quarter of 1933 exports exceeded imports; a deficit of 135 million rubles in 1932 gave way to a surplus of 148 million rubles in 1933.

It is not surprising, therefore, that Stalin's letters of August–October 1933 do not display the anxiety and nervousness which characterized the letters of the previous two years. He was firmly committed—for the moment—to a more moderate rate of investment and industrial growth. In a letter to Molotov dated 12 September, Stalin accepted the proposal, which came from Gosplan via Kuibyshev and Molotov, that capital investment in 1934 should not exceed 21 billion rubles, and that the rate of growth of industrial production should not exceed 15 percent: "this will be for the best," he wrote.[8]

---

5. RGASPI, f. 17. op. 3, d. 922, ll. 58, 58ob. The instruction of 8 May has long been known to historians from the copy in the Smolensk archive (see M. Fainsod, *Smolensk Under Soviet Rule* [1958; rpt. Boston, 1989], 185–88).

6. *Tyazhelaya promyshlennost' SSSR ot XVI k XVII s"ezdu VKP(b)* (Moscow, 1934), 7.

7. *British Documents on Foreign Affairs*, series IIA, vol. XVII (1992), 51.

8. *Stalin's Letters to Molotov*, ed. Lars T. Lih, Oleg V. Naumov, and Oleg V. Khlevniuk (New Haven, 1995), 234.

If Stalin's brief references to the grain procurements in these letters are representative, he was also far more relaxed about the struggle for grain than in 1931 or 1932. On 13 September (document 68) he agreed to a reduction in grain deliveries in the case of those Moscow collective farms where the harvest was lower; on 24 September (document 74) he agreed without question to a similar reduction for the Volga regions, the Urals, and Kazakhstan. Only one paragraph, written on 28 September (document 75), called in general terms for immediate pressure to secure the grain.

Perhaps the most striking feature of Stalin's 1933 letters is the relative *absence* of major economic issues as compared with the previous two years. Instead he dealt with secondary questions—what had been known in Soviet planning circles ever since the civil war as the "vermicelli" of planning. But all Stalin's proposals and strictures on these apparently minor and casual matters were directed toward the increased centralization of authority. In this context Stalin, as in the previous period, clashed with his colleagues in the Politburo who expressed powerful departmental interests. The correspondence in 1933 provides information on several such conflicts. The most significant concerned the supply of combine-harvesters in an incomplete state.

At the end of July 1933 several telegrams were sent from various regions to Molotov in Sovnarkom complaining that the Zaporozhe factory Communard was dispatching new combine-harvesters without a number of essential components.[9] On 28 July, in view of these complaints, Sovnarkom adopted a decree "On the Criminal Dispatch of Incomplete Combine-Harvesters to MTS and State Farms." Sovnarkom required the People's Commissariat of Heavy Industry to cease immediately the dispatch of incomplete combine-harvesters and to furnish the incomplete harvesters already dispatched with the missing parts. It also instructed Akulov, Prosecutor of the USSR, to arrest immediately the managers responsible for the dispatch of incomplete harvesters and put them on trial.[10] This decision led to protests. Khataevich, secretary of the Dnepropetrovsk Regional Committee of the party, sent a special letter addressed to Sovnarkom of the USSR, the Central Committee of the Ukrainian party, and the Prosecutors of both the USSR and Ukraine. He claimed that Communard was working well, and that the incomplete delivery was undertaken in order to pre-

9. GARF, f. R-5446, op. 82, d. 26, ll. 34–36.
10. Ibid. l. 37; the decree was adopted by poll.

vent the theft of components—certain sections of the harvesters were transported separately in special containers. He added: "In general the factory has more successes than failures. In this light the regional committee would consider it expedient not [. . .] to undertake a criminal investigation against the management of the factory."[11] After receiving this letter Molotov wrote to Khataevich: "We are well aware of the achievements of Communard, and so is the prosecutor. This will be borne in mind by the court. This trial is certainly not merely significant just for the factory itself, and to cancel it is entirely inexpedient."[12]

The hearing of the case in the criminal and legal collegium of the Supreme Court of the USSR began on 16 August 1933; criminal charges were brought against officials from several parts of the economic administration and against the managers of Communard.[13] Vyshinsky, Deputy Prosecutor of the USSR, was the prosecutor. His final address, which was published in the press, included the statement "The trial gives us grounds for raising general questions of the work of Soviet economic organizations. [. . .] I refer to the People's Commissariat of Agriculture. [. . .] I refer to the People's Commissariat of Heavy Industry. [. . .] I refer to the republican authorities."[14]

This treatment of the issue angered Ordzhonikidze and Yakovlev, the people's commissars for heavy industry and agriculture. On 24 August in Stalin's absence Ordzhonikidze raised the question for discussion at a sitting of the Politburo. Some points about the discussion are known from the letters of the participants. Kaganovich wrote to Stalin that it emerged at the Politburo that Molotov had arranged both the publication in *Pravda* and the holding of the trial itself (document 60). Molotov gave his own account of these events in a letter to Stalin:

> At the meeting in the Central Committee [i.e. the Politburo meeting] Kaganovich, Kalinin, Ordzhonikidze, Yakovlev, and Vyshinsky were present as well as myself. You know Kalinin's attitude toward these matters—he is always "in favor of the economic leaders," "insulted" by the court and the Workers' and Peasants' Inspectorate, even more so in the present case. Pressed by Ordzhonikidze, Vyshinsky immediately stated that he had made a glaring error, and was generally obsequious. Personal attacks were made on me of a most repugnant kind by Ordzhonikidze, who said that I set this all up, behind the back of

11. Ibid. ll. 18–20.
12. Ibid. ll. 21–22.
13. *Pravda*, 17 August 1933.
14. *Pravda*, 23 August 1933.

the Central Committee, that it was impossible to work with M. [Molotov] and so on. [. . .] In spite of this, and in spite of the fact that Kaganovich tacitly agreed with Ordzhonikidze, I did not give way.[15]

At its sitting on 24 August the Politburo adopted a decision by correspondence condemning the wording (*formulirovka*) of Vyshinsky's speech "which provides a pretext for incorrect accusations against the People's Commissariat of Heavy Industry and the People's Commissariat of Agriculture." The draft of the decision was written by Kaganovich and edited by Molotov. All the members of the Politburo who were present voted for the decision—Kaganovich, Molotov, Kalinin, and Ordzhonikidze.[16]

Having learned of this decision, Stalin sent a telegram to Moscow on 29 August addressed to Kaganovich, Molotov, and Ordzhonikidze, and copied to all the other members of the Politburo: "I learned from Kaganovich's letter that you have found incorrect one point in Vyshinsky's speech, where he refers to the responsibility of the people's commissars for the dispatch and acceptance of incomplete output. I consider this decision incorrect and harmful. The dispatch and acceptance of incomplete output is the crudest of violations of Central Committee decisions, and people's commissars are also bound to be held responsible for a thing of this kind. It is lamentable that Kaganovich and Molotov were unable to stand up against the bureaucratic assault from the People's Commissariat of Heavy Industry."[17] Although Stalin's telegram reached the Central Committee at about 6 P.M. on 29 August, the decision to cancel the condemnation of Vyshinsky was taken by a personal vote only three days later, on 1 September. Kaganovich, Andreev, Kuibyshev, and Mikoian signed the new decision.[18] With the exception of Kaganovich, these were those members of the Politburo who were not involved in the adoption of the previous decision. By a Politburo decision Ordzhonikidze, against whom the reexamination of the matter was implicitly directed, departed on vacation on 1 September. Apparently Kaganovich deliberately delayed the discussion so as not to put Ordzhonikidze in an embarrassing position.

Stalin undoubtedly sensed the tension in the Politburo which resulted from this conflict and decided to use this incident to educate his

---

15. RGASPI, f. 558, op. 11, d. 769, l. 128 (dated 8 September).
16. Ibid., f. 17, op. 163, d. 989, l. 165.
17. Ibid., f. 558, op. 11, d. 80, l. 49.
18. Ibid., f. 17, op. 163, d. 990, l. 70.

colleagues. Although the matter was apparently closed, Stalin returned to it on several occasions in his letters to Kaganovich and Molotov. A week after the decision to reprove Vyshinsky was canceled, Kaganovich had again to justify his behavior (document 65). Then on 12 September Stalin again returned to the question in a letter to Molotov: "The behavior of Sergo [Ordzhonikidze] (and Yakovlev) in the affair concerning 'production with full equipment' can only be characterized as 'antiparty,' since their objective is to defend reactionary party elements against the Central Committee. [. . .] I wrote Kaganovich to express my surprise that he turned out to be in the camp of the reactionary elements in the party."[19]

The conflict about the incomplete harvesters reveals many hidden springs in the relations between members of the Politburo, and in their relative power. As well as showing that Stalin's influence in the Politburo was predominant it also demonstrates that in this period some members of the Politburo had a definite authority and a right to vote in decisions about quite important problems.

As in previous years, in 1933 Stalin's correspondence with his colleagues devoted considerable attention to questions of foreign relations. The autumn of 1933 was a relatively calm period. The letters show that the Soviet leadership was taking a circumspect attitude toward the unfolding of events in Europe. Hitler's growing power did not lead Stalin to make any substantial comments or suggestions. And Kaganovich, who undoubtedly knew Stalin's attitude, remarked that the fascist rulers had been compelled "to 'soften' their attitude toward the USSR" (document 70). He also reported to Stalin that he had instructed the press to deal with the question of the Reichstag fire trial, which began in Leipzig on 21 September 1933, without getting "too artificially worked up" (document 73).

A significant incident in October 1933 illustrates Stalin's wish to avoid an open breach with Germany. Krestinsky was in Vienna for a cure, and Hitler indicated that he was willing to receive him in Berlin. Litvinov argued that this visit would be "unnecessary and even inconvenient," but Kaganovich and Molotov, in a cipher to Stalin on 14 October, stated that "we consider it inexpedient to emphasize the deterioration of our relations with Germany, and think that Krestinsky should go to Berlin and visit Hitler." Stalin concurred.[20] However, at

19. *Stalin's Letters to Molotov,* 234.
20. RGASPI, f. 558, op. 11, d. 81, l. 141.

this point Germany withdrew from the League of Nations, and on 16 October, in a further cipher to Stalin Kaganovich and Molotov stated that "in our opinion, the question of the visit of Krestinsky to Berlin must be dropped."[21] On the same day Stalin replied indignantly in a cipher: "Why should we be concerned with the League of Nations? Why must we demonstrate in honor of the insulted League and against Germany which is insulting it? Perhaps not all the circumstances are known? We learned of Germany leaving the League only from your cipher."[22] But Krestinsky's meeting with Hitler did not take place.[23]

The attitude toward events in the Far East was different. In previous years, the Soviet leadership, extremely alarmed by the Japanese threat, tried on the one hand to play the diplomatic game carefully and cautiously, and on the other hand to increase its military presence in the Far Eastern Region. In the course of 1933, on the basis of their common fear of the role of Japan in the Far East, the beginnings of a rapprochement between the Soviet Union and the United States, already evident in the correspondence of 1932, were greatly strengthened when the new president, Roosevelt, took office. This culminated in the diplomatic recognition of the Soviet Union by the United States after the visit in November by Litvinov, people's commissar of foreign affairs. The greater stability of the internal situation, the success of the military preparations, and the improved relations with the United States all enabled the Soviet Union in the autumn of 1933 to go from appeasement of Japan to a more active role.[24] This was reflected in Stalin's letters to Kaganovich.

On 26 June 1933, as a concession to Japan, negotiations began in Tokyo about the sale of the Chinese Eastern Railroad, which belonged to the USSR. At the negotiations the delegation from Manchukuo (Japanese-occupied Manchuria) disputed the Soviet right of ownership to the railway and proposed its sale at one-tenth of the price demanded by the Soviet government. The Soviet delegation rejected these proposals.[25] The Japanese decided to use force. On 19 September the Japanese ambassador in Manchukuo was informed that it had

21. Ibid., l. 144.
22. Ibid., ll. 144, 144ob.
23. See J. Haslam, *The Soviet Union and the Struggle for Collective Security in Europe, 1933–39* (Basingstoke and London and Basingstoke, 1984), 25–26.
24. See J. Haslam, *The Soviet Union and the Threat from the East, 1933–1941* (Basingstoke and London and Basingstoke, 1992), 22–24.
25. *Dokumenty vneshnei politiki*, vol. XVI (Moscow, 1970), pp. 837–88.

been decided to arrest a group of Soviet employees on the railway. The Soviet leadership learned about this by deciphering the Japanese codes. The People's Commissariat of Foreign Affairs prepared a draft declaration which stated that the Soviet government had acquired information about the intended action of the Manchurian authorities against the Soviet personnel on the railways. The first draft of the document was prepared in fairly mild terms. Kaganovich, who evidently was taking into account Stalin's caution in relation to Japan in the preceding period, particularly emphasized in his letter the mildness of the draft reply (document 69). On this occasion, however, Stalin decided to be firm, and required a sharp paragraph to be included in the text about Japanese responsibility for violating treaties and for preparing the seizure of the railway (document 71). On 20 September 1933 Stalin's version was approved by the Politburo.[26] Stalin's corrections to the September declaration reflected the substantial change which had taken place in the position of the Soviet leadership in relation to Japan.

Following these events, on 24 October, in preparation for the negotiations between Roosevelt and Litvinov, Stalin instructed Molotov and Kaganovich that "if in conversation with Litvinov Roosevelt asks for some rapprochement with us or even a temporary agreement against Japan, Litvinov must take a favorable attitude."[27]

Soon after the diplomatic recognition of the USSR by the United States, the Soviet Union also decided that it was possible to take a firmer attitude toward Germany. At the end of November, after Stalin's return from vacation, the Thirteenth Plenum of the Executive Committee of the Communist International, in a published statement, declared that the fascist government in Germany was "the principal instigator of war in Europe."[28] Then on 19 December the Politburo resolved that the USSR should join the League of Nations on certain conditions, and that it should aim at a regional agreement, within the framework of the League, with France and Poland, and with other European powers, "for mutual defense from aggression on the part of Germany."[29]

The correspondence for 1933 shows that Kaganovich continued in

26. RGASPI, f. 17, op. 162, d. 15, ll. 81–82.

27. Ibid., f. 558, op. 11, d. 82, ll. 44, 440b. This decision was incorporated in a Politburo decision on the following day (ibid., f. 17, op. 162, d. 15, l. 119).

28. See E. H. Carr, *The Twilight of Comintern, 1930–1935* (Basingstoke and London, 1982), 105–20.

29. RGASPI, f. 17, op. 162, d. 15, ll. 154–55 (decision by poll).

his role of executor of Stalin's instructions—an executor who exercised a marked degree of initiative. In addition to his numerous obligations in the Politburo and the Moscow party organization, Kaganovich received a further important post in 1933. On 18 August a special commission on railway transport was established to regulate the railway system, consisting of Molotov (chairman), Stalin, Kaganovich, Voroshilov, Andreev (the people's commissar of transport), Ordzhonikidze, and Blagonravov. On 20 August Kaganovich was appointed deputy chairman of the commission.[30] He was thus made responsible for the numerous problems of one of the most complex and difficult sectors of the economy. On 26 August Kaganovich informed Stalin in detail about the first sitting of the new commission (document 60). Henceforth information about the work of the railways regularly found its place in Kaganovich's letters. Moreover, when the Politburo approved Stalin's leave on vacation on 20 August, it resolved that "during Comrade Stalin's vacation Comrade Kaganovich shall be confirmed as his substitute in the Commission on Defense."[31] In his letters Kaganovich also reported to Stalin about the work of this most important commission, and about major questions of military production raised by Stalin.

Documents 60–85

· 60 ·

Kaganovich to Stalin
26 August
F. 558, op. 11, d. 741, ll. 7–12. Typewritten.

26 August [1933]
Greetings dear Comrade Stalin.

1) We decided to send you the material and proposals on the CER [Chinese Eastern Railroad] matters by airplane rather than in a long cipher. We discussed it for quite a long time, but it is most reliable to send it to you, which is what we are doing.[1]

2) We held the first meeting of the transport commission. We took as the

---

30. *Stalinskoe Politbustro v 30-e gody,* 69.
31. RGASPI, f. 17, op. 162, d. 15, l. 46. A similar decision was taken, on Stalin's proposal, on 4 June 1932 (ibid., f. 558, op.11, d. 77, l. 4)

first item a report on the implementation of the decisions of the CC and Sovnarkom. Although the report was easygoing, as usual, it became clear from the subsequent speeches by Kishkin, Zemliachka and others that the implementation of the CC decisions is proceeding in an obviously unsatisfactory manner. The administration is being restructured in form and in terms of statistics, but first, it is taking a long time, and second, it has not brought about a substantive improvement in the work. The average daily shipment, for example, was lower in July than it was in June. The shipping of grain has been sluggish, although it has picked up in the last few days. There have been a number of instances of sharp resistance to implementation of the decisions of the CC and Sovnarkom, and the struggle is inadequate. The political departments are not yet affecting things, either.[2] We have deemed the work to implement the decisions of the CC and Sovnarkom unsatisfactory and have decided to summon two railroads to the commission—the Kursk and the Yekaterininskaia, for which we will adopt specific decisions.[3] In a few days we will review the entire freight plan so as to send railroad cars to transport the most essential things, above all grain, coal, and ore.[4]

3) With regard to the matter of the shipment of incomplete combines, we had to convene and discuss the issue, not without an acrimonious debate. The trouble was that in Vyshinsky's speech, in the last paragraph of the section "Discipline, Recordkeeping, and Oversight," he gave a broad "hint" pointing the finger not only at the PC of Heavy Industry and the PC of Agriculture but also at the individuals who head them. Comrade Sergo sent in a protest and requested a discussion of the issue. It turned out during the discussion that Comrade Molotov had read this before it was printed in *Pravda* and that Akulov had consulted with him several times during the process. This makes the nature of the discussion understandable, although both tried to show restraint.

We adopted a resolution in which we deemed this section of Comrade Vyshinsky's speech to be incorrect.[5]

4) Now we are working on the issue of warehouses. The main thing is to mobilize additional warehouses, specifically, the textile factories have big cotton warehouses that are largely vacant, we are thinking of putting them to use and so forth. At the next Politburo meeting, which we will convene on the 29th instead of the 25th,[6] we have put down this issue on the agenda and will take practical measures, as you instructed before you left.[7]

5) Comrades Kosior and Postyshev sent in a telegram in which they ask that we speed up the appointment of a secretary for the Donets Basin. I am sending it to you. What should we do?[8]

I am very glad that you had a good trip. Regards to you. Yours, L. Kaganovich.

Regards to Comrade Voroshilov.

26 August

1. See note 1 to document 62.

2. Political departments were established in railroad transport on the basis of a CC resolution dated 10 July 1933 (*KPSS v rezoliutsiiakh* . . . [The CPSU in Resolutions . . .], vol. 6, pp. 80–84).

3. See note 8 to document 70.

4. On 29 August the Politburo adopted a decision on the freight plan for September 1933, which gave top priority to shipments of refractories, fluxes, ores, oil, coke, and coal (RGASPI, f. 17, op. 3, d. 929, l. 6).

5. See documents 62, 64, and 65 and the introduction to this chapter.

6. On 21 August the Politburo postponed its meeting from 25 to 29 August (*Stalinskoe Politbiuro v 30-e gody*, p. 229).

7. See note 5 to document 64.

8. See note 7 to document 64.

· 61 ·

Stalin to Kaganovich (for the members of the Politburo)

27 August

F. 81, op. 3, d. 100, ll. 9–12.

27 August 1933

Greetings, Comrade <u>Kaganovich:</u>

(Show this letter to Comrade Molotov and the other comrades.)

1) I received the response from the three regarding oil shipments along the Volga. It is not a persuasive response. It was clearly drawn up by "smooth operators" at the PC of Heavy Industry or at Gosplan, and out of habit you slapped your signature on it.[1]

If more oil is being produced in Baku this year than last year, exports have been reduced and domestic consumption increased—why are we bringing out less along the Volga than last year? You failed to explain this.

2) I consider it our common crime that the Volga bridge at Nizhny Novgorod is being built for a <u>single track</u>. In about six to eight years, when the Gorky auto plant is expanded and freight traffic increases severalfold, the Moscow—Nizhny Novgorod—Perm railroad line, which runs across this bridge, will literally be slashed, and we will have to build a new bridge helter-skelter. Who needs that? Can one really build large railroad bridges with the intention of having them last for three or four years, <u>rather than 50 to 100 years</u>? Is it truly so hard to grasp that we cannot build such bridges every three or four years? We cannot delegate such issues to the PC of Transport, which cannot see anything beyond its nose. Where is Gosplan, why isn't it raising the issue or sounding the alarm?

I propose that: <u>measures be taken without delay to reconfigure the bridge for two tracks</u> (by building parallel piers or something else).[2]

<u>I will wait for a reply</u>.

3) Who approves for us (which institution) the width and depth of locks in canals, dams, and hydroelectric stations? I am afraid that bunglers (or covert enemies) will get us into a mess with the locks, make them a weak point, and ruin things. Could you report to me (as soon as possible) the projects or resolutions of the appropriate institutions about the dimensions of locks for the Moscow-Volga Canal and the hydroelectric stations under construction on the upper Volga (Yaroslavl, Nizhny Novgorod, Perm). I consider this issue important (the viability of the canals and rivers depends on the dimensions of the locks).[3]

<u>I will wait for a reply</u>.

4) I am afraid that the practical part of the decision on the <u>resettlement</u> committee will get mired in the maze of the bureaucracies just like the decisions on higher technical educational institutions and factory and plant schools. <u>I propose that</u>: the <u>personnel</u> of the resettlement committee be approved <u>without delay</u> and that it be given an <u>operational</u> assignment, also <u>without delay</u>, such as arranging a resettlement by the beginning of next year to the Kuban and the Terek (say, 10,000 heads of households and their families) and to the Ukraine (the steppe, 15,000–20,000). This is an issue of manpower in the south, where there has always been a shortage of workers. Please hurry up with this task.[4]

I will wait for a reply.

Well, that is all for now. <u>Best wishes to you</u>. I. Stalin.

<u>Comrades Kaganovich and Molotov</u>:

I regard Yurkin's "order" to remove Kosko as a disgrace to us. We are removing him (Kosko) not because he is ill but <u>for poor work</u>. That is what should be stated honestly and openly in the "order," rather than trot out <u>a dirty bourgeois, diplomatic lie about Kosko's "state of health."</u>

Yurkin's order <u>must be revoked</u> because it is false and harmful and impairs the proper training of cadres.

Another "order" must be issued from the CC of the VKP(b).

Both of them are to be published.[5]

I. St.

---

1. On 19 August 1933 Stalin and Voroshilov sent Molotov, Kaganovich, and Ord-zhonikidze a telegram that said: "According to a report from Zhdanov, the Volga is supposed to transport 7.5 million tons of Baku oil during the navigation season under the plan, yet on a month-by-month basis it is transporting not only about 20 percent less than the plan, but about 15 percent less than last year. The reason for the lag is ostensibly that there is no oil in Baku. But that is unbelievable, because there is nonetheless more oil in Baku this year than last year. I am afraid that a significant portion of the oil that is designated for the Volga is being transported in tank cars. [. . .] Call in Zhdanov, clear up the situation, verify Zhdanov's report, and put an end to the disgraceful goings-on" (RGASPI, f. 81, op. 3, d. 101, l. 18). In

a cipher in response, dated 22 August, Kaganovich, Molotov, and Ordzhonikidze reported that the reason for the situation was mostly that stocks were low and oil production was lagging, especially in Grozny (ibid., f. 558, op. 11, d. 80, ll. 17–18). On 30 August, in response to Stalin's further complaint, Kaganovich presented more elaborately in a letter the information that in 1933 stocks were lower and production in Grozny was much lower than in the previous year (ibid., d. 741, ll. 13–19).

2. See note 4 to document 64.

3. See note 9 to document 70.

4. See note 1 to document 77.

5. G. K. Kosko was approved as director of the Gigant [Giant] grain-growing state farm at the request of the PC of Agriculture by a decision of the Secretariat of the CC of the VKP(b) on 4 October 1931 (ibid., f. 17, op. 114, d. 264, l. 12). On 31 August, by means of a poll, the Politburo revoked the order of people's commissar of state farms Yurkin to remove Gigant state-farm director Kosko for health reasons "because it covered up the real reason for the removal of Comrade Kosko from his post and thereby impairs the proper training of cadres." A Politburo resolution removed Kosko "because he failed to cope with the tasks entrusted to him by the party and the government" (ibid., op. 3, d. 930, l. 9). On 1 September this decision was published in the newspapers.

· 62 ·

Stalin to Kaganovich
[29 August]

F. 81, op. 3, d. 100, ll. 107–108.

<u>Comrade Kaganovich:</u>

1) I did not find Sokolnikov's "second" directive on the CER [Chinese Eastern Railroad] among the papers. As for the two versions of a response for our delegation in Tokyo, we endorsed your version.[1]

2) I have no objections to Sokolnikov's directives on the conversion rate.[2]

3) It is deplorable and dangerous that you (and Molotov) failed to curb Sergo's bureaucratic impulses with regard to incomplete combine-harvesters and sacrificed Vyshinsky to them. If you are going to train cadres this way, you will not have a single honest member left in the party. It's an outrage. . . .[3]

I. Stalin.

1. The reference is to negotiations in Tokyo on the sale of the CER and negotiations in Harbin regarding the management of the railroad. In Harbin the Manchurian side, in particular, demanded that the authority of the Manchurian assistant manager of the railroad be made equal to that of the Soviet manager. On 1 September 1933 the Politburo resolved to send, on behalf of the PC of Foreign Affairs, a directive to the Soviet delegation in Harbin instructing that the assistant manager's rights be increased, but in such a manner that the Soviet manager's undivided authority over operational issues be preserved (RGASPI, f. 17, op. 162, d. 15, l. 54). On 29 August the Politburo approved a directive by the PC of Foreign Affairs to the Soviet delegation in the negotiations over the sale of the CER, which stated: "You

should not try to persuade the Manchurians to postpone breaking off the negotiations, thereby putting yourselves in the position of the side that is intimidated by a rupture and susceptible to blackmail. Respond to Ohashi's threats to break off the negotiations by saying that you place the entire responsibility for a rupture on the Manchurian delegation" (ibid., l. 51) By all indications, Stalin was alluding to these directives. See also document 60.

2. Stalin is referring to the conversion rate from gold rubles to paper yen to be used in determining the price of the CER (see DVP, vol. XVI, p. 837). According to Sokolnikov the Japanese hoped to treat the gold ruble as equivalent to a paper ruble (see ibid., f. 558, op. 11, d. 80, ll. 51–52).

3. See documents 60, 64, and 65, and the introduction to this chapter.

· 63 ·

Stalin to Kaganovich
1 September

F. 81, op. 3, d. 100, ll. 14–16.

To Comrade Kaganovich.

1) What happened to the decisions on higher technical educational institutions and factory and plant schools? Did they get buried?[1]

2) What happened to the decision on the earnings of playwrights? Isn't it time to put it into final form and print it (in the name of the AUCCTU and the CC)? It would be a good idea to "toughen" it even more.[2]

3) There are reports in the newspapers that Afinogenov's play *Lozh* [The Lie] will be staged during the coming season. Nothing doing. Look over the final version of the play, and if it is unsuitable, I advise banning its production. Don't let Afinogenov and Co. think they can avoid taking the party into account.[3]

4) Why is *Pravda* keeping quiet about Nizhny Novgorod's <u>overfulfillment</u> of the July–August plan for grain deliveries? What is the problem? Bear in mind that Moscow and you will be blamed for this silence, which is unworthy of the party. This must be ended without delay.[4]

Well, that is all for now.

Regards.

1 September 1933   I. Stalin

1. See document 67.

2. See document 68.

3. In April 1933 the playwright Afinogenov sent Stalin *The Lie*. "I will be happy to get any instructions from you, any marginal note, if you find it deserving of attention. In Moscow, Moscow Art Theaters 1 and 2 want to stage it concurrently. I would appreciate hearing your opinion about this point as well," wrote Afinogenov. Stalin's response was negative. After making a large number of critical comments, Stalin wrote: "The play may not be released in this form" (RGASPI, f. 558, op. 1, d. 5088, ll. 1, 121–121ob). On 9 November Afinogenov sent another letter to Stalin: "Comrade Kirshon passed along the message to me that you remained dissatisfied with the second version of the play *The Ivanov Family* (*The*

Lie). Before the play is canceled, I would like to show you the results of the work on it by Moscow Art Theaters 1 and 2 (in the first few days of December). If, however, you find this superfluous, I will immediately cancel the play myself." On 10 November Stalin wrote in a resolution on Afinogenov's letter: "Comrade Afinogenov: I consider the second version of the play to be unsuccessful" (ibid., d. 5087, l.1).

4. On 4 September 1933 *Pravda* published on the front page a telegram from Zhdanov, secretary of the Gorky (Nizhny Novgorod) Regional Committee of the VKP(b), addressed to Stalin and Molotov, which reported that the region had fulfilled the September plan for grain procurements to a level of 106 percent, ahead of schedule, by 1 September.

· 64 ·

Kaganovich to Stalin
2 September

F. 558, op. 11, d. 741, ll. 20–26.

---

2 September [1933]
Greetings dear Comrade Stalin!

1. I received your letter. I have already reported to you by wire that we canceled the resolution on Vyshinsky's speech. The situation with our resolution really did turn out awkwardly. The way it comes out, the prosecutor's office is just starting to get into gear, and we punch it in the nose. That is why you are right in criticizing us.[1] Regarding all the other issues everything has been done, to be specific, we have met the needs of the state horse-breeding farms in accordance with your proposal.[2]

2. Regarding the locks of the Central Volga Canal construction project, Comrade Sergo sent in a report making it clear that they set the same size for the locks—a width of 20 meters, a length of 300 meters, a height of 4 meters, that is roughly the dimensions of the locks of the Mariinsk system. For Volga-Moscow, as I wrote, the width comes out the same, but the length is shorter. I am sending you this report, but I think it is inadequate. The technical specifications will have to be officially discussed and approved either in the Council of Labor and Defense or in the Politburo.[3]

As for the bridge, the question of widening the bridge is being studied at the PC of Transport, in accordance with your assignment, but yesterday I was informed that the PC of Transport staff believes that widening the bridge could jeopardize the bridge already built, but Comrade Andreev has promised to work on the question and report at the next Politburo meeting.[4]

3. Regarding grain procurements this five-day period has yielded a new increase. A total of about 130 million poods [2,129,000 tons] was procured. Right now the main limitation is grain storage—warehouses. Most of our organizations have not prepared themselves for this task. Now we have devised and adopted a number of specific measures. It is planned to

make additional use of warehouse capacity in procurement districts (granaries and storehouses) in the amount of 63 million poods [1,032,000 tons]. The leaders have been made personally responsible for finding this capacity no later than 10 September. There are plans to deliver enough to consumption centers to meet the needs of mills for a year, to this end the industrial regions have been required to find capacities at factory and other warehouses to store 54 million poods [885,000 tons].[5]

We also adopted a number of measures with regard to improving the packing [*buntirovanie*] of grain and speeding up the receiving and safeguarding of grain. I am sending you these resolutions.

The winter sowing is proceeding fairly well. As of 25 August 7,697,000 hectares had been sown, as opposed to 2,780,000 hectares as of the same date last year.

4. The PC of Heavy Industry has requested that we consider the question of ordering a continuous rolling mill, which would entail substantial imports. We decided to defer the issue. Please let me know your opinion, I am enclosing the material.

5. I have done final editing on the resolution on phonographs. I combined all of the appendixes, reducing the sum total by two-thirds. I incorporated all of your criticisms. It seems to me that it would be better to issue this resolution from Sovnarkom and the CC. I am sending you the draft and ask that you let me know.[6]

6. Regarding Sarkis, I have reached agreement with the Ukrainians. We have already formally made him first secretary of the Donets Regional Committee. We did not put down Terekhov as second secretary because the Ukrainians said that neither he nor Sarkis would probably want that. We have put off formalizing his appointment for now.[7]

7. Shubrikov requests that we give him a functionary as second secretary of the regional committee to replace Milkh, whom we took for the political department on the railroad. He requests that we give him either Grichmanov, the current chief of the political sector, or Gorkin, an executive instructor for the CC and a functionary in its agricultural department, or Akulinushkin. All of them are more or less equivalent in quality.

I would not like to give up functionaries from the agricultural department, but the most suitable one of those mentioned would be Gorkin. Please let me know your opinion.[8]

8. In spite of the rain, the parade yesterday on the occasion of International Youth Day went very well—it was lively, spirited, and crowded. For more than two hours dense columns of young people passed through Red Square.

9. Yesterday Sergo left town,[9] and today Molotov left.[10] I will close here. How do you feel, have you already started to relax?

Regards. Yours, L. Kaganovich.

1. See documents 60, 62, and 65 and the introduction to this chapter.

2. On 1 September 1933 the Politburo decided to allocate tractors and motor vehicles to military stud farms in the Northern Caucasus (RGASPI, f. 17, op. 3, d. 930, l. 12).

3. See document 70.

4. On 15 September 1933, on the basis of a report by Andreev, the Politburo considered the Volga and Oka bridges. It was decided that "bridges on main lines must be built with two tracks," and their dimensions and types must be approved by Sovnarkom. Andreev was instructed to arrange an official feasibility study of rebuilding the bridge on the Volga into one with two tracks. In view of a statement by Zhdanov that the bridge builders considered this reconstruction feasible, Zhdanov was instructed to submit the appropriate memorandum within twenty days. Andreev and Zhdanov were instructed to submit to the Politburo by the same deadline draft proposals for railroad crossings on the Oka (ibid., d. 930, l. 3). But on 15 November, after hearing reports from Andreev and Pakhomov, the Politburo, now with Stalin present, deferred the issue of building a two-track bridge across the Volga for a year, and proposed that the issue of building a bridge across the Oka be discussed when the control figures for 1934 were considered (ibid., d. 934, l. 3). See also document 61.

5. On 2 September 1933 the Politburo adopted a series of resolutions that incorporated these measures (ibid., d. 930, ll. 14–17). See document 60.

6. On 15 August 1933 the Politburo adopted a decision to separate the production of phonographs and phonograph records from the PC of Light Industry and to place it under the management of the PC of Heavy Industry. A commission headed by Kaganovich was instructed to rework the draft resolution accordingly. (Ibid., d. 928, l. 3.)

7. On 3 September 1933 the Politburo, by a poll of members, appointed Sarkis first secretary of the Donets Regional Committee (ibid., d. 930, l. 19). See also document 60 and note 4 to document 65.

8. On 9 September 1933 the Politburo granted the request by the Central Volga Regional Committee to transfer Gorkin and appoint him second secretary of the regional committee (ibid., l. 31).

9. On 1 September 1933 the Politburo authorized a vacation for Ordzhonikidze from 1 September through 15 October (ibid., l. 9).

10. On 3 September the Politburo granted Molotov a vacation for a month and a half (ibid., op. 162, d. 15, l. 55).

· 65 ·

Kaganovich to Stalin
7 September

F. 558, op. 11, d. 741, ll. 27–35.

---

7 September [1933]
Greetings dear Comrade Stalin.

1) You know the story of how the Japanese detained the ship *Aleksei Peshkov;* to this day they have not returned it to us. Sokolnikov has sent in a draft protest. The draft is uncontroversial, but since Sokolnikov says that you advised him at one point to wait awhile, we are sending you the draft and ask you to let us know whether this is the right time to send it.[1]

2) I have already reported to you on Sakhatsky-Bratkovsky, right now I

am sending you Comrade Katayama's memorandum, sent in by Akulov, on the circumstances of Sakhatsky's suicide.

3) Preobrazhensky has sent in an article entitled "The Agrarian Program of the Trotskyite Opposition Before the Court of History." This article in my view will not do. The article could be taken as an apology for the Trotskyite agrarian program. He accepts the demagogic points of the Trotskyite platform at face value and fails to expose the hypocrisy and the complete gap between their words and deeds. In short the article shows that he has failed to understand his mistakes, although he is trying to understand them. It is a long article, I am not sending it to you right now, if you want, I will send it to you, but regardless of the article he is calling and waiting for some decision about it, evidently, he wants above all to get a job. Maybe we should give him a job at the PC of State Farms concerned with finance.[2]

4) The Ukrainians report that, according to their information, several members of the Ukrainian Academy of Sciences—Galicians living in Lvov—want to demonstratively divest themselves of the title of members of the Ukrainian Academy. The Ukrainian comrades are raising the question of whether it would be expedient for us expel them ourselves from the Academy right now, without waiting. I think that is right, that is precisely what we should do. Please let me know your opinion.

5) Comrade Blagonravov came to see me, he thinks the situation at the PC of Transport is not very good, that there is no steadfastness in the drive to implement the decisions of the CC and Sovnarkom, etc. But his own mood is also depressed. I criticized him a little and told him that it is already time for him to drop the role of critic, that he is already responsible for everything, because he is already on a level with the people's commissar. He also proposed that a "Railroad Day" be declared and held on behalf of the party—to achieve a turnaround in the implementation of the decisions of the CC and Sovnarkom. I scoffed at him about this Day, because I believe that the key right now is not to have a day of agitation but to conduct an organic, persistent struggle and work. Eventually he agreed and promised to get the work into shape. The condition of the track on the Moscow-Kursk Railroad is very grave.

Akulov wants to hold a trial and prosecute Comrade Petrikovsky, the director of the railroad. A trial can be put on, but this is the least advantageous path for a demonstration, because the railroad workers have always pointed to the track as the objective cause of the wrecks. So if we stage this trial, it must be conducted very carefully and skillfully. Considering that this trial will be of great importance, especially if we put Petrikovsky in the dock, please let me know your thoughts.[3]

6) Regarding the farm machinery affair I agree with your arguments in

both the first and the last letter. I just find it necessary to tell you that the management of this trial was organized incorrectly and therefore I, among others, ended up poorly informed about what was going on. We have a tradition, which you introduced, that if even a less important issue comes up, you convene us, raise it to the level of principle and then whatever is unclear becomes clear and whatever is incomprehensible becomes comprehensible. But in this case Comrade Molotov managed this trial by himself and did not tell anyone anything. This largely accounts for the fact that instead of a direct and simple statement to the effect that the people's commissariats bear responsibility for this matter, hints were given that were so "subtle" that they ended up as explicit raps on the knuckles. I accept your rebuke that I made a mistake and did not realize the importance of this matter, but I cannot agree about the camp and the "feeling of friendship toward some and animosity toward others," etc. You know that "I have one camp and one friendship."

7) Sarkis came to Moscow today and will talk tomorrow about the second secretary. Terekhov needs to be recalled, and he must be given someone else.[4]

8) We buried those who perished in the crash today. It is already clear now that they should not have taken off in such weather, especially since the pilot Dorfman protested.[5]

We have adopted your proposal to forbid responsible functionaries to fly.

We have defined the group of these responsible functionaries as follows: CC members and candidates.

Members of the Central Control Commission and the auditing commission.

The Presidiums of the Central Executive Committees of the USSR and the RSFSR.

The Presidium of the All-Union Central Council of Trade Unions.

Secretaries and chairmen of regional and republican party committees and soviet executive committees.

People's commissars, their deputies, and collegium members.

The directors of chief administrations.

If you have comments, let me know.[6]

Regards. Yours, L. Kaganovich.

1. On 19 July 1933 a Japanese torpedo boat seized the Soviet trawler *Aleksei Peshkov* off the coast of Kamchatka. The Japanese claimed that the *Aleksei Peshkov*, with Soviet border guards on board, had participated in the seizure of a Japanese boat that, according to Soviet authorities, was fishing inside the Soviet coastal zone. Negotiations about the *Aleksei Peshkov* were having no success. On 14 September the Soviet plenipotentiary in Japan handed the Japanese foreign minister a note demanding the release of the vessel. An agree-

ment on this issue was eventually reached eight months later, at the end of May 1934. (DVP, vol. XVI, pp. 515–17, 850–51.)

2. Preobrazhensky, a former leader of the Left opposition, was sentenced in January 1933 to exile for three years and was expelled from the party for the second time in connection with the so-called counterrevolutionary Trotskyite group—I. N. Smirnov, V. A. Ter-Vaganian, Preobrazhensky, and others (see *Izvestiia TsK KPSS,* no. 6, 1991, 73). He was soon released from exile. On 11 September Stalin told Kaganovich in a cipher that Preobrazhensky could be given a post in the PC of State Farms (RGASPI, f. 558, op. 11, d. 80 l. 116). On 20 December the Politburo decided to reinstate him in the party (ibid., f. 17, op. 3, d. 936, l. 5).

3. On 11 September Stalin told Kaganovich in a cipher that "the proposal for a trial of Petrikovsky is mistaken, it is not a matter of a trial, but of checking fulfillment of decisions every day" (ibid., f. 558, op. 11, d. 80, l. 116).

4. On 11 September the Politburo confirmed Vainov as second secretary of the Donets Regional Committee and secretary for coal. Terekhov was appointed chairman of the Central Committee of the metallurgy trade union and recalled from the Donets Basin (ibid., f. 17, op. 3, d. 930, l. 35).

5. On 5 September the director of the Chief Administration of the Civil Air Fleet, Goltsman, and the director of the Chief Administration of the Aircraft Industry, Baranov, were killed in an airplane crash. On the same day the Politburo established a commission to determine the causes of the crash (ibid., l. 26). Kaganovich and Kuibyshev reported the crash and the establishment of a commission to Stalin in a cipher on the same day (ibid., f. 558, op. 11, d. 80, l. 930b.) On the following day Stalin replied that "responsible officials must be forbidden to fly on pain of expulsion from the party" (ibid., l. 93).

6. A Politburo resolution adopted on 11 September forbade responsible functionaries, "on pain of expulsion from the party," to "fly in airplanes without a special decision of the CC in each individual instance." The group of functionaries covered by this decision was based on the proposals in Kaganovich's letter (*Stalinskoe Politbiuro v 30-e gody,* pp. 40–41). Members of the collegia of the people's commissariats were dropped from the list, and it was made specific that the ban covered people's commissars of both the USSR and the RSFSR and their deputies, and the directors of chief administrations of USSR people's commissariats. This correction may have appeared after further comments from Stalin.

· 66 ·

Kaganovich to Stalin
10 September

F. 558, op. 11, d. 741, ll. 36–42.

10 September [1933]
Dear Comrade Stalin

1) We finally finished drawing up the resolution on payments for playwrights. We propose total elimination of the current system of payment, whereby authors enter into a direct agreement with a theater, which has a monopoly on the première, and receive a percentage from the theater, a deduction from the gross receipts based on the number of acts in the play at $1\frac{1}{2}$ percent per act. Consequently, a five-act play yields $7\frac{1}{2}$ percent of the receipts. As a result, given the large theater network and the even larger

demand, authors have raked in 45,000–50,000 rubles apiece in one year, the same thing is being repeated in the following year for the same play. We propose that the state in the form of a special commission or committee acquire a play for a onetime payment, paying between 5,000 and 50,000 depending on the quality, I had doubts about the figure of 50,000, but after all this is a one-time payment and he will not get any more, except a possible royalty for publication of a book version for reading purposes. The writers of course will be displeased, but as an incentive to produce good plays this is a big plus. Just to be on the safe side, in case such a radical change is deemed undesirable, we have prepared a second possible option, leaving the old system altered with a cut in deductions. We could establish a commission or committee attached to the Central Executive Committee or Sovnarkom comprising the following comrades: Yenukidze as chairman or Stetsky as chairman, and Bubnov, Yudin, and Litovsky—the Chief Repertory Committee.

I am sending you our draft resolution. I am very unhappy about burdening you with these papers, but this issue, it seems to me, is not a simple one.

2) At the next Politburo meeting (on the 15th) we will probably discuss the issue of the PC of Water Transport—the commission's proposals.

The question comes up, which we discussed, of who are to be people's commissar and [head of the] political department. The following candidates are possible: Antipov, Muklevich, Zhdanov, Kadatsky. For the post of head of the political department of the PC of Water Transport Ryndin, Vlad. Ivanov, and Zashibaev from Nizhny Novgorod.

3) There is precisely the same question of a dir[ector] of the Chief Administration of the Aircraft Industry to replace Baranov and a dir[ector] of the Civil Air Fleet to replace Goltsman. The following candidates for the aircraft industry are possible from the PC of Heavy Industry: Prokofiev, Khalepsky, or Alksnis, among the functionaries in the aircraft industry Korolyov, Poberezhsky? and . . . Makarovsky are being mentioned. For the post of director of the Civil Air Fleet we could have the following comrades: Yanson (if he is removed from the PC of Water Transport), Zhukov (PC of Communications), Lomov, Unshlikht, and Anvelt (Goltsman's deputy), although they say he is weak.

Please let me know your thoughts on these issues.[1]

4) The situation in the Moscow Region has greatly deteriorated. As a result of totally unprecedented downpours that turned into a literal disaster, there has been a steep drop in crop yields. Oats are turning black and sprouting shoots. We have deployed all forces for hauling from the fields and for threshing, at least the moist sheaves, because there are not enough threshing and drying barns to store the grain in sheaves. There is a similar situation in the Central Black-Earth Region, in the former Oryol Guber-

nia. Vareikis came to town and we increased his allocation for reductions (in addition to the 3 1/2 million poods [57,300 tons] given previously) by another 4 million poods [65,500 tons]. I did not raise the issue of the Moscow Region here, but I am raising it with you Comrade Stalin and I am asking you to help us. Comrade Chernov studied the situation in person and finds it necessary to help us. We have already procured a good amount of grain, 25.5 million poods [418,000 tons]—76 percent of the plan. We definitely would be able to procure not only the basic plan but also a portion of the reserve, but a number of collective farms may end up in a difficult position, especially in districts where oats are the chief crop. That is why I ask you, as secretary of the Moscow Committee, to support us. I am enclosing a proposal formulated by Comrade Chernov, and I ask you to let me know your opinion, by wire if possible.

Regards. Yours, L. Kaganovich.

1. For Stalin's reply to all the issues raised by Kaganovich and the decisions on them, see document 68.

· 67 ·

Stalin to Kaganovich
[before 13 September]

F. 81, op. 3, d. 100, ll. 105–106.

To Comrade Kaganovich.

1) I am not going to read the drafts about higher technical educational institutions and factory and plant schools. I left to get away from paperwork, and you pepper me with a heap of paperwork. Settle it yourselves and settle it as soon as possible, since this matter cannot be put off anymore.[1]

2) Regarding the answer about Manchukuo, I agree.[2]

3) The same goes for the Reichstag fire trial.[3]

Regards.

I. Stalin.

P.S. I urge you to focus in particular on the issue of the timely shipment and delivery of ore, fluxes, refractories, coke, and coal for metallurgy. You have the relevant decision, but the point is not the decision but its implementation. Unless this task is fulfilled, we will cripple the iron and steel industry.[4]

P.P.S. Regarding the sheet mill (the order to the USA), I will write when I sort out the issue.

I. St.

1. On 1 July 1933 the Politburo approved, with revisions, a draft resolution submitted by the Kaganovich commission on improving the organization of cadre training and utilization (at higher technical educational institutions, technicums, and factory and plant schools). It provided that all young specialists who graduate from higher general and technical educational institutions and technicums must work for five years at certain enterprises as specified by the people's commissariats that oversee these educational institutions. Anyone taking a job without authorization was liable to criminal prosecution. Other measures were outlined to increase the number of specialists directly at factories. Similar resolutions were adopted with regard to factory and plant schools, whose graduates were forbidden to transfer to other educational institutions (technicums or higher institutions) after completing their studies . They had to work at a factory for three years, as instructed by the economic organizations responsible. To speed up the training of workers, the academic program at factory and plant schools was shortened from two years to six months (a one-year program was retained for the most complex vocations) (RGASPI, f. 17, op. 3, d. 925, ll. 5, 36–43). The resolutions were published on 15 September. See also document 63.

2. The reference is evidently to coordination over the letter from the USSR's general consul in Harbin, Slavutsky, to the special agent of the Japanese Ministry of Foreign Affairs in northern Manchuria, which was delivered on 11 September 1933. The letter was composed in response to protests by the Manchurian government over the arrest of a group of Russian White Guard émigrés in Manchurian territory. It rejected these charges and lodged a protest "over the fact that the Manchurian authorities are allowing the White gangs to cross into Soviet territory." (DVP, vol. XVI, pp. 502–4.)

3. The Nazis used the burning of the Reichstag in Berlin on 27 February 1933, a month after Hitler was appointed chancellor, to intensify the terror against the Left. Thälmann, the German Communist leader, and Dimitrov, one of the leaders of the Comintern, were arrested. The trial of Dimitrov and others charged with arson began in Leipzig on 21 September 1933. In December Dimitrov was acquitted (see E. H. Carr, *The Twilight of Comintern* [London, 1982], 87–88, 101–2). On 13 September 1933 the Politburo approved a commission to be chaired by Stetsky, to manage the press in connection with the Reichstag fire trial (RGASPI, f. 17, op. 3, d. 930, l. 38). See also document 73.

4. See documents 69, 70.

· 68 ·

Stalin to Kaganovich
13 September

F. 81, op. 3, d. 100, l. 99.

Greetings, Comrade <u>Kaganovich</u>:

1) It would be better to put off the discussions of playwrights[1] and the PC of Water Transport[2] until I arrive.

2) For the aircraft industry, it would be better to promote Poberezhsky or, as a last resort, Korolyov.[3]

3) We can promote Unshlikht to replace Goltsman.[4]

4) I already wired my consent to giving Moscow a reduction on grain deliveries.[5]

That is all for now.
Regards.
13 September[1933]   I. Stalin

1. See documents 63, 66. The draft resolution on playwrights' earnings, with corrections by Stalin, is located in the Kaganovich family files. Stalin expressed doubts over a number of provisions in the document. He wrote over the text: "But it would be better to put off this issue until I arrive" (RGASPI, f. 81, op. 3, d. 93, ll. 99–101).

2. The issue of the people's commissar for water transport was not taken up until 13 March 1934, when the Politburo "acceded to the request" of Yanson to be relieved of his duties as people's commissar and approved Pakhomov as the new people's commissar. Yanson was appointed deputy people's commissar for the maritime section, and Fomin for the river section (ibid., d. 930, l. 6).

3. On 12 September Stalin in a cipher rejected Alksnis and Lominadze as possible candidates, and proposed "Korolyov, Poberezhsky, or someone else linked with production" (ibid., f. 558, op. 11, d. 80, l. 123). On 15 September the Politburo appointed Korolyov, director of the Rybinsk plant, as head of the Chief Administration of the Aircraft Industry. Poberezhsky was appointed the new director of the Rybinsk plant by the same decision (ibid., f. 17, op. 3, d. 930, l. 6).

4. On 21 September the Politburo approved Unshlikht as head of the Chief Administration of the Civil Air Fleet (ibid., d. 931, l. 18).

5. On 15 September the Politburo increased by 4.6 million poods (75,000 tons) the grain placed at the disposal of the authorities of the Moscow Region, so that they could grant cuts in grain deliveries by individual collective farms and independent farms with reduced harvests (ibid., op. 162, d. 15, l. 57).

· 69 ·

Kaganovich to Stalin
13 September

F. 558, op. 11, d. 741, ll. 43–46.

---

13 September [1933]
Greetings dear Comrade Stalin.

1) One of the latest decoded messages contains a very important report on the conference of military officers that took place regarding the de facto seizure of the CER. Li Shao-keng made demands at the meeting of the board for new rights to be granted to the Chin[ese] assistant manager, but so far there have been no moves in this direction. We must, however, be prepared to react. We think that first of all, we should give the newspapers a report roughly along the following lines: "According to reliable information received from Harbin, the Manchurian authorities are contemplating a number of measures aimed at a de facto seizure of the CER through a flagrant violation of the rights of the Soviet manager, whose orders would be validated only by approval of the Manchurian assistant. At the same time police authorities will be instructed to prepare to confront

Soviet staff members of the CER with fabricated accusations, which would serve as a pretext for raids, searches, and arrests."[1] Second, in the future, if they in fact do something, we will have to lodge our own protest. We have composed a draft of such a directive to Yurenev, the end of it is very mild, but for now we feel that the wording should not be sharper. I am sending you this directive and ask that you let us know, by wire if possible, your opinion.[2]

2) With regard to Comrade Karakhan's trip, he has submitted a number of proposals. We cannot resolve them without you. At my proposal he cut his memorandum by about two-thirds, bringing it down to the length of a cipher, which I am sending you, and ask that you let us know your opinion.[3]

3) Regarding ore and the rest [intended] for metallurgy we included it in the Politburo agenda (for the 15th) by way of verification of fulfillment. We will do all that is necessary in accordance with your instructions, I will personally see to this.[4]

Regards to you. Yours, L. Kaganovich.

P.S. We are writing a separate letter about the grain yield.

1. See document 71.

2. On 26 September 1933, after the arrest of Soviet employees of the CER in Harbin, the USSR plenipotentiary in Japan, Yurenev, handed the Japanese foreign minister a sharply worded Soviet statement, along the lines of the statement of 21 September that was adopted at Stalin's insistence (DVP, vol. XVI, pp. 545–46). See also document 71.

3. The reference was to the preparation of a visit by USSR deputy foreign minister Karakhan to Persia. On 19 September 1933 the Politburo approved a resolution on trade with Persia (RGASPI, f. 17, op. 162, d. 15, l. 79).

4. See document 70.

· 70 ·

Kaganovich to Stalin
16 September

F. 558, op. 11, d. 741, ll. 47–54.

16 September [1933]

Greetings dear Comrade Stalin.

1) Comrade Litvinov has proposed the quickest possible consideration of Stomoniakov's memorandum, which he sent in at the end of July, about the trade negotiations and trade agreement with Poland. We could defer this issue until you arrive. If you consider it necessary to speed up consideration of the issue, please let me know.

2) Regarding negotiations with Britain Litvinov has sent out a memorandum, you will get it, it only provides information and does not make

any specific proposals. It merely refers to the desirability of speeding up the negotiations and completing them before the new session of Parliament.[1] This, of course, does not depend on us alone. Our delegation could press a little more persistently there, but that would require that we give them new supplementary directives. If you consider this advisable, please let me know.

3) Interesting materials have been received from Germany, Vinogradov's diary and a memorandum about Hitler's conversation with Nadolny. All these materials are being sent to you. It is clear from them, by the way, how the fascist rulers are forced right now to disguise and "soften" their attitude toward the USSR.

4) Regarding the CER there is no special news so far, either in Harbin or in Tokyo. We will see what the arrival of Hirota brings, it is doubtful that it will be anything serious.[2]

5) You will see from the Politburo minutes that we mainly discussed issues related to verification of fulfillment. We gave a thrashing, to put it bluntly, to the PC of the Timber Industry and the All-Union Corporation for Timber Exports for failing to fulfill the program and for their tardiness in raising the issue.[3] We deemed the progress of construction at the PC of Light Industry to be unsatisfactory, especially the construction of textile factories in Barnaul and Tashkent.[4]

We had a big argument over spare parts. The problem is that last year we had to perform major repairs [*remontirovat kapitalno*] on 90 percent of the tractors. This year again Yakovlev and the people at the PC of State Farms have proposed 80 percent, and we adopted a maximum of 60 percent. Even this figure is large if current and intermediate repairs are normally organized, but since this is the first year of normal operations, we must achieve at least 60 percent major repairs of tractors. The people at the PC of Agriculture and the PC of State Farms did not want this.[5] On the other hand, the PC of Heavy Industry people wanted to take a small program for the first quarter, even though the first quarter is highly important in the preparation for spring. We also chastised them on this issue.[6]

Regarding ore, fluxes, and all the necessities for metallurgy we have taken all the necessary measures, not only in the Politburo.[7] A few days ago we heard a report from the Yekaterininskaia Railroad at the commission on transport and put special emphasis on the hauling of ore. We adopted a tough resolution at the commission on transport regarding both the Yekaterininskaia and Kursk Railroads and we plan to publish it in the name of the CC after approval by the Politburo.[8] Evidently things are getting a little better in transport. For the last few days they have been loading 56,000, 57,000, 55,000 railroad cars.

Regarding the canal locks: we established a commission and instructed it to start with the figures that you recommended. Vinter and Vedeneev said that for the Yaroslavl locks and further up the Volga we should stick with the 20 meter width of the Mariinsk locks, but we, of course, did not adopt their proposals because, as you correctly pointed out, they do not see the prospects for our expansion and the possibility and necessity of the modernization of the Mariinsk system.[9]

6) Shulkin has already admitted his guilt, although he is trying to press the point that during the last phase of his work in Nikolaev he no longer had such a rightwing opportunist attitude, but clearly he is putting on an act here too.[10] From the list of individuals who were in contact with him, he mentions Goldin, the second secretary of the Lower Volga Regional Committee. We need to remove him from there. Please give us your assent and we will remove him.

Well I will close here.

Please let me know how you feel, how your vacation is going.

Regards to you. Yours, L. Kaganovich.

1. For Litvinov's letter to the CC "The Status of Negotiations with Britain as of the Beginning of September 1933," see DVP, vol. XVI, pp. 511–14. The PC of Foreign Affairs, reported Litvinov, deems it necessary to speed up the negotiations and to complete them before the session of the British Parliament, scheduled for 7 November; to do this might require new instructions very soon for the Soviet delegation.

2. Hirota was the new foreign minister of Japan.

3. On 15 September the Politburo noted that "the PC of the Timber Industry and the PC of Foreign Trade were too late in submitting to the Politburo the question of the failure to fulfill the plan for timber haulage and exports." Measures approved for increasing the export of timber included: supplying vehicles for haulage and sending out plenipotentiaries (RGASPI, f. 17, op. 3, d. 930, ll. 5, 55–56).

4. On 15 September the Politburo decided that capital construction by the PC of Light Industry was "unsatisfactory" (ibid., l. 4).

5. See note 4 to document 74.

6. On 15 September the Politburo approved the 1934 plan for production of spare parts at 155 million rubles, including 39 million for the first quarter (ibid., ll. 1–2, 49–50).

7. On 15 September the Politburo adopted a resolution that provided for sending out plenipotentiaries and intensifying supervision of the creation of stocks of ore, fluxes, refractories, and coke at metallurgical enterprises (ibid., ll. 2–3). See also documents 67, 69.

8. The CC resolution on the Kursk and Yekaterininskaia Railroads, dated 17 September 1933, was published in newspapers on 18 September. The director of the Yekaterininskaya Railroad was warned that unless he ensured total fulfillment of the plan for shipments of ore, fluxes, refractories, grain, coke, and coal in the immediate future, "he would not only be removed from his post but would also be expelled from party ranks for violating the party's militant assignment" (ibid., d. 931, ll. 40–42). In the following weeks the press conducted a campaign for fulfillment of the plans for shipments of raw materials for the iron and steel industry. See also document 60.

9. On 15 September the Politburo decided that "the types and overall dimensions of the locks (length, width, depth) must be approved by the USSR Sovnarkom through Gosplan." A commission chaired by Kuibyshev was established to determine the dimensions of the locks of the Mariinsk system, the Volga-Moscow Canal, and the Central Volga construction project. The commission was instructed to proceed on the basis of a compartment length of

250 to 350 meters, a width of 20 to 25 meters, and a height and depth of at least 5 meters (ibid., d. 930, l. 3). See also documents 61, 64.

10. On 2 September a *Pravda* editorial criticized the secretary of the Nikolaev City Party Committee, Shulkin, because in the Nikolaev District of the Odessa Region, which had fulfilled the plan for grain procurements, grain often lay under the open sky despite the availability of warehouses, and robbery was common at warehouses and elevators because of poor security. See also documents 73, 74.

· 71 ·

Stalin to Kaganovich
[18 September]

F. 81, op. 3, d. 100, l. 109.

Comrade Kaganovich:

We are sending you our corrections to Sokolnikov's draft on the CER [Chinese Eastern Railroad]. We insist on our corrections. We believe that the press should lay direct responsibility for all of the outrages in Manchuria on the Jap[anese] gov[ernment].[1]

Stalin.

1. A statement by the government of the USSR to the government of Japan was published in Soviet newspapers on 22 September. It said in part: "The Soviet government believes that direct responsibility for these violations lies with the Japanese Government. Not Manchukuo, which is powerless and unable to take responsibility for events in Manchuria, but the Japanese Government, which is the real master in Manchuria, must bear direct responsibility for all the violations of the pacts on the CER, as well as the seizure of the railroad that is being prepared." See the introduction to this chapter and document 69.

· 72 ·

Kaganovich to Stalin and Voroshilov
19 September
F. 558, op. 11, d. 81, l. 24. Authenticated typewriten copy.

TOP SECRET
BY CIPHER
Copy

To Comrades Stalin, Voroshilov.

At 11 o'clock this morning Pierre Cot and General Barrès paid a visit to Comrade Tukhachevsky. Pierre Cot declared that "two countries in the world do not want war—they are the USSR and France and therefore these countries can, without fear, acquaint each other with their achievements and that he has a proposal that more continuous and closer cooperation be established between French and Soviet aviation, that he is doing this in the most preliminary form, but that, nevertheless, he can propose cooperation in two areas.

"In the area of production—sending our engineers to study the French aircraft industry or inviting French engineers to see our industry, or, if we wish, both together. Second, Pierre Cot proposed that our officers be sent to study French aviation units and to study at French aviation schools."

Pierre Cot was curious to know in which forms Tukhachevsky envisioned cooperation. Tukhachevsky did not give him a definite answer. He promised to report to the government.

They are leaving on 21 September. Please let us know your opinion. Is it advisable to give Pierre Cot and Barrès an affirmative reply on establishing more regular contact between our and their aviation and aircraft industry and on sending our officers and engineers to study French aviation and the aircraft industry.

We would consider it advisable to give an affirmative reply.[1]

No. 35/36/1910/sh.

19 September 1933.

1. The reference is to a visit to the USSR by French Aviation Minister Pierre Cot and the inspector general of French aviation, General Barrès, and other leaders of the Aviation Ministry who were accompanying Cot (see DVP, vol. XVI, pp. 856–57). On 20 September Tukhachevsky sent Kaganovich the following message: "At a luncheon yesterday in honor of the French guests, I had conversations with Pierre Cot, Gen[eral] Barrès, and engineer Caquot on various issues of aviation technology. We touched on issues of flying in poor visibility, the cooling of engines at high altitudes, aircraft armaments, methods of preparing bombers, the preparation of night flights, etc. On all these issues the French very eagerly give answers and openly describe new airplane cannons and machineguns (1,200 rounds per minute). They promise to show us a fighter armed with an automatic cannon in a few months (it is being built right now). The French are very satisfied with their reception, Gen[eral] Barrès in particular says that he has been absolutely charmed by the reception, that he is an old friend of the USSR, and that as far back as 1927 he was trying to arrange with Herriot to make a trip with him to the USSR, but that at the time it did not work out. Until now Barrès had been very reserved. They are earnestly inviting me and Comrade Alksnis to come to France with a group of officers to study aviation and promise to show us all equipment and preparatory procedures" (RGASPI, f. 81, op. 3, d. 101, l. 27).

Stalin's first reaction was very cautious. On 20 September, in a cipher to Kaganovich, he wrote "the French are crawling to us for intelligence purposes"; "collaboration in aviation is acceptable"; but because the Soviet Union was strong in aviation, it should insist that collaboration should be extended to naval matters, especially submarines and torpedo boats (ibid., f. 558, op. 11, d. 81, ll. 22–23).

A month later, on 23 October, in a discussion with people's commissar of foreign affairs Litvinov, the French ambassador to the USSR again raised the question of a visit by Tukhachevsky to France. Litvinov replied that "we have not discussed the issue" and that he did not even know whether Tukhachevsky had received an invitation from anyone. On 30 November a counselor at the French embassy transmitted to Stomoniakov, a member of the collegium of the PC of Foreign Affairs, a memorandum from the French embassy that confirmed the invitation to Tukhachevsky and Soviet pilots to pay a visit to France in response to Cot's visit (DVP, vol. XVI, pp. 555, 859–60). On 10 December the Politburo accepted Cot's proposal that Soviet officers be sent to French aviation schools for advanced training and decided whom to send. Dovgalevsky, the ambassador to France, was instructed to notify the French side of the Soviet intention to send a squadron of airplanes to Paris in response to Cot's visit. (RGASPI, f. 17, op. 162, d. 15, l. 152.) A Soviet aviation delegation headed by the director of the Chief Administration of the Civil Air Fleet, Unshlikht, visited France in August 1934 (DVP, vol. XVII, p. 811).

· 73 ·

Kaganovich to Stalin
20 September

F. 558, op. 11, d. 741, ll. 55–62.

20 September [1933]
Greetings dear Comrade Stalin.

1) As a result of the reduced, and in some places extremely small harvest in the eastern section of the Central Volga, in the northeastern part of the Lower Volga, the southern part of the Urals, and Western Kazakhstan Comrade Chernov proposes that we increase the amount allocated for reductions in grain deliveries for collective farms in the aforementioned regions with reduced harvests.

For the Central Volga	10 million poods [164,000 tons]
For the Lower Volga	6 million poods [98,000 tons]
For the Urals	6 million poods [98,000 tons]
For Kazakhstan	5 million poods [82,000 tons]

For the Lower Volga he also proposes that last year's grain loan be carried over into arrears for '34. I am sending you comrade Chernov's memorandum. I find his proposals acceptable. I would add to this a reduction of 3 million [49,000 tons] for state farms in the Central Volga. The bad harvest hit precisely the districts where state farms are located. There are state farms that gathered only 3 tsentners per hectare. Please let me know your opinion. The latest five-day periods have produced a decrease in grain deliveries, but for now we are not putting on the pressure.[1]

2) Due to the deterioration in work by the textile industry, especially the increase in defective output, which has reached 9 percent in Class 1 defective output and as much as 20–25 percent in Class 2 defective output, the Moscow Committee has convened a regional conference of cotton textile specialists in Orekhovo about the quality of production.

A whole host of outrageous instances of poor management, poor organization of labor and red tape were disclosed. Functionalism has gone so far that after functionalism was eliminated in the work of workers, it was left intact in the so-called specialization of factories. For example: all the support materials—heddles, reeds—used to be produced at each factory and they had what they needed, but now the PC of Light Industry has taken this away from the factories and has established a "specialized" trust called Detalmashina [Machine Parts], and as a result, the factories are groaning because they do not have these so-called parts. On the evening of the 17th I stopped off in Orekhovo, visited the factory, and then the conference. I think, Comrade Stalin, that you will entrust me with the job of rectifying the outrages in the textile industry not only at the Moscow Committee level but also at the CC level. It has reached the point that instead of the normal smoothing-out of the fabrics after trimming they are artificially stretched over and above the norm, the width and length are increased, and they inflate the meter totals for the statistics on plan fulfillment.[2]

3) Regarding the Reichstag fire trial we have given instructions that the coverage in the press should not get too artificially worked up, the intention was to make the coverage of the same nature as for the Gorguloff trial.[3]

4) I have written you about Shulkin, who according to the OGPU memorandum and by his own confession after his arrest was a double-dealer and in effect helped put together the right-wing opportunist group. If you don't have these materials, I can send them to you.[4]

5) Regarding tractors we have made the correction you specified in today's telegram, i.e. 50 percent major repairs instead of 60 percent. This will force them to work even harder to get things into shape.[5]

6) Regarding the Sukharev Tower: after your first telegram I assigned the architects to submit a plan for its reconstruction (the arch) so as to ease traffic.

I did not promise that we were already dropping the demolition idea, but I told them it depends on the degree to which their plan solves the traffic problem. Now I would ask you to permit me to wait awhile so as to get the plan from them. Since it will not satisfy us, of course, we will announce to them that we are demolishing the Sukharev Tower. If you don't think we should wait, then, of course, I will organize this project more quickly, that is right now, without waiting for their plan.[6]

Well I will close here.

Regards. Yours, L. Kaganovich.

P.S. Molotov arrived today.

    L.K.

1. See document 74.

2. The Moscow regional conference of the cotton industry on the quality of output was held on 16–17 September 1933 in Orekhovo-Zuevo. Kaganovich delivered a speech on combating defective output. On 22 September *Pravda* published an editorial that sharply criticized the leadership of the cotton industry. At this time Kaganovich wrote to Ordzhonikidze:

"We had to get into textile issues, things are very bad there. They are producing output of abominable quality, the party will have to tackle this matter vigorously. Things have gone so far that to fulfill the plan in terms of meters they are artificially stretching out fabrics, and that means that when someone buys 5 meters, after washing the shirt he will get a children's shirt instead of an adult's" (*Stalinskoe Politbiuro v 30-e gody*, 137). See also document 74.

3. See note 3 to document 67. Paul Gorguloff, an émigré Russian doctor, who had served in a White army during the civil war, shot and fatally wounded the president of France, Paul Doumer, in Paris on 6 May 1932. At his interrogation Gorguloff described himself as a "Russian fascist," and claimed that he had assassinated Doumer because France was helping the Bolsheviks. His trial was reported at length and in a calm tone in Soviet newspapers at the end of July. He was found by the French court to be of sound mind, and executed by guillotine on 14 September 1932 (*The Times* [London], 7, 9 May, 26, 27, 28 July, 22 August, 15 September 1932.)

4. See note 10 to document 70.

5. In a cipher to Kaganovich dated 20 September, Stalin stated that 50 percent was "entirely sufficient" (RGASPI, f. 558, op. 11, d. 81, l. 26). See note 4 to document 74.

6. See note 5 to document 74.

· 74 ·

Stalin to Kaganovich
24 September

F. 81, op. 3, d. 100, ll. 17–21.

---

24 September 1933
Greetings, Comrade Kaganovich:

1) I have no objections to easing the grain deliveries by both Volga regions, the Urals, and Kazakhstan.[1]

2) You must crack down on the textile industry [in your capacity] both as secretary of the Moscow Regional Committee and as a secretary of the CC. The guilty individuals must definitely be punished, no matter who they are and whatever their "Communist" rank.[2]

3) I have no idea what the Shulkin affair is about.[3]

4) In the repair of tractors (as well as steam locomotives) the most important thing for us is not major repairs [*kapitalny remont*], but current and intermediate repairs. If the latter are well organized, capital repairs cannot exceed 40 percent. Those who demand a 60 or 70 or even 80 percent share for major repairs are not bosses but bunglers or outright enemies, since they are ruining our current and intermediate repairs. The most important thing is to improve current (minor) and intermediate repairs. Without this our tractor fleet will keep limping along, even if we adopt a 100 percent share for major repairs. Yakovlev doesn't understand this, since he is no boss but an empty-headed and puffed-up windbag. And you must understand this. In addition to a decision on a 50 percent share for major repairs, a decision must be adopted to improve current and in-

termediate repairs, to improve them <u>without fail</u>. I repeat, this is the most important thing.[4]

5) I am not going to rush you with regard to the Sukharev Tower.[5]

Regards.

I. Stalin.

1. On 26 September, on the proposal of people's commissar of agriculture Chernov, the Politburo increased the size of the cuts in grain deliveries by collective farms with a reduced harvest in the Central and Lower Volga Regions, the Urals, and Kazakhstan (RGASPI, f. 17, op. 162, d. 15, l. 85). See also document 73.

2. See note 2 to document 73.

3. See note 10 to document 70

4. On 15 September the Politburo approved a draft resolution, submitted by a commission chaired by Kaganovich, on supplying the tractor fleet with spare parts for the spring sowing campaign and for 1934. The resolution provided that the 1934 repair campaign proceed on the basis that no more than 60 percent of the available tractor fleet, as of 1 January 1934, undergo major repairs (ibid., op. 3, d. 930, ll. 1–2, 49–50). On 20 September, at Stalin's demand, the Politburo changed this decision and determined that "no more than 50 percent of the available tractor fleet, as of 1 January 1934, shall undergo major repairs" (ibid., d. 931, l. 18). On 24 September the newspapers published a resolution by the USSR Council of Labor and Defense, dated 21 September, on organizing the utilization of the tractor fleet, which incorporated Stalin's demands. See also documents 70, 73.

5. On 17 August 1933 the newspaper *Rabochaia Moskva* (Working Moscow) published a report on the impending demolition of the Sukharev Tower. In late August a group of well-known architects (I. E. Grabar, I. A. Fomin, I. V. Zholtovsky) sent Stalin and Kaganovich a letter in which they "resolutely objected" "to the destruction of a superb work of art, an act that is equivalent to destroying a painting by Raphael." The architects proposed that a plan for reorganizing Sukharev Square quickly be drawn up, which would make it possible both to preserve the tower and solve traffic problems (*Izvestia TsK KPSS*, no. 9, 1989, 110). On 3 September Stalin sent a cipher to Kaganovich commenting "Perhaps the architects are right about the Sukharev Tower. It is a space question and can be resolved only in Moscow" (RGASPI, f. 558, op. 11, d. 80, ll. 77–80). Kaganovich issued an instruction that a plan should be drawn up. On 18 September Stalin and Voroshilov, who were vacationing in Sochi, sent Kaganovich a further cipher: "We have studied the issue of the Sukharev Tower and have concluded that it must definitely be demolished. We propose that the Sukharev Tower be razed and that the space for traffic be expanded. The architects who object to demolition are blind and short-sighted" (ibid., d. 81, l. 9). On 20 September Kaganovich requested additional instructions on this point (see document 73). The Sukharev Tower was demolished in the spring of 1934.

· 75 ·

Stalin to Kaganovich

28 September

F. 81, op. 3, d. 100, ll. 22–24.

Comrade Kaganovich:

1) Besides airplanes, tanks, artillery, and ammunition, we must also check on the production of submarines. The situation with submarines is

very bad, their production is too slow and outrageously bad. We must push this task hard, day after day, continuously, <u>without a respite</u>. The quality of submarines is bad, very bad.[1]

2) The pressure for grain procurements must be started <u>right now</u>. "In a while" will be too late. Unless you begin to push hard <u>immediately</u>, you will miss an opportunity and demoralize functionaries and collective farmers.[2]

3) We cannot allow "more frequent departures from the country" by foreign correspondents. If they don't like the procedure that has been established for them, they can leave for other countries. All of the current regulations for foreign correspondents must be left intact.

4) Let me know how the development of commercial ("free") bread sales is proceeding.[3]

Regards, I. Stalin.

28 September 1933.

1. See note 6 to document 77. Stalin's comment was in reply to Kaganovich's letter of 24 September in which he reported that the production of military aircraft, tanks, and especially artillery was much less than planned (RGASPI, f. 558, op. 11, d. 741, ll. 63–71).

2. On 24 September Kaganovich wrote to Stalin that grain deliveries in the period 16–20 September were less than planned, and inquired, "Should we react to this decline" (ibid.). See note 3 to document 77.

3. See note 2 to document 77.

· 76 ·

Stalin to Kaganovich
30 September

F. 81, op. 3, d. 100, ll. 25–33.

────────────

<u>Greetings, Comrade Kaganovich:</u>

1) Sergo reports (I am enclosing the cipher) that the shipment of metal is going badly. Be sure to take measures, I urge you.[1]

2) Things in Eastern Siberia are bad. Leonov is weak. He has apparently turned over all practical and organizational matters to the slow-witted bungler Kozlov, while he himself is engaged in "higher theory." They are going to ruin everything. We must carefully prepare the <u>replacement</u> (replacement, and not just removal) of the current leadership. Prepare this move. Do it within a month. You must not delay.[2]

3) In regard to Central Asia it would be better to set up a commission with your participation. It would be better to suspend or limit arrests. Summon Maksum and Khadzhibaev to Moscow. Then they should be replaced.[3]

4) I consider your plan for distributing tractors and trucks to be dan-

gerous. It gives the impression that we have lost our way. The CTP [Cheli-abinsk Tractor Plant] was built primarily and mainly for agriculture, yet you are giving the PC of Agriculture and the PC of State Farms only 600 of the 1,365 crawler tractors [*katerpillery*], i.e. <u>less than half</u>. Why is that, on what basis? One might think that the CTP was built not for agriculture but for the so-called "other customers." Out of 16,000 tire tractors, you again give 3,000 to some sort of "other customers." Why, on what basis? One might think that agriculture doesn't need tractors anymore or won't need them in the near future. Where did you get that idea?

You are giving the PC of Agriculture and the PC of State Farms only 2,000 out of 9,600 trucks. What kind of nonsense is that? Now that actual support points for agriculture have been set up in the provinces through the political departments—and the issues of agriculture and its difficulties are a long way from being eliminated—you are aiming for some unknown reason to shift the focus from agriculture to "other customers." That is jumping the gun. . . .

My opinion:

a) Of the 1,365 crawlers, give 500 to the PC of State Farms and 500 to the PC of Agriculture (1,000 in all), instructing the PC of Agriculture to give crawlers only to MTS [Machine-Tractor Stations] in the <u>steppe</u> (the Ukraine, Northern Caucasus, the Volga region, the Southern Urals, Bashkiria, Siberia, Kazakhstan). We must set the immediate objective of having <u>two</u> to <u>four</u> crawlers <u>in every</u> MTS in the steppe.

Give 250 tractors to the PC of the Timber Industry. Give 20 or 30 to the PC of Military and Naval Affairs (they now have the entire output of Communard tractors from the Kharkov plant) and the same amount or a little more to the PC of Heavy Industry, while leaving ten (ten, and not 135) in reserve.

b) Of the 16,785 tire tractors, give at least 15,000 to the PC of Agriculture and the PC of State Farms.

c) Of the 9,600 trucks, give at least 4,000 to the PC of Agriculture and the PC of State Farms, 2,000 to the PC of Military and Naval Affairs, 1,000 to the Procurements Committee, and the rest to the others (mostly industry).

d) Regarding the distribution of passenger cars, I agree with you.[4]

5) I find it difficult to say anything definite about the subway. We will talk about it when I arrive.

6) You did not report to me what operational assignment was given to the resettlement committee.[5]

Regards, I. Stalin.

30 September 1933.

1. The cipher is missing. See document 79.
2. See note 5 to document 79.

3. On 28 September Kaganovich reported to Stalin that Bauman and Gusarov "are bombarding us about the need to remove Maksum and Khadzhibaev," and that "arrests of officials there are continuously increasing—what is to be done?" (RGASPI, f. 558, op. 11, d. 741, ll. 72–73). On 1 December the Politburo approved a resolution on Maksum, the chairman of the Central Executive Committee of the Tajik SSR, and Khadzhibaev, the chairman of Sovnarkom of the Tajik SSR. The resolution said that "available evidence affords no grounds to charge Comrades Maksum and Khadzhibaev with participating in a counterrevolutionary organization in Tajikistan against Soviet rule." Maksum and Khadzhibaev were accused of making numerous errors: having ties with kulak elements, not doing enough to combat high-handed abuses against the poor by kulaks, and pursuing a bourgeois-nationalist policy in their work. It was decided beforehand to remove both from their posts. Guseinov, the first secretary of the CC of the Communist Party of Tajikistan, was dismissed from his position for failing to take measures. A special resolution dealt with errors by the GPU of Central Asia and Tajikistan ("they exceeded their authority in the fight against anti-Soviet elements by carrying out arrests on a broad, massive scale"). A special commission was assigned to examine the cases of the individuals under arrest and to release those who were "incorrectly" arrested. (Ibid., f. 17, op. 3, d. 935, ll. 21, 67–69.)

4. Kaganovich reported the Politburo proposals to Stalin in a letter dated 28 September (ibid., f. 558, op. 11, d. 741, ll. 72–78). On 1 October Stalin sent a cipher to Kaganovich complaining that "your plan for the distribution of tractors and lorries in the fourth quarter is alarming" (ibid., d. 81, l. 76), and on the same day Kaganovich replied that the plan had not been finally approved—"We await your letter" (ibid., l. 76). Stalin's proposals were incorporated into the Politburo's resolutions "On the Plan for Distribution of Tire and Crawler Tractors in the Fourth Quarter of 1933" and "On the Plan for Distribution of Motor Vehicles and Truck Tractors in the Fourth Quarter," which were adopted on 11 October (ibid., f. 17, op. 3, d. 932, ll. 23–24, 44–47). See also document 79.

5. See note 1 to document 77.

· 77 ·

Kaganovich to Stalin
2 October

F. 558, op. 11, d. 741, ll. 80–89.

---

2 October [1933]
Dear Comrade Stalin.

1) You asked what oper[ational] assignment we gave the resettlement committee for 1933. We gave it an assignment at the end of August of arranging the resettlement by the beginning of 1934 of 10,000 families, and together with the previous instructions it will be 14,000 families in all, to the Kuban and the Terek, and also to the Ukraine (the steppe, 15,000–20,000 families).[1] The other day after Muralov arrived, we summoned him and as a result of our conversation we became convinced that so far they are only recruiting in military units, but at the site they have almost nothing prepared yet. We gave him instructions to work out the entire matter in practical terms: determine the resettlement locations, send out

people to provide housing and all the necessary equipment, set a schedule of departures with precise time frames, provide food, etc.

He will present all this in a couple of days. We don't think he will be able to handle any more in these remaining three months of 1933, so we did not give him an additional assignment for the time being. We may have to arrange a spontaneous resettlement beginning from some districts of the Central Volga. We will have to discuss this.

2) Regarding bread sales I can report [only] preliminary data, because Comrade Mikoian is not here right now, and at the PC for Supply he holds all the threads to bread sales. Here is the situation: stores have been opened in all 151 cities, sales have begun everywhere, but they are selling less than the planned amount of bread. For example, actual daily bread sales for the 61 cities that have been tabulated amount to 3,215 tons as opposed to the 5,649 tons under the sales plan. In Cheliabinsk 30 tons are sold instead of 90 tons, in Tiflis 80 tons instead of 200 tons. In Voronezh 80–85 tons a day are sold instead of 120 tons. Tula sells 55 tons instead of 70 tons. In Moscow too daily sales have been dropping of late: 442 tons in May, 440 tons in June, 412 tons in July, 413 tons in August, 300 tons in September.

There are several reasons here: first, the sales network has not been adequately developed, and often there are many stores in one district of the city and extremely few in another. Second, poor bread delivery. Third, poor quality bread, this pertains especially to provincial cities. Fourth, the appearance of new bread is apparently having an effect, this pertains especially to the south. The word is that a pood [16.4 kilograms] of flour at the market in Ukrainian cities costs up to 30 rubles, and the bread in our stores costs more. When Mikoian arrives we will discuss all the issues related to the above facts. Please do send in your instructions by that time.[2]

3) Regarding grain shipments and deliveries by state farms we are sending out telegrams today to each specific region [*krai*] on an individual basis. We are putting pressure on the Lower Volga in particular. At the same time we are thinking of hitting an individual grain trust and state farm in the press, because things are worst of all on the state farms.[3] On the procurements plan for the fourth quarter we will adopt specific figures tomorrow and will send them to you by wire.[4] The harvesting and carting of beets is going pretty badly, worse than last year, we will have to press the districts harder and evidently we will have to send in an additional quantity of trucks to the beet-growing districts.

4) Regarding the military plants: we specifically heard direct reports by the plants, let's hope that they shape up, but we will have to check on them.[5]

I personally attached myself to Plant 8 in Mytishchi, which flopped with the tank gun, with the anti-aircraft gun, etc. Now in accordance with your instructions we will get to work on submarines.[6]

5) We heard a report at yesterday's Politburo meeting from Piatakov on the Urals Railroad Car Plant. Things are bad there. We rebuked the Urals Regional Committee and instructed it to take measures to provide assistance. We assigned Piatakov to check on fulfillment on a daily basis, so that he will go there again in November, and we will hear a report on the progress of the construction at a Politburo meeting in December.[7]

6) We also heard about the issue of mineral fertilizers, which was raised by the a[gri]c[ultural] department [of the CC]. Yakovlev knows how to put the pressure on so that he is given a little more, but the way the use of fertilizers is organized is outrageous. There are no warehouses, the fertilizers are in bad shape, spoiling and losing their properties, and just turning into soil. The functionaries in the regions have a bad, even hostile, attitude toward fertilizers. We have placed emphasis on this issue and have set up a commission to work out this issue in all its aspects, and most important, to ensure the proper use of fertilizers in practice.[8]

Regards to you. Yours, L. Kaganovich.

P.S. The Komsomol people want to issue a message in connection with the 15th anniversary of the Komsomol, but besides that they want the CC to adopt a resolution. The draft of the message is long and I am not sending it to you, but I am sending you the draft resolution of the CC and ask that you let me know your opinion. In addition they have hinted about giving awards similar to those presented to women for women's day, please let me know your opinion about this as well.[9]

I leave you with a handshake. Yours, L. Kaganovich.

1. On 31 August, by a poll of members, the Politburo confirmed the deputy chairman, secretary and members of the resettlement committee. The resettlement committee was instructed to "arrange the resettlement of at least 10,000 families to the Kuban and the Terek by the beginning of 1934 and of 15,000–20,000 families to the Ukraine (the steppe)" (RGASPI, f. 17, op. 3, d. 930, l. 8). See also documents 61, 76.

2. On 28 February 1933, during the famine, the Politburo decided to start the "free sale" of bread (sale in addition to the ration) in special bread stores at higher prices in Moscow, Leningrad and Kharkov (ibid., d. 916, ll. 31, 92). This decision was gradually extended to other industrial centers. On 16 October, after inquiries from Stalin, Mikoian sent Kaganovich and Molotov a memorandum, which Kaganovich forwarded to Politburo members. Mikoian reported that as of 1 October the free sale of bread was underway in 145 cities and would begin after 1 October in a further 15 cities. Between the start of the free sales in March 1933 and 1 October, 335,000 tons of wheat bread and rye bread were sold for 950 million rubles. After the harvest there was a decline in sales everywhere, especially in the southern regions with the largest harvests. Mikoian therefore proposed that retail prices for the free sale of bread should be reduced by the end of October in a number of southern cities where market prices had fallen to the level of the state prices for free sale. Mikoian proposed that in the other cities prices should not be reduced until November, if at all. (APRF, f. 3, op. 43, d. 46, ll. 2–5.) On 9 November 1933 the Politburo decided to reduce prices for the free sale of bread at state stores (RGASPI, f. 17, op. 3, d. 934, ll. 12–13). Total free sales of bread in 1033 amounted to 2,187,000,000 rubles (*Sovetskaia torgovlia* [1935 (Moscow, 1936)], 74). See also document 75.

3. On 4 October the Politburo approved a decree of the CC and Sovnarkom that dealt with the failure by the Belaia Glina (White Clay) State Farm in the Northern Caucasus Region to fulfill its grain-delivery plan. The state farm director was dismissed and prosecuted. All state-farm directors were warned that in the event of delays in grain deliveries to the state they would be subject to "harsh penalties." At the same time telegrams were approved to the leaders of the Ukraine, the Central Black-Earth Region, and the Lower Volga Region with instructions to renew their efforts to obtain grain procurements (RGASPI, f. 17, op. 3, d. 932, ll. 10–11, 34–37). See also documents 75, 79.

4. The Politburo approved a resolution on the plan for grain deliveries for the fourth quarter on 6 October (ibid., l. 14).

5. On 30 September M. M. Kaganovich, a deputy people's commissar of heavy industry, wrote to Ordzhonikidze: "The thunderstorm of the 29th is over. We heard reports from the directors of the No. 8–92 and Barricades plants at the Defense Commission. So far we have managed to get by without issuing reprimands, but the situation with the program is difficult" (ibid., f. 85, op. 27, d. 214, l. 25).

6. On 5 November the Politburo approved a schedule, drawn up by a commission headed by Gamarnik, for building and delivering 20 M-type submarines in 1933 after correcting their "design flaws that were detected during testing" (ibid., f. 17, op. 162, d. 15, l. 130). See also V. I. Dmitriev, *Sovetskoe podvodnoe korablestroenie* (Soviet Submarine Construction) (Moscow, 1990). See also document 75.

7. On 1 October the Politburo considered the issue of the Uals railroad car assembly plant. Deputy People's Commissar of Heavy Industry Piatakov was instructed "to establish regular, personal supervision of the implementation of all directives for the fulfillment of construction assignments" and to travel to the site in late November or in December. The leaders of the Urals Regional Party Committee also received various assignments. It was decided to consider the issue of the plant again in December. (RGASPI, f. 17, op. 3, d. 931, l. 3.)

8. On 1 October the Politburo adopted in the main a draft resolution, submitted by the agricultural department of the CC, on the use of mineral fertilizers. A commission headed by Kaganovich was instructed to work out the question of fulfilling the program for their production and use (ibid., l. 4).

9. See note 1 to document 78.

· 78 ·

Stalin to Kaganovich
6 October

F. 81, op. 3, d. 100, ll. 34–35.

Greetings, Comrade Kaganovich:

1) I am sending my corrections to the draft resolution of the CC for the jubilee of the Komsomol. The draft has been drawn up in a slipshod manner.

We will have to give 10–15 medals (or 20) to Komsomol members.[1]

2) How long are you going to put up with the abominations at the enterprises of the PC for Supply, especially the canning and bottling plants? They have poisoned more than 100 people again! Why aren't you taking measures against the PC for Supply and Mikoian? How long is the public

going to be abused? Your (i.e. the Politburo's) patience is downright astonishing.[2]

3) It is extremely suspicious that Vangengeim is the top man in the development of materials for the high-altitude balloon,[3] the same Vangengeim who as head of the Weather Bureau promised us a great drought for the summer of 1933 and who established the State Oceanographic Institute in Murmansk, which we later smashed as a nest of German spies. What is going on here? Why such trust for this character?

Well, that is all for now.

Regards, I. Stalin.[4]

6 October 1933

1. On 29 October the Politburo approved the draft resolution of the Central Executive Committee "On Awarding the Order of Lenin to Leaders and Leading Functionaries of Communist Youth." Orders were awarded to 34 people (RGASPI, f. 17, op. 3, d. 933, ll. 29, 58–61). See also document 77.

2. See note 1 to document 80.

3. On 30 September 1933 the crew of the first Soviet high-altitude balloon, *The USSR*, ascended to an altitude of 19,000 meters, setting a world record. Further flights were prepared.

4. A note on the first page states: "Have read. Voroshilov."

· 79 ·

Kaganovich to Stalin
9 October

F. 558, op. 11, d. 741, ll. 90–97.

9 October [1933]

Greetings dear Comrade Stalin.

1) Regarding tractors and trucks I have already sent you a cipher in which I explained that the distribution plan sent to you is an initial plan that was drawn up before your letter was received. Now we have adopted a distribution plan in accordance with your instructions. As for the initial plan, about which I wrote you, we assumed that when we were approving the plan for the third quarter we said that since we gave primarily to the PC of Agriculture and the PC of State Farms in the first three quarters, in the fourth quarter we could to a certain extent satisfy other users, but with trucks and especially with the Cheliabinsk Tractor Plant it turned out to be too much to satisfy other nonagricultural users, which we corrected as soon as we received your instructions.[1]

2) With regard to agricultural campaigns, the harvest is nearing the end, although in a substantial number of districts grain is still lying in windrows in the field not in stacks and not even piled up, so we sent a telegram today to those regions. Now we are putting emphasis on the potato har-

vest, which is not going so well in a number of regions. The harvesting of beets is going poorly, mainly with regard to quality, they are not digging out much and are blaming poor crop yields. Now Mikoian has come to town and tomorrow or the day after we will take specific measures. The winter sowing has not been completed yet. It is chiefly the southern regions that are lagging: the Ukraine, the Northern Caucasus, the Crimea, the Lower Volga.

Regarding grain deliveries we have sent directives for each region individually,[2] and we sent Chernov to the Lower Volga for 10 days.[3] Regarding the Northern Caucasus Mikoian believes they will fulfill the plan, since all they have left is to procure corn, which yielded a pretty good harvest.

3) Regarding the poisonings I can report the following: as soon as we received the report, we gave instructions to the GPU to find the roots of this affair. It has now been determined that a group of wreckers was operating. Evidently, when the investigation ends, a trial must be arranged.

Simultaneously, we will discuss the issue in the Politburo along the lines of your absolutely correct assessment of the management of the canning and bottling plants, which led to unsanitary conditions and made the job easier for the wreckers through poor oversight. We will discuss this issue at the Politburo meeting on the 15th.[4]

4) Regarding Eastern Siberia I completely agree with you, perhaps we should even accelerate things, cipher after cipher is coming in from there, describing how work is breaking down. A possible replacement for Leonov would be Comrade Razumov. He could handle that kind of region. To replace him these people could be nominated: Malinov from the Central Black-Earth Region, Gurevich, one of the secretaries of Central Volga (he did not work well with Shubrikov), Lepa from Central Asia, he could definitely handle Tataria.

In any case, if you consent to Razumov, it will be easier to pick someone for Tataria. Please let me know your opinion.[5]

5) Regarding the shipment of metal, measures have been taken. On the 11th we shall have the commission on transport [on the agenda], we will check on what it has done.[6]

6) We discussed the Gorky Institute in the Orgburo and deferred it so I could find out your opinion. We don't think it should be inflated into a big teaching establishment. This is more of a research institute, where 50 to 100 people can be attached as graduate students, that in short is the crux of the issue. Please let me know your opinion. I would not bother you with it, but they are in a rush with starting arrangements and teaching.

Regards to you! Yours L. Kaganovich.

1. Kaganovich sent the cipher on tractor and vehicle distribution on 9 October (RGASPI, f. 558, op. 11, d. 81, l. 117). On the same day, evidently before he received this cipher, Stalin

in a further cipher to Kaganovich again criticized the former plan. He insisted that in future the draft plan should be submitted to the Politburo not by the PC of Heavy Industry, but by Sovnarkom jointly with the agricultural department of the CC; Kaganovich agreed on the same day. (Ibid., ll. 116, 120.) On 10 October Stalin in a further cipher agreed to the new plan, but proposed that agriculture should receive 16,000 instead of 15,000 tire tractors (ibid., l. 125). See document 76.

2. See note 3 to document 77.

3. On 7 October the Politburo sent People's Commissar of Agriculture Chernov to the Lower Volga Region for ten days to "take all the necessary measures with the regional committee to increase procurements as quickly as possible" (ibid., f. 17, op. 3, d. 932, l.15).

4. See note 1 to document 80.

5. On 18 October the Politburo resolved "to remove Comrade Leonov from the post of first secretary of the Eastern Siberian Regional Committee for failing to cope with his job, recalling him to put him at the disposal of the CC of the VKP(b)." The first secretary of the Tatar Regional Committee, Razumov, was confirmed as the new secretary in Eastern Siberia. Lepa was confirmed as first secretary of the Tatar Regional Committee (ibid., d. 933, l. 7). See also document 76.

6. See document 76.

· 80 ·

Kaganovich to Stalin
16 October

F. 558, op. 11, d. 741, ll. 105–107.

---

16 October [1933]

Greetings, dear Comrade Stalin.

1. At yesterday's Politburo meeting we discussed the poisonings in Dnepropetrovsk. Besides the wrecking activities, the way our economic leaders' work was organized was scandalous. We adopted a rather tough resolution, instructed that criminal proceedings be initiated against the director of the Chief Administration of the Canning and Bottling Industry, Markov, delivered a reprimand to Ukhanov and rebuked Comrade Mikoian. In addition we instructed two commissions to work out the issue: the first on canning and bottling plants and the second on the organization of sanitary measures.[1]

2. Regarding the transport of oil, things are not going very well. We resolved to send both Yanson and Fomin to Baku and to the Volga.[2]

3. We heard a report from Osinsky on crop yields. He reduced his original figures a little, but we still did not adopt them as final. Since the regions require a determination of crop yields as soon as possible so that they can calculate payments in kind, we approved Osinsky's proposals in the main as a basis for calculating payments in kind. We will determine the final figures later.[3]

(Osinsky's figures [in tsentners per hectare]:

winter rye	9.7
winter wheat	11.1
spring wheat	7.3
spring barley	11.1
oats	9.3).

4. Regarding all your assignments the appropriate measures have been taken, specifically the individuals to blame for the crash of the dirigible *Red Star* have been punished.[4]

Regards to you. Yours, L. Kaganovich.

1. The reference is to a mass poisoning in Dnepropetrovsk from canned food produced by the Odessa cannery. On 15 October the Politburo instructed the prosecutor's office to prepare a trial, prosecuting "all the guilty individuals in this matter." USSR people's commissar for supply Mikoian was rebuked for "the absence of proper supervision of the operations of canning and bottling plants and the failure to take all necessary measures to combat the unsanitary condition of the plants." The Politburo established two commissions, which were instructed to devise measures to improve the situation at food-industry enterprises, including sanitary supervision (RGASPI, f. 17, op. 3, d. 932, ll. 3–4). See also documents 78, 79.

2. On 15 October the Politburo adopted a decision on oil transportation. Yanson and Fomin were sent to the regions "to strengthen the hauling of oil" (ibid., l. 5).

3. On 15 October the Politburo considered the issue of crop yields. A commission, comprising Molotov, Kaganovich, and Osinsky, was established to edit the draft resolution submitted by Osinsky (ibid., l. 2).

4. On 15 October the Politburo adopted a resolution on the V-3 dirigible *Red Star*. It said the dirigible disaster on 3 November [1932] was "a consequence of careless and criminal flight preparation of the dirigible." Several functionaries were called to account (ibid., op. 162, d. 15, l. 105).

· 81 ·

Kaganovich and Molotov to Stalin
17 October
F. 558, op. 11, d. 82, ll.6–7. Authenticated typewritten copy.

[By cipher]

Gagry. To Stalin.

Skvirsky has reported that Roosevelt expects to receive a draft of the full text of the reply by the Sov[iet] gov[ernment] to the draft of his message. Once such an acceptable text is received, Roosevelt's official message will be given to Skvirsky. We are sending you two ciphers from Skvirsky[1] and this draft answer from Kalinin.

"I have received your telegram. I have always regarded as abnormal and regrettable the situation that has prevailed for 15 years, in which two great republics—the USSR and the United States of America—do not have customary methods of intercourse and are deprived of the benefits that such intercourse could provide. I am pleased to take note that you too have come to this conclusion. There can be no doubt that difficulties, if they exist or arise between two peoples, can be resolved only if regular relations exist between them, and, on the other hand, they have no chance of being resolved if such intercourse is absent. I will also allow myself to express the belief that the abnormal situation to which you properly refer in your telegram has an unfavorable effect not only on the interests of the two interested states but also on the general international situation, by increasing elements of concern, complicating the process of the consolidation of world peace, and encouraging forces that are aimed at breaching this peace.

"In accordance with the foregoing, I eagerly accept your proposal that a representative of the Soviet government be dispatched to the United States of America to discuss issues of interest to our countries with you. Kalinin."

Please let us know your opinion. In addition I report that Litvinov considers it inadvisable for him to make the trip and proposes that Sokolnikov be sent, but we hold to our previous position and believe that Litvinov should go.[2] No. 86/87/2229/sh.

Kaganovich. Molotov.

16 October 1933

1. The relevant cipher from Skvirsky was as follows: "On the basis of his conversations with the President, Bullitt has again proposed the following procedure: 1) I hand him, for Roosevelt, the draft, which he requested from me, of the full text of Kalinin's reply on the substance of the President's letter, which has already been coordinated with us. 2) If the text of our reply is acceptable, then the President's official letter will be handed to me. 3) Upon receiving this formal letter I will reply to Roosevelt, on Kalinin's instructions, with our letter. 4) After the exchange of letters the question of the day of publication and the content of the statement for the press will be decided. 5) It is assumed that by this time I will receive from you information to pass to Roosevelt on who will represent the USSR in conversation with him. Bullitt's attitude is very optimistic: he states that the President does not wish merely to establish normal relations but also close contact." (RGASPI, f. 558, op. 11, d. 82, l. 8.)

2. On 17 October Stalin and Kalinin sent a cipher to Molotov and Kaganovich agreeing with the draft but insisting that Litvinov should be sent: "act more boldly and without restraint, because the situation is now favorable" (ibid., l. 5). On the same day the Politburo approved the reply from Kalinin to Roosevelt without any changes. Litvinov was appointed as the representative of the Soviet government (ibid., f. 17, op. 162, d. 15, ll. 112, 124). On 19 October Kaganovich and Molotov sent Stalin and Kalinin a further cipher from Skvirsky in which he reported that Roosevelt objected to the phrase which had been translated as "regular relations," because "the opposition would interpret this as recognition of the USSR before the meeting with Litvinov;" Skvirsky had replaced this with the phrase "direct relations" (ibid., f. 558, op. 11, d. 82, ll. 21–22).

· 82 ·

Stalin to Kaganovich
21 October

F. 81, op. 3, d. 100, ll. 37–42.

Greetings, Comrade Kaganovich:

1) I am resolutely opposed to issuing and publishing the material for the report at the party congress that was prepared by the CC apparatus.[1] The writing itch of the "apparatchiks" has caused us quite a bit of harm. The CC apparatus (the departments) should confine itself to providing information to the CC secretaries as material for the secretaries' reports at the congress. And that's all! All the rest is nonsense.

2) The situation with artillery is very bad. Mirzakhanov has demoralized a wonderful plant. Pavlunovsky has messed things up and is ruining the artillery situation. Sergo should be flogged for entrusting a major sector to two or three of his favorite fools, showing that he is prepared to sacrifice the state's interests to these fools. All the Mirzakhanovs and Pavlunovskys must be ousted and demoted. Otherwise the situation will not be rectified.

3) The Baku oil situation is bad. This year we are producing 15 million tons of oil in Baku. Next year we must produce 21 million or 22 million tons. To do this we must step up exploration and intensify current drilling in already explored areas, strengthen Kaspar [the Caspian Shipping Organization], build reservoirs on an urgent basis in Makhach-Kala and Krasnovodsk, and so forth. Unless all of this is done on schedule (i.e. by the end of the winter, with work started immediately), the project will be ruined. In spite of this, the Chief Oil Administration is asleep on the job, and Sergo gets away with pious promises. It will be a disgrace for us if we fail to compel the PC of Heavy Industry to start work immediately and give us a report at every Politburo session on the measures it has taken. I am sending you the relevant explanatory documents from Beria. I consider them to be correct, except for the memorandum about the kerosene pipeline from Makhach-Kala to Stalingrad. Get acquainted with them and act decisively.[2]

4) I am sending you Beria's reports about rare metals in Georgia. We must move this project forward as well.[3]

Well, that is all for now. Regards.

I. Stalin.

21 October 1933

1. The reference is to the XVII Congress of the VKP(b), which took place in January and February 1934. Reports delivered at party congresses were normally accompanied by extensive materials, which were supplied to delegates and sometimes published.

2. Judging by the report in the files of the Molotov Secretariat in Sovnarkom, Beria, the secretary of the Transcaucasian Regional Committee, prepared and apparently handed over to Stalin in person a number of memoranda, including some about the development of the oil industry. He proposed including in the 1934 plan the construction of cracking plants and factories for the primary refining of oil, a pipeline from Makhach-Kala to Stalingrad, and expansion of the oil pipeline from Baku to Batum; conducting geological exploratory operations in new areas in Azerbaijan; and building new vessels for Caspian shipping (GARF, f. R-5446, op. 82, d. 25, ll. 259–260). On 31 October 1933 the Politburo instructed the PC of Heavy Industry to prepare proposals on the issues of Azerbaijan oil by the next Politburo session (RGASPI, f. 17, op. 3, d. 933, l. 31). The issue, however, was not taken up until 5 December, with Stalin's participation. The Politburo approved a resolution on Azerbaijan oil that set new plans for oil production and for major capital projects. The discussion of the oil issue resulted in personnel changes in Azerbaijan. The Politburo dismissed Ruben from the position of first secretary of the CC of the Azerbaijan Communist Party and recommended that Bagirov, chairman of the republican Sovnarkom, should replace him. (Ibid., d. 935, ll. 2, 32–34.) See also document 85.

3. On 31 October the Politburo reviewed Beria's memoranda about rare metals in Georgia. With regard to manganese at Chiatura, the PC of Heavy Industry was instructed to prepare proposals by the next Politburo session. The issues of the molybdenum and lead and zinc deposits and the production of aluminum oxide were postponed "until the control figures for 1934 were examined." (Ibid., d. 933, l. 31.) The problem of Chiatura manganese was not discussed; the issue was taken off the agenda on 3 December, in Stalin's presence (ibid., d. 935, l. 25). See also document 85.

· 83 ·

Stalin to Kaganovich and Molotov
[21 October]

F. 81, op. 3, d. 100, ll. 131–134.

Comrades Kaganovich and Molotov:

In my view, it is time to launch a broad, intelligent (not vociferous!) campaign to prepare and work on public opinion in the USSR and all other countries regarding Japan and directed against Japan's militarists in general. We should develop this in *Pravda,* and partly in *Izvestia.* We should also make use of GIZ [the state publishing house] and other publishers to issue appropriate pamphlets and books. We should acquaint people not only with negative aspects but also with positive aspects of everyday routine, life and conditions in Japan. Clearly, the negative, imperialist, expansionist, militarist aspects should be displayed prominently.

The booklet *Voenno-fashistskie dvizhenia v Yaponii* [Military Fascist Movements in Japan] was published recently. It was published (by [Military] Intelligence) for the Far East and only for selected individuals. Why such a restriction? The pamphlet should be published openly and for everyone without delay with a foreword and some corrections from Radek. This is absolutely imperative. We should also print *Travel Notes on Ja-*

pan and Korea in *Pravda* and in general, we should start an extensive, solid (but not vociferous) preparation of readers against the scum in Japan.[1]

Keep this in mind and move things along.

I. Stalin.[2]

1. See note 1 to document 85.

2. A note by Molotov on the first page reads: "<u>For members of the Politburo</u> for information. V. Molotov," together with the signatures of Andreev, Mikoian, and Ordzhonikidze.

· 84 ·

Kaganovich and Molotov to Stalin
22 October
F. 558, op. 11, d. 82, l. 29. Original. Typewritten.

Cipher.

From Moscow 22 October 1933. 3.05 A.M.   Incoming No. 83.
To Comrade Stalin.

1. Litvinov is leaving in two or three days.[1] In view of the fact that he will travel through Germany, he raised a question with us: does he have to stop in Berlin or pass through without getting out of the train?

We think it is advisable for him to stop in Berlin and not refuse to have a conversation with Neurath or, if Hitler wishes, with him as well. Regarding the substance of the discussions, if they propose signing a protocol to the effect that all conflicts have been settled, we could agree to this on the condition that in some apologetic form they publicly express regret over the improper actions by the German authorities in the conflict over the journalists.[2] If they do not demand an agreement, then he should limit himself to a conversation in a tone that makes clear to them that we do not intend to deepen the conflict, that we are prepared to do everything necessary to restore the previous relations.

2. After Berlin Litvinov will be traveling through Paris. We think that there, too, he should not refuse a meeting with Paul-Boncour if an appropriate proposal is made to Litvinov.

Please let us know your opinion.[3] No. 100

Kaganovich, Molotov.

1. The reference is to Litvinov's visit to the United States. See document 81.

2. On 22 September 1933 the German authorities arrested a TASS representative and an *Izvestia* correspondent in Berlin while they were on their way to the Leipzig trial. The Soviet journalists were released the same day. On 23 September the Politburo instructed the USSR plenipotentiary in Germany, Khinchuk, to deliver a protest to the German government about the arrests, and about the body searches of the Soviet correspondents at the trial. On 26 Sep-

tember the Politburo approved for publication a TASS announcement that Soviet correspondents were being recalled from Berlin and that all German press representatives in Moscow would be deported from the USSR. (DVP, vol. XVI, p. 858; RGASPI, f. 17, op. 162, d. 15, ll. 82, 85.)

3. On the same day Stalin sent his agreement by cipher (ibid., f. 558, op. 11, d. 82, l. 28). On 25 October the Politburo approved without change the directives for Litvinov, outlined in Kaganovich's letter, on meetings in Berlin and Paris (ibid., f. 17, op. 162, d. 15, l. 119).

· 85 ·

Kaganovich to Stalin
24 October

F. 558, op. 11, d. 741, ll. 112–115.

---

24 October [1933]

Greetings, dear Comrade Stalin!

1) I received your letters last night.

Regarding the question of providing more thorough and serious coverage of our relations with Japan in the press you are absolutely right, and the same applies to the situation in Japan itself. Tomorrow we will discuss it and will give the appropriate directives to the press and to the publishing house.[1]

Regarding the question of preparing materials for the party congress I agree with you, we will not publish them, the appropriate instructions will be given to the section heads of the CC.

Regarding the question of oil your criticism has been confirmed in particular in the case of Grozny, where a scandalous attitude toward exploration and drilling has effectively nullified a highly important basin. We distributed Beria's memorandum to the Politburo members and we may take it up at the Politburo meeting on 1 November.[2] The same goes for rare metals in Georgia.[3]

Regarding artillery we have now put on the pressure after your first letter, but we will have to take up the question again.

2) The problem of arranging the proper distribution of [agricultural] incomes is becoming a serious one in practical terms. The regions are underestimating this matter, despite the fact that agricultural work for this year is almost over already. A directive must be issued from the CC and Sovnarkom. We have drawn up such a directive. In view of the importance of this issue I am sending you this draft (it is short—three pages) and ask that you review it and let me know, if possible by wire, your comments and consent to using your signature. Just to be on the safe side I am also sending the draft that was drawn up of the PC of Agriculture instructions, which are more specific. If you find it necessary not to publish the PC of

Agriculture instructions, but rather to put a number of practical points in the directive of the CC and Sovnarkom, please let me know.[4]

Regards to you! I leave you with a handshake.

Yours, L. Kaganovich.

1. See document 83. On 25 October a conference was held in Stalin's office in the Kremlin, attended by Politburo members Molotov, Kaganovich, Ordzhonikidze and Mikoian; Stetsky, the head of the department of party propaganda and agitation of the CC of the VKP(b); Mekhlis, the editor of *Pravda;* and Gronsky, the editor of *Izvestia (Istoricheskii arkhiv,* no. 2, 1995,193). The issue of anti-Japanese propaganda in the press was probably discussed at this conference. On the following day, 26 October, *Pravda* carried a long article, "From Travel Notes on Japan and Korea." Subsequently articles on Japan appeared regularly.

2. See note 2 to document 82.

3. See note 3 to document 82.

4. On 14 November the Politburo considered the draft of the PC of Agriculture instructions on the procedure for distributing incomes. The issue was removed from the agenda, i.e. left unresolved. (RGASPI, f. 17, op. 3, d. 934, l. 19.)

1934

Introduction

IN 1934 Stalin did not receive visitors in his Kremlin office between 30 July and 31 October.[1] The considerable length of his vacation may have been justified on this occasion by the improvement of the general situation in the country.

The year 1934 was the calmest of the thirteen years of Soviet history from the "great breakthrough" of 1929 to the German invasion. In this year the economy began to yield some of the fruits of the painful struggle for industrialization in the previous five years. For the first time the production of heavy industry exceeded the plan; and the production of the food industry also increased substantially. Although the harvest was not outstanding, the amount of grain harvested was probably several million tons greater than in 1933. After the disastrous decline in 1929–33, the number of cattle, sheep, and pigs increased for the first time since 1930. An important bottleneck was the production of cotton, which, in spite of large investments, had not increased since 1931 and even declined slightly in 1934. The Politburo was no longer prepared to import substantial quantities of cotton; and the shortage restricted the production of cotton textiles—the most important light industry. This explains Stalin's close attention to the plans for cotton production in the 1934 series of letters (documents 87, 88, 89, 90).

The improvement in the economy was to some extent both a result and a prerequisite of the political thaw. The XVII Congress of the

1. *Istoricheskii arkhiv*, no. 3, 1995, 141.

Communist Party, convened in January–February 1934, implicitly confirmed the new line—the move away from the extreme policy of the crisis period to a relatively moderate course. In the directives for the second five-year plan approved by the congress, the more balanced economic policy was consolidated. In comparison with the first five-year plan the planned rate of growth of industrial output was considerably reduced, and the priority development of Group B industries (the consumer goods industries) was officially recognized. The verbatim report of the congress is distinguished by relative harmony and restraint as compared with other party meetings in these years. Immediately before and after the congress some leaders of former oppositions were restored to party membership, including Kamenev, Zinoviev, Preobrazhensky, and Uglanov. Bukharin was appointed to the quite important post of chief editor of the newspaper *Izvestia*.

Developments in 1934 followed the general course proposed by the plan. The former strategy of the "great leap forward" was abandoned. In industry various experiments and reforms were introduced. Their aim was to increase the economic autonomy of enterprises and to provide increased material incentives for the workers. The concept that direct product exchange would replace trade was abandoned, and great emphasis was placed on the role of money and economic accounting, and the need to strengthen the ruble. The predilection for asceticism and self-sacrifice, and the view that high earnings were questionable, both characteristic of the first five-year plan, gave way to stress on the notion of a "cultured and prosperous life."

The decision to abolish bread rationing, adopted at the end of 1934, was an important stage in the application of the new approach to the economy.[2] The Stalin-Kaganovich correspondence makes it possible to follow the steps by which this decision was taken. Stalin's letter of 22 October was the first occasion on which he explained his scheme to his colleagues. The state must obtain about 1,500 million poods (24 million tons) of grain "in order to get rid of the <u>rationing system</u> for bread at the end of this year, a system that until recently was necessary and useful but has now shackled the national economy" (document 109).

The Politburo evidently convened several times to discuss this question. On 28 October Stalin's letter was officially placed on the agenda, and the decision about it was recorded under the heading "Letter from

2. This decision is further discussed in O. Khlevnyuk and R. W. Davies, "The End of Rationing in the Soviet Union, 1934–1935," *Europe-Asia Studies,* 52 (1999), 557–610.

Comrade S." The Politburo supported Stalin's proposals about grain deliveries and agreed to the abolition of bread rationing from 1 January 1935. The responsibility for preparing the various measures associated with this reform was delegated to those in charge of the appropriate government departments: Veitser, the people's commissar of internal trade; Zelensky, chairman of the board of Tsentrosoiuz (responsible for the consumer cooperatives); Shvernik, in charge of the trade unions; Grinko, the people's commissar of finance; and Mezhlauk, head of Gosplan. The main problems included: fixing a single price for bread, making arrangements for the expansion of the number of trade outlets, determining the necessary grain stocks and their location, and increasing wages following the increase in bread prices. The decision emphasized that these preparations must be made "in conditions of strict secrecy." It was no doubt in order to preserve secrecy that the decision was not included in the minutes of the Politburo, but recorded "outside the minutes" (*besprotokolno*).[3] Kaganovich informed Stalin about the decision (document 111).

In the agricultural year 1934/35 the amount of grain obtained by "purchases" (*zakupki*), 3.6 million tons (220 million poods), was even greater than Stalin considered necessary. The *zakupki* were collected by the state in addition to the compulsory deliveries but were also largely compulsory in character. In total the state received 26.2 million tons (22.6 million in compulsory deliveries and 3.6 million *zakupki*), in comparison with 23.1 million tons from the previous harvest.[4] We return to the grain collection campaign below. On 25 November 1934 Molotov gave a report about the abolition of bread rationing to the plenum of the party Central Committee, which was published in the press with minor changes. On the following day Stalin spoke to the plenum on the same subject, discussing it in a wider context than in his letter of 22 October. He treated the abolition of rationing as an important stage in the strengthening of the monetary system and trade.[5]

The innovations in the economy were accompanied by some amelioration of the policy of repression. The practical application of some of the most savage laws was modified: thus the number of cases

3. APRF, f. 3, op. 43, d. 51, l. 47.

4. I. L. Strilever, S. A. Khazanov and L. S. Yampolskii, *Khlebooborot i standarty* (Moscow, 1935), 17, 167.

5. *Pravda*, 30 November 1934. The original record of Molotov's report may be found in RGASPI, f. 17, op. 2, d. 528 (printed text), d. 536 (typed text). Stalin's speech may be found in ibid., d. 530, ll. 78–98.

brought under the law of 7 August 1932 was substantially reduced. The use of repression outside the courts, including such practices as sentencing by extraordinary "triumvirates" (*troiki*), was also restricted.[6]

Foreign policy considerations also played an important part in bringing about these changes. The increased threat by the fascist states brought the Soviet Union closer to the Western democracies in resistance to Nazi Germany and imperial Japan. This made it necessary to demonstrate the "democratic achievements" of the Soviet government to the international public, to show that there was a fundamental difference between fascism and communism.

The Soviet leaders were, however, still ready to make use of extraordinary measures, sometimes under the influence of the growing foreign danger. A sign of the times was the decision to detain in the Soviet Union the famous physicist Peter (Pyotr) Kapitsa, who had been working in England at Cambridge University for many years. It has long been known that Kapitsa remained in Moscow in 1934 against his will. The Kaganovich-Stalin correspondence shows that this was a decision at the highest level, directly involving Stalin, Kaganovich, Kuibyshev, and Voroshilov. On 20 September 1934 Kuibyshev and Kaganovich sent Stalin a ciphered telegram setting out the circumstances:

> The physicist Kapitsa, a citizen of the USSR, is again on a visit to Moscow (to the Mendeleev congress). On our instructions comrade Piatakov held discussions with him about working in the USSR. Kapitsa refused on these grounds:
>
> a) the unique conditions for scientific work provided for him in Britain (although comrade Piatakov offered him everything he demanded); b) his personal obligation to Rutherford, the director of the Cambridge institute, who helped him to become a scientist with a world name; c) some research projects started in Britain are incomplete—after completing them, in a few years' time, he is ready to work in the Soviet Union, the citizenship of which he greatly values.
>
> Kapitsa stated that he is ready to give all his inventions to the USSR, and he invites any scientific delegation to his laboratory in Cambridge to take over his inventions, as well as students for training. When he was in Kharkov Kapitsa transferred to the Institute of Physics and Chemistry the drawings of his apparatus for producing liquid helium (liquid helium eliminates any resistance to electric current and thus foreshadows a revolution in electrical engineering).

6. See P. H. Solomon, Jr., *Soviet Criminal Justice Under Stalin* (Cambridge, UK, 1996), 153–95.

We propose: a) to talk with Kapitsa once again in the name of the government; b) if the discussions do not lead to a positive result, to detain Kapitsa for military service, which he has not yet undertaken; c) in any case, not to permit Kapitsa to go abroad even temporarily, as there is every reason to believe that he will not return to the Soviet Union again, and will conceal his inventions; d) in the extreme case, to put him under arrest.

The detention of Kapitsa in the Soviet Union will lead to a great uproar in Britain (his links with Baldwin, Simon, and other British politicians are wellknown), and on these grounds Krestinsky strongly opposes Kapitsa's detention. We think that the situation must be brought to an end in which one of our citizens is furnishing a foreign country with inventions of military significance.

We ask you urgently to inform us of your opinion. Voroshilov is informed about this matter.[7]

Stalin replied affirmatively on the following day.[8] On the same day, September 21, he sent a ciphered telegram to Kaganovich and Kuibyshev confirming this decision, but implicitly rejecting the crude scheme to call up Kapitsa for military service: "Further to my ciphered telegram no. 66, it is possible not to arrest Kapitsa formally, but it is necessary to detain him compulsorily in the USSR and not to let him go to Britain, on the basis of the well-known law about non-returnees. This will be something like house arrest. Then we shall see."[9]

Lord Rutherford sought to secure Kapitsa's return to Britain, and on Litvinov's advice the Politburo agreed that Maisky, the Soviet plenipotentiary in Britain, should explain frankly to Rutherford that Kapitsa was being detained because "the Soviet government considers it necessary to utilize for scientific activity within the country all the Soviet scientists who until now have been working abroad."[10] In due course Rutherford agreed to sell Kapitsa's Cambridge laboratory to the Soviet government for £30,000.[11] Kapitsa did not return to Britain on a visit until over thirty years later.

The reaction of Stalin to the "Nakhaev affair" was a sinister manifestation of the suspicion and cruelty which were deeply rooted in his mentality, together with a conventional image of "the sharpening of

7. RGASPI, f. 558, op. 11, d. 85, ll. 77–78.

8. Ibid., l. 76.

9. Ibid., l. 91.

10. *Akademia nauk v resheniiakh Politbiuro TsK RKP(b)-VKP(b), 1922–1952* (Moscow, 2000), 160–62 (Politburo decision of 23 October 1934).

11. Ibid., 195–96 (Politburo decision of 25 September 1935).

the class struggle." His attitude was supported or accepted by the other leaders. Nothing was known about this affair until the archives were declassified. On 5 August 1934 A. S. Nakhaev, the chief of staff of the artillery division of Osoaviakhim—the Society to Assist Defense, and Aviation and Chemical Development (the organization responsible for civil defense against air and gas attack)—took charge of a detachment of recruits who were undergoing military training in a camp near Moscow. The detachment was brought on to the territory of the barracks of the 2d Infantry Regiment of the Moscow Proletarian Infantry Division, which was located almost in the center of Moscow. He proceeded to address the soldiers. According to the statements of eyewitnesses, he said something like this:

> We were victorious in 1914 and 1917. We seized the factories and the land for the workers and peasants, but they got nothing. Everything is in the hands of the state and a handful of people are in charge of this state. The state is enslaving the workers and peasants. There is no freedom of speech, Semites are ruling the country. Comrade workers, where are your factories, which they promised to give you in 1917? Comrade peasants, where is your land, which they promised to give you? Down with the old leaders, long live a new revolution, long live a new government.[12]

The soldiers were not armed (trainees were not issued with weapons which were completely ready to be fired). Nakhaev ordered them to occupy the guardhouse of the unit and seize the arms which were stored there. But no one obeyed the order, and Nakhaev was arrested almost immediately. Kaganovich's first communication to Stalin on the matter was quite restrained. Explaining that the results of the investigation were not yet available, he did not draw definite conclusions. He also told Stalin that in Voroshilov's opinion Nakhaev was a "psychopath" (document 87). There were more than enough grounds for this conclusion. Nakhaev's actions looked senseless. The information which was assembled about Nakhaev portrayed a sick, isolated thirty-year-old, weighed down with numerous everyday problems and in a state of disarray in his military service. It also emerged that Nakhaev was preparing to commit suicide, but was arrested so quickly that he did not have time to drink the poisoned liquid in the bottle he had prepared.

Stalin, however, pushed the affair in a different direction. When he

12. APRF, f. 3, op. 50, d. 407, l. 5.

received the first very vague records of the interrogation of Nakhaev, he insisted that Nakhaev should be made to confess that he was a member of a whole organization and also a foreign spy, "Polish-German or Japanese." Stalin was not satisfied with the "liberalism" of the Chekists (the OGPU interrogators), and insisted that Nakhaev must be treated with severity—"he must be destroyed" (document 88). Stalin required that in Osoaviakhim and in the military generally the affair should be given the most serious attention; measures to guard military objects should be strengthened. This led to the launching of a campaign to intensify vigilance. Supplementary subdivisions of the NKVD were established to supervise Osoaviakhim; and A. I. Kork was removed from the post of commander of the Moscow Military District. In response to Stalin's directives, the Chekists with a great deal of effort managed to fabricate a case about Nakhaev's links with his former colleague in the Moscow Institute of Physical Fitness, the former tsarist General Bykov (see documents 95, 97). In a memorandum to Stalin dated 15 November 1934, Yagoda informed him that it was Bykov who had instructed Nakhaev to organize the demonstration. Bykov himself was allegedly connected with the Estonian diplomatic mission in Moscow.[13] On 5 December 1934 the Politburo, in accordance with Yagoda's proposal in his memorandum, resolved to forward the Nakhaev case to a closed hearing in the military tribunal of the Supreme Court of the USSR.[14] Nakhaev was probably executed.

The methods used in fabricating the Nakhaev affair were characteristic of the Stalin period. The methods by which the grain campaign of 1934 was carried out in the countryside were equally typical, and often repeated. Stalin had evidently decided that the grain collections must be forced ahead in order to make it possible to abolish bread rationing. Paradoxically but characteristically, the basis for economic reform was laid by draconian means. Stalin raised the issue of the grain collections in no fewer than nine letters in the most energetic terms. "If you display the slightest complacency in grain procurements, we could get into trouble this year," he wrote on 12 August (document 90). On 25 August he accused colleagues of complacency, and again called for organizing, "without delay, a campaign of pressure (pressure as strong as possible!) for procurements," and this should not exclude "some 'voluntary-coercive' measures" in the good-harvest regions to spur

13. *Akademia nauk*, 195–96.
14. RGASPI, f. 17, op. 162, d. 17, l. 87.

purchases of grain (document 96). On 6 September he proposed that 70 percent rather than 60 percent of grain purchases should be in the form of food crops, and ruled that the percentage of purchases retained locally should be reduced. He again warned: "You have no idea what kind of catastrophe is in store for the state if we fail to purchase <u>all</u> 200 million poods [3,276,000 tons] of grain" (document 100). On 13 September he sharply criticized Kaganovich for his proposal to reduce the deliveries from Ukraine, insisting on a turn to a hard policy (document 102).

Under pressure from Stalin the grain collections were again carried out by extraordinary methods, by frontal attack. Numerous plenipotentiaries traveled out from the center, including most members of the Politburo. Those who failed to deliver were frequently subjected to arrests and fines. Decisions were adopted which increased the pressure for taxes applied to individual noncollectivized peasants. Kaganovich actively participated in the campaign. He visited Ukraine, Western Siberia, and the Moscow and Cheliabinsk Regions. These journeys, following the usual pattern, involved the use of repressive measures against local leaders. In the Cheliabinsk Region, for example, following a warning by Stalin that "the situation is really bad" (see document 102), a sitting of the bureau of the regional party committee was convened on 7–9 October; the secretaries of the district committees and the heads of the political departments of the MTS were summoned from "districts lagging in the grain procurements." The subsequent decision noted that "the Cheliabinsk Region is still lagging shamefully in grain procurements and the harvest." It stated that the main mistake of the local authorities was their "indulgent treatment of the opportunist attitudes common in district party committees, district soviet executive committees, and the political departments of MTS and state farms." The regional leaders were accused of "engaging over a long period in attempts at persuasion, and in warnings, instead of adopting practical measures to put pressure on the disrupters of the grain procurements." The decision claimed that "counterrevolutionary elements—followers of Kolchak and Dutov, and kulaks"—were active, and condemned the courts and the prosecutor's office for their inactivity.[15] A large group of local officials were dismissed from their posts, expelled from the party, or put on trial. The regional prosecutor was

15. Admiral A. V. Kolchak (1874–1920) was the leader of the White forces after 1918; Lieutenant-General A. I. Dutov (1879–1921) was an anti-Bolshevik Cossack leader.

ordered to "keep close watch on the progress of cases concerning the violation of the law about grain deliveries and on the actions of counterrevolutionary elements."

Clauses of the decision, not intended for publication, instructed the leadership of the Cheliabinsk regional NKVD to speed up the investigations and transfer to the courts of a number of current cases concerning counterrevolutionary groups. The prosecutor of the region and the chairman of the regional court were to organize in a matter of days "several cases in which the supreme penalty is applied." The sentences were to be published in the press.[16] A communication about this decision was sent to Moscow by telegram and approved by the Politburo on 10 October.[17]

Other members of the Politburo used similar methods. Thus on 19 September the Politburo, on Molotov's proposal, delegated to Eikhe, secretary of the Western Siberian committee of the party, the right to sanction on his own authority sentences to death by shooting; this violated the procedures established earlier to maintain strict control from Moscow over death sentences.[18] Kuibyshev was sent to Central Asia in November to accelerate the collection of cotton. On 7 November, he informed Stalin and Molotov from Uzbekistan that "the direct collusion of sections of the *bai* is playing a major role in the delay in the cotton harvest" (in Central Asia the *bai* were the rich farmers). Kuibyshev reported that "those guilty of direct organized *bai*-kulak resistance" had been put on trial. He also requested the authority to establish a special commission of three persons (Kuibyshev himself, the first secretary of the Uzbekistan party Central Committee, and the chairman of the Sovnarkom of Uzbekistan) with the right to confirm sentences to death by shooting without higher authorization.[19] With the authorization of the Politburo, Kuibyshev introduced similar arrangements in Tajikistan, Kirgizia, and Turkmenia.

The situation in the countryside in 1934 was not as disastrous as in previous years, and in general repression was not as severe. But the actions of the supreme Soviet leaders created conditions for a fresh escalation of terror. This took place shortly after Stalin's return from leave, following the murder of Kirov in Leningrad on 1 December.

16. RGASPI. f. 17, op. 21, d. 5658, ll. 156–161.

17. Ibid. op. 3, d. 953, l. 41. For Kaganovich's impressions of his visit see document 110.

18. *Stalinskoe Politburo v 30-e gody Sbornik dokumentov*, ed. O. V. Khlevniuk, A.V. Kvashonkin, L. P. Kosheleva, and L. A. Rogovaya (Moscow, 1995), 65.

19. GARF, f. R-5446, op. 27, d. 73, l. 3.

5/VIII 1934г 4

Здравствуйте дорогой Сталин!

1) Сегодня у нас было первое заседание П.Б. после вашего отъезда. Утвердили мы ряд постановлений, подготовлявшихся давно как то: с крацицах, о консервах и рыбе, о постройке нового типа плотины по методу инженер Сенькова и т.д. Обсудили мы некоторые вопросы внесеные нар контролем: о бирофеевых операциях Н.К Вейгорга, который вопреки постановлению Ц.К,

Document 87 (first page). Letter from Lazar Kaganovich to Joseph Stalin, 5 August 1934.

Т. Кагановичу

89

19/VIII -35

1) По счет предложения
Бегера я уже послал
вам шифровку.

2) По счет орлов на
башнях посылаю свое
согласие с этим письмом.

3) Предлагаю занять
немедля „Прожектор",
как совершенно неnужный,
а бумагу (освободившую)
а) передать журналу
„Огонек", который ведется

Document 113 (first page). Letter from Stalin to Kaganovich, 19 August 1935.

Кому послана т•т• КАГАНОВИЧУ, МОЛОТОВУ• АРХИВ II СЕКТОРА•

ШИФРОВКА

Из ГАГРИ .... отправлена 22-17•X• ...... 193 3г. Поступила в ЦК ВКП
на расшифрование 17•X• .... 193 3. ч. 10 м. —
Вх. № 1961/ш•

МОСКВА ЦКВКП(б) – т•т•КАГАНОВИЧУ, МОЛОТОВУ•–

Первое• Голосую за Разумова в Сибирь и за Лепу в Татарию•
Второе• Поторопитесь с ответом Рузвельту, обстановка теперь
такова, что наш положительный ответ может дать желательное решение
вопроса• Мы получаем плюс также на Дальвосте•

С Т А Л И Н•

Расшифрована 17•X 193 3 г. в ч. 10 м. 40 *Напечатано* 4 экз. КОЗЛОВ•
Подпись

ИЗВЛЕЧЕНИЕ ИЗ ИНСТРУКЦИИ:

1. Шифротелеграмма должна храниться только в секретных хранилищах.
2. При ссылках на текст шифротелеграмм воспрещается указывать, что цитируемый текст получен шифром, также воспрещается
   указывать и номера шифровок.
3. Ответ на шифровку посылается также в шифрованном виде, текст передаваемого шифром сообщения составляется коротко и ясно:
   пишется только в одном экземпляре, который и передается на расшифрование.

Ciphered telegram from Stalin to Kaganovich and Molotov, 16 October 1933. The telegram was sent from Gagry at 0:22 A.M. on 17 October, received in Moscow at 10 A.M., and deciphered at 10:40 A.M. Four copies were made. Document 81, a cipher sent by Kaganovich and Molotov to Stalin later on 17 October, is a reply to this telegram, which reads:

MOSCOW CC VKP(B). TO COMRADES KAGANOVICH, MOLOTOV.
First. I vote for sending Razumov to Siberia and Lepa to Tataria.
Second. Hurry up with the answer to Roosevelt. The situation now is such that our positive answer may give the solution we want to the question. We will also gain an advantage in the Far East.

STALIN

The printed heading of the cipher reads:

STRICTLY SECRET
Making copies is forbidden

TO BE RETURNED WITHIN 48 HOURS
(Resolution of Politburo, 5 May 1927, protocol 100. para. 5)

The note at the bottom of the cipher reads:

EXCERPT FROM THE INSTRUCTIONS

1. Ciphered telegrams are to be kept only in secret repositories.
2. In references to the text of a ciphered telegram, it is forbidden to state that the text cited was received by cipher; it is also forbidden to state the number of the cipher.
3. Replies to ciphers are also to be sent as ciphers; the text sent by cipher is to be brief and clear. Only one copy is to be written down, and this copy is to be sent for deciphering.

Genia, Kaganovich's mother.

Moisei, Kaganovich's father.

Kaganovich with Maria, his wife, and Maia, their daughter, 1934.

Kaganovich with his wife and daughter, 1934.

Kaganovich with his wife and daughter, 1934.

Kaganovich with his wife and daughter, 1936.

Stalin on holiday in Sochi, 1932.

Stalin and companions traveling by steamer, hunting, and relaxing on vacation in the south, August 1933. From a photo album compiled by the Operational Department of OGPU.

Kaganovich at the opening of the Board of Honor of the collective farms of
the Moscow Region, November 1934.

Kaganovich and Stalin walking in the Kremlin after the parade,
1 May 1934.

A. A. Andreev, 1934.

Kaganovich, 1934 or 1935.

Molotov and Voroshilov, 12 March 1935.

Khrushchev (second from left) and Kaganovich with the builders of the Moscow
metro, spring 1935.

Kaganovich and Mikoyan, December 1935.

Stalin and Kaganovich wearing gift robes at the conference of the vanguard collective farmers of Tajikistan, 4 December 1935.

Ordzhonikidze and Kaganovich, mid-1930s.

Left to right: Molotov, Kaganovich, Stalin, Mikoyan, Kalinin, M. F. Shkiryatov, N. I. Ezhov, Khrushchev, 1936.

Kaganovich, 1936 or 1937.

Documents 86–111

· 86 ·

Stalin to Kaganovich
5 August

F. 81, op. 3, d. 100, ll. 43–46.

Comrade Kaganovich:

I am sending you my criticisms regarding the <u>conduct</u> of the editors of *Bolshevik* related to their commentaries ("From the Editors") on the letter from Engels to <u>Ioan Nedejde</u>.

I don't think the commentaries by the *Bolshevik* editors are an accident. It seems to me that they are the handiwork of Comrade Zinoviev. If the editors point out that they did not receive my previous criticisms, approved by the CC, regarding Engels' article "On the Foreign Policy of Tsarism," that will be a formalistic evasion of the issue, because they certainly were aware of those criticisms through Comrade Adoratsky.[1] I think this is a serious matter. We cannot leave *Bolshevik* in the hands of such blockheads, whom Comrade Zinoviev can always dupe. The guilty individuals must be identified and removed from the staff.

The best thing is to oust Comrade Zinoviev.[2]

Regards.

P.S. <u>Send out my enclosed letter to members of the Politburo and others.</u>

I. Stalin.

5 August 1934.

P.P.S. My criticisms of Engels' article should be shown to Knorin and Stetsky, even though they are familiar with them.

I. St.

---

1. On 22 July 1934 the Politburo decided that it was inadvisable to publish Engels' article in *Bolshevik*. This decision was preceded by a letter from Stalin to Politburo members and Adoratsky, dated 19 July, which gave a critical assessment of the article (see Appendix: document 2).

2. See note 2 to document 90.

· 87 ·

Kaganovich to Stalin
5 August

F. 558, op. 11, d. 742, ll. 4–14.

5 August [1934]
Greetings dear Comrade Stalin.

1) Today we had the first Politburo meeting since your departure. We approved a number of resolutions, which had been in preparation for a long time, namely: on dyes, on canned food, bottled drinks, and fish, on the construction of a new type of dam according to the method of the engineer Senkov, etc.[1] We discussed several issues submitted by the party control people: the transactions on the foreign commodity exchange by the PC of Foreign Trade, which, in violation of the CC resolution that prohibited the purchase of cotton at the exchange and even not of real cotton but of futures, repeated its speculative cotton transaction this year. We issued a rebuke to Boev. We also chastised the PC of Foreign Trade for distortions in the awarding of bonuses, which in effect practiced almost a system of bribery of functionaries. The party Control Commission also submitted the question of electric welding, where along with significant achievements there are also shortcomings, and, most important, this matter needs a new impetus. This issue was discussed rather passionately. As a result of the discussion we established a commission to work on proposals. Sovnarkom submitted the problem of improving seed-growing work for cotton, together with proposals. I considered this draft inadequate, mostly declarative, it contains nothing, for example, about the way the work is organized, no seed-growing districts are specified, there are no measures to provide incentives for collective farms, etc. As a result of the discussion we established a commission to work out proposals. I also had a question about whether this question should be linked to the whole question of cotton in the formulation that you gave. Please do write me, in which direction the issue of cotton should be moved or should we maybe postpone to the fall?[2] We approved the plan for flax and the instructions for the harvesting and processing of flax.

We called in the people from Gorky in connection with the information about outrages and thefts at the auto plant and the workers' supply department. The Gorky people disputed some of the allegations, we decided to send Piatakov, Kosarev, and Sorokin there to investigate on the scene. The situation with regard to management of the plant is bad, we may have to replace Diakonov, of course if we do, we will consult you.[3]

We adopted a resolution today on the second stage of the subway. For the most part the draft that you edited remained intact. Two points have been added, and the resolution has been appended to the Politburo minutes. Please let me know whether to publish it. Comrade Molotov has doubts, and if we publish it, permit us to publish it over your signature.

2) We held a conference of prosecutors.[4] Our impression of them is not very good, it is a rather weak crowd. There are some good functionaries, who with support could develop. They are very pleased, of course, with both the CC decision and the very fact that a conference was convened. They criticized themselves and promised to improve their work. It clearly emerged at the conference that too many people are prosecuted, often people are put on trial for no good reason. There are regions in which more than half of those convicted and prosecuted are later acquitted and the sentences are overturned. The quality of judges and their work are low. So the central issue is the selection and training of people and at the next Orgburo meeting we will take it up.

3) Stetsky proposes that the writers' congress adopt a declaration on the tasks of Soviet writers, so that all of the participants in the congress sign it. We don't think we should compel everybody to sign it, after all there will be various kinds of people there. A declaration could be adopted, but by a simple vote. Please let us know your opinion. In addition there is a plan to adopt a statement against war and fascism.[5]

4) The Ukrainians made a request that we add a reduction of 4 million poods [67,500 tons] for the Dnepropetrovsk Region. Khataevich himself is asking for 6 million. We have not given them an answer yet. Please let me know your opinion. Just in case I am sending you their letter addressed to you.[6]

5) A very unpleasant incident occurred today involving an artillery division of Osoaviakhim [the Society to Assist Defense, and Aviation and Chemical Development]. I will not describe it in detail. The memorandum on this incident is short, and I am sending it to you. We have instructed Yagoda and Agranov to lead the investigation personally. Comrade Voroshilov has reported to us that he (Nakhaev), the chief of staff of the division, is a psychopath. I have just now spoken with comrade Agranov, he told me that in his opinion Nakhaev at the first interrogation conveyed the impression of a normal person, but somewhat distressed. So far he is stingy about giving evidence. We will have a record of the interrogation tonight, and I will send it to you. There must still be clarification as to whether he had accomplices or is a loner. Clearly, Osoaviakhim messed up here. I will inform you in the future on the progress of the investigation.[7]

I will close my letter here. I am very sorry that during the very first days I made two mistakes regarding Florinsky[8] and the publication of the resolution. Today both have already been corrected.

Regards to you.

Yours, L. Kaganovich.

1. All the decisions that Kaganovich goes on to report in his letter were recorded in the minutes of the Politburo meeting of 5 August (RGASPI, f. 17, op. 3, d. 949).

2. See documents 88, 89, 98.

3. The report of the commission to the Gorky auto plant was approved "in the main" by the Politburo on 23 September (ibid., d. 952, l. 6). Nizhny Novgorod was renamed Gorky in honor of the writer in 1932; its old name was restored in 1991.

4. The conference of functionaries of the prosecutor's office took place in the Central Committee on 1 August. See the transcript of the conference in ibid., op. 165, d. 47.

5. See note 2 to document 88.

6. See note 3 to document 88.

7. See documents 88, 89, 90, 91, 95, and 97 and the introduction to this chapter.

8. The head of the protocol section of the PC of Foreign Affairs, Florinsky, was accused by the OGPU of being an active homosexual and a long-term spy (for more detail, see L. Maksimenkov, *Sumbur vmesto muzyki. Stalinskaia kulturnaia revoliutsiia, 1936–1938* [A Muddle Instead of Music: The Stalinist Cultural Revolution, 1936–1938] [Moscow, 1997], 205–6). In a cipher of 4 August Stalin inquired why Florinsky had not been arrested (RGASPI, f. 558, op. 11, d. 73, l. 12), and on the same day Kaganovich replied that he had delayed the arrest for two days at Litvinov's request in view of the visit to Moscow of the Estonian minister of foreign affairs, but "I am to blame" because "the couple of days was extended to six days" (ibid.).

· 88 ·

Stalin to Kaganovich
[8 August]

F. 81, op. 3, d. 100, ll. 135–136.

_____

To Comrade Kaganovich.

I received your letter.

1) Regarding cotton I had in mind a three-year plan for development of cotton growing along the following lines: a) increasing crop yields (with fertilizers, better cultivation, and irrigation) and b) expansion of areas, both in Central Asia and especially in Transcaucasia (Mugan, the Milskaia steppe, etc.). This project must be assigned for study and then a decision adopted.[1]

2) Regarding the writers' congress and the declaration, consult Zhdanov, who will be in Moscow in a few days.[2]

3) I have already communicated in a cipher about Khataevich and the Dnepropetrovsk Region.[3]

4) The Nakhaev affair is about a piece of scum. He is, of course (of course!), not alone. He must be put up against the wall and forced to talk—to tell the whole truth and then severely punished. He must be a Polish-German (or Japanese) agent. The Chekists become laughable when they discuss his "political views" with him (this is called an interrogation!). A venal mutt doesn't have political views—otherwise he would not

be an agent for an outside force. He called on armed people to act against the government—so he must be destroyed.

Apparently, not everything is in good shape at Osoaviakhim.[4]

Regards, I. St.

1. See documents 87 and 89, and note 1 to document 98.

2. On 23 August the Politburo approved a resolution that was to be submitted to the writers' congress (RGASPI, f. 17, op. 3, d. 950, ll. 51, 103). See also document 87 and note 8 to document 95.

3. On 9 August the Politburo granted a petition by the CC of the Ukrainian Communist Party for an additional reduction of 4 million poods (66,000 tons) in the annual plan for grain deliveries in the Dnepropetrovsk Region. The leaders of the Ukraine and Dnepropetrovsk Regions were warned that this plan was final and "is to be fulfilled unconditionally" (ibid., op. 162, d. 17, l. 5). See also document 87.

4. See document 87.

· 89 ·

Kaganovich to Stalin
12 August

F. 558, op. 11, d. 742, ll. 21–27.

---

12 August [1934]

Greetings dear Comrade Stalin!

1) I am sending you yet another letter from Zinoviev and a letter from Adoratsky. They have all gotten panicky, but what is bad is that they grow wise after the event. As for Zinoviev, I think that he did consciously want to draw us into an open debate with Engels so that he could become a defender of Engels. Of course he did not expect such a sharp reaction and is now beating a retreat. Last night the people at *Bolshevik* provided a draft of the article, but since it needs a number of corrections, we will correct it and will send it to you to look at.[1]

2) Regarding the Nakhaev affair you are absolutely right in your assessment both of the substance of the case and of the weaknesses of the interrogation. He is not showing his real roots yet. All of his behavior is confirmation that he is a foreign agent. In a couple of days we will have to settle the issue once and for all along the lines of your instructions. Just in case I am sending you the report of the NKVD. I am sending you another short memorandum from Nik. Kuibyshev on the barracks, very substantive and interesting.[2]

3) The literary issues are growing more serious. Yesterday Comrade Gorky sent *Pravda* an article aimed at Comrades Vareikis and Yudin, where he attacks them with extraordinary harshness. But the problem is not only the harshness but the fact that there are politically incorrect

propositions there, such as the notion that "people from the ancient, tor-mented, still-wild countryside are going to work at factories, plants and to the cities." I gave Mekhlis my consent not to publish this article for the time being.[3] Yesterday Kriuchkov called Comrade Molotov and said that Gorky was asking to come see him [Molotov], and Comrade Molotov in-vited me. I proposed that we postpone it at least until Comrade Zhdanov's arrival, so as to get your guidance through him. Simultaneously a big cam-paign (Kirshon, Afinogenov, Bruno Yasensky) has unfolded against the leadership of the organizing committee. Gorky was insisting on putting in Averbakh to the writers' congress from Moscow, but nothing came of it, which riled him up even more. It seems to me that former RAPP people [members of the Russian Association of Proletarian Writers] are at work here to a large extent. They cannot issue a command, but they are trying to do so through Gorky.[4] According to available information a number of writers are not very happy with the peremptory and decreelike tone of Comrade Gorky's statements.[5] I am sending you the article and Mekhlis's memorandum.

4) As you instructed we have launched appropriate press coverage of the Japanese situation, by printing both dispatches and articles. Yurenev's last cipher shows that Hirota's stance is not as much of an ultimatum as he [Yurenev] depicted it at first. Please indicate whether the dispatches and articles on Japan in recent days were suitable, so that we know how to ori-ent ourselves in the future.

5) On cotton: we will then start to do some work on the issue along the lines of the instructions in your letter, and we will adopt a resolution on seeds without waiting for a conclusion to the issue as a whole.[6]

6) We in the commission considered the Statute on the PC of the Timber Industry. Please give us your instructions on the following question: right now forest conservation and forestry are scattered between the PC of Agriculture, the PC of the Timber Industry, and in part the PC of Heavy Industry, shouldn't we consolidate the whole thing at the PC of the Timber Industry and entrust it with full responsibility for forest preservation and cultivation?[7]

7) An answer to my inquiry came from Yezhov, that so far he does not feel better, he has now been sent to a resort in Austria and is being prom-ised a cure. They reject our doctors' diagnosis and point to gastrointesti-nal disease.[8]

Regards! Yours, L. Kaganovich.

1. See note 2 to document 90.

2. During this time Politburo members and Stalin were sent several memoranda concern-ing the Nakhaev Affair: (1) memoranda from N. Kuibyshev, dated 10 and 11 August, on the inspection of the state of security at the barracks of the Moscow garrison and the disorders in Osoaviakhim, (2) a memorandum from the NKVD on the condition of barracks and mili-

tary camps in Moscow, and (3) an NKVD report on the Nakhaev Affair (APRF, f. 3, op. 50, d. 407, ll. 101–133). See also document 90; note 6 to document 95; and note 6 to document 87.

3. See note 2 to document 91.

4. See note 3 to document 91, and document 105.

5. In the rough draft of Kaganovich's letter, point 3 was worded differently and contained several additional details: "3) Yesterday Comrade Gorky sent *Pravda* an article in which he levels, in passing, rather harsh criticism at Comrades Vareikis and Yudin, the problem, of course, is not the harshness but the substance. The people at *Pravda* requested permission not to publish Gorky's article, we told them that one cannot do that to an article by Gorky, if some corrections are needed, they can be coordinated with him. I gave my consent to hold up publication <u>for the time being</u>, intending to get instructions from you (I am sending you the article). Yesterday Kriuchkov called and said that Comrade Gorky was asking Comrades Molotov and Kaganovich to come see him, we will do that, of course, as soon as we receive your opinion of his article. The preparation for the writers' congress is proceeding on a wide scale and is going pretty well, simultaneously a campaign (Kirshon, Afinogenov, Bruno Yasensky) has developed against the organizing committee. A struggle is being waged in favor of bringing Averbakh to the writers' congress from Moscow, they are even trying to make use of Gorky's authority for this purpose. The RAPP people are seeking to regain their leading position in the Writers' Union, but of course we cannot allow this, not only because this runs directly counter to the opinion and resolution of the party CC, but it would also harm the further development of writers' creativity."

6. See note 1 to document 98.

7. On 18 August Stalin in a cipher to Kaganovich wrote that "forest conservation should not be entrusted to any one agency"; forests of local significance should be transferred from the PC of Agriculture to the NKVD, and conservation of forests of industrial significance should be the responsibility of the PCs exploiting the forests. Forest plantations in the steppes to guard against drought, and their conservation, should be entrusted to the PC of Agriculture. (RGASPI, f. 558, op. 11, d. 83, ll. 95–96.) These proposals were incorporated in a Politburo decision of 15 September (ibid., f. 17, op. 3, d. 952, l. 9).

8. On 31 August Kaganovich sent a telegram to Austria conveying the opinion of the Moscow doctors that Yezhov should not undergo an operation "without acute need" (ibid., f. 558, op. 11, d. 84, l. 67).

· 90 ·

Stalin to Kaganovich

12 August

F. 81, op. 3, d. 100, ll. 48–52.

<u>To Comrade Kaganovich</u>

1) Take note of Comrade Dvinsky's memorandum (enclosed) on short-falls in grain procurements and read my proposals there.[1] If you display the slightest complacency in grain procurements, we could get into trouble this year. Don't forget that the <u>plan</u> for procurements this year is 70 million poods [1,146,000 tons] <u>less than the actual</u> procurements last year.

2) We must include in the resolution on *Bolshevik* a clause removing Comrade Knorin as executive editor [literally, "responsible editor"]. We

cannot pin everything on Comrade Zinoviev. Comrade Knorin is more, not less, responsible than Comrade Zinoviev. Besides, we cannot kick out every member of the editorial board—Knorin and Pospelov can be kept on as regular members. If Mekhlis "rebels," he can be excluded. Make Stetsky the executive editor.[2]

3) Regarding Nakhaev—keep pressing. Call in Kork and his political assistant and give them a tongue-lashing for the heedless and sloppy conduct in the barracks. The PC of Defense must issue an order in every district with regard to sloppy conduct that has been observed. The inspectors must be more vigorous in checking barracks, arms depots, etc.[3]

4) Take note of the daydreamer—Adoratsky, who was familiar with my criticisms of Engels' article and still approved the editorial note in *Bolshevik*. Things at the Institute of Marx, Engels, and Lenin are not in good shape at all. The "scholar" Orakhelashvili proved to be a bumbler (look how many times now!). Where is his "erudition"?

5) Take note of the PC of Internal Trade. Where is it, and in general, does it exist? Where is Veitser? This is a very important matter—keep it in mind.[4]

Regards. I. Stalin.

12 August 1934

1. The second page of Dvinsky's memorandum has survived with Stalin's resolution: "To Comrade Kag[anovich]. I completely agree with Comrade Dvinsky. I propose that: 1) the regions [*kraia*] be given the sternest possible directive on individual peasants [*individualy*], with a requirement that the regions report to the CC every five days on procurements among individuals; 2) Kazakhstan and the Saratov Region be hit hard for their negligence and wastefulness; 3) a campaign to combat ticks be launched, and heedless individuals be severely punished; 4) that fierce pressure be exerted to call in loans. Complacency with regard to procurements is criminal. I. Stalin. P.S. Wherever the situation with regard to procurements, seed loans and ticks, etc. is bad—we should get the secretaries back from vacation and make them rectify matters" (RGASPI, f. 81, op. 3, d. 100, l. 53). These proposals were largely incorporated into the decree of the Sovnarkom and the CC "On the Progress of Grain Procurements," approved by the Politburo on 19 August 1934 (see note 7 to document 95). On 18 August Kaganovich wrote to Stalin that "your directions on the grain procurements are correct and timely" (ibid., f. 558, op. 11, d. 752, ll. 35–40).

2. On 16 August the Politburo adopted a decision "On the Error by the Editors of the Journal *Bolshevik*." The publication of an editorial note on Engels' letter to Ioan Nedejde (*Bolshevik*, nos. 13–14, 31 July 1934), written by Zinoviev, was deemed "an extremely glaring political error." "This note," said the resolution, "falsifies Engels' views on the coming war by alleging that Engels supposedly 'adheres entirely to a defeatist position' and that 'Lenin defended a similar position in the war of 1914' and thereby conceals the indisputable fact that Lenin and Lenin alone laid down a fundamentally new and uniquely correct principle both on the question of the nature of imperialist war and on the question of the policy of Marxists with regard to war." The Politburo deemed "entirely correct" Stalin's criticisms of Engels' article "The Foreign Policy of Russian Tsarism," dated 19 July, and his letter to the Politburo, dated 5 August, on the error by the editors of *Bolshevik* (see Appendix: documents 2, 3). The editors of *Bolshevik* received a reprimand, Zinoviev was removed from the editorial board, and Knorin was dismissed as the journal's executive editor. Stetsky (editor),

Tal, Knorin, and Pospelov were appointed to the new editorial board, and it was instructed to submit to the CC within two days an article criticizing Zinoviev's commentaries. (Ibid., d. 950, ll. 31–32, 82–89.) See also documents 86, 89, 91, 92, 95.

3. See documents 88, 89, 91, 95, 97.

4. See note 7 to document 91.

· 91 ·

Kaganovich to Stalin
14 August

F. 558, op. 11, d. 742, ll. 28–34.

14 August [1934]

Dear Comrade Stalin.

1) Yesterday we reviewed M. Gorky's report to the writers' congress and came to the conclusion that the report is unsuitable in its current form.[1] Above all—the structure itself and the arrangement of the material—three-fourths, if not more, is taken up by historical-philosophical reflections, and incorrect ones at that. Primitive society is presented as an ideal, while capitalism in all of its stages is portrayed as a reactionary force that impedes the development of technology and culture. Clearly, such a position is non-Marxist. Almost no attention is given to Soviet literature, yet the report, after all, is called "On Soviet Literature." In view of the seriousness of our revisions and the danger that the report could fall through we (myself, Molotov, Voroshilov, and Comrade Zhdanov) went to see him and after a rather lengthy discussion he agreed to make corrections and revisions. He obviously is not in a very good mood. For example: he started talking about children, saying, look how bad their education is, it's unequal, as though it were divided into the poor and the rich, some have bad clothing while others have good clothing, a single uniform should be introduced and everybody issued identical clothing. The problem, of course, is not that he started talking about difficulties in this regard but the tone with which it was said. This talk reminded me of Comrade Krupskaia. It seems to me that Kamenev is playing a key role in shaping these attitudes of Gorky's. He cannot talk calmly about Vareikis and Yudin, he reviles them with all his might. His article, although it was not published, is going from hand to hand and according to Kriuchkov about 400 people have read it already. We exchanged opinions today and think that it would be better to publish it after making some corrections than to let it be read as illegal material.[2] The struggle among the small groups in connection with the congress is going hot and heavy. We instructed Comrade Zhdanov to assemble the party group of the organizing committee tomorrow and demand that they stop the squabbling and conduct the congress on a fitting

ideological and political level, and postpone the discussions about the leadership to the end of the congress.[3]

2) At a conference today we completed the editing of the Statute on the Special Conference [attached to the NKVD], I am sending it to you, if you have no corrections or revisions, please let me know by wire.[4]

3) We heard Comrade N. Kuibyshev today on the barracks and on Osoaviakhim (Comrade Voroshilov was already present). The detailed memorandum from Comrade Kuibyshev is being sent to you, you will see in it just how lax the situation regarding passes to the barracks is. This cannot be attributed solely to the fact that the Moscow city council failed to evict all the tenants from the courtyards where the barracks are situated. Of course, they must be evicted, but it is beyond dispute that the military comrades are to blame. Tomorrow we will do some more work on the proposal, which we will send you.[5] So far Nakhaev is not confessing his connections, we gave instructions to conduct the investigation without any debates, but according to all the rules.

4) The article for *Bolshevik* is already finished. As much as I dislike burdening you with paperwork I still find it necessary to send it to you. It seems to me that the article now is basically all right, it was written by Knorin and edited by Stetsky on the basis of our instructions. Please let me know whether to hand it over for publication or redo it.[6]

5) Regarding the PC for Supply the task of dividing it has been delayed, because Veitser was operated on in Berlin and he was detained. He will arrive in a few days and we will divide up the functions, the bureaucracy, the administration, and the people.[7]

6) I am sending you a short memorandum from Litvinov on the Soviet-Turkish-Persian-Afghan-Iraqi pact. We think that Comrade Litvinov's proposal is acceptable. Please let me know your opinion.[8]

Regards to you. Yours, L. Kaganovich.

1. See note 8 to document 95.

2. See document 89. The article was not published. On 15 August Stalin stated in a cipher to Kaganovich "I consider Mekhlis's remarks on Gorky's article correct. [. . .] It must be explained to all Communist literary people that the master in literature, as in other matters, is the CC alone, and that they are obliged to submit themselves to it unconditionally" (RGASPI, f. 558, op. 1, d. 83, ll. 67–69). On 29 December the secretary of the Union of Soviet Writers, Shcherbakov, wrote to Kaganovich about a new article by Gorky that displeased the authorities: "The article is written in the same vein as the one that was held up by the press before the congress" (*"Schaste literatury." Gosudarstvo i pisateli. 1925–1938 gg. Dokumenty* ["The Happiness of Literature": The State and Writers, 1925–1938. Documents], comp. D. L. Babichenko [Moscow, 1997], 185).

3. At the end of August Zhdanov reported to Stalin on the work of the congress (quoted from the rough draft of the letter): "The general tone that was set at the congress somehow immediately precluded the possibility of turning the congress into an arena of factional squabbling. [. . .] An important factor in this regard was a warning that we issued at two meetings of Communists before the congress—the party group of the organizing committee

and the party group of the congress—where we warned of the danger of RAPP-oriented attitudes and that the CC would strike hard at factional attitudes if they crept into the congress" (*"Literaturnyy front": Istoriia politicheskoy tsenzury 1932–1940 gg. Sbornik dokumentov* ["The Literary Front": The History of Political Censorship, 1932–1940. A Collection of Documents], comp. D. L. Babichenko [Moscow, 1994], 13). See also document 89.

4. See note 5 to document 107.

5. See note 6 to document 95, note 2 to document 89, and note 6 to document 87.

6. See note 2 to document 90.

7. On 22 August the Politburo adopted a resolution on the PC of Internal Trade. It instructed Zhdanov, Mikoian, and Veitser to divide up the functionaries and property of the former PC for Supply between the PC of the Food Industry and the PC of Internal Trade. People's commissar of trade Veitser was instructed "to immediately set the work of the PC in motion and receive the administrative apparatus and current business from the PC for Supply," and also to submit a plan within three days for the organizational structure of the PC (RGASPI, f. 17, op. 3, d. 950, l. 46). See also document 90.

8. See note 7 to document 97.

· 92 ·

Stalin to Kaganovich
[after 16 August]

F. 81, op. 3, d. 100, ll. 154–160.

To Comrade Kaganovich.

1) The editorial for *Bolshevik* <u>does not do the job</u>. First, the article complicates matters by introducing the question of Stalin. The comparison should have been between <u>Engels and Lenin</u>. The article complicates matters by adding to this comparison a comparison between Engels and Stalin. This is unreasonable with regard to tactics. It is stupid with regard to the heart of the matter. I made the appropriate change in the article. But then, after I had finished reading the article and mulled over the issue, I came to the conclusion that the article as a whole does not do the job. That Lenin's role cannot be minimized is clear. But one cannot also tear down Engels and minimize his role as a politician. Yet you have left the impression that Engels was a totally worthless politician. That will not do.

I propose that:

a) we don't do an editorial <u>at all</u>, but just confine ourselves to changing the editorial board.[1]

b) the question of an article portraying Lenin's role in the development of Marxist thought be put off until my arrival.

This is a delicate matter and you cannot say everything in a letter. What is needed is a lively and thorough exchange of opinions.

2) Our countercampaign against the Japanese lies and provocations is unsatisfactory and feeble. We must <u>systematically</u> rebut <u>every</u> incorrect report by the Japanese press or officials. This is essential in order to win

over public opinion in Japan, Europe, and the USSR. Yet you are sound asleep and not doing anything. The PCFA [PC of Foreign Affairs] should be flogged for being lethargic, blind, and nearsighted. But instead you are trailing behind the do-nothings at the PCFA.

I propose that we rebut through TASS the enclosed report by *Nichi-Nichi* [*Nichi-Nichi Shimbun*] on a <u>secret</u> pact between the USSR and China.[2]

I propose that we systematically rebut the lies by the Japanese press about the USSR through TASS or in individual articles.

You cannot daydream and sleep when you are in power!

I. Stalin.

1. See note 2 to document 90.
2. On 22 August the Politburo adopted the decision "On Rebutting the Fabrications of the Japanese and Manchurian Press." The PC of Foreign Affairs was instructed "to submit to the CC on a systematic basis rebuttals of false reports disseminated by the Japanese and Manchurian press on questions related to the Chinese Eastern Railroad." Specifically, Stomoniakov was instructed to submit on the same day drafts of commentaries or rebuttals of the report by the Japanese newspaper *Nichi-Nichi Shimbun* on a supposed secret Soviet-Chinese pact and other reports. (RGASPI, f. 17, op. 162, d. 17, l. 12.) See also document 95.

· 93 ·

Stalin to Kaganovich, Voroshilov and Molotov
[before 21 August]

F. 81, op. 3, d. 100, ll. 149–151.

<u>To Comrades Kaganovich, Voroshilov, Molotov</u>.

I have had a chance so far to look through the first part of the "Statute" on the PC of Defense.[1]

I have serious corrections. I don't know whether you carefully read the clauses of the "Statute." It seems to me that our comrades failed to grasp correctly the idea of converting the PC of Military and Naval Affairs into the PC of Defense. This conversion had <u>only one purpose</u>: to <u>formally</u> consolidate every type of defense (they have already been consolidated in practice)—the army, the navy and the air force—in the same hands. Yet the "Statute" provides for the <u>abolition</u> of the STO [Council of Labor and Defense], the <u>conversion</u> of the PC of Military and Naval Affairs to the STO and the <u>transfer of a number of functions</u> from the Central Executive Committee to the PC of Defense. The subclauses "b" (at the end), "d," "e," "h," "i," "m" and "o" in <u>clause 5</u> of the "statute" on the People's Commissariat and <u>subclauses</u> "a," "b," "c" and "d" in clause 6 of the same "Statute" explicitly say this.

I will write the rest of my comments after I study the rest of the "Statute."

It is clear to me that the "Statute" in this form contravenes the Constitution and violates the elementary Leninist concept of the proletarian state in general and of the PC of Defense in particular.[2]

Regards.

I. Stalin.

1. In June the Revolutionary Military Council of the USSR—the collegium of the PC of Military and Naval Affairs—was abolished, and the PC was renamed the USSR PC of Defense.

2. See note 5 to document 95.

· 94 ·

Stalin to Kaganovich and Zhdanov
21 August

F. 81, op. 3, d. 100, ll. 55–59.

To Comrades Kaganovich and Zhdanov.

a) I am returning the "Statutes" on the PC of Defense, the [military] districts and the military council.

I have already written that we cannot convert the PC of Defense either into the Central Executive Committee, which only has the right to call up the public into military service, issue pensions and so forth, or into Sovnarkom or the Council of Labor and Defense, which only have the right to issue directives to all people's commissariats, to mobilize the nat[ional] economy for defense, and so forth.

For the rest of my comments, see the texts of the "Statutes."

All three "Statutes" should be combined into one and shortened where possible.

The Central Military Council should be established attached to the PC of Defense, not attached to the people's commissar. The work plan for the Mil[itary] Council must not be limited to any "individual" issues, the council members should be granted the right to place any issue on the agenda. Otherwise there is no reason to establish a "Mil[itary] Council."

We should set up in the Naval Administration something like a staff (in the manner of the Air Force Administration) that would work out issues of naval operations.

I am not sure that we need a special "administration for fuel supply." That is a luxury.

The "Statutes" in general were drawn up in a slipshod manner, they are encumbered with a whole host of "administrations," "inspectorates," and "departments," the need for which is yet to be proven.

Furthermore. I think the "Statutes" have failed to mention agencies of the PC of Defense that actually exist.

The members of the Politburo and our <u>supervisory</u> bodies should study the "Statutes" in detail, they should brought into line with the actual state of affairs at the PC of Defense, and only after that should a <u>single</u> common Statute on the PC of Defense be adopted.[1]

Comrade Kirov will discuss this in more detail.

b) Focus your attention not only on the Saratov and Stalingrad Regions but also on the Cheliabinsk Region, where something unimaginable is happening with procurements. Send Chernov, Kleiner, and Yakovlev there (i.e. to those regions) and make them procure the grain honestly.[2]

Regards.

I. Stalin.

21 August 1934.

1. See note 5 to document 95.

2. On 25 August 1934 the Politburo dispatched Kleiner to the Stalingrad Region, and Chernov to the Cheliabinsk Region, "to take measures to organize the harvest and grain procurements" (RGASPI, f. 17, op. 3, d. 950, l. 54).

· 95 ·

Kaganovich to Stalin
22 August

F. 558, op. 11, d. 742, ll. 41–51.

22 August [1934]

Greetings Dear Comrade Stalin!

1) You absolutely correctly point out the extreme inadequacy of the reaction in our press to the lying and provocative fabrications by the press in Japan and elsewhere. We have done some things both in our press and even in the press abroad, but this was completely inadequate. Now we are giving the press several items for publication, including a few about the report you sent on the so-called "secret Soviet-Chinese pact." We issued a denial at the time, but it was very brief and only in the foreign press. Now we are going to follow this matter more intensively.[1]

You know about the substance of the situation on the CER and in Japan from the ciphers and TASS. Today there is a report that the Japanese Foreign Ministry has made a statement setting forth the entire course of the negotiations, in their own interpretation, naturally, but citing the same figures. Although they attack us, of course, the tone is such that they seem to be calculating that an agreement can be reached. I am sending this report to you by wire. After discussing the issue we instructed the PC of Foreign Affairs to draft a new TASS announcement, and maybe an interview with someone from the PC of Foreign Affairs leadership as well. As soon as the draft is ready we will send it to you. Comrade Stomoniakov just called and reported that Ota had come to see him. First, he told him of the Japanese government's protest against our publication of the figures—the price of the CER. Second, Ota said that our TASS report gave them the impression that we are cutting off the negotiations for good. Then Ota got to talking about the price itself, saying, basically, that since the construction of one mile in Manchuria costs 100,000 yen, the price of the CER should be 100 million. And if Hirota stated 120 million plus a bonus, that is a good price. Comrade Stomoniakov told him that they are mistaken in their impression that we are cutting off the negotiations, that they are the ones who are pushing things toward a breakdown, that he cannot talk about the price, to which Ota remarked "Yes, the price should be discussed in a businesslike manner." In comparing the [Japanese] Foreign Ministry statement and the conversation with Ota, it is clear that they are sounding out the possibilities. The TASS announcement evidently drove them into a corner. At the same time in Manchuria they are perpetrating all kinds of foul things. Today there is a report that our people under arrest are being tortured and beaten in an effort to make them confess. We decided to give the press today an item about the torturing and beatings, which are aimed at obtaining confessions that they participated in the train crashes. They are now developing an entire anti-Soviet campaign over the issue of the crashes and our supposed participation in them. This confirms that you are right, Comrade Stalin, that we must expose them more vigorously. So we have decided to do one more announcement or interview, including the question of the sale of the CER and the price, so as to deflect their campaign over the crashes.[2]

2) Regarding America—Boev has proposed that since the status of the negotiations right now is unclear, he should stay here awhile. We agreed to delay his departure until we receive a reply from Troianovsky. Please let us know your opinion.[3]

3) We will not print the article in *Bolshevik*.[4]

4) I must admit that before I got your letter I had not read the draft Statute on the PC of Defense. Now, after reviewing it, I agree entirely with your assessment and criticisms. We discussed this issue today. There were references to the fact that it repeats paragraphs from the old 1929 Statute. Yesterday I carefully compared it against the old Statute, and a lot of it really is in the old Statute. But first of all, not all of it is there, and formulations that change the substance have been discarded and revised, and second, even if some of these points were in the old Statute, that does not mean that they are wrong. For example, a) there was nothing in the old Statute about the management of OGPU troops; b) the old Statute said

"management and supervision of the operations of the mobilization staffs of all government agencies" (which is not quite right, either), while the new one gives an even broader formulation: "the management of the mobilization work of the PCs and the mobilization preparations of the national economy."

Then what is the <u>Council of Labor and Defense</u> for?

Or another point: c) the old Statute refers to the issuance of charters and compulsory decrees, and stated at the beginning "The PC of M[ilitary] and N[aval] Affairs proposes matters <u>in compliance with current law</u>," and so forth, whereas "in compliance with current law" was omitted from the new Statute, and so forth. We had an argument, and adopted the foll[owing] resolution: "The commission is to be instructed to rework the draft Statute in accordance with the directions from Comrade Stalin, and Comrade Kaganovich is to be added to the commission." I am continuing to acquaint myself closely with the whole Statute and ask you to inform me of any further comments you may have. We will send you the new draft Statute, or it may be even better to await your return.[5]

5) We adopted a decision on barracks security and on Osoaviakhim. We also sent out Comrade Voroshilov's order. I don't say that it was approved without argument, but I think this decision will help to genuinely correct the shortcomings that were uncovered.[6] We followed all your instructions. Tomorrow I will assemble the military personnel of the Moscow Military District to explain this resolution.

6) Regarding grain procurements—we drew up a short decree in accordance with your instructions and sent it out to the regions (attached), and also through telegrams and telephone conversations pressure must be applied to the localities.[7] This five-day period has yielded a bigger amount than the last period: the last one yielded 84,869,000 [poods; 1,390,000 tons], this one 87,295,000 [poods; 1,430,000 tons]. It's a small step forward. We will have to try to do better.

7) We took measures today regarding your telegram on publishing the speeches and reports at the writers' congress.[8] They are very relevant, because in the first few days the national minorities did not feel comfortable. As a result of certain measures their mood improved, but now with the detailed publication of the reports and speeches they will feel entirely <u>equal</u>. The congress is going well. The discussions are informative and lively.

Best wishes.

Yours, L. Kaganovich.

1. See note 2 to document 92.

2. On 18 August, after the negotiations over the sale of the CER had reached another impasse, a TASS announcement set out in detail the history of the negotiations and revealed the sale prices of the railroad that were at the center of the dispute. The TASS announcement stressed that the Soviet side had done everything it could to achieve progress in the negotia-

tions and had agreed to make numerous concessions. In response to this the Ministries of Foreign Affairs of Japan and Manchuria published statements giving their versions of how the negotiations had developed, which stressed the readiness of the Japanese-Manchurian side for compromises and the intransigence of the Soviet delegation. In addition, the Japanese Ministry of Foreign Affairs instructed the Japanese ambassador to the USSR to protest the Soviet violation of the agreement not to publish information about the negotiations. Meanwhile, Soviet employees continued to be arrested on the CER. From 13 to 21 August 38 people were arrested and charged with complicity in plotting crashes and attacks on trains. (DVP, vol. XVI, pp, 562–70, 815–17.) On 26 August the Politburo resolved to publish a new TASS statement rebutting the allegations made in the statements by the Japanese and Manchurian foreign ministries on 21 and 22 August (RGASPI, f. 17, op. 162, d. 17, ll. 27–28). This TASS statement was published in newspapers on 27 August. See also document 104.

3. The reference is to the Soviet-American negotiations on canceling mutual financial claims. On 13 August the USSR plenipotentiary representative in the United States, Troianovsky, asked Moscow for permission to make new proposals on this issue. On 21 August he was sent a reply in the affirmative. (DVP, vol. XVI, pp. 565, 816.) See also document 104.

4. See note 2 to document 90.

5. See documents 93, 94. On 22 August the Politburo instructed an ad hoc commission of the Politburo "to rework—in accordance with the instructions from Comrade Stalin—the Statute on the PC of Defense." Kaganovich was added to the commission. (RGASPI, f. 17, op. 3, d. 950, l. 44.)

6. On 22 August 1934 the Politburo adopted a resolution "On the Work of Osoaviakhim" that sharply criticized that organization, and its leaders received penalties (ibid., ll. 42, 93–96). On the same day the Politburo approved the resolution "On the State of Security at the Barracks of the Moscow Garrison." It referred to the weak discipline of the sentry services and noted Voroshilov's report that they had been sent a special directive to put barracks security into order (the directive itself, dated 14 August 1934, was appended to the minutes of the Politburo meeting). The Politburo resolution announced penalties to be imposed on the command of the Moscow Military District, on the Moscow Infantry Proletarian Division, and on agents of the special department of the Chief Administration of State Security of the NKVD. The resolution was sent out to military and party leaders in the regions. (Ibid., ll. 41, 97–100.) See also documents 89, 90, and 91 and note 6 to document 87.

7. On 19 August the Politburo approved a decree of Sovnarkom and the CC, "On the Progress of Grain Procurements," which noted that the grain plan was at risk in several regions and republics. The decree instructed that the leaders of these regions should be recalled from their vacations, and that plenipotentiaries should be dispatched to the regions. It listed a number of measures, including a drive against thefts of grain. (Ibid., ll. 36, 91–92.) See also document 90.

8. The First All-Union Congress of Soviet Writers was held from 17 August through 1 September 1934, and Stalin sent several letters to Kaganovich commenting on its progress. In this letter Kaganovich refers to Stalin's telegram of 21 August, in which he commented that "*Pravda* and *Izvestia* evidently do not understand the significance of the writers' congress and do not provide it with enough space" (ibid., f. 558, op. 1, d. 83, ll. 122, 1220b). On 22 August the Politburo ordered *Pravda* and *Izvestia* to intensify coverage of the work of the writers' congress and to publish the reports and speeches on the national minority literatures (ibid., f. 17, op. 3, d. 950, l. 40).

· 96 ·

Stalin to Kaganovich and Zhdanov
25 August

F. 81, op. 3, d. 100, ll. 61–66.

To Comrades Kaganovich and Zhdanov.

It is apparent from the material sent to me that all of you are counting on a good harvest in Siberia, in the Urals, and on the Volga, and while counting on it, you are reassuring yourself with the notion that since the harvest will be good, then the procurements will be good as well.

There is no need to prove that such calculations and expectations are absolutely incorrect, illusory, and dangerous, and can only cause trouble for the state and get it into a mess.

I am convinced of that.

It is necessary:

1) To organize, without delay, a campaign of pressure (pressure as strong as possible!) for procurements both in these regions and in other regions with good harvests by declaring war on . . . a . . . lack . . . of . . . planning.

2) To begin, without delay, to organize grain purchases in all of the good-harvest regions, with the objective of purchasing at least 200 million poods [3,276,000 tons] of grain no matter what, which in turn requires: a) somewhat reducing the share of goods that is allocated to poor-harvest regions in favor of the good-harvest regions, assembling a substantial supplementary commodity reserve for the good-harvest regions right now, and moving it there by the time the purchases of grain get under way;

b) intensifying right now the money-and-tax pressure (seriously intensifying it!) in the good-harvest regions, so as to create there a need for money and the desire to sell grain (I would not object even to some "voluntary-coercive" measures in the good-harvest regions to spur purchases of grain).[1]

All of this is extremely necessary.

Regards. I. Stalin.

25 August 1934

1. See note 1 to document 97 and note 1 to document 100. For grain purchases (*zakupki*) see the introduction to this chapter.

· 97 ·

Kaganovich to Stalin
28 August

F. 558, op. 11, d. 742, ll. 65–74.

28 August 1934
Dear Comrade Stalin.

1. Last night Vasia [Vasily Stalin] gave me your letter in which you wrote about grain procurements. Your warning, your alarm bell is not only timely but is an outright act of salvation for the cause of the successful completion of the grain procurements. Today we convened the Politburo, where we discussed issues of grain procurements and the harvest. The picture is definitely a distressing one. The early harvest in the south led to a leap upward in procurements in July and the beginning of August, but the pace of the second, third, fourth, and fifth five-day periods of August has produced a sharp slowdown in the pace, as follows:

Five-Day Periods in August
[million poods; figures in thousand tons in brackets]

	1st	2d	3d	4th	5th
1933	43.2 [708]	73.9 [1,210]	94.5 [1,548]	94.8 [1,553]	98 [1,605]
1934	75.1 [1,230]	82.9 [1,358]	84.9 [1,391]	87.8 [1,438]	76.4 [1,251]

You are absolutely right that complacency is especially dangerous in the Urals, Bashkiria, the Central Volga and other Volga regions, and West[ern] Siberia.

Yesterday the dir[ector] of the Political Administration of the PC of Agriculture, Comrade Levin, arrived from Siberia and he related a whole host of facts attesting to complacency in Siberia. Today we composed specific telegrams to the regions, but this, of course, is not enough. We have picked people to go to the regions, Comrade Chubar to the Stalingrad Region, Chernov is departing tomorrow for Cheliabinsk, Kalmanovich to Bashkiria, and then we talked about a trip by Comrade Zhdanov to Western Siberia. Comrade Molotov has consented to go either to Western Siberia or to Kazakhstan. Comrade Mikoian will travel to the south regarding the sugar-beet harvest and simultaneously regarding the procurements. Please let us know your opinion by wire about the trip by Comrades Zhdanov and Molotov. I myself could take a trip for about ten days, but then Zhdanov would have to stay. We are instructing the same comrades to take measures regarding the harvest and threshing, because the situation is bad in this respect as well, especially in the eastern regions. In addition we resolved to send to the regions ten members each of the Commissions of Party and Soviet Control regarding the harvest and procurements and to assign all of the representatives of the Commissions of Party and Soviet Control to this work for a month and a half.[1]

Regarding the allocation of consumer goods and the purchase [*zakupka*] of grain we instructed the commission, to which Comrades Chubar and Zhdanov were added as members, to give us their proposals within two days.

2) There is no reply from Japan yet, the arrests are continuing.[2]

I am sending you the cipher received today from Comrade Potyomkin on his conversation with Mussolini.[3] Of course, Mussolini wants to get something from us, but his conversation is very interesting.

I am also sending you a letter from Comrade Stomoniakov about the idea of your receiving the Japanese writer Kawakami (after you return to Moscow).[4]

3) Today Comrades Krestinsky and Surits raised the question with us of the departure of Surits and directives for him. Surits contends that he should not rush right now and upon arriving there should not raise the question of so-called Eastern Locarno. Krestinsky, to the contrary, argues that Surits should leave right now and upon arriving when he meets with Neurath should raise the question of concluding an Eastern Pact. We are inclined toward Krestinsky's proposals and resolved that Comrade Surits should depart on 3 September. Please let us know your opinion by wire. Just in case I am sending you Krestinsky's letter.[5]

4) During the discussion of the question of barracks security Comrade Voroshilov proposed removing Kork. Now Comrade Kork has sent a letter to me personally requesting that I support relieving him of his duties as commander of the Moscow Military District. I personally don't think we should relieve him. Please be sure to let me know your opinion.[6]

5) I wrote to you in one of my letters about Comrade Litvinov's proposal on the Soviet-Turkish-Afghan pact. In a few days the Persian for[eign] min[ister] is arriving—we will have to give an answer. Please be sure to let me know your opinion by wire.[7]

6) As was to be expected Nakhaev confessed his connections with General Bykov, who worked at the Institute of Physical Fitness. And this general is an intelligence agent, according to what has been determined so far, for Estonia. We have to assume of course that it is not just Estonia. These are the initial confessions so far. I will report on what follows.[8]

Regards to you. Yours, L. Kaganovich.

1. See document 96. On 31 August the Politburo adopted a resolution on grain procurements and approved a telegram to the leaders of regions and republics. This demanded that

grain procurements be intensified and that two-thirds of the members of the bureaus of regional committees and members of the presidiums of regional executive committees be sent to rural localities for the whole of September. The resolution demanded that those who failed to deliver grain be fined and held legally accountable. In a departure from previous practice it was decided that the cooperatives should immediately purchase additional grain for the state from collective farms, collective farmers, and individual peasants who had fulfilled the annual plans for grain procurements. The resolution called for more efforts to obtain various payments and arrears. Those whose dispatch to the regions was authorized by the Politburo included Molotov (Western Siberia), Kaganovich (the Ukraine), Kirov (Kazakhstan), Voroshilov (Belorussia and the Western Region), Mikoian (Kursk and Voronezh Regions), Chubar (Central Volga Region), Zhdanov (Stalingrad Region), and Chernov (Cheliabinsk Region). (RGASPI, f. 17, op. 3, d. 951, ll. 16, 81–83.) Zhdanov remained in Moscow until Kaganovich returned (see documents 99, 103).

2. See note 2 to document 95.

3. The cipher is missing.

4. The Japanese ambassador to the USSR, Ota, asked Stomoniakov, deputy people's commissar of foreign affairs, to arrange a meeting with Stalin for the Japanese journalist Kawakami, who was in Moscow. Stomoniakov sent a letter to Stalin and received the latter's consent to a meeting. (DVP, vol. XVII, pp, 586, 820.) On 1 September the Politburo adopted a decision to deem it expedient for Stalin to receive Kawakami after Stalin arrived in Moscow (RGASPI, f. 17, op. 162, d. 17, l. 30). But Kawakami left the USSR in September, and the meeting did not take place.

5. Krestinsky's letter is missing. The reference is to the preparation of the Eastern Pact—a treaty among the countries of Central and Eastern Europe on a collective rebuff to an aggressor. On 30 August Stalin wrote in a cipher to Kaganovich "It is not necessary to rush with Surits's departure for Berlin, it would be better to postpone it" (ibid., f. 558, op. 11, d. 84, ll. 58–59). On 31 August the Politburo decided to postpone Surits' departure for Berlin (ibid., f. l7, op. 162, d. 17, l. 29).

6. See note 6 to document 95. On 30 August Stalin wrote in a cipher to Kaganovich "It is not necessary to remove Kork" (ibid., f. 558, op. 11, d. 84, ll. 58–59). On 5 September Kork was removed from his post as troop commander of the Moscow Military District and appointed director of the Frunze Military Academy.

7. The Persian foreign minister raised the question with Soviet representatives of a nonaggression pact between Persia, Turkey, Afghanistan, and Iraq in the fall of 1933 and in July 1934. On 3 August 1934 Litvinov reported his negative view of this idea in a letter to the CC. (DVP, vol. XVII, pp. 526, 812.) On 30 August Stalin replied in a cipher to Kaganovich "I have already written that it must be postponed" (ibid., f. 558, op. 11, d. 84, ll. 58–59). On 31 August the Politburo, on the basis of Litvinov's proposal, decided to deem negotiations for a Soviet-Turkish-Persian-Afghan-Iraqi nonaggression pact inopportune and to explain to Tehran and Ankara the desirability of deferring the negotiations (ibid., f. 17, op. 162, d. 17, l. 29). See also document 91.

8. See note 7 to document 87 and the introduction to this chapter. On 26 August Agranov sent a telegram to Stalin on the same lines as Kaganovich's letter. Agranov stated that "Bykov has been arrested by us today" (ibid., f. 558, op. 11, d. 84, l. 15).

· 98 ·

Stalin to Kaganovich
28 August

F. 81, op. 3, d. 100, ll. 67–71.

To Comrade Kaganovich.

1. The extremely serious issue of cotton cannot be exhausted (it is impossible) in the Central Commission. All of the cotton-growing experts from the cotton-growing districts and all of the respective regional party secretaries must be called in to the Commission. This will be part commission, part conference. The main task: to guarantee fulfillment of the second five-year plan for cotton (I think it is 40 or 50 million poods [655,000–819,000 tons] of pure cotton) and to prepare this guarantee on a yearly basis by getting to work without delay. The main ways to reach the goal: a) raising crop yields year after year (improving cultivation, maximizing fertilizers, irrigation, etc.); b) expanding crop areas (preparing more and more new areas for crops every year); c) bonuses for high crop yields, special benefits for expanding crop areas, medals for good workers; d) monitoring the implementation of decisions.

Besides an overall guideline decision, specific planning-and-guideline decisions must be adopted for each cotton republic individually.

Without this the decision will turn into a well-intentioned but hollow declaration.[1]

2. It seems to me that the time has come to eliminate the Central Asian Bureau by tying Turkmenia, Uzbekia, and Tajikia directly to Moscow (Karakalpakia can be incorporated into Uzbekia as an autonomous republic, and Kirgizia can be incorporated into the RSFSR). It would be a different matter if there were a federation in Central Asia (as in Transcaucasia)—then the Central Asian Bureau could develop. But since there is no federation there, the Central Asian Bureau cannot last long, and it is already losing (if it has not already lost) its reason for existing. Moreover, the Central Asian Bureau is impeding the growth of the republics and is turning into a regressive factor, a barrier.

It is time to eliminate the Central Asian Bureau, recall Bauman and Maiorov to Moscow and give direct responsibility for the work to the republics.

It will be better without the barrier.[2]

3. Of the 4 million poods [66,000 tons] of grain issued to Kazakhstan to help the weak collective farms and the livestock-raising districts, 600,000 poods [10,000 tons] still remain unused. Kleiner wants to take this entire remainder away from Kazakhstan. I think 150,000 poods [2,500 tons]

could be left for Kazakhstan, and the rest collected for the USSR reserve stock.[3]

That is all for now. Regards.

I. Stalin.

28 August 1934.

1. On 22 August the Politburo set up a commission, chaired by Kaganovich, "to work out issues of the development of cotton growing with regard to raising crop yields (fertilizers, better cultivation, irrigation) and expanding crop areas both in Central Asia and in Transcaucasia" (RGASPI, f. 17, op. 3, d. 950, l. 47). On 23 September the Politburo expanded the commission by adding the leaders of local party organizations and instructed the leaders of the party organizations of the cotton-growing republics and regions to draw up and submit to the CC, no later than 20 October, a concrete plan for the development of cotton growing for 1935–37 (ibid., d. 952, l. 29). See also documents 87, 88, 89.

2. See note 9 to document 99.

3. On 31 August the Politburo approved this proposal by Stalin (ibid., d. 951, l. 15).

· 99 ·

Kaganovich to Stalin
3 September

F. 558, op. 11, d. 742, ll. 75–84.

---

3 September [1934]

Greetings dear Comrade Stalin.

Before our departure we did some work on a number of issues on which we ask that you let us know your opinion.[1]

1) We and the people's commissariats have considered the limits for the national economic plan for the fourth qu[arter]. We are setting the amount of gross output of industry for the Union PCs at 11,170,000,000 rubles, i.e. 28.9 [percent] of the annual plan. We are setting capital investment for the entire national economy at 5,116,200,000 rubles. We are including a point in the resolution to the effect that the all-Union budget should provide for a surplus of revenues over expenditures of 1,500,000,000 r[ubles]. I am sending you the draft resolution.[2]

2) After several reworkings we today finally polished off the resolution on grain purchases, which I am sending you.

The most difficult thing was to set the amount of the goods' allocations. The administration is not especially eager to redistribute the allocations and especially to allocate a suitable assortment of goods. We had to send it back several times and make them recalculate. We have not yet distributed the allocation of 400 million for the fourth qu[arter] among the regions, and the September allocation likewise has not been distributed yet with regard to assortment, only in rubles. This will be done in the next two days. Please let me know your opinion by wire about the resolution itself and about your consent to having your signature on it.[3]

3) We have drafted a resolution on the harvest, haulage, and delivery of sugar beets, it is a very good harvest, but they may take too long to gather it. We are using last year as a standard for setting the deadlines for digging up the beets and hauling them. We are setting the contractual figures as a firm plan for procurements. We are allocating 2,600 trucks for beets, of which 1,200 will be used to haul them in September from the fourth-quarter allocation of the PC of Agriculture and the PC of the Food Industry, 1,100 will be mobilized on grain-growing state farms and at machine-tractor stations, we will mobilize those that have completed procurements and another 300 trucks from the PC of Defense, Comrade Voroshilov is away, he will probably be very angry, but this is feasible and imperative in the Ukraine and the Central Black-Earth Region. We are reporting this to you today by wire. We are not sending you the entire resolution, so as not to overburden you.[4]

4) Pending approval of the final Statute on the PCs of Internal Trade and the Food Industry we approved the structure (Administrations and departments) and the roster of chief personnel yesterday.[5] We are sending them to you and ask you to let us know your opinion. Comrade Zhdanov will write you about this in more detail.

5) Krestinsky has sent us an inquiry with regard to the talks between the French and the Poles about our entry into the League of Nations. I am sending you his paper and ask that you let me know your opinion. We have not determined our final opinion, we think that the most we could agree to is that the French on their own behalf tell them (the Poles) that they take it for granted that the entry of the USSR into the League of Nations does not affect the Riga Peace Treaty, which settled the issue of national minorities, but it would be better not to say even that.[6] A reply will probably come from Litvinov tomorrow, which will be sent to you by wire.

6) We have already replied to Troianovsky denying his request, but we mailed it, so he hasn't received it yet.[7]

7) At the Commission of Defense meeting the question was raised of the orders [*zakazy*—for armaments, etc.] and budget of the PC of Defense for 1935. After some discussion we deferred the matter. We can deal with it in a month or two. Just in case I am sending you the memorandum on these orders and the budget.

8) We adopted relevant decisions regarding all your telegrams, including one on trade unions. A plenum of the All-Union Central Council of Trade Unions is meeting on the 5th and will adopt this resolution. There are certain old-time trade-union officials who are not especially pleased with this breakup into smaller units, they are afraid that there will be less

"respect" and therefore they were delighted at the idea that the issue supposedly encountered a hitch in the Politburo and would be deferred, but
the majority of trade-union people are responding to our decision <u>very</u>
<u>well</u>.[8]

9) Comrade Stalin, please let me know how to work out in practice your
absolutely correct proposals about the Central Asian Bureau and the PC
of Justice, should we wait for a month or two, and then decide? Or move
right now.[9]

10) I wanted to write you in detail about transport matters, but I will do
that after I return from the Ukraine. I must only say that the PC of Transport is simply unable to advance beyond the level of fulfillment it has already achieved with regard to the plan for shipments. In August 57,273
railroad cars were loaded, 92.5 percent of the plan as opposed to July
56,669 cars and June 58,083. Evidently in September and October we will
have to focus in earnest on the preparation for winter.

11) We are leaving today for the grain procurements. Kirov is also leaving tomorrow. Comrades Zhdanov, Kuibyshev, Andreev, and Rudzutak
are staying here. Sergo will arrive from the Urals in a few days.[10]

I will close here.

Regards to you. Yours, L. Kaganovich.

1. For Kaganovich's departure to the Ukraine, see note 1 to document 97.

2. On 11 September the Politburo approved the limits for the national economic plan for
the fourth quarter to which Kaganovich refers (RGASPI, f. 17, op. 3, d. 951, l. 49).

3. See note 1 to document 100.

4. On 4 September the Politburo approved a decision on the harvest, haulage, and delivery of sugar beets from the 1934 harvest, listing the measures to which Kaganovich refers
(ibid., ll. 88–90).

5. A Sovnarkom decree on the central structure of the administrative apparatus of the
PC of Internal Trade and a list of principal officials of the administrations was approved by
the Politburo on 9 September (ibid., ll. 45, 96–98).

6. Following the dispatch of several ciphers to Stalin from Kuibyshev on behalf of the
Politburo and from Litvinov, on 7 September Stalin approved a draft Politburo resolution
which was then adopted formally on the same day. Barthou, the French foreign minister, was
to be given the following answer: Barthou could, on his own behalf, without citing an exchange of opinions with the USSR, reply to Colonel Beck, the Polish foreign minister, that he
did not understand his [Beck's] anxiety over the issue of national minorities, since the Riga
treaty that regulated this issue between the USSR and Poland would remain binding both on
Poland and on the USSR even after the USSR joined the League of Nations. An oral statement was to be made in Warsaw to the Polish Foreign Ministry, or through a Polish representative, that all treaties with Poland remained in force. If Beck insisted on an exchange of
notes, Litvinov was to be permitted as a last resort to agree to this. (Ibid., op. 162, d. 17, ll.
33–34.)

7. The reference is to Soviet-American negotiations on canceling mutual financial claims.
See also documents 95 and 104.

8. The Politburo first considered the restructuring of the trade unions on 3 May 1934,
and passed the question to the Orgburo for its preliminary consideration (ibid., op. 3, d. 944,

l. 36). On 15 July the Politburo instructed a commission headed by Kaganovich to rework the draft resolution on trade unions (ibid., d. 948, ll. 1–2). On 25 August Kaganovich wrote to Stalin that the commission wanted to increase the number of trade unions from 47 to 145–50, but Voroshilov "expressed doubt about the whole matter in principle," while Molotov supported the proposal in principle but added "it is wrong to abolish and create new trade unions every day" (ibid., f. 558, op. 11, d. 742, ll. 56–64). On 29 August the Politburo approved the resolution on the restructuring of the trade unions. The number of trade unions was more than tripled, from the existing 47 to 154 (ibid., f. 17, op. 3, d. 951, ll. 13, 58–66).

9. On 30 October Kaganovich and Molotov wired Stalin a draft resolution on the abolition of the Central Asian Bureau of the CC of the VKP(b) and the Central Asian economic bodies (ibid., f. 81, op. 3, d. 101, ll. 51–52); this incorporated Stalin's proposals as set forth in his letter of 28 August (see document 98). The Politburo approved the resolution in the version proposed by Kaganovich and Molotov, on 2 October 1934 (ibid., d. 953, ll. 22, 91).

10. See note 1 to document 97. On 5 August the Politburo had authorized a trip by Ordzhonikidze to plants and construction projects in the Urals from 7 August until the end of the month (ibid., d. 949, l. 44).

· 100 ·

Stalin to Kaganovich
6 September

F. 81, op. 3, d. 100, ll. 72–75.

To Comrade Kaganovich.

1. We need to set a minimum not of 60 percent <u>food crops</u> in the purchase of grain, but a minimum of 70 percent.

2. The deductions from grain purchases for the *kraiispolkomy* [regional executive committees] should not be set at 20 percent but at 5 percent, and not at 10 percent for the district executive committees, but at 3 percent. You are being too liberal. But you have no idea what kind of catastrophe is in store for the state if we fail to purchase all 200 million poods [3,276,000 tons] of grain. If the regional executive committee takes 20 percent, and the district executive committee takes 10 percent, and the cooperatives collect some as well, what will be left for us? Have you thought about that? Our food situation is worse than you think. You have to drum it into all the regional functionaries that our food situation is catastrophic and that this is precisely the reason we are reducing the deductions. It must be drummed into them that the fate of our food situation depends on the success of the purchases, that the purchases are the combat mission of the day and that we will make an example of any regional committee secretary who fails to fulfill the plan.

An appropriate <u>introduction</u> must be provided for the resolution on grain purchases (the resolution is not being published). It would be better to do <u>separate</u> resolutions <u>for each region</u>.

3. Why wasn't the Stalingrad Region included?

4. We must, without delay, organize grain purchases in the Far East and in the part of Eastern Siberia where special benefits are provided, where there will be no grain procurements, and where grain will be obtainable <u>only</u> on the basis of purchases.[1]

Regards. I. Stalin.

6 September 1934

1. See document 99 and the introduction to this chapter. Stalin's proposals were in large measure incorporated into the decree of the CC and the Sovnarkom "On the Purchase of Grain from the 1934 Harvest," which was approved by the Politburo on 11 September 1934. The minimum plan for grain purchases was set at 200 million poods. (RGASPI, f. 17, op. 3, d. 951, ll. 50, 103–113.) See also documents 96, 109, 111.

· 101 ·

Stalin to Kaganovich
12 September

F. 558, op. 11, d. 85, ll. 44–45.

[Cipher]

For Kaganovich.

I received your letter. I regard any attempts to secure new cuts as a gross violation of the decree of Sovnarkom and the CC of the party. If there is any leadership in the Ukraine, it [the leadership] should know that a decree of Sovnarkom of the USSR and the CC of the party, and one that was adopted with its consent to boot, is binding on it. The plan for grain procurements must be fulfilled completely and unquestioningly.[1]

Stalin.[2]

No. 1. 12 September 1934.

1. See documents 102, 103.
2. This ciphered telegram was sent from Sochi on 12 September at 9:15 pm (RGASPI, f. 81, op. 3, d. 101, l. 46).

· 102 ·

Stalin to Kaganovich, Zhdanov, Molotov, and Kuibyshev
13 September

F. 81, op. 3, d. 100, ll. 76–82.

To Comrades Kaganovich, Zhdanov, Molotov, Kuibyshev.

1) A few days ago I received Comrade Kaganovich's letter (he was writ-

ing from Odessa), where he proposes that we agree to a new cut in grain procurements in the Ukraine (the letter is enclosed).[1] I consider this letter an alarming symptom, since one can tell from it that we may slide onto the wrong road unless we switch to a tough policy in time (i.e. right now). The first cut was necessary. But our functionaries (not just the peasants!) are using it as a first step, which is to be followed by a second step, as a means of pressuring Moscow to obtain a new cut. And people such as Comrade Kaganovich are giving in (or are ready to give in) to this "atmosphere." This could disrupt the procurements for us and destroy their organizing value in a fundamental way.

I propose that:

a) No more cuts be allowed for the collective-farm and peasant sector, and that we brand the demands for cuts as opportunism, as a gross violation of the decisions of the Sovnarkom and the CC (I responded in this vein to Comrade Kaganovich, in the hope that he would read the Ukrainians this reply, the text of which is enclosed with this letter);[2]

b) We demand unconditional fulfillment of the plan, and that those regions that fail to fulfill the plan be held accountable by the CC for poor work and be cited in the press as ineffectual regions that failed to fulfill the plan;

c) An attack be launched in the press (without delay!) against the secretaries and executive-committee chairmen who are doing a poor job with grain procurements.[3]

2) Pay attention to the Cheliabinsk Region, where the situation is really bad. Ryndin is a petty demagogue who panders to the functionaries, trails behind them and does not know how to lead them, to guide them, and is afraid of offending them. He should be told directly: either fulfill the plan completely and on schedule, or you will be removed from your post. Either—or. Let him know that he will be disgraced unless he abandons his trail-behind "policy."[4]

I. Stalin.

13 September 1934

1. The letter is missing.

2. See document 101. Kaganovich sent Stalin's reply by cipher to the regional functionaries concerned, adding, "I consider that Comrades Kosior and Postyshev should travel to Odessa and Dnepropetrovsk Regions for a longer period" (RGASPI, f. 558, op. 11, d. 85, l. 43). See document 103.

3. See note 2 to document 103.

4. On 30 September the Politburo approved a decree of Sovnarkom and the CC on the progress of grain deliveries in the Cheliabinsk Region, which was to be published in the press. The decree laid the blame for the lag in grain deliveries on the regional party committee and its first secretary, Ryndin. Ryndin was warned that, unless he achieved a faster pace of procurements, he would be removed from his post for "failing to measure up to his job." A number of regional functionaries were relieved of their duties and put on trial. The decree

provided for sending to the Cheliabinsk Region a group of leading functionaries from Moscow and heads of political departments from other regions. (ibid., f. 17, op. 3, d. 953, ll. 18, 90.) For later developments see the introduction to this chapter.

· 103 ·

Kaganovich to Stalin
16 September

F. 558, op. 11, d. 742, ll. 85–89.

---

16 September [1934]
Greetings Dear Comrade Stalin.

1) I arrived in Moscow on the 14th—one day I spent at collective farms in the Moscow Region. I received your telegram after I left Kharkov, so it was too late for me to show it to the Ukrainian comrades.[1]

Nobody knew about my letter to you—neither Kosior nor Postyshev. I received your letter today, I showed it to all the comrades. We consider your instructions correct and are adopting them as guidelines. I would just like Comrade Stalin for you to be sure that now just as in the past I have not eased the pressure now in the struggle for grain deliveries. The functionaries in the Ukraine from those in the center down to the lowest level did not feel in my pressure any sentiment toward reductions, the result of this was that this five-day period yielded almost 2 million poods [32,800 tons] more than the previous one. The Kiev Region has already completed the entire plan. I hope the Kharkov and Vinnitsa Regions will complete by sometime between the 1st and the 5th. As for the Odessa and Dnepropetrovsk Regions, I have sent a telegram saying that Comrades Kosior and Postyshev should spend some more time there and exert pressure to fulfill the plan.

We thought we would receive information on the five-day period by this evening, but it will come in tomorrow. Tomorrow we will also draw up practical measures for all the regions and will provide appropriate press coverage according to your instructions.[2]

This five-day period is yielding less than the previous one, so we will have exert strong pressure. Comrade Zhdanov is leaving tomorrow for the Stalingrad Region. If it were possible, I would travel to one of the regions again.[3] Regarding individual peasants we wired you our proposals today.[4] Tomorrow we will consider the proposal on the tax and will report to you.[5]

2) We have set the plan for distribution of tractors and trucks for the fourth quarter. I am sending you this draft and we ask that you let us know your opinion. We had to force tractors on the PC of Agriculture and the PC of State Farms, oddly, they refuse to take that many of their own voli-

tion. The PC of Agriculture wanted to take 10,000 instead of 12,500 wheeled tractors. We told them off for this and gave them 12,500, the same thing happened with the PC of State Farms.[6]

3) This year we have had a magnificent beet harvest, without precedent in all these years. We have added some more trucks for the beets. The most important thing is to ensure full utilization of the harvest. When I was in the Ukraine, the Ukrainians and I took appropriate measures there.

Regards. L. Kaganovich.

1. See document 101.

2. See document 102. On 18 September 1934 a *Pravda* editorial, "Fulfill the Grain Procurements Plan Unconditionally," criticized the leaderships of the Eastern Siberian, Western Siberian, Stalingrad, Central Volga, Cheliabinsk, Odessa, and Dnepropetrovsk Regions.

3. See note 1 to document 97 and note 4 to document 108.

4. On 17 September the Politburo approved a decree of the Central Executive Committee and Sovnarkom that increased the fines to be imposed on individual farms that failed to fulfill obligations to the state both for deliveries in kind and for money payments (RGASPI, f. 17, op. 3, d. 952, l. 14).

5. On 17 September the Politburo submitted the proposals of the PC of Finance on taxation of individual farms for consideration by a commission headed by Zhdanov (ibid., d. 952, l. 14).

6. On 25 September the Politburo approved a plan for distribution of trucks and tractors for the fourth quarter of 1934. The resolution indicated that the reason for the reluctance of the PC was its lack of money to cover the costs of the tractors: "The statement by the USSR PC of Agriculture to the USSR Gosplan refusing a portion of the tractors designated under the plan for distribution of tractors, supposedly because of financial difficulties, is to be deemed unfounded, and particularly harmful from the standpoint of the interests of agriculture." (Ibid., d. 953, l. 7.)

· 104 ·

Kaganovich to Stalin
20 September

F. 558, op. 11, d. 742, ll. 90–98.

20 September [1934]
Greetings dear Comrade Stalin.

1) Today we finished editing the instructions for the delegation to the Mongolian congress.[1] These instructions contain no new political principles.

The delegation is being instructed to proceed on the basis of old directives that have stood the test of time. The emphasis in the organizational matter is being placed on raising the role and the proportionate weight of the party and proceed on the basis of retaining Gendung [as prime minister of Mongolia] under all circumstances. We are sending you the draft of the instructions and ask that you let us know your opinion by wire, since we will have to send it to Irkutsk to be delivered to the delegation, which has already departed Moscow.[2]

At the same time Comrade Sokolnikov has raised a number of questions. The most important one is the issue of reducing the Mongolian Republic's indebtedness to us and of deferring payments. They owe us around 95 million tugriks, this large debt, according to Eliava and Sokolnikov, came about as a result of prices in trade with the [Soviet] Union that were disadvantageous to Mongolia. So they have proposed reducing the indebtedness by 34 million tugriks and deferring the military loans of 28 million until 1945. That would leave 33 million tugriks to be paid in the next few years.

We adopted a brief draft resolution without revising the figures, authorizing Comrade Sokolnikov only to hold conversations in this direction. The remaining resolutions derive from already extant CC resolutions that have not been fulfilled by the PC of Foreign Trade. I am sending them to you just to be on the safe side. Please let us know your opinion on deferring the payments and reducing the indebtedness.[3]

2) A cipher has come in from Comrade Troianovsky in America, in which he again raises the question of making concessions and proposes his own plan. In it he already completely retreats from the loan and speaks only of a long-term credit. Krestinsky sent him an answer on his own without talking with anyone. I am sending you the telegrams of Troianovsky and Krestinsky and ask that you give us instructions on what to do?.[4]

3) A telegram has come in from Yurenev saying that it is imperative to make the point to Hirota that the Japanese government must guarantee that for six months the orders we place are set at export prices for export goods and at world prices for equipment. We doubt that it is advisable right now to complicate the negotiations all over again. I am sending you Yurenev's cipher and we ask that you let us know your opinion.

He has probably already delivered our conditions. The delivery to Hirota was delayed somewhat because of distortions in the cipher.[5]

4) The Comintern people have sent us an inquiry about an appeal to them by the British Independent Labour Party to hold an international conference against fascism and war. We are inclined to feel that this is inadvisable. It is not out of the question and is even likely that the Trotskyites are at work here and, while muddying the waters or even acting against a united front in France, want to seize the "initiative" here.

We are sending you the material and ask that you let us know your opinion.[6]

5) Regarding grain procurements we are exerting specific pressure in each region, in accordance with your instructions. There are no data yet today on the fourth five-day period. We expect an increase in West[ern]

Siberia, in the Cheliabinsk Region, in the Central Volga, and in Saratov, but apparently there will not be a sharp increase in all procurements, since several regions are already near the end, and some have already finished their procurements. Comrade Zhdanov left yesterday for the Stalingrad Region.

Comrade Molotov has left West[ern] Siberia for Moscow. In the Ukraine everybody is busy with procurements, there may be some increase in this five-day period. We are pressing all of the regions that have completed the plan to make sure that all the remaining obligations for individual peasants and collective farmers be fulfilled without fail,[7] and that grain purchases move into gear simultaneously. We will try to finish the plan of grain purchases for the Moscow Region as soon as possible.

Regards to you. Yours, L. Kaganovich.

P.S. I have just received a cipher from Yurenev that he has handed our conditions to Hirota. I will send the cipher to you.

1. On 16 September Kaganovich sent a cipher to Stalin proposing the names of the Comintern delegates to the congress, and that Sokolnikov should also be sent in spite of his objections; on the same day Stalin agreed (RGASPI, f. 558, op. 11, d. 85, ll. 41, 40). On 17 September the Politburo approved the delegation from the VKP(b) and the Comintern to the congress of the MPRP (Mongolian People's Revolutionary Party); Sokolnikov was confirmed as representative of the CC of the VKP(b) (ibid., f. 17, op. 3, d. 952, l. 13).

2. On 22 September Stalin wrote in a cipher to Kaganovich: "The instructions to the delegation to Mongolia are not solid but are acceptable" (ibid., f. 558, op. 11, d. 85, ll. 103, 1030b). The Politburo approved the instructions to the delegation on 23 September. The instructions confirmed the old instructions of the Comintern Executive Committee to the Mongolian Communists, called for improved coordination in the top leadership of the Mongolian Republic, and gave recommendations for elections to the CC of the MPRP (ibid., op. 162, d. 17, ll. 46, 50–51).

3. On 22 September Stalin wrote in a cipher to Kaganovich: "The reduction in indebtedness and the deferment of payments may be agreed to" (ibid., op. 11, d. 85, ll. 103, 1030b). On 23 September a Politburo resolution on Mongolia authorized Sokolnikov, in a discussion with representatives of the Mongolian People's Republic, to raise the question of a possible reduction in indebtedness and deferment of payments without mentioning specific figures. It was decided to postpone official negotiations until Mongolian representatives came to Moscow. (Ibid., f. 162, d. 17, ll. 46, 50–51.)

4. The telegrams are missing. Reference is to the Soviet-American negotiations to settle financial claims (see note 3 to document 95) and the Soviet attempt to obtain a loan from the United States. On 22 September Stalin wrote in a cipher to Kaganovich that "such serious questions cannot be settled in an exchange of telegrams," and proposed that Troianovsky should be recalled to Moscow and "the question should be decided after serious discussion in which Litvinov participates" (ibid., f. 558, op. 11, d. 85, ll. 103, 1030b). On 23 September the Politburo instructed the PC of Foreign Affairs to recall Troianovsky to Moscow for a report (ibid., f. 17, op. 162, d. 17, l. 45).

5. Reference is to the negotiations over the sale of the CER. On 19 September 1934 the USSR plenipotentiary in Japan visited Hirota, the Japanese foreign minister, and transmitted the Soviet government's new proposals to him (a lower purchase price in combination with a number of additional conditions) (DVP, vol. XVII, pp. 601–3). See also document 95.

6. On 22 September Stalin sent a cipher to Kaganovich: "In my opinion the proposal of

the Independent [Labor] Party to hold a conference against war and fascism may be agreed to. However, it must be arranged that anti-Soviet people like Trotsky do not have access to the conference" (RGASPI, f. 558, op. 11, d. 85, ll. 103, 1030b).

7. See note 1 to document 97. On 20 September the Politburo adopted a resolution on grain-procurement work in regions that had fulfilled the annual assignments for grain procurements as a whole. The resolution set the objective of achieving in these regions complete fulfillment of assignments by each collective farm and by each individual peasant (ibid., f. 17, op. 3, d. 952, l. 18).

· 105 ·

Stalin to Kaganovich
23 September
F. 71, op. 10, d. 130, l. 218. Typewritten copy.

___

To Comrade Kaganovich.

23 September 1934

1) Do read the letter from Comrade Ehrenburg.[1] He is right. We must abolish the traditions of RAPP[2] in MORP.[3] This is imperative. Get to work on this matter with Zhdanov. It would be a good idea to expand the framework of the MORP (a) the struggle against fascism, b) active defense of the USSR) and have Comrade Ehrenburg head MORP. This is a major project. Give it your attention.[4]

2) Read the report by Comrade Gromov and others. In my view, Gromov should be awarded the title of Hero of the Soviet Union and be given an Order of Lenin, and Filin and Spirin should just be awarded Orders of Lenin. These are remarkable people, and we must not leave them unrecognized. The appropriate explanation can be prepared (without disclosing any military secrets).[5]

Regards. I. Stalin.

P.S. I will await your reply.

1. See Appendix: document 4.

2. The Russian Association of Proletarian Writers, founded in 1925. It was abolished in 1932. It came under criticism for sectarianism and an uncompromising attitude toward other writers' groups.

3. The International Association of Revolutionary Writers (1930–35).

4. See note 1 to document 108.

5. On 28 September the Politburo adopted Stalin's proposal and approved the appropriate draft decree by the Central Executive Committee. The awards were presented "for heroism and selfless work displayed in setting a world record in a nonstop flight along a closed course over a distance of 12,411 kilometers [7,707 miles] for 75 hours." (RGASPI, f. 17, op. 3, d. 953, ll. 12, 82; see also the *New York Times*, 30 September 1934.)

· 106 ·

Kaganovich to Stalin
24 September

F. 558, op. 11, d. 742, ll. 99–104.

---

24 September [1934]
Greetings dear Comrade Stalin.

1) The Politburo met yesterday.

We discussed a number of practical questions, including the question of attaching enterprises to the PCs of the all-Union industries and to the PC of Local Industry.[1] Although we argued for local industry, there was no alternative to taking a number of enterprises from the regions and transferring them to a Union PC. For example, the PC of the Food Industry previously had had almost none of its own Union enterprises, now we had to give it a number of enterprises.

I must say that Moscow, which has a lot of light industry and food industry, especially suffered. We heard a report by Comrade Veitser on the progress of the shipment of goods for purposes of grain purchases.[2] It is clear that extra supervision is necessary here to ensure that shipments proceed in accordance with the plan and most importantly, that the proper assortment is provided. Purchases of grain have already begun. People are very eagerly selling grain for trucks, in the Moscow Region, for example, we sold 120 trucks for grain in two days, we collect 4,000 poods [67 tons] for a 1.5-ton vehicle.

2) There is some alarm again over transport, the latest fourth five-day period is resulting in a decrease in shipments, and there has been an inordinate increase in the number of crashes.

We are now exerting pressure for the repair of locomotives and track in preparation for winter. In approving the plan of shipments for October we had to cut back both the military department and the PC of Heavy Industry in order to increase the freight of foodstuffs, grain, and vegetables, and we added some extra railroad cars for firewood.

3) Comrade Fridrikhson arrived from Germany, but we have not heard him yet. Comrade Dvinsky has sent you his [Fridrikhson's] report. Please let me know your opinion. I am also sending you Comrade Eliava's memorandum on the sale of gold to the Germans.[3]

4) On your instructions Comrade N. Kuibyshev reviewed the material related to Yaffe's statement on military bacteriological work. The situation there is very bad. I am sending you his memorandum.[4]

Evidently we will not be able to discuss it until you return.

5) I am sending you Comrade Umansky's memorandum on the corrections by Wells. We cannot make these corrections, of course, without you.

Comrade Dvinsky is also sending you the text of the conversation with the corrections inserted.[5]

6) The grain procurements so far are not producing a sharp increase.

The Urals and Western Siberia are still doing poorly, things are also poor in the Saratov Region. I think it would be advisable for me to travel out to the procurements again and for a longer period, either to the Saratov Region or to the Cheliabinsk Region.[6]

Please let me know your opinion.

7) Regarding all your telegrams with instructions we have adopted the relevant decisions.

Regards to you. Yours, L. Kaganovich.

1. On 23 September the Politburo approved the list of enterprises that were to come under local industry (RGASPI, f. 17, op. 3, d. 952, ll. 1–2). All-Union enterprises were those subordinate to the PCs of the Heavy, Timber, Light, and Food Industries.

2. On 23 September the Politburo heard a report by the PC of Internal Trade on the shipment of goods to stimulate grain procurements. Allocations of goods and measures for delivering them were determined (ibid., ll. 32–34).

3. The memorandum is missing.

4. The memorandum is missing.

5. Stalin's conversation with the British writer H. G. Wells took place on 23 July 1934 from 4 to 7 PM (*Istoricheskii arkhiv*, no. 3, 1995, 140). On 30 August Stalin sent the transcript with his corrections to his assistant Dvinsky with a note: "Comrade Dvinsky! I am sending you the examined transcript of the conversation with Wells. Make copies (leave the original in the files—mine) and give three copies to Umansky (show Umansky the original and my corrections in the text)—one of them for Wells, another for Maisky, the third for himself, and send out the rest of the copies to the Politburo members for their information. This must all be done without delay (I am already late with the transcript). Regards!" (RGASPI, f. 558, op. 1, d. 3151, ll. 2–3).

On 21 September Stalin sent a cipher, in reply to a query from Kaganovich, that the conversation could be published in *Bolshevik* if Wells did not object, but "it is not worthwhile to publish it in *Pravda*" (ibid., op. 11, d. 85, l. 85). On 22 September the Politburo adopted a decision to publish Stalin's conversation with Wells in the journal *Bolshevik* (ibid., f. 17, op. 3, d. 952, l. 23).

Toward the end of September Dvinsky sent Stalin the text as prepared for the press, and enclosed the following note: "Comrade Stalin! I am sending you Comrade Umansky's memorandum with Wells's corrections attached. On the basis of the material sent by Comrade Umansky, I prepared the text of the conversation for the press in the form it would appear in the event that you accept the corrections. [. . .] The next issue of *Bolshevik* is scheduled for publication on 30 September. We could get the conversation with Wells into that issue upon receiving your instructions" (ibid., f. 558, op. 1, d. 3151, l. 52). On 28 September Stalin replied to Dvinsky: "You can print the conversation with Wells in the form—with the corrections by Wells and Umansky—in which you sent it to me. The headline should be changed from 'A Conversation with a British Writer' to 'Comrade Stalin's Conversation with a British Writer,' etc. Strike out the byline 'I. Stalin' over the heading. At the end of the conversation you should keep the note: 'Transcribed by K. Umansky.' On page 21 line 4 from the bottom add the phrase: 'We call this,' etc. (See text.) Tell Umansky about this final correction so he can pass it along to Wells. I. Stalin" (ibid., l. 53). (For all versions of Stalin's correction of the text of the conversation, see ibid., f. 558, op. 1, d. 3151.) The conversation was published in *Bolshevik*, no. 17, 1934.

The Stalin-Wells interview was published in various editions in English and is extensively described in H. G. Wells, *An Experiment in Autobiography* (London, 1934), 799–807.

6. See note 4 to document 108.

· 107 ·

Kaganovich to Stalin
28 September

F. 558, op. 11, d. 742, ll. 105–114.

---

28 September [1934]
Greetings dear Comrade Stalin.

1) I received your letter. Regarding both questions I have replied by wire.

Regarding MORP and Ehrenburg's proposal I will send you the draft resolution as soon as Comrade Zhdanov arrives and we do some work on it together.[1]

2) The question of the I-16 plane, based on the memorandum from N. Kuibyshev and Beriozin, has been raised with the Commission on Defense, which will meet on the 3d.[2]

3) I am sending you our resolution on the disclosure of the flight by the RD plane. You properly write in your letter that we should word it so as to avoid revealing a military secret, but Comrades Alksnis and others tried on the very day of the flight to transmit the report to all countries without asking anybody. We established a commission, investigated, and punished them.[3]

4) You already know from the ciphers about the beating of our military attaché's secretary by agents of the police [*defenziva*]. Our mission was dilatory and failed to deliver a protest against this.

We had to send an urgent written protest. I am sending it to you for review.[4]

5) On the Special Conference attached to the NKVD, we long ago already drafted a Statute. I am sending it to you and ask that you let me know your opinion.[5]

6) Regarding geographical maps we concluded that this matter must be transferred to the NKVD. They don't want it themselves, but this is the best solution. I am sending you a brief draft resolution and ask that you let me know your opinion.[6]

7) I am sending you material on our two planes that got lost during a night flight and ended up on the territory of Manchukuo.[7] One was at the Manchuria station, that one was forced to stay there, i.e. it was detained, the second one ended up in Eastern Manchuria near Grodekovo. Since the

Japanese were not there at the time, the population helped our pilots and our pilots flew back home.

A report has now come in that the Japanese arrived at that village two hours later and took repressive measures against the villagers. Since they are also raising a ruckus over this matter, we decided to make a brief statement to the Japanese authorities about the incident itself, indicating that the pilots will be punished. We also approved Comrade Tamarin's order imposing punishments in relation to this incident.

8) The subway construction is now going pretty well, unfortunately there was a fire a few days ago in one shaft where they are working with a shield. The causes have not yet been determined, so far the investigation has found that the cord on a hoist caught fire.

What made it catch fire was either a spark from a knife switch or from smoking, or arson, this has not been established yet. The effort to put it out was very intensive, and the fire did not spread. The only thing that happened was that because of the forced release of compressed air from the air locks, the ground began to shift and near the Metropole [Hotel] behind the Chinatown wall a little old two-story house collapsed, the tenants were evacuated beforehand. The situation in the shaft has now been put right and work will start tomorrow.

We have drawn conclusions from this lesson and have tightened up on discipline, vigilance, and careful work. I must mention that Comrade Abakumov displayed superb orientation, energy, and selflessness in dealing with putting out the fire and the complex technical matter of the air lock and the shifting ground. Now we are preparing for operation and installation and are getting the construction of stations into gear.

I will stop here.

Regards to you. Yours, L. Kaganovich.

1. See note 1 to document 108.

2. The I-16 was a fighter created by designer N. N. Polikarpov, and first produced in December 1933.

3. See document 105. On 15 September the Politburo ordered an urgent investigation of the fact that a report on the flight of the plane was distributed abroad and published in the Soviet press without the permission of the CC and Sovnarkom (RGASPI, f. 17, op. 3, d. 952, l. 6). On 23 September the Politburo approved a resolution on this matter that announced that punishments for disclosure of information on the flight had been imposed on Alksnis, the chief of the air force, and a number of leading press and censorship officials (ibid., l. 51). The RD plane (an ANT-25) was constructed with the aim of achieving a nonstop flight record (RD—*rekord dalnosti,* "distance record") (see V. S. Shavrov, *Istoriia konstruktsii samoletov v SSSR do 1938 g.* [The History of Airplane Building in the USSR Until 1938] [2d ed., Moscow, 1978], 484–89). It achieved a record for the European territory of the USSR on 10–12 September 1934.

4. On 27 September the Politburo approved the draft of a protest to the Polish government, submitted by the PC of Foreign Affairs, over the beating of an attaché from the Soviet mission by police (RGASPI, op. 162, d. 17, l. 54).

5. The Politburo approved the Statute on the Special Conference attached to the NKVD on 28 October (ibid., op. 3, d. 954, ll. 8, 38). See also document 91. The Special Conference had the right to sentence "socially dangerous" persons to exile or imprisonment in a labor camp for up to five years (see *Sobranie zakonov* [Collection of Laws], *1935*, art. 84, dated November 5, 1934).

6. A decree of Sovnarkom on 15 July 1935 established the Chief Administration of State Surveying and Cartography (*Lubianka, 1917–1960: Spravochnik* [Lubianka, 1917–1960: A Reference Book], comp. A. I. Kokurin and N. V. Petrov [Moscow, 1997], 14).

7. The document is missing.

· 108 ·

Kaganovich to Stalin
3 October

F. 558, op. 11, d. 742, ll. 115–123.

3 October [1934]
Greetings dear Comrade Stalin!

1. We called in representatives of the International Association of Revolutionary Writers [MORP]. They will now prepare a draft resolution for their presidium in which they will have to acknowledge that they have elements of RAPPism and that because of this they have slowed down the recruitment of broader circles of writers who advocate positions of combating fascism and war and defending the Soviet Union. And it is clear from the discussion with them how timely your proposal is.

Their resolution must contain direct wording about disbanding the MORP.

Simultaneously drafts are being prepared for a statement by the Soviet delegation and by the French and American delegations proposing that the MORP be disbanded and that an international writers' conference be convened. Before that it will evidently be necessary to hold a meeting, best of all in Paris, which would also be attended by the kind of writers Ehrenburg refers to. At this meeting an Organizing Committee could be established for convening a conference or congress of writers who advocate positions of combating fascism and war and defending the USSR. None of these drafts has been prepared anywhere yet, and as soon as they are ready they will be sent to you or will wait in Moscow until a joint discussion with you.[1]

2. Yesterday there was a conference of operational workers at the PC of Transport, where issues of preparation for the winter were discussed, true it wasn't completely prepared, but it was beneficial. I visited them and briefly pointed out to them that we are especially concerned about the following questions:

1) Why the number of crashes has increased.

2) Why the idle periods of railroad cars are not diminishing—6.03 days out of 9.05 turnarounds.

3) Why a poor job is being done on routing.

4) A number of specific points in CC resolutions on stations that are not being carried out.

I warned them that for the past six months the CC and Sovnarkom have been lenient toward them, giving them help, but now, if they prepare poorly for the winter, we will thrash them.

The conference proceeded in a businesslike manner. Andreev gave a pretty good speech. They are now preparing practical proposals, which I planned to approve through the transport commission or directly from the PC of Transport.

3. We have already confirmed the chair[men] of the CC of the trade unions, there was a special commission under Comrade Zhdanov.[2]

On the 1st all of the new chair[men] 150 people gathered at the All-Union Central Union of Trade Unions, half of them are from the regions. We went to see them, Comrade Zhdanov and I. Some of the old chairmen did not do very well in speaking about their tasks. I had to dwell in detail on the purpose and significance of this reorganization, and develop the instructions that you have repeatedly issued that they must get closer to real life, closer to production, and to the workers' needs, and I gave them a number of items of practical advice about how they should work.

4. The latest five-day period produced 64,101,000 poods [1,050,000 tons] as opposed to 55,849,000 [915,000 tons] in the previous fifth five-day period. September as a whole yielded 412,200,000 poods [6,751,000 tons] as opposed to 391,600,000 [6,414,000 tons] in September of last year.

The West[ern] Sib[erian], Stalingrad, Sverdlovsk and Cheliabinsk Regions increased procurements. There was a drop of 1 million [poods; 16,400 tons] in the Ukraine. Kharkov completed the plan. Dnepropetrovsk produced an increase, although Khataevich simultaneously sent in a memorandum that you have probably received. In all, the Ukraine has done 92.6 [percent] of the entire plan, they have about 20 million poods [328,000 tons] left to procure.

We are going to hit them in the newspapers tomorrow. Today in accordance with your telegram I berated *Pravda* about why they have left out the Ukraine.[3] With regard to grain purchases we have 18 million poods [295,000 tons]. The Moscow Region has already purchased 3 million poods [49,000 tons]. Things are already moving with more difficulty now, but we will try to finish in October. I am taking 15 heads of political departments and [party] secretaries from Moscow to Siberia. We have already sent 30 people to Cheliabinsk.

As I wired you I will make a stop in Cheliabinsk. Yagoda will not go, since Comrade Prokofiev is there in Siberia, and he, Comrade Yagoda, says he has a lot of different matters to attend to here.[4]

Regards. Yours, L. Kaganovich.

1. See documents 105, 107. An international writers' congress in defense of culture was held in Paris on 21–25 June 1935. It was attended by 230 writers from 35 countries, including a large Soviet delegation. A decision was adopted at the congress to establish the International Association of Writers, which was known in the West as the International Association of Writers for the Defense of Culture. The American section was called the League of American Writers (see *The Writer in a Changing World*, ed. H. Hart [London, 1937], 201–2). The International Association of Revolutionary Writers was disbanded in December 1935.

2. On 25 September the Politburo confirmed the chairmen of the central committees of the newly established trade unions (RGASPI, f. 17, op. 3, d. 953, ll. 71–81). See also note 8 to document 99.

3. On 4 October *Pravda* published an editorial headed "The Ukraine Must Accelerate Grain Deliveries," which said that the Ukraine, after receiving a not very challenging plan, was dragging out the delivery of grain to the state.

4. On 2 October the Politburo adopted a decision to send Kaganovich and Yagoda to Western Siberia on 4 or 5 October in order to intensify grain procurements (ibid., l. 24). On 3 October the Politburo rescinded this decision with regard to Yagoda because his deputy Prokofiev was already in Western Siberia with a group of functionaries (ibid., l. 25). On 4 October the Politburo instructed Kaganovich to make a stop in the Cheliabinsk Region about the grain procurements (ibid., l. 26). See also documents 106 and 110 and the introduction to this chapter.

· 109 ·

Stalin to Kaganovich
22 October

F. 81, op. 3, d. 100, ll. 83–87.

To Comrade Kaganovich.

The plan for grain procurements will apparently be fulfilled for the USSR as a whole. But it would be foolish to rest easy because of this. To cope with all the economic needs, we must still fulfill the plan for grain purchases. As the material makes clear, the plan for grain purchases by regions, as it was drawn up, contains defects (it is obviously too low for the Ukraine, the former Central Black-Earth Region, the Moscow and Gorky Regions, Bashkiria, the Cheliabinsk Region, and the Western Region). These defects must be corrected right away. The plan needs to energize and spur people forward rather than trail behind events, behind the purchases of grain. . . .

We must have in the state's hands 1.4 billion to 1.5 billion poods [22.9 million to 24.6 million tons] of grain in order to get rid of the rationing system for bread at the end of this year, a system that until recently was necessary and useful but has now shackled the national economy. We must get rid of the rationing system for bread (perhaps for groats and macaroni as well) and the related "bartering" of industrial crops and some animal-husbandry products (wool, leather, etc.). By reducing the commerc[ial] price and raising the ration price, we will set an average price for bread and flour, stabilize it at that level, and vary it from zone to zone. This will necessitate a wage increase, and price increases for cotton, flax, wool, leather, tobacco, etc.

This reform, which I consider an extremely serious reform, should be prepared right away, so that it can begin to be implemented in full in January 1935.

But in order to carry out this reform, we must have a sufficient reserve of grain.

That is why we cannot rest easy based on the success of the procurements, and the plan for grain purchases must also be carried out in full.

Consult the Politburo members, read them this letter and—if they agree—start preparing things. We will discuss the details of the plan when I arrive in Moscow.[1]

Regards. I. Stalin.

22 October 1934

1. The first page of the letter contains the resolution "Members of the Politburo to assemble today at 5 o'clock. L. Kaganovich" and the signatures of Zhdanov, Molotov, Kuibyshev, Kalinin, and Andreev.

Kaganovich reported to Stalin in a letter dated 28 October on the decisions regarding grain purchases and the abolition of the rationing system for bread (see document 111). See also the introduction to this chapter.

· 110 ·

Kaganovich to Stalin
23 October

F. 558, op. 11, d. 742, ll. 124–131.

23 October [1934]

Greetings dear Comrade Stalin!

1) I am very grateful to you for sending me to the Cheliabinsk Region and the Western Siberian Region. I immersed myself again in agricultural matters and made real use of my experience in grain procurements. I must tell you that the problem in both the Cheliabinsk and the Western Siberian Regions is not only the inability to organize procurements in a practical and timely manner, but also an incorrect political approach to procure-

ments. Our functionaries, including those in the regions, have not seen the resistance to procurements and have taken an unprincipled, "economical," as they now admit themselves, approach to procurements. That is precisely why they allowed a conflict to occur between procurements and the stacking of grain. And on the site at the grass roots all the draft animals have in effect been switched to stacking and merely in a formal sense at that, because labor discipline in reality is poor and in general many of the horses are poorly utilized. The harvest is excellent, but if we did not exert pressure for the grain procurements, they would not gather the harvest and would foul up the procurements.

Most of the secretaries of district committees and heads of political departments are approaching the procurements like unprincipled pragmatists and do not see, for example, that kulaks and White Guards are sitting in the collective farms pretending to be Partisans [of the civil war]. There is no political work among collective farmers, no explanations. I will set out all the facts and ideas for you in person, both about the lessons from the mistakes in grain procurements and about some questions of agriculture. On the scene in Siberia and the Cheliabinsk Region I had to lash out, of course, as harshly as I could against the opportunists and blind leaders. The results don't seem to be too bad, Siberia will finish by the 1st, and Cheliabinsk at the latest by the 25th.[1]

2) We have intensive work under way in Moscow to clear a number of streets from the subway construction operations, simultaneously we are leveling out a number of streets, we are tearing down part of the China-town wall and then from the CC to the Metropol hotel we are leveling out and widening the street. We are moving the statue of Ivan the Printer at the same site, but are taking it up to the site of the former church that used to stand behind the Chinatown wall. We are tearing down the house opposite the National [Hotel], about which you gave your instructions. As a result a new square will form in front of the Manezh. We expanded Arbat Square, removed a piece of the boulevard up to the Gogol statue, as you instructed, and opened it [the boulevard] up to Arbat Square. As for the subway, the project is going pretty well. The tunnel is almost finished, just a little piece is left where they proceeded with a shield in the vicinity of the Neglinka River, there is shifting ground there every step of the way.

We have now gotten work on the stations into gear. In a number of places we will not use marble, but something like artificial marble, cheap concrete plates, but done well and beautifully. There will be escalators, moving stairs, some of them are finished already. There are some difficulties with the subway cars, the workers are having problems learning to use them. This car, it is a little more complicated than an ordinary railroad car, but I think we will manage to achieve 40 cars, and for the initial period that will not be bad. The electrical substations will be ready on schedule.

Very hard work is required now. We have to keep people away from distractions and conceitedness. For example, we opened a trial section of 2.5 kilom[eters] so as to train the personnel and pandemonium breaks out, some are ready to conjure up the idea that the subway is virtually done already, and the newspapers are ready to exaggerate any report without grasping the substance of the matter. At this point such complacency is especially harmful. Even so, by February we will have a subway, thanks to your assistance and concern.

3) I did not want to burden you, but in view of its importance I am sending you the draft of the slogans and ask that you let me know your opinion by wire.[2]

After arriving from Siberia I wanted very much to come to visit you for a couple of days, but I could not bring myself to do it.

Regards. Yours, L. Kaganovich.

1. See note 4 to document 108; see also the introduction to this chapter.
2. The slogans for the seventeenth anniversary of the October revolution with Stalin's correction were approved by the Politburo on 31 October (RGASPI, f. 17, op. 163, d. 1044, ll. 72–80).

· 111 ·

Kaganovich to Stalin
28 October

From the Kaganovich family archive.

---

28 October 1934
Greetings dear Comrade Stalin.

1) After receiving your letter we drew up proposals on grain purchases [*zakupki*], which I sent and wired to you.[1] Today we gave a number of assignments to Veitser, Kleiner and others on preparing the dissolution of the rationing system, and on new prices and wages.[2] It will be a big and fine project. As for grain, we trust we will end up well. We will have to do a really good job, of course, of organizing purchases.

The entire plan for grain procurements has already been fulfilled, but we are not announcing it in the press yet, because procurements of reserve obligations will still be collected.

2) Things are still going poorly with regard to cotton. Comrade Kuibyshev will leave for Tashkent on the 30th to exert pressure for cotton procurements.[3]

Regards to you Comrade Stalin.
Yours, L. Kaganovich.

1. See document 109. On 2 November the Politburo approved a resolution on a supplementary plan for grain purchases in the amount of 43.7 million poods [716,000 tons]. These purchases had to be made in the fourth quarter in addition to the plan for grain purchases that was approved by a decree of the CC and Sovnarkom on 11 September (see note 1 to document 100). (RGASPI, f. 17, op. 3, d. 954, ll. 39–40.)

2. See document 109 and the introduction to this chapter.

3. On 23 October the Politburo resolved: "In view of the slow progress of cotton procurements, Comrade V. Kuibyshev is to be sent to Central Asia" (ibid., d. 953, l. 1).

1935

Introduction

IN 1935, as in the previous year, Stalin's vacation was lengthy: his appointment book contains no entries between 10 August and 2 November.[1] But the letters he exchanged with Kaganovich and the other Soviet leaders in these weeks were insignificant. Instead of letters Stalin and Kaganovich mainly exchanged strictly businesslike short telegrams and phonegrams in cipher. As the introduction to this book pointed out, there were two main reasons for this change. First was the new situation at the top level of power after the murder of Kirov in Leningrad on 1 December 1934. Stalin paid less and less attention to the opinions of his colleagues, and gradually strengthened his system of personal power, freeing himself from the remaining restrictions of collective leadership. Second, this was also the time when telephone communication between Moscow and the south became safer and more reliable.

Stalin also used the Leningrad murder as a pretext for finally dealing with his former political opponents—the leaders and participants in the oppositions of the 1920s and the early 1930s—and for strengthening the policy of repression generally. A mere few hours after the news of Kirov's murder Stalin prepared in his own handwriting the decree of the Central Executive Committee (TsIK) of the USSR, which became known as the Law of 1 December. This extraordinary document included several major new provisions. The investigation of cases con-

1. *Istoricheskii arkhiv,* no. 3, 1995, 173.

cerned with terrorist acts should be completed within ten days. The indictment should be handed to the accused only twenty-four hours before the case was heard. Cases should be heard without the participation of the parties concerned. No references to the court of appeal and no pleas for mercy were to be allowed. The sentences to death by shooting should be carried out immediately after they were announced. The procedures of the Law of 1 December were an excellent basis on which extensive terrorist actions could be carried out by the state itself, and they were used very widely in the course of 1937–38.

The former opposition leaders Kamenev and Zinoviev and their supporters were accused of the murder of Kirov with entirely inadequate justification. At the same time former rank-and-file supporters of the oppositions began to be exiled to Siberia and the Far North. What became known as the "Kremlin Affair" directly continued the repressive policy against former supporters of the oppositions. Between January and April 1935 the agencies of the PC of Internal Affairs (NKVD) arrested a group of employees of government institutions located in the Kremlin (including cleaners, librarians, and staff members of the secretariat of TsIK and of the office of the Kremlin Commandant). They were accused of organizing a terrorist group which had prepared to assault government leaders, particularly Stalin himself. Those arrested included relatives of Kamenev, and he was accused of being one of those who had inspired the conspiracy. Yenukidze, the secretary of TsIK, who was in charge of the Kremlin household, was dismissed on the grounds that he had protected the conspirators.[2] He was demoted to the post of a plenipotentiary in Kislovodsk on 13 May. In June he was expelled from the party. On 7 September Stalin objected that "he does not recognize his decline and does not suffer from modesty," and insisted that he should be further demoted.[3] In 1937 he was executed. Yenukidze was an old friend of Stalin and other members of the Politburo, so the Yenukidze Affair provided a further indication of Stalin's antipathetic and even hostile attitude to the old Bolsheviks, as is clearly shown in document 120.[4]

At this time Stalin began to reveal his dissatisfaction with the present structure of the NKVD. A prisoner escaped in the course of being

2. *Izvestiia TsK,* no. 7, 1989, 86–93.

3. RGASPI, f. 558, op. 11, d. 89, ll. 71–76.

4. For further details of the Yenukidze affair, see J. A. Getty and O. V. Naumov, eds., *The Road to Terror: Stalin and the Self-Destruction of the Bolsheviks, 1932–1939* (New Haven, 1999), 161–79, 234–35.

transferred in a special rail coach, and on 25 October Stalin complained in a cipher to Molotov, Kaganovich, and Yagoda that "the Chekist [i.e. former OGPU] section of the NKVD does not have sufficient leadership and is undergoing a process of degeneration. [. . .] [It] suffers from a serious illness. It is time for us to engage in curing it."[5]

The wave of terror organized after the murder of Kirov spread beyond the former members of the oppositions. At the end of 1934 and the beginning of 1935 the Politburo authorized the exile as well as the mass confinement in camps of "kulaks" and "anti-Soviet elements" from Azerbaidzhan, Ukraine, and the Leningrad Region. So-called socially alien elements were exiled en masse from Moscow and Leningrad. This term referred to such people as the surviving members of the nobility and the bourgeoisie and those who had been sentenced to imprisonment in the past. Then between May and December 1935 a "verification" (*proverka*) was carried out in party organizations of the existence and authenticity of party documents; in practice this turned into a party purge (*chistka*), in the course of which people were arrested.

It seemed as if the outburst of state terror in the first few months after Kirov's murder had destroyed forever all the moderate initiatives of the previous period. In fact, however, two tendencies coexisted in 1935 and 1936: certain elements of the moderate policy remained, even while state terror intensified.

The continuation of the moderate course of policy was primarily due to the need to consolidate the emergence of the economy from crisis. After the lengthy travails of collectivization and dekulakization considerable concessions were made to the peasants. The documents of the second Congress of Collective-Farm Shock Workers, convened in February 1935, were approved by the Soviet government as a law. These gave definite rights to cultivate and expand the "personal auxiliary economies" (i.e. the private plots) of the collective farm households. The private plots developed rapidly at this time, as did agricultural production in the socialized sector of the collective farms. This enabled an improvement in the life of the peasants and in the food situation in the country as a whole. The overcoming of the crisis in agriculture was reflected in the success of the grain deliveries to the state.

During his leave in 1935 Stalin, together with his deputies in Moscow, devoted great attention—not for the first time—to the need

5. RGASPI, f. 558, op. 11, d. 92, ll. 67–68.

to accumulate grain stocks. On 4 September, in a cipher to Molotov and Kaganovich, he insisted on increasing the purchases (*zakupki*) of grain, made in addition to the compulsory grain deliveries: "Bear in mind that we will not have a good harvest every year. It is necessary to have 400–500 million poods [6.55–8.19 million tons] of untouchable transitional stock, if we want to secure ourselves against a bad harvest or external complications. The present Untouchable Reserves [*fondy*] are inadequate, as they are current Reserves, and not permanent."[6] On 27 September Kaganovich and Molotov explained in a cipher to Stalin that on 1 July 1935 the total stock of grain had been 400 million poods (6.55 million tons), including 200 million (3.28 million tons) in Untouchable and other reserve Funds. They anticipated that the 200 million could be increased to 500 million (8.19 million tons) by 1 July 1936. Stalin replied on the following day that the Funds could be restricted to only 350 million poods (5.73 million tons), but this must be "an absolutely Untouchable Grain Reserve," "transferred without change in size from year to year and renewed each year"; three-quarters of the total must be food grains.[7] These efforts were on the whole successful. In the course of the agricultural year 1935/36 total stocks increased from 6.55 million tons on 1 July 1935 to 9.92 million on 1 July 1936.[8] When the country suffered particularly bad weather conditions and a very poor harvest in 1936, widespread famine was avoided by using a substantial part of these stocks.

Industry developed very rapidly in these years. The investment projects started during the first five-year plan continued to be brought into operation, and further substantial investments in industry were undertaken. The availability of an increased supply of agricultural raw materials enabled the expansion of the consumer goods industries. At the same time, planning was to a considerable extent based on the use of economic methods and the renunciation—at least in an extreme form—of the former policy of attempting to advance by great leaps. The more balanced and better coordinated economic policy gave reasonable results. Among historians of the Soviet economy the years 1934–36 are known as "the three good years" (the phrase was coined by the Russian-American economist Naum Jasny). This was the most successful period of the prewar five-year plans, which may be why eco-

6. Ibid., d. 89, l. 35.
7. Ibid., d. 90, ll. 105, 101–104.
8. Estimated from data in a memorandum from Kleiner to Stalin dated 15 November 1936 (GARF, f. R-5446, op. 26, d. 84, ll. 34–29).

nomic problems occupy less space in the Stalin-Kaganovich correspondence than in previous years. The one exception is that Kaganovich, having been appointed people's commissar of transport at the beginning of 1935, now more frequently wrote to Stalin about the situation on the railways, to which considerable resources were devoted throughout 1935.

As in 1934, the threatening external situation played a major role in Soviet policy. On 2–3 October 1935 Mussolini invaded Abyssinia (now Ethiopia).[9] The Soviet Union drew closer to France, Great Britain, and the United States. In May Franco-Soviet and Czechoslovak-Soviet pacts were signed, and in July–August the Seventh Congress of the Communist International, reversing previous revolutionary policies, strongly supported the formation of Popular Fronts against fascism in the Western democratic countries.

Before the Italian invasion of Abyssinia Stalin took an extremely cautious attitude to the dispute between the two countries, and restrained Litvinov's growing inclination to take a strong stand. He was anxious not to destroy the Soviet Union's long-standing good relations with Italy, and he was suspicious of Britain and France. On 2 September, a cipher from Stalin to Kaganovich and Molotov displayed a wholly inadequate realization of the fascist threat. Stalin insisted that the PC of Foreign Affairs "does not understand the international situation":

> The conflict is not so much between Italy and Abyssinia as between Italy and France on the one hand, and Britain on the other hand. The old Entente no longer exists. Instead two Ententes are emerging: the Entente of Italy and France, on the one hand, and the Entente of Britain and Germany on the other hand. The fiercer the struggle between them, the better for the USSR. We can sell grain to both of them, so that they can fight each other. It is not at all advantageous to us that one of them should now defeat the other.[10]

Nine days later Litvinov proposed that he should walk out of the Assembly of the League of Nations in connection with the failure of the Assembly to elect the representative of the USSR (himself) as one of the six vice-presidents—"linking this with my speech at the Council [of the League] against an Abyssinian war." Stalin forthwith agreed.[11]

---

9. On the Abyssinian conflict, see J. Haslam, *The Soviet Union and the Struggle for Collective Security in Europe* (Basingstoke and London and Basingstoke, 1984), 60–79.

10. RGASPI, f. 558, op. 11, d. 89, ll. 2, 20b.

11. Ibid., ll. 92–93.

Meanwhile, after a little maneuvering, the Assembly voted to elect Litvinov as vice-president. This incident led Stalin in a further cipher to Kaganovich and Molotov dated 12 September to criticize Litvinov as guided "not so much by the interests of the USSR as by his own overwhelming pride," and to object to his speech at the League:

> He separates himself from Italy, from the supporters of aggression and war. That is good of course. But he does not separate himself even by a weak hint from the position of those powers which have a sphere of influence in Abyssinia and thus convert the independence of Abyssinia into a hollow specter. [. . .] Litvinov wants to follow the British line, but we have our own line.[12]

Eleven days later, in a cipher dated 23 September, Kaganovich and Molotov sent Stalin the draft of a letter which the Comintern proposed to send to the Labour and Socialist International, stating that "war in Abyssinia may flare up at any moment," and calling for a joint conference to discuss measures to preserve peace in face of the "fascist criminals." Evidently taking into account Stalin's previous caution, Kaganovich and Molotov commented about the Comintern draft letter "we doubt whether it is expedient," but on the following day Stalin replied, "I do not object."[13] This shift in Stalin's position towards taking a stand against Italian aggression was consolidated a few days later. On 27 September, the Soviet trade union leaders together with Dimitrov, the general secretary of Comintern, proposed to recommend to Sir Walter Citrine, general secretary of the British Trade Union Congress, then in Moscow, "the establishment of a contact committee [. . .] to coordinate joint action in the struggle against the attack of Italian fascism on Abyssinia," and Stalin agreed on the same day.[14] Then on 4 October, immediately after the Italian invasion, Litvinov, who was visiting Moscow, proposed that the USSR should agree to sanctions against Italy providing this was supported by the other members of the League. Stalin immediately agreed.[15] For further developments see documents 123 and 124. The Council of the League branded Italy an aggressor, and the member states agreed to impose sanctions. Throughout the winter of 1935–36 the Politburo, with Stalin's agreement, continued to support sanctions.

12. Ibid., ll. 99–102.
13. Ibid., d. 90, ll. 59–60, 58.
14. Ibid., ll. 88, 87.
15. Ibid., ll. 143–144, 142. Kaganovich, Molotov, and Andreev reported the proposal to Stalin in a cipher, and themselves endorsed it.

These internal and external factors served to limit the growth of terror in the USSR. In spite of the increased number of arrests in 1935, and the "verification" in the party, attempts were also made at reconciliation with at least part of those strata of the population which had been subject in previous years to discrimination and repression. At the beginning of 1935 the government promised to introduce a new constitution that would restore the civil rights of some categories of the population (such as former kulaks). The convictions of many collective farmers were annulled. The cases of those convicted under the law of 7 August 1932 were reexamined. The departure of the children of former kulaks from exile was made less difficult. The previous restrictions on the recruitment of Cossacks for the Red Army were canceled, and Cossack cavalry units were created. At the beginning of December Stalin launched a significant fresh political appraisal at a conference of combine-harvester operatives. A. Gilba, a Bashkir collective farmer, stated from the platform that "although I am the son of a kulak, I will fight honestly for the cause of the workers and peasants and for the construction of socialism." Stalin called out a phrase which became famous: "A son is not responsible for his father."[16] This was followed by an extensive propaganda campaign.

Towards the end of Stalin's 1935 vacation an event occurred which portrayed him to the Soviet public as a man of the people with normal human feelings. On 17 October he paid a rare visit to his mother in Georgia. The visit was reported in *Pravda* and other newspapers on 27 October. Behind the scenes, however, Stalin displayed both his capriciousness and his anxiety to maintain a modest appearance before his colleagues. On 21 October, Poskrebyshev, on behalf of Kaganovich, sent Stalin by cipher for his approval the proposed press communication about the visit. It was written in flowery language and included an account of Ekaterina (Keke) Dzhugashvili's admiration for her "model son." Stalin wrote on the telegram "I will not approve or deny it. It is not my concern. Stalin."[17] Kaganovich understandably took this as a signal that the report of the visit could be published. But on 29 October, following the publication of the report, Stalin reacted angrily in a cipher to Molotov, Kaganovich, Andreev, Zhdanov, and Tal (the editor of *Pravda*): "I ask you to put a stop to the philistine riffraff invading our central and local press, placing in the newspapers an 'interview'

16. *Pravda*, 2 December 1935.
17. RGASPI, f. 558, op. 11, d. 92, ll. 22–23.

with my mother, and every other kind of rubbishy publicity, even pictures. I ask you to spare me from the importunate ballyhoo of the publicity of these scoundrels."[18] This was the last telegram sent by Stalin before his return from vacation.

Documents 112–125

· 112 ·

Kaganovich to Stalin
16 August

F. 558, op. 11, d. 743, ll. 1–4.

---

16 August [1935]
Greetings Dear Comrade Stalin!

1) Several districts in the Odessa Region have found themselves in a difficult situation with the harvest. Veger and the CC of the KP(b)U [Communist Party (Bolsheviks) of Ukraine] are requesting a reduction of 12 million [poods; 197,000 tons] for the Odessa Region in the plan of grain deliveries for the rural sector and a seed loan for the winter sowing of 1.5 million poods [25,000 tons]. We would consider it possible to grant their request, Kleiner will arrive in two days and we will hear his report.[1]

Please let me know your opinion. Just in case I am sending you Veger's letter.[2]

2) Regarding the removal of the eagles from the Kremlin towers, we have planned the enclosed brief decision by the CC and Sovnarkom, based on the drawings of the stars that you approved. Please: first, approve this design, second, specify whether the one on the top of the Historical Museum should be removed as well, and third, whether an item should be published in the newspapers about the fact that a decision has been made to remove the eagles and replace them with stars.[3]

3) Comrade Stomoniakov insisted today on discussing the note to Hirota in reply to his note. We instructed him to shorten it and soften it a little. When it is ready, we will ask you, of course, whether it should be delivered at all. This question came up today, but we still instructed him to redo it.[4]

I will not burden you anymore for now.

I leave you with a handshake and hope you have a good vacation. L. Kaganovich.

18. Ibid., l. 82.

Greetings to our boss Svetlana! I await her instructions, and will carry out whatever she asks, even a request to delay attending school for 15–20 days.

One of the secretaries L. M. Kaganovich.

Greetings to my colleague Vasya—secretary of boss Svetlana. L.K.[5]

1. See note 1 to document 113.
2. The letter is missing.
3. See note 2 to document 113.
4. See note 2 to document 114.
5. Vasya (Vasily) and Svetlana were Stalin's fourteen-year-old son and nine-year-old daughter. For Stalin's long-standing joke that Svetlana was a major political figure, see S. Alliluyeva, *Twenty Letters to a Friend* (New York, 1967).

· 113 ·

Stalin to Kaganovich
19 August

F. 81, op. 3, d. 100, ll. 89–90.

<u>Comrade Kaganovich</u>

19 August 1935

1) I have already sent you a cipher regarding Veger's proposals.[1]

2) Regarding the eagles on the towers, I am sending you my agreement with this letter.[2]

3) I propose that we <u>shut down</u> *Prozhektor* [Spotlight] without delay <u>because it is totally unnecessary</u> and transfer the paper (that becomes available) to the magazine *Ogonyok* [Little Flame], which is managed much better and which should be expanded.[3] Vasilievsky should be assigned to a different job (as editor of *Prozhektor* he proved to be obtuse and good for nothing).

Regards. I. Stalin.

<u>P.S.</u> Svetlana the boss will be in Moscow on 27 August.[4] She is demanding permission to leave early for Moscow so that she can check on her secretaries.

I. St.

1. Stalin's cipher of the same date described Veger's proposal as "a minimum" (RGASPI, f. 558, op. 11, d. 88, l. 29). On 20 August the Politburo adopted a decision to lower the grain-delivery plan for the Odessa Region and to release seed loans for winter sowing to the collective farms in the region that had had crop failures (ibid., f. 17, op. 162, d. 18, l. 115). See document 112.

2. On 22 August 1935 the Politburo approved a decree of the CC and the Sovnarkom that provided for the removal by 7 November 1935 of the eagles on the towers of the Kremlin wall and the Historical Museum building and the erection of five-point stars on the towers of

the Kremlin (ibid., op. 3, d. 970, l. 57). On 23 August an announcement to this effect was published in the newspapers. On 29 September the Politburo approved the allocation of 30 kilograms of gold to manufacture the Kremlin stars (ibid., op. 162, l. 18, l. 137). See documents 112, 117.

3. See note 1 to document 114.
4. See note 5 to document 112.

· 114 ·

Kaganovich to Stalin
22 August

F. 558, op. 11, d. 743, ll. 5–9.

22 August [1935]
Greetings Dear Comrade Stalin!

1) I received your letter. We adopted a decision on *Prozhektor* today. At the same time we instructed Comrade Tal to submit to the Secretariat of the CC his proposals on expanding and improving *Ogonyok*.[1]

2) The latest five-day period yielded 237 million poods [3,882,000 tons] of grain. As a result, although the Ukraine ended up with a small decrease, we still have an increase in procurements thanks to other regions. Still lagging at present are Bashkiria, the Sverdlovsk and Omsk Regions, and some others, but we will see what the next five-day period produces. All the regions are lagging in the repayment of grain loans, we are thinking of putting pressure on this aspect. Procurements as a whole this year are going very well, of course. Because of this, and also to push closer to 80,000, we have adopted for September a plan to load 73,000 railroad cars.

3) I am sending you a new draft of the note in reply to Hirota. Please review it and let me know your opinion.[2]

4) Comrade Voroshilov has submitted a draft resolution on reducing the draft age. Although Comrade Voroshilov has spoken with you about this, in view of the importance of this decision I am sending you the draft and ask that you let me know your opinion.[3]

5) We are sending you with today's mail a memorandum from Comrade Agranov on the arrest of the editor of the French-language newspaper *Journal de Moscou,* which is published in Moscow, Lukianov (a former émigré and adherent of the Change of Landmarks movement [*smenovekhovets*]). The PC of Foreign Affairs entrusted the entire staff and publication of the newspaper to him. The newspaper was conducted incorrectly, and evidently Change of Landmarks elements, and perhaps spy elements as well, clustered around it. Today people from the PC of Foreign Affairs came in to protest the arrest. It would have been better of course, if

the NKVD had requested authorization for the arrest and we had removed him as editor before the arrest, but in essence they acted properly. Unfortunately, we got into an acrimonious argument with Comrade Voroshilov today over this. We still resolved not to release this Lukianov and to remove him as editor. As for the direction of the newspaper, we instructed Comrade Tal to review in detail the content of a whole host of issues of the newspaper, draw up proposals, and report to us.

Evidently we will have to search for a nonparty person as editor, but first of all a Soviet person and second the secretary of the newspaper must be a Communist. Incidentally Vinogradov—the writer whose letter you left for me—was mentioned as a candidate for editor. Please let me know your opinion.[4]

Warm regards to you. How are you enjoying your vacation? Yours, L. Kaganovich.

Regards to Svetlana the boss.[5] We are looking forward to seeing her.

L. Kaganovich.

1. See document 113. On 22 August the Politburo adopted a decision to close the journal *Prozhektor* and transfer the allocation of paper that was freed up to the magazine *Ogonyok* (RGASPI, f. 17, op. 3, d. 970, l. 59).

2. On 1 July the plenipotentiary of the USSR in Japan had delivered to the Japanese foreign minister, Hirota, a note from the Soviet government on violations of the USSR border by Manchukuo that resulted in casualties among Soviet border guards (DVP, vol. XVIII, pp. 430–34). On 20 July, in a note in reply, the Japanese side rejected these complaints. On 27 August Stalin noted in a cipher that he did not object to the draft (RGASPI, f. 558, op. 11, d. 88, l. 97). The new Soviet note, sent to Hirota on 2 September, expressed dissatisfaction with the statement by the Japanese government and reiterated the protest over intrusions into Soviet territory (DVP, vol. XVIII, pp, 480–82). See also documents 112, 125.

3. On 27 August Stalin stated in a cipher that he did not object to the draft resolution (RGASPI, f. 558, op. 11, d. 88, l. 97). In 1936 the qualifying age for call-up into the Red Army was lowered from 21 years of age to 19.

4. See note 1 to document 116. *Vekhi* (Landmarks) was a book of essays criticizing the Russian intelligentsia for its support of revolution, published in 1909. In 1921 a group of émigrés in Prague published *Smena vekh* (A Change of Landmarks), in which they argued for reconciliation between the Soviet regime and the intelligentsia, and the supporters of this movement became known as the *smenovekhovtsy* (adherents to the "Change of Landmarks").

5. See note 5 to document 112.

· 115 ·

Stalin to Kaganovich
[after 22 August]

F. 81, op. 3, d. 100, ll. 95–97.

To Comrade Kaganovich.

1) The NKVD had no right to arrest Lukianov without the approval of the CC. Agranov should get a dressing-down.[1] Vinogradov will probably be suitable.

2) <u>You must push hard</u> on the grain procurements and on getting the [grain] loans repaid. You must especially push the Ukrainians, who have been corrupted by our concessions, as well the Omsk Region and other eastern regions. Send Kleiner to the Omsk Region, somebody else to the Bashkir Region and push hard.[2]

3) Why was Trilisser replaced with Moskvin as a candidate for the executive committee of the Comintern? What is the problem?[3]

4) We should satisfy Yevdokimov (Northern Caucasus) (see enclosed letter).[4] Regards.[5]

I. Stalin.

1. See note 1 to document 116.
2. See note 2 to document 116.
3. On 10 August the Politburo approved Manuilsky, Stalin, and Trilisser as members of the presidium of the executive committee of the Comintern (RGASPI, f. 117, op. 162, d. 18, l. 110). See also document 116.
4. The letter is missing.
5. In the upper right-hand corner of the letter Mikoian wrote: "Have read."

· 116 ·

Kaganovich to Stalin
27 August

F. 558, op. 11, d. 743, ll. 10–15.

27 August [1935]

Greetings Dear Comrade Stalin!

I received your letter.

1) Regarding the arrest of Lukianov, evidently Comrade Yezhov gave his consent, but at the meeting I personally pointed out to Comrade Agranov that they did not have the right to carry out an arrest without officially raising the question in the CC. But Comrade Stalin, I want to tell

you that the main argument we had was not so much over this as over the merits of the issue. Voroshilov denied in advance Lukianov's guilt and the newspaper's errors, without having read either the newspaper or the materials. In my view, he is wrong, and when I began to try to prove he was wrong, we got into an acrimonious argument.

In any case, we will give Agranov a dressing-down, but if we have to discuss the merits of the issue, permit me to defend the position I have taken.[1]

2) Regarding grain procurements you are absolutely right, tomorrow already we will do everything you propose.[2]

3) Trilisser was renamed Moskvin because his surname is known as that of an NKVD functionary.[3]

4) An interesting letter came in from Tairov in Mongolia. It describes the attitudes of Gendung and the entire leadership. Evidently, Gendung is detaching himself more and more from us. Just in case I am sending you this letter.[4]

5) Comrade Andreev's draft, which you left, called for verification of the Komsomol beginning in September. I think, Comrade Stalin, that this is inadvisable. A verification of party cards is under way now. Naturally, a Komsomol verification would suffer. It would be better to postpone it until 1936, when the verification of party cards will be over. Please let me know your opinion.[5]

6) The Commission on Defense met yesterday. Unfortunately, the issue I asked to have raised for discussion was not included in the agenda, that was the memorandum by Prokofiev that you left, on the condition of military artillery depots and the storage of artillery shells. It is clear from this memorandum that this area is very poorly organized, but now we will have to discuss it at the next meeting.

We discussed the question of the construction of TsAGI [the Central Aerodynamic Institute] in Ramenskoe.[6] We decided not to build a dam and to build a facility for hydroplane construction at another site. In Ramenskoe we will build a facility for land-based aircraft.

Just in case I am sending you the minutes of the Commission on Defense.[7]

Well I will close here.

I will write about my PC of Transport business in the next letter.[8]

Warm regards to you Yours L. Kaganovich.

1. See documents 114, 115. On 22 August the Politburo decided to dismiss Lukianov, the editor of the newspaper *Journal de Moscou*. The PC of Foreign Affairs was instructed to select another candidate for the position (RGASPI, f. 17, op. 3, d. 970, l. 64). On 28 August the Politburo pointed out to the NKVD the "incorrectness" of arresting Lukianov without CC approval. An extract from the minutes containing this decision was sent to Agranov (ibid., op. 162, d. 18, l. 123). On 13 September Raevsky was confirmed as editor of the newspaper (ibid., op. 3, d. 971, l. 35).

2. See document 115. On 28 August the Politburo sent Kleiner to the Omsk Region and Tyomkin to Bashkiria "to assist local organizations in intensifying grain procurements" (ibid., d. 970, l. 72).

3. See note 3 to document 115.

4. The letter is missing.

5. An inspection began in May 1935 to verify that party members had party cards and record cards and that they were authentic. In effect this continued the party purge that had been underway since the end of 1932. On 31 August in a cipher to Kaganovich and Molotov Stalin agreed that the inspection of the Komsomol should be delayed until 1936 (ibid., f. 558, op. 11, d. 88, ll. 139–141).

6. TsAGI was established in 1918. Ramenskoe is a town near Moscow.

7. The minutes are missing.

8. Kaganovich was appointed people's commissar of transport, in addition to his other responsibilities, on 28 February 1935.

· 117 ·

Kaganovich to Stalin
29 August

F. 558, op. 11, d. 743, ll. 20–22.

29 August [1935]

Greetings Dear Comrade Stalin!

1) We are sending you the resolution on the Volga-Moscow Canal. I edited the introductory section along the lines of the exchange of opinions at the Politburo meeting. Please let me know whether to publish it in the newspapers after you sign it.[1]

2) What should we do with the draft resolution on the Intelligence Administration that Comrade Gamarnik sent in? Should we postpone it until the fall? Please let me know your opinion.[2]

3) Mirzoian sent a telegram about the celebration of the 15th anniversary of the Kazakh Republic on 24 October. In it he raises a number of economic issues: the construction of houses of culture, of a library, etc. He also raises the question of awards. Please let me know your opinion.[3]

4) Today we saw mock-ups of the stars. They came out very nice and attractive. I am sending you photographs of the mock-ups and the draft resolution with corrections. Please let me know your opinion, preferably by wire, in view of the need to start work.[4]

5) A Politburo meeting has been scheduled for the 31st, and the agenda for the meeting is being sent to you. I will write to you after the meeting.[5]

Regards. Yours, L. Kaganovich.

1. The decree of Sovnarkom and the CC "On the Construction of the Moscow-Volga Canal" was approved by the Politburo on 7 September 1935 (RGASPI, f. 17, op. 3, d. 971, ll. 21, 95–99). On 9 September it was published in *Pravda*.

2. On 27 November the people's commissar of defense approved the new staff of the Intelligence Administration of the Red Army (see Ye. Gorbunov, "Voennaia razvedka v 1934–1939 godakh" [Military Intelligence, 1934–1939], in *Svobodnaia Mysl* [Free Thought], no. 2, 1998,106).

3. After a second appeal from Mirzoian, dated 5 September, the Politburo adopted the proposal of the republic to postpone the celebration of the 15th anniversary of Kazakhstan from 4 to 14 October (RGASPI, f. 17, op. 163, d. 1078, l. 8). On 22 October the Politburo approved a draft decree of the presidium of the Central Executive Committee on the development of Kazakhstan over the past 15 years, which also provided for the construction of houses of culture (ibid., op. 3, d. 972, ll. 42, 147–155).

4. See note 2 to document 113.

5. See document 118.

· 118 ·

Kaganovich to Stalin
31 August

F. 558, op. 11, d. 743, ll. 23–28.

---

31 August [1935]

Greetings Dear Comrade Stalin!

We had the Politburo meeting today.

1. We discussed the proposals of Comrade Antipov's commission regarding the report of the PC of Light Industry on the cotton, linen, and wool industries. The commission became preoccupied with one aspect of the situation—technical re-equipping, the replacement of machinery, imports, and an injection of money. All this is essential, but based on the proposals that you made at the time of the report, it is essential to stress the section on rectifying current blatant shortcomings and questions of the improvement of management. This is just what was missing from the resolution. So the Politburo instructed the commission to improve the resolution, after which we will do final editing on it and send it to you.[1]

2. Regarding the issue of the hydro-complex on the Volga the Politburo adopted the construction project located at Rybinsk instead of Yaroslavl.[2]

3. We discussed the question of the beet harvest, and Comrade Kosior attended. We set up a commission headed by Mikoian, which we instructed to submit proposals within three days. Everybody says that the harvest is 25–30 percent larger than last year's, i.e. about 120–125 tsentners per hectare. Everything depends on the quality of the harvest. The opportunities now are better than they have ever been, because in the Ukraine grain procurements will be finished by 5 September, so vehicles and manpower will become available. We want to emphasize this in the directive and point out that all resources must be redeployed toward beets, in order to have a lot of sugar.[3]

4. The situation is again not very good regarding grain storage, ticks are beginning to infect the grain. Today we heard a report on this issue for verification purposes, it turned out that with regard to the construction of warehouses as well, despite the fact that a lot has been built already, 259 out of 1712 warehouses under construction have still not been completed.[4]

Therefore we put a little pressure on Kleiner today. Tomorrow he leaves for Omsk.

5. For verification purposes we also heard a report on the issuance of state certificates granting collective farms permanent (perpetual) use of the land. Unfortunately, your directive and the CC decision have not been carried out. Everyone points to someone else. The PC of Agriculture people cite the fact that Goznak has not printed the actual certificates. We instructed them to ensure that certificates are issued to 40,000 collective farms before 1 October, and to 120,000 collective farms before the end of the year.[5]

6. We discussed proposals on providing schools with writing supplies. Since you are very interested in school matters and this was done based on your instructions, I am sending you the draft of this resolution.[6]

7. The cotton situation is not too bad. According to available information the harvest in Uzbekistan is 10.5 tsentners [per hectare], as opposed to 8.2 last year. In the new regions (the Ukraine, Northern Caucasus), the harvest is 5–6 tsentners. So according to preliminary assumptions we can draw up a procurements plan of 30–31 million poods [491,000–507,000 tons]. After the discussion in a few days we will determine the level and will consult you.[7] Regards to you. Yours, L. Kaganovich.

P.S. Today I reported to our boss Svetlana on our work, she seemed to deem it satisfactory. She feels well. Tomorrow she is already going to school. L.K.

---

1. On 31 August the Politburo adopted only the first section of the resolution proposed by the commission, the section dealing with the provision of equipment for light industry. The commission was instructed to undertake additional work on the two further sections, on the organization of work at enterprises, current tasks, and the quality of output. The final editing was to be carried out by a commission consisting of Molotov, Kaganovich, Antipov, Yezhov, Zhdanov, and Liubimov. (RGASPI, f. 17, op. 3, d. 970, l. 2.)

2. On 31 August the Politburo approved a proposal for construction of a hydro-power complex at Rybinsk. The construction was assigned to the NKVD. (Ibid., d. 971, l. 2.)

3. A decree of the CC and Sovnarkom on harvesting sugar beet and on the wages of tractor drivers and others was approved by a poll of Politburo members on 3 September. The plan for procurements of sugar beet in 1935 was approved at 15.2 million tons. The Politburo also approved the text of a telegram from Sovnarkom and the CC to local leaders. (Ibid., ll. 8–10.) On 5 September the resolution was published in *Pravda*.

4. On 31 August the Politburo established a commission to prepare a draft resolution on grain storage (ibid., d. 970, l. 3), and the resolution was approved on 3 September (ibid., d. 971, ll. 7, 84–85).

5. The state certificate for perpetual use of land by collective farms was approved by the Politburo on 7 May. Goznak (Chief Administration for Production of State Symbols, Coins and Orders) was instructed to print 600,000 copies of these documents during 1935 and 1936. (Ibid., d. 963, l. 25.)

6. See note 5 to document 120.

7. A few days later Kaganovich and Molotov reported to Stalin about the plan for cotton procurements (ibid., f. 558, op. 11, d. 89, ll. 57–58). On 9 September a plan to procure 30,058,000 poods (492,000 tons) of cotton fiber in 1935 was approved unchanged by the Politburo (ibid., f. 17, op. 3, d. 971, ll. 23, 109–113).

· 119 ·

Kaganovich to Stalin
5 September

F. 558, op. 11, d. 743, ll. 29–36.

---

5 September [1935]
Greetings dear Comrade Stalin!

1) Kandelaki arrived and gave a brief report on the placing of orders against the 200 million German credit. We have placed orders for 25 million marks. According to him things are made more difficult by the nature of our orders—the complexity of the equipment and the specific character of a certain segment of the orders. We did not decide anything, I advised Kandelaki to write you a brief report, I am sending it to you.[1]

2) The PC of Foreign Affairs has submitted a draft of the agreement between the Mongolian People's Republic and Manchukuo on the border commission. We exchanged opinions and find it acceptable. We are sending it to you and ask that you let us know your opinion.[2]

3) Our grain procurements are going well. What we have this year with regard to grain is really a great victory for the party—a victory for your line Comrade Stalin! Today we adopted your proposal and set the plan for grain purchases at 300 million poods [4.9 million tons].[3] You are absolutely right in saying that we must look ahead. We rejected the proposal of the Commission on Procurements for 150 million [2.5 million tons] (which Comrade Molotov also supported by the way), but we also set a minimum figure of 200 million [3.3 million tons].

Regarding the sale prices for bread we will report to you today by wire. As soon as the draft as a whole is ready, we will send it out to you or we will consult you by wire.[4]

4) A draft resolution is being sent to you today regarding economic measures on the Khorezm oasis, this primarily affects the Turkmenians.[5] I believe this resolution is of great importance for a substantial segment of the Turkmenians and Uzbeks, and therefore it would be a good idea for this to be issued from the CC over your signature. Incidentally I promised

them I would report to you and told them you would help them. In general they left Moscow completely changed people.

5) A few words about PC of Transport affairs. The brunt of the work at present revolves around locomotive management, questions of wages, and the rearrangement of railway schedules on new principles. A few days ago I heard reports by the railroad directors and even some depot heads on the special phone. Clearly the stagnant marsh is on the move. The leaders are being forced to shape up because they are pressured not only from above but also from below—by the engineers and conductors. Most gratifying is the spirit of the locomotive brigades and the conductors. On the Donets Railroad, for example, the engineers, not waiting for 1 October, when the new norms will be introduced are already beginning to produce good speeds. There are some engineers who in eight hours return from a one-way trip of 100 kilometers, a round trip of 200 kilometers. The engineers at Liman depot spoke and said that "for the first time we feel ourselves organized people—for the first time," an engineer said, "I have dinner at a definite time with my family." And when one engineer came home on the first day of work under the new system after eight hours, his wife began to ask him whether the train had been canceled and refused to believe that he had already made the trip. The average daily journey of a locomotive on the Donets Railroad increased from 184 to 220 kilometers.

Levchenko has already cooled off and put 100 locomotives in reserve. But there are big problems in organizing the work of the depots under a new system. This is primarily in a section of the central railroads and all the eastern railroads. There are particularly big difficulties in drawing up the schedules so that when one locomotive arrives the next locomotive is ready at the depot on time. A few days ago I had a conference with low-level schedule makers and it turned out that they are left to themselves, nobody guides them, and whatever they draw up is approved automatically without anybody even reading it. Now we will consider the schedule of each railroad at the PC of Transport, coordinating the railroads, and by 15 September we will approve the new schedules. We are putting on the pressure, especially in preparing for the winter. We have dispatched a number of heads of the administrations of the PC of Transport and their deputies to the regions, particularly to the east. On 1 September we had a sharp reduction in loading as compared with the 31st—a drop of 10,000 railcars, showing that the erratic performance in loading is still going on. I had to rebuke a number of railroad directors. We have to be alert. I have a number of questions: about the division of the railroads, about investment in 1936, etc. But I am not raising them now. I would be very happy if at least by the end of September I could visit you for at least a day or two.

Regards to you. Yours, L. Kaganovich.

1. See note 3 to document 120. "The specific character of a certain segment of the orders" is a reference to orders for military goods.

2. See note 1 to document 120.

3. On 5 September the Politburo adopted a plan for purchases of 300 million poods (4.9 million tons) of grain from the 1935 harvest (RGASPI, f. 17, op. 3, d. 971, l. 16).

4. On the same day Molotov and Kaganovich sent a cipher to Stalin on the reduction of the retail prices of bread and flour. They proposed "to tie in the whole question with the abolition of the rationing of meat, sugar, and fish," recommended reduced prices for Central Asia, and proposed to prepare a complete draft of the decree on prices and rationing within five days (ibid., f. 558, op. 11, d. 89, ll. 55–56). On 6 September Stalin replied that to avoid profiteering, prices should be reduced in all regions simultaneously but not until 1 October (ibid., l. 52). On 20 September Kaganovich and Molotov sent Stalin a long cipher with proposals about the reduction of bread prices and the abolition of other food rationing (ibid., d. 90, ll. 6–12). On the same day Stalin replied "instead of a draft you have sent me general propositions; send the draft decree when it is ready" (ibid., ll. 2–3). On 22 September Kaganovich and Molotov sent the draft decree to Stalin, who approved it with minor changes (ibid., ll. 45–46, 44). See note 1 to document 122.

5. The decree of Sovnarkom and the CC "On Measures to Develop Cotton Growing and the Production of Seed Alfalfa at the Khorezm Oasis" was approved by the Politburo on 14 September; Stalin agreed to the draft without change (ibid., op. 163, d. 1078, ll. 136–139). See also document 120.

· 120 ·

Stalin to Kaganovich
8 September

F. 81, op. 3, d. 100, ll. 91–94.

8 September 1935

To Comrade Kaganovich.

1) I am returning the draft agreement between the MPR [Mongolian People's Republic] and Manchukuo. I have made corrections, on which I insist.[1]

2) I vote for the draft on Khorezm.[2]

3) I have read Kandelaki's letter. Things in Germany are apparently not going too badly for us. I am sending it to you. Give Comrade Kandelaki my regards and tell him to insist on getting from the Germans <u>everything</u> that we need for the military and with regard to dyes.[3]

4) I am sending you Agranov's memorandum on Yenukidze's group of "old Bolsheviks" ("old farts" in Lenin's phrase). Yenukidze is a person who is alien to us.[4] It is strange that Sergo and Orakhelashvili continue to be friends with him.

That is all for now. Regards. I. Stalin.

P.S. I am returning the draft on materials for school and writing. I have made minor corrections. I vote in favor.[5]

I. St.

1. The text of the agreement between the MPR and Manchukuo on a border commission was approved by the Politburo on 13 September (RGASPI, f. 17, op. 162, d. 18, l. 141). See also document 119.

2. See note 5 to document 119.

3. See document 119. On 9 April Soviet-German agreements were signed in Berlin: on the settlement of Soviet payment obligations; on Soviet shipments to Germany and current orders by the USSR; and on additional orders by the USSR in Germany (DVP, vol. XVIII, pp. 270–74). On 3 September Kandelaki, the USSR trade representative in Germany, sent Stalin a letter informing him of the successful conclusion of these agreements and on difficulties with placing military orders (APRF, f. 3, op. 64, d. 663, ll. 128–129).

4. Agranov's memorandum is missing. At the beginning of 1935 the NKVD fabricated the "Kremlin Affair"—see the introduction to this chapter.

5. The draft decree of Sovnarkom and the CC of the party on school writing materials, submitted by the CC department of schools, was adopted in principle by the Politburo on 31 August. A commission chaired by Zhdanov was instructed to undertake the final editing (RGASPI, f. 17, op. 3, d. 970, l. 3). On 14 September the Politburo approved the decree in its final form (ibid., d. 971, ll. 37, 118–125). See also document 118.

· 121 ·

Kaganovich to Stalin
17 September

F. 558, op. 11, d. 743, ll. 37–39.

17 September [1935]

Greetings dear Comrade Stalin.

1) I am sending you the TASS announcement and the draft proposal of the PC of Foreign Affairs on the pamphlet issued by the Japanese War Ministry with smears against the USSR. Please let me know your opinion. We had doubts whether it is advisable to put out such a statement now with publication in the press.[1]

2) I am sending you Stomoniakov's proposal on the expected attempt by Japanese ships to pass by Khabarovsk in order to avoid the Kazakevich channel. Please let us know your opinion by wire.[2]

3) I am also sending you two memoranda from the PC of Foreign Trade on the negotiations with world oil companies and on the list of items to be ordered in France.[3]

4) I implore you to support me on the following issue: our passenger rail transportation has deteriorated, mainly with regard to the discipline of the service personnel and the maintenance of rail terminals, train cars, cleanliness, and order. The current head of the passenger department is not up to this. Since a good organizer is needed here, I would ask you to give me Comrade Olsky. He will agree to this himself, and to replace him we can confirm his deputy Kamensky, who did an outstanding job in the Donets Basin in food services.[4]

5) We gave Comrade Yezhov a vacation with a trip abroad.[5]

6) The Chekists have designed a new uniform, they were supposed to show it to you. Please let me know your opinion.[6]

Regards to you. How are you enjoying your vacation and how do you feel?

Yours, L. Kaganovich.

1. On 22 September the Politburo instructed Radek to publish an article analyzing the pamphlet and coordinating it with Stomoniakov (RGASPI, f. 17, op. 162, d. 18, l. 150).

2. On 21 September Stalin sent a cipher to Kaganovich and Molotov commenting on Stomoniakov's proposal (ibid., f. 558, op. 11, d. 90, ll. 33–34) ; and in accordance with Stalin's cipher on 22 September the Politburo resolved "to take measures to seize vessels if they attempt to pass over our internal waters" (ibid., f. 17, op. 162, d. 18, l. 150).

3. The memoranda are missing. On 21 September Stalin wrote in a cipher to Kaganovich and Molotov that "I do not object to negotiations with the world oil trusts" and that "it would be good to add to the orders from France items for submarines and minelayers, i.e. electrical equipment, diesels, turbines, etc." (ibid., f. 558, op. 11, d. 90, ll. 33–34). On 23 September the Politburo authorized the PC of Foreign Trade to enter into negotiations with world oil trusts "on the sale abroad of our own retail and warehouse oil facilities," whose cost was determined to be 6 million rubles (ibid., f.17, op. 162, d. 18, l. 151). On 29 September the Politburo approved the list of items to be ordered in France (ibid., l. 155).

4. On 23 September Stalin sent a cipher to Kaganovich and Molotov stating that Olsky's work in public catering was a "major responsibility" and that he should not be removed (ibid., f. 558, op. 11, d. 90, ll. 50–51).

5. On 10 September Stalin wrote to Yezhov: "You should leave on vacation as soon as possible—for a resort in the USSR or abroad, whichever you prefer, or whatever the doctors say. Go on vacation as soon as possible, unless you want me to raise a big ruckus" (ibid., d. 755, l. 39). On 19 September the Politburo granted Yezhov a two-month vacation beginning on 1 October, sending him abroad for treatment accompanied by his wife. A total of 3,000 rubles in foreign currency was allocated for these purposes. When Kaganovich sent out the draft resolution for a vote, he attached a note to it: "To Members of the Politburo. Comrade Stalin specified in a letter to Comrade Yezhov that it was imperative he [Yezhov] go on vacation" (ibid., f. 17, op. 163, d. 1079, l. 63). On 29 September, modifying the decision of 19 September, the Politburo granted Yezhov a vacation from 26 September (ibid., op. 3, d. 971, l. 57).

6. On 4 October the Politburo adopted a resolution, "On Military Titles, Uniforms, and Decorations for the NKVD" (ibid., d. 972, l. 9).

· 122 ·

Kaganovich to Stalin
26 September

F. 558, op. 11, d. 743, ll. 40–64.

---

26 September [1935]

Greetings Dear Comrade Stalin!

1) Today we published the resolution on price reductions for bread and

the abolition of the ration-card system for meat, etc.[1] Today as well there were meetings at all the plants and talks on this topic. The workers and clerical staff are in a very good mood. Everybody welcomes this decision, because above all it clearly points to a path of price reductions and increases in real wages. Many workers are immediately doing calculations and pointing out themselves that since they had been buying meat and butter at the market to supplement the rations, this now benefits them. Evidently we will now have to focus attention on the stores and on how the sale of goods is organized.

2) After several reworkings the PC of Transport has drawn up an engineering design and cost estimate for the construction of the Moscow–Donets Basin Railroad. We based it on your instructions that this should not be a super-trunk line but a regular, normal type of railroad. In terms of technical specifications (the ruling grade and so forth) it will still be better than the Moscow-Kursk Railroad. As a result of reducing a number of operations, the estimate has been drawn up for a total of 790 million [rubles] instead of 1.17 billion. If 490 million had not already been spent as of today, we could have built it at a lower cost. Now 300 million is left for all of the remaining operations—145 million for the total completion of the Moscow-Valuiki section and 155 million for Valuiki to Nesvetai. We are stretching out all this work over two years '36–'37. In '36 we must finish the section from Moscow to Valuiki and begin work from Valuiki to Kondrashovka.

In '37 all operations will be totally completed. I am sending you a brief memorandum and implore you Comrade Stalin to let me know your opinion.[2]

3) Comrade Berman has arrived from the Far East. He reports that the track from Karymskaia to Urusha has been completed, although with a very thin (15–20 centimeters) layer of ballast, which will have to be filled out later.[3] In addition, civil and technical structures have not been completed (residential buildings, stations and depots, and the water pipeline is not finished) on this section. On the section from Bochkarevo to Khabarovsk, the track bed has not yet been laid and, apparently, it will not be possible to make real use of the second tracks on this section until next spring. The quality of work in terms of all specifications is not bad.

Ten days ago I dispatched a group of high-level functionaries to inspect the railroads' readiness for operation. The worst aspect there (Berman reports this too) is the housing situation, so we will have to accelerate housing construction in the fourth quarter. Please let me know your opinion on the construction of Khabarovsk-Norilsk-Ussuriisk in 1936. I instructed the administrators to bear in mind that this section will be built in 1936. As a result of his trip, Berman and I are now working out practical measures for the construction of two tracks.

4) The people's commissar of transport was granted the right to award people a Badge of the Honored Railroad Worker. Comrade Andreev has awarded many employees. Since I have not yet exercised this right, I decided to ask your opinion. Just in case I am also sending you the list. Please do let me know your opinion. The situation with loading is going fairly well. Now we have to put on the pressure again to fight against crashes.

That's it. Warm regards to you. Yours, L. Kaganovich.

1. See document 119. The decree of the CC and Sovnarkom on the reduction of bread prices from 1 October 1935 and the simultaneous elimination of the ration-card system for meat and fish products, sugar, animal fats, and potatoes, was approved by the Politburo on 25 September (RGASPI, f. 17, op. 3, d. 971, ll. 61, 140–149), and was published in newspapers the following day.

2. The memorandum is missing. On 28 October the Politburo considered the general estimate and construction plan for the Moscow—Donets Basin Trunk Line and approved the main technical specifications as submitted by the PC of Transport. The estimated cost of construction was approved at 780 million rubles. (Ibid., d. 972, ll. 53, 54.)

3. On 27 March 1934 Sovnarkom had adopted a decree on the construction in 1934 of second tracks for the Karymskaia-Bochkarevo Railroad in the Khabarovsk Region. The OGPU and the PC of Transport were assigned to manage the construction. (GARF, f. R-5446, op. 57, d. 30, ll. 21–22.)

· 123 ·

Kaganovich to Stalin
[before 9 October]
F. 81, op. 3, d. 101, l. 73. Typewritten copy.

To Comrade Stalin.

Today we received the following report from Rozenberg by telephone: "According to the estimates of the Secretariat of the League of Nations the plenary session of the Assembly opening on 9 October will last at least four days. The British delegation even believes that the session may last a whole week. Right after the Assembly the Coordination Committee will convene. The plan is for it to consist of 25 members (all the members of the Council plus a number of states chosen by the Assembly). The first delegates of most countries have arrived in Geneva to participate in the work of the Assembly and the Committee (specifically, France is represented by Lavalle and Britain by Eden)." In this connection, according to Rozenberg, League circles are expressing a certain amount of puzzlement over the absence of the head of the Soviet delegation. According to his information, this absence lays the groundwork for some journalistic circles to spread false rumors concerning the position of the USSR in the Italo-Abyssinian conflict.[1]

We would think that Litvinov should leave urgently for Geneva. Please let us know your opinion.[2]

1. On 2–3 October 1935 Italian troops invaded Ethiopia (see the introduction to this chapter).
2. See document 124.

· 124 ·

Kaganovich to Stalin
9 October

F. 558, op. 11, d. 743, ll. 49–51.

9 October [1935]
Greetings Dear Comrade Stalin!

1. Today Comrade Litvinov raised the question of directives for him during further discussion in Geneva of the Italo-Abyssinian war. He formulated his brief "theses" in seven points. We disagreed with him, because we consider them incorrect and at odds with the instructions you gave. We instructed him to stick to the directives already given him on the basis of your telegrams. I am sending you his seven points and please let us know your opinion.[1]

2. We exchanged opinions today on the issue of French credits. Litvinov proposes that we do not reject the French proposals, including the Seligman bank. The PC of Foreign Trade on the contrary proposes we reject them and agree to negotiate only if a group of major banks is organized. We are leaning toward Litvinov's proposal, because we think that the major banks will participate. They are not acting now, but are letting out the Seligmans in order to maintain their fundamental position on debts. I am sending you both memoranda and ask that you let me know your opinion.[2]

3. Comrade Litvinov has raised the question of rejecting the proposals of the Persian government on abrogation of art. 6 of the Soviet-Persian Treaty of 1921.

We agree with him. I am sending you the memorandum and ask that you let me know your opinion.[3]

4. Today we considered the plan of distribution of tractors and motor vehicles for the fourth quarter. I am sending you this distribution and ask that you let me know your opinion.[4]

5. Regarding my trip to the eastern railroads, if you deem it possible, I would leave around 15 October, Comrades Andreev and Zhdanov are already here,[5] otherwise I will have to do it in November. Please let me know your opinion.[6]

That is all for now. Warm regards. Yours, L. Kaganovich.

1. The memorandum is missing. On 8 October the Politburo agreed with Litvinov on sending a directive to Potyomkin, which said in part: "State the readiness of the USSR to fulfill, on an equal footing with other League members, the obligations imposed on them by the League charter. Do not refuse to participate in the Committee to Determine the Nature and Amount of Sanctions" (RGASPI, f. 17, op. 162, d. 18, l. 175). On 15 October the following directive was given to Litvinov in Geneva: "Follow an independent Soviet line in the spirit of your last speech in Geneva and avoid anything that could be interpreted as a subordination of our line to the position of Britain. Do not show any more zeal with regard to sanctions than other countries, and maintain contact with France as much as possible" (ibid., l. 178).

2. The memoranda are missing. On 21 October the Politburo adopted a decision to enter into negotiations with the French banks (ibid. l. 181).

3. The memorandum is missing. On 20 October the Politburo accepted the proposal of the Iranian government to eliminate article 6 from the Soviet-Iranian Treaty of 1921 (ibid., l. 180). The article permitted Soviet troops to be brought into Persia "in the event that attempts are made by third countries through armed intervention to carry out an expansionist policy in Persian territory or to turn Persian territory into a base for military action against Russia, if this endangers the borders of the Russian Soviet Federated Socialist Republic or powers allied with it" (DVP, vol. XVIII, pp. 538–89).

4. The distribution plan was approved by the Politburo on 21 October (RGASPI, f. 17, op. 3, d. 972, ll. 41, 138–146).

5. On 9 August Andreev had been granted a vacation for a month and a half beginning on 15 August (ibid., d. 970, l. 28); on 5 September Zhdanov had been granted a vacation for a month beginning on 7 September (ibid., d. 971, l. 12).

6. On 4 September 1935 Kaganovich reported in a letter to Ordzhonikidze: "I couldn't go to Siberia, the boss said: 'When Sergo arrives, you can go.'" Not until 4 January 1936 did the Politburo authorize Kaganovich to leave on 7 January to visit the Siberian and Far Eastern Railroads (*Stalinskoe Politbiuro v 30-e gody* [Stalin's Politburo During the 1930s], 146–47).

· 125 ·

Stalin to Kaganovich and Molotov
13 October

F. 81, op. 3, d. 101, l. 69. Typewritten copy.

[Phonegram]
Moscow
CC of the VKP(b)
To Kaganovich and Molotov.

The directive you gave to Sangursky and Deribas,[1] in my view, is wrong, because the result will be that the Japanese will occupy, unimpeded, our sector where the fighting took place, take the Japanese bodies and then say that the Japanese were killed in Manchurian territory, accusing us of violating the borders and crossing into Manchurian territory. It would have been better to give them an immediate directive to occupy this sector of ours with our troops, take the Japanese bodies, and secure material evidence for ourselves. But now you can't correct the directive, since you have already sent it to there.

I also don't like the part of the directive where you give the Japanese the opportunity to prance freely around our territory to a depth of 3 kilometers from the Manchurian-Soviet border. Have you thought about the position in which our border guards, and possibly the fortified areas, will find themselves? What is the reason for such magnanimity toward the Japanese scum?

The note to Hirota and the TASS report were obviously written too hastily and sloppily, but nothing can be done—there is very likely no chance, being so far away, of making corrections. We will have to leave them in the form in which you transmitted them to Sochi.[2]

Stalin.[3]

1. On 12 October the Politburo instructed Gamarnik and Yagoda to cancel the order to Deribas and Sangursky "not to expand armed clashes under any circumstances in connection with the incident at Novo-Alekseevka. In the event of a new attack by the Japanese detachment, you are not to join battle within 3 kilometers from our border and only after the Japanese advance beyond 3 kilometers are you to properly repulse the attack, though without allowing our units to cross the border under any circumstances" (RGASPI, f. 17, op. 162, d. 18, l. 176).

2. The note of 12 October delivered to Hirota discussed the attack on a Soviet border detail on 6 October by a Manchurian detachment under the command of a Japanese officer and new intrusions into Soviet territory in subsequent days (DVP, vol. XVIII, pp. 526–27). A TASS report on border violations by the Japanese-Manchurian detachments and on the protests lodged with the Japanese government was published in the newspapers on 13 October. On 20 October Kaganovich and Molotov sent Stalin the draft of a telegram from Khabarovsk reporting that many Japanese military items had been found on Soviet territory (RGASPI, f. 558, op. 11, d. 92, l. 37). Stalin replied that it would just cause laughter—"the only serious proof would be Japanese bodies, but our glorious frontier troops kindly overlooked the Japanese bodies, handing them to the Japanese" (ibid., ll. 34–36).

3. The document contains the notation "Phonegram received by Comrade Dvinsky at 4:50 A.M. on 13 October 1935."

1936

Introduction

FOR INDUSTRY the year 1936 was perhaps the most successful in the whole of the 1930s. With the exception of coal and oil, all industries expanded rapidly. According to official figures, the production of heavy industry increased by as much as 30 percent. The production of armaments, which formed part of heavy industry in the statistics, increased, according to a Western estimate, by at least 60 percent.[1] This was in sharp contrast with the growth of armaments in 1935, when armaments expanded less rapidly than the rest of industry owing to the difficulty of switching to more advanced technology.

The increase in the production of consumer goods by 27 percent almost equaled that of heavy industry. This was a year of significant expansion in the standard of living of a large section of the urban population. On the other hand, owing to particularly unfavorable weather conditions, the grain harvest of 1936 was extremely low. But large grain stocks had been accumulated in previous years, and these were drawn upon to avoid widespread hunger—a sharp contrast with the famine of 1933.

In 1936 capital investment (measured in current prices) increased by as much as 30 percent, twice as rapidly as in the previous year. These large investments were directed not only to the capital goods industries and armaments but also to the consumer goods industries, and to edu-

---

1. See Harrison's index in *Europe-Asia Studies,* 49 (1997), 374, 391 (article by M. Harrison and R. W. Davies). The real increase is underestimated in the index, as it is in terms of numbers of weapons, without allowing for technical improvements.

cation and the social services. But the expansion in investment resulted in financial difficulties, and in July 1936, before Stalin's departure on vacation, the Politburo approved a much more moderate investment plan for 1937. Paradoxically, the increasing violence of the purges was accompanied by a more balanced economic policy. But in 1937 and 1938 competent economic planning and the expansion of the economy were temporarily crippled by the disruption caused by the arrest and execution not only of leading political figures but also of many managers, engineers, and ordinary workers and collective farmers.

In 1936 Stalin was on leave from 14 August to 25 October.[2] The period of his leave saw the launching of the first stage of the 1936–38 purges, and much of his correspondence with Kaganovich in these months was devoted to the political repression. By the time Stalin departed on vacation, the preparation of the first major Moscow political trial was complete. This was the trial of the "Anti-Soviet United Trotskyite-Zinovievite Center," known in the West as the Kamenev-Zinoviev trial.[3] In view of the importance of the trial we have included in this book all the relevant ciphered telegrams exchanged between Stalin and Kaganovich.

For several months Stalin had been personally in charge of fabricating the case against a group of old Bolsheviks who had been opposition leaders, including Zinoviev, Kamenev, I. N. Smirnov, Mrachkovsky, and Bakaev. The turning point in preparing the trial was the arrest and interrogation of Dreitser, a well-known Trotskyist, and Pikel, the former head of Zinoviev's secretariat. During the interrogation they "revealed" the existence of a "terrorist center" of Trotskyites and Zinovievites. Kaganovich received the records of their interrogation while he was on vacation in Kislovodsk in July. He wrote to Stalin from Kislovodsk supporting the retribution which Stalin was preparing against former members of the oppositions, and bluntly said they should be executed (see document 127).

When he returned from vacation, Kaganovich was made responsible for the final preparations for the trial during Stalin's own absence, and he managed the trial itself. It was to Kaganovich that V. V. Ulrikh, president of the Military Collegium of the Supreme Court, presented various draft versions of the sentences to be imposed; Kaganovich passed

2. See *Istoricheskii arkhiv*, no. 4, 1995, 31 (Stalin's Kremlin appointment book).
3. See also J. A. Getty and O. V. Naumov, eds. *The Road to Terror: Stalin and the Self-Destruction of the Bolsheviks, 1932–1939* (New Haven, 1999), 247–57.

them on to Stalin. Changes in the final version of the sentence were made by Kaganovich in his own hand: he added Ordzhonikidze and himself to the list of persons against whom terrorist acts had allegedly been attempted.[4]

This first public trial of opposition leaders took place from 19 to 24 August 1936. It was carefully managed by Kaganovich and the absent Stalin. On the eve of the trial, Kaganovich settled final details with Ulrikh and with Vyshinsky, the prosecutor (see document 130). Stalin ordered that the trial should be in public and that foreign correspondents should be invited. He was anxious to convince foreign observers present at the trial, and the Soviet population, that the former oppositionists really pursued terrorist aims, participated in terrorist actions, and acted as agents of the Gestapo and of foreign intelligence services. He also sought to discredit and isolate Trotskyist organizations in the West. The "confessions" of the accused, obtained by the NKVD in the course of several months, were directed towards these purposes. In informing Stalin in some detail about the progress of the trial, Kaganovich and Yezhov emphasized the reaction of the foreign correspondents (see document 134, item 5, and document 136, item 4).

In pursuit of his aim of discrediting the oppositionists at home and abroad Stalin postponed the arrest of some of the former leading supporters of Trotsky, including Rakovsky, Radek, and Piatakov. Their function at this stage, according to Stalin, was to write articles condemning Trotsky, Kamenev, and Zinoviev, in order to "deprive our enemies of the opportunity to depict the trial as a show and as a factional reprisal by the CC against the Zinoviev-Trotsky faction" (document 143). On 21 August the newspapers carried articles by Rakovsky, Radek, and Piatakov sharply condemning Trotsky, Kamenev, and Zinoviev, and demanding that they should be executed. To achieve maximum publicity abroad Stalin instructed that the proceedings of the Kamenev-Zinoviev trial should be translated into foreign languages (see document 150).

The correspondence of Stalin and Kaganovich about the trial clearly confirms that Stalin was the principal inspirer of the retribution against his former political opponents, and personally sanctioned the death sentences imposed on them. Document 143 shows Stalin at work preparing the "evidence" of the accused. In this cipher he or-

4. See *Reabilitatsiia: Politicheskie protsessy 30–50-kh godov* (Moscow, 1991), 187–88.

dered Kaganovich to summon Kamenev's wife, already under arrest, for further interrogation, and specifically indicated that testimony was to be obtained from her on how Kamenev had reported to foreign ambassadors his "plans for the conspiracy and assassinations of the VKP leaders."

The Kamenev-Zinoviev trial gave the signal for repressive acts against other former opposition leaders. Testimony at the trial itself referred to the participation of the former Left oppositionists Piatakov, Radek, Sokolnikov, and Serebriakov in "terrorist organizations," and to the links between the "Trotskyite-Zinovievite bloc" and the former Right-wing leaders, including Tomsky, Rykov, Bukharin, and Uglanov. The blow also fell on many highly-placed leaders of government departments, and on the assistants of members of the Politburo. Thus the NKVD falsified confessions claiming that Ya. A. Livshits, one of Kaganovich's deputies in the People's Commissariat of Transport, had participated in a "terrorist Trotskyite center." Livshits was arrested shortly afterwards. Later, in January 1937, Livshits was arraigned at the second major Moscow trial, together with Piatakov, who was Ordzhonikidze's deputy, and a group of economic officials.

The evidence against Piatakov began to be prepared long before the Kamenev-Zinoviev trial. Several of the accused testified to the existence of a further "parallel anti-Soviet Trotskyite center" in which Piatakov participated. Information arrived from Kiev that N. V. Golubenko and others had testified that Piatakov headed a Ukrainian Trotskyite center. In reporting this news about Piatakov to Stalin on 17 August, Kaganovich inquired "what to do with him?" (See document 130.) Stalin decided not to arrest him immediately. By agreement with Ordzhonikidze Piatakov was sent on a visit to the Urals.

As we have seen, Stalin's decision may have been due to his anxiety to use Piatakov to testify in the press against Trotsky. The delay in Piatakov's arrest may also have been due to Stalin's need to cope with objections from Ordzhonikidze. Though our knowledge about this is so far incomplete, there is a great deal of evidence that Ordzhonikidze tried to persuade Stalin to cease the repression of those who managed the economy. This eventually led to a conflict between Stalin and Ordzhonikidze, and to Ordzhonikidze's death on 18 February 1937. Kaganovich undoubtedly knew about Ordzhonikidze's views and probably sympathized with them, both because he was friendly with Ordzhonikidze and because he had himself been harmed by the arrest of officials in the Commissariat of Transport.[5] It seems clear from various documents that Kaganovich never openly dissented from the arrests ordered by Stalin, but he did help Ordzhonikidze as long as he could. Probably the two documents approved on 31 August 1936 were the outcome of their joint efforts. These were the Politburo decision to rescind the expulsion from the party of the director of the Magnesite factory in Satka (Cheliabinsk Region), and the directive sent to party leaders forbidding them from dismissing senior economic officials or expelling them from the party without the knowledge and agreement of the party Central Committee. Kaganovich sent both documents to Stalin for his approval (document 152). On 8 September Kaganovich ordered the heads of the political departments of the railways to familiarize themselves with the directive.[6] This is further indirect evidence that he sympathized with it.

From the beginning of September 1936 Ordzhonikidze was on vacation in Kislovodsk, and wrote letters to Stalin in which he tried to persuade him to moderate the repression. Thus on 7 September he wrote: "Some people think that all former [oppositionists] should be driven out of the party, but this is irrational and should not be done— but our people do not always have enough patience and ability to look things over and sort them out." In this context Ordzhonikidze again tried to mitigate the fate of Piatakov. While trying not to anger Stalin, Ordzhonikidze carefully expressed his doubts about the accuracy of the evidence against Piatakov and proposed a way of avoiding his arrest: "The new testimony of Sokolnikov, Piatakov's wife, Golubenko, and Loginov broadens the people involved still further. I have no doubt that in the main their testimony was correct, but it is difficult to know who they have wrongly involved in the matter. Whatever we decided, it is absolutely impossible to leave him [Piatakov] as deputy [people's commissar of heavy industry], now this would be harmful. If we do not arrest him, let us send him somewhere, or leave him in the Urals as at present."[7] But Ordzhonikidze failed to prevent the arrest of Piatakov, which took place in the night of 12 September.[8]

5. See O. Khlevniuk, *In Stalin's Shadow: The Career of "Sergo" Ordzhonikidze* (New York, 1995), and E. A. Rees, *Stalinism and Soviet Rail Transport, 1928–1941* (Basingstoke and London, 1995).

6. APRF, f. 3, op. 22, d. 150, ll. 128–129.

7. RGASPI, f. 558, op. 11, d. 779, ll. 99–107.

8. *Reabilitatsiia*, 218–19.

The scenario for the case against the former Right-wing leaders Rykov, Bukharin, and Tomsky followed similar lines. After the accusations at the Kamenev-Zinoviev trial, Tomsky committed suicide (see document 138). Then the NKVD obtained a "confession" from Sokolnikov that the "Right wing" was linked with the "terrorist Trotskyite-Zinovievite center." Stalin, to demonstrate his objectivity, and following his usual practice of reaching his goal by gradual steps, approved a personal confrontation between Sokolnikov, and Rykov and Bukharin. This took place on 8 September in the presence of Kaganovich, Yezhov, and Vyshinsky.[9] Two days later, on 10 September, the newspapers announced, with Stalin's approval, that the investigation of Rykov and Bukharin had been closed (document 162).

This delay was only temporary. Kaganovich was already clear about Stalin's true intentions. In reporting the personal confrontation with Sokolnikov to Stalin, he wrote that "the role of Rykov, Bukharin, and Tomsky will yet be uncovered" (document 166). Stalin inexorably pushed for the escalation of the terror. On 25 September 1936 Stalin and Zhdanov sent a phonegram from Sochi to Moscow calling for the dismissal of Yagoda from the post of people's commissar of internal affairs and his replacement by Yezhov. This famous document has so far always been cited from Khrushchev's secret report at the XX party congress in 1956.[10] In the present volume it appears in full for the first time as a translation from the original (document 169). The full version shows that Stalin had agreed to the changes of personnel in the NKVD in advance with Yezhov.

On the day after this telegram was sent Kaganovich formalized it as a decision of the Politburo.[11] Three days later, on 29 September, on Stalin's instructions, Kaganovich prepared a further decision, "On How to Deal with Counterrevolutionary Trotskyite-Zinovievite Elements." This embodied much of the approach set out by Stalin in his telegram three weeks earlier (document 158). It stated: "Until recently the party Central Committee regarded the Trotskyite-Zinovievite scoundrels as a leading political and organizational detachment of the international bourgeoisie. Recent facts testify that these gentlemen have sunk even further, and they must now be regarded as intelligence agents, spies, saboteurs, and wreckers of the fascist bourgeoisie in Eu-

9. *Izvestiia TsK*, no. 5, 1989, 71.
10. N. Khrushchev, *The Secret Speech Delivered at the Closed Session of the 20th Congress of the CPSU* (London, 1956), 35–36.
11. RGASPI, f. 17, op. 3, d. 981, l. 50.

rope. [...] In this connection it is necessary to deal with the Trot-skyite-Zinovievite scoundrels, including not only those who have been arrested, and whose investigation is already completed, and those un-der investigation [...] whose cases are not yet completed, but also those who were previously sent into exile."[12] In practice this was a di-rective to eliminate all former members of the oppositions. Rykov and Bukharin were in due course arrested, and they were put on trial in March 1938.

There is a great deal of evidence, including the present correspon-dence, that Kaganovich fully supported the new line, and the activity of the NKVD under Yezhov's leadership (see document 177). The ter-ror began with the former members of the oppositions, and spread to wider and wider sections of the population, reaching its peak between mid-1937 and the end of 1938.

The repressions followed their own logic, but were undoubtedly in-fluenced by the worsening international situation and the growing danger of war. In March 1936 German troops marched into the demil-itarized zone of the Rhineland, claiming that this action was justified because the Franco-Soviet alliance was directed against Germany. In July 1936 Spanish troops headed by General Franco rose against the republican government with the support of Germany and Italy. We have already referred to the huge expansion of Soviet arms production in 1936. As early as the beginning of September Stalin raised the ques-tion of supplying arms to Spain via Mexico (see document 159). On 29 September the Politburo approved a plan to supply arms to the Span-ish government. It has already been pointed out in the literature that this decision coincided with the appointment of Yezhov as people's commissar of internal affairs, which was followed by a new wave of repressions.[13] On 7 October on Stalin's instructions the representative of the USSR on the Nonintervention Committee made a statement to the president of the committee which indicated that the USSR was abandoning nonintervention. The Spanish question is prominent in the Stalin-Kaganovich correspondence.

Simultaneously the Soviet leaders continued to give careful attention to the situation in the Far East. The USSR countered the closer accord between Japan and Germany by itself moving closer to China. Signifi-

12. Ibid., l. 58. See also Getty and Naumov, *Road to Terror*, 273.

13. See M. T. Mescheriakov's article in *Otechestvennaia istoriya*, no. 3, 1993, 85; and M. M. Gorinov's in *Istoria Rossii: XX vek* (Moscow, 1996), 293–94.

cantly, the decision of 8 September about the operations of the Chinese Red Army (see document 160) assumed that it was necessary to avoid a clash between the Chinese communists and the Nankin (Nanking) government. A year later, on 21 August 1937, this approach was consolidated by the signing of a nonaggression pact between the USSR and the Chinese government.

Documents 126–177

· 126 ·

Kaganovich to Stalin
[26 January]
F. 17, op. 163, d. 1092, l. 70. Original typescript.

———————

[Cipher]
Moscow. CC of the VKP(b)
To Comrade Stalin.

I got acquainted with the work of the Krasnoiarsk hub and the locomotive and railroad-car repair shop. Dozens of eastbound trains have become backed up in the approaches to Chernorechenskaia, at the station itself and in Krasnoiarsk. Besides the disgraceful work by the operations employees, this is caused by the breakdown of the locomotive stock at the Krasnoiarsk depot. Half of all the freight locomotives are out of service because of breakdowns. The quality of repairs is disgraceful, often downright criminal. The depot and the shop are contaminated with wrecker elements who are connected with the Japanese and Poles. With the connivance of some pseudo-Communists, they have set up a system of repairs that has led to the [word unintelligible] of communications and the failure of boilers, injectors, and pumps. A group of Trotskyites has been uncovered at the shop—they were engaging in wrecking activity with regard to repairs, baiting the Stakhanovites and demoralizing the workers. The party organizers and party organizations of the depot and shop are doing an abominable job, the party organizations are, to all intents and purposes, demoralized, the Stakhanovites are treated like dirt, and the workers' mood is pretty poor. I took immediate measures on the spot to rectify the situation, transferred 15 locomotives from the PC of Transport reserve in Irkutsk, gave the shop an assignment to help the depot with repairs, and a repair train has already arrived from Moscow. All this will make it possible in the days to come to bring the locomotives back to health and undo the bottlenecks in Chernorechenskaia and Krasnoiarsk and move the trains without hindrance from Tomsk to the east.

I request that the CC adopt the following resolution:

1) To dispatch a senior official of the NKVD from Moscow to the Krasnoiarsk hub and shop in order to completely uncover the subversive work of spy and hostile-class elements.

2) In view of the poor work and extensive contamination of the party organizations of the Krasnoiarsk hub and shop, to conduct a second verification of party documents there.

3) To confirm as party organizer of the Krasnoiarsk locomotive and railroad-car repair shop A. I. Khonin, a functionary of the regional committee who previously worked in the political department of a machine-tractor station and as secretary of the district committee, and to relieve Ignatovich of the duties of party organizer.

4) To confirm as party organizer of the Krasnoiarsk locomotive depot P. M. Pereverzev, a functionary of the regional committee who previously worked in the political sector of an MTS in Western Siberia.

5) To dismiss from his job the head of the Krasnoiarsk locomotive section, Tarakanov, and appoint Sokolov (a functionary of the Administration of Locomotive Operations of the PC of Transport and an engineer) as head of the locomotive section.

L. Kaganovich.[1]

1. This cipher was sent at 8:15 P.M. on 26 January from Irkutsk to Stalin in Moscow, reaching Moscow at 10:00 A.M. on 27 January. On 28 January the Politburo heard a report on the work of the Krasnoiarsk rail hub and adopted all of Kaganovich's proposals (RGASPI, f. 17, op. 3, d. 974, l. 63). Kaganovich's cipher from Irkutsk is marked "In favor. I Stalin, V. Molotov, K. Voroshilov, S. Ordzhonikidze," as well as with a notation by a Politburo secretary indicating the assent of Andreev, Chubar, Kalinin, and Mikoian.

· 127 ·

Kaganovich to Stalin
6 July

F. 558, op. 11, d. 743, l. 53.

6 July [1936]

Greetings dear comrade Stalin!

1) When I set off I left 4 memoranda with draft CC resolutions on imports for the PC of Transport.[1] These questions have not yet been decided. I assure you, Comrade Stalin, that if you had entrusted this to me in the past as head of the transport department of the CC,[2] I would not have

been so nonpartisan as I am now—I have severely cut the requests from the administrations of the commissariat by 80 to 90 percent. I will not repeat here the arguments in the memoranda. I request that you examine and satisfy these modest requests of the PC of Transport. Comrade Livshits can explain things further.[3]

2) I read the testimonies of those swine Dreitser and Pikel. Although this was clear even earlier they have now revealed the true bandit face of those murderers and provocateurs Trotsky, Zinoviev, Kamenev, and Smirnov. It is already absolutely clear that the main instigator of this gang is that venal scum Trotsky. It is time to declare him an outlaw, and to execute the rest of the lowlifes we have in jail.

Regards as ever. Your L. Kaganovich.

Kislovodsk

6 July [1936]

1. Kaganovich was on leave from 15 June to 1 August (RGASPI, f. 17, op. 3, d. 978, l. 51).

2. The transport department of the CC was established by the XVII Congress of the Communist Party. Kaganovich was appointed its head on 10 March 1934 (ibid., d. 941, l. 14), and from 28 February 1935 to 22 August 1937 was also people's commissar of transport.

3. On 16 July Sovnarkom decided to import equipment and materials for the PC of Transport (GARF, f. R-5446, op. 1, d. 487, ll. 109, 111, 113).

· 128 ·

Kaganovich, Chubar, and Ordzhonikidze to Stalin
17 August
F. 558, op. 11, d. 93, l. 14. Original typescript. Signed by the authors.

From Moscow, telegram No. 11925

To Comrade Stalin

The Kharkov and Stalingrad tractor plants must cease operations in the fourth quarter, by decision of the CC, to prepare for the changeover in January 1937 to the production of crawler tractors. The renovation of the plants is one quarter [three months] behind schedule. The PC of Heavy Industry proposes that:

1) A fourth-quarter program be assigned to the plants, in addition to the annual plan, for the production of 11,000 tractors, 13,000 motors and 1,000 truck tractors;

2) The plants not stop operating in the first quarter [of 1937] and produce tire tractors for the spring sowing period;

3) Both plants stop operating in the second quarter and that preparations begin in July for their changeover to the production of crawler tractors, providing for the production of 30,000 crawler tractors.

We request your assent.

Kaganovich. V. Chubar. Ordzhonikidze.

17 August 1936
7:25 P.M.

1. Transmitted to Stalin by a telegram on which Stalin noted his assent (RGASPI, f. 558, op. 11, d. 93, l. 13). The appropriate Politburo decision was dated 19 August (ibid., f. 17, op. 3, d. 980, l. 48).

· 129 ·

Yezhov and Kaganovich to Stalin
17 August
F. 558, op. 11, d. 93, l. 21. Original typescript.

Cipher
From Moscow 17 August 1936 at 9:52 P.M.
Incoming No. 2
To Comrade Stalin, Sochi.

We have planned the press coverage of the trial of the counterrevolutionary Trotskyite-Zinovievite terrorist group as follows:

1) *Pravda* and *Izvestia* will publish daily full-page reports on the trial. Other newspapers will publish reports on the trial covering up to half a page. The indictment and speech by the prosecutor will be published in full. All the reports will be distributed through TASS, which is equipped for this. In addition, newspapers will publish articles and comments as the trial proceeds (resolutions, etc.). All material will go to press with the approval of Comrades Stetsky, Tal, Mekhlis, Vyshinsky, and Agranov. Overall supervision is to be entrusted to Comrade Yezhov.

2) The press representatives who will be admitted to the trial are: a) the editors of the major central newspapers and correspondents for *Pravda* and *Izvestia;* b) functionaries of the Executive Committee of Comintern and correspondents to serve foreign communist press employees; c) correspondents of the foreign bourgeois press.

Several embassies are requesting admission. We consider it appropriate to issue tickets only for ambassadors to attend in person.

We request your assent. No. 2.[1]

Yezhov, Kaganovich.

1. Stalin replied with his assent by cipher from Sochi on 18 August at 6:42 P.M. (ibid., l. 20).

1936

· 130 ·

Kaganovich to Stalin
17 August

F. 558, op. 11, d, 743, ll. 54–55.

17 August [1936]
Greetings Dear Comrade Stalin!

1) Comrade Litvinov has sent in the draft of a letter to the League of Nations, I am sending it to you, we will not adopt any decisions until we get your reply.[1]

2) Golubenko, Loginov, and Mrachkovsky have given very serious evidence about Piatakov, the minutes have been sent to you. They all testify that he was the leader of a Ukrainian terrorist center. They also point to Livshits as a participant. We don't think that Piatakov's article should be allowed in the press now,[2] and in general what should we do with him? Sergo arranged with him (before the testimony was taken) that Piatakov would travel now to the Urals, and later arrangements could be made with the Far Eastern Region. Please let us know your opinion, both about the article and in general, what to do with him?[3]

3) We had a discussion today with Comrade Vyshinsky and Ulrikh and determined: (1) to begin the hearing of the case on the 19th at 12 noon with the intention of ending the trial on the 22nd. (2) to conduct the interrogation in the following sequence: 1) Mrachkovsky, 2) Yevdokimov, 3) Dreitser, 4) Reingold, 5) Bakaev, 6) Pikel, 7) Kamenev, 8) Zinoviev, 9) Smirnov, 10) Olberg, 11) Berman-Yurin, 12) Goltsman, 13) M. Lurie, 14) N. Lurie, 15) Ter-Vaganian, 16) Fritz David.

(2) [*sic*—should be (3)] To reveal the full extent of the role of the Gestapo.

(3) [*sic*—should be (4)] Not to interfere with the accused if they identify Piatakov and others. If you have instructions regarding these points, please let us know.

Regards to you. Yours, L. Kaganovich.

P.S. Comrade Yezhov is writing to you about some news.[4]

1. See document 135. On 22 August Litvinov sent the general secretary of the League of Nations a letter proposing measures that would promote the use of the principles of the Statute of the League of Nations regarding collective security and sanctions against aggressor states. Sanctions could be applied if at least three-quarters of the members of the Council of the League who were present voted for them. (DVP, vol. XIX, pp. 399–401.)

2. This evidently refers to Piatakov's article against Trotsky, Kamenev, and Zinoviev in connection with the preparation of the trial of the "Trotskyite-Zinovievite terrorist center." See note 1 to document 143.

3. For further details see the introduction to this chapter.

4. In the upper left-hand corner of the first page is the notation, "My files. St[alin]."

· 131 ·

Stalin to Kaganovich and Chubar
18 August

F. 558, op. 11, d. 93, ll. 29–30.

By cipher.
To Kaganovich, Chubar. CC of the VKP(b), Moscow.

I consider it necessary to sell oil to the Spaniards immediately on the most favorable terms for them, at a discounted price, if need be. If the Spaniards need grain and foodstuffs in general, we should sell all that to them on favorable terms. Let me know how much oil we have already delivered to the Spaniards. Make it incumbent on the PC of Foreign Trade to act quickly and precisely.

Stalin.
No. 4
18 August 1936[1]

---

1. The number and date were entered by the secretary. The cipher was sent from Sochi at 2:42 P.M. (RGASPI, 558, op. 11, d. 93, l. 28). See also document 132.

· 132 ·

Kaganovich, Ordzhonikidze, and Chubar to Stalin
18 August

F. 558, op. 11, d. 93, l. 31. Authenticated typewritten copy.

By cipher
Top secret
Copy
To Comrade Stalin

We heard Comrade Sudin's progress report on the sale of oil to the Spaniards. It was determined that 6,000 tons of fuel oil has been sold as of 18 August, and another tanker has been ordered to fill up with oil.

In accordance with your telegram, the PC of Foreign Trade has been instructed to sell oil to the Spaniards immediately at a reduced price in the necessary amount on the most favorable terms. As for grain and foodstuffs, instructions have been issued to ascertain their needs on an urgent basis. After they are ascertained, we will report to you again. No. 1132/sh.
Kaganovich. Ordzhonikidze. Chubar.
18 August 1936[1]

---

1. See document 131.

· 133 ·

Stalin to Kaganovich and Yezhov
19 August

F. 558, op. 11, d. 93, l. 35.

[Cipher]
To Kaganovich, Yezhov. CC of the VKP(b), Moscow.

I read Radek's letter addressed to me about his situation in connection with the Trotskyite trial. Although the letter is not very persuasive, I propose anyway that the question of arresting Radek be dropped for now and that he be allowed to publish an article over his byline against Trotsky in *Izvestia*. The article will have to be reviewed beforehand.

Stalin.

No. 5
19 August 1936[1]

1. The number and date were entered by the secretary. The cipher was sent from Sochi at 3:56 P.M. (RGASPI, f. 558, op. 11, d. 93, l. 34). See also document 143.

· 134 ·

Kaganovich and Yezhov to Stalin
19 August

F. 558, op. 11, d. 93, ll. 32–33. Original typescript. Signed by the authors.

[By cipher]
To Comrade Stalin

We are sending you our first report [on] the trial.

1. The trial opened [at] 12 noon with a formal interrogation of the accused about the indictment handed down against them.

When the court chairman asked the accused whether they were familiar with the material of the accusation and the indictment, they all replied in the affirmative. No statements were made in this regard.

2. When the court chairman asked the defendants whether they had any challenges to raise against the makeup of the court, they all replied that they had no challenges.

3. When the defendants were asked whether they had any statements, a reply came from Zinoviev and Kamenev.

Zinoviev and Kamenev made the following statements:

a) Zinoviev stated that he confirmed the entire testimony of Bakaev that the latter reported to Zinoviev that a terrorist act was being prepared against Kirov and, in particular, that Nikolaev would be the direct perpetrator. In addition, Zinoviev also reported that on the day of Kirov's assassination, Mandelshtam, a member of the Leningrad center, traveled to deliver a report to Zinoviev in person. Mandelshtam reported all the circumstances of Kirov's assassination to Zinoviev.[1]

b) Kamenev asks to be allowed to cross-examine the witness Yakovlev, only after he, Kamenev, is questioned.

4. The indictment was read. After the indictment was read, all of the defendants were asked whether they pleaded guilty, and all of them replied, "Yes we do."

Three of them made qualifying statements:

a) Smirnov stated:

he was a member of the united center;

he knew that the center had been organized with terrorist objectives;

he had received a personal directive from Trotsky to proceed to terrorism. But he himself did not personally take part in the preparation of acts of terrorism.

b) Goltsman stated that he pleads guilty. He confirmed that he had received a written directive from Trotsky to proceed to terrorism and to pass on this directive to the center and specifically to Smirnov. At the same time he stated that he personally did not take part in the preparation of acts of terrorism.

c) Ter-Vaganian pleaded guilty only to the extent of the statements he gave (he was a member of the terrorist center and so forth, according to his statements in the transcript).

5. The guilty pleas by all the defendants made a stunning impression on the foreign correspondents.

6. After the recess the direct examination of Mrachkovsky began. His demeanor was calm. He confirmed and clarified all of the statements. He totally buried Smirnov. Smirnov, under pressure from the statements and the prosecutor, was compelled to confirm most of Mrachkovsky's testimony. It is actually good that he is expressing a little discontent. Because of that he has put himself [in] a stupid situation. All the defendants are attacking Smirnov.

7. We will report on further trial proceedings this evening.

Kaganovich. Yezhov.[2]

1. Point a) has been checked off with a red pencil in the left margin.

2. The telegram contains the following notation on the top margin, "send through Comrade Volovich. 12008." A telegraph tape has been pasted to the bottom of the first page. It reads: "Transmitted on 19 August 1936 at 7:15 P.M. Transmitted by Zakharov rec[eived] by Afonin."

· 135 ·

Stalin to Kaganovich
19 August

F. 558, op. 11, d. 93, ll. 37–38.

[Cipher]

To Kaganovich. CC of the VKP(b). Moscow.

Received your letter. Litvinov's draft on the League of Nations is acceptable. I have one correction to make: regard three-fourths, rather than four-fifths, as a necessary majority.

With regard to Piatakov and Radek, I have already spoken with you on the phone. With regard to the trial procedure, I agree.

Stalin.

No. 6

19 August 1936[1]

    1. The number and date were entered by the secretary. The telegram was sent by cipher from Sochi on 20 August at 12:15 A.M. (ibid., l. 36). See document 130.

· 136 ·

Kaganovich and Yezhov to Stalin
20 August

F. 558, op. 11, d. 93, ll. 42–46. Original typescript. Signed by the authors.

[By cipher]

Sochi. To Pauker.

To Comrade Stalin.

    1. During the morning and evening sessions the following were examined: Mrachkovsky, Yevdokimov, Dreitser, Reingold, Bakaev, and Pikel.

    2. The most essential parts of their examinations were the following:

    a) Mrachkovsky confirmed in full the entire factual aspect of his statements from the pretrial investigation and clarified these statements. His testimony with regard to the role of Trotsky and Smirnov was especially convincing. This was the most important part of Mrachkovsky's testimony.

    b) Yevdokimov fully confirmed the statements from the pretrial investigation and added a number of important details. What was most convincing in his testimony were the details of Kirov's assassination on the direct instructions of Trotsky, Zinoviev, Kamenev, himself—Yevdokimov—and others.

    c) Dreitser confirmed all the statements from the pretrial investigation.

He dwelt in particular on the roles of Trotsky, Smirnov, and Mrachkovsky. He gave very detailed testimony about them. He especially attacked Smirnov for the latter's attempt to play down his role in organizing the terror.

d) <u>Reingold</u> confirmed in full the statements made during the pretrial investigation and clarified them in a number of places. The most essential parts of his testimony were:

a detailed account of the two variants of the plan to seize power (double-dealing, terrorism, military plot);

a detailed statement on communications with rightists and on the existence of terrorist groups among the rightists (Slepkov, Eismont), of which Rykov, Tomsky, and Bukharin were aware;

a statement about the existence of a reserve center consisting of Radek, Sokolnikov, Serebriakov, and Piatakov;

a statement about a plan to expunge the trail of the crime by destroying any Chekists who knew anything about the crime as well as their own terrorists;

a statement about the theft of state funds for the needs of the organization with the aid of Arkus and Tumanov.

e) <u>Bakaev</u> confirmed in full the statements from the pretrial investigation. He gave a very detailed and convincing account of Kirov's assassination and the preparation for Stalin's assassination in Moscow. He especially insisted that Trotsky, Zinoviev, Kamenev, and Yevdokimov were direct accomplices in this affair. While he minimized his own role somewhat, he was resentful that they had not told him everything earlier.[1]

f) <u>Pikel</u> confirmed in full the statements from the pretrial investigation. For the most part, he repeated Reingold's testimony. He gave particular attention to Bogdan's suicide, stating that, in effect, they had murdered Bogdan, that he had committed suicide at Bakaev's insistence. The day before Bogdan's suicide, Bakaev spent the entire night at his home and told him that either he had to commit suicide himself in the morning or they would destroy him themselves. Bogdan chose Bakaev's first suggestion.

3. We are taking special note of the behavior of the following defendants at the trial:

a) <u>Smirnov</u> has taken the line that, while he was a member of the Trotskyite-Zinovievite center and knew about its terrorist principles, he did not himself participate in the organization's practical activities, did not participate in the preparation of acts of terrorism and did not share the principles of Trotsky-Sedov. The cross-examinations of all the defendants immediately and repeatedly exposed Smirnov's lies. Under pressure from the other defendants' testimonies, Smirnov was compelled at the evening session to admit a number of facts that incriminated him and he became less active.[2]

b) <u>Zinoviev</u>, when questioned by the prosecutor on redirect examination about whether the facts set forth by the defendants were accurate, admitted to the overwhelming majority of them. He disputed minutiae, such as whether it was precisely those particular individuals or others who were present during the discussions of plans for terrorism, and so forth. His demeanor was more depressed than anyone else's.

c) <u>Kamenev,</u> when questioned by the prosecutor on redirect examination <u>about whether the facts disclosed by the defendants</u> were accurate, <u>confirmed the overwhelming majority of them. His demeanor was more provocative than Zinoviev's. He tried to show off.</u>[3]

4. Several defendants, especially Reingold, spoke in detail about ties with rightists, referring by name to Rykov, Tomsky, Bukharin, and Uglanov. Reingold, specifically, testified that Rykov, Tomsky, and Bukharin knew about the existence of rightist terrorist groups.

This made a particular impression on the foreign correspondents. All of the foreign correspondents dwelled specifically on this point in their dispatches, calling it especially sensational testimony.

We believe that when the report on Reingold's testimony is published in our newspapers, the names of the rightists should not be deleted.

5. Many defendants identified the reserve center as consisting of Radek, Sokolnikov, Piatakov, and Serebriakov, identifying them as convinced supporters of the Trotskyite-Zinovievite bloc. All of the foreign correspondents in their dispatches pounced on this testimony as a sensation and are transmitting it to their press. We believe that[4] when the report is published in our press these names should not be deleted, either.[5]

Yezhov. Kaganovich.[6]

1. Item "e" has been checked off with a red pencil in the left margin.

2. A further phrase has been stricken: "on the whole, it must be said that his situation is more foolish."

3. A further phrase has been stricken: "portraying himself as a supreme leader."

4. The sentence originally read: "We believe that it is impossible to conceal this testimony in our press."

5. The draft of the letter also contained an item 6, which has not survived in full: "The trial has had a stunning impression on every foreign correspondent without exception. According to a report from Tal, Astakhov, and the Chekists, the foreign correspondents have no doubts about the guilt of all the defendants, and in particular Trotsky, Zinoviev, and Kamenev. They were particularly impressed by the redirect examination of Kamenev, Zinovie[v] [text breaks off]"

6. The text of the letter contains Kaganovich's corrections. A telegraph tape has been pasted to the end of the letter. It reads: "20 August 1936 2:50 A.M. Transm[itted] by Zakharova rec[eived] by Afonin."

· 137 ·

Kaganovich and Chubar to Stalin
21 August
F. 558, op. 11, d. 93, l. 51. Original typescript.

Telegram.
From Moscow 21 August 1936 at 11:50 P.M.
To Comrade Stalin. Sochi.

1) Because of the poor harvest in a number of areas of Kazakhstan (Ak-tiubinsk and Western Kazakh regions), the Kazakh Regional Committee is requesting that grain deliveries be reduced by 5,650,000 poods [92,830 tons]. We are planning to put at Kazakhstan's disposal a fund of reductions for grain deliveries in the amount of 3,575,000 [58,740 tons], including 1.5 million poods [24,650 tons] from the reserve of assigned obligations and 2 million poods [32,900 tons] from the plan, with the reductions carried over as arrears to be collected from the 1937 harvest. If our proposal is adopted, Kazakhstan must deliver 39.2 million poods [644,100 tons] in the peasant sector. Last year Kazakhstan delivered 41.6 million poods [683,500 tons].

2) The Kirov Region is requesting a deferment on grain deliveries and payment in kind in the amount of 6 million poods [98,600 tons] and to re-lease 500,000 poods [8,200 tons] of rye seeds on loan. We plan to put at the disposal of Kirov Region a fund of reductions for grain deliveries by collective farms in the amount of 2.5 million poods [41,100 tons]. to be carried over as arrears and subject to collection from the 1937 harvest, to reduce the plan for payment in kind for MTS services in Kirov Region by 500,000 poods, and to release to the collective farms of Kirov Region 300,000 poods [4,900 tons] of rye as a seed loan. If our proposal is adopted, Kirov Region must deliver 27.2 million poods [446,900 tons] from the peasant sector. Last year Kirov Region delivered 33.5 million poods [550,400 tons].

3. Gorky Regional Committee is requesting a reduction on grain deliveries in the amount of 1.5 million poods [24,650 tons]. We plan to give it a reduction of 1 million poods [16,430 tons]. If our proposal is adopted, Gorky Region must deliver 20 million poods [328,600 tons] in the peasant sector. Last year Gorky Region delivered 21 million poods [345,000 tons].

Please let us know your opinion.[1] No. 12111.
Kaganovich, Chubar.

1. Stalin wrote his reply alongside the text of the telegram: "With regard to reductions for the Kazakhstan, Kirov, and Gorky regions, I agree. St." On 22 August Stalin's reply was sent

as a cipher from Sochi at 12:50 A.M. (ibid., l. 50). It was formalized as a Politburo decision the same day.

· 138 ·

Kaganovich, Yezhov, and Ordzhonikidze to Stalin
22 August
F. 558, op. 11, d. 93, l. 55. Original typescript.

Cipher.
From Moscow 22 August 1936 at 5:46 P.M.
Incoming No. 6.
To Comrade Stalin. Sochi.

Tomsky committed suicide by gunshot this morning. He left a letter addressed to you, in which he tries to prove his innocence. Just yesterday, in his speech at the meeting of OGIZ [Corporation of State Publishing Houses], Tomsky admitted to a number of meetings with Zinoviev and Kamenev and to being discontented and peevish. We have no doubt that since Tomsky, just like Lominadze,[1] knew that he could no longer hide his connection with the Zinovievite-Trotskyite gang, he decided to cover his tracks by committing suicide.

We think: 1) He should be buried right there in Bolshevo. 2) Publish the following announcement in the newspaper tomorrow:

"The CC of the VKP(b) announces that M. P. Tomsky, candidate member of the CC of the VKP(b), having become weighed down by his ties to the counterrevolutionary Trotskyite-Zinovievite terrorists, committed suicide on 22 August at his dacha in Bolshevo."[2]

Please convey your instructions. No. 7.
Kaganovich, Yezhov, Ordzhonikidze.

1. V. V. Lominadze was removed from his post as secretary of the Transcaucasia Regional Party Committee in 1930 for participation in the "Syrtsov-Lominadze group" and was later appointed secretary of the Magnitogorsk party committee. In January 1935 he committed suicide after he learned that the NKVD had concocted material on his participation in a "counterrevolutionary organization."

2. Tomsky's suicide was reported in *Pravda* on 23 August.

· 139 ·

Kaganovich and Chubar to Stalin
22 August
F. 558, op. 11, d. 93, l. 58. Original telegraph tape.

Telegram from Moscow. No. 48.
To Comrade Stalin. Sochi.
We received the following telegram today from the Second International:

"To the Chairman of Sovnarkom. We regret that, at a time when the world working class is united in its feelings of solidarity with Spanish workers in their defense of the democratic republic, a major political trial has begun in Moscow. Despite the fact that the accused in this trial—Zinoviev and his comrades—have always been sworn enemies of the socialist Labor and Socialist International and the International Federation of Trade Unions, we cannot refrain from requesting that the accused be assured of every judicial guarantee, that they be permitted to have defense lawyers who are completely independent of the government, that they not receive death sentences, and that, in any case, no procedure be employed that would preclude the possibility of appeal. Chairman of the Labor and Socialist International De Brucker. Secretary Adler. Chairman of the International Federation of Trade Unions Citrine. Secretary Chevenels."

We don't think we should answer them. Please let us know your opinion.

Kaganovich. Chubar.[1]

1. See document 140. A telegraph tape attached to the letter read: "Transmitted 22 August 1936 at 6:15 P.M. Transm[itted] by Zakharova. Rec[eived] by Afonin.

· 140 ·

Stalin to Kaganovich
22 August
F. 558, op. 11, d. 93, ll. 55–550b.

[By cipher]
To Kaganovich.
Regarding your 7, I agree.[1] I also agree that we shouldn't answer the Second International. But I think we should publish the telegram from the Second International, and say in the press that Sovnarkom does not deem it necessary to reply, since the sentence is the business of the Supreme Court, and ridicule and stigmatize in the press the snakes who signed the

telegram as defenders of the gang of assassins and Gestapo agents—Trotsky, Zinoviev, Kamenev—and sworn enemies of the working class.

Stalin.

No. 10
22 August 1936[2]

1. See document 138.
2. The number and date were entered by the secretary. The cipher was sent from Sochi the same day (RGASPI, f. 558, op. 11, d. 93, l. 54). See document 139. Soviet newspapers published the telegram from the Labor and Socialist International (the Second International) and the International Federation of Trade Unions on 23 August with an abusive commentary, under the heading "Despicable Defenders of Murderers and Gestapo Agents."

· 141 ·

Kaganovich, Ordzhonikidze, Voroshilov, Chubar, and Yezhov to Stalin
22 August
F. 558, op. 11, d. 93, l. 65. Authenticated typewritten copy.

Copy.
Secret.
By cipher.
To Comrade Stalin.

Following Vyshinsky's speech at the evening session, all of the defendants declined to make speeches in their defense. The final remarks by the defendants are now being delivered in court. The trial will end tomorrow.

We are transmitting the text of the verdict to you by cipher, leaving out the formal part—the enumeration of names.[1] Please let us have your instructions.

No. 1181/sh.

Kaganovich. Ordzhonikidze. Voroshilov. Chubar. Yezhov.

22 August 1936

1. The text of the verdict is not published in the present volume. The final verdict is available in English in *Report of Court Proceedings* . . . (Moscow, 1936), pp. 174–80 (for a full reference to this publication see document 150, note 1).

· 142 ·

Stalin to Kaganovich
23 August

F. 558, op. 11, d. 93, ll. 62–64.

[By cipher]
CC of the VKP, Moscow.
To Kaganovich.

First, the draft of the verdict is essentially correct, but it needs stylistic polishing. Second, we must mention in a separate paragraph of the verdict that Trotsky and Sedov are subject to prosecution or are on trial or something like that. This is of great importance for Europe, both for the bourgeois and for the workers. We simply cannot fail to mention Trotsky and Sedov in the verdict, because such an omission will be interpreted to mean that the prosecutor wants to try these gentlemen but that the court supposedly disagrees with the prosecutor. Third. We should strike out the concluding words: "the verdict is final and is not subject to appeal." These words are superfluous and make a bad impression. An appeal should not be allowed, but it is not smart to write about this in the verdict. Fourth, the titles of Ulrikh and the members of the court must be reproduced in full, and we should say about Ulrikh that he is the chairman not of some unknown institution but of the Military Collegium of the Supreme Court.[1]

Stalin.

No. 11
23 August
23–10[2]

1. On 24 August Poskrebyshev transmitted a telegram to Sochi for Stalin: "Chechulin. On the instructions of Comrade Kaganovich I am reporting that the titles of Ulrikh, '*armvoeniurist* [army military jurist],' and of the members of the court, '*divvoeniurist* [divisional military jurist],' according to competent individuals, do not expand. Poskrebyshev. 24 August 1936 9:40 P.M." (RGASPI, f. 558, op. 11, d. 93, l. 81).

2. The number, date and time were entered by the secretary. The cipher was sent from Sochi at 5:07 P.M. (ibid., l. 61).

· 143 ·

Stalin to Kaganovich
23 August

F. 558, op. 11, d. 93, ll. 77–80.

[By cipher]
CC of the VKP.
<u>To Kaganovich.</u>

First. The articles by Rakovsky, Radek, and Piatakov came out pretty well.[1] Judging by the correspondent summaries, the foreign correspondents are keeping quiet about these articles, which are of great significance. They must be reprinted in newspapers in Norway, Sweden, France, and America, at least in the Communist newspapers. What makes them important, by the way, is that they deprive our enemies of the opportunity to depict the trial as a show and as a factional reprisal by the CC against the Zinoviev-Trotsky faction. Second. It is obvious from Reingold's testimony that Kamenev, through his wife Glebova, sounded out French Ambassador Alphand about the possible attitude of the French government toward a future "government" of the Trotskyite-Zinovievite bloc. I think Kamenev also sounded out the British, German, and American ambassadors. This means that Kamenev must have disclosed to those foreigners the plans for the conspiracy and assassinations of the VKP leaders. This also means that Kamenev had already disclosed these plans to them, because otherwise the foreigners would not have agreed to talk with them about a future Zinovievite-Trotskyite "government." This is an attempt by Kamenev and his friends to form an outright bloc with the bourgeois governments against the Soviet government. This is also the key to the secret of the well-known advance obituaries by American correspondents. Obviously, Glebova is well informed about this whole filthy subject. Glebova must be brought to Moscow and subjected to a series of meticulous interrogations. She might reveal a lot of interesting things.

Stalin.

No. 12 and 13
23 August 1936[2]

1. These articles, sharply condemning Trotsky, Zinoviev, and Kamenev, and demanding their execution, were published in the newspapers on 21 August.

2. The number and date were entered by the secretary. The cipher was sent from Sochi at 11:36 P.M. (ibid., l. 76).

· 144 ·

Kaganovich, Ordzhonikidze, Voroshilov, and Yezhov to Stalin
24 August
F. 558, op. 11, d. 93. l. 90. Original typescript.

By cipher
From Moscow 24 August 1936 at 8:48 P.M.
Incoming No. 11
To Comrade Stalin. Sochi.

The presidium of the Central Executive Committee of the [Soviet] Union has received petitions for clemency from all of those sentenced except for Goltsman. The presidium will assemble today at 9 P.M. The Politburo has instructed that the petitions be denied and that the sentence be carried out tonight. Tomorrow we will publish announcements in the newspapers that the petitions by the convicted individuals were denied and the sentence was carried out. No. 21.

Kaganovich, Ordzhonikidze, Voroshilov, Yezhov.[1]

1. Stalin replied with his assent by cipher from Sochi at 11:30 P.M. (RGASPI, f. 558, op. 11, d. 93, l. 89).

· 145 ·

Kaganovich to Stalin
24 August
F. 558, op. 11, d. 93, l. 93. Original typescript.

Telegram.
From Moscow 24 August 1936 at 9:05 P.M.
To Comrade Stalin. Sochi.

Twelve thousand people have been dismissed from the aircraft industry this year by way of a purge, and 13,500 people are being drafted into the army. Ordzhonikidze has made a request that the aircraft industry be completely exempted from this year's call-up. Voroshilov agrees to exempt 5,000. In view of the fact that workers are being recruited for the aircraft industry by a special procedure and the departure of 13,500 people will badly impair the operation of the plants, I consider it possible to exempt 8,000–10,000 people from the draft.

Please let me know your opinion. No. 12225.

Kaganovich.[1]

1. A rough draft of the telegram has been preserved in the file—with Ordzhonikidze's sig-

nature (RGASPI, f. 558, op. 11, l. 94). On 24 August Stalin replied that 10,000 people could be exempted from the draft (ibid., l. 93), and on 25 August the Politburo resolved to exempt 10,000 workers, engineers, technicians, and clerical staff of the factories and organizations of the aircraft industry (ibid., f. 17, op. 3, d. 980, l. 65).

· 146 ·

Kaganovich to Stalin
26 August
F. 558, op. 11, d. 93, l. 98. Original typescript

Telegram (through NKVD)
From Moscow 26 August 1936 at 2:17 P.M.
To Comrade Stalin. Sochi.

A number of our engineers, permanent representatives of our industry, are on the scene in America.

Troianovsky, supported by Litvinov, asks that we make up a delegation out of these engineers to attend the Energy Congress without delivering papers. They feel that by doing so we will avoid giving the impression of boycotting the congress. We find it possible to agree. Please let us know your opinion.[1]

Kaganovich.

1. Sent the same day by telegram to Sochi. Stalin replied with his assent (RGASPI, f. 558, op. 11, d. 93, l. 98).

On 26 August the Politburo authorized the PC of Heavy Industry to form such a delegation, which would attend "without delivering papers" (ibid., f. 17, op. 3, d. 980, l. 69).

· 147 ·

Kaganovich to Stalin
27 August
F. 558, op. 11, d. 93, ll. 110–111. Original typescript.

Cipher.
From Moscow 27 August 1936 at 4:30 A.M.
Incoming No. 12
To Comrade Stalin. Sochi.[1]

I am transmitting to you the draft of a message to the Norwegian government. Please give me your instructions.

Kaganovich.

"On the instructions of my[2] government, I have the honor of stating the following: on 1 December 1934 S. Kirov, secretary of the regional committee of the Communist Party[3] and a member of the presidium of the Central Executive Committee of Soviets[4] was assassinated in Leningrad. A court investigation determined that the assassination was committed by a member of a terrorist organization that had set the objective of perpetrating acts of terrorism against members of the Soviet government and other leaders. This was admitted in court[5] by Kirov's assassin himself, as well as his accomplices. An additional investigation, as well as a court inquiry on 19–23 August of this year,[6] further determined that the aforesaid terrorist organization was established at the initiative of L. Trotsky, currently a resident of Norway, who issued detailed instructions to his accomplices in the USSR for the assassination of Stalin, Voroshilov, Kaganovich, Ordzhonikidze, and other members of the government and local organizations.[7] To this end Trotsky sent special agents from abroad.[8] All of the above facts were confirmed at an open court inquiry[9] by all of Trotsky's accomplices and agents, who were on trial.

"Therefore it may be regarded as proven that L. Trotsky, a resident of Norway, is the organizer and leader, and inspirer,[10] of acts of terrorism aimed at assassinating members of the Soviet governments and the leaders of the Soviet people.

"In bringing the foregoing to the notice of the Norwegian government, the Soviet government believes that continuing to afford asylum to L. Trotsky, an organizer of acts of terrorism, may cause damage to the friendly relations between the USSR and Norway and would run counter to modern concepts of the norms of international relations. It may be recalled on this occasion that, in regard to the assassination of the Yugoslav king Alexander and the French foreign minister Barthou, the attitude of governments toward the preparation within their territory of acts of terrorism against other governments was a subject of discussion in the Council of the League of Nations on 10 December 1934, when the obligation of members of the League to assist one another in the fight against terrorism was established and it was even deemed desirable that an international convention for this purpose be concluded.

"The Soviet government firmly[11] expects that the Norwegian government will not fail to take appropriate measures to deprive Trotsky of a continued right of asylum in Norwegian territory." Nos. 22, 23.[12]

1. In the upper left-hand corner Stalin wrote "The draft is sloppy" and made numerous notations alongside the text.
2. Stalin corrected "my" to "the Soviet."
3. Stalin corrected "secretary of the regional committee" to "a member of the Central Committee."
4. Stalin inserted "of the USSR."
5. Stalin inserted "at the end of 1934."
6. Stalin crossed out the words "of this year" and inserted "1936."
7. Stalin replaced "local organizations" with "leading officials."

8. Stalin inserted "to the USSR."

9. Stalin inserted "in August 1936."

10. Stalin crossed out "and inspirer."

11. Stalin crossed out "firmly."

12. See documents 148 and 149. The draft is marked "In favor. M. Kalinin" (Kalinin was president of the Central Executive Committee) (RGASPI, f. 558, op. 11, d. 55, l. 57).

· 148 ·

Kaganovich to Stalin

27 August

F. 558, op. 11, d. 93, l. 115. Original typescript.

Cipher.

From Moscow 27 August 1936 at 9:52 P.M.

Incoming No. 14

To Comrade Stalin. Sochi.

Sedov is now living in Paris, so Litvinov proposes that Girshfeld be instructed to declare to Delbos in less official form, but with the same substance as to the Norwegians, that Sedov should be stripped of the right of asylum, but without publication in the press.

Please let me know your opinion. No. 25.

Kaganovich.[1]

1. Stalin replied with his assent on the same night by cipher from Sochi at 12:00 midnight. (ibid., l. 114). See documents 147 and 149.

· 149 ·

Stalin to Kaganovich

27 August

F. 558, op. 11, d. 93, ll. 108–109. Signed by Stalin and Chechulin.

[Phonegram]

Moscow

CC of the VKP(b)

To Kaganovich.

I think we can agree with Litvinov on delivering our note to the Norwegian government orally rather than in writing, but with the idea that a report on this will be issued in the press.[1]

I think the same note should be sent orally to the German government about Sedov, Trotsky's son.

*Simultaneously with the delivery of the note to the Norwegian govern-
ment we must go on the attack against the leadership of the Norwegian
Labor Party. This leadership is apparently privy to all of Trotsky's secrets,
and as a result it vigorously defends Trotsky in its newspaper. We should
openly fling in the face of these Norwegian vermin the accusation that
they are backing Trotsky's criminal, terrorist schemes. Stalin.[2]*

1. On 27 August the Politburo decided to deliver orally to the Norwegian government a
note on depriving Trotsky of the right to asylum, and to have a report issued in the press
(RGASPI, f. 17, op. 162, d. 20, l. 60). Under Soviet pressure, the Norwegian government initially decided to intern Trotsky, but then it deported him to Mexico on 19 December 1936.
For these events see I. Deutscher, *The Prophet Outcast: Trotsky, 1929–1940* (London, 1963),
324–54.
2. The italicized text was recorded by Chechulin, and at the bottom of the letter is his notation "Completed by dictation from Comrade Stalin. 27 August 1936." The phonegram
was sent from Sochi the same day (ibid., f. 81, op. 3, d. 101, l. 79). See also documents 147
and 148.

· 150 ·

Stalin to Kaganovich
28 August

F. 558, op. 11, d. 93, l. 118.

[By cipher]
CC of the VKP. Moscow.
To Kaganovich.
The report on the trial should be translated into European languages in
the form in which it was published in *Pravda* and *Izvestia*. The indictment
will have to be included, the prosecutor's speech as well, and certainly the
final statements by the accused. It should be issued not by the Party Publishing House or by *Pravda* but by the USSR PC of Justice. This should be
done as soon as possible and widely disseminated abroad.
Stalin.
No. 20
28 August 1936[1]

1. The number and date were entered by the secretary. The cipher was sent from Sochi at
2:15 P.M. (RGASPI, f. 558, op. 11, d. 93, l. 117). On the same day the Politburo approved the
corresponding decision (ibid., f. 17, op. 3, d. 980, l. 72). The report of the trial, with an ab-
breviated version of the cross-examination of the defendants, was published in English as
*Report of Court Proceedings. The Case of the Trotskyite-Zinovievite Terrorist Center Heard
Before the Military Collegium of the USSR Supreme Court. Moscow, August 19–24, 1936*
(Moscow, 1936). The trials of January 1937 and March 1938 were published in full in English.

· 151 ·

Stalin to Kaganovich
28 August

F. 558, op. 11, d. 93, ll. 120–123.

[By cipher]
CC of the VKP. Moscow.
To Kaganovich.
cc: Ordzhonikidze
  I am against the plan of orders for the remaining portion of the British credit as approved by Sergo. I insist that three-fourths of the remaining credit be used for the needs of naval shipbuilding, for turbines or turbine parts for destroyers, cruisers, battleships, for models of large naval artillery or even entire batteries, and for equipment for the Arkhangelsk plant. The argument that the design for the Arkhangelsk plant is not ready and that this supposedly makes it impossible to place orders is a hollow, formalistic evasion. We have big shipyards in Nikolaev and Leningrad, from which it can be determined what orders must be placed for the Arkhangelsk plant. Please keep me posted about the resolution of this question and don't make concessions to those who favor the method of formalistic evasions.

Stalin.

No. 21
28 August 1936[1]

1. The number and date were entered by the secretary. The cipher was sent from Sochi at 11:45 P.M. the same day (RGAPSI, f. 558, op. 11, d. 93, l. 119).

· 152 ·

Kaganovich and Yezhov to Stalin
29 August

F. 558, op. 11, d. 93, ll. 135–136. Original typescript.

Telegram
From Moscow 29 August 1936 at 10:40 P.M.
To Comrade Stalin. Sochi.
  1) In accordance with your instructions we have drawn up the following draft directive:
  "To all secretaries of regional committees, and of central committees of nationality-based Communist Parties: With regard to the fact that respon-

sible functionaries and especially directors of enterprises who were appointed by decision of the CC have been dismissed from their jobs and expelled from the party recently in a number of party organizations without the knowledge or consent of the CC of the VKP(b), the CC points out that such actions by local party organizations are improper. The CC directs regional committees and the central committees of nationality-based Communist Parties to cease this practice and, in any instance in which local party organizations possess material that raises doubts about the possibility of retaining in the party a functionary appointed by decision of the CC, to submit this material for consideration by the CC of the VKP(b).

"CC of the VKP(b)."[1]

2) In addition, with regard to the publication in today's issue of *Izvestia* of an incorrect item about the director Comrade Tabakov headed "An Exposed Enemy," we have prepared the following decision:

On the Item "An Exposed Enemy" (*Izvestia* of 29 August 1936). The CC of the VKP(b) deems incorrect the charge by the party organization of the Magnesite plant in Satka, Cheliabinsk Region, against the plant director, Comrade Tabakov, of aiding and abetting and protecting the executed Trotskyite terrorist Dreitser.

The CC of the VKP(b) resolves:

1. To rescind the decision of the party organization at the Magnesite plant in Satka to expel Comrade Tabakov from the party.

2. To point out to the editor of the newspaper *Cheliabinsky Rabochy* [Cheliabinsk Worker], Comrade Syrkin, that he acted incorrectly in publishing the decision of the plant's party organization on Comrade Tabakov without verifying the accuracy of the charges against him.

3. To deem correct the removal by the editors of *Izvestia* of the newspaper's Cheliabinsk correspondent, Comrade Dubinsky, from his post for reporting to *Izvestia* without verification the information on Comrade Tabakov taken from the local newspaper.

4. To instruct the editors of *Izvestia* to publish, together with a notice about this decision of the CC of the VKP(b) on this matter, an editorial note acknowledging the error of having printed the aforementioned item in *Izvestia*.

Please let us know your opinion.[2] No. 3.

Kaganovich, Yezhov

1. The directive was sent out to the regions on 31 August (APRF, f. 3, op. 22, d. 150, l. 129).

2. Stalin replied with his assent on 30 August (RGASPI, f. 558, op. 11, d. 93, l. 126.) The Politburo approved this resolution on 31 August (ibid., f. 17, op. 3, d. 980, l. 79). The following day it was published in the newspapers.

· 153 ·

Kaganovich to Stalin
1 September

F. 558, op. 11, d. 94, l. 2. Original typescript.

Telegram (through the NKVD).
From Moscow 1 September 1936, at 4:25 P.M.
To Comrade Stalin. Sochi.

TsUNKhU [the Central Administration of National Economic Account-
ing] has come to Sovnarkom with a petition to conduct the All-Union Livestock Census on 1 February 1937 rather than 1 December 1936, as the CC
and Sovnarkom previously scheduled it, basing the petition on the argument that conducting a livestock census a month before the population census will divert census-takers from preparing for the population census and
that the 1 December data will supposedly not provide an accurate picture of
the state of animal husbandry. Sovnarkom concurred with TsUNKhU and
proposes that the livestock census be moved to 1 February 1937.

I don't think the arguments of the TsUNKhU are valid. Therefore the
proposal to postpone the livestock census should, in my view, be rejected
and the previous decision of the CC should be retained, i.e. the All-Union
Livestock Census should be taken on 1 December 1936.

Please let me know your opinion.[1] No. 6.

Kaganovich.

1. See document 154

· 154 ·

Stalin to Kaganovich
2 September

F. 558, op. 11, d. 94, l. 2.

[By cipher]
CC of the VKP. Moscow.
To Kaganovich

It is better to postpone the livestock census to 1 February 1937.
Stalin.

No. 23
2 September 1936[1]

1. The number and date were entered by the secretary. The cipher was sent from Sochi at
1:50 A.M. the same day (RGASPI, f. 558, op. 11, d. 94, l. 1). See document 153. On 3 Sep-

tember the Politburo decided. modifying the Sovnarkom and CC decree of 28 May 1936, to hold the livestock census on 1 February 1937 (ibid., f. 17, op. 3, d. 981, l. 5).

· 155 ·

Kaganovich and Molotov to Stalin
2 September
F. 558, op. 11, d. 94, ll. 7–8 Original typescript. Signed by the authors.

[By cipher]
To Comrade Stalin.

We discussed the question of the national economic plan for the fourth quarter with the people's commissars. We set the volume of output for Union and local industry for the fourth quarter at 19.7 billion rubles, which yields an increase of 17.3 percent over the third quarter. The PCs were instructed to draw up, for each chief administration, trust, and enterprise, assignments to manufacture finished, complete products and a detailed assortment of these products, ensuring that they are of high quality and conform to established standards.

The Council of Labor and Defense is being instructed to approve a detailed assortment plan for goods, broken down by industrial PCs.[1]

The average daily loading of rail transport was set at 91,000 cars; freight traffic in commercial trains, at 131 million tons; and the volume of passenger transportation, at 18 billion passenger-kilometers. We are setting the volume of river cargo shipments at 12 million tons, and maritime shipments at 7.8 million tons.

We are setting the volume of capital investments at 7,909,037,000 rubles; the financial provision, adjusting for a decrease in the cost of investment, amounts to 7,048,002,000 rubles.

Retail sales in state and cooperative trade will amount to 28 million rubles [*sic*—should be billion]. The market allocation of grain in terms of flour, 3,100,000 tons; groats, 230,000 tons; sugar, 360,000 tons; vodka and spirits, 20,300,000 decaliters.

Please let us know your opinion. No. 6.

Kaganovich, Molotov.[2]

---

1. The "assortment plan" showed the type, variety, and quality of goods to be produced.
2. A telegraph tape has been pasted to the bottom of the letter. It reads: "2 September 1936 6:50 P.M." The text of the letter contains corrections by Molotov and Kaganovich, as well as the secretary's notations that it was sent. The proposals were incorporated in a Politburo resolution of 3 September (RGASPI, f. 17, op. 3, d. 981, l. 8).

· 156 ·

Stalin to Kaganovich and Molotov
5 September
F. 558, op. 11, d. 94, ll. 14–140b.

[By cipher]
CC of the VKP. Moscow.
To Kaganovich, Molotov.

I think the grain procurements are going pretty well. We cannot demand that the pace keep increasing if there is a drought on the Volga and the harvest in Siberia is a full 20 days behind last year owing to climatic conditions. We will collect the grain in Siberia, but it will be late. I consider the directive to newspapers that they criticize the regions "more strongly" to be tactically wrong, since such criticism will only benefit the fascists' agitation about "famine" in the USSR. We should not get nervous and give in to Kleiner's screaming. We will collect the grain in any case. We may collect a tiny bit less than last year, but we don't even need any more. We can just send people, but there is no reason to raise a clamor in the press.[1]

Stalin.

No. 26
5 September 1936[2]

1. This is a reply to a cipher from Kaganovich and Molotov dated 4 September, in which they proposed a list of high officials to be sent to lagging regions, and also that "we give a directive to *Pravda* and *Izvestia* to criticize these regions more strongly" (RGASPI, f. 558, op. 11, d. 94, l. 14). On 5 September the Politburo agreed to send the officials to the regions, including Kleiner, Kalmanovich, and Chernov (ibid., f. 17, op. 3, d. 98, l. 14).

2. The number and date were entered by the secretary. The cipher was sent from Sochi at 2:37 A.M. (ibid., f. 558, op. 11, d. 94, l. 13).

· 157 ·

Kaganovich to Stalin
6 September
F. 558, op. 11, d. 94, l. 47. Original typescript.

Telegram.
From Moscow 6 September 1936 at 12:50 A.M.
To Comrade Stalin. Sochi.

The situation on the Moscow-Donbass Railroad is not improving, the way it is operating is completely unsatisfactory. Yemshanov is not up to the job, he must be removed. At the same time, Rozental, the head of the railroad's political department, must also be dismissed.

We are thinking of promoting [A. N.] Andreev as director of the railroad. Andreev is an engineer, he used to work on military communiqués, for the past year he has been an inspector and dispatcher for the PC of Transport, he made trips to problem sections on the railroads and distinguished himself as an efficient functionary. Andreev is now Yemshanov's deputy.

We are designating Lapidus as the head of the political department of the railroad, he is now an instructor for the Political Administration of the PC of Transport, he is an experienced party functionary.

I ask for your approval.[1]

The situation is also very bad on the Southern Urals Railroad under Kniazev and on the Kuibyshev Railroad under Kovylkin, as soon as we find candidates, I will report to you.[2] No. 12.

Kaganovich.

1. The same day Stalin replied by cipher at 7:38 P.M. with his assent (RGASPI, f. 558, op. 11, d. 94, l. 46.) On 7 September the Politburo decided to remove Yemshanov from his position as director of the Moscow-Donbass Railroad for failing to cope with his job. A. N. Andreev was confirmed as the new director. I. V. Lapidus was confirmed as head of the political department of the railroad, replacing Ya. D. Rozental (ibid., f. 17, op. 3, d. 981, l. 16).

2. By a Politburo resolution dated 5 October 1936, Kniazev and Kovylkin were relieved of their duties as railroad directors (ibid., l. 74). See also document 173.

· 158 ·

Stalin to Kaganovich and Molotov
6 September

F. 558, op. 11, d. 94, ll. 32–39.

[By cipher]

To Kaganovich, Molotov.

Pravda fell flat on its face with its articles about the trial of the Zinovievites and Trotskyites. *Pravda* failed to produce a single article that provided a Marxist explanation of the process of degradation of these scum, their sociopolitical complexion, and their real platform. It reduced everything to the personal element, to the notion that there are evil people who want to seize power and there are good people who hold power, and fed this paltry mush to the public.

The articles should have said that the struggle against Stalin, Voroshilov, Molotov, Zhdanov, Kosior, and others is a struggle against the Soviets, a struggle against collectivization, against industrialization, a struggle, consequently, to restore capitalism in the towns and villages of the USSR. Because Stalin and the other leaders are not isolated individuals but the personification of all the victories of socialism in the USSR, the personification of collectivization, industrialization, and the blossoming of culture in the USSR, consequently, the personification of the efforts of workers, peasants, and the working intelligentsia for the defeat of capitalism and the triumph of socialism.

They should have said that whoever fights against the party and the government in the USSR stands for the defeat of socialism and the restoration of capitalism.

They should have said that talk that the Zinovievites and Trotskyites have no platform is a fraud on the part of these scum and a self-deception by our comrades. These scum had a platform. The gist of their platform was the defeat of socialism in the USSR and the restoration of capitalism. It wasn't to these scum's advantage to talk openly about such a platform. Hence their claim that they don't have a platform, which our bumblers took at face value.

They should have said, finally, that the degradation of these scum to the level of White Guards and fascists is a logical outgrowth of their moral decline as opposition leaders in the past.

As far back as the X party congress, Lenin said that if a faction or factions persist in their errors in their struggle against the party, under the Soviet system they will, without fail, slide down to the level of White Guardism, the defense of capitalism, a struggle against the Soviets, and must, without fail, merge with the enemies of Soviet rule. This proposition by Lenin has now been brilliantly confirmed. But *Pravda,* unfortunately, failed to make use of it.

That is the spirit and direction in which agitation should have been conducted in the press. All this unfortunately has been missed.

Stalin.[1]

Nos. 29 and 30
6 September 1936

1. The cipher was sent from Sochi on 6 September at 4:05 A.M. (RGASPI, f. 558, op. 11, d. 94, l. 31).

· 159 ·

Stalin to Kaganovich
6 September

F. 558, op. 11, d. 94, ll. 53–54.

———————

[By cipher]
CC of the VKP. Moscow.
<u>To Kaganovich.</u>

It would be good to sell Mexico 50 high-speed bombers, so that Mexico can immediately resell them to Spain. We could also pick about 20 of our good pilots to perform combat functions in Spain and at the same time give flight training on the high-speed bombers to Spanish pilots. Think this matter over as quickly as possible. It would be good to sell by the same means 20,000 rifles, 1,000 machine guns, and about 20 million rounds of ammunition. We just need to know the calibers.

Stalin.

No. 34
6 September 1936[1]

    1. The number and date were entered by the secretary. The cipher was sent from Sochi at 11:58 P.M. the same day (RGASPI, f. 558, op. 11, d. 94, l. 52). See also document 176.

· 160 ·

Kaganovich and Molotov to Stalin
8 September

F. 558, op. 11, d. 94, ll. 68–69. Original typescript.

———————

Cipher.
From Moscow 8 September 1936 at 1:55 A.M.   Incoming No. 26
To Comrade Stalin. Sochi.

The command of the Chinese Red Army has reported two options for further operations by the Red Army.

Under the first option, after the Huang River freezes the first army line of advance occupies the Ningxia area (400 km from the southern border of the Mongolian People's Republic) by December 1936; the fourth army line advances and occupies Lanzhou and later advances to Suzhou (the western part of Gansu Province); the second army line consolidates the southern part of Gansu.

The Chinese comrades consider the objective of this operation to be consolidation of the current Soviet base at Shaanxi and Gansu, moving closer to the USSR, creation of a single anti-Japanese front, and countering Japan's attempts to cut communications between the USSR and China. Implementation of this option for operations is made dependent on whether assistance is forthcoming from the USSR.

The second option, which is proposed in the event that it is impossible to receive assistance from the USSR, calls for directing the operations of all three army lines of advance to the southern parts of Gansu and Shaanxi Provinces, the northern part of Sichuan Province, and the western part of Henan and Hubei. "In order to postpone fulfillment of the plan to advance westward from the Huang River until the winter of next year."

In the opinion of the command of the Chinese Red Army, the second option is disadvantageous in view of the need to abandon current Soviet areas and the inevitability of a military clash with Nanking. This option "will not be a line of advance against Japan but a line of advance that leads to civil war." Next year the militarists will intensify their blockhouse tactics and will rely even more on Japan, and as a result the difficulties for the advance of Chinese Red Army units will increase.

The CC of the Chinese Communist Party and the command of the Chinese Red Army regard the first option as the main one and are asking for approval and assistance with armaments, money, and men, and they indicate that issues of finance, food, and armaments have become extremely grave.

We consider it possible:

1) To agree to the first option for a plan of operations by the Chinese Red Army, specifically: to occupy the Ningxia area and the western part of Gansu Province. At the same time, we should categorically state that it is unacceptable for the Chinese Red Army to advance further in the direction of Xinjiang, which could cut off the Chinese Red Army from the principal Chinese regions.

2) To predetermine that after the Chinese Red Army occupies the Ningxia area, assistance will be provided with weapons in the amount of 15,000–20,000 rifles, eight cannons, ten mortars, and a commensurate amount of foreign-type ammunition. The weapons should be concentrated on the southern border of the Mongolian People's Republic by December 1936 and sold through a foreign firm that Uritsky knows, after preparing trucks to carry them to Ningxia.

Please let us know your opinion. Nos. 38, 39, 40.

Kaganovich, Molotov.[1]

---

1. Stalin replied from Sochi by cipher on 9 September at 7:17 P.M. with his agreement (RGASPI, f. 558, op. 11, d. 94, l. 65).

· 161 ·

Kaganovich to Stalin
[after 8 September but before 20 September]

F. 81, op. 3, d. 101, l. 96. Typewritten copy.

[Cipher]
To Stalin.

1. Litvinov proposes that concessions be made to the Japanese on the question of the time frame for allotting the fishing zones, and specifically that they be leased for five years, with the leases to be automatically renewed for three years, if the Japanese agree in turn to shorten the term of the convention itself from 12 to 8 years.

We consider Litvinov's proposal acceptable.[1]

2. Stomoniakov has submitted for approval drafts of the agreements on the redemarcation of the Soviet-Manchurian boundary and on the settlement of border conflicts. Litvinov proposes that these drafts be approved with minor corrections that he has formulated. We sent you Stomoniakov's drafts and Litvinov's corrections on 8 September. We consider Litvinov's proposal acceptable.[2]

Please let me know your opinion on both these issues.

1. On 20 September 1936 the Politburo decided, conditional upon the assent of the Japanese government, "to shorten the term of the new convention by four years and to deem it possible to promise the Japanese that at the end of a five-year period, during which we agree to allow them to lease without any negotiation the zones they are currently exploiting, we will be prepared to instruct our authorities that petitions by the lessees of these zones to extend the term of the lease on the same conditions for not more than three years be granted, provided that the lessees have conscientiously fulfilled their obligations" (RGASPI, f. 17, op. 162, d. 20, ll. 78, 79).

2. On 20 September the Politburo resolved to raise no objections to the counterdrafts submitted by Stomoniakov for the agreements on the redemarcation of the Soviet-Manchurian boundary and on border conflicts (ibid., l. 78).

· 162 ·

Kaganovich to Stalin
9 September

F. 558, op. 11, d. 94, l. 64. Original typescript.

[Cipher]
To Stalin.

I am sending you the exact text of an announcement by the Prosecutor's Office in the press. No. 15. Kaganovich.

"At the USSR Prosecutor's Office. The USSR Prosecutor's Office has now completed an investigation concerning references made by several defendants on 19 and 20 August during the trial of the Trotskyite-Zinovievite terrorist center in Moscow to the complicity in one degree or another of N. I. Bukharin and A. I. Rykov in their criminal counterrevolutionary activities.

"The investigation did not establish legal grounds for initiating judicial proceedings against N. I. Bukharin and A. I. Rykov, and as a result the investigation of this case was closed."[1]

1. A telegraph tape has been pasted to the bottom of the cipher. It reads: "Transmitted 9 September 1936 at 10:35 P.M. Transm[itted] by Zakharova receiv[ed] by Afonin."

· 163 ·

Kaganovich to Stalin
11 September
F. 558, op. 11, d. 94, l. 84. Original typescript.

[Phonegram]
To Comrade Stalin.

We take for granted the necessity of immediately removing Piatakov from his post as deputy people's commissar of heavy industry. We just think that there is no need to report the removal in the newspapers until the announcement of the prosecutor's office on the results of the investigation is published.

Please give me your instructions.

Kaganovich.

11 September 1936[2]

1. See document 164.
2. Below the date is noted: "Received by telephone."

· 164 ·

Stalin to Kaganovich
11 September
F. 558, op. 11, d. 94, l. 84.

[Phonegram]

It is better to remove Piatakov now from the deputy's post, without waiting for the results of the investigation.

Stalin.[1]

1. Below is the secretary's notation: "Transmitted by telephone 11/9/36." The same file contains a note by the secretary: "Dvinsky to Chechulin. Comrade Kaganovich asks whether or not to publish right now. Chechulin passed on Comrade Stalin's words: 'Don't publish'" (RGASPI, f. 558, op. 11, d. 94, l. 87).

A little earlier on 9 September, Dvinsky sent a cipher to Sochi for Stalin's vote: "From Moscow 9 September 1936 at 11:10 P.M. Incoming No. 29. Sochi. To Comrade Stalin. For voting purposes. 'It has been determined on the basis of indisputable information that CC member Yu. L. Piatakov maintained close ties with the terrorist groups of Trotskyites and Zinovievites. The Politburo believes that such behavior by Piatakov is not compatible with membership in the CC or the VKP(b), and submits for a vote by CC members a proposal that Piatakov be expelled from membership in the CC and the VKP(b). Secretariat of the CC of the VKP(b).' Dvinsky" (ibid., l. 75). Stalin wrote on the cipher "In favor." On 11 September the Politburo resolved to remove Piatakov without publishing the decision in the press (ibid., f. 17, op. 3, d. 980, l. 26).

· 165 ·

Stalin to Kaganovich
14 September

F. 558, op. 11, d. 94, l. 101.

[Phonegram]
CC of the VKP.
To Kaganovich
If you have a women's rally in Moscow and a resolution by the rally, the resolution should be sent to President Azaña of Spain, Prime Minister Caballero and a woman well known to us, Dolores Ibarruri.
Stalin
14 September 1936.[1]

1. The date was entered by the secretary. The reverse side of the sheet contains the notation "Transmitted to Moscow by telephone." The copy notes the time of transmission as 8:45 P.M. (RGASPI, f. 558, op. 11, d. 94, l. 100). A citywide meeting of the women of Moscow was held in the Bolshoi Theater on the evening of 14 September. On 15 September newspapers published the resolution of the meeting, which was formulated in accordance with Stalin's instructions. See also document 167.

· 166 ·

Kaganovich to Stalin
14 September

F. 558, op. 11, d. 743, ll. 56–63.

---

14 September [1936]

Greetings dear Comrade Stalin!

1) On the basis of a cipher from Surits, Litvinov has proposed that a protest note be sent to Germany with regard to the insulting and harshly worded speeches at the Nuremberg congress of fascists. We <u>don't think this should be done</u>.[1]

The experience of the past month shows that our tactics of barring hysterical outbursts and maintaining calm and self-control have proved to be completely justified.

Please let us know your opinion. I am sending you Litvinov's memorandum. I am also sending you his two memoranda concerning his visit to Geneva.[2]

In these memoranda he raises the fol[lowing] questions:

1) Putting an international air force of 1,000 planes at the disposal of the League of Nations.

2) Countering capitulationist sentiment in Czechoslovakia.

3) Formalizing our relations with Tur[key].

4) The question of a large, unified, anti-German defensive bloc.

None of these questions is of pressing importance at present. We promised to let you know anyway. If you find any of these questions to be significant for this moment, please let me know your opinion.

2) The Iranian government has informed our trade representative of its desire to negotiate our delivery to and installation in Iran of equipment for various enterprises: six cotton mills, a meat plant, six sugar mills, and a few others, the total cost of the equipment and its installation would be about $60 million. Delivery would take six to seven years.

The government deliveries would be paid for with raw materials. The Germans are now trying to worm their way into this business. The PC of Foreign Trade is asking our opinion. We have not settled on any draft of a decision, but it seemed to me that we should probably not turn down the negotiations.

<u>Please let us know your opinion.</u>

3) A few days ago we discussed the question of limits on the use of flour. Komzag [the Procurements Committee] and the PC of Internal Trade have submitted proposals that we restrict the issue of bread and flour to any single individual. We did not think this should be done. Maybe this can still be allowed in the rural districts of regions with poor harvests, and

then in limited quantities, but on the whole this cannot be allowed. In taking this view we proceeded from your instructions that enemies not be given any grounds for fabrications or slander.[3]

I would ask you to let me know if our position on this question is correct, especially since this question will probably come up again.

4) A few words about the confrontation between Sokolnikov, Rykov, and Bukharin [as part of their interrogation]. Sokolnikov makes an impression of an embittered criminal bandit who lays out the assassination plan and their work in this direction without the slightest embarrassment.

Rykov was fairly composed and kept trying to find out from Sokolnikov whether he knew about Rykov's participation only from Tomsky or from someone else as well. Evidently, after he found out that Sokolnikov knew about Rykov's connection with Zinoviev and Kamenev only from Tomsky and Kamenev, he, Rykov, completely settled down and went on the offensive. But both Rykov and Bukharin put their main emphasis on recent years, as for '31–'32–'33, they were both obviously evasive. Although Rykov had to admit that in 1934 Tomsky had already asked him whether he should go to Zinoviev's dacha, i.e. in the year of Kirov's assassination. All Rykov said was that he had advised Tomsky against it, but had not told anyone about it.

Bukharin, he argued more with Sokolnikov, although he had to admit that in response to Sokolnikov's request that his article be published in *Izvestia* Bukharin replied: "Write with your full signature, you need to fight for your legality, I am telling Rykov this, too." For the most part, he, Bukharin, confirmed this. After Sokolnikov left, Bukharin turned on the tears and asked to be believed. I am left with the impression that they may not have maintained a direct organizational tie with the Trotskyite-Zinovievite bloc, but in '32–'33, and perhaps in the following years as well, they were informed about the Trotskyites' affairs. Evidently they, the rightists, had their own organization, allowing united action from below. Just the other day the transport bodies of the GPU gave me the list of a Trotskyite group of railroad employees under arrest in Moscow, but when I took a look at the list, there were some pretty prominent former Moscow functionaries of Uglanov's, and I think it is a rightist-Trotskyite organization of railroad employees. At any rate, we must search for the rightist underground organization, it exists. I think the role of Rykov, Bukharin, and Tomsky will yet be uncovered.

Piatakov is not giving testimony yet. A confrontation will be arranged both for him and for Radek. It's good that we are completely smashing all of these Trotskyite-Zinovievite rats.[4]

5) I informed you about Spanish affairs by telephone.

Warm greetings and best wishes to you.

Yours L. Kaganovich.

1. In a telegram to the PC of Foreign Affairs on 11 September, Surits, the Soviet plenipotentiary in Germany, wrote, "We must give a sharp, strong response to Nuremberg, so that it meets with understanding and approval in many countries—but not a reply that plays into the hands of the warmongers." On 19 September Krestinsky, deputy people's commissar of foreign affairs, informed Surits of the directive of the Soviet leadership: "It has been decided not to send a note. As for the press reaction, as you have seen, our press reacted quite decisively to the party congress, even giving sharp characterizations of members of the government" (DVP, vol. XIX, p. 762).

2. Litvinov's memoranda about his Geneva visit are not in the file, and the decisions about his proposals in the memoranda have not been traced.

3. On 11 September a Politburo decision about trade in grain in the fourth quarter proposed that priority in the allocation of flour and bread should be afforded to the trade network in urban centers (RGASPI, f. 17, op. 3, d. 980, l. 26).

4. See the introduction to this chapter.

· 167 ·

Kaganovich to Stalin
24 September
F. 558, op. 11, d. 94, l. 121. Original typescript.

[Phonegram]
To Stalin. Sochi.

The rally at Dynamo Stadium for assistance to the women and children of Spain just ended. More than 100,000 people attended the rally.

The rally was very enthusiastic.

The speakers were: Nikolaeva; Zotov, an engineer from the Stalin Motor Vehicle Plant; USSR People's Artist Kachalov; Astakhova, a teacher at the Radishchev School; Fokin, a medal-winning locomotive engineer at the Ilyich Depot; Kapustina, a weaver at the Trekhgorka mill; and Zhorov, a physician at Clinical Hospital 1.

A message to Azaña and Caballero and a greeting to Comrade Stalin were adopted at the rally.

There will be a similar rally tomorrow in Leningrad.

Regards.

L. Kaganovich.[1]

1. The secretary noted in the upper left-hand corner of the document: "Transmitted by telephone via Comrade Chechulin. 24 September 1936."

· 168 ·

Kaganovich to Stalin
25 September
F. 558, op. 11, d. 94, l. 122. Authenticated typewritten copy.

Top Secret.
Copy.
By cipher.
To Comrade Stalin. Sochi.

   Despite instructions to Litvinov that he not take the position of fighting for the seats of the delegates of the Abyssinian state, which is effectively defunct, and that in voting he either abstain or vote for nonrecognition, depending on the situation, Litvinov pursued the opposite line there.[1] We have demanded an explanation of his behavior from him. Upon receiving it, we will report to you. No. 1427/sh.

Kaganovich.

25 September 1936

   1. The Italian government made it a condition of its participation in the Assembly of the League of Nations that the Abyssinian delegation should be removed, in view of the fact that the Abyssinian state had ceased to exist. According to Litvinov, the French and British governments preferred to resolve the question in Italy's favor. In order not to admit openly that Abyssinia had ceased to exist as an independent state, they proposed that the authorizations signed by the Emperor should not be recognized. The question had to be resolved by the Mandate Commission. On 21 September Litvinov informed Moscow: "I stated in the Mandate Commission that I did not agree that the question of Abyssinia should be discussed in a roundabout way; the question should be openly posed: do we continue to consider Abyssinia an independent state or do we recognize the annexation." On 23 September he reported that the Mandate Commission had "unanimously agreed to the right of the Abyssinians to sit in the Assembly" of the League (DVP, vol. XIX, pp. 673, 434).

· 169 ·

Stalin and Zhdanov to Kaganovich, Molotov,
and other members of the Politburo
25 September
F. 558, op. 11, d. 94, ll. Signed by Zhdanov.

[Cipher]
CC of the VKP(b). Moscow.
To Comrades Kaganovich, Molotov and other members of the Politburo.

   First. We consider it absolutely imperative and urgent that Comrade Yezhov be appointed people's commissar of internal affairs. Yagoda has clearly turned out not to be up to his task in the matter of exposing the Trotskyite-Zinovievite bloc. The OGPU was four years late in this matter. All the party functionaries and most of the regional representatives of the NKVD say this. Agranov can be retained as Yezhov's deputy at the NKVD.[1]

Second. We consider it imperative and urgent that Rykov be removed from the PC of Communications and Yagoda be appointed people's commissar of communications.[2] We don't think this matter needs any justification, since it is clear as it is.

Third. We consider it absolutely urgent that Lobov be removed and Comrade Ivanov, secretary of the Northern Regional Committee, be appointed people's commissar of the timber industry. Ivanov knows forestry, he is an efficient man, and Lobov as people's commissar is not getting the job done and fouls it up every year. We propose that Lobov be retained as Ivanov's first deputy at the PC of the Timber Industry.

Fourth. As for the Party Control Commission [PCC], Yezhov can be retained in his second job as chairman of the PCC so that he gives nine-tenths of his time to the NKVD, and Yakov Arkadievich Yakovlev could be promoted to Yezhov's first deputy at the PCC.

Fifth. Yezhov agrees with our proposals.

Stalin. Zhdanov.

No. 44

25 September 1936

Sixth. Needless to say, Yezhov remains a secretary of the CC.[3]

1. Point 1 was included without the last sentence in Khrushchev's secret speech to the XX party congress in February 1956. The phrase "The OGPU was four years late" was not underlined in the text of the cipher, as shown in some versions of the speech, but inserted.

2. Preserved in the file is a memorandum from Stalin to Yagoda dated 26 September, taken down by Chechulin: "To Comrade Yagoda. The PC of Communications is a very important matter. It is a defense-oriented PC. I have no doubt that you will be able to get this PC on its feet. I urge you to agree to take the PC of Communications job. Without a good PC of Communications we feel as though we have no hands. The PC of Communications cannot be left in its present condition. We must urgently get it on its feet. I. Stalin" (RGASPI, f. 558, op. 11, d. 94, l. 132). A copy of this memorandum notes that Kaganovich and Molotov have seen it and that the text was transmitted by telephone from Sochi on 26 September at 9:30 P.M. (ibid., l. 131).

3. The number, date, and point 6 were entered by Chechulin. The personnel changes proposed in the telegram were approved by the Politburo on 26 and 29 September (ibid., f. 17, op. 3, d. 981, 49, 50, 51).

The reverse side of the cipher reads: "This c[iph]er was sent to Comrade P. N. Pospelov on 8 February 1956, and returned on 13 September 1957" (ibid., f. 558, op. 11, d. 94, l. 123).

· 170 ·

Kaganovich and Molotov to Stalin
27 September
F. 558, op. 11, d. 94, ll. 133–135. Original typescript.

Telegram.
From Moscow 27 September 1936 at 7:35 P.M.
To Comrade Stalin. Sochi.

US Secretary of the Treasury Morgenthau yesterday made an outrageous anti-Soviet statement, which we are sending you (enclosure 1).

We consider it imperative to give the following Gosbank [State Bank] statement (enclosure 2) to the press as early as today.[1]

In addition, we are instructing Svanidze to summon the British and American correspondents and to give them detailed factual material that demonstrate the irreproachability of Gosbank and the crookedness of Chase Bank, which indeed bought at a lower exchange rate for the pound than the Gosbank directive specified.

Please let us know your opinion.[2] No. 20.

Kaganovich, Molotov.[3]

Enclosure 1 (via TASS)

Morgenthau statement.

New York, 26 September. The Associated Press reports from Washington that Treasury Secretary Morgenthau called in members of the press and told them that Gosbank is seeking to drive down the exchange rate of the pound sterling, but that he, Morgenthau, with the aid of the American monetary stabilization fund, had staved off any impact from the Gosbank actions by buying up the 1 million pounds sterling that the Soviet government had offered in the money markets "at any price."

According to the Washington dispatch, Morgenthau then called in members of the press a second time and said that the US intervention had averted a decrease of the pound-sterling exchange rate as a result of the Gosbank moves. In Morgenthau's words, the United States intends to utilize all the resources of the stabilization fund to prevent sharp currency fluctuations.

The United Press reports from Washington: "Experts say the Gosbank's actions could have killed the hopes of establishing international currency equilibrium if the United States had not intervened. At a time when the New York Stock Exchange is calm, as was the case today, and the London and Paris exchanges are closed, pounds thrown onto the market by the Soviet Union could have caused a significant decrease in the pound's exchange rate."

The Pound's Exchange Rate Drops in the US

According to the United Press, US Treasury Secretary Morgenthau told members of the press: "My investigation has shown that the USSR Gosbank issued an order to sell 1 million pounds at any price. When I learned of this, I bought the 1 million pounds. I used our stabilization fund to buy what they wanted to sell. The USSR Gosbank used the pounds to drive down their exchange rate. This is the only instance to date in which any government, bank or private individual attempted to artificially influence the foreign currency market in the United States. I sincerely hope that this incident will not happen again." According to the agency, when Morgenthau was asked how the Soviet government had hoped to benefit from this sale, he replied: "You should ask the Soviet government that." The agency went on to say that Morgenthau had called the attention of the members of the press to yesterday's statement by the Treasury Department, which says that the United States, Britain, and France invited other countries to cooperate and expressed the hope that the other countries would not make attempts to achieve "abnormal competitive and foreign-currency gains and thereby impede efforts to restore more stable economic relations." According to the agency, as Morgenthau read this quotation, he put particular emphasis on the words "cooperate," "abnormal," and "impede."

Morgenthau's statement about the USSR Gosbank, the agency goes on to state, "is considered unprecedented in the history of the American Treasury Department. Morgenthau asked the correspondents to transmit their dispatches as soon as possible before the stock exchange closed."

Morgenthau's statements, in which he accuses the Soviet government of acting counter to the "gentlemen's agreement" among the United States, Britain, and France and depicts the United States as the savior of British currency from attacks by the Soviet Union, was presented in the Scripps-Howard press under the headline "Soviet Union Attacks the Dollar and Pound," which is what Morgenthau was seeking. Morgenthau stated that the USSR Gosbank sold 1 million pounds in New York because the London and Paris stock exchanges were closed. Morgenthau hastily held two special conversations with members of the press in order to make them act against the Soviet Union.

1. The draft of the USSR Gosbank statement (RGASPI, f. 558, op. 11, d. 94, l. 136) was adopted without revisions. The statement, which declared that the sale of 1 million pounds sterling via the Chase bank was a normal transaction, was published in Soviet newspapers on 28 September, and is reprinted in DVP, vol. XIX, p. 450. It is not published in the present volume.

2. Stalin agreed on 28 September (RGASPI, f. 558, op. 11, d. 94, l. 136).

3. The rough draft of the document was written by Kaganovich, and corrections were made by Molotov (ibid., l. 143). The US press reports, and Mogenthau's statement, have been retranslated from the Russian.

· 171 ·

Kaganovich and Molotov to Stalin
5 October
F. 558, op. 11, d. 95, ll. 19–20. Original typescript.

Telegram.

From Moscow 5 October 1936 at 12:30 A.M..

To Comrade Stalin. Sochi.

The plan for grain purchases has been set by separate decisions of the CC and Sovnarkom for the Ukraine, Azov–Black Sea Region, Northern Caucasus, the Crimea, Western Siberia, and the Far Eastern Region in the amount of 116,500,000 poods [1,926,000 tons].

For the remaining regions, we are setting the following plans for grain purchases:

Northern Region	500,000 poods
Leningrad Region	500,000 "
Kalinin Region	500,000 "
Western Region	2.5 million poods
Moscow Region	2 million poods
Ivanovo Region	600,000 poods
Yaroslavl Region	500,000 "
Gorky Region	2 million poods
Kirov Region	3 million "
Sverdlovsk Region	3 million "
Cheliabinsk Region	4 million "
Bashkir ASSR	1 million "
Tatar ASSR	1 million "
Kuibyshev Region	1 million "
Orenburg Region	1 million "
Kursk Region	2.5 million poods
Voronezh Region	3 million poods
Saratov Region	1 million "
Stalingrad Region	1 million "
Kazakh ASSR	7.5 million poods
Kirgiz ASSR	2 million poods
Omsk Region	2.5 million poods
Krasnoiarsk Region	8 million poods
Belorussian SSR	3 million poods
Transcaucasian SFSR	1.5 million poods

Uzbek SSR	1 million poods
Turkmen SSR	100,000 poods
Tadzhik SSR	500,000 poods

In all, we plan to purchase 56,700,000 poods [929,000 tons] from these regions. As a result, the total plan for grain purchases this year will total 173,200,000 poods [2,837,000 tons], as against actual grain purchases last year of 218 million poods [3,570,000 tons]. Please let us know your opinion. No. 25.

Kaganovich, Molotov.[1]

1. Grain purchases (*zakupki*) were nominally voluntary, and were supplied in addition to the compulsory procurements. See also document 172.

· 172 ·

Stalin to Kaganovich and Molotov
5 October

F. 558, op. 11, d. 95, l. 20.

[By cipher]
CC of the VKP. Moscow.
To Kaganovich, Molotov.

Here are my amendments to the plan for grain purchases: add 5 million poods to the Ukraine, 1.5 million to the Azov Region, 1 million each to the Northern Caucasus and Kuibyshev regions, 1.5 million to Western Siberia, and 500,000 poods each to the Stalingrad Region, Moscow Region, Orenburg Region, and the Crimea.

Stalin.

No. 51
5 October 1936[1]

1. The number and date were entered by the secretary. The telegram was sent from Sochi at 1:56 P.M. (RGASPI, F. 558, op. 11, d. 95, l. 18). See document 171. The plan for grain purchases proposed by Kaganovich, as corrected by Stalin, was approved by the Politburo on 5 October (ibid., f. 17, op. 3, d. 981, ll. 70, 71).

· 173 ·

Kaganovich to Stalin
5 October
F. 558, op. 11, d. 95, l. 25. Original typescript.

Telegram.
From Moscow 5 September 1936 at 6:15 P.M.
To Comrade Stalin. Sochi.

1) To replace Kniazev as director of the Southern Urals Railroad, I nominate Bodrov, a maintenance engineer who was dispatched a few months ago to be Kniazev's deputy, he got to know the railroad and now, after a check I conducted, I am sure that he will be up to the job.

2) To replace Kovylkin as director of the Kuibyshev Railroad, I nominate Khrustalev, the deputy director of the Transcaucasian Railroad. He is an outstanding functionary and will definitely be up to the job, and the work of the Transcaucasian will not be affected by his departure.

3) Please give your assent to the dismissal of Livshits as my deputy. Regardless of the future clarification of his position, his authority and capacity for work have been so undermined that it is impossible and inadvisable for him to work as deputy. At present he could be given a job on one of the eastern railroads.

Please let me know your opinion. No. 26

Kaganovich[1]

1. See document 157. Stalin replied by cipher from Sochi at 9:08 P.M. with his assent (RGASPI, f. 558, op. 11, d. 95, l. 24). Kaganovich's proposals on points 1 and 2 were approved by the Politburo on 8 October (ibid., f. 17, op. 3, d. 981, l. 75). On the same day Livshits was removed and placed at the disposal of the PC of Transport (ibid.).

· 174 ·

Kaganovich and Molotov to Stalin
9 October
F. 558, op. 11, d. 95, ll. 40–41. Original typescript.

Telegram.
From Moscow 9 October 1936 at 1 A.M.
To Comrade Stalin. Sochi.

The Sverdlovsk and Bashkir Regional Committees and the Saratov, Kirov, and Gorky Regional Committees have submitted requests for a reduction in the grain-procurement plans. We heard reports by the secretaries of each of these organizations.[1]

1) The Sverdlovsk Regional Committee requests a reduction in the grain-procurements plan of 10,500,000 poods [172,000 tons], including a decrease in payments in kind of 4,500,000 poods, a deferment for the collection of the payment in kind of 1 million poods, a decrease in grain deliveries of 3,800,000 poods, and a deferment for the repayment of loans of 1,200,000 poods. The region has 27 districts with poor harvests.

We intend to reduce the plan for Sverdlovsk Region by 7,800,000 poods [128,000 tons], including a decrease in the plan for payment in kind of 4,000,000 poods, to defer the payment in kind of 800,000 poods, to reduce the grain-delivery plan by 2 million poods, and to defer the repayment of loans of 1 million poods.

2) The Bashkir Regional Committee requests an additional reduction in the grain-delivery plan of 6 million poods [98,000 tons], a deferment for the payment in kind along with last year's arrears of 1,445,000 poods, a deferment until the 1937 harvest for the repayment of the loan of 600,000 poods received last year for the winter planting, and a reduction in the potato-delivery plan for collective farms from 140,000 tons to 50,000 tons.

We intend to reduce the plan for grain deliveries by an additional 5 million poods [82,000 tons], to defer the collection of the payment in kind of 700,000 poods and the arrears in payment in kind of 300,000 poods until the 1937 harvest, to defer until the 1937 harvest the repayment of the loan of 600,000 poods received in 1936, and to reduce the plan for potato deliveries to 60,000 tons.

3) The Saratov Regional Committee has posed the question of an additional reduction in the grain-procurement plan of 6,600,000 poods [108,000 tons], including a decrease in the plan for payment in kind of 2,500,000 poods, a deferment in the collection of the payment in kind of 1,300,000 poods, a reduction in grain deliveries of 1,800,000 poods, and a reduction in the plan for grain deliveries by state farms of 1 million poods. Saratov previously already received a reduction in the plan of 16,485,000 poods [270,000 tons].

We intend to reduce the plan for payment in kind by 2 million poods, to defer until 1937 the collection of the payment in kind of 1 million poods, to carry over 1 million poods of grain deliveries into arrears until 1937, and in all to reduce the grain-procurements plan for the Saratov Region by 4 million poods [66,000 tons].

4) The Kirov Regional Committee requests a reduction in the plan for payment in kind of 2,500,000 poods and a decrease in the grain-delivery plan of 2,500,000 poods, an overall reduction in grain procurements of 5 million poods [82,000 tons]. The Kirov Region has already received a reduction of 3 million poods.

We intend to reduce the plan for payment in kind by an additional 2 million poods and to carry over 1,500,000 poods of grain deliveries into arrears.

5) The Gorky Regional Committee requests a reduction in the plan for payment in kind of 1,770,000 poods, a reduction in the plan for grain deliveries of 180,000 poods, a loan of 4,158,000 poods, the return to collective farms of 600,000 poods that was overdelivered by collective farms as a result of the reduction that was granted, and a credit of 3 million rubles for monetary assistance to collective farms.

We intend to carry over 180,000 poods of grain deliveries into arrears, to reduce the plan for payment in kind by 1,500,000 poods and to provide a credit of 3 million rubles to collective farms. We plan to defer the question of the loan until the first quarter [of 1937] and to resolve the question of releasing the loan of 600,000 poods based on what was overdelivered as a result of the deferment granted to collective farms on grain deliveries.

Please let us know your opinion. No. 29.
Kaganovich. Molotov.

1. "Payment in kind," made in return for the services of Machine-Tractor Stations, was in effect a supplement to compulsory grain deliveries. See document 175.

· 175 ·

Stalin to Kaganovich and Molotov
9 October

F. 558, op. 11, d. 95, l. 49.

[By cipher]
CC of the VKP. Moscow.
To Kaganovich, Molotov.

Sverdlovsk Region has a good harvest. There is little basis for Kabakov's demands. We can give a total reduction of not more than 5 million [82,000 tons]. In regard to Bashkiria, Saratov, and the Kirov and Gorky Regional Committees, I agree.

Stalin.

No. 55
9 October 1936[1]

1. The number and date were entered by the secretary. The cipher was sent from Sochi at 12:45 P.M. (RGASPI, f. , op. 11, d. 95, l. 48). See document 174.

· 176 ·

Kaganovich to Stalin
11 October
F. 558, op. 11, d. 95, l. 97. Original typescript.

Phonegram.[1]
To Comrade Stalin.

First. We have still not told Caballero anything about our shipments. We think Gorev should be instructed to inform Caballero about the assistance officially, but in a conspiratorial manner. For the moment he should be informed, with all the details, about what has already arrived, and he should be informed in the future as the ships arrive.

Second. Considering that five ships are already headed for southern ports and that the further dispatch of new ships with special cargoes along this route may be dangerous, we would deem it possible to send some of the cargoes along the northern route, to a port on the Bay of Biscay, for example, Bilbao or Santander. At present all of Asturias is in our friends' hands, except for Oviedo.[2]

Kaganovich.

1. At the bottom of the letter is the notation: "Transmitted 11 October 1936 to Chechulin by telephone at 9:15 P.M."

2. On the same day Stalin replied to Kaganovich: "I received your phonegram about shipments to Caballero. I agree with you about everything" (RGASPI, f. , op. 11, d. 95, l. 96). On 29 September the Politburo had decided to begin arms deliveries. By 22 October five ships had been dispatched to Spain containing 50 tanks, plus fuel and ammunition, 30 high-speed bombers, and artillery (see *Rodina*, no. 9, 1996, 67). Further Soviet arms shipments to Spain were made in larger quantities.

· 177 ·

Kaganovich to Stalin
12 October
F. 558, op. 11, d. 743, ll. 64–71

---

12 October [1936]
Greetings Dear Comrade Stalin!

1) Yesterday we had a Politburo meeting. Among a number of questions we discussed: a) the progress of automobile production at the Gorky auto plant, about which you gave instructions on the telephone. It turned out that a number of important parts are indeed different from Ford parts: the wheels, the steering wheel, springs, shock absorbers, the frame, the air filter, and others. Most of these parts are closer to those for the Buick. Dia-

konov argued that this will not cause any incompatibility in the design of the vehicle. Since there was no chance to clarify this at the meeting itself, we instructed the PC of Heavy Industry to do a technical analysis of this issue and report to the CC within ten days. In addition, it was learned that apart from the fact that the plan is not being fulfilled quantitatively, a number of parts being produced are defective, and are being allowed onto the assembly line. As a result, the engine, clutch, transmission, and rear-axle assembly have major defects due to which a number of accidents have occurred in Moscow. We gave Diakonov a tough talking-to (Dybets unfortunately was not in Moscow) . We also had to mete out some harsh criticism to Pramnek, who is having trouble grasping the plant's failure and is blaming most of the problem on the supplier plants. In ten days, when we receive the proposals from the PC of Heavy Industry, we will report to you.[1]

b) We had to put pressure on the Ukrainians regarding the digging up and haulage of sugar beets, because Comrade Mikoian is not here, there has been barely a peep out of Belenky and unless we hurry up with the digging up and haulage, we may lose a great deal in both the quantity and the quality of beets. We hope you will not condemn us for this pressure.[2]

2) Regarding the issue of seeds, on which you gave instructions, the agricultural department of the CC is now doing a lot of work. It turned out that for buckwheat there are no people at the institutes or at the PC of Agriculture who work on varieties of buckwheat or are even so much as familiar with this question. The same picture applies to millet, there proved to be not a single worker at the PC of Agriculture dealing with millet. Regarding spring wheat it has already been determined that there is no regionalization of varieties. The PC of Agriculture recommended the cesium 0111 variety for the entire central zone, including Siberia. It has now been determined that this variety is most prone to smut and is inferior to varieties of lutescens 062 for the European zone and the milturum 0321 variety for the east.

The novinka variety recommended by the PC of Agriculture becomes badly infected by rust fungus and smut. It is not out of the question that we are dealing here not only with ordinary bungling but also with wrecking activities. By the end of the month the issue will be prepared and then we will report to you. The same goes for the question of the cost of constr[uction] of the MTS.

3) Regarding the Spanish situation we are acting in strict compliance with your instructions. The statement that you proposed making proved to be extremely timely and well-formulated, as the responses make clear.[3] After the luncheon with the Spanish ambassador Pascua I told him in a conversation that you personally devote extraordinary attention to revolutionary Spain and take their difficulties and needs close to heart. He

earnestly requested that we convey his regards and gratitude to you. He said that the Spanish revolu[tionary] masses know about this and are very appreciative, and that you are very popular in Spain, that your writings have been translated into Spanish and are read together with Lenin's writings by the broad masses. He himself is apparently depressed over the danger of losing Madrid. The fact that he is not a real Bolshevik revolutionary but a Menshevik, is, of course, having an effect on him. Nevertheless, it seems to me that out of a desire to spur his optimism we pressured him too much. But in general the conversation went pretty well.

4) In connection with the 50th birthday of Sergo [Ordzhonikidze] the Northern Caucasus Regional Committee raised the question of renaming the region and the r[ail]r[oad] after Comrade Ordzhonikidze. Please let us know your opinion. In addition, we are thinking of providing appropriate coverage in the press and issuing a congratulatory message from the CC. We will send you the text of the message beforehand.

5) Comrade Yezhov is doing well. He has started off firmly and energetically on rooting out the counterrevolutionary bandits, and conducts interrogations in a superb and politically literate manner. But apparently a segment of his administration, even though it has quieted down now, will be disloyal to him. Take, for example, this question, which it turns out is of great importance for them, that is the question of rank. There is talk that as Yagoda is still the general commissar, that Yezhov will not be given this rank, and so forth. It is odd, but this "problem" is of importance to his staff. When we were deciding the question of the people's commissar, this question somehow was not raised. Comrade Stalin, do you find it necessary to raise this question?[4]

Well I will close here.

On everything else we are trying to correct the shortcomings and mistakes that you point out, and we are working at the top of our effort. We are very glad that you feel well. Warm regards to you and best wishes.

Yours, L. Kaganovich.

P.S. A letter came in from Comrade Mikoian in which he sends you fervent greetings. L. Kaganovich.[5]

---

1. On 11 October the Politburo decided: "a) To instruct the PC of Heavy Industry to investigate the reasons for the unsatisfactory quality of the M-1 vehicles being manufactured by the Gorky auto plant both with regard to the organization of production, work methods and supplies to the plant and with regard to flaws in the design of the vehicle. b) To instruct Comrades Rukhimovich and Pramnek to submit their proposals for improving the quality of the vehicle within ten days" (RGASPI, f. 17, op. 3, d. 981, l. 1). On 14 January 1937 the Politburo adopted a resolution on the construction of the Gorky auto plant directing that work begin on a new engine for cars and trucks. Construction work to expand the plant was scheduled for completion at the end of September 1939. (Ibid., d. 983, ll. 26, 113–16.)

2. On 11 October the Politburo approved the plan for delivery of beets from the 1936

harvest. The Ukraine was instructed to finish digging up the beets—by 1 November 1936—and to complete the haulage of the beets—by 10 November (ibid., d. 981, ll. 3, 92–94).

3. On 7 October 1936 the Soviet representative in the Nonintervention Committee read a declaration on the assistance given to the Spanish insurgents by the governments of Portugal, Germany and Italy, which were parties to the nonintervention agreement. According to the declaration, "unless the violations of the nonintervention agreement cease immediately," the Soviet government "will consider itself exempt from the obligations arising from the Agreement" (DVP, vol. XIX, pp. 463–64).

4. The title of general commissar of state security was conferred on Yezhov on 27 January 1937 (*Lubianka, 1917–1960: Spravochnik* [Lubianka, 1917–1960: A Reference Book], comp. A. I. Kokurin and N. V. Petrov [Moscow, 1997], 14).

5. In the upper left-hand corner of the first sheet of the letter is the notation: "My files. I St[alin]."

Appendix
Glossary of Terms and Abbreviations
Brief Biographies
Index

Appendix

· 1 ·

Kuibyshev to Kaganovich
10 August 1931
F. 558, op. 11, d. 739, ll. 26–27.

To Comrade Kaganovich, secretary of the CC of the VKP(b).

1. On the directives for the second five-year plan.

Only today I will send the CC the draft of "the basic lines of the second five-year plan" and a special memorandum on metal. I propose that a conference be convened after Comrade Stalin, who should be sent the material immediately, has his say. If you still find it necessary to convene a conference before Comrade Stalin's comments, then I propose convening it on 14 August at 8 P.M.

2. On the directives for 1932 control figures.

The commission that was selected by the Politburo has effectively disbanded in view of the departure of Comrades Stalin and Molotov. The exchange of opinions at the first session of the commission and the failure with regard to the convening of the subcommission (representatives of the most important economic organizations—Vesenkha, Tsentrosoiuz, municipal services, etc.—did not come) compels me to submit the following proposal:

a) Confine ourselves to the directives that have already been adopted by the Politburo (a 35 percent increase in output, 20–22 billion [rubles] in capital investment, the concentration of resources [*fondy*] on metal, coal, transport, and mechanization, the import of metal and equipment below last year);

b) Capital investment should not be allocated at present by agencies and organizations, but a limit of 20–22 billion rubles should be set on capital investment for the entire national economy;

c) On the basis of these general directives, agencies should submit their draft control figures to Gosplan by 25 October, and the republics should submit theirs by 10 November 1931 (the deadlines set by the Sovnarkom decree of 21 July);

d) Gosplan should be required to submit its consolidated national economic plan for 1932 to the Politburo and the government by 1 December 1931;

e) The directives drawn up by Gosplan should be sent out solely as [informational] material to agencies and republics.

Comrades Mikoian, Grinko, Rukhimovich, and Odintsov are in agreement with these proposals.

3. <u>Regarding my vacation.</u>

I request that I be granted a vacation from 20 August until 5 October in view of my illness.

4. <u>On my future work.</u>

Since I clearly cannot manage the duties of head of Gosplan, I request that I be relieved of this job and provided with a job that I can handle (it would be better if it were in a region or a district).

V. Kuibyshev.

10 August 1931

· 2 ·

Stalin to Ordzhonikidze
9 September 1931
F. 81, op. 3, d. 99, ll. 27–28. Authenticated typewritten copy.

---

9 September 1931   Copy.
Greetings, Sergo!

I received your letter. Zina [Ordzhonikidze's wife] has arrived. I suggested that she move to Puzanovka, where there is much more space than at Zenzinovka, but she didn't want to and stayed at Zenzinovka.

1) At long last the Politburo has revoked its decisions on additional imports of steel. That is very good. It is time to realize that we face a financial and monetary storm that the USA is organizing against us and against which we Bolsheviks are duty-bound to take the most ferocious measures. Must we end up bankrupt in a year or two and thereby wreck all of the economic plans, or must we prevent bankruptcy—that is the question that the Politburo settled by revoking the additional steel imports. Now, at last, we can hope that the Bolsheviks (Bol-she-viks!) will attempt (will at-

tempt!) to take the first (first!) step in the direction of fulfilling the <u>numer-ous</u> decisions by the party congresses and the party's CC on <u>build-ing up</u> hard-currency <u>reserves</u>.

2) It is also clear that we, especially members of the CC, must not and cannot dupe one another. There is no need to prove that the proposal for additional imports of steel and other items—without a straightforward and honest proposal to revoke the July decision of the Politburo—was an attempt to dupe the CC (Kaganovich, Rudzutak, etc.) It is not hard for the Piatakovs to take a similar non-Bolshevik path, since for them Bolshevik law is not mandatory. Bolsheviks cannot take such a path, unless, of course, they want to turn our Bolshevik party into a conglomerate of de-partmental gangs. The Politburo has made things clear here as well.

3) You say: give us a solution, tell us where we can get steel, railroad-car axles and wheels, etc. I don't think we will <u>ever</u> find a solution or <u>ever</u> have an adequate amount of steel, axles, wheels, etc., <u>unless</u> we minimize the imports of these items <u>now</u>, unless we set up production of these items <u>in our country right now</u>, <u>unless</u> we pressure our own economic apparatus <u>right now</u> and <u>compel</u> it to fulfill the numerous decisions of the CC on or-ganizing steel production on a large scale at <u>our own</u> plants. Why is the modernization [*rekonstruktsiia*] of the Urals steel mills proceeding in such an outrageously sloppy manner? Why aren't military plants being put to <u>maximum</u> use to produce high-quality steels? Because the economic appa-ratus is <u>counting</u> on the stupidity and bungling of the CC, the economic apparatus is <u>counting</u> on the CC to give its consent to additional imports. The task is to do away with this counting on the CC's stupidity. What is better: putting pressure on the state's reserves of foreign currency while preserving the peace of mind of the economic apparatus, or putting pres-sure on the economic apparatus while preserving the interests of the state? I think the latter is better than the former.

Well, that is all for now. Don't dress me down for being rude and, per-haps, overly direct. Still, you can dress me down as much as you want.

Your I. Stalin.

· 3 ·

Stalin to the members of the Politburo and Adoratsky
19 July 1934
F. 17, op. 3, d. 950, ll. 82–86. Typewritten original.

To the members of the Politburo and Comrade Adoratsky.

In sending out Engels' article "The Foreign Policy of Russian Tsarism," I find it necessary to preface it with the following comments.

Comrade Adoratsky is proposing to publish in the next issue of *Bolshevik,* which is devoted to the 20th anniversary of the imperialist world war, Engels' well-known article "The Foreign Policy of Russian Tsarism," which was first published abroad in 1890. I would consider it quite normal if the proposal was to print this article in a collection of Engels' works or in one of the historical journals. But the proposal to us is that it be printed in our militant journal, in *Bolshevik,* in an issue devoted to the 20th anniversary of the imperialist world war. Therefore this article is evidently considered to be a source of guidance, or at any rate profoundly instructive for our party functionaries with regard to clarifying the problems of imperialism and imperialist wars. But unfortunately, despite its merits, the content of Engels' article makes clear that it does not possess these qualities. Moreover, it has a number of shortcomings that, if published without criticism, may confuse the reader.

I would therefore consider it inadvisable to publish Engels' article in the next issue of *Bolshevik.*

But what are the shortcomings?

1. In describing the expansionist policy of Russian tsarism and doing justice to the abominations of that policy, Engels does not attribute it primarily to the "need" of Russia's military-feudal-mercantile leaders for outlets to the seas and seaports, for an expansion of foreign trade and control of strategic locations. Instead he gives more weight to the notion that Russia's foreign policy was led by a supposedly all-powerful and very talented gang of foreign adventurists, which for some reason was lucky everywhere and in every endeavor, which surprisingly managed to overcome each and every obstacle on the path to its adventurist goal, which duped all of the European rulers with surprising dexterity and finally reached the point where it had made Russia the most militarily powerful state.

This treatment of the issue by Engels may seem more than incredible, but it is, unfortunately, a fact.

Here are the relevant sections of Engels' article.

"Foreign policy," Engels states, "is unquestionably the realm in which tsarism is very, very strong. Russian diplomacy constitutes a kind of new Jesuit Order, which is powerful enough to overcome, when necessary, even the tsar's whims and, while spreading corruption far beyond itself, is capable of stopping corruption in its own midst. At first it was primarily foreigners who were recruited for this Order: Corsicans, such as Pozzo di Borgo; Germans, such as Nesselrode; and Ostsee [Baltic Sea] Germans, such as Liven. Its founder, Catherine II, was also a foreigner."

"To this day only <u>one</u> full-blooded Russian, Gorchakov, has held a high post in this order. His successor, von Girs, again bears a foreign surname."

"It was this secret society, whose members were recruited originally from among foreign adventurists, that elevated the Russian state to its present might. With iron perseverance, steadfastly pursuing its objective, not stopping at perfidy, treachery, or assassination from around a corner, or fawning—unstinting with bribes, refusing to become intoxicated by victories, refusing to lose heart after defeats, stepping across millions of soldiers' corpses and at least one tsar's corpse—this gang is as unscrupulous as it is talented, and has done more than all the Russian armies to expand Russia's borders from the Dnieper and the Dvina beyond the Vistula, to the Prut, the Danube, and to the Black Sea, from the Don and the Volga beyond the Caucasus, to the sources of the Amu Darya and the Syr Darya. It has made Russia great, mighty, and fear-inspiring, and has opened its way to world domination" (see Engels' above-mentioned article).

One might think that in the history of Russia, in the history of its foreign relations, diplomacy was everything, and tsars, feudal lords, merchants, and other social groups were nothing, or almost nothing.

One might think that if Russia's foreign policy had been led by Russian adventurists such as Gorchakov and others, rather than foreign adventurists such as Nesselrode or Girs, Russia's foreign policy would have taken a different course.

Never mind the fact that an expansionist policy with all of its abominations and filth was by no means the monopoly of Russian tsars. Everyone knows that an expansionist policy was also associated—at least as much, if not more—with the kings and diplomats of every country in Europe, including an emperor in a bourgeois mold such as Napoleon, who, despite his nontsarist background, successfully practiced intrigue, deceit, perfidy, flattery, atrocities, bribery, assassinations, and arson in his foreign policy.

Clearly, it could not have been otherwise.

In his criticism of Russian tsarism (Engels' article is a good piece of militant criticism), Engels evidently was somewhat carried away and, once carried away, he forgot for a minute about some elementary facts that were well known to him.

2. In describing the situation in Europe and analyzing the causes and portents of the approaching world war, Engels writes:

"The present-day situation in Europe is defined by three facts: 1) Germany's annexation of Alsace and Lorraine; 2) tsarist Russia's yearning for Constantinople; 3) the struggle between the proletariat and the bourgeoisie, which is growing hotter and hotter in every country—a struggle, for which the ubiquitous upsurge of the socialist movement serves as a thermometer."

"The first two facts account for the present division of Europe into two large military camps. The annexation of Alsace-Lorraine turned France into an ally of Russia against Germany, and the tsarist threat to Constantinople is turning Austria and even Italy into an ally of Germany. Both camps are preparing for a decisive struggle—a war such as the world has never seen, a war in which 10 to 15 million armed warriors will face one another. Only two factors have until now prevented the eruption of this terrible war: first, the unprecedently rapid development of military technology, in which every newly invented type of weapon is overtaken by new inventions before it can even be introduced in a <u>single</u> army, and second, the absolute impossibility of calculating one's chances, the complete uncertainty as to who will ultimately emerge victorious from this gigantic struggle."

"This entire danger of world war will disappear the day when affairs in Russia take such a turn that the Russian people are able to do away with the traditional, expansionist policy of their tsars and, instead of fantasies of world domination, pursue their own vital interests inside the country, interests that are threatened by extreme danger."

". . . The Russian National Assembly, which will want to deal at least with the most urgent internal tasks, will have to decisively put an end to any efforts toward new conquests."

"Europe is sliding with increasing speed, as though down a slope, into the abyss of a world war of unprecedented scope and force. Only one thing can stop it: the replacement of the Russian system. That this must occur in the next few years is beyond all question."

". . . On the day tsarist rule, that last bastion of European reaction, falls, on that day a completely different wind will begin to blow in Europe" (ibid.).

One cannot help but notice that in this description of the situation in Europe and the list of factors leading to world war a very important point is omitted that later played a decisive role, i.e. the <u>imperialist</u> struggle for colonies, for markets, and for sources of raw materials, which was already of extraordinary importance then; it omits the role of England as a factor in the coming world war, and the conflicts between Germany and England, conflicts that were also of substantial importance and that later played an almost decisive role in the outbreak and development of the world war.

I think this omission is the main shortcoming of Engels' article.

This shortcoming leads to other shortcomings, of which the following should be noted:

a) An <u>overestimation</u> of the role of tsarist Russia's yearning for Constantinople in paving the way for the world war. True, at first Engels judges Germany's annexation of Alsace-Lorraine to be the leading war factor, but later he relegates that aspect to the background and gives priority to the expansionist ambitions of Russian tsarism by asserting that "<u>this entire danger of world war will disappear the day</u> when affairs in

Russia take such a turn that the Russian people are able to do away with the traditional, expansionist policy of their tsars."

This is, of course, an exaggeration.

b) An <u>overestimation</u> of the role of the bourgeois revolution in Russia and the role of the "Russian National Assembly" (the bourgeois parliament) in preventing the approaching world war. Engels asserts that a collapse of Russian tsarism is the only means of preventing a world war. This is an obvious exaggeration. A new, bourgeois system in Russia, with its "National Assembly," could not have prevented the war, if only because the mainsprings of the war lay in the realm of the imperialist struggle between the principal imperialist powers. The point is that ever since Russia's Crimean defeat (in the 1850s), the autonomous role of tsarism in European foreign policy began to decline significantly, and by the time the imperialist world war drew near, tsarist Russia was essentially playing the role of an auxiliary reserve for the main European powers.

c) An <u>overestimation</u> of the role of tsarist rule as "the last bastion of European reaction" (Engels' words). The fact that tsarist rule in Russia was a powerful bastion of European (as well as Asian) reaction cannot be disputed. But that it was the <u>last</u> bastion of this reaction—this is a matter of doubt.

It should be noted that these shortcomings in Engels' article are not only of "historical value." They were, or should have been, of great practical importance. Indeed, <u>if</u> the imperialist struggle for colonies and spheres of influence is disregarded as a factor in the approaching world war, <u>if</u> the imperialist conflicts between England and Germany are also disregarded, <u>if</u> Germany's annexation of Alsace-Lorraine is minimized as a war factor in comparison with the yearning of Russian tsarism for Constantinople, which is depicted as a more important and even decisive war factor, <u>if</u>, finally, Russian tsarism represents the last bulwark of European reaction—then isn't it clear that, say, the war of bourgeois Germany against tsarist Russia is not an imperialist war, not a predatory war, not an antipopular war, but a war of liberation or almost a war of liberation?

There can scarcely be any doubt that this way of thinking must have contributed to the betrayal by German social democrats on 4 August 1914, when they decided to vote for military credits and proclaimed the slogan of defending the bourgeois fatherland against tsarist Russia, against "Russian barbarism" and so forth.

Characteristically, in the sections of his letters to Bebel in 1891 (a year after Engels' article was published) that dealt with the prospects of imminent war, Engels says outright that "victory for Germany, therefore, is victory for the revolution," that "if Russia starts a war, then onward against the Russians and their allies, no matter who they are!"

It is clear that this way of thinking leaves no room for revolutionary defeatism, for the Leninist policy of transforming the imperialist war into a civil war.

Those are the facts with regard to the shortcomings in Engels' article.

Engels, alarmed by the French-Russian alliance that was being formed at the time (1890–1891) and was aimed against the Austrian-German coalition, apparently set himself the goal of attacking the foreign policy of Russian tsarism in his article and stripping it of any credibility in the eyes of public opinion in Europe, and above all in England. But in pursuing this goal he overlooked a number of other highly important and even crucial points, which resulted in the one-sidedness of the article.

After all of the foregoing, is it worthwhile to print Engels' article in our militant organ, *Bolshevik*, as a source of guidance, or at any rate as a profoundly instructive article, since it is clear that printing it in *Bolshevik* is tantamount to tacitly giving it precisely this kind of recommendation?

I don't think it is worthwhile.

I. Stalin.

19 July 1934.

· 4 ·

Stalin to members of the Politburo, Adoratsky, Knorin, Stetsky,
Zinoviev, and Pospelov
5 August 1934
F. 17, op. 3, d. 950, ll. 87–89. Typewritten original.

To members of the POLITBURO,
Comrades Adoratsky, Knorin, Stetsky, Zinoviev, Pospelov.

Issue 13–14 of *Bolshevik* carried the article "From the Editors" (pages 86–90), which comments on F. Engels' letter to Ioan Nedejde in January 1888 and in which Engels' views on the future war have been obviously falsified.

The editors of *Bolshevik*, using Engels' letter to the Romanian Ioan Nedejde in 1888 in improper and tricky ways, assert in their article that:

a) Engels "fully adheres to a defeatist position," a position favoring the defeat "even of his bourgeois fatherland";

b) "Lenin advocated a similar position in the war of 1914";

c) Lenin, therefore, did not provide anything substantially new in the matter of defining the character of the war and the policy of Marxists toward the war.

Consequently:

1. The editors of *Bolshevik* concealed from readers the fact that Engels

failed to comprehend the imperialist character of the future war, which is clear both from Engels' letter to Ioan Nedejde (1888) and from his article "The Foreign Policy of Russian Tsarism" (1890), as well as his well-known letters to Bebel (1891). To comprehend the depth of the difference between the views of Lenin and Engels on the character of the war, one need only compare with these works by Engels the tables compiled by Lenin and entitled "An Experiment in Consolidating the Main Data of World History Since 1870," which were printed in the same issue of *Bolshevik* and in which Lenin cites the imperialist struggle among the great powers (including Germany) for <u>colonies and spheres of influence</u>, as early as the beginning of the 1880s, as a cause of the war.

2. The editors of *Bolshevik* <u>concealed</u> from readers the fact that two or three years after his letter to Ioan Nedejde, when the French-Russian alliance had begun to take shape as a counterweight to the alliance of Germany, Austria, and Italy, Engels <u>changed</u> his attitude toward the war and began no longer to speak out in favor of Germany's defeat but rather in favor of its <u>victory</u> (see especially Engels' letters to Bebel in 1891), and Engels retained this attitude, as is well known, until the end of his life.

3. The editors of *Bolshevik* <u>concealed</u> from readers the fact that there is no way to equate the <u>passive</u> defeatism of Engels ("wishing for all of them to be beaten"), which he later repudiated, as has been mentioned, in <u>favor of defensism</u>, with the <u>active</u> defeatism of Lenin ("transformation of the imperialist war into a civil war").

4. The editors of *Bolshevik* <u>concealed</u> from readers the indisputable fact that Lenin and Lenin alone provided a <u>fundamentally new</u> and uniquely correct orientation both on the question of the <u>character</u> of the war and on the question of the policy of Marxists toward the war.

Those are the facts with regard to the tricks by the editors of *Bolshevik*.

Only idiots can harbor any doubts that Engels was and remains our teacher. But this by no means implies we must paper over Engels' mistakes, that we must conceal them and—especially—pass them off as incontestable truths. That kind of policy would be a policy of lies and deceit. Nothing is so contrary to the spirit of Marxism and the precepts of Marx and Engels as such a policy, which is unworthy of Marxists. Marx and Engels said themselves that Marxism is not a dogma but a guide to action. This accounts for the fact that Marx and Engels themselves repeatedly amended and supplemented various propositions in their works. Hence Marx and Engels regarded as paramount in their doctrine not the letter or individual propositions but the spirit of this doctrine, its method. It could not be otherwise, since if Marxism had a different orientation its <u>further development</u> would be inconceivable, because Marxism would turn into a mummy. It could not be otherwise because in that case Lenin would not be the person who not only restored Marxism but also <u>developed it further</u>.

And if Lenin developed it further, then is it not clear that we must not be afraid of crediting the <u>new propositions</u> on the war to Lenin, which rightfully belong to him and which he provided, in the interests of the further development of Marxism?

There can be no doubt that only disrespect for Marxism and its founders could have prompted the editors of *Bolshevik* to pursue a policy of papering over and clouding the facts, a policy of belittling Lenin's role in working out a <u>new</u> orientation for Marxism on the issues of the character of the war and the policy of Marxists toward the war.

I think the editors of *Bolshevik* in their article tacitly proceed from a Trotskyite-Menshevik orientation, according to which Engels is alleged to have said <u>everything</u> that needed to be said about the war, its character and the policy of Marxists toward the war, and all Marxists need to do is restore what Engels said and apply it in practice. Lenin is alleged to have done precisely that by taking "a similar position in the war of 1914," and whoever disagrees with this [the editors imply] is revising Marxism and is not a genuine Marxist.

As is well known, the Trotskyite-Menshevik gentlemen proceeded from the same orientation when they rejected the possibility that socialism could triumph in a single country, by referring to the fact that Engels in *The Principles of Communism* (1846) rejects such a possibility; Engels, according to them, had already said everything that needed to be said, and whoever continued to insist on the possibility that socialism could triumph in a single country was revising Marxism.

It is hardly necessary to prove that this orientation is completely rotten and anti-Marxist, because it dooms Marxism and its method to stagnate and vegetate by sacrificing it to a literal interpretation.

I think this incorrect orientation is the root of the error by the editors of *Bolshevik*.

It seems to me that the journal *Bolshevik* is falling (or has already fallen) into unreliable hands. Even the fact that the editors attempted to publish Engels' article "On the Foreign Policy of Russian Tsarism" in *Bolshevik* as a source of guidance—even this fact does not speak in favor of the editors. The CC of the VKP(b), as is known, intervened in time and halted the attempt. But this event did not have a beneficial effect on the editors. Even the opposite happened: evidently out of spite at the instructions from the CC, the editors published, already <u>after</u> the warning from the CC, an article that can only be characterized as an attempt to mislead readers with regard to the actual position of the CC. And after all, *Bolshevik* is an organ of the CC.

I think the time has come to put an end to this situation.

I. Stalin.

5 August 1934.

· 5 ·

Ehrenburg to Stalin
13 September
F. 558, op. 1, d. 4591, ll. 4–7. Typewritten original.

Odessa, 13 September [1934]
Esteemed Iosif Vissarionovich!

I hesitated for a long time about whether I should write this letter to you. Your time is precious not only to you but to all of us. If I finally decided to write to you, it is because the issue of organizing the Western and American literature that is dear to us can hardly be resolved without your participation.

You have probably noticed the extent to which the makeup of the foreign delegations that attended the Writers' Congress failed to measure up to the weight and significance of the event.[1] With the exception of two Frenchmen—Malraux and J.-R. Bloch—the Czech poet Nezval, the two German fiction writers (not first-rate, but still gifted) Pluvier and O. M. Graf, and, finally, the Dane [Andersen] Nexö, there were no representatives of Western European or American literature of any importance. This is partly attributable to the fact that the invitations to the congress, which for some reason were sent out not by the Organizational Committee but by MORP [International Association of Revolutionary Writers], were composed in an extraordinarily inept manner. The people they invited were by no means those who should have been invited. But the main reason for the low-level makeup of the foreign delegations at our congress is the entire literary policy of MORP and its national sections, which can only be described as typical of RAPP [Russian Association of Proletarian Writers].

The "International Congress of Revolutionary Writers," which was held in Kharkov a few years ago, proceeded from start to finish under the influence of RAPP. Since then 23 April has occurred.[2] For us this is a sharp boundary between two eras of our literary life. Unfortunately, 23 April has failed to change the policy of MORP.

Who is running MORP? A few third-rate Hungarian, Polish, and German writers. They have been living in our country for a long time, but this settled way of life has had no effect either on their psyche or on their creative work. And they have lost touch with Western life once and for all, and they do not see the profound changes that have taken place in the mainstream of the Western intelligentsia since the fascist offensive.

I will cite several examples. The "RAPP-ites" in America are alienating from us such significant writers as Dreiser, Sherwood Anderson, and Dos Passos. They rebuke novelists for the "inconsistent" political line of some characters in their literary works, and I am not talking about criticism but about charges of renegadism and so forth.

The organ of the French section of MORP, the journal *Commune,* conducted a survey among writers. The writers responded, but the responses were printed this way: twenty lines by the writer, and then forty of clarifications by the editors in extremely crude and comprehensive personal attacks. Such conduct by the MORP section alienates from us even the writers we hold most dear: André Gide, Malraux, Roger Martin du Gard, Fernandez, and others. Suffice it to say that even Barbusse is in the position of someone barely tolerated.

As for the Germans, Radek in his concluding remarks at the congress clearly displayed the narrow-mindedness and, worse, the self-conceit of the literary circles that have seized the leadership of German revolutionary literature.

I could add that the same thing is occurring in other countries as well. In Czecho-Slovakia, Vančura and Olbracht have been repudiated. In Spain, there are a few snobs and adolescents in the organization. In the Scandinavian countries, antifascist writers are treated as "mortal enemies." And so on.

The situation in the West right now is extremely favorable: the majority of the most important, talented, and best-known writers will sincerely follow us against fascism. If a broad, antifascist writers' organization existed instead of MORP, the writers who would immediately join it would include Romain Rolland, André Gide, Malraux, J.-R. Bloch, Barbusse, Vildrac, Durtain, Giono, Fernandez, Roger Martin du Gard, Geenaux, Chanson, Alain, Aragon; Thomas Mann, Heinrich Mann, Feuchtwanger, Leonhard Frank, Glezer, Pluvier, Graf, Mehring; Dreiser, Sherwood Anderson, Dos Passos, Gold, and others. I have listed only three countries, and those authors who are well known in our country from the translations of their books. I will say it more succinctly—with rare exceptions, such an organization would unite all important and uncorrupted writers.

The political program of such an organization must be very broad and at the same time precise:

1) A struggle against fascism
2) Active defense of the USSR.

The Western European and American intelligentsia pays heed to "big names." So the value of a large antifascist organization that is headed by famous writers would be extremely high.

But the establishment of such an antifascist writers' organization requires, first, the approval of our leading bodies and, second, the dissolution or radical reorganization of both MORP and its national sections.

The All-Union Writers' Congress will play an enormous role in attracting the Western European intelligentsia to us. The full range of issues on

culture and craftmanship were raised for the first time at the congress, commensurate with the growth of our country and its right to worldwide spiritual hegemony. At the same time the congress showed the extent to which our writers, both nonparty people and party members, have united around the party in its creative work and its preparations for the country's defense. The way our writers greeted the delegates of the Red Army will enable the Western intelligentsia to comprehend our position inside the country and our organic connection with the task of defending it.

Similarly, the disagreements that occurred at the congress on questions of creativity and technique will show the same intelligentsia how amazingly fast we have grown in recent years. The majority of the congress warmly applauded the reports or speeches that insisted on raising the cultural level, on overcoming provincialism, and on the necessity of exploration and inventiveness. These speeches and applause also generated warm sympathy among the foreign writers who attended the congress. One can safely say that the work of the congress paved the way for the creation of a large, antifascist organization of Western and American writers.

Forgive me, Iosif Vissarionovich, for taking up so much of your time, but it seems to me that, as well as its importance for our literature as such, an organization of this kind will now be of militant, general political importance.

With deep respect, Ilya Ehrenburg.

1. See note 8 to document 95.
2. See document 89.

Glossary of Terms and Abbreviations

APRF	Arkhiv prezidenta Rossiiskoi Federatsii (Archive of the President of the Russian Federation)
Cheka	Chrezvychainaia komissiia (Extraordinary Commission) [predecessor to OGPU]
Chekist	Functionary of Cheka, used of OGPU functionaries generally
delo (d., plural dd.)	file (in an archive)
DVP	*Dokumenty vneshnei politiki SSSR* (Documents of Foreign Policy of USSR), (Moscow, 1968–73), vols. XIV–XIX
fond (f.)	collection (in an archive)
GARF	Gosudarstvennyi arkhiv Rossiiskoi Federatsii (State Archive of the Russian Federation)
Gosbank	Gosudarstvennyi bank SSSR (State Bank of the USSR)
Gosplan	Gosudarstvennaia planovaia komissiia SSSR (State Planning Commission of the USSR)
GPU	Gosudarstvennoe politicheskoe upravlenie (State Political Administration), (local or republican) political police
Komsomol	Kommunisticheskii soiuz molodyozhi (Young Communist League)
list (l., plural ll.)	folio
MORP	Mezhdunarodnoe obedinenie revoliutsionnykh pisatelei (International Association of Revolutionary Writers)
NKVD	Narodnyi komissariat vnutrennykh del (People's Commissariat of Internal Affairs), incorporating the political police from 1934

OGIZ	Obedinenie gosudarstvennykh izdatelstv (Corporation of State Publishers)
OGPU	Obedinyonnoe gosudarstvennoe politicheskoe upravlenie (Unified State Political Administration), political police
opis (op.)	catalogue or inventory (for an archival collection)
Orgburo	Organizational Bureau of the Central Committee of the Communist Party
Osoaviakhim	Obshchestvo sodeistviia oborone, aviatsionnomu i khimicheskomu stroitelstvu v SSSR (The Society to Assist Defense, and Aviation and Chemical Development)
RAPP	Rossiiskaia assotsiatsiia proletarskikh pisatelei (Russian Association of Proletarian Writers)
RGASPI	Rossiiskii gosudarstvennyi arkhiv sotsialno-politicheskoi istorii (Russian State Archive of Social and Political History); formerly RTsKhIDNI; formerly Central Party Archive
RSFSR	Rossiiskaia Sovetskaia Federativnaia Sotsialisticheskaia Respublika (Russian Soviet Federative Socialist Republic)
Sovnarkom	Sovet narodnykh komissarov (Council of People's Commissars of the USSR or of a republic)
STO	Sovet Truda i Oborony SSSR (Council of Labor and Defense of the USSR), a subcommittee of Sovnarkom of the USSR
TASS	Telegrafnoe agentstvo Sovetskogo Soiuza (Telegraph Agency of the Soviet Union), the main Soviet news agency
Tsentrosoiuz	Vsesoiuznyi tsentralnyi soiuz potrebitelskikh obshchestv (All-Union Central Union of Consumer [Cooperative] Societies)
TsIK	Tsentralnyi Ispolnitelnyi Komitet SSSR (Central Executive Committee [of Soviets] of the USSR)
Vesenkha	Vysshii sovet narodnogo khoziaistva SSSR (Supreme Council of the National Economy of the USSR), responsible for the administration of industry until the end of 1931
VKP(b)	Vsesoiuznaia kommunisticheskaia partiia (bolshevikov) (All-Union Communist Party [Bolsheviks])

RUSSIAN TERMS AND ABBREVIATIONS GIVEN IN ENGLISH

| AUCCTU | All-Union Central Council of Trade Unions (Vsesoiuznyi tsentralnyi sovet professionalnykh soiuzov) |
| CC | Central Committee (of the Communist Party) (Tsentralnyi komitet) |

CCC	Central Control Commission (of the Communist Party) (Tsentralnaia kontrolnaia komissiia)
Central Executive Committee—*see* TsIK	
CER	Chinese Eastern Railroad (Kitaisko-Vostochnaia zheleznaia doroga)
chief administration	*glavnoe upravlenie (glavk)*, subdivision of a PC
collective farm	*kollektivnoe khoziastvo* (kolkhoz)
Comintern	Communist International (Kommunisticheskii internatsional)
Commission of Defense	Komissiia oborony, a joint commission of Politburo and Sovnarkom
Committee of Reserves	Komitet rezervov, a subcommittee of Sovnarkom
corporation(s)	*obedinenie* (pl. *obedineniia)*—replaced chief administrations and syndicates in 1930; later gradually replaced again by chief administrations
Council of Labor and Defense	Sovet Truda i Oborony, a subcommittee of Sovnarkom
deliveries	*postavki* (compulsory deliveries [of agricultural products])
district	*raion*
executive committee	*ispolnitelnyi komitet* (usually of a soviet)
Far Eastern Commission	Dalnevostochnaia komissiia (of the Politburo)
Fulfillment Commission	Komissiia ispolneniia (of Sovnarkom)
labor-day	*trudoden* (unit of remuneration for collective farmers)
mobilization reserve	*mobilizatsionnyi fond*
MPR	Mongolian People's Republic (Mongolskaia narodnaia respublika)
MTS	*mashino-traktornaia stantsiia* (Machine-Tractor Station)
PC	People's Commissariat (Narodnyi komissariat)
PC for Supply	Narodnyi komissariat snabzheniia
PC of Agriculture	Narodnyi komissariat zemledeliia
PC of Communications	Narodnyi komissariat sviazi
PC of Defense	Narodnyi komissariat oborony
PC of Finance	Narodnyi komissariat finansov
PC of Foreign Affairs	Narodnyi komissariat inostrannykh del
PC of Foreign Trade	Narodnyi komissariat vneshnei torgovli
PC of Heavy Industry	Narodnyi komissariat tiazheloi promyshlennosti

PC of Internal Trade	Narodnyi komissariat vnutrennei torgovli
PC of Justice	Narodnyi komissariat iustitsii
PC of Light Industry	Narodnyi komissariat legkoi promyshlennosti
PC of Local Industry	Narodny komissariat mestnoi promyshlennosti
PC of Military and Naval Affairs	Narodnyi komissariat po voennym i morskim delam
PC of State Farms	Narodnyi komissariat zernovykh i zhivotnovodcheskikh sovkhozov
PC of the Food Industry	Narodnyi komissariat pishchevoi promyshlennosti
PC of the Timber Industry	Narodnyi komissariat lesnoi promyshlennosti
PC of Transport	Narodnyi komissariat putei soobshcheniia
PC of Water Transport	Narodnyi komissariat vodnogo transporta
PCC	Party Control Commission (Komissiia partiinogo kontrolia)
pood	16.38 kilograms (0.01638 tons)
procurements	*zagotovki* (of agricultural products)
purchases	*zakupki* (of agricultural products)—see the introduction to Chapter 4
region	*oblast* or *krai*
Special Conference	Osoboe soveshchanie, attached to the NKVD
state farm	*sovetskoe khoziaistvo* (sovkhoz)
Transport Commission	Transportnaia komissiia (of the Politburo)
tsentner	0.1 ton
untouchable reserve	*neprikosnovennyi fond*

Brief Biographies

Abakumov, Ye. T. (1895–1953)—Became party member, 1918. Appointed deputy director of Metrostroy (the Subway Construction Project), 1933; director, 1935–39.

Adler, Friedrich (1879–1960)—Leader of the Austrian Social Democrats and a leader of the Labor and Socialist International.

Adoratsky, V. V. (1878–1945)—Became party member, 1904. Director of the Institute of Marx-Engels-Lenin under the CC, 1931–39.

Afinogenov, A. N. (1904–1941)—Became party member, 1922. Russian, Soviet playwright.

Agranov, Ya. S. (1893–1938)—Became party member, 1915. First deputy people's commissar of internal affairs, 1934–37. Executed.

Agranovsky, A. D. (1896–1951)—Journalist. Worked for the newspapers *Pravda* and *Izvestia* in the 1920s and 1930s.

Akulinushkin, P. D. (1899–1937)—Became party member, 1917. Appointed a deputy head of the personnel assignment department (*raspredotdel*) of the CC, July 1932. Representative of the Party Control Committee in the Odessa Region, 1934. Appointed first secretary of the Krasnoiarsk Regional Party Committee, December 1934. Executed.

Akulov, I. A. (1888–1937)—Became party member, 1907. Appointed a deputy people's commissar of the Workers' and Peasants' Inspectorate and a member of the presidium of the party Central Control Commission, 1929. Appointed a deputy chairman of the OGPU, 1931. Appointed a prosecutor of the USSR, 1933. Executed.

Alain (Emile-Auguste Chartier)—French literary critic and philosopher.

Aleksandrovsky, S. S. (1889–1949)—Soviet diplomat. Counselor at the Soviet mission in Germany, 1931–33.

Alksnis, Ya. I. (1897–1938)—Became party member, 1916. Appointed commander of the air force of the Workers' and Peasants' Red Army, June 1931. Executed.

Alliluyeva, N. S. (1901–1932)—Became party member, 1918. Wife of Joseph (I. V.) Stalin. Student at the Industrial Academy, 1929–32. Committed suicide.

Alliluyeva, S. I. (b. 1926)—Daughter of Joseph (I. V.) Stalin.

Alphand, Charles—French ambassador to the USSR, 1936.

Anderson, Sherwood (1876–1941)—American writer.

Andreev, A. A. (1895–1971)—Became party member, 1914; member of the Politburo, 1932–52. Chairman of the Central Control Commission and people's commissar of the Workers' and Peasants' Inspectorate, 1930–31. People's commissar of transport, 1931–35.

Andreev, A. N. (1901–38)—Inspector-dispatcher, then deputy director, of the southern section of the Central Operations Administration of the PC of Transport. Appointed director of the Moscow–Donets Basin Railroad, September 1936. Executed.

Andreichin, G. I. (1894–?)—Became party member, 1920. Manager of the Moscow office of Amtorg, the Soviet trading corporation in the United States, 1932.

Anisimov, I. I. (1899–1966)—Became party member, 1939. Soviet literary critic.

Antipov, N. K. (1894–1938)—Became party member, 1912. People's commissar of postal and telegraph services, 1928–31. A deputy people's commissar of the Workers' and Peasants' Inspectorate, 1931–34. Appointed a deputy chairman of the Soviet Control Commission, 1934; appointed chairman, 1935. Executed.

Anvelt, Ya. Ya. (1884–1937)—Appointed a deputy chairman of the board of the Civil Aviation Corporation, November 1930. Repressed.

Aragon, Louis (1897–1982)—French writer and public figure.

Arkus, G. M. (1896–1936)—A deputy chairman of the board of Gosbank, 1931–36. Executed.

Averbakh, L. L. (1903–1938)—Became party member, 1919. Appointed editor of the journals *Na literaturnom postu* (At the Literary Post) and *Vestnik inostrannoy literatury* (Herald of Foreign Literature), 1929. Executed.

Azaña (y Díaz), Manuel (1880–1940)—Head of government of the Spanish Republic, 1931–33 and February–May 1936; president, 1936–39.

Babel, I. E. (1894–1941)—Russian, Soviet writer. Executed.

Bagdatiev—Member of the presidium of Gosplan, 1931.

Bagirov, M.-D. A. (1896–1956)—Became party member, 1917. Appointed an executive instructor of the CC and chairman of the Sovnarkom of the Azerbaijan SSR, 1932. First secretary of the CC of the Communist Party (Bolsheviks) of Azerbaijan, 1933–53. Executed.

Bakaev, I. P. (1887–1936)—Became party member, 1906. A leader of the opposition, 1925–27. Expelled from the party, 1927; after his reinstatement in the party he did economic work. Expelled again from the party and convicted in 1935 of complicity in the assassination of Kirov. Sentenced to death at the Kamenev-Zinoviev trial, August 1936.

Balitsky, V. A. (1892–1937)—Became party member, 1915. A deputy chairman of the OGPU, 1931–32. Appointed chairman of the Ukrainian GPU, 1933; people's commissar of internal affairs of the Ukrainian SSR, 1934–37. Executed.

Baranov, P. I. (1892–1933)—Became party member, 1912. Commander of the air force, 1924–31. Appointed deputy chairman of Vesenkha for the Main Administration of the Aircraft Industry, December 1931. Died in an airplane crash.

Barbusse, Henri (1873–1935)—French writer and public figure.

Barrès, General—Inspector general of French aviation in 1933.

Barthou, Jean-Louis (1862–1934)—Minister of foreign affairs of France, 1934.

Basseches, Nikolaus—Correspondent for the Austrian newspaper *Neue Freie Presse.*

Bauer, Otto (1882–1938)—A leader of the Austrian Social Democrats and the Second International.

Bauman, K. Ya. (1892–1937)—Became party member, 1907. First secretary of the Central Asian Bureau of the CC, 1931–34; head of the planning, trade, and finance department, then of the science department of the CC, 1934–1936. Died in prison.

Bebel, August (1840–1913)—A founder and the leader of the German Social-Democratic Party and the Second International.

Beck, Colonel Josef (1894–1944)—Minister of foreign affairs of Poland, 1932–39.

Bedny, Demian (1883–1945)—Became party member, 1912. Russian, Soviet writer.

Belenky, M. N. (1891–1938)—Became party member, 1920. A deputy people's commissar of supply, 1931–34. A deputy people's commissar of the food industry, 1934–36. Executed.

Bergavinov, S. A. (1899–1937)—Became party member, 1917. First secretary of the Far Eastern Regional Party Committee, 1931–33. Died in a prison hospital.

Beria, L. P. (1899–1953)—Became party member, 1917. Appointed first secretary of the CC of the Communist Party of Georgia, 1931; appointed, concurrently, secretary of the Transcaucasian Regional Party Committee, 1932. Executed.

Berman-Yurin, K. B.—Functionary of the Communist Party of Germany, 1923–33; after moving to the USSR, was consulting editor for the foreign department of the newspaper *Za industrializatsiiu* (For Industrialization), 1933–36. Sentenced to death at the Kamenev-Zinoviev trial, August 1936.

Blagonravov, G. I. (1895–1943)—Became party member, 1917. A deputy people's commissar of transport, 1931–35. Executed.

Bliukher, V. K. (1890–1938)—Became party member, 1916. Commander of the Far Eastern Army, 1929–38. Died while under investigation.

Bloch, Jean-Richard (1884–1947)—French writer and public figure.

Boev, I. V.—A deputy people's commissar of foreign trade, 1932–33; trade representative in the United States, 1934–36. Executed.

Bogdanov, P. A. (1882–1939)—Became party member, 1905. Head of Amtorg, Soviet trade corporation in the United States, 1930–34. Executed.

Bologoi—Soviet military attaché in Japan.

Boncour, Paul—*see* Paul-Boncour.

Bron, S. G. (1887–1938)—Trade representative in Great Britain, 1930–31; chairman of the All-Union Chamber of Commerce, 1932. Executed.

Brüning, Heinrich (1885–1970)—German chancellor, March 1930–May 1932.

Bubnov, A. S. (1884–1938)—Became party member, 1903. People's commissar of education of the RSFSR, 1929–37. Executed.

Bukharin, N. I. (1888–1938)—Became party member, 1906. Member of the Politburo, 1924–29, a leader of the "right deviation." Appointed head of the science and technology sector of Vesenkha, 1929; member of the collegium of the PC of Heavy Industry, 1932–34; and editor of *Izvestiia*, 1934–36. Executed.

Bullitt, William Christian (1891–1967)—American diplomat. First US ambassador to the USSR, 1933–36.

Bykov, L. N.—Major general in the tsarist army. Instructor at the Moscow Institute of Physical Fitness during the 1930s. Executed.

Caballero—*see* Largo Caballero.

Caquot, A.—French scientist and engineer.

Chechulin, S. F. (1897–1970)—Appointed a staff member of the secret department of the CC, 1930.

Chernov, M. A. (1891–1938)—Joined the Social-Democratic movement, 1909; became party member, 1920. Chairman of Komzag, the Committee for Procurements of Agricultural Products attached to Sovnarkom, 1933–34; people's commissar of agriculture, 1934–37. Executed.

Chesheiko-Sokhatsky, Ye. (1892–1933)—Appointed first secretary of the Communist Party of Western Ukraine, a member of the Politburo of the CC of the Communist Party of Poland, and party representative in the Executive Committee of the Comintern under the pseudonym Yu. Bratkovsky, 1929. Repressed.

Chubar, V. Ya. (1891–1939)—Became party member, 1907; elected candidate member of the Politburo, 1926; member of the Politburo, 1935–38. Chairman of the Sovnarkom of the Ukraine, 1923–34; appointed a deputy chairman of Sovnarkom of the USSR and the Council of Labor and Defense, 1934. Executed.

Cooper, Colonel Hugh L.—American engineer, consultant to Dnieper dam project. Chairman of the Russian-American Chamber in New York, 1932.

Cot, Pierre (1895–1977)—French minister of aviation, 1933–34 and 1936–38.

Delbos, Yvon (1885–1956)—French government and political leader. Leader of the Radical Party, 1932–40. Minister of foreign affairs, 1936–38.

Deribas, T. D. (1883–1938)—Became party member, 1903. NKVD plenipotentiary in the Far East Region, 1935–37. Executed.

Diakonov, S. S. (1898–1938)—Became party member, 1920. Appointed director of the Gorky auto plant, 1932. Executed.

Dimitrov, Georgi (1882–1949)—Leader of the Bulgarian and international Communist movement. Principal defendant in the Reichstag fire trial, 1933. After his acquittal he moved to the USSR. Appointed general secretary of the Executive Committee of the Comintern, 1935.

Dirksen, Herbert (1882–1955)—German ambassador to the USSR, 1928–33; German ambassador to Japan, 1933–38.

Dos Passos, John (1896–1970)—American novelist.

Dovgalevsky, V. S. (1885–1934)—Became party member, 1908. Plenipotentiary of the USSR to France, 1927–34.

Dreiser, Theodore (1871–1945)—American writer.

Dreitser, Ye. A. (1894–1936)—Became party member, 1919. Active participant in the opposition during the 1920s. Expelled from the party, 1928. After his reinstatement in the party in 1929 he did economic work; before his arrest in July 1936 he was deputy director of the Magnesite plant in the Cheliabinsk Region. Sentenced to death at the Kamenev-Zinoviev trial, August 1936.

Durtain, Luc (1881–1959)—French writer.

Dvinsky, B. A. (1894–1973)—Became party member, 1920. Aide to Stalin, 1928–30, a deputy head of secret department of the CC VKP, 1930–34, and of the special sector of the CC, 1934–37.

Dybets, S. S. (1887–?)—Became party member, 1918. Director of the Chief Administration of the Automobile and Tractor Industry of the PC of Heavy Industry, 1935. Repressed.

Eden, Anthony (1897–1977)—Lord Privy Seal, 1934–36; British foreign secretary, 1935–38.

Ehrenburg, I. G. (1891–1967)—Russian, Soviet writer.

Eikhe, R. I. (1890–1940)—Became party member, 1905. First secretary of the Siberian and Western Siberian Regional Party Committees, 1929–37. Executed.

Eisenstein, S. M. (1898–1948)—Soviet film director.

Eismont, N. B. (1891–1935)—Became party member, 1907. People's commissar of trade of the RSFSR, 1926–33; concurrently a deputy people's commissar of foreign and internal trade, 1926–30; a deputy people's commissar for supply, 1930–33. Arrested, 1933. Released, 1935. Died in an automobile accident.

Eliava, Sh. Z. (1883–1937)—Became party member, 1904. A deputy people's commissar of foreign trade, 1931–36; a deputy people's commissar of light industry, 1936–37. Repressed.

Filin, A. I. (1903–1941)—Became party member, 1922. Test pilot, crew member on M. M. Gromov's record-setting flight.

Florinsky, D. T. (1899–?)—Manager of the protocol section of the PC of Foreign Affairs, 1933–34. Repressed.

Fomin, I. A. (1872–1936)—Soviet architect.

Fomin, V. V. (1884–1938)—Became party member, 1910. A deputy people's commissar of water transport, 1931–35. Executed.

Fridrikhson, L. Kh. (1889–1937?)—Became party member, 1908. Appointed deputy trade representative for exports in Berlin, January 1932; trade representative in Germany from 1933. Repressed.

Fritz-David (Krugliansky), I. I.—Member of the Communist Party of Germany. Arrived in the USSR in 1933 and until his arrest in 1936 worked for the Executive Committee of the Comintern and as a consultant for *Pravda*. Sentenced to death at the Kamenev-Zinoviev trial, August 1936.

Frumkin, M. I. (1878–1938)—Became party member, 1898. A deputy people's commissar of finance, 1926–29. Member of the presidium of Vesenkha, 1931; then member of the collegium of the PC of Transport; a deputy people's commissar of foreign trade, 1932–35. Executed.

Gamarnik, Ya. B. (1894–1937)—Became party member, 1916. Chief of the Political Administration of the Workers' and Peasants' Red Army, 1929–37; first deputy people's commissar of military and naval affairs, 1930–34; first deputy commissar of defense, 1934–37. Under threat of arrest, he committed suicide.

Gide, André (1869–1951)—French writer.

Giono, Jean (1895–1970)—French writer.

Girs, N. K. (1820–1895)—Russian diplomat. Appointed minister of foreign affairs of Russia, 1882.

Glebova-Kameneva, T. I. (1895–?)—Became party member, 1923. Staff member of the Academy Publishing House. Wife of L. B. Kamenev. Repressed.

Gogol, N. V. (1809–1852)—Russian writer.

Gold, Michael (1894–1967)—American Communist writer.

Goldin, Ya. G.—Became party member, 1917. Appointed second secretary of the Lower Volga Regional Party Committee, January 1933; second secretary of the Stalingrad Regional Party Committee, 1934–37.

Goloshchokin, F. I. (1876–1941)—Became party member, 1903. First secretary of the Kazakh Regional Party Committee until January 1933. Executed.

Goltsman, A. Z. (1894–1933)—Became party member, 1917. Head of state Civil Aviation Corporation, from October 1930. Died in an air crash.

Goltsman, E. S. (1882–1936)—Became party member, 1903. Staff member of the PC of Foreign Trade. Sentenced to death at the Kamenev–Zinoviev trial, August 1936.

Golubenko, N. V. (1897–1937?)—Became party member, 1914. Head of construction of the Bogolepsk By-Product Coking Integrated Works (Donets Region), 1935–36. Repressed.

Gorchakov, A. M. (1798–1883)—Russian diplomat. Minister of foreign affairs of Russia, 1856–1882.

Gorkin, A. F. (1897–1988)—Became party member, 1916. Appointed a sector head and deputy head of the organizational and instructional department of the CC, 1932; appointed a sector head in the agricultural department of the CC, March 1933; first secretary of the Orenburg Regional Party Committee, 1934–7.

Gorky, A. M. (1868–1936)—Russian, Soviet writer.

Grabar, I. E. (1871–1960)—Soviet painter and art critic; academician of the Academy of Sciences of the USSR.

Graf, Oskar Maria (1894–1967)—German writer.

Grichmanov, A. P. (1896–1939)—Became party member, 1917. Second secretary of the Far Eastern Regional Party Committee, February 1932–July 1933; head of the political sector of the MTS and deputy head of agricultural administration, Central Volga Region, 1933–36. Repressed..

Grinko, G. F. (1890–1938)—Became party member, 1919. People's commissar of finance, 1930–37. Executed.

Gromov, M. M. (1899–1985)—Became party member, 1941. Soviet aviator. In 1934 set world long-distance record for a single flight (more than 12,000 kilometers).

Gronsky, I. M. (1894–1985)—Became party member, 1918. Executive editor of the newspaper *Izvestia*, 1931–February 1934.

Gubkin, I. M. (1871–1939)—Became party member, 1921. Geologist, academician of the Academy of Sciences of the USSR.

Guéhenno, Jean (Marcel Jules Marie) (1890–?)—French writer.

Gurevich, A. I. (1896–1937?)—Became party member, 1916. Appointed a member of the presidium of Vesenkha, 1930; director of the Chief Administration of the Metallurgical Industry, 1932–36; a deputy people's commissar of heavy industry from December 1936. Repressed.

Gurevich, D. S. (1899–?)—Became party member, 1917. Appointed a secretary of the Central Volga Regional Party Committee, 1930.

Gurevich, M. G. (1890–?)—Became party member, 1919. Head of the foreign-policy sector of Vesenkha, 1929–31; trade representative in France, 1931–34.

Guseinov, Mirza D. B. ogly (1894–1938)—Became party member, 1918. First secretary of the CC of the Communist Party of Tajikistan, then worked at the PC of Education of the RSFSR, 1930–33. Repressed.

Hayashi—Appointed war minister of Japan, January 1934.

Herriot, Edouard (1872–1957)—Leader of the French Radical Party; prime minister of France, 1932.

Hirota, Koki (1878–1948)—Japanese ambassador to the USSR, 1930–32; minister of foreign affairs, 1933–38; concurrently prime minister of Japan, 1934–38.

Hoover, Herbert (1874–1964)—President of the United States, 1929–33.

Iaffe—scientist, staff member of the Military Medical Institute at Vladikha (Moscow Region).

Ibarruri, Dolores ("La Pasionaria") (1895–1991)—A secretary of the CC of the Communist Party of Spain, 1932–42.

Ilyin, N. I. (1884–1957)—Became party member, 1910. Member of the presidium of the Central Control Commission, 1925–34.

Ioan Nadejda—*see* Nedejde, Ion.

Iofan, B. M. (1891–1976)—Became party member, 1924. Soviet architect; designer of the plan for the Palace of Soviets in Moscow.

Isaev, U. D. (1899–1938)—Became party member, 1921. Chairman of the Sovnarkom of the Kazakh Autonomous Republic from 1931. Repressed.

Ivanchenko, Ya. P. (1891–?)—Became party member, 1917. Manager of the Eastern Steel Corporation, 1931–35.

Ivanov, V. I. (1893–1938)—Became party member, 1915. First secretary of the Northern Regional Party Committee, 1932–36. Executed.

Kabakov, I. D. (1891–1937)—Became party member, 1914; member of the CC, 1925–37. Appointed first secretary of the Urals Regional Party Committee, 1929 (which became the Sverdlovsk Regional Committee in 1934). Executed.

Kachalov, V. I. (1875–1948)—People's Artist of the USSR.

Kaganovich, M. M. (1888–1941)—Became party member, 1905. A deputy people's commissar of heavy industry, 1932–36. Under threat of arrest, he committed suicide.

Kalinin, M. I. (1875–1946)—Became party member, 1898; elected member of the Politburo, 1926. Chairman (President) of the All-Russian Central Executive Committee and the Central Executive Committee of the USSR, 1919–38.

Kalmanovich, M. I. (1888–1937)—Became party member, 1917. Chairman of the board of Gosbank and deputy people's commissar of finance, 1930–April 1934. People's commissar of state farms, 1934–37. Executed.

Kamenev, L. B. (1883–1936)—Became party member, 1901; member of the Politburo, 1919–25; an opposition leader. Repeatedly repressed. After his last reinstatement in the party in December 1933, until his arrest in December 1934, he was director of the Academy Publishing House. Sentenced to death at the Kamenev-Zinoviev trial, August 1936.

Kamensky, G. I. (1905–38)—Chief of the political department of the Moscow-Belorussian-Baltic Railroad, 1934; chief of the political department of the Moscow subway, 1935. Executed.

Kandelaki, D. V. (1892–1938)—Became party member, 1919. USSR trade representative in Germany, December 1934–April 1937. Executed.

Karakhan, L. M. (1889–1937)—Became party member, 1904. Deputy people's commissar of foreign affairs, 1927–34. Repressed.

Kartvelishvili, L. I. (1890–1938)—Became party member, 1910. Appointed secretary of the Transcaucasian Regional Party Committee, 1931; second secretary of the Western Siberian Regional Party Committee, 1932. Executed.

Katayama, Sen (1859–1933)—Cofounder of the Communist Party of Japan.

Kautsky, Karl (1854–1938)—A leader of the German Social Democrats and the Second International.

Kavtaradze, S. I. (1885–1971)—Became party member, 1903. First deputy prosecutor of the Supreme Court, 1924–27. Expelled from the party in 1927 for participating in the Trotskyite opposition; repressed. Reinstated in the party, 1941.

Kawakami—Japanese writer.

Kawoshe—Japanese naval officer.

Khalatov, A. B. (1896–1938)—Became party member, 1917. Chairman of the board of the State Publishing House and the Corporation of State Publishing Houses of the RSFSR, 1927–32. Executed.

Khalepsky, I. A. (1893–1938)—Became party member, 1918. Director of the Administration of the Motorization and Mechanization of the Red Army, 1929; appointed a member of the Revolutionary Military Council, 1932; director of the Motor Vehicle and Armored Tank Administration of the Red Army, 1935. Repressed.

Khataevich, M. M. (1893–1937)—Became party member, 1913. Secretary of the Central Volga Regional Party Committee, 1930–32; appointed first secretary of the Dnepropetrovsk Regional Party Committee, 1933. Executed.

Khinchuk, L. M. (1868–1944)—Became party member, 1920. USSR plenipotentiary in Germany, 1930–34. People's commissar of internal trade of the RSFSR, 1934–37. Executed.

Khlopliankin, M. I. (1892–1937)—Became party member, 1914. Deputy people's commissar for supply, 1930–34; head of the department for industrial goods and first deputy people's commissar of internal trade, 1832–36. Executed..

Kirov, S. M. (1886–1934)—Became party member, 1904, elected a member of the Politburo, 1930. Appointed first secretary of the Leningrad Regional and City Party Committees, 1926; concurrently a secretary of the CC, 1934. Murdered, 1 December 1934.

Kirshon, V. M. (1902–1938)—Became party member, 1920. Soviet writer and playwright. Executed.

Kishkin, V. A. (1883–1938)—Chief of the transport department of the OGPU, 1931; a deputy people's commissar of transport, October 1931–33; appointed director of the Chief Railroad Administration of Siberia and the Far East, March 1932; head of the transport department of OGPU, 1933–35; head of inspection group, then a deputy people's commissar of transport, 1935–37. Executed

Kleiner, I. M. (1893–1937)—Became party member, 1920. Appointed deputy chairman of Komzag, the Committee for Procurements of Agricultural Products attached to Sovnarkom, 1933; chairman, 1934–37. Repressed.

Kniazev, I. A. (1893–1937)—Became party member, 1918. Director of the Southern Urals Railroad, 1935–36. Repressed.

Knorin, V. G. (1890–1938)—Became party member, 1910. Director of the Party History Institute of Red Professors, 1932. Appointed deputy head of the department of party propaganda and agitation of the CC, 1935. Worked at the Executive Committee of the Comintern, 1928–35. Executed.

Kodatsky, I. F. (1893–1937)—Became party member, 1914. Appointed chairman of the Executive Committee of the Leningrad City Soviet, 1932. Repressed.

Koltsov, M. Ye. (1898–1940)—Became party member, 1918. Soviet journalist. Member of the editorial board of *Pravda,* 1934–35. Executed.

Komarov, N. P. (1886–1937)—Became party member, 1909. People's commissar of municipal economy of the RSFSR, 1931–37. Executed.

Koo, Dr Wellington (Ku Wei-chun)—Chinese diplomat.

Kork, A. I. (1887–1937)—Became party member, 1927. Troop commander of the Moscow Military District, 1929–35; appointed director of the Frunze Military Academy, 1935. Executed.

Korolyov, G. N. (1890–1938)—Became party member, 1919. Appointed director of the Chief Administration of the Aircraft Industry of the PC of Heavy Industry, September 1933–35; appointed director of the Rybinsk aircraft engine plant, 1935. Executed.

Kosarev, A. V. (1903–1939)—Became party member, 1919. Appointed general (first) secretary of the CC of the Komsomol, 1929. Executed.

Kosior, S. V. (1889–1939)—Became party member, 1907, elected a member of the

Politburo, 1930. General (first) secretary of the CC of the Communist Party of the Ukraine, 1928–38. Executed.

Kosko, G. K.—Director of the Gigant grain state farm, 1931–33.

Kovylkin, S. T. (1887–1943)—Became party member, 1905. Director of the Samara-Zlatoust Railroad; director of the Orenburg Railroad, 1936–37. Repressed.

Kozlov, I. I. (1896–?)—Became party member, 1918. Secretary of the Krasnaya Presnya district party committee, Moscow, 1930–31; secretary of the Eastern Siberian Regional Party Committee, 1932–33.

Kozlovsky, B. I. (1899–1975)—Became party member, 1918. Manager of Eastern Department 2 of the PC of Foreign Affairs, 1932.

Krestinsky, N. N. (1883–1938)—Became party member, 1903. A deputy people's commissar of foreign affairs, July 1930–March 1937. Executed.

Krinitsky, A. I. (1894–1937)—Became party member, 1915. A deputy people's commissar of the Workers' and Peasants' Inspectorate, 1930–32; appointed chief of the Political Administration and deputy people's commissar of agriculture, 1933. Executed.

Kritsman, L. N. (1890–1938)—Became party member, 1918. A deputy chairman of Gosplan, January 1931–January 1933. Repressed.

Kriuchkov, P. P. (1889–1938)—Secretary to A. M. Gorky. Executed.

Krupskaia, N. K. (1869–1939)—Became party member, 1898. Appointed deputy people's commissar of education of the RSFSR, 1929.

Ku Wei-chun—*see* Koo, Dr Wellington.

Kuibyshev, N. V. (1893–1938)—Became party member, 1918. Appointed head of the military inspectorate of the Workers' and Peasants' Inspectorate, November 1930. Appointed head of the naval group of the Party Control Commission, April 1935. Executed.

Kuibyshev, V. V. (1888–1935)—Became party member, 1904, elected a member of the Politburo, 1927. Chairman of Gosplan and deputy chairman of Sovnarkom and the Council of Labor and Defense, 1930–34; appointed chairman of the Soviet Control Committee and first deputy chairman of Sovnarkom and the Council of Labor and Defense, 1934.

Kurchevsky, L. V. (1891–1937)—Soviet artillery designer.

Kviring, E. I. (1888–1937)—Became party member, 1912. A deputy chairman of Gosplan, 1927–31; a deputy people's commissar of transport, 1931. Executed.

Lancaster, William—A director of the National City Bank of New York.

Lapidus, I. V.—Chief of the political department of the Moscow–Donets Basin Railroad, September 1936–June 1937.

Largo Caballero, Francisco (1869–1946)—Prime minister and minister of war of the Spanish Republic, 1936–37.

Laval, Pierre (1883–1945)—Prime minister of France, January 1931–January 1932 and June 1935–January 1936; minister of foreign affairs, October 1934–June 1935.

Leonov, F. G. (1892–1938)—Became party member, 1914. First secretary of the Eastern Siberian Regional Party Committee, 1930–33. In the CC reserves, 1933–34. Appointed deputy director for politics of the Northern Caucasus All-Union Grain Trust in Piatigorsk, April 1934. Executed.

Lepa, A. K. (1896–1938)—Became party member, 1914. First secretary of the Tatar Regional Party Committee, 1933–37. Executed.

Levchenko, N. I. (1894–1941)—Became party member, 1919. Director of the Donetsk Railroad, 1934; a deputy people's commissar of transport, 1936–37. Executed.

Levin, A. A. (1903–1938)—Became party member, 1919. Deputy head of the agricultural department of the CC until 1934, then deputy people's commissar of agriculture for politics. Second secretary of the Central Volga and Kuibyshev Regional Party Committees, 1934–37. Executed.

Levin, R. Ya. (1898–1937)—Became party member, 1915. Deputy people's commissar of finance, 1930–37. Executed.

Li Shao-keng—Chairman of the board of the Chinese Eastern Railroad, 1933.

Likhachev, I. A. (1896–1956)—Became party member, 1917. Director of the Moscow auto plant, 1926–39.

Litovsky, O. S. (1892–1971)—Became party member, 1918. Director of the Chief Administration for Supervision of Spectacles and Repertories, 1930–37. Repressed.

Litvinov, M. M. (1876–1951)—Became party member, 1898. People's commissar of foreign affairs, 1930–39.

Litvinov, Savely M.—Became party member, 1915. Brother of M. M. Litvinov. Staff member of USSR trade office in Berlin. Was prosecuted by French authorities in 1930 for fraud.

Liubimov, I. Ye. (1882–1937)—Became party member, 1902. A deputy people's commissar of foreign trade and trade representative in Germany, 1930–31, people's commissar of light industry, 1932–37. Executed.

Liven, Kh. A. (1777–1838)—Russian diplomat.

Livshits, Ya. A. (1896–1937)—Became party member, 1917. From 1930, successively director of the Southern, Northern Caucasus, and Moscow-Kursk Railroads. A deputy people's commissar of transport, 1935–36. Executed.

Lobov, S. S. (1888–1937)—Became party member, 1913. A deputy people's commissar for supply, 1930–32. People's commissar of the timber industry, 1932–36. People's commissar of the food industry of the RSFSR, 1936–37. Executed.

Loganovsky, M. A. (1895–1938)—Became party member, 1918. A deputy people's commissar of foreign trade, 1932–37. Executed.

Loginov, V. F. (1897–1938?)—Became party member, 1917. Manager of the Coke Trust in Kharkov, April 1933–36. Repressed.

Lominadze, V. V. (1897–1935)—Became party member, 1917; member of the CC, 1930. First secretary of the Transcaucasian Regional Party Committee, 1930. Did economic work, 1931–32. Secretary of the Maginitogorsk City Party Committee, 1933–35. Committed suicide under threat of arrest.

Lomov (Oppokov), G. I. (1888–1938)—Became party member, 1903. A deputy chairman of Gosplan, 1931–33; member of the Bureau of the Commission of Soviet Control, 1934–37. Executed.

Lukianov, S. S. (1889–?)—Editor in chief of the newspaper *Journal de Moscou*, April 1934–August 1935.

Lurie, M. I.—Became member of the Communist Party of Germany, 1922. Arrived in the USSR, 1933; appointed a professor at Moscow University, 1933. Sentenced to death at the Kamenev-Zinoviev trial, August 1936.

Lurie, N. L.—Member of the Communist Party of Germany from 1922. Arrived in the USSR, 1932. Chief physician at the infirmary of the Cheliabinsk tractor plant, 1933–36. Sentenced to death at the Kamenev-Zinoviev trial, August 1936.

Lytton, V. R. (2d Earl of Lytton)—British chairman of the League of Nations commission established in September 1931 to examine the situation in northeast China.

Ma Chang-shang—Chinese general, a leader of the anti-Japanese resistance in Manchuria. Received weapons and ammunition from the USSR.

Maiorov, M. M. (1890–1938)—Became party member, 1906. Secretary of the Central Asian Bureau of the CC, 1933–34. Appointed a deputy chairman of Tsentrosoiuz, 1934. Executed.

Maisky, I. M. (1884–1975)—Plenipotentiary of the USSR in Finland, 1929–32, and in Great Britain, 1932–43.

Makarovsky, S. I. (1880–1934)—A deputy chairman of the All-Union Corporation of the Aircraft Industry, 1932.

Maksum—*see* Nusratulla, Maksum

Malinov, M. M. (1894–?)—Became party member, 1918. Secretary of the Central Black-Earth Regional Party Committee, 1930–32.

Malraux, André (1901–1976)—French writer and political figure.

Mamulia, Ya. I.—Became party member, 1917. Secretary of the Transcaucasian Regional Party Committee, 1930.

Mandelshtam, S. O. (1895–?)—Became party member, 1917. Until his arrest in 1936, was deputy head of the economic sector of the State Institute for the Design of Metallurgical Plants.

Mann, Heinrich (1871–1950)—German writer and public figure.

Mann, Thomas (1875–1955)—German writer.

Mariasin, L. Ye. (1894–1937)—Became party member, 1915. A deputy chairman of the board of Gosbank 1931–34; chairman, 1934–36. Executed.

Markov, N. I.—Member of the collegium of the PC for Supply, 1930–34.

Martin du Gard, Roger (1881–1958)—French writer.

Meerzon, Zh. I. (1894–1939)—Became party member, 1919. Manager of the organizational and instructional department of the CC, 1931. Secretary of the Transcaucasian Regional Party Committee, 1932–34. Executed.

Mekhlis, L. Z. (1889–1953)—Became party member, 1918. Editor of *Pravda*, 1930–37.

Menzhinsky, V. R. (1874–1934)—Became party member in 1902. Chairman of the OGPU, 1926–34.

Mezhlauk, V. I. (1893–1938)—Became party member, 1917. First deputy chairman of Gosplan, 1931–34; chairman of Gosplan and a deputy chairman of Sovnarkom and STO, 1934–37. Executed.

Mikoian, A. I. (1895–1978)—Became party member, 1915; elected a candidate member of the Politburo, 1926; member of the Politburo (presidium) of the CC, 1935–66. Appointed people's commissar for supply, 1930; people's commissar of the food industry, 1934–38.

Milkh, L. R.—Became party member, 1917. Second secretary of the Central Volga Regional Party Committee, 1931–32; head of the political department of South-Western Railroad from 1933. Repressed.

Mirzakhanov, I. A. (1888–1960)—Became party member, 1905. Director of Artillery Plant 8 until 1936.

Mirzoian, L. I. (1897–1939)—Became party member, 1917. First secretary of the Kazakh Regional Party Committee, February 1933–June 1938. Executed.

Molotov, V. M. (1890–1986)—Became party member, 1906; member of the Politburo (presidium) of the CC, 1926–57. Chairman of Sovnarkom, 1930–41.

Morgenthau, Henry (1891–1967)—US secretary of the treasury, 1934–45.

Moskvin, I. M. (1890–1937)—Became party member, 1911. Head of the cadres sector of Vesenkha, 1930–31; member of the collegium of the PC of Heavy Industry, 1932–34. Appointed head of the heavy industry group of the Soviet Control Commission, 1935. Executed.

Mrachkovsky, S. V. (1888–1936)—Became party member, 1905; an active participant in the Left opposition. Expelled from the party, 1927. In 1928, after reinstatement in the party, did economic work; was construction chief of the Baikal-Amur Railroad before his next arrest in 1933. Sentenced to death at the Kamenev-Zinoviev trial, August 1936.

Muklevich, R. A. (1890–1938)—Became party member, 1906. Appointed inspector of the navy, 1931; appointed director of the Chief Administration of the Shipbuilding Industry of the PC of Heavy Industry, December 1933; a deputy people's commissar of the defense industry, 1936–37. Executed.

Münzenberg, Wilhelm (1889–1940)—Member of the CC of the Communist Party of Germany; chairman of the Communist Youth International.

Muralov, A. I. (1886–1937)—Became party member, 1905. A deputy people's commissar of agriculture, 1933–36. Executed.

Myshkov, N. G. (1894–1937)—Became party member, 1917. Chairman of the steel corporation *Stal* and a member of the presidium of Vesenkha of the USSR, 1930; director of the Vesenkha Administration for Construction Projects in the Iron and Steel Industry and chief of construction of the Kharkov tractor plant, 1931–32; director of the Magnetogorsk iron and steel combine, 1933; first deputy of the PC of Light Industry 1934–37. Repressed.

Nadolny, R. (1873–?)—German ambassador to the USSR, 1933–34.

Nakhaev, A. S. (1903–1935)—Was party member, 1927–28; resigned from the party out of sympathy with the opposition. Graduated from the Leningrad Artillery School, 1925; discharged from the army owing to illness, 1928. Until the end of 1933, worked at enterprises and construction projects in Odessa and Moscow, then was an instructor in military subjects at the Moscow Institute of Physical Fitness and chief of staff of the artillery division of the Society to Assist Defense, and Aviation and Chemical Development. Executed.

Nedejde, Ion (Ioan) (1854–1928)—Romanian public-affairs writer, Social Democrat, translator of Engels' works into Romanian.

Nesselrode, K. V. (1780–1862)—Minister of foreign affairs of Russia, 1816–56.

Neumann, Heinz (1902–1937)—Became member of the Communist Party of Germany, 1919. Candidate member of the presidium of the Executive Committee of the Comintern (ECCI), 1931–32. Instructor of the ECCI in Spain, fall of 1932–November 1933. Hired as a translator at the Foreign Workers Publishing House in the USSR, October 1935. Repressed.

Neurath, Constantin von (1873–1956)—Minister of foreign affairs of Germany, 1932–38.

Nexø, Martin (1869–1954)—Danish writer.

Nezval, Vitezslav (1900–1958)—Czech poet.

Niedermayer, Oskar von—German officer. From 1921, a principal representative of Wehrmacht in secret Soviet-German military collaboration.

Nikolaeva, K. I. (1893–1944)—Became party member, 1909. Head of sections of the CC, 1930–33; second secretary of the Western Siberian Regional party committee, 1933; second secretary of the Ivanovo Regional party committee, 1934–36; a secretary of AUCCTU from 1936.

Nusratulla, Maksum (1881–1938)—Became party member, 1920. Chairman of the Central Executive Committee of the Tajik SSR, 1929–33. Began studies in Moscow, December 1933. Repressed.

Ohashi, T. (1893–1975)—General consul of Japan in Harbin, 1931; deputy minister of foreign affairs of Manchukuo from 1933.

Ohlberg, W. P.—*see* Olberg, V. P.

Okhtin, A. Ya. (1891–1938)—Became party member, 1908. Plenipotentiary of the USSR in Mongolia, 1927–31; representative of the CC of the VKP(b) in Mongolia, 1932–33. Executed.

Olberg, V. P. (1907–1936)—Member of the Communist Party of Germany; expelled from party, 1932, for factional activities. Arrived in the USSR, 1935; until his arrest in 1936 was a teacher at a pedagogical institute in the city of Gorky. Sentenced to death at the Kamenev-Zinoviev trial, August 1936.

Olbracht, Ivan (1882–1952)—Czech writer.

Olsky, Ya. K. (1898–1937)—Became party member, 1917. Appointed chief of the special department of the OGPU, October 1930. Appointed chairman of Moscow Public Catering Corporation, August 1931; director of the Chief Administration of Canteens of the PC of Internal Trade, 1934–37. Executed.

Orakhelashvili, M. D. (1881–1937)—Became party member, 1903. Chairman of the Sovnarkom of the Transcaucasian Soviet Federative Socialist Republic,

1931, then first secretary of the Transcaucasian Regional Party Committee. Deputy director of the Institute of Marx, Engels, and Lenin attached to the CC of the VKP(b), 1932–37. Repressed.

Orakhelashvili, M. P. (1887–1938)—Became party member, 1906. People's commissar of education of Georgia, September 1931–June 1932, then a department head at Tiflis University. Director of the Administration of Higher Education of the PC of Education of the RSFSR, 1933–37. Repressed.

Ordzhonikidze, G. K. ("Sergo") (1886–1937)—Became party member, 1903, and a member of the Politburo, 1930. Appointed chairman of Vesenkha, 1930; appointed people's commissar of heavy industry, 1932. Committed suicide as a result of a conflict with Stalin.

Ordzhonikidze, Z. G. (1894–1960)—wife of G. K. Ordzhonikidze.

Osinsky, N. (V. V. Obolensky) (1887–1938)—Became party member, 1907. Deputy chairman of Gosplan and director of the Central Administration of National Economic Accounting, January 1932–August 1935. Appointed director of the Institute of the History of Science and Technology of the Academy of Sciences of the USSR, August 1935; member of the editorial board of the newspaper *Izvestia,* 1931–35. Executed.

Ota, T (1880–1956)—Japanese ambassador to the USSR, 1932–36.

Ozyorsky, A. V. (1891–1938)—Became party member, 1917. A deputy people's commissar of foreign trade, 1930; trade representative in Great Britain, September 1931. Executed.

Pakhomov, N. I. (1890–1938)—Became party member, 1917. Chairman of the Gorky Regional Executive Committee, 1928–34; people's commissar of water transport, March 1934–April 1938. Executed.

Papen, F. von (1879–1969)—German statesman and diplomat. Chancellor of Germany, July–November 1932.

Pascua, M.—Spanish ambassador to the USSR, 1936.

Pashukanis, Ye. B. (1891–1937)—Became party member, 1918. Director of the Institute of Soviet Construction and Law of the Communist Academy, 1931–36. Repressed.

Patek, S. (1866–1945)—Defense lawyer. Polish ambassador to the USSR, 1926–33; appointed Polish ambassador to the United States, 1933.

Paul-Boncour, Joseph (1873–1972)—Prime minister and minister of foreign affairs of France, 1932–33; minister of foreign affairs, 1933–34.

Pavlunovsky, I. P. (1888–1940)—Became party member, 1905. Appointed deputy chairman of Vesenkha for military industry, July 1931; appointed a deputy people's commissar of heavy industry, 1932. Executed.

Petrikovsky, A. A.—Director of the Moscow-Kursk Railroad, 1933; director of the Moscow District Railroad, 1934. Director of the Moscow subway, 1934–37. Repressed.

Petrovsky, G. I. (1878–1958)—Became party member, 1897; candidate member of the Politburo, 1926–39. Chairman (President) of the All-Ukrainian Central Executive Committee, 1919–38.

Piatakov, Yu. L. (1890–1937)—Became party member, 1910; a leader of the Left opposition. Expelled from the party, 1927. After reinstatement in the party in 1928, appointed chairman of Gosbank. A deputy people's commissar of heavy industry, 1932–36 (first deputy from June 1934). Executed.

Piatnitsky, O. A. (1882–1938)—Became party member, 1898. Appointed a member of the Executive Committee of the Comintern, 1921. Transferred to the staff of the CC of the VKP(b) in 1935; became head of the political and administrative department. Executed.

Pikel, R. V. (1896–1936)—Became party member, 1917; aide to Zinoviev. Expelled from party, 1927; after reinstatement in 1929, worked at cultural establishments. Sentenced to death at the Kamenev-Zinoviev trial, August 1936.

Pilsudski, Jozef (1867–1935)—Effectively dictator of Poland, 1926–35. Temporarily prime minister in 1930.

Poberezhsky, I. I. (1897–1944)—Became party member, 1920. Appointed director of the All-Union Corporation of the Aircraft Industry, February 1932; appointed director of Rybinsk factory, September 1933, and of Aircraft Plant 19, May 1934. Executed.

Pokrovsky, M. N. (1868–1932)—Became party member, 1905. Soviet historian and academician of the Academy of Sciences of the USSR. Member of the Central Party Control Commission, 1930–32.

Poliudov, Ye. V. (1887–?)—Became party member, 1907. Member of the collegium of the PC of Transport, 1931. Sector head at the PC of Finance of the RSFSR, October 1931–34.

Polonsky, V. I. (1893–1937)—Became party member, 1912. Appointed first secretary of the CC of the Communist Party of Azerbaijan and secretary of the Transcaucasian Regional Party Committee, 1930; appointed head of the organizational department of the CC, February 1933. A deputy people's commissar of transport for politics, 1933–35. A secretary of the AUCCTU, 1935–37. Executed.

Pope, Frederick—Colonel and president of the Nitrogen Engineering Corporation of New York, which concluded technical assistance agreements with the Soviet chemical industry.

Popov, N. N. (1891–1938)—Became party member, 1919. Member of the editorial board of *Pravda*, 1922–32; head of the department of culture and propaganda and then a secretary of the CC of the Communist Party of the Ukraine, 1933–37. Executed.

Pospelov, P. N. (1898–1979)—Became party member, 1916. A member of the editorial board and manager of the party-life department of the newspaper *Pravda*, 1931–34; head of the press group of the Commission of Party Control, 1934–37.

Postnikov, A. M. (1886–1937)—Became party member, 1904. Director of the Mobilization Administration of Vesenkha, 1930. A deputy people's commissar of transport, July 1930–October 1931; appointed director of the Moscow-Belorussian-Baltic Railroad, October 1931; appointed director of the Moscow-

Kazan Railroad, January 1932. Second and first deputy people's commissar of transport, 1934–37.

Postyshev, P. P. (1887–1939)—Became party member, 1904; candidate member of the Politburo, 1934–38; a secretary of the CC, 1930–34. From 1933 to 1937, was second secretary of the CC of the Communist Party of the Ukraine and first secretary of the Kharkov Regional Party Committee and City Committee (until 1934) and the Kiev Regional Committee (from 1934). Executed.

Potyomkin, V. P. (1874–1946)—Plenipotentiary of the USSR in Italy, 1932–34; plenipotentiary of the USSR in France, 1934–37.

Pozzo di Borgo—Corsican leader.

Pramnek, E. K. (1899–1938)—Became party member, 1917. First secretary of the Gorky Regional Party Committee, 1934–37. Appointed first secretary of the Donetsk Regional Party Committee, May 1937. Executed.

Preobrazhensky, Ye. A. (1886–1937)—Became party member, 1903; a leader of the Left opposition. Worked in Gosplan and in various commissariats and in diplomatic functions during the 1930s. Executed.

Prokofiev, G. Ye. (1895–1937)—Became party member, 1919. Appointed chief of the special department of the OGPU, August 1931; a deputy chairman of the OGPU and director of the Chief Administration of the Workers' and Peasants' Militia attached to the OGPU, November 1932–July 1936. A deputy people's commissar of internal affairs, July 1934–September 1936. Executed.

Pylaev, G. N. (1894–1937)—Became party member, 1902. Chairman of the Leningrad Regional Economic Council and a member of the presidium of the RSFSR Vesenkha, 1930–31. Repressed.

Rabinovich, F. Ya. (1885–1937)—Became party member, 1902. Member of the collegium of the PC of Foreign Trade, 1930–37. Executed.

Radek, K. B. (1885–1939)—Became party member, 1903; a leader of the Left opposition. Expelled from the party, 1927; reinstated, 1930. Manager of the bureau of international information of the CC, 1932–September 1936. Killed in prison.

Raevsky, S. A. (1885–1937)—Became party member, 1906. Head of the foreign department of the newspaper *Izvestia*, 1929–35; editor of the newspaper *Journal de Moscou*, 1935. Executed.

Rakovsky, Kh. G. (1873–1941)—Became party member, 1917. A leader of the Left Opposition; expelled from the party, December 1927. Head of the administration of the teaching establishment of the PC of Health of the RSFSR, 1934. Chairman of the Union of Red Cross and Red Crescent Societies, 1936. Executed.

Razumov, M. O. (1894–1937)—Became party member, 1913. First secretary of the Tatar Regional Party Committee, 1932–33, then of the Eastern Siberian Regional Committee, from November 1934. Executed.

Redens, S. F. (1892–1940)—Became party member, 1914. Plenipotentiary of the OGPU in the Ukraine, then chairman of the GPU of the Ukraine, 1931–33;

plenipotentiary of the OGPU for the Moscow Region, 1933–34; director of the NKVD administration for the Moscow Region, 1934–38. Executed.

Reingold, I. I. (1887–1936)—Became party member, 1917; a participant in the Left opposition. Expelled from the party, 1927; after reinstatement, was deputy people's commissar of agriculture, 1929–34; head of the Chief Administration of Cotton Growing of the PC of Agriculture, 1934–35. Sentenced to death at the Kamenev-Zinoviev trial, August 1936.

Rewentlow, Count Ernst zu—German journalist and political figure; member of a right-wing party, then joined the Nazi Party in 1927; supporter of an Eastern orientation. Maintained regular contact with the Soviet embassy in Germany from 1923 until the beginning of the 1930s.

Riabovol, K. S. (1894–1938)—Became party member, 1919. Chairman of the board of Soiuznefteeksport (All-Union Corporation for Oil Exports), 1931–33. Executed.

Rolland, Romain (1866–1944)—French writer; public figure.

Roshal, G. G. (1898–?)—Became party member, 1917. Executive instructor of the mass-agitation department of the CC, 1930–May 1931; appointed head of the personnel department and a member of the collegium of the PC of Agriculture of the RSFSR, 1931.

Royzenman, B. A. (1878–1938)—Became party member, 1902. Member of the collegium of the PC of the Workers' and Peasants' Inspectorate, 1926–32. Appointed a deputy executive editor of a journal of the PC, November 1932. Repressed.

Rozenberg, M. I. (1896–1938)—Became party member, 1919. Appointed a counselor at the Soviet mission in Paris, 1931; plenipotentiary of the USSR in Spain, 1936–37. Repressed.

Rozengolts, A. P. (1889–1938)—Became party member, 1905. People's commissar of foreign trade, 1930–37. Executed.

Rozental, K. Ya. (1900–?)—Member of the presidium of Gosplan, 1930–31; a deputy people's commissar of the timber industry, 1932–35. Repressed.

Rozental, Ya. D. (1897–1938)—Became party member, 1917. Member of the collegium of the PC of Transport, head of the political department of the Northern Caucasus Railroad, member of the bureau of the Azov–Black Sea Regional Party Committee, 1931–34. Head of the political department of the Moscow–Donets Basin Railroad, then worked at the PC of Transport, 1935–36. Executed.

Ruben, Rubenov, R. G. (1884–1937)—Became party member, 1917. First secretary of the CC of the Communist Party of Azerbaijan, 1933. Appointed plenipotentiary of the Party Control Committee for the Kiev Region, 1934, then the Leningrad Region. Repressed.

Rudzutak, Ya. E. (1887–1938)—Became party member, 1905; member of the Politburo, 1926–32; candidate member of the Politburo, 1934–37. A deputy chairman of Sovnarkom and the Council of Labor and Defense, 1926–37; concurrently chairman of the Central Control Commission and people's commissar of the Workers' and Peasants' Inspectorate, 1931–34. Executed.

Rukhimovich, M. L. (1889–1938)—Became party member, 1913. People's commissar of transport, 1930–31, then manager of Kuzbassugol (the Kuznets Basin Coal Trust). Appointed deputy people's commissar of heavy industry for fuel, June 1934. People's commissar of the defense industry, 1936–37. Executed.

Ryklin, G. Ye. (1894–1975)—Became party member, 1920. Soviet writer.

Rykov, A. I. (1881–1938)—Became party member, 1898. Chairman of Sovnarkom of the USSR, 1924–30, and Sovnarkom of the RSFSR, 1924–29. People's commissar of communications (posts and telegraph), 1931–36. Executed.

Ryndin, K. V. (1893–1938)—Became party member, 1915. Second secretary of the Moscow Regional Party Committee, 1932–34; first secretary of the Cheliabinsk Regional Committee, 1934–37. Executed.

Saito Makoto (1858–1936)—Prime minister of Japan, 1932–34.

Sakhatsko-Bratkovsky—*see* Chesheiko-Sokhatsky, Ye.

Sangursky, M. V. (1894–1937)—Became party member, 1909. Chief of staff, 1930–34; deputy commander of the Special Far Eastern Military District, 1934–36. Executed.

Sarkis, Sarkisov, S. A. (1898–1937)—Became party member, 1917. Director of Zagotzerno (the Grain Procurement Corporation) and a member of Komzag, the Procurements Committee for Agricultural Products, 1932. Appointed first secretary of the Donetsk Regional Party Committee, 1933. Executed.

Sedov, Lev (1906–1938)—Son of L. D. Trotsky. While in exile, actively participated in the work of an organization of Trotsky supporters; an organizer of Trotsky's journal *Biulleten oppozitsii* (Bulletin of the Opposition).

Senkov—Soviet engineer.

Serebriakov, L. P. (1888–1937)—Became party member, 1905. Director of the Central Administration of Highways and Motor Transport, 1931–35; deputy director of the Chief Administration of Highways of the NKVD, 1935–36. Executed.

Sergo—*see* Ordzhonikidze, G. K.

Sewering, Karl (1875–1952)—Minister of internal affairs of Prussia, 1930–32.

Shcherbakov, A. S. (1901–1945)—Became party member, 1918. Appointed assistant head of a department of the CC, 1932, then head; concurrently first secretary of the Union of Soviet Writers, 1934–36.

Shchusev, A. V. (1873–1949)—Soviet architect and academician of the Academy of Sciences of the USSR.

Sheboldaev, B. P. (1895–1937)—Became party member, 1914. First secretary of the Northern Caucasus Party Regional Committee, 1931–34, and the Azov–Black Sea Regional Committee, 1934–37. Executed.

Sholokhov, M. A. (1905–1984)—Soviet writer.

Shubrikov, V. P. (1895–1937)—Became party member, 1917. Secretary of the Central Volga Regional Party Committee and the Kuibyshev Regional Committee, 1932–37. Repressed.

Shulkin—Secretary of the Nikolaev City Committee in the Ukraine.

Shvernik, N. M. (1888–1970)—Became party member, 1905. Chairman of the All-Union Central Council of Trade Unions, 1930–44.

Skvirsky, B. Ye. (1887–1941)—Counselor at the Soviet mission in the United States, 1933–36. Executed.

Slavutsky, M. M.—Consul general in Harbin, 1930–33.

Slepkov, A. N. (1899–1937)—Became party member, 1919. Supporter of Bukharin. Member of the bureau and head of agitation and propaganda work of the Central Volga Regional Party Committee, 1928–32. Repressed, 1932. Exccuted.

Smirnov, I. N. (1881–1936)—Became party member, 1899; a leader of the Left opposition. Expelled from the party, 1927; reinstated, May 1930; occupied industrial posts, 1929–32. Expelled again in 1933 and received a prison sentence. Sentenced to death at the Kamenev-Zinoviev trial, August 1936.

Sokolnikov, G. Ya. (1888–1939)—Became party member, 1905. USSR plenipotentiary in Great Britain, 1929–32, then a deputy people's commissar of foreign affairs. First deputy people's commissar of the timber industry, 1935–July 1936. Killed in prison, 1941.

Sorokin, M. L. (1892–1941)—Became party member, 1921. Deputy manager of the department of the CC for assignment of administrative, economic, and trade union cadres, 1933–35; deputy manager of the industrial department of the CC from March 1935. Executed.

Spirin, I. T. (1898–1960)—Became party member, 1920. Aviator and participant in a number of record flights to the north, China, and Europe.

Stalin, V. I. (1921–1962)—Son of Joseph (I. V.) Stalin.

Stetsky, A. I. (1896–1938)—Became party member, 1915. Head of the department of the CC for party propaganda and agitation, 1930–38; concurrently, in 1934, became editor in chief of the journal *Bolshevik*. Executed.

Stimson, Henry L. (1867–1950)—US secretary of state, 1929–33.

Stomoniakov, B. S. (1882–1941)—Became party member, 1902. Member of the collegium of the PC of Foreign Affairs, 1926–34; a deputy people's commissar of foreign affairs, 1934–August 1938. Executed.

Strumilin, S. G. (1877–1974)—Became party member, 1923. Economist, statistician, and academician of the Academy of Sciences of the USSR. Worked at the Gosplan of the RSFSR and the USSR, 1921–37.

Sudin, S. K. (1894–1938)—Became party member, 1918. Deputy people's commissar of foreign trade, 1932–34. Deputy group head of the Soviet Control Commission, 1934–35. Appointed first deputy people's commissar of foreign trade, March 1935; acting people's commissar, June–October 1936. Executed.

Sukhishvili, V. A. (1888–?)—Became party member, 1904. Chairman of the Sovnarkom of Georgia, 1931. Repressed.

Sulimov, D. Ye. (1890–1937)—Became party member, 1905. Chairman of the RSFSR Sovnarkom, 1930–37. Executed.

Surits, Ya. Z. (1882–1952)—Became party member, 1903. Plenipotentiary of the USSR in Turkey, 1930–34; in Germany, 1934–37.

Svanidze, A. S. (1884–1941)—Became party member, 1904. Deputy trade repre-

sentative in Germany, 1930–31; member of the board of Gosbank, January–
November 1931. Appointed chairman of the board of the Foreign Trade Bank,
December 1931. Appointed deputy chairman of the board of Gosbank, 1935.
Repressed.

Svetlana—*see* Allilueva, S. I.

Syrkin—Editor of the newspaper *Cheliabinsky rabochy* (Cheliabinsk Worker).

Syrtsov, S. I. (1893–1937)—Became party member, 1913; candidate member of
the Politburo, 1929–30. Chairman of Sovnarkom of the RSFSR, 1929–30. Dismissed on charges of factional activity and assigned to economic work: was
deputy chairman of the board of the Eksportles (Timber Export) joint-stock
company, manager of a trust for equipment and explosives, and a plant director.
Executed.

Tabakov, Z. Ya.—Became party member, 1919. Director of the Satka magnesite
plant in the Cheliabinsk Region during the 1930s.

Tairov, V. Kh. (1894–1938)—Became party member, 1915. Member of the Revolutionary Military Council of the Special Far Eastern Army, 1932–35. Plenipotentiary of the USSR in Mongolia, 1935–37. Executed.

Tal, B. M. (1898–1938)—Became party member, 1918. Deputy manager of the
department of agitation and propaganda, 1929–37; head of the science sector
of the department of culture and propaganda; manager of the department of the
press and publishing houses of the CC; member of the editorial board of *Pravda;*
editor of *Za industrializatsiiu;* appointed deputy editor of the newspaper *Izvestia,* 1936. Executed.

Terekhov, R. Ya. (1889–?)—Became party member, 1912. Secretary of the Donetsk Regional Party Committee, responsible for coal, February–September 1933;
chair of the central committee of the trade union of the iron and steel industry
from November 1933.

Ter-Vaganian, V. A. (1893–1936)—Became party member, 1912; a leader of the
opposition. Repeatedly repressed. Sentenced to death at the Kamenev-Zinoviev
trial, August 1936.

Thälmann, Ernst (1886–1944)—Leader of the Communist Party of Germany. Arrested by the Nazis, 1933; died in prison.

Tolokontsev, A. F. (1889–1937)—Became party member, 1914. Held senior posi-
tions in military industry. Appointed manager of the All-Union Corporation of
Machine Building of the PC of Heavy Industry, July 1931. Head of the Chief
Administration of Precision Engineering, 1933–34. Repressed.

Tomsky, M. P. (1880–1936)—Became party member, 1904; member of the CC,
1919–34; member of the Politburo, 1922–30. Manager of the Corporation of
State Publishing Houses, 1932–36. Committed suicide.

Trilisser (Moskvin), M. A. (1883–1940)—Became party member, 1901. Deputy
people's commissar of the Workers' and People's Inspectorate of the RSFSR,
1930–34; member of the Soviet Control Committee and representative in the
Far Eastern Region, 1934–35. Appointed to the presidium of the Executive
Committee of the Comintern from the VKP(b), August 1935. Executed.

Troianovsky, A. A. (1882–1955)—Plenipotentiary of the USSR in Japan, 1927–33; in the United States, 1933–38.

Trotsky, L. D. (1879–1940)—Joined the revolutionary movement, 1897; became party member, 1917. A leader of the October Revolution. Member of the Politburo and one of Stalin's chief political opponents, 1919–26. Exiled from the USSR. Engaged in intensive political activities while in exile. Assassinated in Mexico on Stalin's orders by an NKVD agent.

Tukhachevsky, M. N. (1893–1937)—Became party member, 1918. Appointed deputy chairman of the Revolutionary Military Council and director of armaments for the Red Army, 1931; appointed a deputy people's commissar of military and naval affairs, 1934, and first deputy people's commissar of defense, 1936. Executed.

Tumanov, N. G. (1887–1936)—Became party member, 1917. Member of the presidium of Vesenkha, 1931–32. Chairman of the board and manager of the USSR Industrial Bank, 1932–36. Executed.

Tyomkin, M. M. (1895–?)—Became party member, 1914. Appointed a member of the Party Control Commission, 1934; head of the agricultural group of the Party Control Commission, 1935. Repressed.

Ukhanov, K. V. (1891–1937)—Became party member, 1907. Deputy people's commissar for supply, 1932–34; people's commissar of light industry of the RSFSR, 1934–36, and of local industry of the RSFSR, 1936–37. Executed.

Ulrikh, V. V. (1889–1951)—Chairman of the Military Collegium of the USSR Supreme Court, 1926–48; concurrently deputy chairman of the USSR Supreme Court, 1935–48.

Umansky, K. A. (1902–1945)—Deputy manager, then manager, of the department of the press and information of the PC of Foreign Affairs, 1931–36. Counselor at the Soviet mission in the United States, 1936–38. Died in a plane crash.

Unshlikht, I. S. (1879–1938)—Became party member, 1900. Deputy chairman of Vesenkha for the military industry, 1930; a deputy chairman of Gosplan, 1930–32; chief arbitrator attached to Sovnarkom, 1933; head of the Chief Administration of Civil Aviation, 1933–35. Executed.

Vainov, A. R. (1899–?)—Became party member, 1918; secretary of Donetsk Regional Party Committee from July 1932; deputy head of the industry department of the party Central Committee, March–April 1936. Repressed.

Vančura, Vladislav (1891–1942)—Czech writer.

Vangengeim, A. F. (1881–1942)—Became party member, 1928. Appointed first head of the Hydrometeorological Service, 1929.

Vangère—French industrialist, director of the Petrofine company.

Vareikis, I. M. (1894–1938)—Became party member, 1913. First secretary of the Central Black Earth Regional Party Committee, 1928–34; of the Voronezh Regional Committee, 1934–35; of the Stalingrad Regional Committee, 1935–36. Executed.

Vasia—_see_ Stalin, V. I.

Vasilievsky, V. N. (1893–1957)—Became party member, 1912. Executive editor of the magazine _Prozhektor_ (Spotlight), 1935.

Vasilkovsky, G. O. (1903–38)—Became party member, 1921. Deputy head of the economics department of *Pravda*, responsible for engineering, 1928–34; editor of the newspaper *Za industrializatsiiu*, 1935–37. Executed..

Vedeneev, B. Ye. (1884/1885–1946)—Soviet hydroelectric engineer, academician of the Academy of Sciences of the USSR, and a leader of the construction of the Volkhov and Dnieper hydroelectric stations.

Veger, Ye. I. (1899–1938)—Became party member, 1917. Appointed first secretary of the Odessa Regional Party Committee, 1933. Executed.

Veitser, I. Ya. (1889–1938?)—Became party member, 1914. Trade representative in Berlin, 1931. A deputy people's commissar of foreign trade, 1932–33; people's commissar of internal trade, 1934–37. Executed.

Vildrac, Charles (1882–1971)—French writer.

Vinogradov, A. K. (1888–1946)—Russian, Soviet writer.

Vinogradov, B. D. (1903–38)—First secretary of the Soviet mission in Germany, 1932–33.

Vinter, A. V. (1878–1958)—Soviet power engineer, academician of the Academy of Sciences of the USSR, and construction chief of the Dnieper hydroelectric station; a deputy people's commissar of heavy industry, 1932–34.

Volovich, Z. I.—Deputy section head for the NKVD, 1937. Repressed.

Voroshilov, K. Ye. (1881–1969)—Became party member, 1903; member of the Politburo (Presidium of the CC), 1926–60. Chairman of the Revolutionary Military Council and people's commissar of military and naval affairs, 1925–34; people's commissar of defense, 1934–40.

Vyshinsky, A. Ya. (1883–1954)—Joined the Social-Democratic movement, 1903 (as a Menshevik); became a Communist Party member, 1920. Appointed prosecutor of the RSFSR and a deputy people's commissar of justice of the RSFSR, 1931; deputy prosecutor of the USSR, 1933; prosecutor of the USSR, 1935–39.

Wang Tseng-ssu—Member of the Chinese delegation at the Soviet-Chinese conference of 1932.

Wellington Ku—*see* Koo, Dr Wellington

Yagoda, G. G. (1891–1938)—Became party member, 1907. Appointed deputy chairman of the OGPU, 1924; people's commissar of internal affairs, 1934–36; people's commissar of communications, 1936–37. Executed.

Yakovlev, A. I. (1900–1937)—Became party member, 1917. Chairman of the Transcaucasian Control Commission, 1930. Repressed.

Yakovlev, Ya. A. (1896–1938)—Became party member, 1913. People's commissar of agriculture, 1929–34; appointed head of the agricultural department of the CC, April 1934. Appointed first deputy chairman of the Party Control Commission, 1936. Executed.

Yanson, N. M. (1882–1941)—Became party member, 1905. People's commissar of water transport, 1931–34; appointed deputy people's commissar of water transport, 1934, and a deputy head of the Chief Administration of the Northern Sea Route.

Yaroslavsky, Ye. M. (1878–1943)—Became party member, 1898. Member of the

Central Control Commission of the party, 1923–34; member of the editorial board of *Pravda* until June 1932; appointed chairman of the Society of Old Bolsheviks, 1931.

Yemshanov, A. I. (1891–1941)—Became party member, 1917. Director of operations of the Moscow–Donets Basin Railroad, 1934–36. Repressed.

Yenukidze, A. S. (1877–1937)—Became party member, 1898; secretary of the presidium of the Central Executive Committee, 1922–March 1935. Removed from the CC and expelled from the party "for political and moral degradation," June 1935. Assigned to economic work. Executed.

Yeryomin, I. G. (1895–1937)—Became party member, 1917. Appointed to the presidium of Vesenkha, 1931. A deputy people's commissar of light industry, 1932–37. Repressed.

Yerzinkian (Yerzikiants), S. Ye. (1881–?)—Became party member, 1918. Trade representative in Finland, 1928–early 1930. In summer of 1934 he refused to return to the USSR. He was accused of forgery by the Soviet authorities and, following a request from the Soviet plenipotentiary in Finland, was arrested and imprisoned by Finnish authorities.

Yevdokimov, G. Ye. (1884–1936)—Became party member, 1903. Chairman of the Samara Region Union of Agricultural Cooperatives, 1929–34; then, until his arrest in December 1934, was director of the Main Administration of the Dairy Industry of the PC of the Food Industry. Sentenced to death at the Kamenev-Zinoviev trial, August 1936.

Yudin, P. F. (1899–1968)—Became party member, 1918. Director of the Institute of Red Professors of the Communist Academy, 1932–34; deputy head of the press department of the CC, 1935.

Yurenev, K. K. (1888–1938)—Became party member, 1905. USSR plenipotentiary in Japan, 1933–37. Repressed.

Yurkin, T. A. (1898–1986)—Became party member, 1919. People's commissar of grain and livestock state farms, 1932–34; first deputy people's commissar of grain and livestock state farms, 1932–36; people's commissar of state farms of the RSFSR from October 1936.

Zashibaev, A. S. (1895–1938)—Became party member, 1917. Secretary for transport of the Nizhny Novgorod Regional Party Committee and secretary of the Party Committee of the Gorky auto plant, 1932–34. Executed.

Zelensky, I. A. (1890–1938)—Became party member, 1906. Appointed chairman of the board of Tserntrosoiuz, 1931. Executed.

Zemliachka, R. S. (1876–1947)—Became party member, 1896. Staff member of the PC of the Workers' and Peasants' Inspectorate and the PC of Transport, 1926–33; member of the Committee of Soviet Control from 1934.

Zetkin, Klara (1857–1933)—A cofounder of the Communist Party of Germany. Elected a member of the presidium of the Executive Committee of the Comintern, 1921.

Zhdanov, A. A. (1896–1948)—Became party member, 1915. Department head, then first secretary of the Nizhny Novgorod (later Gorky) Regional Party Committee, 1922–34; appointed a secretary of the CC, 1934; concurrently first secretary of the Leningrad Regional and City Party Committees, 1934–44.

Zholtovsky, I. V. (1867–1959)—Soviet architect.

Zhukov, I. P. (1889–1937)—Became party member, 1909. Chairman of the All-Union Corporation of the Electrical Equipment Industry, 1930; a deputy people's commissar of heavy industry, 1932; a deputy people's commissar of communications, 1933–36. Executed.

Zinaida Gavrilovna—*see* Ordzhonikidze, Z. G.

Zinoviev, G. Ye. (1883–1936)—Became party member, 1901; member of the Politburo, 1921–26; chairman of the Executive Committee of the Comintern, 1919–26. A leader of the opposition; repeatedly repressed. After his last reinstatement in the party in late 1933 and until his next arrest in December 1934, was a member of the editorial board of the journal *Bolshevik*. Sentenced to death at the Kamenev-Zinoviev trial, August 1936.

Znamensky, A. A. (1887–1943)—Became party member, 1905. USSR consul in Mukden, May 1930–October 1932.

Index

417

BOOKS IN THE ANNALS OF COMMUNISM SERIES

The Fall of the Romanovs: Political Dreams and Personal Struggles in a Time of Revolution, by Mark D. Steinberg and Vladimir M. Khrustalëv

The Last Diary of Tsaritsa Alexandra, introduction by Robert K. Massie; edited by Vladimir A. Kozlov and Vladimir M. Khrustalëv

The Unknown Lenin: From the Secret Archive, edited by Richard Pipes

Voices of Revolution, 1917, by Mark D. Steinberg

Stalinism as a Way of Life: A Narrative in Documents, edited by Lewis Siegelbaum and Andrei K. Sokolov

The Road to Terror: Stalin and the Self-Destruction of the Bolsheviks, 1932–1939, by J. Arch Getty and Oleg V. Naumov

The Diary of Georgi Dimitrov, 1933–1949, introduced and edited by Ivo Banac

Enemies Within the Gates? The Comintern and the Stalinist Repression, 1934–1939, by William J. Chase

Stalin's Letters to Molotov, 1925–1936, edited by Lars T. Lih, Oleg V. Naumov, and Oleg V. Khlevniuk

The Stalin-Kaganovich Correspondence, 1931–36, compiled and edited by R. W. Davies, Oleg V. Khlevniuk, E. A. Rees, Liudmila P. Kosheleva, and Larisa A. Rogovaya

Dimitrov and Stalin, 1934–1943: Letters from the Soviet Archives, edited by Alexander Dallin and Fridrikh I. Firsov

Spain Betrayed: The Soviet Union in the Spanish Civil War, edited by Ronald Radosh, Mary R. Habeck, and G. N. Sevostianov

The Secret World of American Communism, by Harvey Klehr, John Earl Haynes, and Fridrikh I. Firsov

The Soviet World of American Communism, by Harvey Klehr, John Earl Haynes, and Kyrill M. Anderson

Stalin's Secret Pogrom: The Postwar Inquisition of the Soviet Jewish Anti-Fascist Committee, edited by Joshua Rubenstein and Vladimir P. Naumov